Evidence-Based Practices for Educating Students with Emotional and Behavioral Disorders

Mitchell L. Yell
University of South Carolina

Nancy B. Meadows
Texas Christian University

Erik Drasgow
University of South Carolina

James G. Shriner
University of Illinois at Urbana–Champaign

Merrill
is an imprint of

PEARSON

Upper Saddle River, New Jersey
Columbus, Ohio

Library of Congress Cataloging in Publication Data

Evidence based practices for educating students with emotional and behavioral disorders/Mitchell L. Yell . . . [et al.].
   p. cm.
  Includes bibliographical references and index.
  ISBN-13: 978-0-13-096823-4
  ISBN-10: 0-13-096823-4
  1. Problem children—Education—United States.　2. Mentally ill children—Education—United States.　3. Emotional problems of children—United States.　4. Behavior disorders in children—United States.　I. Yell, Mitchell L.
  LC4802. E95 2009
  371. 94—dc22

2007042417

Vice President and Executive Publisher: Jeffery W. Johnston
Executive Editor: Ann Castel Davis
Editorial Assistant: Penny Burleson
Senior Managing Editor: Pamela D. Bennett
Production Editor: Sheryl Glicker Langner
Production Coordination: Carol Singer, GGS Book Services
Design Coordinator: Diane C. Lorenzo
Cover Designer: Heather Miller
Cover Art: SuperStock
Production Manager: Laura Messerly
Director of Marketing: Quinn Perkson
Marketing Manager: Kris Ellis-Levy
Marketing Coordinator: Brian Mounts

This book was set in Garamond Book by GGS Book Services. It was printed and bound by Hamilton Printing Company. The cover was printed by Phoenix Color Corp.

Pearson Education Ltd., London
Pearson Education Singapore, Pte. Ltd.
Pearson Education Canada, Inc.
Pearson Education—Japan

Pearson Education Australia PTY, Limited
Pearson Education North Asia, Ltd., Hong Kong
Pearson Educación de Mexico, S.A. de C.V.
Pearson Education Malaysia, Pte. Ltd.
Pearson Education Upper Saddle River, New Jersey

Merrill
is an imprint of

10 9 8 7 6 5 4 3 2 1
ISBN 13: 978-0-13-096823-4
ISBN 10:　　0-13-096823-4

Dedication

Mitchell Yell: To my wife, Joy, my three sons, Nick, Eric, and Alex, and the memory of my parents, Erwin and Vonnet.

Nancy Meadows: To Mike, Dan, Andrew, Adrienne, and Corey for their love and support, and to the memory of Ron Meadows.

Erik Drasgow: To my family for their support, Doug Hinton for his guidance, and Paul Sabato for his enduring friendship.

James Shriner: To my family, Cheryl and Marshall, who have been patient and supportive throughout this effort.

Preface

Our purpose in this textbook is to help readers become effective teachers of students with emotional and behavioral disorders (EBD). Effective teachers assess, plan, organize, and deliver individualized academic and behavior programming and they collect data on actual student performance to inform instructional decisions. This textbook presents, describes, and gives examples of evidence-based educational practices that are effective for teaching students with EBD.

We have organized the text in the following manner. In the first section we provide the foundation for the field of EBD and cover characteristics of students with these disorders, discussing assessment, law, applied behavior analysis, positive behavior support, cognitive behavioral interventions, and social skills training. In the second section we expand on evidence-based classroom and behavior management strategies and procedures that teachers use to (a) prevent the occurrence of problem behavior, (b) intervene with students who exhibit problem behavior by teaching alternative and replacement behavior, and (c) respond to problem behavior when it occurs. In the third section we address academic interventions for students with EBD. To do this, we review the principles of effective instruction; examine the research on teaching reading, writing, mathematics, and study skills; and emphasize the importance of planning instruction and collecting data to monitor student progress.

Our major goal in this textbook is communicating to teachers and teacher trainers that it is their professional obligation to rely on evidence-based educational practices for teaching students with EBD. The laws, No Child Left Behind and the Individuals with Disabilities Education Improvement Act, require that educators use practices and procedures supported by research. Moreover, if teacher programs are to improve the quality of the lives of the students with whom they work, they are ethically obligated to base instruction on this body of evidence.

Acknowledgments

We are grateful to many people who were so helpful during the completion of this project. We thank Ann Davis, our editor, who provided direction and encouragement from the inception of this textbook and then returned to cheer us on to the finish line. We thank Allyson Sharp, who was our editor for a while during the middle stages of the project. Thanks also to Penny Burleson, Ann Davis's editorial assistant, for her persistence and good cheer and also to the reviewers who helped improve this textbook: Lisa Bloom, Western Carolina University; Amelia E. Blyden, The College of New Jersey; Lisa R. Churchill, California State University–Chico; Greg Conderman, Northern Illinois University; Sharon Cramer, Buffalo State College; Coleen Klein-Ezell, University of Central Florida; Elizabeth Deane Heins, Stetson University; Thomas F. McLaughlin, Gonzaga University; Robert Michael, State University of New York–New Paltz; Maureen R. Norris, Bellarmine University; David Dean Richey, Tennessee Tech University; Lorraine S. Taylor, State University of New York–New Paltz; and Pamela H. Wheeler, Lewis University.

We also are grateful for the guidance and friendship of our mentors: Frank Wood and Stan Deno (Mitchell Yell), Rick Neel (Nancy Meadows), James W. Halle (Erik Drasgow), and James Ysseldyke (James Shriner).

Brief Contents

Contents

4   Applied Behavior Analysis   62
BY ERIK DRASGOW, MITCHELL L. YELL, AND JAMES HALLE

5 Functional Behavioral Assessments and Behavior Intervention Plans   92

BY ERIK DRASGOW, CHRISTIAN A. MARTIN, ROBERT E. O'NEILL, AND MITCHELL L. YELL

6 Cognitive Behavioral Interventions   124

BY MITCHELL L. YELL, T. ROWAND ROBINSON, AND NANCY B. MEADOWS

7 Social Skills Instruction 155
By Nancy B. Meadows

8 Meeting the Needs of Students with EBD Through Collaborative Teaming 176
By K. Alisa Lowrey, Mitchell L. Yell, and D. Clark Cavin

9 Developing Educationally Meaningful and Legally Sound Individualized Education Programs 190
By Mitchell L. Yell

Part 2 Classroom and Behavior Management   215

10 Schoolwide Positive Behavior Support   217
By Mitchell L. Yell and M. Renee Bradley

11 Classroom and Behavior Management I: Preventing Problem Behavior in the Classroom   235
By Mitchell L. Yell

12 Classroom and Behavior Management II: Responding
to Problem Behavior   261
By Mitchell L. Yell

13 Classroom and Behavior Management III: Intervening
with Problem Behavior   282
By Mitchell L. Yell

16 Teaching Students with EBD III: Planning Instruction and Monitoring Student Performance   379

By Mitchell L. Yell, Todd W. Busch, and David C. Rogers

NOTE: Every effort has been made to provide accurate and current Internet information in this book. However, the Internet and information posted on it are constantly changing, and its is inevitable that some of the Internet addresses listed in this textbook will change.

PART 1

Foundations

Introduction to Emotional and Behavioral Disorders

Christine A. Christle and Mitchell L. Yell

Focus Questions

- Why are emotional and behavioral disorders (called EBD) so difficult to define?
- How are students with EBD classified?
- What are the prevalence rates of EBD?
- What are the characteristics of students with EBD?
- What is the history of the field?
- Why do children have these disorders?
- What are the risk factors?
- How do teachers intervene with students who have EBD?
- Where are students with EBD educated?

The focus of this textbook is on a segment of the student population that poses serious challenges to school personnel. Some of these students may be described as noncompliant, disruptive, defiant, aggressive, violent, and hostile. On the other hand, some may be depicted as anxious, depressed, and suicidal. What is it about these students that make their behavior so challenging and so resistant to change?

Often, in addition to exhibiting problem behavior, these students also struggle with school assignments. Furthermore, these students typically have problems in relationships with other students and adults. The ultimate challenge for teachers of students with emotional or behavioral disorders (EBD) is to intervene using evidence-based instructional and behavioral strategies so that these students can be successful in school and maintain satisfactory peer and adult relationships.

In this chapter, we provide an overview of EBD in students. First we address what constitutes an emotional or behavioral disorder. We begin by discussing the definition of EBD and the continuing controversy and misunderstanding surrounding the definition. Second, we explore the nature of different categories within the field of EBD by looking at the major classification systems. Third, we examine the history of this disability category and the various conceptual models that shaped the field. Subsequently, we explore the common characteristics of this group and the causal or risk factors related to EBD. Fourth, we discuss the referral and identification process for students to receive special education and related services for emotional and/or behavioral disorders. Fifth, we briefly explain the issues regarding interventions that will be covered in later chapters. Finally, we describe the various placement options for students identified with EBD.

DEFINITION OF EBD

Prior to the 1997 reauthorization of the Individuals with Disabilities Education Act (IDEA) the term for the special education category for children with EBD was *serious emotional disturbance (SED)*. In the IDEA Amendments of 1997, the word "serious" was dropped from the definition; thus federal terminology was changed to *emotional disturbance (ED)*. There were no changes to the definition in the Individuals with Disabilities Education Improvement Act of 2004 (hereafter IDEA 2004). Federal law defines emotional disturbance as including one or more of the following characteristics over a long period of time and to a marked degree, and which adversely affects educational performance:

   a. An inability to learn that cannot be explained by intellectual, sensory, and health factors.

   b. An inability to build or maintain satisfactory interpersonal relationships with peers and teachers.

   c. Inappropriate types of behavior or feelings under normal circumstances.

   d. A general pervasive mood of unhappiness or depression.

   e. A tendency to develop physical symptoms or fears associated with personal or school problems. (IDEA Regulations, 34 C.F.R. § 300.7(c)(4))

The IDEA definition also includes schizophrenia but does not apply to children who are socially maladjusted, unless it is determined that they have an emotional disturbance.

Problems of Definition

There has been considerable criticism regarding the terms and definition in the federal law due to several factors, including the ambiguity of terms; the possibility of misinterpretation; stigma; and a lack of a common understanding about the nature of ED (Forness & Kavale, 2000; Hunt & Marshall, 2005). Forness and Kavale (2000) discussed five problematic criteria for eligibility in the IDEA definition. The first is inability to learn, which confuses ED with the definition of learning disability (LD). The second is inability to build or maintain satisfactory relationships with teachers or peers, which suggests social adjustment problems. However, the ED definition is confusing and contradictory in that it excludes children who are socially maladjusted. Professionals in the field have discussed the impossibility of reliably distinguishing social from emotional maladjustment, especially since it is more common for problems to co-occur with others rather than singly (Merrell & Walker, 2004). The other three criteria (i.e., inappropriate types of behavior or feelings, pervasive mood of unhappiness, and tendency to develop physical symptoms or fears) classify a student as exhibiting a type of ED before eligibility is even determined. In addition to typecasting prior to eligibility, these types no longer reflect recent educational research and current clinical diagnoses.

Several terms in the federal definition are ambiguous. For example, how long is a *long period of time*? How do we measure a *marked degree*? Professionals argue that the terms are too vague as diagnostic markers that give rise to concerns of underidentification of students needing services (Hunt & Marshall, 2005). Thus, school personnel may mistake certain types of ED for social maladjustment, resulting in the exclusion of students needing services (Kauffman, Brigham, & Mock, 2004). The problems in defining behavioral deviation also are compounded by several factors, including the difficulty in measuring emotions and behavior; the variance in cultural values and what is considered acceptable and unacceptable behavior; and the diversity of conceptual models (Gargiulo, 2006). The terms in the definition are so imprecise that interpretation can vary among individuals, school districts, and states. In addition, what is considered unacceptable behavior changes over time, from generation to generation, and varies from rural area to inner city.

An Alternative Definition

In an effort to establish a more functional definition, the Mental Health and Special Education Coalition in 1990 advocated for changes to be made in the federal definition (McIntyre & Forness, 1997). The group proposed the change in terminology to provide a label that has more utility, is less stigmatizing, and is more representative of the students who experience problems with emotions and/or behavior. The coalition proposed the following definition:

The term "emotional or behavioral disorder" means a disability that is characterized by behavioral or emotional responses in school programs so different from appropriate age, cultural, or ethnic norms that the responses adversely affect educational performance, including academic, social, vocational or personal skills; more than a temporary, expected response to stressful events in the environment; consistently exhibited in two different settings, at least one of which is school-related; and unresponsive to direct intervention applied in general education, or the condition of a child is such that general education interventions would be insufficient.

The term includes such a disability that co-exists with other disabilities.

The term includes a schizophrenic disorder, affective disorder, anxiety disorder, or other sustained disorder of conduct or adjustment, affecting a child if the disorder affects educational performance as described in paragraph (1). (*Federal Register*, 1993, p. 7938)

Forness and Kavale (2000) outlined six advantages of the proposed definition over the current ED definition:

1. It emphasized a two-step diagnostic process determining symptoms and impairment that is essentially similar to that for the LD and mental retardation (MR) categories.

2. It included ethnic or cultural considerations in identification.

3. It stressed the need for multiple sources of case data.

4. It enhanced the possibility of early identification and intervention.

5. It listed examples of clinical diagnoses that could create eligibility if educational performance is impaired, so as to facilitate referrals to and from mental health, but does not necessarily require such diagnoses.

6. It did not require meaningless distinctions between social and emotional maladjustment, distinctions that often waste diagnostic resources when it is already clear that serious problems exist.

The National School Boards Association (NSBA) objected to the proposed definition, however, and it was not adopted. The members of the NSBA feared that the proposed definition would result in dramatic increases in students identified for special education services for ED, resulting in huge costs to states and local school districts. There was widespread support among special educators, however, for adoption of the proposed definition. Unfortunately for practitioners, parents, and students, the controversy on the definition may continue for some time, a factor that may prohibit greater potential for advancement in the field (Forness & Kavale, 2000; Merrell & Walker, 2004).

In spite of the federal definition's use of the term *emotional disturbance*, most professionals in the field have adopted the term *emotional or behavioral disorders*; thus we will use the abbreviation *EBD* throughout this text. In an effort to help practitioners with such an ambiguous definition and vague terms such as *marked degree* and *long period of time*, a good guideline to use is that by definition, students with EBD exhibit problem behaviors that are *extreme* according to social norms, and *chronic*, lasting more than 6 months. The problem behaviors interfere with their academic achievement and with their social relationships at school, at home, and in the community (Jensen, 2005). However, students with EBD exhibit a wide range of behavior patterns that require different interventions.

CLASSIFICATION OF STUDENTS WITH EBD

Classifying students with EBD is a challenge because most behavior problems co-occur with other problems and disabilities. However, students with EBD often exhibit behaviors that are related in some way or are part of a syndrome. In an effort to group related behaviors and help distinguish the behavioral patterns or types of EBD, two classification systems are generally used: psychiatric and dimensional.

Psychiatric Classification

The most widely used psychiatric classification system is the one developed by the American Psychiatric Association (2000) published in the *Diagnostic and Statistical Manual of Mental Disorders, 4th ed. rev. (DSM–IV–TR)*. Conditions from the *DSM–IV–TR* that commonly result in classification for EBD include (a) anxiety disorder, (b) mood disorder, (c) oppositional defiant disorder, (d) conduct disorder, and (e) schizophrenia (Turnbull, Turnbull, Shank, & Smith, 2004). The *DSM–IV–TR* includes descriptions of symptoms for each of these categories of disorders that may help in diagnosis. These psychiatric categories, however, are not aligned with the criteria for special education and related services under IDEA. Thus, a psychiatric diagnosis does not necessarily mean that a child qualifies for special education.

Dimensional Classification

Educators generally rely on a dimensional system, such as the Child Behavior Checklist (CBCL) developed by Achenbach and Edelbrock (Achenbach & Edelbrock, 1991) that broadly groups behaviors into two dimensions, externalizing (acting out) and internalizing (withdrawal) (Nelson, Rutherford, & Wolford, 1996). Externalizing behaviors are those that are overt and appear to be directed toward others or the environment. These behaviors are also referred to as "undercontrolled" and characterized by aggressiveness, noncompliance, and outbursts such as temper tantrums. Externalizing behaviors are disruptive and usually disturb the classroom routine. These are the youth that gain public attention because they display behaviors that cannot be ignored. Students who exhibit externalizing behaviors seem to lack self-control (Jensen, 2005).

On the other hand, internalizing behaviors are covert and self-directed. These behaviors are also referred to as "overcontrolled" and are characterized by avoidance, compulsiveness, anxiety, and depression. Youth who exhibit internalizing behavior disorders may be extremely troubled but often are overlooked by school personnel and mental health professionals because they rarely act out. For this reason they are in danger of not receiving services for their developmental deficits (Heward, 2000). However, at some point such youth may exhibit externalizing behaviors in the form of suicide or targeted violence. Sadly, suicide is the third leading cause of death among youth. In fact, the Centers for Disease Control and Prevention (CDC; Thornton, Craft, Dahlberg, Lynch, & Baer, 2000) reported the suicide rate for youth aged 15–19 increased by 11% between 1980 and 1997; during the same period, the rate for youth aged 10–14 escalated by 109%. Although rare, acts of targeted violence (e.g., multiple homicides) by youth are horrific and traumatize the communities in which they occur.

Thus, classifying EBD is difficult due to the co-occurrence of other dimensions, or types of behaviors, and the co-morbidity with other disabilities. For example, a student with EBD may be diagnosed with depression and with conduct disorder, while also having an identified learning disability. This same student, whose initial behavior problems were classified as internalizing, may also have outbursts that would be classified as externalizing. It is apparent that the psychiatric classification system may help professionals with diagnosing EBD, whereas the dimensional classification system seems most helpful to educators with intervention planning. Given the problematic definition, the ambiguity of terms, the lack of consensus on what is considered socially acceptable, and the difficultly in classifying EBD, how do we determine the prevalence of EBD in our public schools?

PREVALENCE OF EBD

Prevalence estimates (e.g., the number or percentages of individuals exhibiting a disorder at or during a given time) for EBD vary greatly. Figures from the U.S. Department of Education indicate that less than 1% (0.73%) of students in public schools was identified as having EBD during the 2002–2003 school year. This represents 8.1% of all students aged 6–21 receiving special education services, making EBD the fourth largest of the disability categories (U.S. Department of Education, 2005). However, many professionals consider EBD an underserved category as prevalence estimates range as high as 21% (Forness & Kavale, 2000; Kauffman, 2005).

CHARACTERISTICS OF STUDENTS WITH EBD

Students with EBD make up a diverse group of students who exhibit a wide range of characteristics. Nonetheless, several common characteristics of this group were summarized by Bradley and her colleagues from three national longitudinal studies supported by the Office of Special Education Programs (OSEP; Bradley, Henderson, & Monfore, 2004). They found that the majority of students identified with EBD are male with a disproportionate number African American. Compared to other students with disabilities, students with EBD are identified later; begin receiving services later; and are placed in more restrictive settings. Students with EBD also are likely to take prescribed psychiatric medication, and to receive psychological, mental health, counseling, or social work services at school. Results from these studies also found that as a group, students with EBD experience worse educational, behavioral, and social outcomes than any other disability group. Students with EBD also have the lowest postsecondary attendance and graduation rates of any disability groups (Bullis & Cheney, 1999; Kauffman, 2001).

Cognitive Characteristics

Intellectually, these students span a large range of ability, from mental retardation to gifted and talented, with most scoring in the average to above average range on IQ tests (Jensen, 2005). Despite their average intellectual ability, students with EBD often perform below their expected level in school (Nelson, Benner, Lane, & Smith, 2004). As noted previously, most emotional and behavioral disorders co-occur with other disabilities (Cullinan & Epstein, 2001). In fact, many students with EBD also meet the definition of learning disabilities (Glassberg, Hooper, & Mattison, 1999; Hunt & Marshall, 2005) and attention-deficit hyperactivity disorder (ADHD) (Gresham et al., 2001).

Academic Deficits

Many students with EBD have serious academic deficits (Coleman & Vaughn, 2000; Gunter & Denny, 1998; Lane, 2004). In fact, low academic achievement and school failure are primary characteristics exhibited by students with EBD (Coleman & Webber, 2002; Foley & Epstein, 1992; Kauffman, 2005). According to Scruggs and Mastropieri (1986), research findings support the notion that students with EBD are deficient in all areas of academic functioning and that with respect to academic performance there are few differences between students with EBD and students with learning difficulties. Moreover, in addition to high rates of academic failure and low grades, many students with EBD experience grade retention, school avoidance, and school dropout, which lead to major adjustment problems later in life (Bullock, Gable, & Melloy, 2005; Lane, 2004.) Difficulties in reading have been found to be extremely prevalent among children and youth with EBD (Coleman & Vaughn, 2000).

Unfortunately, the work of Knitzer, Steinberg, and Fleisch (1990) revealed that many classrooms of students with EBD are characterized by (a) boring repetitive academic lessons consisting primarily of worksheets; (b) irrelevant instructional programs that are not matched to students' abilities; (c) low rates of active academic responding and engagement; and (d) very little, if any, thought given to instructional planning. This may be because teachers devote so much attention to managing disruptive behavior that the questions regarding what and how students with EBD should be taught are not afforded careful consideration (Levy & Chard, 2001). In Chapters 14 through 16 we examine the crucial area of providing effective instruction to students with EBD.

Language Deficits

It is not surprising that language disorders accompany EBD because behavior is a form of communication. Before children learn language they communicate their needs and desires through their behavior (e.g., crying, throwing, spitting). Children who have not developed speech, such as children who are born deaf, often communicate using inappropriate behaviors until they learn more appropriate means of communicating (e.g., sign language). As Gunter and Denny (1998) pointed out, many teachers of students with EBD use instructional language that requires the very language skills in which their students are deficient. For example, teachers often use figurative speech and multiple-meaning words, elements of pragmatic language that many students with EBD have difficulty interpreting.

Receptive and expressive language disorders also are common among students with EBD (Benner, Nelson, & Epstein, 2002), as are pragmatic language disorders (i.e., difficulties using language and nonverbal communication in social situations) (Landrum, Tankersley, & Kauffman, 2003). This may be one explanation for the inability of many students with EBD to cope with the behavioral demands and expectations in the school setting. Thus, it is imperative for teachers to assess the language difficulties of their students, to use appropriate instructional language, and to discover the communicative intent of the students' behaviors to teach appropriate alternative forms of communicating.

School Discipline Infractions

Other school problems result from the behavior of students with EBD and school discipline policies. Recent incidents of school violence and a focus on high-stakes accountability have led many schools to develop zero tolerance policies for disruptive students (Imich, 1994; Leone, Mayer, Malmgren, & Meisel, 2000). Data from longitudinal studies indicate that three quarters of secondary students with EBD have been suspended from school and over one third have been arrested while in secondary school (Bradley et al., 2004). Unfortunately, the finding that many students are suspended multiple times demonstrates that suspension does not meet the goal of reducing the probability that students will commit or recommit infractions that lead to suspension (Raffaele-Mendez, Knoff, & Ferron, 2002).

Social Skill Deficits

Students with EBD also experience difficulties with social relationships. They are often rejected by classmates and by adults (Gresham & MacMillan, 1997; Walker, 1995; Walker, Colvin, & Ramsey, 1995). Researchers have studied teacher interactions with students with EBD and results demonstrate that the most consistent and predictable interactions between teachers and students occurred around events of student inappropriate behavior rather than appropriate behavior (Wehby, Lane, & Falk, 2003). Overall, teachers of students with EBD provided significantly more reprimands than praise and provided infrequent instruction, estimated at less than 30% of teacher–student interactions (Shores & Wehby, 1999; Van Aker, Grant, & Henry 1996; Wehby, Symons, Canale, & Go, 1998). These researchers suggest that ineffective instruction by teachers followed by inappropriate behavior by students may set up a negative reinforcement cycle in which both teachers and students engage in escaping behaviors. Consequently, both teachers and students may unconsciously agree to leave each other alone, an arrangement termed the "curriculum of non-instruction" (Gunter, Denny, Jack, Shores, & Nelson, 1993).

Problem Behavior

Fraser (1996) noted that family processes may shape students' aggressive behaviors in interpersonal relationships, which in turn lead to social rejection by peers at school. Young children at risk for EBD begin to use antisocial and aggressive behaviors with their peers as early as preschool, and an aggression-rejection pattern develops that maintains and supports the continuation of their antisocial behavior (Farmer & Cadwallader, 2000). Conroy and Brown (2004), in their discussion of the research on behavior problems in early childhood, cited research involving emerging problem behaviors of 1- and 2-year-old children. They pointed out that over half of these children continued to show maladaptive behaviors 1 to 2 years later. Without effective interventions, these children who lack social and emotional competence in early childhood continue to exhibit problems throughout their school career, leading to chronic disabling conditions in adulthood.

Wehby and his colleagues observed the behaviors of first-grade students rated as high and low risk for aggression (Wehby, Dodge, & Valente, 1993). They found that the high-risk students spent more time alone during unstructured time, whereas low-risk students interacted with peers. Peers are important as sources of social learning and behavioral development, especially during adolescence. Unfortunately, many students with EBD have not developed social competence. The social pattern for students with EBD may begin with a tendency to engage in conflict with peers, followed by frequent rejection by peers. Students with EBD then gravitate toward deviant peers. This development of a negative social pattern for students with EBD implies continuing problems with relationships and maladjustment throughout life. For this reason, Kauffman (2005) stated that teachers need to include the peer culture in addressing behavioral interventions for students with EBD.

At times, some students with EBD may become physically aggressive toward others or themselves. They may engage in behaviors that are self-injurious, assaultive, violent, or that cause serious property damage. These behaviors usually require interventions beyond the instructional and behavioral interventions used for most students with EBD. In such cases, teachers and individualized education program (IEP) teams must work together to develop crisis prevention and management programs (Gargiulo, 2006). A sample crisis emergency plan form can be found on the Web site of the Center for Effective Collaboration and Practice at http://cecp.air.org/fba/ problembehavior3/appendixd.htm. For the safety of all concerned, it is imperative that teachers know the district and state regulations and guidelines regarding interventions that may be used in response to dangerous behaviors. In order to better understand these characteristics and other issues facing us today, it may help to look back at the evolution of the field of EBD.

HISTORY AND DEVELOPMENT OF THE FIELD

Teachers have faced the problem of students' disturbing behavior throughout history. However, students with EBD were typically segregated from public schools and ostracized by society. Students with EBD have been included in public schools for less than six decades (Whelan & Kauffman, 1999). During the 18th century religious beliefs and superstition dominated the attitudes toward persons with disabilities. Emotional or behavioral disorders were considered to be caused by demon possession and children and youth exhibiting deviant behaviors were neglected, abused, and punished as adults under the law (Kauffman, 2005). The first half of the 19th century was characterized by a movement toward moral treatment for individuals with EBD and mental retardation. Many youth described as deviant or troubled were housed in asylums or institutions for the feebleminded or insane. It wasn't until 1886 that EBD was distinctly separated from mental retardation (Gargiulo, 2006). The focus appeared to shift in the later half of the century from treatment to the development of theories and the diagnosis of the psychological disturbances in children and youth (Kauffman, 2001).

Little progress was made toward recognizing and treating individuals with EBD until the 20th century. In 1909 the National Committee for Mental Hygiene was established by Clifford Beers, Adolph Meyer, and William James. This began what became known as the mental hygiene movement. Several clinics were established in the United States, with treatment centered on Freudian psychodynamic methods. William Healy founded the Juvenile Psychopathic Institute in Chicago in 1909 and studied the psychological and sociological conditions of delinquents. The growing concern for children's mental and physical health resulted in the creation of the U.S. Children's Bureau in 1912. Professional organizations such as the Council for Exceptional Children (CEC), founded in 1922, and the American Orthopsychiatric Association (AOA), founded in 1924, did much to promote the education and treatment of children and youth with EBD. Although the CEC was instrumental in lobbying for federal funding and legislation for all children with disabilities, the AOA promoted research and development of therapies and education for children and youth with EBD (Bullock & Mendez, 1999).

The 1930s saw the growth of child psychiatry as a field with the opening of psychiatric hospitals, clinics, and schools, and the first textbook on child psychiatry was published by Leo Kanner. Bruno Bettleheim was instrumental in the 1940s with his psychoanalytical method. In 1946 New York City established 600 schools specifically to educate students described as maladjusted and disturbed (Kauffman, 2001). Before 1950 a classification system of behavioral disorders had been devised, but programs and intervention strategies were not evident until after 1950.

By the 1950s education of students with EBD had become a distinct field of specialization. The first private day school for students with EBD in the United States, the League School, was founded by Carl Fenichel. The first book on teaching students with EBD, by Leonard Kornberg, was published in 1955. By this time researchers were working on systematic procedures to identify students with EBD (Kauffman, 2001).

During the 1960s the field of EBD grew considerably. In 1963 Congress passed P.L. 88-164, which provided funding for teacher preparation for students with EBD. In 1964 a new division of CEC, the Council for Children with Behavioral Disorders, was formed (Bullock & Mendez, 1999). By the end of the 20th century the majority of students identified with EBD were being educated in public school special education classrooms. Treatment for EBD focused on education, prevention, and early identification. By this time, several distinct conceptual models representing theoretical approaches and strategies for students with EBD had emerged. Many of these conceptual models remain prominent in special education programs today and teachers use a variety of models in working with students with EBD.

CONCEPTUAL MODELS

A number of theoretical or conceptual models developed over the years to explain why behavioral disorders exist. These conceptual models serve a number of purposes including (a) guiding assessment and evaluation, (b) providing methods by which teachers can intervene with students, and (c) allowing professionals to communicate with each other. Whereas conceptual models may help in developing interventions, the fact that these conceptual models exist may stem more from our desire to understand the cause or causes of EBD. Next we briefly explain the most common of these models.

Psychodynamic

This model is based on a psychoanalytic approach influenced by Sigmund Freud. The belief is that emotional and behavioral problems are caused by pathological imbalances in mental states. Treatment involves individual psychotherapy and a permissive classroom environment with an accepting teacher. Psychodynamic theory is based on the assumption that the unconscious motivation for behavior must be understood before the problems can be resolved (Kauffman, 2005).

Psychoeducational

Similar to the psychodynamic model, this approach also includes a psychotherapy component to uncover underlying internal conflicts. However, this model also includes an analysis of behavior within the context in which it occurs. The Life Space Interview is a treatment used in this model, whereby a teacher conducts an interview with a student who has just had a behavioral outburst. The interview questions are geared to help the student understand what triggered the problem and to plan for the future to prevent the problem from occurring again. The focus of the psychoeducational model is on helping students acquire self-control by reflecting on past behavior and planning future behavior (Kauffman, 2005).

Ecological

The ecological approach considers the student's behavior in context with the environment (home, school, community). Problems are caused by an imbalance or failure to match the person and the environment. Treatment involves altering the environments as well as the student's behavior and transactions within the environments. An example of this model is Project Re-ED, a residential program established by Nicholas Hobbs in the 1960s in which children are taught and reinforced for appropriate behaviors. Re-ED staff also work closely with significant individuals in the social system to achieve a better fit between the child and his or her social milieu (Gargiulo, 2006).

Humanistic

This model is person-centered, stressing individual freedom, self-direction, self-fulfillment, and self-evaluation. The view of abnormal behavior is the result of societal pressures to conform to behaviors that clash with a person's self-actualization needs. The treatment approach is one of guidance within a loving and supportive environment, wherein the student is encouraged to solve his or her own problems (Kauffman, 2005).

Biophysical

The belief underlying the biophysical model is that physiology directs how a person behaves. These physiological influences, which include genetic, biochemical, and temperament factors, can cause emotional or behavioral disorders. Thus the biophysical view represents a medical orientation in which the problem lies within a student. A basic tenet of this mode, therefore, is that it is extremely important to recognize the underlying biological cause of the problem behavior (Kauffman, 2005). Treatment is often conducted primarily by medical personnel and often includes psychopharmacology or drug treatment and the teacher's role is to monitor and observe student behavior.

Behavioral

Proponents of the behavioral model posit that behavior is a function of environmental events. Because behavior exists in a social context, in order to successfully change behavior, one must understand and change the context.

Problem behaviors are seen as inappropriate learned responses to the environment that are maintained and reinforced. Treatment is based on precise behavioral targeting—teaching appropriate behaviors, then controlling the environmental antecedents—and consequences (Bradley et al., 2004). The behavioral model gave rise to the methodology of applied behavior analysis (ABA), which includes strategies such as differential reinforcement, chaining, modeling, shaping, token economies, time-out, and response cost (Nelson, Scott, & Polsgrove, 1999). (For further explanation of the behavioral model, see Chapter 4.)

Cognitive

Cognitive psychologists believe that behavior is influenced by what we think (i.e., cognitions). Adherents of cognitive psychology believe the main determinants of human behavior are within the individual. Proponents of this model believe that EBD arises from flawed cognitions and that by directly altering the flawed thoughts, perceptions, beliefs, and attributions, individuals change their emotional and behavioral responses. (See Chapter 6 for further explanation of the cognitive and cognitive-behavioral model.)

CAUSAL AND RISK FACTORS

A major challenge in the field of EBD is identifying and understanding cause. On the one hand, identifying cause can lead to the development of effective intervention and prevention strategies, whereas on the other hand, identifying cause can lead to attributing blame. The issue of responsibility for one's actions remains controversial regarding students at risk for and identified as having EBD, especially when the cause is not clearly related to biological factors, such as with students who are diagnosed with schizophrenia or Tourette's syndrome. Overall, popular opinion seems to attribute the behavior of students with EBD as willful and deserving of punishment. This is evidenced by the overrepresentation of youth identified as having EBD in juvenile corrections. Teachers and school personnel have the difficult task of carefully weighing the evidence to determine which students have the ability to control their actions and which students truly have a disability or EBD.

Although various factors have been suggested as possible causes of EBD, research has not shown any specific factors to be the direct cause. However, several *risk factors* have been identified that seem to coincide with EBD. Risk factors are described as conditions or situations that are empirically related to particular outcomes (Reddy et al., 2001).

Risk factors that are related to EBD are grouped into two major categories: internal or biological, involving individual characteristics; and external, involving family, school, community, and peer group characteristics. Risk factors also exert different effects at different stages of development. Just as individuals develop through complex interactions with their environments, risk factors operate in combinations, and the more risk factors to which a youth is exposed, the greater the likelihood he or she will exhibit EBD.

Internal Risk Factors

Internal risk factors are described as within the self, and can be further divided into physiological and psychological characteristics. Physiological characteristics may involve organic factors, as in dysfunctions of the central nervous system; genetic factors, such schizophrenia; and syndromes, such as Tourette's (Hunt & Marshall, 2005).

Psychological characteristics include cognitive deficits, hyperactivity, concentration problems, restlessness, risk taking, aggressiveness, early involvement in antisocial behavior, and beliefs and attitudes favoring deviancy. Limited intelligence also has been associated with poor problem-solving skills, poor social skills, and risk for behavioral deviation (Calhoun, Glaser, & Bartolomucci, 2001). Other cognitive deficits, such as low levels of abstract and moral reasoning and inappropriate interpretation of others' behaviors, have been found to correlate with problem behaviors in youth (Kashani, Jones, Bumby, & Thomas, 1999). In addition, many investigators agree that early involvement in antisocial activity has been a stable and strong predictor of later antisocial behavior (Arllen, Gable, & Hendrickson, 1994; Hawkins et al., 2000; Laub & Lauritsen, 1998; Reilly, 1999; Walker, Stieber, Ramsey, & O'Neill, 1991). Early exposure to patterns of inappropriate and antisocial behavior seems to act like a virus, lowering the immune system and making the person vulnerable to a host of other negative behavior patterns (Sprague & Walker, 2000).

External Risk Factors

External risk factors are variables present in the environment that create contexts for daily living, and can be divided into four domains: the home or family environment, the school setting, the neighborhood or larger community environment, and the persons with whom children associate (e.g., peer groups).

Family Risk Factors Several conditions in the home can create risk factors for EBD in children and youth. These factors include (a) parental criminality, (b) harsh and ineffective parental discipline, (c) lack of parental involvement, (d) family conflict, (e) child abuse and/or neglect, and (f) rejection by parents (Patterson, Forgatch, & Stoolmiller, 1998; Walker et al., 1991). The impact of these situations on a child's social and behavioral learning is obvious. Children who are exposed to patterns of coercive interactions at home are likely to repeat them in school, increasing their risk for school failure and exclusion (Sprague & Walker, 2000). A strong association also exists between poverty and behavior problems. In fact, low socioeconomic status may be the single most common denominator for risk of behavioral deviation (Scott & Nelson, 1999a; Walker & Sprague, 1999a). Other risk factors for children disadvantaged by poverty may include race (particularly Black and Hispanic), and family structure (female-headed households).

School Risk Factors Certain factors in the school may be considered risk factors for EBD. In fact, some inappropriate social behaviors may be learned or reinforced at school while appropriate behaviors are ignored. For example, when teachers or school personnel take a "hands-off" approach and ignore bullying and harassment, they inadvertently condone such behaviors (Furlong & Morrison, 2000). The absence of clear rules and school policies governing student behavior, and few allowances for individual differences may also contribute to EBD. Additionally, the range of behaviors school personnel consider acceptable for students is narrow and often unknowingly biased (Hunt & Marshall, 2005). Zero tolerance policies and an authoritarian discipline style that engages staff in power struggles also may pose risks for EBD (Skiba & Peterson, 2000). Classroom practices such as teachers' lack of instructional interactions and low rates of praise, along with few opportunities for students with EBD to correctly respond, negatively affect academic and behavioral performance of students (Gunter & Denny, 1998; Sutherland & Wehby, 2001b).

Community Risk Factors. Community factors that put youth at risk for EBD include living in high-poverty neighborhoods with high levels of disorganization (e.g., crime, drug selling, gangs, and poor housing). Communities with a high turnover of residents, with few adults to supervise or monitor children's and teenagers' behavior, also pose risks for the development of EBD (Flannery, 1997). Limited opportunities for youth recreation or employment, the availability of firearms, and violence in the neighborhood are other risk factors that have been associated with the community (Loeber & Farrington, 2000).

Peer–Related Risk Factors Youth involvement with peers who exhibit EBD poses a risk factor. Adolescents who are unpopular with prosocial or conventional peers, and thus rejected by them, may find acceptance only in antisocial or delinquent peer groups. In fact, Farmer and Cadwallader (2000) found that preschool children who exhibit antisocial behavior begin to interact with their peers in ways that maintain and support the continuation of their antisocial behavior. In effect, children who associate with deviant peer groups go through a process of deviancy training in which their peers teach them deviant norms and values. These relationships become stronger and more reinforcing over the years and the antisocial patterns and beliefs become more resistant to change.

Risk factors do not occur in isolation; rather, they are multifaceted, interrelated, and change over time. There is a constant and progressive interplay between the individual (internal risks) and his or her environment, such as family, school, community, and peers (external risks) (Hanson & Carta, 1995). The larger the number of risk factors to which a child is exposed, the greater the likelihood that he or she will engage in antisocial behavior (Hawkins et al., 2000). In addition, the earlier the onset of problem behaviors, the more resistant they are to intervention.

Understanding risk factors and the complex interplay between various factors during one's life is one step that may facilitate identifying which students have EBD.

INTERVENTIONS

The identification and understanding of risk factors can lead to the development of more effective intervention and prevention strategies. Moreover, systematic prevention is more efficient and effective than intervening after the problem is well developed. No single strategy works with all students; therefore, teachers need to be proficient in both proactive and pre-corrective strategies (antecedents) and reactive or corrective strategies (consequences) in addressing academic and nonacademic needs of their students. In this section we discuss both proactive and reactive interventions. First we address schoolwide and classwide comprehensive interventions (i.e., positive behavioral support); then we discuss more specific academic, behavioral, and social interventions.

Positive Behavioral Support

A three-tiered model that incorporates strategies of prevention and intervention at graduated levels of intensity has shown preliminary success in dealing with problem behavior (Horner, Todd, Lewis-Palmer, Irvin, & Boland, 2004). This model is based on a proactive framework developed by the Institute of Medicine in response to

public health epidemics (Greenberg, Domitrovich, & Bumbarger, 1999; Leone et al., 2000). The three-tiered model of prevention and intervention provides an appropriate context for applying a wide range of strategies across multiple life domains to reduce risks and increase protective factors. The method used in schools to minimize problem behaviors and foster positive, appropriate behaviors is called positive behavioral support (PBS). It is described in terms of primary, secondary, and tertiary strategies (Fitzsimmons, 1998; Guetzloe, 1999; Sprague & Walker, 2000; Walker et al., 1995). (See chapter 10 for more information on schoolwide positive behavioral support.)

Primary strategies are applied through universal interventions and the focus is to prevent initial occurrences of a problem. Primary prevention programs may be more readily accepted and adopted than other intervention approaches because they are positive, proactive, and their potential for stigmatizing participants is minimal (Greenberg et al., 1999). Primary prevention strategies are the foundation of effective prevention, because protective factors can be best learned, performed, and maintained when they are ingrained in youths' daily routines. For example, teaching basic literacy, problem-solving, social skills and rules to all students encourages academic success and discourages the development of problem behaviors. Primary strategies that target change in the social context appear to be more effective than those that attempt to change individual attitudes, skills, and behaviors alone (Scott & Nelson, 1999a; Sprague, Sugai, & Walker, 1998; Todd, Horner, Sugai, & Sprauge, 1999). An example of a primary prevention strategy that addresses problem behavior may be a schoolwide system of positive student discipline that is applied across all individuals through the efforts of all school staff, such as a schoolwide bullying prevention program (Olweus, Limber, & Mihalic, 1998). Successful prevention programs must demonstrate stability and they must be extensive. That is, such programs should include many components and target the general youth population as well as those at risk for antisocial behavior (Mendel, 2000).

Secondary strategies are applied through targeted interventions and include efforts geared to specific problems or individuals for which primary prevention strategies have not been effective. This selected group is at a heightened risk of problem behavior, and strategies are aimed at preventing reoccurrences of such undesired behavior. Secondary prevention strategies are aimed at providing extra protection for those individuals who are exposed to multiple risk factors for EBD (Guetzloe, 1999). Examples of secondary or targeted prevention activities may include providing support to at-risk children and youth through a mentoring program and providing social skills instruction to small groups of students.

Tertiary strategies are applied through intensive interventions and include efforts to address those individuals for whom secondary prevention strategies have not been effective. Tertiary prevention and intervention techniques usually are applied to a problem that is already out of control (Yell & Rozalski, 2000), and the goal is rehabilitation and preventing the condition from overwhelming the person and his or her environment. Youth who exhibit serious problems that constitute a chronic condition are candidates for strategies at this level. An example of tertiary prevention is a wraparound plan coordinated by the school for a student who also is being served by the juvenile justice system. This plan could involve services across school, home, and community life domains (Eber, Nelson, & Miles, 1997). Families may receive such support as training on behavior management skills as well as how to meet their own continuing needs. (See Chapter 10 for a more thorough explanation of school-wide PBS.)

Academic Interventions

Poor academic performance is a characteristic of students with EBD, and researchers have concluded that their academic achievement scores seem to worsen over time (Gable, Hendrickson, Tonelson, & Van Aker, 2002; Gunter & Denny, 1998; Nelson et al., 2004). Yet until fairly recently, special educators focused primarily on behavioral interventions for students' problem behavior often to exclusion of academic instruction. In fact, most behavior management practices emphasized the systematic application of consequences after the behavior rather than the antecedents or environmental settings present before the behavior (Kerr & Nelson, 2006). We now realize that quality educational instruction (i.e., antecedents) may be the most desirable and economical prevention and intervention strategy for EBD (Gable et al., 2002).

Currently there is little information in the literature on effective academic interventions for students with EBD (Gargiulo, 2006; Wehby, Lane, and Falk, 2003). However, we do know that we must examine the specific academic problems of students with EBD while paying attention to the behavioral characteristics that may further inhibit their school performance. Students with EBD typically have problems with behaviors related to academic engagement, such as attending to academic tasks, completing independent assignments, and participating in class activities. Academic interventions for students

with EBD should incorporate modifications and adaptations to the curriculum that target learning strategies; attention to instruction and task engagement; retention of information; and successful application of knowledge in appropriate contexts (Gunter, Denny, Kenton, & Venn, 2000; Kauffman, 2005).

Academic interventions for students with EBD can be divided into two broad areas: academic curriculum and instructional delivery (Gargiulo, 2006). Academic curriculum encompasses the content to be learned, including specific programs and materials. Instructional delivery includes the strategies used to facilitate learning of the content. Teachers must be aware that students often display frustration in acting-out or withdrawal behaviors when the curriculum and the instructional delivery styles do not match their abilities and needs. This mismatch may perpetrate a failure cycle in which academic frustrations foster behavior problems, resulting in disciplinary practices (e.g., time-out, suspension) that remove the student from academic instruction. The student falls further behind academically and receives fewer opportunities to learn appropriate behaviors. This pattern is repeated and repeated, eventually becoming a chronic situation in which the student falls hopelessly behind academically and exhibits behavior problems that may lead to delinquency and possible incarceration (Christle, Nelson, & Jolivette, 2004). (See Chapters 14, through 16 for an in-depth examination of teaching and students with EBD.)

Academic Curriculum Whereas students with EBD must have access to the general education curriculum to the maximum extent possible, modifications and supports may be necessary to allow access. Teachers must ensure that the content is at the correct level of difficulty for their students—not too easy, yet not too difficult. For example, the curriculum for a high school student with EBD who reads at a fourth-grade level may need to be modified to match her reading ability level. However, we would not recommend using fourth-grade materials as these would not match her interests and experiences. Conversely, a fourth-grade student who reads at a high school level would become bored if asked to use fourth-grade materials. Yet we must take care to match the curriculum materials with her interests and experiences. Curriculum-based measurement (CBM) is an effective means to assess students' performance levels based on the curriculum in which students are working (Deno, 1998; Scheuermann, 1998).

Teachers also may need to modify the number of items or length of material that a student is expected to complete, or substitute part or all of the curriculum for a more functional or appropriate curriculum (Gunter et al., 2000). For example, many students with EBD need focused instruction in school survival skills (e.g., appropriately requesting assistance).

Instructional Delivery Instructional delivery must address teacher–student instructional interactions. As Wehby and his colleagues (1998) discovered, the rates of teacher–student instructional interactions in classrooms for students with EBD are very low. Teachers must monitor their instructional interactions to provide high levels of academic engagement for their students. Indeed, educational research has shown that the academic engagement rate, or the time students spend engaged in learning, is positively related to academic achievement (Greenwood, 1991). Thus, teachers should rely on evidence-based instructional methods that increase students' academic engaged time such as direct instruction (Hunt & Marshall, 2005; Landrum et al., 2003). The elements of direct instruction—including structure, sequencing, pacing, frequent corrective feedback, and practice of newly acquired skills—promote student academic engagement, which leads to increased academic achievement (Landrum et al., 2003).

Another means of increasing task engagement, which also has shown increased academic outcomes and decreased inappropriate and disruptive behaviors for students with EBD, is increased opportunities to respond (Lewis, Hudson, Richter, & Johnson, 2004; Sutherland & Wehby, 2001b). Several strategies have been successful in increasing active student responding and academic success, such as choral responding (i.e., all students verbally respond simultaneously), and response cards (i.e., all students use cards or boards to respond by holding them up for the teacher to see) (Heward, 2000). Christle and Schuster (2003) demonstrated increased opportunities to respond, increased time-on-task, and increased academic achievement using response cards in a fourth-grade classroom. Classwide peer tutoring, in which students respond in a gamelike format and peers provide correction or reinforcement, is another method that has shown positive results for increasing students' opportunities to respond and academic engagement (Greenwood, Horton, & Utley, 2002).

Other effective instructional strategies include advanced preparation and planning; rapid pacing; smooth transitioning; providing interesting, hand-on activities; and offering choices. Teaching students how to learn through strategy instruction (e.g., organizational skills, study skills, mnemonics) and how to self-monitor academic behaviors and progress also are considered effective instructional practices (Landrum et al., 2003). The importance of teacher behaviors in relation to student academic outcomes cannot be understated. Researchers have demonstrated that when teachers changed their behavior and used effective instructional procedures, students' desirable behaviors increased and undesirable behaviors decreased (Gunter & Denny, 1998; Gunter et al., 2000).

Whereas many of the behavioral problems in classrooms may be due to the mismatch of students' ability with curriculum or ineffective instructional delivery, other problem behaviors may be due to social skills deficits. Thus, interventions for students with EBD need to include behavioral and social skills development as well as academics if they are to achieve success in school.

Behavioral Interventions

Although there are a myriad of complex and unpredictable problem behaviors students with EBD exhibit, we can broadly group them as either behavioral excesses or deficits. That is, students may exhibit too many inappropriate behaviors, not enough appropriate behaviors, or a combination of both. Thus, behavioral interventions for students with EBD consist of behavior enhancement or reduction interventions. Behavioral interventions can be applied either prior to the behavior (i.e., as an antecedent) or after the behavior (i.e., as a consequence).

Throughout the discussion on behavioral interventions, teachers should keep in mind the importance of assessment. That is, assessment should be done prior to any intervention to identify factors associated with the occurrence and nonoccurrence of specific behaviors. Functional behavioral assessment (FBA) looks beyond the student and the target behavior to other significant, social, cognitive, and/or environmental factors that may explain the function or purpose behind student behavior (Ryan, Halsey, & Matthews, 2003; Walker & Sprague, 1999a). Researchers have successfully promoted desirable behavior of students with EBD using FBA procedures (Kern, Delaney, Clarke, Dunlap, & Childs, 2001; Ryan et al., 2003). Although the FBA process may vary, according to O'Neill et al. (1997) an FBA should achieve five outcomes: (a) an operational definition(s) of the problem behavior(s); (b) a description of the setting events and antecedents (e.g., times, places, activities) that predict the occurrence and nonoccurrence of the problem behaviors; (c) a description of the consequences responsible for the problem behavior; (d) verification of the predictors and consequences through direct observation; and (e) a summary hypothesis statement that serves as the basis for designing the positive behavior support plan.

Using FBA procedures helps combine contextual and individual factors in developing assessment-based interventions, such as behavior intervention plans (BIPs). A BIP is a proactive plan that outlines steps to teach a replacement behavior that matches the function of the target behavior. It should describe when and how the intervention will be used. O'Neill et al. (1997) suggested that behavior support plans (a) be based on the functional assessment data; (b) be consistent with fundamental principles of behavior; (c) be a good contextual fit with the values, skills, and resources of all people in the setting; (d) include an operational definition of the behavior; (e) include summary statements resulting from the FBA; (f) be consistently implemented as planned; and (g) include a monitoring and evaluation plan. Moreover, ongoing formative assessment should be an integral part of any intervention plan to monitor the effectiveness of the intervention and the student's progress, whether using behavior enhancement, reduction, or a combination of both interventions. (Chapters 4, 5, and 13 further discuss applied behavior analysis, functional behavioral assessment, and behavioral interventions.)

Behavior Enhancement Interventions Interventions to increase appropriate behaviors, such as compliance with teacher directions, can be applied as antecedents or as consequences. Examples of successful antecedent interventions for increasing student compliance include precision requests and behavioral momentum strategies. Precision requests are specific teacher directions that include predictability, specific consequences for compliance and noncompliance, and an appropriate amount of time for the student to comply (De Martini-Scully, Bray, & Kehle, 2000; Landrum et al., 2003). For example, a teacher first explains and posts the classroom rules along with consequences for compliance and noncompliance. One rule may be that students come into the room and sit in their assigned seats when the bell rings. If a student fails to comply, the teacher makes eye contact with the student and, using a quiet and unemotional tone of voice says, "Roberta, please sit down in your chair." If the student does not comply within 5 seconds the teacher again makes eye contact and, using a quiet and unemotional tone of voice says, "Roberta, you need to sit down in your chair to earn a token for free time." Behavioral momentum describes a hierarchy of teacher directions whereby the teacher delivers directions that have a high probability of student compliance and then continues with directions that have a lower probability of student compliance (Belfiore, Lee, Scheeler, & Klein, 2002; Landrum et al., 2003). For example, if given a choice, a student chooses to do single-digit division problems rather than two-digit division problems. In order to encourage compliance with practicing two-digit problems the teacher gives three single-digit problems before each two-digit problem. The advantage of antecedent interventions (e.g., precision requests and behavioral momentum strategies) over consequence-based interventions is that teachers do not need to wait and observe students and then deliver consequences. Instead, they can use proactive teaching measures to increase the probability of compliance (Belfiore et al., 2002; Gable et al., 2002).

Consequence interventions involve providing a contingent consequence that maintains or strengthens a behavior, a principle known as reinforcement. For example, a student named Curtis is often late getting to class. The next time he arrives on time the teacher acknowledges his on-time behavior by saying, "Curtis, thank you for getting to class on time." Curtis arrives on time more frequently; thus the teacher's praise functioned as positive reinforcement for Curtis. The effectiveness of contingent, positive teacher attention on the behavior of students with EBD is well documented, yet this easy-to-implement technique is rarely used by teachers (Wehby et al., 1998). Perhaps many teachers fail to realize that to effectively change students' behaviors they also must change their own behaviors. Many teachers are unaware of the powerfully reinforcing value of simple behaviors such as eye contact, smiles, kind words, physical proximity, and social interaction (Maag, 2001). The techniques based on positive reinforcement, such as applications of token economies, behavioral contracts, and group-oriented contingencies, will be discussed in detail in Chapter 13. Maag offers five easy-to-implement recommendations for using positive reinforcement (Maag, 2001):

1. *Catch Students Being Good:* Praising students occasionally can maintain high rates of students' appropriate behaviors.

2. *Think Small:* Set small goals and do not expect students with EBD to behave better than students without disabilities.

3. *Have a Group Management Plan:* It is easier to manage specific students with challenging behaviors when the entire class is well behaved.

4. *Prevent Behavior Problems:* Establish classroom rules, provide engaging academics, seat students with EBD next to well-behaved students, constantly monitor students, and provide high levels of praise and reinforcement.

5. *Use Peer Influence Favorably:* Students with EBD often misbehave to get peer attention. Teachers may use group management plans and elicit peers to reinforce appropriate behaviors.

Behavior Reduction Interventions Behavior reduction interventions can be grouped into four levels of intrusiveness from least to most intrusive (Alberto & Troutman, 2006). Level I includes strategies based on differential reinforcement. For example, differential reinforcement of other behavior (DRO) is a strategy in which a teacher provides reinforcement to a student who has not exhibited the problem behavior for a specified period. Level II includes strategies for withholding a reinforcement that seems to be maintaining the problem behavior. Teacher and peer attention are often highly reinforcing for students. For instance, when Joey makes fartlike noises in class his peers giggle and the teacher calls his name. When the teacher and peers ignore Joey's noises he stops making them. They consistently withheld the reinforcement maintaining the behavior and the problem behavior was extinguished. Level III involves the removal of desired stimuli or reinforcement as in response cost and time-out. Teachers often use response-cost strategies within token economies, in which students may earn tokens for desired behavior and lose them for undesired behavior. Time-out procedures have become increasingly popular with both general and special education teachers. However, the basic principles of time-out are frequently misunderstood and the procedures implemented improperly. Most notably, teachers often assume that their classroom is reinforcing for the students. If this is not the case for a student then time-out from the classroom will not be effective. Level IV requires the presentation of aversive stimuli, such as a verbal reprimand or a physical spanking. Levels III and IV are most often described as punishment.

Punishment is viewed by this society as a highly effective means to control its members, yet it is grossly misunderstood by most people. For example, many believe that spanking or paddling a student constitutes punishment, and in schools, spanking and paddling are often referred to as corporal punishment. However, if a student is paddled for shouting in the cafeteria and her shouting in the cafeteria continues and even increases in frequency, the paddling did not serve as punishment but rather as reinforcement. On the other hand, if a student is paddled for shouting in the cafeteria and her shouting in the cafeteria stops or decreases in frequency, the paddling served as punishment for the student. Remember that in order for a consequence to be a punishment it must result in the decrease of the behavior it follows.

In an educational system that is based on a punishment mentality, teachers of students with EBD need to be acutely familiar with the issues surrounding punishment. Although punishment may be effective for most students in public schools, it is ineffective for about 5% of students who engage in the most challenging behaviors (Maag, 2001). It is important to remember that teacher attention or adult attention is a powerful reinforcer—even if it is negative. This is especially the case for students with EBD who typically receive very little positive attention (Maag, 2001). Behavior reductive procedures such as punishment may be popular because they often can produce quick results; however, the results are often temporary, and they do not teach appropriate behavior. Punishment should be the last intervention considered, not the first. Teachers first must be sure they have designed and implemented an appropriate instructional program and tried Level I and Level II strategies before resorting to more intrusive Level III or Level IV strategies (Darch, Miller, & Shippen, 1998).

Teachers are responsible for knowing and following their school district policies regulating behavior reductive procedures. In addition, effective teachers are aware of the procedures for properly implementing behavioral reduction interventions, as well as the legal and ethical guidelines regarding their use. Guidelines for implementing behavior reduction interventions in a correct and legally sound manner are explained in Chapter 13. The Council for Exceptional Children provides policy guidelines for using behavioral interventions on its Web site (http://www.cec.sped.org/pp/polcreate.html).

Besides problems with academics and with inappropriate behaviors, many students with EBD fail to normally develop social competence. Several barriers exist that may hinder this development such as exposure to risk factors, problems interpreting social cues, difficulty with the pragmatic use of language, beliefs and attitudes favoring deviancy, and limited opportunities to learn and practice social skills. In spite of these barriers various social skill training methods have proven successful in enhancing social skills for students with EBD.

Social Skills Training

Gresham (1998b) defined social skills as "socially acceptable learned behaviors enabling individuals to interact effectively with others and avoid or escape socially unacceptable behaviors exhibited by others" (p. 20). The inability *to build or maintain satisfactory interpersonal relationships with peers and teachers* is a criterion included in the federal definition of emotional disturbance. Whereas most children seem to just "pick up" social skills, many children with EBD have difficulty learning those skills necessary to develop interpersonal relationships. They also have difficulty determining which social skills to use in different situations. Thus, the success of students with EBD in school, at home, and in the community depends on their acquisition of social skills.

Teachers have provided social skills training (SST) over the past several years using both formal and informal instructional methods. The research on the success of social skills training has produced mixed results, at best suggesting that SST is a weak intervention strategy (Gresham, 1998b; Landrum et al., 2003). Gresham cited several reasons for such weak results including (a) the use of invalid and insensitive measures, (b) a generic approach to teaching groups of students as opposed to focusing on specific deficits of individual students, and (c) the failure to program for functional generalization. He suggested four primary objectives for SST: (a) promote skill acquisition, (b) enhance skill performance, (c) reduce or remove competing behaviors, and (d) facilitate maintenance and generalization. Darch and colleagues (1998) described an instructional classroom management (ICM) program that involves strategically teaching all that is required to have the necessary social skills to behave appropriately in the classroom setting. Potential behavior problems are viewed as instructional problems in ICM. Social skills training involving both formal and informal methods will be covered in detail in Chapters 14 and 15. Keep in mind that SST should be an integral part of a comprehensive treatment program and not just an intervention standing on its own.

PLACEMENT OPTIONS FOR STUDENTS WITH EBD

Schools traditionally have been responsible for determining the educational placement for most students with EBD. However, school systems need to work more collaboratively with public agencies, as students with EBD present multiple needs within the community (Robertson et al., 1998). The continuum of placement options ranges from full-time in a general education classroom to segregated schools and homebound or hospital environments. Compared to all students with disabilities, students with EBD are placed in more restrictive, segregated settings. According to the 25th Annual Report to Congress, during the 2000–2001 school year 32% of students with EBD who attended public schools spent more than 60% of the day outside the regular class either in resource rooms or in self-contained classrooms, compared to 20% for all disabilities. During that same period 13.1% of students with EBD were placed in separate school facilities compared to 3% of all students with disabilities. More students with EBD were placed in residential facilities during the same period (3.7%) compared to 0.7% of all students with disabilities. Also, a greater percentage of students with

EBD were placed in either a hospital or homebound setting (1.3%) compared to 0.5% of all students with disabilities (U.S. Department of Education, 2003).

Educational placement decisions for students with EBD are usually based on the severity of the behavior. However, some researchers suggest that placement decisions for students with EBD are based more on non-relevant, subjective variables rather than on objective characteristics such as behavior, risk factors, and student and family need (Kauffman, Cullinan, & Epstein, 1987; Kauffman & Lloyd, 1995; Robertson et al., 1998). Teachers who are most familiar with the student may have little input into the placement decisions as opposed to district and school administrators. Unfortunately, the availability of placement options often takes precedence over the student's psychoeducational evaluation data. A popular placement option for students with EBD is the alternative education program.

ALTERNATIVE EDUCATION PROGRAMS

The term *alternative education* refers to any type of program that differs from traditional public schooling, ranging from unique classes offered in a general education school building to "last chance" schools—separate schools where students are sentenced as a last step before expulsion. The number of alternative education programs is growing tremendously nationwide (Hosley, 2003). It is estimated that approximately 20,000 alternative education programs and schools are currently in operation, with the majority designed for students at risk for school failure or those with challenging behavior (Lange & Sletten, 2002). However, Katsiyannis and Smith (2003) raised concerns with placing students with EBD in alternative settings due to the variability in policy and mandates regarding these programs across states, as well as the lack of monitoring and evaluation on their efficacy. It is unfortunate that we know very little about their effectiveness as few large-scale studies of alternative programs have been conducted (Tobin & Sprague, 2000).

One study on alternative education was conducted by the University of Minnesota in 2001 in which state special education directors across the country were interviewed regarding alternative schools. Camilla Lehr (2004) from the National Center on Secondary Education and Transition summarized the findings of these interviews. She outlined three major issues that were apparent from these interviews, including (a) there are limited data on the number of students served, especially since most states do not collect data on students with disabilities attending alternative schools; (b) there is a perception that students with disabilities are being pushed out of traditional public schools into alternative schools because of strict district and school policies (c) there are serious concerns about the quality of special education services available for students with disabilities in alternative schools.

The state of Kentucky is developing and testing an Alternative Education Program Evaluation Instrument. Preliminary results from 2001 to 2002 and 2002 to 2003 show that alternative education programs in Kentucky rated highest in learning environment, leadership, and planning. On the other hand, assessment, curriculum, and instruction received the lowest ratings (Swarts, 2003–2004).

Although there is a lack of research on the effectiveness of current alternative education programs, we do have information on effective school-based interventions for students with EBD (Tobin & Sprague, 2000). Table 1-1 lists Tobin and Sprague's recommended practices for alternative education strategies for students who are at risk for or have EBD. Teachers and school personnel who consider referring students with EBD to alternative programs should evaluate the intended program based on these strategies. They also should ask questions regarding the program's entry criteria, teacher qualifications, and the supports available to address students' IEP provisions (Katsiyannis & Smith, 2003).

Students with EBD are often placed in alternative education settings as a last chance before expulsion for infractions of school rules. When alternative education programs fail to address the complex mental health needs and the behavioral and academic deficits of students with EBD, these students often are "dumped" into the juvenile justice system (Burns et al., 2003).

JUVENILE JUSTICE

Indeed, when we look at the prevalence of disabilities in the juvenile justice system, it is clear that this has become the default system for youth who have reading, writing, or socializing problems, as well as those with mental health problems, and those who are forced out or drop out of school (Nelson, 2000). Compared to the EBD prevalence rate of less than 1% in public schools, students with EBD are extremely overrepresented in juvenile correctional facilities. The average prevalence of

Table 1–1   Summary of research-based alternative education strategies

Low ratio of students to teachers	More personal time for each student
	Better behavioral gains
	Higher quality of instruction
Highly structured classroom with behavioral classroom management	Level systems provide predictable structure
	Self-management skills are taught
	High rates of positive reinforcement
	High academic gains
	Students are able to move to less restrictive settings
Positive rather than punitive emphasis in behavior management	Rewards for acceptable behavior and compliance
	Directly teach clear classroom rules
	Begin with rich reinforcement and then "fade" to normal levels when possible (four positives to one negative)
Adult mentors at school	Mentor must use positive reinforcement
	Mentor takes special interest in child
	Mentor tracks behavior, attendance, attitude, grades
	Mentor negotiates alternatives to suspension and expulsion
Individualized behavioral interventions based on functional behavioral assessment	Identify causes of the behavior
	Identify what is "keeping it going"
	Identify positive behaviors to replace problems
	Interview and involve the student
	Use multicomponent interventions
Social skills instruction	Problem solving
	Conflict resolution
	Anger management
	Empathy for others
High-quality academic instruction	Direct instruction plus learning strategies
	Control for difficulty of instruction
	Small, interactive groups
	Directed responses and questioning of students
Parental involvement	Frequent home–school communication
	Parent education programs, provided either at school or in the community

Source: Based on Tobin & Sprague, 2000.

youth with disabilities in juvenile correction facilities is 33.5% and of those, 47% are identified as having EBD. According to a recent survey of correctional facilities across the country, prevalence estimates of youth with disabilities in juvenile correction facilities range from 9.1% to 77.5% (Mears & Aron, 2003; Quinn, Rutherford, Leone, Osher, & Poirer, 2005).

Moreover, the odds are good that high school dropouts will become involved with the juvenile justice system, as dropouts comprise 85% of all juvenile justice cases (Stanard, 2003). What is more alarming is the evidence that most dropouts with EBD (73%) were arrested 3–5 years after they left high school (Wagner, D'Amico, Marder, Newman, & Blackorby, 1992). The real crime is that incarceration is a dramatically unsuccessful treatment, especially for youth who are adjudicated to adult correctional facilities by current "get tough" policies on youth crime (Leone et al., 2003).

Explanations for the overrepresentation of youth with disabilities in juvenile correctional facilities often include issues involving school failure, susceptibility, and problem-solving deficits (Quinn et al., 2005). As described earlier, many youth exposed to multiple risk factors enter public school socially, emotionally, and academically behind their age peers. Their lives also may involve multiple family stressors (e.g., drugs and alcohol, divorce, abuse). Academic deficits often foster behavior problems, which result in disciplinary practices (e.g., time-out, suspension) that remove the students from academic instruction. This perpetuates a failure cycle in which these students fall further behind academically and receive fewer opportunities to learn appropriate behaviors (Christle et al., 2004). This cycle continues with an ever increasing magnitude with chronic disciplinary problems in school often leading to delinquency and incarceration (Walker & Sprague, 1999b), a pathway often referred to as the school-to-prison pipeline (Wald & Losen, 2003).

Youth with EBD also are thought to have personality and cognitive deficits that predispose them to criminal or delinquent behavior. In many cases young people with EBD may have poorly developed impulse control, inability to anticipate consequences, inadequate perception of social cues, and a high degree of suggestibility. These characteristics make them susceptible to criminal influence and criminal behavior. In addition, youth with EBD often have deficits in problem-solving strategies and may not mentally process consequences and alternative strategies. Thus, an inadequate social-cognitive development increases the risk of delinquent and criminal behavior (Quinn et al., 2005). Kauffman (2005) identified the following characteristics of delinquent youth that are strongly correlated with EBD: (a) problems in school; (b) low verbal intelligence; (c) parents who are alcoholic or who are frequently arrested; (d) family reliance on the welfare system or poor income management; (e) broken, crowded, or chaotic homes; (f) inadequate or erratic parental supervision; (g) parental and sibling hostility or indifference toward the youth; and (h) substance abuse.

It is no mystery how youth with EBD become clients of the juvenile justice system. Unfortunately, the longer their deficits and behavior problems persist, the less likely that remediation in public schools or alternative programs will be successful. Consider that students who do not read by the fourth grade have only a .12 probability of ever learning to read (Adams, 1988). Likewise, Walker and colleagues (1995) observed, "if antisocial behavior patterns are not changed by the end of grade 3, they should be treated as a chronic condition, much like diabetes" (p. 6). Just as a person with diabetes needs professional medical services in order to survive and maintain a normal life, youth with chronic EBD need professional special education and related services.

Despite the need for intensive remediation and professional special education and related services, evidence suggests that these needs are not being met for youth with disabilities in juvenile corrections (Leone & Cutting, 2004; Mears & Aron, 2003; Meisel, Henderson, Cohen, & Leone, 1998; Quinn, Rutherford, & Leone, 2001). In fact, the Urban Institute concluded in its report on youth with disabilities in the juvenile justice system that these facilities have shifted their focus over the years, from treatment and rehabilitation to punishment (Mears & Aron, 2003). Rather than treating and rehabilitating youth with chronic EBD, the juvenile justice system appears to be exacerbating their problems. These youth are entitled to a comparable academic program they would receive in public school and instruction by highly qualified teachers. Yet most of these young people do not make adequate progress due to a lack of access to the general education curriculum for prolonged periods of disciplinary isolation (Leone & Cutting, 2004). As is the case in public schools, youth with EBD in juvenile justice facilities are more likely to be excluded from education and placed in isolation or other confinement due to disciplinary issues than those youth without EBD.

Whereas the overall academic instruction in juvenile justice educational programs lacks rigor and qualified teachers, it should be noted that many students in juvenile correction facilities report positive experiences in correctional educational programs. Some students make significant academic progress and have attributed this to the empathy of their teachers, small class sizes, and the highly structured environment (Leone, Rutherford, & Nelson,

1991). On the other hand, many teachers in correctional educational facilities lack expertise and certification in their fields. For example, a survey of juvenile justice facilities revealed that only 17% of the teachers were fully certified to teach special education (Quinn et al., 2001).

The same laws (i.e., Individuals with Disabilities Education Act, Section 504 of the Rehabilitation Act of 1973, and Title II of the Americans with Disabilities Act) that protect students with disabilities in public schools extend to youth in juvenile justice facilities. The Department of Justice, under the Civil Rights of Institutionalized Persons Act (CRIPA), has the authority to enforce these laws. It is unfortunate that there has been much litigation in recent years to ensure that students with disabilities in juvenile correctional facilities receive the special education and related services for which they are entitled. Many of the problems of students with EBD within the juvenile justice system parallel and are a part of the issue of meeting the mental health needs of students with EBD.

MENTAL HEALTH

The surgeon general's 2002 report on children's mental health (*Report of the surgeon general's conference*, 2001) revealed that mental disorders among youth in the general population were significantly higher than what was previously believed. The report stated that approximately 20% of children and adolescents in the general population are experiencing a mental disorder; approximately 10% of these children and youth experience mental illness severe enough to cause impairment at home, in school, and in the community. The report suggested that less than half of those with mental disorders will receive the treatment they need. In addition, 27% of children who are involved with the child welfare system show high levels of behavioral and emotional problems, yet nearly one third have not received mental health services (Kortenkamp & Ehrle, 2002). Results from a client–patient survey conducted by the U.S. Center for Mental Health Services indicated that most youth who are severely emotionally disturbed are placed in residential care programs (Warner & Pottick, 2003), and many have been living apart from relatives (i.e., in group homes and foster care).

The difficulty for children with mental health needs and their families to receive appropriate services stems from the fact that this country has not developed a formal policy to ensure the provision of comprehensive mental health services for troubled youth (Lourie & Hernandez, 2003). Family problems, depression and anxiety, school coping problems, and aggression are reasons most often

given for youth who are admitted for mental health services. It is imperative that mental health services and supports be developed and made available to youth and their families within their communities, and particularly within schools. However, one of the few mandates for providing mental health services to children and youth in schools is contained in IDEA for children identified as having ED. Both psychological services and counseling are listed as related services that may be required to assist a child with a disability to benefit from special education. Whereas students with EBD do receive services from school psychologists and school counselors, many students require intensive long-term interventions. Parents have been forced to pursue legal due process procedures in order to get mental health services for their children with EBD. In some cases, parents have relinquished custody of their children to the child welfare system to obtain services (U.S. General Accounting Office, http://www.gao.gov/new.items/d03397.pdf); other parents have been relieved when their children are labeled delinquent so that they may obtain mental health services within juvenile corrections (Lourie & Hernandez, 2003). Although mental health services are offered in most juvenile correction facilities, the nature and effectiveness of such services have been in question.

The National Center for Mental Health and Juvenile Justice (NCMHJJ) was established in 2001 to assist in developing improved policies and programs for youth with mental health disorders involved with the juvenile justice system. The NCMHJJ has outlined six key issues (Cocozza, 2005):

1. There is a growing awareness of mental health disorders among youth in the general population.

2. The prevalence of mental disorders among youth in the juvenile justice system is two to three times higher than among youth in the general population (60% to 70 % have a diagnosable mental disorder).

3. There is an increasing sense of awareness and crisis surrounding the care and treatment of youth with mental disorders in the juvenile justice system (a trend known as the criminalization of mental illness).

4. There are a number of factors that are contributing to the sense of crisis, such as an increase in the number of youth with mental disorders entering the juvenile justice system.

5. Despite this bleak picture, we are seeing signs of improvement with the availability of new and effective tools and services that are demonstrating real promise for youth involved with the juvenile justice system. These include improved screening

and assessment tools and the use of evidence-based practices, such as multisystemic therapy (MST) and functional family therapy (FFT).

6. There is certainly much activity under way, but more needs to happen. For example, reentry programs for youth transitioning out of residential placement need to be strengthened.

Although mental health and the juvenile justice systems often serve the same youth, these systems as well as the education system operate under separate mandates, philosophies, goals, practices, and funding streams. What is needed is an integrated system of enhanced partnerships where policy and practice are aligned across agencies with the goal of improving the lives of children and youth. As Walker and Sprague said, "To divert students at risk for behavioral disorders from an at-risk life path, it is essential that the key social agents in the student's life be directly involved in the intervention" (1999b).

Chapter Summary

Students with EBD pose serious challenges to school personnel and a better understanding of this disorder may provide guidance in helping you become effective teachers of these students. The definition of EBD is surrounded by ongoing controversy and although the federal definition uses the term *emotional disturbance* (*ED*), most practitioners in the field use the term *emotional and behavioral disorders* (*EBD*). There are two major classification systems used to help distinguish behavior patterns or types of EBD, psychiatric and dimensional.

Prevalence estimates indicate less than 1% of students in public schools are identified as having EBD and many professionals consider this to be a gross underestimate. Whereas students with EBD show a wide range of characteristics, these students generally are identified later and receive services later than any other disability group. Unfortunately, students with EBD tend to experience the worst educational, behavioral, and social outcomes of any disability group.

It wasn't until the 20th century that students with EBD were recognized and treated as a disability group in public schools. The desire to determine a cause of EBD led to the emergence of several conceptual models over the years to address the needs of students with EBD.

Although various internal and external risk factors have been related to EBD, research has not identified a direct cause.

Early screening and identification of EBD is crucial, as the symptoms increase in intensity over time and become more and more resistant to remediation. Interventions for students with EBD include systematic prevention and academic, behavioral, and social skills training. Academic interventions include providing a rich curriculum and delivering effective instruction. Behavioral interventions include behavior enhancement and reduction programs. Teachers should be cognizant of federal, state, and district policies regarding physical interventions. Research indicates that the most effective social skills training occurs in context rather than in isolation.

Although the placement options for students with EBD range from the general education classroom to residential care programs, more students with EBD are found in the most restrictive setting, such as mental health facilities and juvenile correction programs. To effectively educate and improve the outcomes for students with EBD, an integrated system of enhanced partnerships is needed where policy and practice are aligned across agencies.

CHAPTER 2

Legal Issues in Educating Students with Emotional and Behavioral Disorders

Mitchell L. Yell

Focus Questions

- What is the Individuals with Disabilities Education Act and how does it affect the education of children and youth with EBD?

- Are there special rules and procedures that educators should follow when disciplining students with EBD?

- What responsibilities do special education teachers have when managing their student records?

- Should teachers report suspected instances of child abuse and neglect?

- Can teachers be held liable for a student's injury or misconduct?

Federal and state laws exert a profound influence on the education of students with emotional and behavioral disorders (EBD). The most important of these laws is the Individuals with Disabilities Education Act (IDEA), which was recently amended and reauthorized in the Individuals with Disabilities Education Improvement Act of 2004 (hereafter IDEA 2004). States and school districts must adhere to the requirements of IDEA when educating students with disabilities in special education programs. In addition to IDEA, other federal and state laws also affect special education programs for students with EBD.

The purpose of this chapter is to provide an overview of IDEA, and to examine the ways that these important laws affect the education of students with EBD and teachers of students with disabilities. Additionally, I will examine four other areas of importance to teachers of students with EBD: (a) disciplining students with disabilities, (b) keeping student records confidential, (c) reporting child abuse and neglect, and (d) supervising students with disabilities. It is important that teachers of students with EBD understand their rights and responsibilities under these laws. To gain a thorough understanding of how individual states interpret IDEA and other laws, readers should know their state's laws and regulations regarding students with disabilities. This is important because of the flexibility the federal government gives states to determine how they will implement the law. Additionally, issues regarding the supervisory responsibilities of teachers are matters that are left entirely to the states.

THE INDIVIDUALS WITH DISABILITIES EDUCATION ACT

In this section I first review the major purpose of the Individuals with Disabilities Education Act (IDEA). Second, I explain the major principles of the law. Third, I offer recommendations to teachers to help them meet the requirements of IDEA.

The Purpose of IDEA

In 1975 President Gerald Ford signed the Education for All Handicapped Children Act (EAHCA)[1] of 1975. The law, often referred to as P.L. 94–142, promised to provide states with federal financial support if states would pass laws enacting the provisions of P.L. 94–142 at the state level. The heart of the law was a set of procedures that set forth an educational bill of rights for students with

---

[1]In 1990 the EAHCA was renamed the Individuals with Disabilities Education Act (IDEA).

disabilities. These procedures required states to develop policies ensuring that all qualified students with disabilities receive an appropriate special education. The purpose of the law was as follows:

To assure that all children with disabilities have available to them. . . . a free appropriate public education which emphasizes special education and related services designed to meet their unique needs, to assure that the rights of children with disabilities and their parents or guardians are protected, to assist states and localities to provide for the education of all children with disabilities, and to assess and assure the effectiveness of efforts to educate children with disabilities. (IDEA, 20 U.S.C. § 1400(c))

On December 3, 2004, President George W. Bush signed the Individuals with Disabilities Education Improvement Act (IDEA 2004) into law. This law, numbered P.L. 108–446, was passed to reauthorize and amend the IDEA. In passing the law, Congress sought to increase schools' accountability for improving the academic and functional performance of students in special education. The U.S. Department of Education issued regulations implementing IDEA 2004 on August 3, 2006.

Members of Congress believed that IDEA had successfully ensured access to educational services for millions of children and youth with disabilities. Nevertheless, implementation of the law had been impeded by low expectations and an insufficient focus on applying scientifically based research on proven methods of teaching children and youth with disabilities. The focus of the 2004 reauthorization, therefore, was on increasing the quality of programs for students in special education by increasing accountability for results. Moreover, IDEA 2004 sought to support high-quality, intensive preservice preparation and professional development based on scientific research. Congress, in passing IDEA 2004, also sought to encourage schools to develop schoolwide approaches based on research-supported reading programs and positive behavioral interventions and supports, to reduce the need to label children as disabled and to provide assistance to all children in need of support.

The Major Principles of IDEA

IDEA contains a number of provisions to ensure that all qualifying students with disabilities receive a free and appropriate education in the least restrictive environment, and that procedural protections are granted to students and their parents. The major provisions of IDEA determine what constitutes an appropriate special education for students with disabilities. Some scholars have divided IDEA into major principles for discussion purposes (e.g., Turnbull et al., 2004); however, neither IDEA's

Table 2–1 Principles of IDEA

Principle	Requirement
Zero reject	Locate, identify, and provide services to all eligible students with disabilities
Protection in evaluation	Conduct an assessment to determine if a student has an IDEA-related disability and if he or she needs special education services
Free appropriate public education	Develop and deliver an individualized education program of special education services that confers meaningful educational benefit
Least restrictive environment	Educate students with disabilities with nondisabled students to the maximum extent appropriate
Procedural safeguards	Comply with the procedural requirements of IDEA
Parental Participation	Collaborate with parents in the development and delivery of their child's special education program

statutory language nor the U.S. Department of Education's Office of Special Education Programs (OSEP) have recognized the division of the law into these principles (Yell, Drasgow, Bradley, & Justesen, 2004). Nevertheless, this division is a useful tool for introducing the law; therefore, I use a similar division in this chapter. These provisions are zero reject, protection in evaluation, free appropriate public education, least restrictive environment, and procedural safeguards. Underlying all of these provisions is the idea of parental participation. Table 2-1 lists and briefly describes each of these principles.

Zero Reject The zero reject principle requires that states provide special education services to all students with disabilities who are eligible for services under IDEA, regardless of the severity of the disability. According to the zero reject principle, schools must locate and serve all students who have a disability covered by IDEA. Additionally, the disability must adversely affect a student's educational performance. The premise of IDEA is that all students with disabilities, no matter how severely disabled, can benefit from an education and are entitled to receive it (Norlin & Gorn, 2005).

Protection in Evaluation Because a fair and accurate evaluation is extremely important to ensure an appropriate education, IDEA includes protection in evaluation procedures (PEP). These procedures mandate that school districts gather accurate information to determine (a) whether a student has a disability covered by IDEA, (b) whether a student requires special education and related services, and (c) what educational services should be included in the student's individualized education program (IEP).

When students are suspected of having a disability, they are referred to school teams to determine if they may qualify for special education services under IDEA. These teams, often called multidisciplinary teams (MDTs), usually receive student referrals from teachers, school personnel, or parents. When a student is referred, the MDT must decide if the student should be evaluated for special education services. Figure 2-1 depicts this process.

If the MDT decides to conduct an evaluation, a student's parents must give written consent to conduct the evaluation. If the parents refuse to give consent for evaluation, and the IEP team believes the child needs special education services, the school district may go to a due process hearing to obtain permission to conduct the evaluation. The trend in the courts in such cases has been to rule that the school district has a duty to evaluate a child suspected of having a disability even if it requires a hearing (Bateman & Linden, 2006).

The evaluation must be conducted within 60 days of receiving parental consent. States may have shorter timelines, in which case the state timelines must be followed. When parental consent is received, the MDT appoints a person or persons to conduct a full and individualized evaluation of the student. The evaluation must be conducted in accordance with the requirements listed in IDEA (see Table 2-2). Additionally, parents must be a part of the evaluation process.

Once the evaluation is completed, the MDT decides if the student is eligible for special education services. This decision is based on the results of the evaluation. The MDT determines if (a) the student has a disability covered by IDEA, and (b) the disability adversely affects his or her educational performance. If both criteria are met, the student is eligible for special education services. If the student is eligible to receive special education services, the school must convene a team within 30 calendar days to develop an IEP. Parents must give their consent to services. If parents do not give consent for their child to receive services, the school cannot provide services, nor can they go to a due process hearing to contest the parents' refusal.

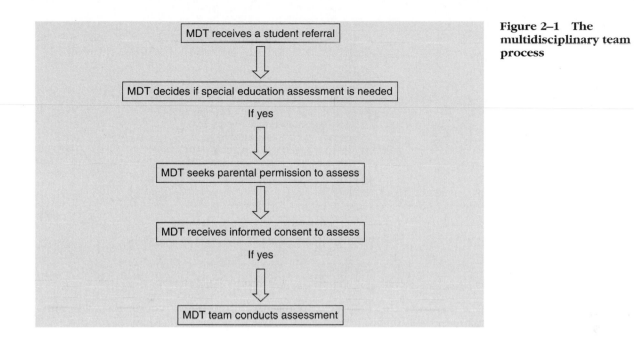

Figure 2–1 The multidisciplinary team process

Table 2–2 Procedural safeguards of IDEA

Procedural Safeguard	Requirement
Prior written notice	A school must provide parents with prior written notice whenever it proposes or refuses to initiate or change the (a) identification, (b) evaluation, (c) educational placement, or (d) provision of a free appropriate public education for a student.
Consent	A school must obtain informed parental consent before initiating the (a) preplacement evaluation, (b) initial placement in a special education program, or (c) reevaluation.
Independent educational evaluation	Parents have a conditional right to obtain an independent educational evaluation (IEE) at public expense if the parents disagree with the local educational agency's (LEA's) evaluation. Parents notify the LEA when they request that the district pay for an IEE. The LEA must either agree to fund the IEE or request a due process hearing to show that its evaluation was appropriate. The results of an IEE must be considered by the LEA.
Opportunity to examine records	A school shall afford the parents of a student with a disability an opportunity to inspect and review all educational records regarding the student's (a) identification, (b) evaluation, and (c) educational placement.
Mediation	Mediation is an intervening step that may be used prior to going to a due process hearing. Mediation is a voluntary dispute resolution forum in which an impartial mediator sits down with both parties in a special education dispute and assists them to resolve the problem. If the problem is resolved through mediation the parties must execute a binding agreement that contains the terms of the resolution.
Resolution session	The resolution session is a step between a formal filing for a due process hearing and the actual hearing. The LEA is required to convene a meeting between the parents and relevant members of the IEP team. During the meeting the parents have an opportunity to discuss their complaint and the LEA is afforded an opportunity to resolve the complaint. If the complaint is not resolved to the parents' satisfaction within 30 days of receiving the hearing request, the due process hearing may commence.
Due process hearing	A due process hearing is the primary forum for resolving disputes between parents of children with disabilities and concerning matters involving the (a) identification, (b) evaluation, (c) or the provision of a free appropriate public education. In the hearing, an impartial due process hearing officer hears both sides of the dispute, examines the issues and the relevant section of the law, and issues his or her decision.

Figure 2–2   The IEP process

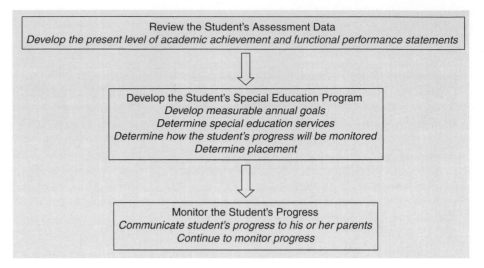

In IDEA 2004 Congress added a provision that requires that when MDTs make eligibility decisions they cannot determine that a student is disabled under the IDEA if his or her problem is primarily due to lack of appropriate instruction in reading, including in the essential components of reading instruction (i.e., phonemic awareness, phonics, vocabulary development, reading fluency, reading comprehension), lack of instruction in math, or limited English proficiency (IDEA, 20 U.S.C. § 1414(b)(5)). This section of the reauthorized IDEA is an indication of the emphasis that Congress placed on the use of evidence-based practices when it reauthorized the law.

In IDEA 2004 significant changes were made in eligibility criteria for students with learning disabilities. Although Congress did not change the definition of a learning disability, it did add provisions regarding how schools may determine if a student has a learning disability. The new provision states that school districts cannot be required to use a discrepancy formula to determine if a child has a learning disability. Districts, however, may use a discrepancy model if they so choose. Additionally, a district may use a process that determines if a child responds to scientific, research-based interventions as part of the evaluation process. Clearly, Congress encouraged, but did not require, school districts to begin using a response to intervention model as part of the eligibility process in learning disabilities.

Free Appropriate Public Education States are required to provide a free appropriate public education (FAPE) to students who are eligible to receive special education services under IDEA. A FAPE consists of special education and related services that are provided

(a) at public expense, (b) in accordance with state standards, and (c) in conformity with his or her IEP.

The IEP is the cornerstone of special education because it is the blueprint of a student's special education program. The IEP document contains the educational needs of a student, the goals and objectives that direct his or her program, the educational programming and placement, and the evaluation and measurement criteria that were developed during the IEP process. Indeed, the IEP is the document and process that formalizes the FAPE for a student with disabilities. Figure 2-2 depicts the IEP process. Congress made significant changes to the IEP in IDEA 2004. (These changes are explored in detail in Chapter 9.)

Related Services. To ensure that students with disabilities receive a FAPE, it is often necessary to provide related services. Related services are supportive aids and services provided by a school to assist a student with disabilities to benefit from the special education program. IDEA defines related services as "services that may be required to assist the child with a disability to benefit from special education" (IDEA, 20 U.S.C. § 1401 (17)). Although Congress provided a list of related services in IDEA, the list is not exhaustive. This means that related services are not only those services listed by Congress, but may be any service the IEP team determines necessary to provide a FAPE. Examples of related services include occupational and physical therapy, parent counseling and training, psychological services, school health services, social work services, interpreting services, and transportation. According to the U.S. Supreme Court in *Cedar Rapids v. Garret F.* (1999), related services can include extremely complex health services, even those which would require a full-time nurse (Katsiyannis & Yell, 2000). Related services do not include medical services provided by a physician or medical devices that are surgically implanted (e.g., cochlear implants).

In a number of cases, courts have held that schools were required to provide counseling and psychological services to provide students with EBD a FAPE. That is, in addition to their education program the students also needed counseling from counselors or psychologists to benefit from their education programs. Regulations to IDEA define counseling services as "services provided by qualified social workers, psychologists, guidance counselors, or other qualified personnel" (IDEA Regulations, 42 C.F.R. § 300.16(2)). Furthermore, counseling and training of a student's parents may also be a related service. If parents need training or counseling to assist them with understanding the special needs of their child, the school may have to provide this service (IDEA Regulations, 42 C.F.R. § 300.16(2)(6)). If these services were not provided by a school, and a court determined that counseling or psychotherapy was a necessary related service, the school would have to pay for the services (Maag & Katsiyannis, 1996; Yell, 2006). Maag and Katsiyannis (1996) recommended that IEP teams should consider including counseling as a related service in the IEPs of students with EBD who may require such services.

FAPE and the IDEA Reauthorizations of 1997 and 2004. When the EAHCA was passed in 1975, Congress intended that the law open the doors of public education to students with disabilities (Yell et al., 2004). Thus, the original emphasis of FAPE was on access to education programs rather than on any particular level of educational benefit (Eyer, 1998; Yell & Drasgow, 2000). This emphasis, however, was altered substantially by the IDEA reauthorizations of 1997 and 2004. The theme of both reauthorizations was to improve the effectiveness of special education programs by requiring measurable and demonstrable improvement in the academic achievement and functional performance of students with disabilities.

Least Restrictive Environment IDEA mandates that students with disabilities are educated with their peers without disabilities to the maximum extent appropriate. Students in special education can be removed to separate classes or schools only when the nature or severity of their disabilities is such that they cannot receive an appropriate education in a regular education classroom with supplementary aids and services. When students are placed in segregated settings, schools must provide opportunities to interact with their peers who are not disabled where appropriate (e.g., art class, physical education).

To ensure that students are educated in the least restrictive environment (LRE), school districts must ensure that a complete continuum of alternative placements is available. The continuum represents an entire spectrum of placements where a student's special education program can be implemented (Norlin & Gorn, 2005). The purpose of the continuum is to ensure that students with disabilities are educated in the LRE that is most appropriate for their individual needs. Figure 2–3 depicts the continuum of alternative placements.

The less restrictive settings on the continuum are those settings that are closest to the regular education classroom or mainstream. It is very important that schools use the continuum of placements when students are educated in more restrictive settings. This means that schools should not move students to a more restrictive placement (e.g., a special school) without first attempting to educate the student in a less restrictive setting (e.g., a special class). For example, students should not be moved from the regular classroom to more restrictive settings unless education in the regular classroom with supplementary aids and services will not provide a FAPE. On the other hand, schools must not substitute a policy of "full inclusion" for the continuum of placements (Bateman & Linden, 2006). Such an action would be illegal under IDEA. As Bateman and Linden (1998) aptly stated, "there is not now and never has been a requirement in the IDEA that all children with disabilities be included or mainstreamed into the regular classroom" (p. 13).

Disagreements between parents and schools over LRE have led to numerous court cases. A number of the LRE cases have made their way to U.S. courts of appeals. These decisions have set forth tests that will be used by a court to apply the law to the facts of the case. The federal

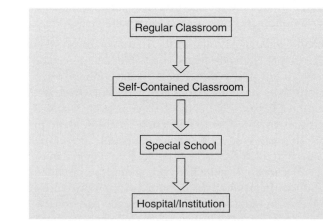

Figure 2–3   The continuum of placements

statutes, regulations, and these LRE cases provide a number of consistent principles that schools must adhere to in promoting inclusive educational practices (Yell, 2006).

Individualization. A central principal of IDEA is that a student's individual needs are the most important consideration when determining educational services. This is also true of placement. To make placement decisions requiring that *all* students will be in the general education classroom, therefore, is just as illegal as placing *all* students with disabilities in special schools. Rather, the planning team that develops a student's IEP must first determine what educational services are required and then where they can be most appropriately delivered. The one caveat to this principle concerns disruptive behavior. If a student's presence in a particular setting would significantly impair the education of other students, whether by disruptive behavior or by requiring an inordinate amount of the teacher's time, thus depriving other students, that setting would not be appropriate (IDEA Regulations, 34 C.F.R. § 300.552, comment). Similarly, if a student's presence in a general education classroom threatens the safety of other students or poses a danger, a general education setting would not be appropriate (*Clyde K. v. Puyallup School District*, 1994).

Presumptive Right to an Integrated Education. The LRE mandate in IDEA sets forth a clear preference for integrated placements. That is, students with disabilities have a right to be educated with students who are not disabled to the maximum extent appropriate. Thus, IEP teams must make good-faith efforts to educate students with disabilities in integrated settings. Before school personnel conclude that a student should be educated in a more restrictive setting, they must consider whether supplementary aids and services would permit an appropriate education in the general education setting. Supplementary aids and services might involve educational options such as a resource room, itinerant instruction, a paraprofessional, a behavior intervention plan, or assistive technology.

Appropriateness. Nothing in the statutory or case law indicates that LRE considerations are intended to replace considerations of appropriateness. To the contrary, when determining a student's special education and related services, the IEP team's first consideration must be what will constitute an appropriate education for the student. In determining a student's special education, therefore, questions of *what* educational services are required must precede questions of *where* they should be provided (Yell, 2006). In making considerations of appropriateness, the IEP team must address both academic and nonacademic needs (e.g., modeling, social development, communication). The law's clear preference for educating students with disabilities in general education classrooms indicates that when an appropriate education can be provided in an integrated setting and the placement will not disrupt the classroom setting, inclusion is generally required (Norlin & Gorn, 2005).

Options. When an IEP team determines that placement in general education with supplementary aids and services will not meet the needs of a student, the team must have the entire continuum of alternative placements from which to choose the appropriate setting. This does not mean that school districts must have all alternative placements within their boundaries. What it does mean is that schools must be able to access the appropriate placement if required to meet the needs of a particular child. A school district could use alternative means, such as contracting with larger school districts for services, to obtain the alternative placement required.

When IEP teams determine a student's appropriate placement, therefore, LRE must be considered. A student should not be placed in any setting, however, unless it is appropriate for him or her. This means that when developing an IEP program, appropriateness is the primary consideration and the LRE is secondary (Bateman & Linden, 1998; Champagne, 1993; Yell, 2006). Therefore, IEP teams should first determine a student's goals, objectives, and the special education and related services that will provide a meaningful education for him or her. Then, the team should determine the placement in which those goals and objectives can be met, keeping in mind the LRE mandate of IDEA. The continuum of educational services should be used to determine the least restrictive placement that will provide a FAPE. The IEP team must ensure that a student is educated with nondisabled students to the maximum extent appropriate.

Procedural Safeguards Congress included an extensive system of procedural safeguards in IDEA. These safeguards are administrative requirements that are designed to protect the interests of students with disabilities and ensure their access to special education services. The procedural safeguards require that school districts and parents be equal partners in the special education process. For example, parents have the right to participate in all meetings about their child's special education including meetings regarding (a) identification, (b) evaluation, (c) programming, and (d) placement. Parents must also be notified before the school can initiate or change the student's identification, evaluation, or educational placement. Additionally, parents must give their consent before the school can conduct the initial evaluation, place their child in special education, or administer any new tests during a reevaluation. IDEA's procedural safeguards are listed and briefly explained in Table 2-2.

When there is a disagreement between the school and the parents on matters concerning the (a) identification, (b) evaluation, (c) education, or (d) placement of the child, parents may request a due process hearing. Schools may also request a due process hearing regarding the same issues. A due process hearing must be conducted by either the state educational agency (SEA) or the local educational agency (LEA) responsible for providing special education services to a student. A due process hearing is a forum in which both sides present their arguments to an impartial third party, the due process hearing officer.

Any party in the hearing has the right to be represented by counsel, present evidence, compel the attendance of witnesses, and examine and cross-examine witnesses. Following the hearing, the hearing officer announces his or her decision, which is binding on both parties. Either party, however, may appeal the decision. In most states, the appeal is to the SEA. The decision of the agency can then be appealed to state or federal court.

When IDEA was reauthorized in 1997, Congress attempted to alleviate the overly adversarial nature of special education by encouraging parents and educators to resolve their differences by using nonadversarial methods (Hodge & Shriner, 1997). Specifically, the law was amended to require states to offer mediation as a voluntary option to parents and educators as an initial process for dispute resolution. In mediation, the parents and school personnel meet with an impartial mediator to attempt to resolve their differences. If mediation is not successful either party may request an impartial due process hearing. Congress again attempted to lessen the adversarial nature of the special education process when they reauthorized IDEA in 2004. Congress did this by developing a resolution session as an intermediary step between a meditation session and the due process hearing. According to this provision, within 15 days of receiving a parent's complaint, the school district must convene a meeting with the parents and relevant members of the IEP team, including the school representative, to discuss the complaint and attempt to resolve it. Essentially, the parents give the school district a 30-day period in which to resolve the issue. If no resolution is reached within 30 days of filing the complaint, the due process hearing may take place. If the complaint is settled, both parties will sign a legally binding agreement. Moreover, this settlement agreement is enforceable in any state or federal court that has jurisdiction.

In an attempt to stop frivolous special education lawsuits, Congress included language in IDEA 2004 that allows school districts to collect attorney's fees from parents if the case brought by the parents was frivolous or unreasonable. If the parents attorney continues to litigate a case after it is clearly without foundation, the school can also recover attorney's fees.

A significant change made in IDEA 2004 is the "no harm no foul" doctrine included in the statute. According to this standard, due process hearing officers must base their decisions on substantive grounds. This means that the hearing officer must determine whether the student in question received a free appropriate public education (FAPE) that provided meaningful educational benefit (Yell, 2006). A hearing officer can rule against a school on procedural grounds only if the procedural violation (a) impeded the student's right to receive a FAPE, (b) impeded the parents opportunity to participate in educational decision making, or (c) caused a deprivation of educational benefits.

A very important set of provisions within the procedural safeguard section of IDEA concerns the discipline of students with disabilities. This has been a very controversial and confusing issue (Conroy, Clark, Gable, & Fox, 1999; Yell, 2006). Legal requirements in the discipline of students with disabilities are covered later in this chapter.

IDEA 2004 and Research-Based Practices

A primary goal of Congress in passing IDEA 2004 was to align the IDEA with the No Child Left Behind (NCLB) Act of 2001. Clearly, one area in which this alignment can be seen is the emphasis both laws placed on the use of research-based practices. Specifically, IDEA now requires that the services on which teachers develop their IEPs should "be based on peer reviewed research." This means that teachers should use educational or behavioral procedures when there is reliable evidence that the programs or interventions are effective.

Although IDEA 2004 does not define peer-reviewed research, NCLB does provide a definition of scientifically based research. "Scientifically based research means research that involves the application of rigorous, systematic, and objective procedures to obtain reliable and valid knowledge relevant to education activities and programs" (NCLB, 20 U.S.C. § 7801 (37)). No Child Left Behind further defines the term to include

research that (i) employs systematic, empirical methods that draw on observation or experiment; (ii) involves rigorous data analysis that are adequate to test the stated hypotheses and justify the general conclusions drawn; (iii) relies on measurements or observational methods that provide reliable and valid data across evaluators and observers, across multiple measurements and observations, and across studies by the same or different investigators; (iv) is evaluated using experimental or quasi-experimental designs in which individuals, entities, programs, or activities are assigned to different conditions and with appropriate controls to evaluate the effects of the condition of interest, with a preference for random-assignment experiments, or other designs to the extent that those designs contain within-condition or across-condition controls; (v) ensures that experimental studies are presented in sufficient detail and clarity to allow for replication or, at minimum, offer the opportunity to build systematically on their findings; and (vi) has been accepted by a *peer-reviewed* [emphasis added] journal or approved by a panel of independent experts through a comparable rigorous, objective, and scientific review. (NCLB, 20 U.S.C. § 7801(37))

This language change is very significant. It means that special education teachers need to know the research in the field of EBD and be able to apply these research findings in their special education programs. Teachers should also be able to discuss research-based practices in IEP meetings. For example, if a parent questions a certain methodology or program, teachers will need to be able to discuss the research base of the particular practice. Walsh (2005) asserted that this language also gives school districts a framework for considering parent requests for particular methodologies. This means that if a parent requests that a teacher use a particular methodology, an IEP team may determine if the methodology has empirical support before deciding if it will be used. If there is no empirical support for the parentally suggested methodology, the team could decide not to use the methodology on grounds that it is not supported by peer-reviewed research. Similarly, if a parent inquires about the research regarding the methods or practices that the teacher uses or if the parent disputes these methods because he or she doesn't believe the research supports the methods, the teacher needs to know and be able to explain the peer-reviewed research behind his or her choice of educational practices and be able to defend the use of the particular practice. This area will no doubt be the subject of future litigation.

Implications for Administrators and Teachers

In this section I offer suggestions to assist teachers in meeting the requirements of IDEA. These suggestions will be useful for teachers in working with their students to help them receive an education that confers meaningful educational benefit.

Understand Your Responsibilities Under IDEA

Since the original passage of the law in 1975, IDEA has been the major force for improving educational opportunities for children and youth with disabilities. IDEA is a complex law and teachers need to be aware of their responsibilities and duties if they are to meet both the

Table 2–3   Websites with special education law information

Name of Site	URL
Council for Exceptional Children	http://www.cec.sped.org
Department of Education	http://www.ed.gov
Law and Special Education	http://www.ed.sc.edu/spedlaw/lawpage.htm
Special Ed Connection (fee-based)	http://www.specialedconnection.com
Wrightslaw	http://www.wrightslaw.org

letter and spirit of the law. Additionally, because IDEA is reauthorized, and often amended, every 4 or 5 years, it is important that administrators and teachers keep abreast of new developments in special education law. (Table 2-3 contains the Web addresses of some free Internet sites that are devoted to special education law.) IDEA's dispute resolution mechanisms can be costly, emotionally trying, and time-consuming. If teachers understand their duties under the law, they will be more likely to help prevent such disputes by developing special education programs that are educationally meaningful and legally correct.

Involve Parents in the Special Education Process in Meaningful Ways

A central principle of IDEA is that parents are to be involved in helping develop special education programs for their children. Special educators must ensure that parents are meaningfully involved in the IEP process. Beyond merely involving parents to ensure that the legal requirements of IDEA are met, there are many other ways that parents can be involved in their children's educational programs. For example, parents can work cooperatively with their children's teachers to implement school- and home-based intervention systems such as token economies and contingency contracts.

Understand and Implement Research-Based Practices

IDEA puts teachers and school districts under pressure to improve student achievement by using educational practices based on peer-reviewed research. Special education teachers, therefore, must make empirically supported practices the core of their instructional procedures if they are to provide meaningful educational programs to their students. Unfortunately, there is a huge gap between (a) what we know works from scientifically based research, and (b) educational and behavioral procedures that are used in many classrooms (Landrum, 1997; Tankersley, Landrum, & Cook, 2004). Scientifically based research on instructional practices will not impact students' academic achievement unless such practices are actually used in classrooms. To remedy this problem, IDEA 2004 requires that research-based programming be written into IEPs and used in classrooms.

Develop Educationally Meaningful and Legally Sound IEPs IDEA requires that schools further the educational achievement of students with disabilities by developing IEPs that provide a special education program that confers measurable and meaningful educational progress. To ensure that IEPs meet both the letter and spirit of IDEA, teachers must be able to (a) conduct relevant and meaningful assessments, interpret these assessments, and match special education programs and strategies to the assessment results; (b) develop special education programming that includes meaningful and measurable annual goals and that includes research-based procedures and strategies; and (c) collect meaningful data on a frequent and regular basis on their students' progress to ensure that their instructional programs are working, and to make accurate decisions regarding when programmatic changes must be made.

Summary of IDEA

It is very important that teachers of students with EBD understand their rights and responsibilities under IDEA. IDEA sets forth a number of principles that teachers must follow when providing special education services to their students (i.e., zero reject, protection in evaluation, free appropriate public education, least restrictive environment, and procedural safeguards). The primary objective of the law is to ensure that all eligible students with disabilities receive a free appropriate public education specifically designed to meet their unique needs. Moreover, a student's parents should be meaningfully involved in developing their child's programs. It is crucial that the special education programs confer meaningful educational benefit on students. Subsequent chapters address aspects of the special education process in greater detail (e.g., conducting assessments, developing IEPs).

DISCIPLINING STUDENTS WITH EBD

The discipline of students with disabilities has been a very controversial and confusing issue (Conroy et al., 1999; Yell, 2006). Much of the confusion has been caused by the lack of federal guidance in IDEA prior to 1997. In the IDEA Amendments of 1997, Congress addressed discipline for the first time. In doing so, it attempted to balance school officials' obligation to ensure that schools are safe and orderly environments conducive to learning, and the school's obligation to ensure that students with disabilities receive a FAPE. In IDEA 2004, procedures to discipline students with disabilities were modified.

Generally, school officials may discipline students with disabilities in the same manner as they discipline students without disabilities. In fact, most types of disciplinary procedures that are used as part of a schoolwide discipline plan may be used with students in special education. For example, procedures such as verbal reprimands; warnings; contingent observation; exclusionary and seclusionary time-out (TO); response cost; detention; in-school suspension (ISS); or the temporary delay or withdrawal of goods, services, or activities (e.g., recess, lunch) are permitted as long as these procedures are used with all students, and the procedures (a) do not interfere significantly with the student's IEP goals, (b) do not change a student's placement, or (c) are not applied in a discriminatory manner (Yell, 2006). The exceptions to this general rule are procedures that result in a student with disabilities being suspended or expelled from school or having his or her placement unilaterally changed.

In the following section, I (a) explain IDEA's requirements regarding the discipline of students with disabilities, (b) discuss the importance of addressing problem behavior in a student's IEP, (c) explain legal considerations when using behavior reduction procedures, and (d) offer suggestions to administrators and teachers so that when they discipline students with disabilities they do so in a legally correct manner.

Short-Term Disciplinary Removals

When students with disabilities violate a school's code of student conduct, IDEA authorizes school officials (i.e., building-level administrators) to unilaterally suspend students with disabilities, or place students in an alternative educational program for up to 10 school days to the same extent that such sanctions are used with students without disabilities. To react quickly to such situations, the building-level administrator can remove a student with disabilities from school without having to convene an IEP team, conduct a manifestation determination, or seek permission to do so from a student's parents. School officials, however, must afford a student his or her due process rights (i.e., oral or written notice of the charges, an explanation of the evidence that support the charges, and an opportunity to present his or her side of the story).

IDEA does not establish a specific limitation on the number of days in a school year that students with disabilities can be suspended from school. Nevertheless, there are two critical points that school officials must keep in mind when using short-term suspensions. First, 10 consecutive days is the upper limit on out-of-school suspensions. If a suspension exceeds this limit, it becomes a change of placement. In this situation, if school officials do not follow IDEA's change of placement procedures (e.g., written notice to the student's parents, convening the IEP team), the suspension is a violation of the law.

Second, when the total number of days that a student has been suspended equals 10 cumulative days, educational services must be provided. At this point the IEP team has to meet and take the following actions: (a) the team must determine what services will be provided and where; (b) the team must conduct an FBA and develop a BIP (if an FBA and BIP are already a part of the IEP, they must be reviewed); (c) the team has to examine the previous suspensions to see if they amounted to a unilateral change of placement; and (d) the team should conduct a manifestation determination. I briefly review these requirements in the following sections.

Providing Educational Services   Educational services must be provided after the 10th cumulative day of removal. For example, if a student is suspended for 10 cumulative days in the fall semester, and is then suspended for 3 more days in the spring term, educational services must be provided from the first day in which cumulative suspensions exceed 10 days or, in this case, the first day of suspension in the spring.

When suspensions amount to over 10 cumulative days, the IEP team must determine the educational services that will be provided to the student. The educational services must allow students to (a) progress in the general education curriculum, (b) receive special education and related services, and (c) advance toward achieving their IEP goals. Often these services will be offered in an interim alternative educational setting (IAES). School officials may implement additional short-term suspensions for separate incidents of misconduct, that is, as long as they provide educational services to the suspended student.

Because there are limits on the number of days in which a student with disabilities may be removed from the school setting, school officials should use out-of-school suspensions judiciously and in emergency situations. Moreover, school personnel should keep thorough records of the number of days in which students with disabilities are removed from schools for disciplinary reasons so they do not inadvertently violate the provisions of IDEA.

The frequency and number of short-term removals, if they are excessive, may be indicative of a defective IEP.

Martin (1999) asserts that the greater the number of short-term disciplinary removals, the greater the likelihood that a hearing officer will find that the behavior portion of the IEP is inappropriate and a deprivation of the student's right to a FAPE. Indeed, if a student is approaching 10 cumulative days of suspension, the IEP team should be convened to review the student's behavioral plans, conduct a functional behavioral assessment, and develop or review the student's BIP. Martin (1999) also suggests that the IEP team conduct a manifestation determination prior to the 11th day of accumulated short-term removals.

Conducting FBAs and Developing BIPs   When a student is removed for more than 10 days in a school year, 10 consecutive days in a row, or placed in an IAES for 45 days, a functional behavioral assessment (FBA) must be conducted, and a BIP must be revised or developed if it does not exist (IDEA, 20 U.S.C. § 1415(k)(1)(B)(i); IDEA Regulations, 34 C.F.R. § 300.520(b)(1)). Readers should note that the term *behavior intervention plan* has been removed from IDEA. The law now uses the phrase *behavioral intervention services and modifications* (IDEA, 20 U.S.C. § 1415(k)(I)(D)). For clarity I will continue to use the abbreviation *BIP*.

IDEA does not describe the components of an FBA or a BIP beyond stating that when conducting an FBA following a 10-day suspension or 45-day removal, the FBA and BIP must address the behavior that led to the removal. The reason for not providing more specific information about conducting FBAs and developing BIPs was to leave the specifics of the FBA and BIP requirements of the law to state and local educational agencies.

Based on the results of the FBA, the IEP team develops a BIP. The BIP is a behavior change program that emphasizes teaching prosocial behaviors to replace a student's inappropriate behaviors (Drasgow, Yell, Bradley, & Shriner, 1999). The key component of the BIP is the use of positive behavioral interventions and supports. Chapter 5 explains the FBA and BIP processes in detail.

Determining When Disciplinary Sanctions Become a Change of Placement   The determination of what constitutes a change of placement is important to understanding the limits of discipline under IDEA (Tucker & Goldstein, 1992). Minor changes in the student's educational program that do not involve a change in the general nature of the program do not constitute a change in placement. For example, a change in the location of the program, in and of itself, did not constitute a change of placement (*Concerned Parents and Citizens for Continuing Education at Malcolm X v. The New York*

City Board of Education, 1980). A change in the educational program that substantially or significantly affects the delivery of education to a student constitutes a change in placement and is not permissible.

A suspension that lasts over 10 consecutive days is a change of placement under IDEA. Because such a suspension is a change of placement, the school district must follow IDEA's change of placement procedures. This means that a school district must provide the parents of the suspended student with written notice prior to initiating the change, which should include an explanation of the applicable procedural safeguards (*OSEP Questions and Answers*, 1999). The purpose of such a notice is to give the parents an opportunity to object if they disagree with the placement change. If a student's parents object to the change of placement, the school district may not suspend the student beyond the 10 consecutive days. The only exceptions are when a student (a) brings a weapon to school or a school function; (b) uses, possesses, or sells illegal drugs; or (c) causes serious bodily injury. In such situations, school officials may immediately and unilaterally move a student to an interim alternative educational setting. Additionally, when the IEP team conducts a manifestation determination and decides the student's misconduct is not related to his or her disability, a student may be removed from school for more than 10 days (see the later section for elaborations on the manifestation determination).

A series of short-term suspensions may also become a change in placement. The question of when disciplinary removals amount to a change of placement, however, can be determined only by a student's IEP team. To determine if a series of short-term suspensions have become a change in placement, an IEP team must determine the circumstances surrounding the suspension, including (a) the length of each removal, (b) the total amount of time that the student is removed, and (c) the proximity of the removals to one another (IDEA Regulations, § 300.520, Note 1). Nevertheless, neither IDEA nor the regulations implementing the law provide clear guidance as to when repeated short-term suspensions of fewer than 10 school days amount to a change of placement. Ultimately, this question will be answered by due process hearing officers and judges. The decision to classify a series of suspensions as a change in placement can be decided only on a case-by-case basis. It is important, therefore, that when a series of short-term suspensions amount to over 10 *cumulative* school days, the IEP team be convened to determine whether these suspensions may be a change in placement.

Removal of a student for fewer than 10 cumulative or 10 consecutive school days probably will not amount to a change in placement. Similarly, if a series of short-term suspensions of not more than 10 days each are used for separate incidences of misbehavior, they probably will not be a change of placement, as long as the suspensions do not create a pattern of exclusions. However, school officials must not assess repeated short-term suspensions as a means of avoiding the change of placement procedures that are required when using long-term suspensions. According to Gorn (1999), subterfuge of this nature, if detected, will invariably result in a finding that a school district violated the procedural requirements of IDEA.

Readers are cautioned that state law regarding suspensions of students with disabilities should be consulted because some states put a ceiling on the number of days that students with disabilities can be suspended during a school year. If state law allows fewer days of suspension than does IDEA, then school officials must adhere to the state guidelines.

Holding the Manifestation Determination If a student violates a school rule and is suspended because of the disciplinary infraction for more than 10 days, or the student's placement is changed to an interim alternative educational setting (IAES) because of the infraction, IDEA 2004 still requires that the parents and relevant members of the IEP team (as determined by a parent and a school's administration) conduct a manifestation determination. The purpose of the manifestation determination is to decide if (a) the student's misconduct was caused by, or had a direct and substantial relationship to the student's disability; or (b) the student's misconduct was the direct result of the school district's failure to implement the IEP.

When the IEP team conducts the manifestation determination, the team's task is to review all relevant information in the student's file, including the student's IEP, and then meet to determine if a student's misbehavior was caused by or was related to his or her disability. The team member who is responsible for collecting and interpreting the data should be qualified and knowledgeable regarding the student, the misbehavior, and the disability. Additionally, the data used to assist the team in the determination should be recent, and collected from a variety of sources. Data collection procedures may include review of records of past behavioral incidences, interviews, direct observation, behavior rating scales, and standardized instruments. Finally, the team must consider any other relevant information supplied by the parents of the student. Moreover, the review must be completed within 10 days of the disciplinary infraction.

The IEP team should then consider the behavior subject to the disciplinary action, the evaluation information, and answer the following questions to assess the relationship between the misconduct and the disability:

First, was there a direct and substantial relationship between the misconduct and the disability? A direct and substantial relationship is a very rigorous standard; therefore, proving that a student's misconduct was a manifestation of his or her disability may be a very difficult standard to meet.

Second, was the IEP properly implemented? If the IEP is not being implemented as written, the determination is essentially over because such problems indicate that the misbehavior is a manifestation of the disability.

If the team determines that either the disability was not related to the misbehavior, or that the IEP was properly implemented, the student can be disciplined like any other student would be disciplined. For example, the student could be placed on a long-term suspension, expelled, or placed in an IAES. When a student is placed in an IAES, he or she must continue to receive a FAPE. That is, a student must continue to work on the IEP goals and be involved in the general curriculum, although in a different setting. The IAES is determined by the IEP team. Additionally, the school should conduct an FBA and develop and implement behavior intervention services and modifications that are designed to address the behavior so that it does not recur.

If the team determines that a relationship between behavior and disability exists or that a student's IEP was not properly implemented, the student may not be expelled, although school officials will still be able to initiate change-of-placement procedures. The standard specifies that if a relationship exists between a student's misbehavior and the school's failure to implement the IEP, the IEP team must conclude that the misbehavior was a manifestation of the student's disability. In such a situation, the student's IEP team must conduct an FBA and develop and implement a BIP for the student, or review the BIP if one was already in place. Also, the student must be returned to the setting from which they were removed, unless the IEP team and the parents agree to a change in placement when they develop the new BIP. When conducting the determination, it is important that teams keep thorough documentation of the process.

Long-Term Disciplinary Removals

Long-term suspensions and expulsions qualify as a change of placement. Because such actions would result in a placement change, the procedural safeguards of IDEA would automatically be triggered. IDEA does not establish a specific limitation on the number of days in a school year that students with disabilities can be suspended from school for disciplinary reasons. Thus, there is no clear answer in the law as to the number of days that a student can be suspended before schools change a student's placement by using long-term suspensions. Neither is there an absolute limit on the number of school days that students with disabilities can be removed from their current placement in a school year (*OSEP Questions and Answers*, 1999).

Removal for 45 School Days School officials may unilaterally exclude a student with disabilities from school for up to 45 *school* days without regard to whether the misbehavior was a manifestation of the student's disability if the student (a) brings, possesses, or acquires a weapon at school, on school premises, or a school function (e.g., school dances, class trips, extracurricular activities); (b) knowingly possesses, uses, or sells illegal drugs, or sells a controlled substance at school, on school premises, or at a school function; or (c) has inflicted serious bodily injury to another person while at school, on school premises, or at a school function (IDEA, 20 U.S.C. § 1415(k)(1)). A weapon is defined as a "weapon, device, instrument, material, or substance. . . . that is used for, or is readily capable of, causing death or serious bodily injury" (IDEA, 20 U.S.C. § 615(k)(10)(D)). (For a list of weapons covered under IDEA see the Federal Criminal Code, 18 U.S.C. § 930(g).) A controlled substance refers to a legally prescribed medication (e.g., Ritalin) that is illegally sold by a student. (For a list of controlled substances covered by IDEA see the Controlled Substances Act, 21 U.S.C. § 812(c).) Serious bodily injury refers to physical injuries that result in risk of death, physical pain, disfigurement, or loss or impairment of a bodily function. In the event of such exclusions for these offenses, students may be placed in an appropriate interim alternative educational setting (IAES).

Interim Alternative Educational Settings IDEA requires that a FAPE must be made available to all eligible students with disabilities, even those who have been suspended or expelled from school (IDEA, 20 U.S.C. § 1412(a)(1).) According to the regulations (IDEA Regulations, 34 C.F.R. § 300.520(a)(1)(ii)) and Department of Education guidance (*OSEP Questions and Answers*, 1999), when a student is suspended *in excess of 10 cumulative days* in a school year, the school district must continue to provide a FAPE. This means that on the 11th cumulative day of a student's removal from school, educational services must begin. These services are provided in an IAES (IDEA, 20 U.S.C. § 1415(k)(3)).

IDEA describes three specific circumstances when an IAES may be used for disciplinary purposes. First, an IAES may be used for a short-term disciplinary removal from school for 10 days or less. School officials may unilaterally impose a short-term suspension on a student with a disability for less than 10 consecutive days for violating school rules, and for additional removals for not more than 10 consecutive days in a school year for separate incidences of misconduct, as long as these removals do not constitute a change in placement. After 10 days of removal in a school year, educational services must be provided to suspended children. An alternative to out-of-school suspension is placement in an IAES. There is not an absolute limit on the total number of short-term placements in an IAES, as long as FAPE is provided, and the proximity and pattern of removals does not constitute a change in placement (Telzrow & Naidu, 2000). Second, an IAES may be used in situations when a student with disabilities is removed from school for a longer term (e.g., long-term suspension, expulsion). Third, an IAES placement can be ordered by a hearing officer.

Although the use of homebound instruction or tutoring as an IAES is not specifically prohibited by IDEA, homebound placements are problematic (Katsiyannis & Maag, 1998). This is because school districts must continue to provide the services listed in a student's IEP while he or she is in the IAES. For example, if a student receives related services such as counseling, physical therapy, or speech, these services must be part of the student's program in the IAES. Clearly, providing these services in a homebound setting would be difficult. Furthermore, a comment in the proposed regulations suggests that a homebound placement will usually be appropriate for a limited number of students, such as those who are medically fragile and not able to participate in a school setting (IDEA Regulations, 34 C.F.R. § 300.551, Note 1). In answers to a series of questions regarding discipline, the Office of Special Education and Rehabilitative Services (OSERS) noted that in most circumstances homebound instruction is inappropriate as a disciplinary measure; however, the final decision regarding placement must be determined on a case-by-case basis ("Department of Education Answers Questions," 1997).

Telzrow and Naidu (2000) suggested that for short-term IAES placements, schools should develop and use in-school suspension programs as their IAESs. Some advantages of using such programs for an IAES is that students can continue to work on their individualized goals and objectives and receive the special education, related services and behavioral programming that are required by their IEPs (Yell, 2006). These authors also suggest that school districts consider the use of alternative programs or schools for long-term IAES placements, as long as these programs include the academic and behavioral programming and parental involvement as required in a student's IEP.

Problem Behavior and the IEP

IDEA requires that if a student with disabilities exhibits problem behaviors that impede his or her learning or the learning of others, then the student's IEP team shall consider strategies, including positive behavioral interventions and supports, to address problem behavior (IDEA, 20 U.S.C. § 1414 (d)(3)(B)(i)). Additionally, comments to the 1999 IDEA federal regulations indicate that if a student has a history of problem behavior, or if such behaviors can be readily anticipated, then the student's IEP must address that behavior (IDEA Regulations, 34 C.F.R. § 300 Appendix A question 39). This requirement applies to all students in special education, regardless of their disability category.

It is up to the IEP team to determine what behaviors are significant enough to require interventions formally written into the IEP. Drasgow and colleagues (1999) inferred from previous hearings and court cases that these problem behaviors may include (a) disruptive behaviors that distract teachers from teaching and students from learning, (b) noncompliance, (c) verbal and physical abuse, (d) property destruction, and (e) aggression toward students or staff.

These problem behaviors should be addressed in the following manner: First, when a student exhibits problem behavior, the IEP team must determine if the behavior impedes his or her learning or other students' learning; second, if the team decides that the problem behavior does interfere with the student's learning, then it must conduct an assessment of the behavior; and third, the IEP team must develop a plan based on the information gained from the assessment that reduces problem behaviors and increases socially acceptable behaviors.

The results of the team's decisions must be included in the IEP. This means that the IEP of a student with serious problem behaviors must include the information from the assessment in the present levels of academic achievement and functional performance section of the IEP. Because educational needs must be addressed by developing appropriate special education programming, the IEP must also include (a) measurable goals and objectives, and (b) special education and related services that address the problem behavior. Moreover, if the student's behavioral program involves modifications to the general education classroom or supplementary aids and services, these modifications and services must be included in the IEP.

Behavior Reduction Procedures

Although the law and best practice indicates that behavior programs should be based on positive behavior interventions designed to teach and enhance appropriate behaviors, teachers of students with EBD and administrators frequently find it necessary to use behavior reduction procedures, such as seclusion or isolation time-out and in-school suspension. There have been many empirical and ethical issues raised regarding these procedures (Braaten, Simpson, Rosell, & Reilly, 1988; Maag, 2001); nonetheless, these procedures are often used in response to behavioral crises. Legal problems with the use of these procedures have also been examined (Yell, 2006; Yell & Peterson, 1995). (Readers should note that there are no legal problems regarding procedures such as response cost, contingent observation, or exclusion time-out as long as they are used in an appropriate and nondiscriminatory manner.)

The use of seclusion time-out and in-school suspension can be legally problematical if not used appropriately (Yell, 2006; Yell & Peterson, 1995). The difficulty with these practices is that if they are used in an inappropriate manner, they can result in interference with IEP goals or objectives or in a unilateral change in placement (Yell, 2006).

Seclusion/Isolation Time-out
Timeout is a disciplinary procedure frequently used by teachers of students with disabilities. Time-out generally involves placing a student in a less reinforcing environment for a period of time following inappropriate behavior. A type of time-out that should be classified as a controlled procedure is seclusion/isolation time-out (Yell, 1994). In this type of time-out the student, contingent on misbehavior, is required to leave the classroom and enter a separate time-out room for a brief duration.

In-School Suspension
In-school suspension (ISS) programs require the suspended student to serve the suspension period in the school, usually in a classroom isolated from schoolmates. During ISS, the student works on appropriate educational material provided by the teacher. Several advantages of using ISS are that (a) it avoids the possibility of the suspended student roaming the community unsupervised; (b) the student being disciplined is segregated from the general school population; and (c) the student continues to receive an education during the suspension period (Yell, 1990).

Implications for Administrators and Teachers

Disciplining students with disabilities has long been a controversial and confusing area. With the inclusion of a section on discipline in IDEA 1997 and IDEA 2004, teachers'

responsibilities in this area became clearer. It is extremely important to understand these responsibilities and act accordingly. The following is a list of principles that administrators and teachers should follow.

Implement a Schoolwide Discipline System
Schools should develop and implement schoolwide discipline systems. Moreover, these systems should focus on teaching and supporting appropriate behavior (see Chapter 10). In schoolwide systems, the school's administration, faculty, and staff develop rules that teach and regulate student conduct. This is necessary to maintain discipline and to operate efficiently and effectively. This means that students should clearly know which behaviors are acceptable and which behaviors are prohibited. If students violate reasonable school rules by behaving in ways that are prohibited, they will be held accountable. Student accountability to rules implies that violators will be subject to disciplinary sanctions or consequences (Yell, Rozalski, & Drasgow, 2001).

Many school officials mistakenly assume that because of IDEA's restrictions on suspensions and expulsions, regular school district discipline policies do not apply to students with disabilities. Students with disabilities who attend public school, however, are subject to a school district's regular discipline policies and procedures (Gorn, 1999; Yell, 2006). Gorn (1999) suggests that if a student's IEP team determines that (a) he or she will be subject to the school district's regular disciplinary policy, and (b) the policy *does not* violate the requirements of IDEA, the team may use the student's IEP or BIP to affirm that the student will be subject to the district's regular discipline policies and procedures. The U.S. Department of Education seemingly supported such a view in a comment to the final IDEA regulations, "in appropriate circumstances the IEP team . . . might include specific regular or alternative disciplinary measures that would result from particular infractions of school rules" (*OSEP Questions and Answers*, 1999, p. 12589). If an IEP team decides that a student will be subject to an alternative discipline plan, then this plan should be included in the student's IEP or BIP.

Include Positive Behavior Interventions and Supports in Students' IEPs
IDEA requires that if a student with disabilities exhibits problem behaviors that impede his or her learning or the learning of others, then the student's IEP team should consider positive behavioral interventions and supports to address that behavior. For example, if a student has a history of problem behavior, or if such behaviors can be readily anticipated, then the student's IEP must address that

behavior (IDEA Regulations, 34 C.F.R. § 300 Appendix A question 39).

When an IEP team addresses a student's problem behavior, the needs of the individual student are of paramount importance in determining the behavior strategies that are appropriate for inclusion in the child's IEP (*OSEP Questions and Answers*, 1999). If teachers of students with EBD fail to address a student's problem behaviors in the IEP, then that failure may deprive the student of a FAPE (Drasgow et al., 1999). This could result in legal actions against the offending school district.

Document Disciplinary Actions and Referrals

When disciplining students with disabilities it is crucial to keep written records of all disciplinary actions taken. An examination of court cases and administrative rulings in disciplinary matters indicates that in many instances, decisions turned on the quality of the school's records (see *Cole v. Greenfield-Central Community Schools*, 1986; *Dickens v. Johnson County Board of Education*, 1987; *Hayes v. Unified School District No. 377*, 1987; and *Oberti v. Board of Education of the Borough of Clementon School District*, 1993). As Baird (2005) asserts, if it is not written down, legally it did not happen. It is crucial, therefore, that teachers keep thorough records of incidences that lead to the use of disciplinary procedures, the particular actions that were taken, and the results of the action. Figure 2–4 is an example of a record-keeping form for recording disciplinary actions.

Evaluate the Effectiveness of Behavior Reduction Procedures and Disciplinary Actions

It is important that teachers evaluate the effectiveness of disciplinary procedures that are used with their students. There are two major reasons for collecting data on effectiveness on an ongoing basis. First, such data should be used to make decisions about whether an intervention is reducing target behaviors. If the data show that an intervention is successfully reducing the problem behavior, the procedures or interventions may be continued. If, however, the procedure is not having the desired results, its use should be discontinued. If formative data of this nature are not collected, teachers will not know with certainty if a given procedure is actually achieving the desired results. Second, teachers are accountable to supervisors and parents, and data collection is useful for accountability purposes. From a legal standpoint, it is imperative that teachers collect such data. Anecdotal information is not readily accepted by courts, but data-based decisions certainly would be viewed much more favorably.

Summary of Disciplining Students with Disabilities

Disciplining students with disabilities is a complex issue. In addition to observing the due process rights that protect all students, administrators and teachers have to be aware of the additional safeguards afforded students with disabilities by the IDEA. Teachers must collect formative data to determine if the procedures are having the desired effect on student behavior. Moreover, when disciplinary procedures such as exclusion time-out, suspension, or expulsion are used, teachers should keep written records because proper documentation may be important if these actions are challenged. Finally, disciplinary procedures should be used reasonably and for legitimate educational purposes; they must not compromise a student's FAPE or be applied in a discriminatory manner.

MANAGING STUDENT RECORDS

Teachers and administrators frequently have questions about managing student records. With whom may they share information contained in a student's cumulative file, what records or information may parents gain access to, and what information must the school or teacher keep private? The federal law that governs all educational records in public schools is the Family Educational Rights and Privacy Act (FERPA). The requirements of FERPA were included in IDEA.

In this section of the chapter, I first review FERPA. Second, I explain the major principles of the law. Third, I offer recommendations to teachers to help them meet the requirements of FERPA.

Family Educational Rights and Privacy Act

Until 1974 it was common for schools to deny parental access to their child's educational records. Granting access to parents was considered time-consuming, costly, and a potential source of liability because it increased a school's accountability by opening up the educational process to public scrutiny (Thomas & Russo, 1995). In addition to denying parental access, schools sometimes used student records inappropriately. For example, often school officials provided access to student records to outside agencies and persons. In 1974, Congress enacted the Family Educational Rights and Privacy Act (20 U.S.C. § 1232, *et seq.*). The law was passed to correct this situation.

The purpose of FERPA was to guarantee parental access to student records while prohibiting access to these records by persons without legitimate reasons to

FIGURE 2-4

Record-keeping form for behavior incidences

Behavior Incident Report

Student: _____   Date: _____

Teacher: _____   Time: _____

Description of behavior incident (e.g., precipitating factors, students involved, incident description, etc.):

Did the student's behavior endanger the safety of the student or others? If so, how?

Description of interventions used to manage the problem:

Reason for actions taken:

Results of actions taken:

Reported to administrators and parents (incident must be reported to administrators and parents as soon as possible):

Signature of teachers: _____   _____

Signature of witness(es): _____   _____

_____   _____

Signature of parents: _____   _____

Signature of administrators: _____   _____

know their contents. This federal law required schools to (a) allow parents to view their child's educational records on demand and (b) prohibit access to educational records to people who did not have a legitimate educational reason to see the records. FERPA applied to all students attending institutions receiving federal financial assistance. Table 2–4 lists the requirements of FERPA.

Records Covered by FERPA FERPA covers all records, files, documents, and other materials that contain personally identifiable information directly related to a student that are maintained by the educational agency or by a person acting for that agency. Records that are not covered by the FERPA disclosure rules include those records made by educational personnel that are in sole possession of the maker and are not accessible or revealed to other persons except substitutes (e.g., personal notes made by a child's teacher), and records of the law enforcement unit of an educational agency (e.g., school's police liaison officer) that are maintained solely for law enforcement purposes.

Parental Access Rights Under FERPA Parents and students who are 18 years of age or older have the right to see, inspect, reproduce, and challenge the accuracy of educational records. Additionally, if the parents request that the school officials explain and interpret their child's records, school officials must do so. If the parents believe that the educational records are misleading or inaccurate, they may request that the school amend the records. The school may deny the parents' request; however, this refusal may be contested in a due process hearing.

Additionally, access to student records must be granted to *both* parents, even when only one parent has legal custody unless a court order has been issued denying access to the noncustodial parent.

Confidentiality of Student Records Access to educational records by third parties is permitted only if the parents consent in writing to the request. Such consent forms must be signed, dated, and include the specific records to be disclosed, to whom they are to be disclosed, and the purpose of disclosure. Schools must keep records of requests for access, including the person or agency's name and reasons for requesting access, along with parental consent. The exceptions to these confidentiality provisions include (a) school officials with legitimate educational reasons for seeing this information (e.g., the student's teachers, counselors, principals, school psychologists, school nurses, school social workers or other school officials that need to access the student's files); (b) officials representing schools to which the student has applied; (c) persons responsible for determining eligibility for financial aids; (d) persons acting under judicial orders; and (e) in emergency situations, persons who act to protect the health and safety of the student. Finally, it is again important to note that nothing in FERPA prohibits administrators from sharing information with teachers who have legitimate educational interests in accessing the information, or with anyone for whom the information is required to protect the health and safety of the student, or of the student's teachers (Fischer, Schimmel, & Stellman, 2002).

Table 2–4   Requirements of the Family Educational Rights and Privacy Act (FERPA)

Requirement	Explanation
Confidentiality of information	Third-party access to educational records is permitted only if a student's parents provide written consent. The exceptions to these confidentiality requirements include (a) school personnel with a legitimate education interest, (b) persons responsible for determining eligibility for financial aid, (c) officials representing schools to which the student has applied, (d), judicial orders to release records, and (e) persons who act to protect a student's health and safety (in emergency situations). School officials may use and make public directory information such as names and addresses.
Accessibility rights	Parents and eligible guardians over 18 years old have the right to see, inspect, reproduce, and challenge the accuracy of educational records. These rights include custodial and noncustodial, unless a court order terminates the noncustodial parents' rights regarding the student.
Amending of records	If parents believe that their child's educational records are misleading or incorrect, they may request that the school amend the records. School officials may deny the request; however, the parents may challenge this denial in a due process hearing.
Destruction of Records	When the school district no longer needs educational records, school officials must notify the parents. The parents may request copies of the records or request that the records be destroyed. If the parents request destruction, the school district may retain a permanent record of the student's name, address, grades, etc.

Violations of FERPA

If a school that receives federal financial assistance denies parents their rights to inspect and review records, or if third parties are allowed to view records without parental permission, the school is in violation of FERPA. The Family Policy and Regulations Office of the Department of Education enforces the law and has the power to investigate and review complaints concerning possible violations of FERPA. If a complaint is filed, the agency will notify the school and provide an opportunity to respond. Following an investigation, the agency will send its findings to the school and the person(s) filing the complaint. If the Department of Education finds that a school has violated FERPA, the school will be provided with steps to remedy the situation. If a school does not take steps to voluntarily remedy the violation, the Department of Education may terminate federal aid.

FERPA and IDEA

IDEA contains many of the components of FERPA and both laws apply to the educational records of students with disabilities. In fact, IDEA requires that state and local educational agencies formulate policies regarding the educational records of students with disabilities that are consistent with FERPA (Yell, 2006). If teachers maintain student IEPs, assessment data, evaluation reports, or other educational records, they should be kept in a locked file. Access should be granted only to educational personnel with a legitimate reason to access the information. Personnel that are involved in the student's education, such as administrators (e.g., principal, assistant principal), the student's counselor, the school psychologist, the student's regular education teacher(s), the school social worker, or personnel from a school in which the student is to be transferred, certainly may have a legitimate need to read the student's files and should be granted access.

Implications for Administrators and Teachers

Train Special Education Teachers on Confidentiality Requirements Because special education teachers often have access to sensitive personal information (e.g., testing information), it is important that they receive training on confidentiality requirements. Moreover, this is required by IDEA (IDEA Regulations, 34 C.F.R. § 572(c)). Such training should include a teacher's responsibilities under FERPA and IDEA.

Ensure That Student Records Are Kept Confidential IDEA and FERPA guarantee that parents and persons with a legitimate reason have the right to see educational records; however, a student's records must not be available to persons without a right to know. It is important, therefore, that students' educational records that are kept by the teacher (e.g., the IEP, test protocols) are kept in a secure location. Moreover, only administrators, teachers, and staff members (e.g., counselors, psychologists, nurses, social workers) should be allowed to view these materials. To ensure that records are kept confidential, teachers should develop a record-keeping system to track people who examine student records. These records should contain the names and signatures of persons reading the files, and the times the files were taken and returned.

Keep a Personal Notes File for Information Not Included in the Educational Records Often teachers keep personal records on students. If these records are for the teachers' use only, such records are permitted under FERPA, *as long as these records are not shared with other educators* (with the exception of a substitute teacher). Personal records of this nature should not be included with a student's educational records because if they are included, they become part of the official record and can be seen by parents.

Summary of Managing Student Records

Schools are required to grant parental access to their child's school records. It is important that teachers guard the confidentiality of their students' educational information. In addition to not allowing records access without parental permission, activities such as "lounge talk" or conversations with others in which students are personally identified and information is divulged may be in violation of students' rights under FERPA.

A positive result of the passage of FERPA is that schools are less likely to keep inaccurate information based on opinion rather than fact in a student's file. Although fears of parents and students being able to sue schools for false information contained in the files are unfounded, it is important that student files are (a) accurate, (b) based on facts and firsthand observation, and (c) educationally relevant (Fischer et al., 2002).

REPORTING SUSPECTED CHILD ABUSE AND NEGLECT

In 1991 the United States Advisory Board on Child Abuse and Neglect issued a report indicating that child abuse had reached the level of a national emergency. The report also stated that the nation's educational system had the potential to be the linch-pin of efforts to protect children from abuse and neglect. Currently all 50 states and the District of Columbia require persons, such as teachers, counselors, social service providers, mental health professionals, and physicians to report suspected cases of child abuse and neglect. To fully understand reporting requirements, readers should consult state requirements regarding reporting child abuse or neglect.

Legal Requirements to Report Suspected Child Abuse and Neglect

In 1974 the National Child Abuse Prevention and Treatment Act became law (42 U.S.C. §§ 5101–5107). This federal law provided funds to states that met its guidelines for reporting and dealing with child abuse and neglect. For purposes of the law, child abuse and neglect were defined as:

Physical or mental injury, sexual abuse or exploitation, negligent treatment, or maltreatment of a child under the age of eighteen or the age specified by the child protection law of the state in question, by a person who is responsible for the child's welfare, under circumstances which indicate that the child's health or welfare is harmed or threatened. (42 U.S.C. § 5106g(4))

Federal involvement in child abuse and neglect was increased by the passage of the Child Abuse Prevention, Adoption, and Family Services Act of 1988 (42 U.S.C. § 5101 et seq.) and the Child Abuse Prevention and Treatment Act of 1992 (42 U.S.C. § 5101 et seq.). Although these federal laws provided funding for efforts to prevent and treat child abuse and neglect, it is important that teachers understand that child abuse and neglect are state crimes. The 50 states and the District of Columbia have child protection service agencies that investigate reports of child abuse, offer services to at-risk families, and bring charges against abusive parents. Although there are similarities among the state laws requiring that teachers report suspected child abuse, there are also differences. It is important, therefore, that teachers know of the definitions and reporting requirements of the states in which they reside.

No states require that reporters of child abuse or neglect be absolutely certain that such abuse is occurring, but rather that they have a suspicion that such abuse is, in fact, taking place (Brooks, 1996; Cates, Markell, & Bettenhausen, 1995). That is, because child abuse is seldom witnessed, if individuals see evidence of what they and most people would believe to be possible child abuse, they have an obligation to report their suspicions. Absolute proof is not needed in a report of suspected child abuse or neglect. Waiting to gather proof prior to reporting child abuse may involve grave risk to the child and could, if the child is subsequently injured, subject the teacher to criminal or civil litigation (Cates et al., 1995).

Reporting Requirements

State laws mandate the procedures for reporting suspected child abuse and neglect. Typically states require that reports be made in a timely manner. The definition of "timely" varies among the states but is often between 24 hours and 3 days. In making the report, certain information is often required. Usually report forms are available from schools, social service agencies, or the state.

Because of their administrative roles, often the principal of a school will be the party who actually reports suspected abuse or neglect to child protective services. These reports will often form the basis for civil or criminal investigations so the report should be as detailed as possible. For example, reports should contain direct quotes, reports from a school nurse, and photographs of the suspected abuse if it is readily apparent.

Immunity from Lawsuits

Every state also provides immunity from civil suit and criminal prosecution that may arise from reporting suspected child abuse or neglect (Fischer et al., 2002). This immunity applies to reporters who act in "good faith" or "without malice"; therefore, teachers or counselors who report honest suspicions of abuse cannot be sued. States grant immunity for good-faith reports to encourage reporting because it is believed that reporters will more likely act if they have no fear of civil or criminal liability.

Liability for Failure to Report

In most states, failure to report suspected child abuse or neglect may result in criminal prosecution (Cates et al., 1995). Furthermore, all states provide for civil liability for damages related to the failure to report abuse (Fischer et al., 2002). In these states teachers or counselors who fail to report abuse can be sued for monetary damages if the failure was directly related to the actual abuse.

Legal Action

If teachers or counselors file a report of suspected child abuse or neglect, the statutes and regulations of the state in which the report is filed determine the specific steps that will follow. Typically after a report has been made, the state's social services agency will determine if the allegations warrant investigation and activation of the child protection services (Mahoney, 1995). All states have rules that set a time limit in which the accuser may request that the report be expunged, and have administrative procedures that protect the due process rights of the accused. If it is determined through investigation that abuse or neglect has taken place, an action may be undertaken in criminal, civil, or family court (Brooks, 1996).

Implications for Administrators and Teachers

Be Aware of the Signs of Child Abuse and Neglect Teachers of students with EBD should attend training on the signs of potential abuse or neglect. In addition to training, teachers should also know their schools' procedures for reporting suspected abuse and neglect.

School Districts Should Develop Policies and Provide Training on Reporting Suspected Child Abuse and Neglect The policies that the school district develops must be in writing and made available to the public as well as employees. Additionally, school district employees should be trained on these policies and how they can meet the standards of state law. Appropriate training will help ensure that school district employees meet their state's requirements for reporting suspected child abuse or neglect.

Teachers Should Keep Thorough Records of Suspected Abuse and Neglect The importance of keeping thorough records cannot be stressed too much. Anecdotal records can be crucial in abuse and neglect cases. Whenever possible, records should include the signatures of witnesses.

Summary of Reporting Suspected Child Abuse and Neglect

Teachers and counselors are clearly in positions of great sensitivity regarding child abuse and neglect. Outside of a child's parents, few people have as extensive contacts with the child as do educators. In cases involving potential cases of child abuse, teachers' responsibilities are clear. State laws require that suspected cases be reported to the appropriate authorities. Failure to respond appropriately to this responsibility could result in termination, criminal prosecution, civil suits and continued abuse of the child. Additionally, educators are offered protection from suits by immunity granted in instances of good-faith reporting of child abuse. If teachers file a report in good faith (i.e., a report filed because of honest concern and without malice or intention to do harm), they will not be held liable if the report turns out to be false.

TEACHER LIABILITY FOR STUDENT INJURY AND MISCONDUCT

In the past decade there has been a substantial increase in the number of lawsuits filed on behalf of students with disabilities seeking compensation for injuries while at school. Usually these cases involve student injuries, either physical or emotional, that occur either accidentally or intentionally. Although these cases usually occur on school grounds or at school functions, teachers have also been found liable when they assign students dangerous activities, even if a resulting injury occurs away from school grounds (*Simmons v. Beauregard Parish School Board*, 1975). Teachers have also been held liable in situations in which a student has injured another student or teacher *if* the student's teacher knew beforehand or should have known that the student was likely to try and harm another student, and the teacher did nothing to prevent it (*Ferraro v. Board of Education of the City of New York*, 1961). In such suits, plaintiffs (the person bringing the action) usually seek some form of monetary awards for the injury.

Although courts have acknowledged that schools cannot guarantee the safety of all students, school officials may face legal liability when a teacher injures a student by a either deliberate action or negligence. Usually student injury suits involve tort claims of negligence.

Tort Laws

Tort laws offer remedies to individuals harmed by the unreasonable actions of others. Tort claims usually involve state law and are based on the legal premise that individuals are liable for the consequences of their conduct if it results in injury to others (Fischer et al., 2002). Tort laws involve civil suits, which are actions brought to protect an individual's private rights. There are two major types of tort violations that involve teachers: intentional and negligence torts.

Intentional Torts Intentional torts are usually offenses committed by a person who attempts or intends to do harm. For intent to exist, the individual must be aware that injury will be the result of the act. Two common type of intentional torts are assault (i.e., an overt attempt to physically injure a person or create a feeling of fear and apprehension of injury) and battery (i.e., an actual physical contact is made in an attempt to injure). Both assault and battery can occur if a person threatens another, causing apprehension and fear, and then actually strikes the other, resulting in physical injury.

The courts typically give teachers accused of assault and battery a great deal of leeway (Valente & Valente, 2005). This is because assault and battery cases often result from attempts to discipline a student or stop a student from injuring someone. Courts are generally reluctant to interfere with a teacher's authority to discipline students (Valente & Valente, 2005). Courts have found teachers guilty of assault and battery, however, when a teacher's discipline has been cruel, brutal, excessive, or administered with malice, anger, or intent to injure.

In determining if a teacher's discipline constitutes excessive and unreasonable punishment, courts will often examine the age of the student; the instrument; if any, used to administer the discipline; the extent of the discipline; the nature and gravity of the student's offense, the history of the student's previous conduct; and the temper and conduct of the teacher.

Negligence Torts   The second type of tort law violation, which is encountered frequently in education related cases, is negligence. The difference between negligence and an intentional tort is that negligent acts leading to injury are neither expected nor intended. Students who bring negligence claims must prove that school personnel should have foreseen and prevented the injury by exercising proper care. Accidents that could not have been prevented by reasonable care do not constitute negligence (Fischer et al., 2002).

There are four elements that must be present for negligence to occur: (a) the teacher must have a duty to protect students from unreasonable risks, (b) the teacher must have failed in that duty by not exercising a reasonable standard of care, (c) there must be a causal connection between the breach of the duty to care and the resulting injury, and (d) there must be an actual physical or mental injury resulting from the negligence. In a court, all four elements must be proven before damages will be awarded for negligence.

The Teacher Had a Duty to Protect Students. The first element, the duty to protect, is clearly part of a teacher's responsibilities. Teachers have a duty to anticipate foreseeable dangers and take necessary precautions to protect students in their care (Fischer et al., 2002). Specifically, teacher duties include adequate supervision, maintenance of equipment and facilities, and heightened supervision of high-risk activities. Clearly this duty applies to activities during the school day; however, courts have also held that this duty may extend beyond regular school hours and away from school grounds (e.g., after school activities, summer activities, field trips, bus rides).

The Teacher Failed to Exercise a Reasonable Standard of Care. The second element that must be proven in cases of negligence occurs when teachers fail to exercise a reasonable standard of care in their duties to students. If a teacher fails to exercise reasonable care to protect students from injury, then the teacher is negligent. Courts in negligence cases will gauge a teacher's conduct on how a "reasonable" teacher in a similar situation

would have acted. The degree of care exercised by a "reasonable" teacher is determined by factors such as (a) the training and experience of the teacher in charge, (b) the student's age, (c) the environment in which the injury occurred, (d) the type of instructional activity, (e) the presence or absence of the supervising teacher, and (f) a student's disability, if one exists (Fisher, Schimmel, & Stellman, 2002; Mawdsley, 1993). For example, a primary-grade student will require closer supervision than a secondary school student; a physical education class in a gymnasium or an industrial arts class in a school woodshop will require closer supervision than a reading class in the school library; and a student with EBD will require closer supervision that a student who doesn't have behavior problems.

A number of cases have held that the student's IEP, disability, and unique needs are all relevant factors in determining the level of supervision that is reasonable (Daggett, 1995). Additionally, school officials may be liable for damage claims resulting from a failure to supervise a student with disabilities when that student injures another student.

The Teacher's Negligence Was Causally Connected to the Student's Injury. The third element that must be proven in a negligence case is whether there was a connection between the breach of duty by the teacher and the student's injury; that is, the teacher failed to exercise a reasonable standard of care (element two) and this breach of duty resulted in the subsequent injury to the student (element four). This element, referred to as proximate cause, often hinges on the concept of foreseeability. That is, could a teacher have anticipated the student's injury? If the injury could have been foreseen and prevented by a teacher, and if a reasonable standard of care had not been exercised, a logical connection—negligence—may exist. To answer questions regarding proximate cause, courts will attempt to ascertain if the injury was a natural and probable cause of the wrongful act (i.e., failure to supervise), and if it should have been foreseen in light of the attendant circumstances. Negligence claims will not be successful if the accident could not have been prevented through the exercise of reasonable care.

The Student Was Injured by the Teacher's Negligence. The final element that must be proven in negligence cases is that there was an actual physical or mental injury. Moreover, although the injury does not have to be physical, it must be real as opposed to imaginary (Mawdsley, 1993). Even in instances where there is negligence, damage suits will not be successful unless there is provable injury.

Implications for Administrators and Teachers

One of educators' most important obligations is to provide a reasonable standard of care for all students (Mawdsley, 1993). School districts should take actions to make certain that administrators, special and regular education teachers, and other personnel are aware of their care and supervisory duties under the law (Daggett, 1995; Mawdsley, 1993). The following suggestions were offered by Yell (2006) to assist administrators and teachers in meeting these responsibilities.

School Districts Should Develop Policies and Provide Training on Standards of Care and Supervision The policies that the school district develops must be in writing and made available to the public as well as employees. Additionally, school district employees should be trained on these policies and how they can meet the standards of state law. Appropriate training will help ensure the safety of all students, teachers, and staff. Such training should stress supervisory responsibilities, especially in activities that could foreseeably result in an accident or injury to a student. Because this area of law changes rapidly, legal developments should be monitored and school policies should be updated when necessary.

The IEP Team Should Address Potential Safety Risks and Plan for Them When Appropriate The IEP should include actions that will be taken to minimize these risks. In addition to members of the IEP team, regular education teachers and other personnel (e.g., paraprofessionals) involved with student care should be aware of any safety issues, potential problems, or required supervisory issues.

School Officials Should Not Rely on Waivers Educators sometimes assume that teachers and schools can release themselves from damages by having parents sign waivers or releases. This is untrue because parents cannot waive their children's claim for damages (Fischer et al., 2002; Yell, 2006). Teachers always have a duty to their students to prevent foreseeable injury by providing appropriate supervision. Parental releases, waivers, or permission slips do not relieve teachers or schools of liability if they fail to discharge their duties in an appropriate manner.

Teachers Should Keep Thorough Records As previously mentioned, teachers must keep thorough records. Thorough records can prove crucial in liability cases. The records should include the signatures of witnesses and administrators, as well as supervisory personnel. Parents should be notified of any situations that could result in liability claims. Figure 2–4 depicts an example of such a form.

Summary of Teacher Liability for Student Injury and Misconduct

Teachers and other school officials may be held liable for student injuries that occur because of their actions or negligence, but this liability also applies to all other citizens and professions (Fischer et al., 2002). Because educators work with children, they are likely to be involved in situations that in which students may be injured. The possibility of liability is especially acute for special educators who work with students, who because of their disabilities, have a greater likelihood of not recognizing danger and dangerous situations, and thus being injured, or injuring others. In fact, schools, school officials, and teachers may have a heightened standard of care for students with disabilities, especially those with cognitive and behavioral disabilities (Mawdsley, 1993). Special educators should not worry needlessly about liability; however, they need to recognize the heightened standard of care the teaching profession brings.

Chapter Summary

It is important that teachers of students with EBD understand their responsibilities under IDEA and other laws affecting the education of students with disabilities, including FERPA. Teachers need to know the laws of the states in which they work regarding students with disabilities, confidentiality of educational records, state liability laws, and reporting requirements when abuse or neglect is suspected.

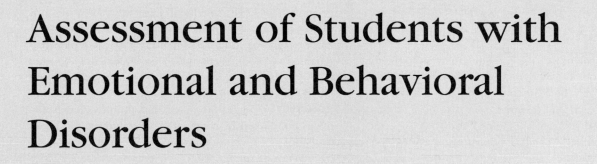

CHAPTER 3

Assessment of Students with Emotional and Behavioral Disorders

James G. Shriner, Scott P. Ardoin, and Mitchell L. Yell

Focus Questions

- What legal requirements must be followed when assessing students with emotional and behavioral disorders?

- What kinds of instruments are used to assess students with EBD?

- What do all the different scores on tests mean?

- Why is assessment important for determining interventions that will be used with students with EBD?

- How can teachers shown student progress by conducting an assessment?

According to Salvia and Ysseldyke (2007), assessment is "the process of collecting data for the purpose of making decisions about individuals and groups" (p. 5). Huefner (2000) noted that the importance of the assessment process cannot be overstated because an accurate picture of the student's strengths, weaknesses, and current levels of academic achievement and functional performance is the basis of all educational programming that will follow. Special education programming is based on a thorough and individualized evaluation.

The assessment process provides answers to the following questions: (a) who should receive special education services (i.e., eligibility and classification decisions); (b) what instructional programming should a student receive (i.e., instructional planning); and (c) how effective are a student's special education services (i.e., progress monitoring). The assessment process, thus, is central to learning and teaching (Kauffman, 2001; Reschly, 2000).

Assessing students with emotional and behavioral disorders (EBD) is an especially complex subject (Landrum, 2000). In this chapter we examine this process. First, we discuss the assessment requirements in the Individuals with Disabilities Education Act (IDEA). Second, we look at the assessment of students in special education. Third, we investigate how assessment and intervention are linked. Fourth, we examine the issue of accountability in special education.

IDEA AND ASSESSMENT

The formal assessment and evaluation procedures of IDEA are intended to ensure that (a) special education services are provided to children and youth who demonstrate the need for such services, (b) decisions for service provision are fair and defensible, and (c) all requirements for evaluations are implemented consistently in all districts and states and monitored for appropriateness and compliance (Shriner & Spicuzza, 1995).

Most of the assessment practices that we use in special education are the result of federal legislation or litigation (Salvia & Ysseldyke, 2004; Yell, 2006). This is because prior to the passage of the Education for All Handicapped Children Act (EAHCA) in 1975 (renamed IDEA in 1990), many students with disabilities were excluded from school entirely and many others were provided with an education that did not meet their unique educational needs (Yell & Drasgow, 2000). Early court cases, such as *Pennsylvania Association of Retarded Citizens* (PARC) v. *Pennsylvania* (1972) and *Mills* v. *Board of Education of the District of Columbia*

(1972) addressed the importance of a thorough assessment of a student's educational needs as a prerequisite for appropriate educational programming.

In the EAHCA, Congress required that all students with disabilities who were referred for special education services would receive an individualized assessment to determine if they were eligible to receive special education services, and if so, the content of their educational program. The EAHCA included eight specific provisions to ensure that assessment procedures were nondiscriminatory, equitable, and fair. When the EAHCA, which was renamed the Individuals with Disabilities Education Act (1990) in 1990, was reauthorized in the Individuals with Disabilities Education Act Amendments of 1997 (hereafter IDEA 1997), Congress required that all individual assessments conducted by a school include information about the student's involvement and progress in the general curriculum or, for preschoolers, in appropriate activities (IDEA Regulations, 34 C.F.R. § 300.532(b)). Table 3–1 lists the protection in evaluation Procedures (PEP) of IDEA.

In IDEA 1997 Congress made a few other important changes in the assessment procedures to clarify parents' rights to information. Parental consent for assessment of their child has always been required by IDEA regulations; however, IDEA 1997 puts consent in the legislative language and stresses that consent for evaluation is *not* consent for placement of a child. Furthermore, IDEA 1997 also required parental consent for reevaluations unless the school can determine that the parents failed to respond to reasonable attempts to obtain their consent. This information, in addition to existing rules that parents be provided with prior notice and explanations

Table 3–1   Protection in evaluation procedures

- Tests are to be selected and administered in such a way as to be racially and culturally nondiscriminatory.
- To the extent feasible, students are to be assessed in their native language or primary code of communication.
- Tests must be valid for the specific purpose for which they are used.
- Tests must be administered by trained personnel in conformance with the instructions provided by the test producer.
- Tests used with students must include those designed to provide information about specific education needs, and not just a general intelligence quotient.
- Decisions about students are to be based on more than performance on a single test.
- Assessment tools and strategies provide relevant information that directly assists persons in determining the educational needs of the child.
- Students are to be assessed in all areas of suspected disability.

of all assessment procedures, tests, records, and reports, helps ensure that parents are provided with a more complete picture of what the school is doing for their child. Assessment procedures were altered in the Individuals with Disabilities Education Improvement Act of 2004 (hereafter IDEA 2004). The assessment requirements that were added in IDEA 2004 are depicted in Table 3-2.

Next we discuss the assessment process.

Referral for Special Education

In a sense, special education begins with the referral and assessment process that may lead to the provision of services. As such, this process is a useful beginning point for our description of assessment as it relates to students with EBD.

School districts have an affirmative duty under the child find requirements of IDEA (IDEA, 20 U.S.C. § 1412(a)) to identify, locate, and assess all children with disabilities residing within the district's jurisdiction who (a) have disabilities and need special education as a result, or (b) are suspected of having a disability and need special education services. This includes children who attend private school, children who are homeless, and children from migrant families. Because it is an affirmative duty, parents are not required to request that a school district identify and assess their child, nor does a failure to request an assessment by parents relieve a school district of its child find obligations. Many, perhaps most, students with disabilities are identified when a teacher initiates a request for a special education evaluation, often called the referral process. In addition to teachers, other school personnel (e.g., counselors) and parents can also make referrals. In fact, IDEA 2004 specifically states that parents may request an evaluation for special education services.

The request for assessment usually goes to a school-based team, often called a multidisciplinary team (MDT). This team should consist of members of the individualized education program (IEP) planning team and other qualified personnel. Parents must be included in the eligibility determination process. The team's task is to determine if under IDEA the student may qualify for special education services by teachers.

Procedural Safeguards and Assessment

If the MDT decides to conduct an assessment of a student, the team must receive informed consent from the student's parents before the assessment can be conducted. Moreover, IDEA requires that school districts send parents a full explanation of all procedural safeguards available during the assessment process, a description of what a district plans or refuses to do, and a description of any additional options considered and reasons that were rejected. For testing purposes, a description of all evaluation and assessment procedures, records, or reports the district used to make a decision, and any additional information that may be relevant to a district's proposal or refusal to provide special education services is to be provided to the student, parent, or guardian (Yell, 2006). IDEA, however, does not require the identification of specific tests that will be administered.

Table 3–2 Assessment in IDEA 2004

Differences	Explanation of Changes
Timelines	Eligibility determinations to be completed within 60 days of receiving parental consent for the evaluation or within the state-established timeframe, if applicable.
Parental refusal to consent	LEA cannot request dispute resolution to override a parent's refusal to consent for special education and related services. In these circumstances, the LEA is not responsible to provide FAPE, convene an IEP meeting, or develop an IEP.
Eligibility for special education	A child shall not be eligible because of lack of appropriate instruction in reading, including in the essential components of reading instruction (as defined in section 1208(3) of the Elementary and Secondary Education Act of 1965); lack of instruction in math; or limited English proficiency.
Learning disabilities	LEAs shall not be required to consider whether a child has a severe discrepancy between achievement and intellectual ability (discrepancy formula).
	LEAs may use a process that determines if the child responds to scientific, research-based intervention as a part of the required evaluation procedures.
Change of eligibility	LEA shall provide the child with a summary of the child's academic achievement and functional performance, including recommendations regarding the child's postsecondary goals (for students no longer eligible because of earning a regular high school diploma or exceeding the age of eligibility).

The procedural safeguards must be presented to students and parents in language that is easy to understand and, when necessary, interpreters must be made available for non-English-speaking individuals or persons with sensory impairments. After parents grant consent for the district to conduct an assessment, IDEA 2004 requires that the initial assessment take place within 60 days. If the state has established a shorter timeframe in which to conduct the assessment (e.g., 45 days), school personnel must follow the state timelines.

Conducting the Assessment

When conducting an assessment, school-based personnel must attend to the previously mentioned protection in evaluation procedures (see Table 3–1). Furthermore, they must ensure that the assessment meets the following four requirements. First, the team must conduct a full and individualized assessment. Second, all assessment decisions regarding the assessment must be made by a group of knowledgeable persons. Third, the assessment data must be linked to a student's educational programming. Fourth, the assessment must include procedures that can be used to monitor a student's progress in his or her program. Next we review these requirements.

IDEA requires that the school-based team conduct a full and individualized examination. According to Reschly (2000), the assessment must be individualized. Additionally, the assessment must address (a) the referral concerns, (b) the nature of the problem, (c) the characteristics of the student, (d) the student's learning and behavior patterns, and (e) the concerns of the student's parents (Yell & Drasgow, 2000). Reschly (2000) contended that assessing students by always using a standard battery of tests is poor practice. In addition to standardized achievement and intelligence tests, Reschly asserted that assessments should consist of interviews, direct observation, curriculum-based assessments, and similar measures.

Clearly, when a student who exhibits problem behaviors is being assessed for special education services, the assessment must address his or her behavioral needs. Regardless of the possible disability category that the student may be served under, the team must address the problem behaviors if the student's behaviors impede his or her learning or the learning of others (IDEA, 20 U.S.C. § 1414 (d)(3)(B)(i)). Assessment of problem behaviors requires that the team collect and interpret functional information from a variety of sources (see Chapter 5 on functional behavioral assessments).

Additionally, a team of knowledgeable persons should make decisions regarding the assessment. Persons on the assessment team should have expertise in the specific areas being assessed. For example, if the team needs an assessment of a student's assistive technology needs, someone on the team must be qualified to assess the student in that area. When school districts do not have personnel who have expertise in a required area of assessment, the school district officials should ensure that school-based personnel receive proper training or hire an outside consultant to perform the assessment.

The assessment information must also lead to educational programming. That is, if an assessment indicates an area of need, this area must be addressed in the present levels of academic achievement and functional performance. The present levels statement describes the student's performance in areas that are affected by his or her disability (Yell & Drasgow, 2000). The present levels statement, in turn, must lead to educational programming to address that particular need. This is done in the IEP through the measurable annual goals, the special education services, or both goals and services.

Finally, the assessment must include procedures that will allow a student's teacher to continue to collect assessment data during the course of instruction to monitor the student's progress. Thus, the assessment becomes the baseline by which the student's instructional or behavioral progress is determined. IDEA requires monitoring of a student's progress during the course of instruction (i.e., formative assessment) so that educators can modify his or her program, if necessary.

Reevaluating Students in Special Education

The reevaluation process is generally understood to be a comprehensive evaluation, similar to the initial assessment that was conducted by the MDT (Norlin & Gorn, 2005). In the reevaluation, the MDT should address four issues: (a) whether the student still has the disability, (b) what the student's level of academic achievement and functional performance are, (c) whether the student continues to need special education and related services, and whether any changes in the student's IEP are required (IDEA Regulations, 34 C.F.R. § 300.533(a)(2)). Eligible students in special education programs should be reevaluated at least every 3 years (IDEA, 20 U.S.C. § 1414(a)(2)). Language in IDEA 2004 requires that a reevaluation be conducted if the student warrants a reevaluation, or if the student's teachers or parents request a reevaluation (IDEA, 20 U.S.C. § 1414(a)(2)(A)).

The reevaluation process was streamlined when IDEA was reauthorized in 1997 and in 2004. Under the new law, a 3-year evaluation may rely on existing information and assessments. If the local educational agency

(LEA) believes that no additional data are needed and the parent agrees, it is possible that the reevaluation can be conducted with no new assessments being given. In this regard, the reevaluation process is more purposeful—seeking to assess only when valid reasons exist.

ASSESSING STUDENTS IN SPECIAL EDUCATION

Achievement Tests

Achievement tests evaluate knowledge and skills in numerous areas. These tests are used to compare one student's achievement in an area to other students in the same area. Many of these tests are *norm referenced* or *criterion referenced*. Some achievement tests are designed to be group administered, whereas others are designed to be administered by a qualified adult in a one-to-one setting with a student (individually administered). There are many different achievement tests on the market, with many designed to evaluate knowledge and skills in multiple areas; for example in math, reading, spelling, social studies, science, and so on. Other tests are designed to test knowledge and skills in a specific domain; for example, in writing.

Norm-Referenced Testing Norm-referenced tests (NRTs) are tests in which a student's current achievement or performance level is compared to the performance level of a national sample of students administered the same test by the test author. This population of students is typically called the norm or standardization sample. For norming tests, authors generally attempt to select a sample of students that are representative of the population, often using the most recent census data collected. It is important that an NRT is used only with students whose demographics (e.g., age, gender, first language) are represented in the norm or standardization sample.

The purpose of NRTs is to compare, in a rank order fashion, the degree to which a student has characteristics (e.g., reading skills, language skills, behavior) similar to other students of the same age or grade. Students' raw scores are generally converted into an equivalence, percentile, or standard score in order to describe students' performance in a fairly objective but global manner. NRT scores provide information regarding the degree to which a student's skill, behavior, or ability level is similar or dissimilar from a comparison group of interest (norm-referenced group). Group-administered NRTs are best used for screening purposes because they allow for the identification of students whose academic achievement, behavior, speech, or intellectual ability are substantially below or above the normative sample and are therefore in need of supplemental services.

Whereas the primary purpose of group-administered NRTs is to screen students, individually administered NRTs are used to obtain broad-based knowledge of what characteristics a student does and does not have. Because individually administered NRTs are administered in a one-to-one setting, a variety of response types beyond multiple choice or fill in the blank are possible, and thus the range of skill levels assessed can be individualized. Individually administered NRTs typically have examiners give easier or more difficult problems based on a student's response accuracy. Test authors provide examiners with detailed instructions on how to establish a basal (level below which the student is likely to get all of the questions correct) and a ceiling (level at which the student is not likely to get any more questions correct) on the test to decrease the number of items examiners must administer. Considering that NRTs are generally developed to assess the level of ability of a wide age range of students, administering all items of a test to a student would likely result in extreme frustration for both the examiner and student.

Individually administered NRTs or norm-referenced scales are currently the most widely used model for determining whether a student has an educational or behavioral disorder, and is thus eligible for special education. Typically students are administered intelligence tests in order to determine their predicted level ability; that predicted level is compared to their level of achievements as determined by their performance on individually norm-referenced achievement tests. This model is generally referred to as the IQ-achievement discrepancy model, and is based on the philosophy that if a student has an emotional or behavioral disability his or her achievement should be significantly below his or her ability level. When a discrepancy is found between predicated and actual achievement and factors such as inappropriate education, visual problems, and auditory problems are ruled out as causes of the discrepancy, it is generally determined that the student has an exceptionality and should thus receive special education services. Behavioral and social emotional rating scales are often administered along with interviews of parents and teachers as a means of determining whether the discrepancy is due to a specific learning disability or emotional and behavioral disability. IDEA 2004 prohibits states from mandating that discrepancy formulas be used when determining whether a student has a learning disability, although schools are free to choose a discrepancy model. The law now encourages the use of a response to intervention model.

Unfortunately, because individual NRTs are developed to assess students of multiple ages and grades, the number of skills assessed in a specific domain (e.g., mathematics) is relatively large and thus individual skills are assessed using a relatively small number of items. The limited number of observations of a student's performance on specific skills (e.g., adding two-digit numbers with regrouping) decreases the utility of conducting error analysis and developing interventions using the data collected from NRTs. Other characteristics of NRTs that limit their utility to develop and monitor intervention effectiveness and monitor students' progress include (a) being able to administer the test only after several months have passed; (b) most NRTs have only two alternate forms and therefore, if used more than twice in a relative short period of time, students may improve due to practice effect; (c) they are time-consuming and costly to administer; and (d) examiners require training in order to administer, score, and interpret the results.

Equivalent Scores. NRTs generally yield several types of scores. The first type is *equivalence scores*, often either age-equivalent or grade-equivalent scores, and for reasons to be discussed later should be interpreted with extreme caution. Age scores compare a student to other students of the same chronological age. For example, a student earning a score on an age-equivalent scale of 9-2 obtained a raw score approximately equal to the mean raw score of students in the normative sample who were of that age. This could be on an achievement test of reading, spelling, or on some behavior scale or social skills rating. Similarly, grade scores compare a student to students in the normative sample at certain points in the academic year. For example, if a student obtains a grade score of 4.3, he or she has performed as well as a typical student in the third month of fourth grade. An important point to remember is that any equivalent score is simply a way of describing the average or median performance for a particular grade or age group and is not an indication that the student can perform the same skills as students of the specified age or grade equivalent.

Equivalent scores themselves are a way to give the information about a student in a developmental level that seems easy for most people in the school to understand but which actually has serious shortcomings. First, both age-and grade-equivalent scores are subject to rather systematic misinterpretation. Students who earn an equivalent score of 12-0 on an age scale have answered the same number of items correctly, responded the same, or been rated as similar to the average 12-years-old. This does not mean that the student has done or can do exactly the same behaviors as the average 12-year-old, nor does it

mean the task was completed in the same way. The information provided is simply a way of describing the performance of an average person who does not exist and therefore should not be used as a means of placing a student in a curriculum. Second, there is often a need for the interpolation of scores, which is the estimation of the value between two given scores. Scores are established when a test is normed. Children are rarely tested at every point on an age scale or grade scale, meaning that children are not tested at the 1st month of third grade, the 2nd month of third grade, the 3rd month of third grade, and so forth. Nor are they tested in the first month of their 12th year of life, 2nd month, and so forth. Consequently, a child who earns a score of 3.2 is assigned a score for which no children may have been tested at age 3.2. Equivalent scores may also be derived through extrapolation, which is the extension of scores to age or grade not actually administered in the norming process. Tests developed to assess the skills of first through fourth graders may actually produce grade-equivalent scores of kindergarten and sixth grade, even though no kindergarten or sixth-grade student was ever administered the test for normative purposes. For this reason extreme equivalent scores should be interpreted with even greater caution.

This process helps promote typological thinking (Salvia & Ysseldyke, 2004). In other words, the average child does not exist. Equivalent scores encourage the comparison of students to inappropriate groups. For example, it is inappropriate to suggest that a third grader who obtains a 5.5 grade equivalent score can perform middle-of-the-year fifth-grade work. The third grader simply obtained the same raw score as the average mid-year fifth grader. No other attributes are shared between the third-grade student and the average fifth grader. Third-grade students should be compared with other third-grade students who have had similar educational opportunities.

Finally, there is an important difference between age- and grade-level scores in that they are more ordinal, and not equal interval in nature. There is not always an equal degree of change in behavior or performance from one month to the next at any grade level, nor from one month to the next at any age. It should also not be expected that every student will make an increase in one grade-or age-equivalent score per year.

Percentile Ranks. A second commonly used score provided by NRTs is the percentile rank, which is an indication of the percentage of students who score at or below a certain raw score on a test or assessment. Depending on the test administered or the desire of the person reporting the score, a percentile rank can refer to age- or grade-based norm groups. For example, if a student who is 11 years old obtains a raw score that converts to a percentile rank of 75% the student has scored as well as or better than 75% of the 11-year-olds who took that particular test or who were assessed on that particular rating scale. In addition, if a fourth grader takes a test and his raw score translates to a percentile rank of 99, then the student did as well as or better than 99% of the fourth graders taking the test or performing on that rating scale.

Percentile ranks are not the same as percentage correct on any given test. Percentile ranks are also sometimes divided into deciles which are bands of 10 possible percentile ranks, or quartiles, which are bands of 25 percentile ranks within width. Percentiles, deciles, and quartiles are indications of relative standing, and are derived from the raw scores on any test or rating scale.

Standard Scores. Finally, scores from NRTs can also be expressed as standard scores, which tell how far above or below a student's performance is from the mean performance of students in the normative sample who are of a student's approximate age. Percentile ranks are one type of standard score, but more commonly we hear of standard scores being used in intelligence testing where the mean is 100 and the standard deviation is 15. Someone scoring at the 50th percentile on a typical intelligence test, therefore, would be assigned an IQ of 100. Other commonly used standard scores include z-scores (mean of 0; standard deviation of 1) and T-scores (mean of 50; standard deviation of 10).

Standard scores allow for the evaluation of a student's relative strengths and weaknesses across different tests. For instance, an 11-year-old may be administered an achievement test that assesses basic reading comprehension skills that was developed to assess the achievement of students between the ages of 6 and 12 years, and a test developed to assess math computation skills of students between 10 and 18 years of age. Knowing that the student obtained a raw score of 28 on the reading achievement tests and a score of 10 on the mathematics achievement tells nothing regarding how the student compares to other students of the same age. It is first of all unlikely that the same numbers of items were administered across the tests and the level of difficulty of the test would likely differ drastically, considering the differences in the age levels the tests were developed to assess. Whereas the reading test would likely have several problems that most 6-year olds could easily answer, the mathematics test would likely have few if any that a 6-year old could answer. NRTs therefore provide standard scores, so that a student's performance on one NRT can be compared to his performance on another NRT. Using the student's age and the normative tables provided by the test authors, the examiner can determine that the reading raw score of 28 was equivalent to a T-score of 45 and the mathematics raw score of 10 was equivalent to a T-score of 60. Differences in these T-scores suggest that math computation is a relative strength for the student. This student performed half a standard deviation below same-age peers (T-score of -0.5 = percentile score of 32) on the reading achievement test and one standard deviation above same-age students on the mathematics achievement test (T-score of $+1.0$ = percentile score of 84).

Standard scores within one standard deviation above and below the mean (e.g., T-scores between 40 and 60) include one half of the population and are typically considered scores in the average range. Standard scores above and below one standard deviation from the mean are considered in the above- and below-average range, respectively. Depending on the test or subscale being examined, being above or below average can be positive or negative. A T-score of 65 on a writing achievement test is a positive thing, whereas a T-score of 65 on a scale of hyperactivity may be reason for concern.

Criterion-Referenced Assessment Seldom do we describe a student's performance relative to a group of other students as the only information upon which we will base decisions for placement or instruction. NRTs only provide us with rankings, but a criterion-referenced assessment is not concerned with the rankings of students compared to one another. Criterion-referenced assessments are used in making judgments about a student's performance in comparison to a predetermined criterion or standard. The major purpose of criterion-referenced assessment is to look at the performance of a student relative to some scale that has been established as providing a meaningful description of student learning or attainment. It helps to describe exactly what the student has and has not learned, and can give more exact information about how a student performs on specific academic or behavioral tasks.

The scores obtained from the administration of criterion-referenced tests (CRTs) differ from NRTs. Rather than providing equivalence or standard scores, which provide information regarding a student's standing in comparison to a normative sample, CRTs typically provide percentages correct, number correct, or a rate-per-minute score. They might also give global ratings of performance such as overall ratings of a project or portfolio. CRTs provide scores relative to a standard beginning at the low end of performance, meaning that the student has not accomplished the tasks or behaviors that are being measured, and to the high end, meaning that the student has the ability to demonstrate all of the skills that are being measured. In contrast to NRTs, CRTs compare a student's performance to a skill level, not to other people. In criterion-referenced testing there is a greater concern about the degree to which a student has learned what has been taught than about how well other students have done. To a greater extent than NRTs, students' performance on CRTs can be linked to curriculum and/or intervention development for a particular student.

ASSESSMENT AND INTERVENTION

Many different types of assessment information are gathered on and about students with EBD. But testing must serve a purpose and tests are valid only in terms of the purposes for which they are evaluated. Programming choices for students with emotional and behavioral disorders ought to be data based. It is also extremely important that assessment has an instructional purpose in mind. CRTs, even though they are intended to be objectively referenced, do not always provide significant help with the assessment intervention link. This is because sometimes the tests that are administered do not have a high degree of correspondence with the information that is taught or with the curriculum in which the student is enrolled. As a matter of fact, most commercially prepared criterion-referenced and norm-referenced tests do not adequately cover the content that is part of the instruction of most students (Good & Salvia, 1988; Jenkins & Pany, 1978; Shapiro & Derr, 1987; Shriner & Salvia, 1988). The most direct application of CRT to address the assessment–intervention link is curriculum-based assessment (CBA) in which the student's progress is based on samples of ongoing performance within existing course curriculum content. The idea of CBA is that the local school curriculum is the domain from which samples of student behavior are collected and against which student progress is judged.

Basics of Curriculum-Based Assessment

Curriculum-based assessment (CBA) is defined as a set of assessment procedures that use "direct observation and recording of a student's performance in the local curriculum as a basis for gathering information to make instructional decisions" (Deno, 1987). CBA is important because it has been shown to produce reliable and valid information relating to student performance and can answer questions such as how effective a particular instructional program is for a specific student (McLoughlin & Lewis, 2007). Some distinguishing features of CBA do address the shortcomings of traditional standardized norm-referenced

or criterion-referenced instruments that were discussed earlier. The issue of content validity is addressed in CBA because all items are taken directly from a student's curriculum. There is virtually 100% overlap between what is taught and what is tested. The information that is collected in CBA is also relevant to instructional planning, so the assessment intervention link is made very explicit. In addition, teachers find that CBA gives timely feedback on student performance and teachers' behaviors that can change student performance.

The various models of CBA include Gickling's accuracy-based model (Gickling & Havertape, 1981; Gickling & Thompson, 1985), Blankenship and Idol's criterion-referenced model (Blankenship, 1985; Idol, Nevin, & Paolucci-Whitcomb, 1986), and a fluency-based model known as curriculum-based measurement (CBM); (Deno, 1985). Although these models differ, they are similar in that they are derived from material used in the classroom, are quick and easy to administer, allow for repeated measurements, and allow for student performance to be graphed and systematically monitored (Frisby, 1987). Although they do differ, they do not have to be used independently of each other.

Gickling's (Gickling & Havertape, 1981; Gickling & Thompson, 1985) accuracy-based CBA model incorporates primarily production-type responses taken directly from the student's curriculum with the primary outcome measure being percentage correct. Obtained levels of accuracy are intended to be used to place students in the appropriate level of instruction. Emphasis is placed on analyzing the task demands of the instructional material and is based on assessment results; teachers are expected to develop their own instructional material. Due to these expectations, this model may be viewed more as an intervention rather than an assessment model.

Similar to Gickling's model, the criterion-referenced model of CBA (Blankenship, 1985; Idol et al., 1986) may be viewed more as a teaching rather than testing model, as the primary purpose of the criterion-referenced model is to provide teachers with information for instructional planning. Criterion-referenced models of CBA use direct and frequent measures of student performance on sequentially arranged objectives derived from the classroom curriculum. Students' mastery of these sequential objectives is evaluated using various response types including production (e.g., written answers to math problems) and selection-type responses (e.g., selecting words that don't belong in a set of rhyming words). Mastery of skills by students may be assessed using either or both accuracy and fluency, depending on the skill being assessed. Although this model is primarily designed for continuous assessment of short-term objectives,

Blankenship (1985) suggests that maintenance of skills can also be assessed through the intermittent readministration of the CBA probes throughout the year.

Curriculum-Based Measurement

The fluency-based model of CBA, CBM (Deno, 1985), differs from the previous two models in several ways. First, the previous models lack standardized administration procedures, whereas CBM has standardized procedures for assessing students' mathematics, reading, spelling, and writing skills. For example, in mathematics, students are administered multiple skill mathematics calculation probes. Students are told that they are to work across rows and then down to the next row, and that they are to put an "X" through any problem they do not know how to complete. Rather than scoring probes based on number of problems correct as is typically done in the classroom, probes are scored based on number of digits correct. For example, if a student answered that $5 + 8 = 15$ the student would receive 1 digit correct for the one in the ten's column.

Standardized procedures have facilitated extensive evaluation of the CBM model, especially in the area of reading (see Shinn, 1989, for a review). The technical adequacy of CBM for identifying students in need of intervention, being sensitive to intervention effects, and providing teachers with reliable information for making instructional decisions is abundant. CBM was judged to have sufficient evidence to be used for both progress monitoring and formative evaluation of reading fluency by the Reading First Academy Assessment Committee (Kame'enui, 2002), which reviewed a large number of assessment practices in various areas of reading (i.e., screening, diagnosis, progress monitoring, and outcome assessment) (Francis et al., 2005). Although many instruments evaluated by the committee were approved for summative evaluation of various reading components (e.g., phonemic awareness, comprehension), only a few were considered sensitive to instructional growth and intervention effects.

Whereas other CBA models use accuracy or accuracy and fluency as their primary measure, CBM always uses fluency. Fluency is the combination of accuracy plus speed. Reasons for measuring fluency rather than accuracy include: (a) accuracy alone does not mean that a student has mastery of a skill; (b) accuracy has a ceiling (i.e., students cannot exceed 100% accuracy); (c) measuring fluency facilitates the graphing of data in time series fashion toward a long-term goal; and (d) in order to perform complex skills it is necessary to be fluent in the component skills. Whereas teachers may sometimes question the utility of assessing fluency (Fuchs, Fuchs, and Maxwell, 1988), fluency has repeatedly been shown to be a necessary component of comprehension and consistently correlates as high or higher with standardized measures of comprehension than does any alternative (Ardoin et al., in press; Deno, Mirkin, & Chiang, 1982; Fuchs et al., 1988; Jenkins & Jewell, 1993). Although a student's comprehension of a text may be poor after the first reading, comprehension generally improves with each successive reading as the student's attention is spent less on decoding and to a greater extent on comprehending the text. White and Haring (1980) pointed out that students who are slow yet accurate have not mastered the skill; however, others who are faster but less accurate may have mastered the skill.

Another dimension of CBM that distinguishes it from other forms of CBA is that it integrates components of traditional and behavioral assessment. Rather than measuring specific skills, each CBM probe assesses a relatively broad range of skills (i.e., a construct), sampled from the annual curriculum. Sampling broadly from the curriculum results in a broad dispersion of scores when students within a class or grade are assessed. Students' scores can be viewed as a performance indicator, representing their global level of competence within the domain assessed (Fuchs & Fuchs, 2002). The performance of students within a grade or class can be compared in order to identify students in need of intervention. This is a form of peer referencing (Deno, 1985) and gives an idea of how well a student is performing in relation to similarly functioning peers who have had the same educational opportunities (i.e., same teachers, taught in same curriculum, exposed to same school resources or lack thereof). Special education teachers can also use data collected by regular education teachers to determine how discrepant a student's performance is from regular education students, who are of the same age or grade equivalence. CBM data collected on students in regular education can also be used to establish long-term goals for students in special education.

The integration of traditional and behavioral assessment also facilitates CBM's use for measuring and graphing progress over extended periods of time. Establishing a long-term goal, continually monitoring progress toward that goal, and using a line graph to plot the data in time series fashion enables teachers to visually determine whether a student will attain an established long-term goal. Goals are increased for students whose data suggest that they will exceed their goal. Thus, if a long-term goal for a student in special education is that in 6 months the student will be reading end-of-the-year fourth-grade material at a rate of 100 words correct per minute and the student appears as if he will exceed that goal, the goal should be raised. Increasing a student's long-term goal helps ensure that instruction is continually provided at a level that will maximize the student's potential. Goals are generally established using researched or school-based normative rates of growth. If a student can exceed that rate of growth, then that rate of growth should always be expected from the student while monitoring progress toward that goal.

When students' scores on CBM probes differ substantially from their peers, teachers should begin implementing interventions and monitoring the effects of those interventions using CBM procedures. Students who do not respond adequately to interventions implemented in the regular education classroom—meaning when provided with interventions their rate of growth remains substantially below the rate of growth of their classmates—may need more assistance than can be provided in the regular education classroom (i.e., special education). The data collected through CBM progress monitoring of the student should be used in the decision-making process regarding whether the child needs special education. If a student becomes eligible for special education, CBM progress monitoring should continue and be used to monitor progress toward IEP goals, to evaluate whether the student makes greater gains while in special versus regular education, and to determine what interventions are effective for a student. For a thorough discussion of CBM, see Chapter 16.

Although there is a long history of formative evaluation in special education, such evaluation required by NCLB is relatively new to general education professionals. Potentially, CBM can be used as a common measurement process and thus assist in the integration of regular and special education services. The federal government is encouraging such integration in order to ensure a continuum of interrelated services for children at risk as they move from instruction in a general education classroom to placement in special education (National Association of State Directors of Special Education, 2002).

A computerized version of CBM called Monitoring Basic Skills Progress (MBSP) (Hamlet, Fuchs, & Fuchs, 1997) is available in the areas of basic reading, spelling, and mathematics. The computer programs are used to monitor student progress, identify students who require intervention, and to suggest changes and improvements to instructional programs. The programs can track student progress from Grades 1 through 7. The computer software administers and scores tests, provides students with feedback regarding their performance, and summarizes student performance in graphic form. The goals of most of the MBSP programs include describing student

progress and formulating appropriate instructional goals for students. They can also be used to compare effectiveness of different types of teaching used with students and to determine how to improve the students' overall educational program. The important feature of the computerized version of MBSP is that it does the record keeping and helps the teachers with decision making.

Organizing Data

In most situations when CBA is used with students, the data that result from student assessments are put onto graphs. The advantage of using graphs is that they help with the decision-making process related to how a student is progressing or not progressing through a curriculum. (For a discussion of making graphs, see Chapter 4.) When students have desired levels of performance established for them, graphs are a way to illustrate for students, teachers, and possibly parents how student are performing in relation to the desired level of performance that has been set. Deno and Fuchs (1987) recommended that when graphing student data, a relatively small unit of mastery such as number of pages mastered or number of words read correctly be used instead of larger units (e.g., chapters or levels of a curriculum completed). The reason is that larger units are less likely to represent equal units of progress and may not assist in showing small changes in performance. When student progress through a curriculum is planned, the teacher might consult the curriculum sequence for the materials being used and plot a line on a graph that shows the expected (goal) level of performance. This line is used as a reference point for decisions about instructional programming. The expected progress lines connect the student's current level of performance to the goal level that is determined. For example, a student may be assessed to answer 5 digits correct in 2 minutes, the student's progress will be monitored for 15 weeks, and a goal level of 50 digits correct in 2 minutes is established. This goal level may be determined based on local norms, class norms, or research norms. Based on previous data the teacher may know that her students typically gain 3 digits correct per 2 minutes weekly, thus she multiplies 3 times the number of weeks the student will be monitored and adds that to the student's current functioning ($3 \times 15 + 5 = 50$).

After data are plotted it is important to assess whether the student is progressing in a particular instructional or behavioral program. In order to assess whether a student is progressing, a *trend line* can be drawn. A trend line is a line that can be drawn on a graph that shows a student's progress or decline in a specific area. If the student's trend line is flatter than the expected trend line or is not showing change toward the desired terminal behavior, then the teacher should consider a change in the instructional program. Changes can include a different type of teaching procedure (e.g., increased modeling, increased opportunities to practice), student grouping (i.e., size and makeup of instructional group), increased time allocated to instruction, a change in materials, or motivational strategies (e.g., goal setting). If the trend line of the student's actual performance is equal to or steeper than the expected trend line or shows significant progress toward the desired terminal behavior, then the program should probably be left intact and a loftier goal considered. This type of goal-oriented approach can help students understand how they are doing, and prompt the special education teacher to adjust goals upward when students are making adequate progress.

Deno and Fuchs (1987) and Fuchs, Hamlet, and Fuchs (1997) recommended—as an easier, but not necessarily better, alternative to calculating a trend line—that changes to an instructional program be considered when three consecutive data points are below the expected trend line. When evaluating academic performance, however, these changes should not take place until a minimum of six data points are collected. Also, it is possible that changes could be made if a student's performance is becoming highly variable or unstable. A high degree of variability might indicate that the teacher should analyze exactly how a particular student is responding to an instructional approach.

Performance Assessment

According to the Office of Technology Assessment (1992), performance assessments have three key features: (a) The assessment tasks require students to construct rather than select responses, (b) the assessment tasks allow teachers to observe student behavior as they engage in "real-world" activities, and (c) scoring methods examine students' thinking as well as their ability to analyze the product created. Performance assessments in content areas involve students *actively* doing things that allow them to show what they know. Students might perform tasks individually or in groups. Baron (1991) listed several types of performance assessments that are being used more frequently and include open-ended questioning, investigative tasks and projects, extended writing activities, observations and interviews, and portfolios. The use of *portfolio* assessment has gained popularity in recent years in many content areas (McLoughlin & Lewis, 2005).

In contrast to traditional paper-and-pencil assessments, portfolios are thought by some to be better reflections of student thinking and understanding. Portfolios also allow teachers to assess student dispositions such as curiosity, persistence, and risk taking (Pandey, 1991). Portfolios yield a permanent record of student achievement because they are collections of student work, but proponents argue that the assembly of a portfolio provides valuable learning and assessment opportunities. Stenmark (1991), in a discussion of mathematics portfolios, remarked that they can improve self-confidence because students can be engaged at their own level of ability and experience.

Portfolios might be either working collections for the student to continually refine or assessment collections for evaluation purposes. Regardless of which orientation is used, the intended purpose must be decided and defined in advance. The context and categories of portfolio entries (e.g., answers to open-ended questions, reports, computers, products, etc.) should reflect the students' work over time.

Portfolios usually are scored using holistic, rubric-based decision-making processes. An individual entry and/or a complete portfolio often is assigned scores on a scale from 1 (beginning work, inadequate) to 4 (distinguished work, exemplary).

Several disadvantages of portfolios have been listed by both proponents and detractors (e.g., Kleinert, Kearns, & Kennedy, 1997; Salvia & Ysseldyke, 2007). Among the most important for teachers to consider are (a) the time commitment and constraints of assembling and evaluating portfolio entries, (b) the relative "grossness" of portfolio scoring methods and the variability that is introduced when multiple persons evaluate portfolios, (c) the instructional utility of portfolio assessment results, and (d) the difficulty of communicating portfolio assessment results to students, teachers, and parents.

Data Sources for Behavioral Assessment

Behavior of all types, including problem behavior, is often influenced by each specific environment the student encounters (Bronfenbrenner, 1979; Greenwood, 1999). When the student is observed in one environment, teachers are seeing a contextually defined sample of behavior. It is possible that what we see is representative of all of the student's behavior, but it is more likely that we see an incomplete picture. It is often recommended that we "aggregate" data by some method, perhaps by observing the student more than once (Merrell, 1994) or using different assessment methods. Martin (1998) referred to the aggregation process and subsequent broadening of available information as "multi-setting, multi-source, multi-instrument assessment" (p. 86). The assessments consist of some combination of methods,

Table 3–3   Methods, contexts, and data sources for social-emotional assessment

Method	Context	Data Source
Rating scales	Classroom	Child
Self-reports	Playground	Parent/Surrogate
Situational measures	Home	Extended family members
Observation procedures	Work	Teachers

context, and data source. For example, we could gather data by observing a student on the playground, having the teacher rate the behavior of the student in the classroom, or by having a parent report on the student's behavior at home. Table 3–3 shows some of the possible breakdowns of each category of a multi-factored assessment.

The multifactor approach takes into account that a student's behavior is often unstable, and that it changes as a function of the environment. Therefore, a variety of different data collection strategies, including those that gather information from the parent(s), should be encouraged (Achenbach & Edelbrock, 1991, Martin, 1988; IDEA, § 1414(b)(2)(A)). We must be mindful, however, that multiple data sources may increase error and confusion when incongruent information is obtained (Merrell, 1994). Reconciling contradictory information can be a difficult task, especially when different types of data collection (e.g., rating scales and interviews) are completed by different observers or raters (e.g., teachers and parents) (Achenbach & Edelbrock, 1991; Elksnin & Elksnin, 1997). Still, because no one approach can provide all the answers about a student's behavior, it is important that teachers know about various ways of collecting social and behavioral data.

Rating Scales

There are several types of rating scales. Generally a parent, teacher, or peer of the student must rate the extent to which that child demonstrates certain desirable and/or undesirable behaviors. Evaluators must make qualitative judgments about the presence or absence of a particular behavior (checklists) or to quantify the amount or frequency of the behavior (Likert-type). The important concept to remember is that rating scales provide an index of someone's *perception* of the student's behavior. Raters are likely to have different views of acceptable and unacceptable expectations or standards for behavior, and thus their different perceptions of the same student's behavior are likely to provide different ratings of him or her. Gresham and Elliott (1990)

reminded us that rating scales are inexact and do not consider environmental influences (e.g., behavior of other students in the environment, demands placed on students, reinforcement available for appropriate or inappropriate behavior, specificity of rules, consistency of consequences); therefore, they should be supplemented by other data collection methods if possible.

Rating scales are popular because they are easy to administer and useful in providing basic information about a student's level of functioning. They offer some structure to an assessment or evaluation, and can be used in almost any environment to gather data from almost any source. Elliott, Busse, and Gresham (1993) considered rating scales to be efficient because they can be used (a) to describe a variety of student behaviors with input from many sources, and (b) to provide information very soon after a concern about a student has been raised. Because of their expediency, rating scales are likely to be the centerpiece of the initial step of a behavioral assessment of a student with EBD.

Observational Procedures

Observational procedures used to assess behavioral characteristics of students are useful because they allow the evaluator to gather data on several important factors at once (e.g., social behavior, deficits, and excesses). Merrell (1994) asserted that naturalistic observation is often the most direct and desirable way to assess child and adolescent behavior. Most often we observe students in classroom and other school settings, but there are times when observations should be done in the home, work, or other natural settings. As you will read in the chapter on functional assessment of behavior, sometimes it is necessary to manipulate a situation for an observation of a student in order to determine what role the behavior plays in getting the student what he or she wants. The process of manipulating the student's environment for direct observations takes much time and effort, but may be important enough to obtain clearer or stronger evidence about what is causing or promoting a student to engage in particular behaviors (O'Neill et al., 1997). Observations are generally very reliable and valid measures (Gresham & Lambros (1998)), and help teachers make connections between assessment and intervention. Good observations, although more demanding of the teacher in terms of effort and scheduling, provide useful data on the student's overt behavior, environmental influences, consequences of the behavior, and peer reactions. Data collected from observations also tend to be more useful when evaluating the effects of an intervention.

Self-Report Measures

When individuals are asked to reveal common behaviors in which they engage or to identify inner feelings, *self-report* measures are being used. Self-reports of beliefs and attitudes are important, regardless of the viewpoint of the evaluator. The benefits of obtaining students' input are largely based on two unique and important contributions of the self-report data. First, the utility of an assessment measure is that it provides essential information but does not identically replicate data provided by other methods. Self-reporting on aspects of treatment, for example, that cannot be obtained through other methods (e.g., side effects of medication) is one way in which students can self-report and provide information that cannot necessarily be obtained through any other method. Second, although there is potentially bias in self-report data, it is also "correct" in an important sense (Witt, Cavell, Heffer, Carey, & Martens, 1988). Students' self-perceptions provide insight into how they are interpreting their actions or the actions of others, the consequences of behaviors, and possible future actions. Students who have inaccurate beliefs and attributions of their own behavior may be following implicit rules that can delay their access to reinforcement or prevent them from making the connection between their behavior and consequences (compare Hayes, Brownstein, Haas, & Greenway, 1987).

Self-reports might include checklists or rating scales completed by the student. They also may include student ratings of how they performed in a certain situation. Self-reports, however, are susceptible to misinformation from the student and, therefore, should be part of a more comprehensive assessment plan.

Interview Techniques

Interviews are most often used to get information about the student's perspective on a variety of issues and to gain insight into overall patterns of thinking and behaving. An interview is different from a discussion or conversation because it is more purposeful and directive. The interviewer needs some level of expertise for keeping the session focused throughout. There are many variations on the interview method—most distinctions are made along a continuum of structured to unstructured or formal to informal. Regardless of the format, Merrell (1994) suggested that interviews, through a series of predetermined questions probe for information in one or more of the following areas of functioning and development: medical/developmental history, social-emotional functioning, educational progress, and community involvement. Occasionally, as in the case of early intervention programs, the family as a unit (or family members) may be the focus of

interviews that seek to identify salient home environment factors that may be having an impact on student behavior (Broderick, 1993).

Situational Measures

Situational measures of social and behavioral functioning include peer acceptance nomination scales and sociometric techniques. Both types of measures provide an indication of an individual's social status and may help describe the attitude of a particular group (e.g., class) toward the target child. Peer nomination techniques require that students identify other students whom they prefer on some set of criteria (e.g., whom they would most or least like to have as a study or play partner). Students who receive a high number of positive ratings might be viewed as "accepted." Those who receive mostly negative ratings might be "rejected," and those who receive only a few nominations or median ratings are viewed as "neglected" (Elksnin & Elksnin, 1997). Overall, sociometric techniques provide a contemporary point of reference for comparisons of a student's status among members of a specified group.

Defining Behavior

Data are collected using a standardized format. It is important that behaviors are operationalized so that if two different people rate the behavior, there is consistency in their rating. Operationalizing behavior also helps ensure that the student and teacher understand precisely what behavior is to be increased or decreased. For instance, in-seat behavior may be defined by a teacher as the student having his buttocks on the chair and his weight being supported by the chair. A student might understand in-seat behavior as having his knees on his chair or just having one knee on the chair, while standing up doing work. As well as helping to ensure the reliability of data collection, defining behavior can often decrease conflicts between teachers and students when implementing and monitoring interventions.

Within the field of social-emotional assessment, behaviors are defined by frequency, duration, latency, and amplitude (Salvia & Ysseldyke, 1998). Defining behavior in these observable terms enables others to understand the outcomes of the assessment.

Frequency measures the number of times that an event takes place.

- Jamie was out of his seat during instruction 10 times in 20 minutes.

- Marcus talked out 9 times in 20 minutes.

Duration measures the length of time during which an event occurs.

- Tina looked out the window for 13 of 20 minutes.
- Jose was sitting in the corner for 20 of 20 minutes.

Latency measures the time between a given instruction and a response.

- After being told, Darrell took 11 minutes to get out his pencil.
- After a given direction it took Laura 5 minutes to start working.

Amplitude measures the force of a behavior. This can be measured qualitatively or quantitatively. Quantitative measurement of amplitude involves the calculation of the force (i.e., the speed of a thrown ball or the decibels of a yell). In a classroom setting it is most often measured in a qualitative manner.

- Quang kicked the locker, leaving a dent.
- Vicki hit the window with a stick; there was no visual damage.

The Concept of Multiple Gating

The assessment of students with, or at risk for developing, behavior problems has been characterized by the use of ambiguous and subjective assessment methods. Additionally, the choice of assessments is often idiosyncratic to the person conducting the evaluation (Wehby, et al., 1993). The need for accurate and efficient assessment and identification of children in need of emotional or behavioral services has been partially addressed by a process known as *multiple gating*. Walker & Severson (1990) explained multiple-gating assessment as a procedure that consists of a series of progressively more precise assessments that systematizes the multimethod assessment concept to assist in reliable decision making. Multiple-gating assessment forces the decision maker to use some of the different types of data collection tools discussed previously in a systematic manner. Table 3–4 is a list of the basic components of the multiple-gating process.

Essentially, all students are initially in the "pool" of students who may be at risk for some learning or behavior problem(s). Multiple gating progressively narrows the larger pool, until those individuals who are "highly likely to exhibit the [learning or behavior problems] in question are identified" (Merrell, 1994, p. 37). The selection is accomplished through the use of more sensitive (and thus more time-consuming and expensive) procedures and measures. Almost all of the methods of assessment discussed could be used in multiple-gating systems.

Table 3–4 Multiple-gating procedures

Gate	Who Is Involved	What Is Done
1—Primary	All classrooms students	Teacher screening of all students for problem behavior
2—Secondary	Highest ranked students on problem behaviors	Teacher rating on specific behavior
3—Tertiary	Students who exceed established criteria	Direct observation of behavior in different ecologies
Completed screening	Students with observed behavioral deficits or excesses and who pass through all gates	Prereferral intervention or formal evaluation

One of the purposes of assessment is to make decisions that affect the lives of students with and without disabilities. As we have described, students with disabilities are often subjected to more testing than their nondisabled peers. For students with emotional behavioral disorders this is even more the case because it is not only these students' academics deficits that are assessed, but also their social-emotional functioning. Decisions about how to teach and what to teach are made for academics and for behavioral planning by teachers and by multidisciplinary teams. In the next section we talk about the types of tests that might be given to students with EBD.

Assessing the Instructional Environment

It is always important to assess the student's behavior and performance in school settings and in other settings in which he or she might be experiencing difficulty. But it is also important to assess the environments themselves. For example, some students' behaviors are not the problem of the child. Rather, some behaviors may originate due to specific ecological or environmental factors (e.g., lack of classroom structure, inconsistent implementation of classroom rules, failure of teacher to teach classroom rules, lack of reinforcement provided for appropriate behavior, failure of teacher to provide quality instruction, too much unstructured time given to students, home environment). Once these factors can be identified it may be found that they provide either no opportunity for appropriate behavior or promote inappropriate behavior. We have discussed in great detail the assessment of student-specific behaviors and achievement factors. It is also important that we look at the extent to which the student's instructional environment is supporting the appropriate behaviors and academic performance that we want to foster in schools. Again, it is very important that we use direct observation of a student's instructional environment in assessing our overall approach to the instructional programs that we provide. Direct observation will give an analysis of what the student does in specific environmental conditions and how he or she might interact and behave when the teacher presents certain instructional tasks (challenging vs. frustrational, mathematics vs. reading) or instructional settings (e.g., individual grouping, groups of 3-5 students, classwide instruction). One method of assessing the total ecology of the child is to use a scale designed to evaluate the effectiveness of the instructional environment in which the student is being asked to perform.

The Instructional Environment Scale, second edition (TIES-II) (Ysseldyke & Christianson, 1993) is a comprehensive system geared toward examining the elements of a student's instructional environment for determining how different factors relate to the student's performance both in school and in home situations. This scale evaluates 12 instructional environment components and 5 home support for learning components. These components are collected via direct observation in the classroom, an interview with the student, and an interview with the student's teacher. All data collection activities are important to provide a broad enough view of the student's characteristics, the teacher's characteristics, and the ecology in which the student is being educated. The 12 instructional environment components and the home support for learning components are listed in Table 3-5.

Data from the classroom observation are collected in a narrative manner on a record form. The student interview that follows the classroom observation has two main purposes: to provide information on the student's perception and an understanding of the instructional environment, and to check on the student's progress and rate of success in those environments. Last, the teacher interview is conducted followed by a parent interview of the home support for learning characteristics. All of the interviews and observations are summarized in qualitative ratings that are in fact judgments by the person doing the interviews regarding the extent to which the factors found to be important for supporting effective instruction are available for an individual student's instructional environment.

One important advantage of using a system such as TIES-II is that data are gathered in an instructionally relevant context and appropriate interventions that meet student needs and that are feasible for the teacher to implement can be planned using the data from the observations

Table 3-5   Components of the Instructional Environment Scale–II (TIES–II)

Component	Key Points
Instructional Match	• The student's characteristics and instructional delivery are considered simultaneously.
Teacher Expectations	• High, realistic goals are set and communicated.
Classroom Environment	• Rules and routines are identified.
	• Transitions are brief.
	• Atmosphere is cooperative.
	• Misbehavior is handled promptly.
Instructional Presentation	• Demonstrate-Prompt-Practice-Prove sequence is used.
	• Cues, concrete examples, and modeling are used.
	• Class pace is brisk, with immediate feedback and high rates of teacher–student interaction.
Cognitive Emphasis	• Learning strategies are taught directly.
	• Emphasis is on problem solving.
	• Student explanations are encouraged.
Motivational Strategies	• Extrinsic and intrinsic strategies are balanced.
Relevant Practice	• Guided and independent practice is used.
	• Success rates on practice tasks are high.
	• Tasks are related to goals.
Informed Feedback	• Feedback is task specific and explicit.
	• Error correction is used.
Academic Engaged Time	• Instruction is continuous and well-paced.
	• Student behavior is monitored.
	• "Down time" is minimized.
Adaptive Instruction	• Student goals are appropriate.
	• Materials and methods are matched to student needs.
Progress Evaluation	• Monitoring is direct and frequent.
	• Students are informed of performance.
Student Understanding	• Students' perceptions of goals match their instruction.

and interviews. TIES-II is important in that it fulfills the assessment intervention link that is critical to effective instructional programming for students with EBD. One of the important characteristics of TIES-II is that it helps with the consultation between regular education and special education teachers and collaborative efforts to work with the student's overall instructional program. Not all components of TIES-II need to be used for all students. It may be that the parent interviews and the evaluation of the home supports for learning are not essential. It could also be that only the classroom context needs to be evaluated and the student interview could be skipped. The important factor to consider in using TIES-II is that it is an evaluation of the instructional environment of a particular student. It is not an evaluation of the student, nor is it an evaluation of the teacher or the parents, in particular. TIES-II is meant to enhance instructional programming, not to be used as an assessment of student, teacher, or parent behavior.

Error Analysis

Another means of student and curriculum evaluation is error analysis. Surely, the use of error analysis will be discussed in other courses and books, but it is a process of looking at a student's paper in a diagnostic manner. In this process the teacher looks for error patterns, hypothesizes why the errors are occurring, and then tests the hypothesis (Ashlock, 1998). The use of error analysis will help assess the way a student is developing within a specific curriculum. It promotes the detection of consistent errors made by a student in a systematic way or pattern. Many times these error patterns occur due to overgeneralization or overspecialization and take place in any subject matter, from math to spelling. Error patterns can be as simple as adding when the student is supposed to be subtracting, or as complicated as trying to use the distributive property with exponents (see Figure 3–1).

Error analysis is especially useful while monitoring students' performance using CBM. Because students are given probes of the same difficulty across an extended period of time, consistently made errors can be detected, intervention to correct these errors can be made, and the effects can be noticed through both further error analysis

FIGURE 3–1

The distributive property

Correct	Error
$3 - 2 = 1$	$3 - 2 = 5$
$2(a + b) = 2a + 2b$ and $(a + b)^2 = a^2 + 2ab + b^2$	$(a + b)^2 = a^2 + b^2$

(determining if the certain type of error decreases) and increases in fluency. It is important to learn how to perform error analysis in all core subject areas.

ACCOUNTABILITY IN SPECIAL EDUCATION

Throughout the last 20 years the need for accountability in education has grown. Most accountability is determined through the process of student assessment. Special education has slowly moved along the same path as the rest of the education system. In IDEA 2004 local educational agencies (LEAs) and state educational agencies (SEAs) were required to assess the progress of students receiving special education services. Additionally, IDEA 1997 and 2004 required that all students with disabilities participate to the greatest extent possible in state and local achievement testing. It also means that if a student is not going to participate in the general state and local tests, IEP teams have to determine another approved form of assessment in which the student will participate. Most state and local assessments are developed through a standards-referenced assessment process. That is, states and local districts develop goals or standards that students should obtain by certain grade levels. These goals should generate what curriculum is taught in classrooms. Usually, at the end of school year, students are then assessed on how they have mastered these set standards. Students with special needs are to participate in these assessments.

Chapter Summary

Assessment has always been a critical component of special education and education reforms. Although the stakes have been raised significantly in recent federal education reforms, assessment of students with disabilities typically focuses on eligibility determination for special education services and estimates of student performance to ascertain learning needs. In this chapter, we have provided a systematic overview of the assessment practices for students categorized EBD under IDEA. We began this chapter by examining the assessment provisions under recent federal laws and regulations (IDEA 1997 and IDEA 2004). Assessment, in most cases, begins with a simple referral process initiated either by the teacher, other school personnel, or the parents. Subsequently, a school-based multidisciplinary team comprised of teachers, parents, and other relevant professionals participates in the assessment process for initial eligibility determination and subsequent educational programming. Key concepts during these assessment procedures include individualization, multiple measures, identification of students' strengths and needs, linking of assessment to programming, and nondiscriminatory and progress monitoring.

The assessment of students with EBD is complicated by co-occurrence of both learning and behavioral needs. The remaining portion of the chapter focused exclusively on the methods of assessing academic and social-behavioral needs of students with EBD along with their corresponding strengths and limitations. Although psychometrically sound norm-referenced measures exist, they need to be supplemented with criterion-referenced measures for the purposes of effective educational planning and intervention. We discussed distinguishing features and examples of some commonly used criterion-referenced measures for academic achievement and social-behavioral deficits such as curriculum-based assessment, curriculum-based measurement, performance assessment, rating scales, self-reported measures, interviews, situation measures, and so on. With increased emphasis on student outcomes in recent times, understanding the assessment procedures is critical to meeting the academic and social-behavioral needs of students with EBD. Good assessment information will enable teachers, parents, and other decision makers to make the most appropriate decisions for students in question.

CHAPTER 4

Applied Behavior Analysis

Erik Drasgow, Mitchell L. Yell, and James Halle

Focus Questions

- What are the major characteristics and principles of applied behavior analysis?

- How can teachers of students with emotional and behavioral disorders increase their students' appropriate behavior while decreasing their inappropriate behavior?

- What are the problems with using punishment?

- What is generalization and how can teachers of students with EBD help ensure that it occurs?

Applied behavior analysis (ABA) is the branch of psychology that is devoted to understanding and improving socially important human behavior (Cooper, Heron, & Heward, 2007). Although this is a goal of many disciplines, ABA has a particular history, philosophy, and methodology that make it different from other approaches. The purpose of this chapter is to describe that history, philosophy, and methodology, with a special emphasis on applying the methodology to understand and change the behavior of students with emotional and behavioral disorders (EBD).

HISTORY

The history of applied behavior analysis can be traced back more than 100 years. One person who made significant contributions to the early development of the field was the Russian, Ivan Pavlov (1849-1936). Pavlov studied the digestion of animals by observing their physiological reactions to food before they began to eat. During his research, he noticed that the physiological processes of animals (c.g., salivating) began when they saw food or heard it being prepared but before they had started to eat. Pavlov believed this was a learned response that resulted from the animals' laboratory experience with food. Pavlov then shifted his research to studying how animals acquired connections between an environmental stimulus and such reflex actions as salivating. *Stimulus* refers to any "condition, event, or change in the physical world" (Cooper, Heron, & Heward, 2007, p. 18) and reflex actions (i.e., involuntary behaviors) are referred to as *respondents*. Pavlov's contributions to the field included the scientific examination of learning mechanisms and of the relationship between the environmental stimuli and involuntary behaviors.

Pavlov's work influenced many other scientists, including the American psychologist John Broadus Watson (1878-1958). Watson argued that the study of behavior ought to consist of the direct observation of relationships between the environment and behavior instead of relying on subjective reports of mental processes or states of mind. He incorporated Pavlov's methods and focus on environmental events into a broader theory of behavior. Watson's contribution to the field was to examine learning from a behavior-environment perspective, and to apply rigorous methods from the natural sciences to understand the relationship. Watson's approach to understanding learning was called *behaviorism*.

B. F. Skinner (1904-1990) is most directly responsible for creating the field of behavior analysis for a number of important reasons. First, he shifted the emphasis on learning from reflexes (i.e., respondents) to voluntary or *operant*

behavior (Skinner, 1938). Second, he demonstrated that the frequency of operant behavior is determined by the consequences that follow the behavior. The different types of consequences that influence operant behavior are called the principles of learning. Third, he developed a precise methodology to examine the relationship between environmental consequences and their effects on the frequency of operant behavior. He named this approach the experimental analysis of behavior. Fourth, Skinner (1953) emphasized that the principles of learning could be used to improve social conditions and to solve social problems. Fifth, his approach to public education stressed the use of positive consequences to increase desirable behavior rather than the reliance on aversive procedures to control and motivate students (Skinner, 1968). Skinner was responsible for describing how consequences affect behavior and how a society could use these principles to improve the lives of its citizens.

Contemporary applied behavior analysis (ABA) was established in 1968 by two significant events. First, the *Journal of Applied Behavior Analysis (JABA)* was created. *JABA* extended the methodology developed in the experimental analysis of behavior to humans and to problems of social significance. Second, Baer, Wolf, and Risley (1968) described the scope, purpose, and procedures of ABA in a paper published in the first issue of *JABA*. They also defined each word of applied behavior analysis: *Applied* refers to changing behavior that is of immediate use to the person and to society. For example, we could teach a person to hop on one leg, but this is not as useful as teaching a person to cross the street safely. *Behavior* means that the focus is on only that which can be directly seen and reliably measured. For example, we can see a person fidget and grimace, but we cannot see "negative emotional energy." *Analysis* refers to identifying the cause-and-effect relationship (called a *functional* relationship) between environmental events and a particular behavior. The rest of this chapter is devoted to describing ABA and its application to students with EBD.

CHARACTERISTICS OF ABA

ABA is based on Skinner's behavioral theory. Behavioral theory is comprised of three fundamental assumptions (Wolery, Bailey, & Sugai, 1988). First, a behavioral sequence has three components that consist of *antecedents, behavior*, and *consequences*. Second, the way a person behaves at any given time is the result of the existing antecedents and the person's history of consequences associated with those antecedents. Third, teachers must manage and control antecedents and consequences to facilitate the learning of socially desirable skills by their students. We now provide a more thorough description of antecedents, behavior, and consequences.

Antecedents are conditions, events, or stimuli that set the occasion for behavior to occur because they signal that certain consequences are available for the behavior. For example, the telephone ringing is the antecedent for answering it. Antecedents trigger or cue a behavior. Thus, antecedents serve as the "when" in the behavioral sequence.

Behavior is the response to the antecedent and serves as the link to the consequence. Behavior is the observable action of a person. For example, answering the phone is the observable response to the sound of it ringing. Behavior occurs after the antecedent. Behavior is the "what" in the behavioral sequence.

Consequences occur after the behavior, are contingent on the behavior, and influence the probability of the behavior occurring in the future under similar antecedent conditions. Some consequences increase the likelihood of behavior and other consequences decrease the likelihood of behavior. For example, a consequence of answering the phone that would increase the future likelihood of answering the phone is the voice of a close friend. A consequence of answering the phone that may decrease the future likelihood of answering the phone is the voice of a pushy salesperson. Consequences are the "why" behavior occurs or does not occur in the behavioral sequence. The different types of consequences serve as the principles of behavior. The principles of behavior will be described later in the chapter.

The antecedent-behavior-consequence sequence is at the center of ABA. But ABA also includes additional assumptions and characteristics (Cooper, Heron, & Heward, 2007; Miltenberger, 2004; Turnbull, Turnbull, Shank, & Leal, 1995). These assumptions and characteristics are listed in the following text.

Most behavior is learned. Both desirable and undesirable behavior is learned through a person's interaction with the environment.

Behavior is influenced by consequences. An increase or decrease in behavior is a result of the environmental consequences that follow the behavior.

Behavior can be changed. Because behavior is learned, new behavior can be taught by changing the learning environment and by altering existing antecedents and consequences for desirable and undesirable behavior.

Teaching is based on behavioral principles. ABA is the application of basic principles that are based on almost 50 years of research with people.

Behavior is the focus. ABA is intended to change behavior, not characteristics or traits. For example, we cannot change "autism," but we can change the behavior of a person labeled as having autism.

Precise description of a "game plan" for changing behavior. ABA procedures must be used consistently to be effective, so ABA game plans are very specific about what to teach, when to teach, where to teach, and how to teach.

Precise measurement of behavior change. Behavior targeted for change is precisely defined and consistently assessed to assess progress.

Rejection of hypothetical underlying causes of behavior. Some areas of psychology are interested in "guessing" about the underlying causes of behavior (e.g., a bad emotional relationship with your mother makes you hit other people). ABA rejects this view because "emotional relationships" are not observable or measurable, and are not environmental events (i.e., they are not consequences) that we can alter.

These assumptions and characteristics will be reflected in each section throughout the rest of this chapter. We now proceed with a discussion of the principles of behavior and other foundational concepts of ABA.

PRINCIPLES OF BEHAVIOR

ABA is based on the fact that consequences influence behavior. That is, what happens after a behavior and occurs because of the behavior determines whether that behavior is *more likely* or *less likely* to occur in the future under the same antecedent conditions. Thus, there are two categories of consequences: consequences that maintain or strengthen behavior and consequences that weaken behavior. The two categories of consequences are referred to as the *principles of behavior* (e.g., Malott, 2008; Malott & Suarez, 2004). The principles of behavior that strengthen the future occurrence of behavior consist of positive reinforcement and negative reinforcement. The principles of behavior that weaken the future occurrence of behavior consist of punishment and extinction. We first examine positive and negative reinforcement and then extinction and punishment.

Principles That Increase Behavior

Reinforcement is defined as a consequence that occurs contingent on a behavior and maintains or strengthens that behavior (Skinner, 1969). *Positive reinforcement* is defined as a contingent consequence that maintains or strengthens a behavior because a person *gets something*. The things a person gets could be attention, activities, events, or any type of object or item. For example, you walk (i.e., the behavior that is strengthened) to the cafeteria to get lunch (i.e., the consequence). Lunch makes walking to the cafeteria more likely when the antecedent, hunger, is present. *Negative reinforcement* is defined as a contingent consequence that maintains or strengthens a behavior because a person avoids or escapes something.

Escape behavior terminates an ongoing situation. For example, if you are in an unpleasant social situation, you may excuse yourself (i.e., the behavior that is strengthened) to go to the bathroom. In this situation, you are escaping the unpleasant social situation. Avoidance behavior prevents the occurrence of an unpleasant situation. For example, you may walk the long way around your neighborhood to avoid contact with an unfriendly neighbor. Figure 4–1 contains examples of reinforcement and its association with antecedents.

FIGURE 4–1

Types of reinforcement

Positive Reinforcement

Antecedent	Behavior	Consequence	Future Effect
The phone rings	You answer the phone	The caller is your friend	You are more likely to answer the phone in the future
It is time for your favorite television program	You turn on the television	You watch your favorite program	You are more likely to turn on the television at the same time in the future
Your homework is due soon	You complete your homework	The teacher gives you an A	You are more likely to do your homework in the future
It is time to go to work	You go to work	You get a paycheck	You are more likely to go to work on time in the future

Negative Reinforcement

Antecedent	Behavior	Consequence	Future Effect
You have a headache	You take an aspirin	Your headache goes away (escape)	You are more likely to take aspirin in the future when you have a headache
People in a movie theater are talking during the movie	You move away from them	You can watch the movie in silence (escape)	In the future, you are more likely to move away from people who talk in the theater during a movie
Your homework is due and you have not done it	You don't go to class	You do not get scolded nor get dirty looks from your teacher (avoidance)	You are more likely to avoid class in the future when you don't do your homework
It is raining outside	You open your umbrella	You do not get wet (avoidance)	You are more likely to open your umbrella in the future when it is raining outside

Identifying Positive and Negative Reinforcement

Positive and negative reinforcement are similar in that they both strengthen behavior, but are different in that each has a different type of consequence that follows behavior. Figure 4-2 provides a decisional flowchart for determining whether positive or negative reinforcement is in effect.

It is important to remember that the principles of behavior are determined by their effect on behavior. We know that a consequence is positive or negative reinforcement only when we can demonstrate that the behavior it follows is maintained or strengthened (i.e., increases in frequency of occurrence). For example, if a teacher praises a student for joining in class discussions, and the student reduces the number of times that she joins in class discussions after the teacher praises her, then praise is *not* a reinforcer. Conversely, if a teacher scolds a student each time he talks out in class and the rate of outbursts increases, then scolding is, in fact, reinforcement because (a) it occurs after each outburst, and (b) the rate of outbursts has been strengthened.

Types of Reinforcers   There are two types of reinforcers. A primary (or unlearned or unconditioned) reinforcer contributes to survival and does not have to be learned. Examples of primary positive reinforcers include food, water, sexual stimulation, shelter, and warmth. Examples of primary negative reinforcers include escape from heat, cold, or pain. In sum, primary reinforcers usually have biological importance (Cooper, Heron, & Heward, 2007).

Secondary (or conditioned) reinforcers are learned. They acquire reinforcing properties through the contingent and repetitive pairing with a primary reinforcer. For example, when infants are born, food is reinforcing and verbal praise is not. But every time a parent feeds the infant, they are likely to talk to the infant and make comments about how well the child is eating. Thus, over time verbal praise acquires reinforcing properties of its own because it has been paired with a primary reinforcer (i.e., food). Other examples of secondary reinforcers may include attention, tokens, and grades.

There are two special classes of secondary reinforcers. The first class is called the Premack Principle (Premack, 1959, 1965). The Premack Principle occurs when a preferred activity is used to reinforce behavior. For example, a parent may tell a child that if the child cleans his room, then he can watch his favorite television program. The child is then more likely to clean his room because the consequence for cleaning is the highly preferred activity of watching television. In technical terms, the Premack Principle is based on the fact that low-probability behavior (e.g., cleaning one's room) increases in frequency when it is followed by high-probability behavior (e.g., watching television). The second class is called generalized conditioned reinforcers. Generalized conditioned reinforcers provide access to a wide range of primary or secondary reinforcers. The most common example of a generalized conditioned reinforcer is money. Money can be exchanged for an unlimited variety of primary (e.g., lunch at McDonald's) and secondary (e.g., video games) reinforcers.

Making Reinforcement Work   A number of factors influence the effectiveness of reinforcement. These factors consist of the immediacy and consistency of the reinforcer, deprivation and satiation, the characteristics of the reinforcer, and the schedule of reinforcement (Alberto & Troutman, 2006; Cooper, Heron, & Heward, 2007; Kazdin, 2001; Miltenberger, 2004).

Immediacy. The most effective consequences are those that occur immediately after the behavior. The longer the time period is between a behavior and a reinforcer,

Figure 4–2   Decisional flowchart

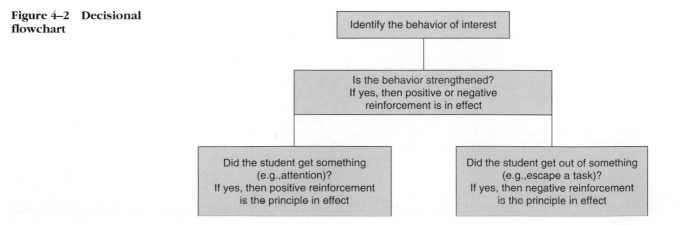

the more likely it is that the association between the two will be weakened. If the time between the behavior and the reinforcer is too long, then the reinforcer will have no effect on the behavior. For example, when you drive your car, you use the gas pedal or brake, turn the steering wheel, and use the turn signals. The car responds with immediate reinforcing consequences to your driving behavior. Imagine what would happen if you turned the steering wheel and the car responded 30 seconds later!

Contingency. Contingency refers to the consistent relationship between a response and the consequence it produces (Skinner, 1969). Contingent reinforcement means that the response (or behavior) occurred before the consequence and resulted in the consequence. Contingent also means that the consequence is available only when the response occurs. Consider the following example: You enter an elevator and push the button to get to your floor. Pushing the floor button (a response or behavior) causes the elevator to go to the floor that you want (the consequence). In this case, pushing the floor button occurred before the elevator moved and caused the elevator to take you to your floor. Moving the elevator also occurs only when you push the button. Thus, getting to the floor that you want is contingent on you pushing the right elevator button.

Deprivation and Satiation. Deprivation and satiation influence the value of the reinforcer. Deprivation increases and satiation decreases the value of a reinforcer. Deprivation occurs when a person has not had access to a reinforcer for some time. For example, the reinforcing value of food increases when you have not eaten for a long time. Satiation occurs when a person has consumed or had excessive exposure to a reinforcer. For example, the reinforcing value of food decreases when you have just finished a meal.

Characteristics of the Consequence There are two important characteristics of reinforcing consequences. First, reinforcers are often individualized and variable. For example, some people may find every type of music reinforcing, some may find only a particular type (e.g., classical or alternative) reinforcing, others may find only a particular song or tune reinforcing, and some people may not find any music reinforcing. Thus, we should never assume that something will be reinforcing for a person because it is reinforcing to us. Second, the amount or intensity of a reinforcer influences its value. For example, many people find praise reinforcing, but a single "good work" once a week may not be enough. Another example will help illustrate how the characteristics of reinforcers

influence behavior. Suppose that you are looking for a job. You are looking because you are in a state of financial deprivation. You begin by looking for jobs that you like or that you would find fulfilling. In other words, you know that reinforcers are individualized and that you want to select a job that is reinforcing to you. But you also realize that if your state of financial deprivation is fairly significant, then many types of jobs may take on reinforcing characteristics. You finally select a job. You are curious to know how much you will get paid, or, in other words, you are curious about the amount of reinforcer that is contingent on your work behavior. In the end, you accept the job because (a) your state of financial deprivation is great, (b) the work that you will be doing is individually reinforcing to you, and (c) the amount of your wage is adequately reinforcing considering your current state of financial deprivation.

Schedules of Reinforcement A schedule of reinforcement refers either to the *number of responses* that have occurred since the preceding reinforcement or to the *amount of time* that has elapsed since the last response was reinforced (Ferster & Skinner, 1957). Schedules of reinforcement that are based on the number of responses that have occurred since the preceding reinforcement are called ratio schedules. Schedules of reinforcement that are based on the amount of time that has elapsed since the last response was reinforced are called interval schedules.

Ratio Schedules. Ratio schedules refer to reinforcement that is delivered after a specific number of behaviors have occurred. One type of ratio schedule is called a continuous reinforcement (CRF) schedule. A CRF schedule means that reinforcement is delivered after every occurrence of the behavior. One example of a CRF schedule in everyday life is the use of a television remote. Each time you push a button (the behavior) the channel changes (the reinforcement). Teachers also use CRF schedules when a student is acquiring a new behavior or is engaging in a behavior for the first time. For example, when students are beginning to read, the teacher may present some sight words (the antecedents). Each time a student responds correctly (the behavior) to the presented sight words, the teacher may praise the student (the reinforcement).

Another type of ratio schedule is called an intermittent schedule of reinforcement. An intermittent schedule of reinforcement means that reinforcement is delivered only after the behavior has occurred a number of times. Thus, reinforcement is delivered occasionally. If reinforcement is delivered after the behavior has occurred a specific and consistent number of times, then this schedule is called a fixed ratio (FR) schedule of reinforcement.

For example, if a teacher praises a student after completing five math problems, then the teacher is using an FR-5 schedule of reinforcement. If reinforcement is delivered after a certain number of responses, but that number varies from time, then this schedule is called a variable ratio (VR) schedule of reinforcement. When a teacher praises a student for completing on the average of five math problems (e.g., praise after the student completes the first four math problems and after the student completes the next six problems), then the teacher is using a VR schedule of reinforcement.

Ratio schedules are effective for maintaining behavior after it is acquired. To illustrate how ratio schedules maintain behavior, we will return to our example of teaching students to read. A teacher starts out by reinforcing a student each time (CRF) the student correctly reads a sight word. As the student acquires the sight words, the teacher may then deliver praise only after the student correctly reads a sentence that consists of multiple words. Thus, the teacher is delivering reinforcement on an intermittent schedule because he or she has moved from praising the student for reading each word to praising the student for reading multiple words. And if the number of words in the sentences that the student reads varies, then the teacher is using a VR schedule of reinforcement.

Interval Schedules. Interval schedules refer to reinforcement that is delivered when a behavior occurs after a certain amount of time has elapsed. One type of interval schedule is called a fixed interval (FI) schedule of reinforcement. A FI schedule means that reinforcement is available after a certain and consistent amount of time (i.e., an interval) has passed. For example, a teacher may reinforce students each time they have stayed on task for 5 minutes. Another type of interval schedule is called a variable interval (VI) schedule of reinforcement. A VI schedule means that the duration of each interval varies, but reinforcement is available after an average amount of time has passed. For example, a teacher may reinforce students for staying on task after 6 minutes have passed, after 4 minutes have passed, after 7 minutes have passed, and after 3 minutes have passed. In this case, the teacher is using a VI 5-minute schedule of reinforcement (i.e., 6 minutes + 4 minutes + 7 minutes + 3 minutes = 20 minutes); 4 reinforcements = reinforcement every 5 minutes on the average).

Using reinforcement effectively requires that a teacher meet several requirements. First, the teacher must select a consequence that, in fact, increases the likelihood of the future occurrence of the behavior. Second, the teacher must deliver the reinforcer immediately after the behavior

and contingent on the behavior. Third, the teacher must understand that reinforcers often are individualized and that the value of a reinforcer varies across people and within people. Finally, a teacher must deliver reinforcement more frequently during the early stages of learning and then ought to reduce the frequency of reinforcement as a student becomes more proficient at the skill.

Behavior Principles That Decrease Behavior

There are two principles of behavior that decrease the future occurrence of behavior: extinction and punishment.

Extinction Extinction reduces the future occurrence of a behavior by withdrawing, terminating, or preventing access to the reinforcement that served as the consequence maintaining the behavior. Consider the following examples:

> You try to start your car. The battery is dead. You try to start the car seven or eight times. You finally "give up" and leave your car.

> Your friend is watching a football game on TV. You ask him a question. He doesn't answer. You try to get an answer by asking him the question five or six times. Finally, you "give up" and go do something else.

> You go into the bathroom. You turn on the light. Nothing happens. You flick the switch several times more. Finally, you "give up" and go to a different bathroom.

In each of these examples, the individual's behavior (e.g., turning the car key in the ignition) did not result in reinforcement (e.g., the car starting) and eventually the behavior stopped. Behavior stopped fairly quickly and quite smoothly in the examples. Although behavior stopped quickly in the examples, this may not be the case when a teacher decides to use extinction to stop the problem behavior of her students. For example, a teacher may decide to "ignore" problem behavior with the hope that it will "go away." The problem behavior in this case may stop if the teacher ignores it, but then again, it may not. To decide whether ignoring a behavior is likely to be an effective approach for reducing its occurrence, the teacher needs to consider the answers to the following questions.

Has the Reinforcer Maintaining the Problem Behavior Been Identified? For extinction to be successful, the reinforcer maintaining a behavior has to be accurately identified and then access to that reinforcer must be systematically and consistently prevented. Consider the following scenario: A student acts silly (e.g., makes odd sounds and weird faces) during reading class. The teacher may assume that the student is behaving that way to get her attention. Thus, she decides to ignore the student (i.e., prevent access to the consequence of her attention) every time the student makes an odd sound or weird face. If the teacher ignores the student in this case, the problem behavior may or may not go away for several reasons.

First, it may not be the teacher's attention that is the maintaining consequence for the problem behavior. Perhaps the maintaining consequence is the reaction that the behavior gets from other students. Or it could be the reaction from one particular student. Second, the maintaining consequence could be escape from the academic work demands of reading. In this case, the problem behavior is not maintained by positive reinforcement (i.e., access to attention) but rather is maintained by negative reinforcement (i.e., escape or avoidance from academic work). If the teacher ignores the student, the student's behavior is not likely to be affected because the teacher is spending less time attending to the student and that allows the student to avoid reading. For extinction to work, the first actual reinforcer maintaining the behavior must first be identified, and then access to the reinforcer must be eliminated. Chapter 5 describes procedures to identify reinforcers that maintain problem behavior.

Can Access to Reinforcement Be Prevented? Once the reinforcer maintaining behavior is identified, the key to using extinction successfully is to prevent access to it. This is often very difficult to do, especially if peers deliver it (Kazdin, 2001). For example, if problem behavior is maintained by the response it gets from a variety of peers in different settings, then it is virtually impossible to prevent access consistently to all of these sources of reinforcement. It also is difficult to prevent access to reinforcement when it is negatively reinforced by escape or avoidance. For example, a student may avoid or escape academic demands by sharpening his pencil, requesting to go to the bathroom, arguing with the teacher, or saying that he has a headache and then putting his head down on the desk. Each of these behaviors results in at least temporary escape or avoidance regardless of the teacher's response to them. In addition, ignoring them enables the student free access to escape or avoidance. Thus, before deciding to use extinction, a teacher must decide if he can reliably prevent access to the reinforcer maintaining the problem behavior.

Does the Behavior Need to Be Stopped Immediately? One characteristic of extinction is that its effects are not immediate. Extinction may take a fairly long time before

the behavior is reduced or eliminated, and some behaviors are quite resistant to extinction. One factor that determines how long extinction will take is the current schedule of reinforcement that is maintaining the behavior (Ferster & Skinner, 1957). Variable ratio and variable interval schedules of reinforcement that have been maintaining behavior will result in the behavior continuing for long periods of time after extinction has begun. Thus, the teacher must decide whether the behavior needs to be reduced immediately, (in which case, extinction is not the best approach), or whether a gradual reduction in behavior is acceptable.

Is the Behavior Likely to Get Worse Before It Gets Better? Extinction often causes behavior to increase in frequency, intensity, or both before the behavior improves. Behavior will likely increase in frequency during the initial stages of extinction. This increase is referred to as an extinction burst. Our earlier scenario described a student who made odd sounds and weird faces. If teacher attention was the consequence of maintaining those behaviors and the teacher ignored them, then there would likely be an increase in the occurrence of those behaviors immediately following the beginning of the extinction period.

Extinction may cause an increase in the intensity of the behavior, or it may cause an increase in other aggressive behavior during the early stages of extinction. This phenomenon is referred to as extinction-induced aggression (Azrin, Hutchinson, & Hake, 1966). When individuals cannot access reinforcement, they may become "frustrated," and this frustration is likely to lead to the emotional response of anger and the behavioral response of aggression. Aggression may occur in an effort to obtain lost reinforcement. Consider this common experience: You place money in a vending machine, but it just falls through and ends up in the change return slot. You are likely to put the money in a few more times. The amount of times that you put the money in again depends on (a) how much you want the items (i.e., deprivation), and (b) what your previous schedule of reinforcement with vending machines is. After you put the money in a few times, but it just comes back out (i.e., the vending machine has put you on extinction), you may yell or swear at the machine, or you may even slap, hit, or kick the machine. Your response may be even more aggressive if the machine takes your money and gives you nothing.

Extinction may lead to the occurrence of more severe problem behavior during its early stages. This puts the teacher in an undesirable position. To return to our earlier scenario, let's consider what might happen if the student's odd noises and weird faces are maintained by teacher attention and the teacher decides to ignore the student. Being ignored by the teacher might frustrate the student. This makes him angry and so he decides that he will increase his problem behavior in an effort to access the lost reinforcement, or he may take out his frustration on another student. So, the student ends up shouting and ultimately hits a student next to him. The teacher now cannot ignore these new and more intense problems, so she intervenes after shouting and hitting have occurred to talk to the student and try to calm him down. The teacher in this case is now inadvertently reinforcing shouting and hitting with her sustained and individualized attention. Thus, extinction has resulted in the student escalating to more severe problem behavior, and because the teacher cannot ignore these more severe forms, she reinforces them with her attention. This situation makes it more likely that the student will shout and hit in the future to get teacher attention: A situation has been created that is worse than before.

A teacher must carefully consider the effects of extinction before deciding to use it to decrease behavior. The best approach when using extinction is to combine the extinction of problem behavior with the reinforcement of other or alternative behavior. For example, if the teacher determines that a student's odd sounds and weird faces are being reinforced by her attention, then she may decide to use extinction for these behaviors while also using her attention as reinforcement provided contingently on the student getting her attention in appropriate ways (e.g., raises his hand, says "Am I doing a good job on my work?").

Punishment Punishment is any consequence that occurs after a behavior, is contingent on a behavior, and rapidly reduces the likelihood that the behavior will occur in the future. There are two types of punishment. *Positive punishment* (also called Type 1 punishment) is defined as the contingent presentation of an aversive stimulus that reduces the occurrence of behavior. *Negative punishment* (also called Type 2 punishment) is defined as the contingent removal of a desirable stimulus that reduces behavior. We now examine each.

Positive Punishment. Consider the following examples:

> You reach over a fence to pet a dog. The dog bites your hand. You never try to pet the dog again.

> You go to the bathroom. You turn on the light. You get a bad shock. You refuse to touch that switch again.

> You say something during a meeting. People laugh at you. You never say another thing at a meeting.

Each of these consequences is positive punishment because a consequence was presented that (a) occurred after the behavior, (b) reduced its future occurrence, and (c) reduced the behavior rapidly (i.e., the behavior rarely occurred again after a single presentation of the consequence).

Positive punishment consists of two types of aversive stimuli. The first type of aversive stimuli does not need to be learned and are called primary aversive stimuli. Primary aversive stimuli include such things as electric shock, physical assault, loud noises, and bright lights. The second type of aversive stimuli are learned through being paired with existing aversive stimuli and are called secondary or conditioned aversive stimuli. The word "no" is a good example of a secondary aversive stimulus because it often acquires its aversive properties through being paired with a loud voice.

Overcorrection is a positive punishment procedure and consists of two components. The first component is called restitution and consists of an individual restoring or correcting an environment beyond its original condition. For example, if a student makes a mess during an activity, the teacher may require that the student clean the entire classroom. Cleaning the entire classroom would meet the criteria of positive punishment if it (a) is presented following the occurrence of a behavior (i.e., making a mess), and (b) rapidly reduces the future occurrence of making a mess. The second component is called positive practice and consists of requiring an individual who has engaged in problem behavior to engage in an exaggerated or repeated practice of the desirable behavior. For example, if a student runs in the school halls, the teacher may require the student to practice walking very slowly throughout the school for an hour. Walking very slowly throughout the school for an hour would meet the criteria of positive punishment if it (a) is presented following the occurrence of a behavior (i.e., running in school), and (b) rapidly reduces the future occurrence of running.

Negative Punishment. Consider the following examples:

> A child is sent to his room for being silly at the dinner table. The child no longer acts silly at the dinner table.

> A student talks out during class and, in response, his teacher takes away his computer time. The student does not talk out in class the next day.

> A driver is fined $75 for exceeding the speed limit. The driver does not exceed the speed limit again.

Each of these consequences is negative punishment because a desirable stimulus (e.g., computer time, money) (a) was removed after the behavior, (b) reduced its future occurrence, and (c) reduced the behavior rapidly (i.e., the behavior rarely occurred again after a single presentation of the consequence).

There are two negative punishment procedures. The first procedure is called response cost and this consists of the contingent loss of desirable stimuli (i.e., positive reinforcers). Token systems often use response-cost procedures in which the teacher provides students with tokens that can be exchanged for access to reinforcers, and then takes away tokens contingent on the occurrence of bad behavior. There is no time limit regarding how long the teacher removes reinforcers in response-cost procedures. The second procedure is called "time-out from reinforcement" and consists of preventing access to positive reinforcement for a period of time contingent on bad behavior. For example, a teacher may have a student sit on the bleachers during recess if the student is misbehaving. It is important to remember that time-out from reinforcement acquires its punishing properties only when access to reinforcers is prevented. For example, if a student misbehaves during academic times to escape work, then sending the student to time-out is not going to reduce misbehaving because the student is not being removed from a reinforcing situation. In fact, it is likely that sending the student to time-out for misbehaving is likely to increase the frequency of misbehavior because it may function as negative reinforcement for the misbehavior.

Making Punishment Work A number of factors influence the effectiveness of punishment. These factors consist of the immediacy and contingency of the punisher, deprivation and satiation, the characteristics of the punisher, and reinforcement of alternative behavior (Alberto & Troutman, 2006; Cooper, Heron, & Heward, 2007; Kazdin, 2001; Miltenberger, 2004).

Immediacy. Consequences are most effective when they are delivered immediately after the occurrence of the behavior. Thus, to be most effective, punishment must occur as quickly as possible after the undesirable behavior. For example, if a student misbehaves in class and the teacher provides an immediate unpleasant consequence, then that consequence is likely to be effective. Conversely, if a student misbehaves and the teacher sends the student to see the principal, but the student has to wait outside his office for an hour, then the consequence that the principal gives is less likely to be effective at changing the misbehavior.

To be effective, punishment must occur immediately after the problem behavior but before the problem behavior can access reinforcement. For example, if a student acts out to get attention, but punishment is delivered after the student has gotten the attention of the whole class (i.e., has already accessed reinforcement), then any punishment is likely to be less effective. In this case, punishment is being delivered after the behavior of acting out already has been reinforced. Punishment that follows reinforcement is not as effective as punishment that immediately follows the behavior *and* prevents access to reinforcement. Consider the following example: A student steals another student's money. To be effective, punishment must occur after the student has stolen the money but *before* he has the opportunity to spend it. Punishment would be much less effective if the student stole the money, spent it all on his favorite candy, ate the candy, and then got punished.

Contingency. Punishment must occur contingent on the problem behavior and every time the problem behavior occurs. Contingent means that punishment is delivered soon after the behavior occurs and never delivered during times when the behavior does not occur. Consistency may be the most important aspect of punishment for two reasons. First, a continuous schedule of punishment is more effective for reducing behavior than is an intermittent schedule of punishment. Second, problem behavior occurs because there is some occasional source (i.e., intermittent schedule) of positive or negative reinforcement that is maintaining the behavior. Thus, problem behavior that is intermittently punished is also being intermittently reinforced when punishment is inconsistent.

When problem behavior is intermittently punished and intermittently reinforced, the problem behavior is likely to continue (Azrin, Holz, & Hake, 1963). Consider the following example: A student talks out and fools around during seat work. Talking out and fooling around is negatively reinforced because by doing this the student escapes or avoids doing the work. When the student talks out and fools around, the teacher reprimands (i.e., positive punishment) the student and takes away his computer time (i.e., negative punishment). By being inconsistent, the teacher is not likely to reduce talking out and fooling around because sometimes the student is punished for these behaviors but on other occasions, the student is reinforced for the same behaviors. To be effective and reduce the problem behaviors, the teacher would have to punish *every* occurrence of them.

Deprivation and Satiation. States of satiation and deprivation influence the effectiveness of both reinforcers and punishers. Deprivation and satiation can make punishment either more or less effective. For example, taking away computer time (i.e., negative punishment) contingent on problem behavior may not be an effective punisher if the student has spent the entire previous evening playing video games at home or surfing the Web. Conversely, taking away computer time may be a more effective punisher if the student has not had access to computers for some time and thus is in a state of "computer game deprivation."

Characteristics of the Punisher. Punishers, like reinforcers, vary from person to person. Thus, punishers must be individualized. For example, getting scolded may serve as a punisher for one student, yet serve as a reinforcer for another person. Conversely, a student may do well on a test. In response to this, you might publicly praise him and show everyone in the class his test. If he leaves the next test blank, then your actions have punished him.

Often punishers lose their effectiveness over time, especially if the punisher is used frequently. Scolding a student often loses its effectiveness over time, and scolding may in fact come to serve as a reinforcer. To maintain the effectiveness of punishment, punishers have to be varied. Sending a student to time-out for each occurrence of problem behavior is not as effective as using verbal reprimands, overcorrection, response cost, and other assorted strategies. One important thing to remember, however, is that punishment is defined only by its effect on behavior. If a teacher uses a variety of strategies (e.g., response cost, time-out), but the problem behavior does not decrease, then by definition those strategies are not punishment.

Reinforcement of Alternative Behavior

Perhaps the most effective approach to problem behavior is to combine punishment with the reinforcement of alternative socially desirable behavior. Using punishment alone reduces the opportunity for an individual to access reinforcement. By reinforcing desirable behavior, a teacher increases the frequency of those behaviors. The more time a student spends engaging in socially desirable behavior, the less time he has to engage in problem behavior. Indeed, most applied behavior analysts would agree that any application of punishment must include reinforcement for desirable behavior. For example, any program that uses punishment to reduce the number of times a student talks out in class ought to include positive reinforcement for being quiet in class.

Problems with Punishment

The presentation of aversive stimuli is the most familiar form of punishment (Kazdin, 2001) and teachers often turn to this form of punishment almost by reflex (Alberto & Troutman, 2006). Thus, applied behavior analysts are greatly concerned with the improper or excessive use of

punishment. In fact, the excessive use of punishment may be one of the causes of EBD (Kazdin, 1995; Wolfe, 1999). Punishment is also associated with a variety of ethical and behavioral concerns.

Teachers may use punishment for several reasons (Drasgow, 1997). First, punishment is quick, easy to administer, and may result in an immediate decrease in some undesirable behaviors. For example, a simple verbal reprimand such as "stop!" might reduce inappropriate talking or whispering during class time. Second, teachers may feel that punishment will "teach the student a lesson" or "give the student what he has coming." A teacher may have a student clean all the desks in the room because he wrote on his own desk, or send a student to in-school suspension for "talking back." Taken together, these reasons could lead a teacher to assume that punishment is a good consequence for reducing undesirable behavior because of its ease, its immediate effects, and the feeling that the student somehow is making "retribution" for his behavior. But is punishment really the best option for reducing undesirable behavior? Although teachers often feel that punishment is "good medicine" for bad behavior, is it really the most effective option for reducing undesirable behavior? The following review of punishment suggests that it is generally not an effective consequence for a variety of reasons.

First, because punishment is quick and easy to administer, teachers may come to rely on it as their first line of defense for undesirable behavior. This may result in the misuse, or especially the overuse, of punishment. When teachers use punishment frequently, they become closely associated with negative consequences. Thus, the teacher's relationship with students suffers. Students may come to fear or avoid the teacher or even the entire setting where punishment typically occurs (e.g., the classroom). We all have seen classrooms where students cringe or flinch whenever the teacher walks by, or have known students who dread going to school because the teacher is "mean" or "hollers" all day.

Second, when teachers use punishment, a student has four options, three of which are negative:

1. The undesirable behavior may be reduced.

2. The student may strike back (e.g., a teacher restrains a student; the student bites the teacher's arm).

3. The student may become withdrawn, may "tune out" the punisher (e.g., quits listening to verbal reprimands), and may remain tuned out the rest of the day or school year, thus learning nothing.

4. The student may engage in escape or avoidance behavior that is worse than the initial behavior

getting punished (e.g., the student is sent to time-out for talking out, then refuses to go to the time-out area; the teacher then also must punish the student's refusal).

Thus begins the vicious cycle of escalating undesirable behavior followed by escalating punishing consequences.

Third, one of the most basic and powerful forms of student learning takes place through observation and imitation (Bandura, 1965; Bandura & Walters, 1963). Because the teacher is a prominent figure in the classroom, students closely attend to his or her behavior. The teacher is the model of adult behavior for students. The teacher who constantly yells, threatens, or even hits (i.e., relies on punishment) is, in effect, saying to students that this is how an adult reacts to undesirable behavior in the environment. A punishment-oriented teacher may actually increase the level of undesirable behavior in the classroom, as students begin to copy the teacher's "aggressive" forms of behavior (Sobsey, 1990; Timberlake, 1981).

Fourth, the effects of punishment may not last or may not generalize (Kazdin, 1994; Rolider, Cummings, & Van Houten, 1991). That is, the effects may be temporary and highly specific. Students often adapt to milder forms of punishment (e.g., verbal reprimands, time-out) so that the punishing effects are lost over time, or when the teacher stops punishment of a particular behavior (e.g., talking out), that behavior may return to the original, or even higher, rates of occurrence. Students also may learn quickly where they will be punished, as well as where they can get away with the undesirable behavior. This lack of generalization is reflected in the old saying "When the cat's away, the mice will play." Moreover, research has shown that when any behavior is successful even very infrequently, it will continue to be used (Ferster & Skinner, 1957). Thus, to achieve enduring and generalized results in reducing undesirable behavior, *punishment may need to occur in multiple settings and be administered by multiple people.*

Finally, and perhaps most importantly, punishment involves very little student learning. Teachers punish students in an attempt to reduce undesirable behavior, but punishment does not result in the student learning any *acceptable* (alternative) forms of behavior. Teachers often say a student should "know better" when engaging in undesirable behavior, but this seems contrary to educational philosophy. If he knows better, why does the behavior occur? Isn't the role of teachers to teach new and acceptable ways of behaving so that they have proof that students do know better, and thereby eliminate the burden placed on the student to spontaneously and

independently discover how to behave? Teachers must pave the way for students to learn acceptable behavior, and to do this teachers need (a) to select alternative forms of desirable and acceptable behavior to teach, and (b) to provide consequences for desirable behavior that motivate students to master the alternative forms.

SUMMARY

The principles of behavior refer to consequences that occur after behavior and as a result of the behavior. Positive and negative reinforcement are the two types of consequences that maintain or strengthen the behavior they follow. Punishment is a consequence that reduces the likelihood of a behavior occurring in the future. Extinction reduces the future occurrence of a behavior because the reinforcement that was maintaining the behavior is *no longer* accessible.

APPLYING THE PRINCIPLES OF BEHAVIOR

The principles of behavior are consequences that influence the future occurrence of behavior. Just about all behavior has consequences. For example, if you go to work (behavior), you get paid (reinforcement). If you frequently arrive to work late (behavior), you may get fired (punishment). If you study hard (behavior), you may get a good grade (positive reinforcement) or may avoid the embarrassment of a bad grade (negative reinforcement). If you talk to a friend during class (behavior), the teacher may glare at you (punishment). A very important thing to understand about the principles of behavior is that they occur naturally as a result of our behavior and thus constantly influence how we behave. In other words, much of our behavior is a product of our constant interaction with the environment and people, and thus the principles of behavior influence everyone's behavior.

Our behavior is shaped by the environment and by other people. Often the consequences the environment and other people provide are inconsistent or unsystematic. For example, sometimes we exceed the speed limit when we are driving and do not get a ticket. Another time we do get a ticket. Or we study hard for a test and sometimes get a good grade but at other times we may get a bad grade even though we studied hard. For a teacher to be effective at changing a student's behavior, she must apply the principles of behavior consistently and systematically. Applied behavior analysis provides the technology that enables a teacher to apply the principles of behavior consistently and systematically so that she can effectively change a student's behavior. The remainder of this chapter describes the procedures of ABA.

DEFINING AND DESCRIBING BEHAVIOR

Changing behavior begins by identifying the behavior, by defining it so that it can be measured, and by specifying the desirable change in the behavior. We now describe each of these areas.

Identifying the Target Behavior

The *target behavior* is the behavior that needs to be changed. Some target behaviors need to be increased. For example, a teacher may want to increase the number of times a student answers questions in class, or the number of times a student completes his homework, or the amount of time a student stays on task during seat work. In these examples, the target behavior is answering questions, completing homework, and staying on task. Some target behaviors need to be decreased. For example, a teacher may want to decrease the number of times a student sharpens his pencil, the number of times a student talks out, or the amount of time a student takes to get started working. In these examples, the target behavior is sharpening a pencil, talking out, and getting to work.

Teachers should select or identify target behaviors because of their importance to a student's life. That is, changing a target behavior means that the student's life will be improved because of the change. In addition, it is important to select a target behavior that is observable (e.g., hitting) and not one that refers to internal states (e.g., anger). Internal states cannot be accurately measured to record progress, and internal states are inferred from observable behavior. Thus, it is more parsimonious and precise to record observable behavior.

Defining the Target Behavior

Describing a target behavior in precise terms is referred to as an *operational definition*. The operational definition of the target behavior should meet three criteria: objectivity, clarity, and completeness (Kazdin, 2001). Objectivity refers to the observable characteristics of the target behavior. Clarity refers to an unambiguous definition that someone unfamiliar with the student could read, understand, and paraphrase. Completeness refers to defining the target behavior in a way that explains which behaviors are included in the target behavior and which behaviors are excluded. Table 4-1 provides examples of operational definitions of common target behaviors of students with EBD.

The purpose of an operational definition is to move away from subjective impressions or interpretations of underlying causes of behavior and to move toward

Table 4–1   Operational definitions

Behavior	Operational Definition
Hitting	Making forceful contact with any part of the hand, or with any object held in the hand, on any part of another person's body
Kicking	Making forceful contact with any part of the foot on any part of another person's body
Destruction	Disrupting the physical environment by breaking or tearing objects (e.g., furniture, books)
Out of place	Moving beyond the explicitly defined boundaries in which the student is allowed to move, without getting permission from the teacher or paraprofessional

objective, direct, and accurate measurement of the occurrence of the target behavior. Operational definitions are necessary for assessing the target behavior and thus necessary for evaluating the effectiveness of an intervention. In sum, an operational definition takes the guesswork out of teaching (Alberto & Troutman, 2006).

Writing Behavioral Objectives

A behavioral objective provides the context for the target behavior and, in essence, is an instructional road map that specifies the intended instructional outcome or behavioral destination. By clearly specifying an instructional outcome in observable and measurable terms, a teacher can compare current performance to desired performance, collect information that demonstrates progress toward the desired outcome, and determine when improvements in the target behavior match the specified behavioral destination. By specifying an outcome, a teacher then can plot the most efficient route to achieve the desired behavioral destination for a student.

Behavioral objectives have a particular format and structure that includes four distinct components. The components include

1. The student
2. The target behavior
3. The conditions
4. The criteria for desired performance

The *student component* reflects the individualization of desired outcomes for each student. Thus, every behavioral objective begins with the student's name. The *target behavior component* consists of an observable

Figure 4–3 Behavioral objectives with components noted

By May 2008 when observed playing with peers during structured play time, John will interact without hitting for 10 consecutive days.

In 32 weeks, when presented with a randomly selected reading passage from Merrill Reader, book 4, Jeremy will read aloud 60 words correctly in one minute.

In 24 weeks, when observed during history class for five consecutive 45-minute sessions, Robbie will be on task for 90% of the intervals observed.

Student ——————
Target behavior ====
Conditions [ ]
Criteria for desired performance ⬭

and measurable verb that describes the target behavior. The target behavior component must have an operational definition, but the definition is not necessarily included in the objective itself as that would result in a long and cumbersome objective. The *conditions component* refers to the antecedent stimulus that sets the occasion for the behavior to occur. In essence, the target behavior tells a student *what* to do, but not *when* to do it. Thus, it is just as important for a student to know when to do the behavior, and the conditions component provides this information to the student. The conditions component and target behavior of the objective form the first two parts of our A-B-C behavior sequence. The entire A-B-C relationship will be created by the teacher who provides the reinforcement (the "C" of the sequence) for the target behavior (i.e., the target behavior component of the objective, or the "B" of the sequence) under the appropriate antecedents (i.e., the conditions component of the objective, or the "A" of the sequence). The *criteria component* states the acceptable level of student performance of the selected target behavior under the specified conditions. The teacher must select the acceptable level of performance by considering such factors as nature of the content (i.e., basic vs. advanced), ability of the student, and the level of performance necessary for the skill to be functional in natural and everyday settings. Moreover, the law requires that skills be ambitious and meaningful, but also reasonable.

Figure 4-3 provides examples of behavioral objectives in which these components are identified. Figure 4-4 is a form that teachers can use to construct behavioral objectives.

One important guideline to follow when writing behavioral objectives for students with EBD is the *fair-pair* rule (White & Haring, 1982). The fair-pair rule states that any objective aimed at reducing a problem behavior (e.g., throwing schoolwork on the floor) needs to be accompanied by an objective aimed at increasing either an incompatible behavior or a replacement behavior. An incompatible behavior is one that cannot physically occur at the same time as the problem behavior. For example, doing schoolwork is incompatible with throwing it on the floor. A replacement behavior is one that results in the same outcome as the problem behavior. For example, if a student throws work on the floor because it is too difficult, the replacement behavior may be to ask for a break from the work, or to ask for assistance with the work. Thus, a behavioral objective to reduce throwing work on the floor should be accompanied by a behavioral objective that either increases the incompatible behavior of doing schoolwork or the replacement behavior of asking for a break or for assistance with the work. The idea behind the fair-pair rule is that reducing

FIGURE 4-4

Form for constructing objectives

Student	Behavior	Conditions	Criterion

Table 4–2 Examples of the fair pair

Inappropriate Behavior	Fair Pair
Talking out of turn	Raising hand for permission to talk
Leaving assigned seat	Staying in assigned seat
Pushing when in line	Standing with hands at side when in line
Being off task during independent schoolwork	Attending to independent schoolwork
Being noncompliant	Being compliant

one behavior (e.g., problem behavior) does not mean that another behavior (e.g., a desirable behavior) will spontaneously occur or increase. Table 4-2 provides examples of fair pairs.

ASSESSING BEHAVIOR

Once a teacher has written a behavioral objective, the next step is to assess the target behavior. Assessment is necessary during both *baseline* and *intervention*. Baseline means that no teaching has yet occurred. Baseline assessment serves two purposes: First, it provides information about the current levels of the target behavior. Second, baseline serves to predict the continued level of the target behavior if no teaching occurred. Intervention means that teaching is occurring. Intervention assessment enables the teacher (a) to compare baseline and intervention levels of the target behavior to determine the effectiveness of her teaching, (b) to make objective decisions about progress toward mastering the behavioral objective, and (c) to know when the student has met the criteria for the behavioral objective.

The most important aspect of assessing behavior is to collect objective information, called data, about the occurrence of the target behavior during intervention. Data are required for teachers to make objective decisions about the effectiveness of teaching and to guide decisions about revising or changing teaching strategies. Thus, assessment consists of two components: a recording system that accurately and efficiently documents the occurrence (i.e., data) of the target behavior, and a graphing system that allows a visual inspection of data to guide teaching decisions.

RECORDING SYSTEMS

A recording system is a data collection system that is used for the assessment of a target behavior. This assessment must produce numerical data that quantify the occurrence of the target behavior. Each recording system is comprised of three components: a recording method, a recording instrument, and a recording schedule (Miltenberger, 2004).

Recording Method

A recording method is an observational strategy or procedure that is used to count the occurrences of the behavior. There are several strategies and procedures for counting behavior and we will present the strategies that teachers are most likely to use. Although there are different strategies, they all share the common characteristic: that data are collected by a person directly observing a student and then writing down or counting some aspect of the target behavior.

Frequency measures simply count the number of times a behavior occurs. Frequency is best to measure behaviors that have a clear beginning, a clear ending, and take a similar length of time to perform. For example, hitting, swearing, and saying "excuse me" are examples of behavior that is best measured by frequency recording. Frequency should be used when (a) a behavior can be easily counted, (b) the observation periods are constant, and (c) the most important aspect of the behavior is the number of times it occurs. If observation periods vary in time, then frequency data can be changed to rate of response data by dividing the number of responses by the number of minutes in the observation period. For example, if a teacher uses frequency recording to determine the number of math problems a student completes, but each day the time for work changes, then the teacher would divide the number of responses by the amount of time. For example, if a student completes 10 problems in 20 minutes, then he completes 0.5 problem *a minute*. If he completes 18 problems in 30 minutes, then he completes 0.6 problem *a minute*.

Latency and *duration* recording focus on the time aspect of behavior. Latency refers to the amount of time it takes from when a behavior should start until when it actually starts. For example, how long it takes for a student to get settled down and start working during work time is an example of a behavior that is best measured by latency recording. Duration refers to how long a behavior occurs from when it starts until when it stops. How long a student has a tantrum or stays out of his seat is an example of behavior that is best measured by duration recording. Latency and duration measure the time dimension of behavior.

Interval recording consists of observing a student behavior for a block of time (e.g., 30 minutes). The block of time is divided into equal intervals of shorter time (e.g., 2 minutes) and then the observer records either the occurrence or nonoccurrence of the target behavior -during each interval. Interval recording is appropriate for behavior that occurs too rapidly to be counted, does not have a clear beginning or ending, or does not have a constant time duration. For example, measuring the amount of time that a student is on task is a behavior that is best measured by interval recording.

There are two types of interval recording: partial interval recording and whole interval recording. In partial interval recording, a person simply marks the behavior as occurring if the target behavior occurred *at any time* during the interval. In whole interval recording, the behavior must occur throughout the entire interval in order to be recorded. Interval recording is a very accurate recording method, but it is also labor intensive because it requires that someone observe a student for the duration of the observation block.

Time sampling is a variation of interval recording. In time sampling recording, a block of time is divided into intervals just like in whole and partial interval recording. During time sampling, however, the observer records only during a specific time of an interval. For example, if a block of time is divided into 15 one-minute intervals, the observer could record if the behavior is occurring or not occurring at the end of each interval. That is, the observer would quickly look at the student at the end of each minute, determine if the behavior is or is not occurring, and then record the observation. In this case, the observer would have 15 separate observations and the total direct observation time over the 15-minute block would be less than a minute. Time sampling is appropriate for the same behaviors as interval recording, but is much less labor intensive at the cost of some accuracy.

A recording method is an observational strategy that enables an observer to measure the relevant aspect of the target behavior accurately and reliably. Teachers must be careful to select the method that is best suited to the target behavior and to use that method throughout baseline

and intervention. One way to guide the selection of an appropriate method is to apply the A-B-C sequence to determine which component of the sequence is the relevant aspect of the target behavior (see Figure 4–5).

Recording Instruments

Recording instruments are what teachers use to document the occurrence or nonoccurrence of the target behavior. Most often, recording instruments are data sheets that teachers have prepared to collect numerical information about the target behavior in a quick, efficient, and accurate manner. Data sheets can take many different forms, but they usually consist of an organized format on paper that lets the observer register the occurrence or nonoccurrence of the target behavior by marking the appropriate place on the paper with a pencil.

Figure 4–6 provides an example of a data sheet that can be used to record the frequency of a target behavior.

Each time the behavior occurs, the observer makes a "+" in the box of that day. Figure 4–7 provides an example of a data sheet that can be used to record both the duration and frequency of a target behavior.

The observer writes down when the behavior started in one box and when it stopped in the next box. This format allows the observer to determine the average duration of each occurrence of the target behavior, the cumulative duration of all occurrences, and the number of times (or frequency) that the target behavior occurs. Figure 4–8 provides an example of a data sheet that can be used for whole and partial interval recording, as well as time sampling.

For whole interval recording, the observer places a "+" in the interval box when the behavior occurs for the entire interval. For partial interval recording, the observer places a "+" in the interval box when the behavior occurs

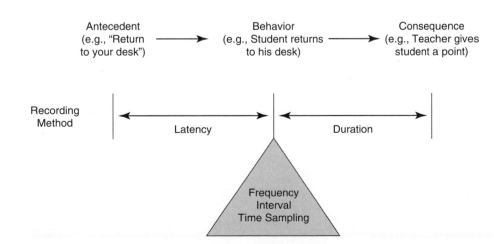

Figure 4–5   Using the A-B-C sequence to select an appropriate recording method

Adapted from Alberto & Troutman (2006).

FIGURE **4-6**

Data sheet to record the frequency of a target behavior

Data Collection Sheet

Student's name _____   Observer's name _____

Teacher's name _____   Date _____

Behavior _____   Setting _____

Time	Behavior #1 (e.g., Hitting)	Behavior #2 (e.g., Kicking)	Behavior #3 (e.g., Swearing)	Behavior #4 (e.g., Out of Seat)

FIGURE **4-7**

Data sheet to record both the frequency and duration of a target behavior

Student's name _____   Observer's name _____

Teacher's name _____   Date _____

Behavior _____   Setting _____

Date	Time			Duration
	Start Time	Stop Time		
4/5/08	2:30 p.m.	2:40 p.m.	10 minutes	
4/6/08	2:48 p.m.	2:56 p.m.	6 minutes	
4/7/08	2:24 p.m.	2:28 p.m.	4 minutes	
4/8/08	2:32 p.m.	2:36 p.m.	4 minutes	
Cumulative frequency 4 (e.g., 1 on 4/5, 1 on 4/6, etc.)			Cumulative duration 24 minutes (e.g., 10+6+4+4)	

FIGURE 4-8

Data sheet for recording whole and partial interval recording and time sampling data

Student's name _____   Observer's name _____

Teacher's name _____   Date _____

Behavior _____   Setting _____

Time	1	2	3	4	5	6	Total
9:00–9:01 a.m.	+	+		+	+		4
9:01–9:02 a.m.		+	+	+	+		4
9:02–9:03 a.m.			+		+	+	3
9:03 9:04 a.m.	+	+		+	+	+	5

Recording method: <u>Partial interval</u> Interval length: <u>10 seconds</u> Total time observed: <u>4 minutes</u>

at any time during the interval. For time sampling recording, the observer places a "+" in the interval box if the behavior is occurring at the end of each interval.

One important thing to note is that people (including students) often behave differently when they know they are being observed. This is referred to as *reactivity*. Teachers should realize that reactivity decreases over time and that to minimize reactivity, teachers should record behavior as part of their normal and daily teaching activities. In addition, teachers should record behavior as unobtrusively as possible and never use recording as a threat or a punishment system (e.g., "You're being bad. I'm writing that down.").

Recording Schedule

A teacher must collect information about the target behavior to make valid judgments about the effectiveness of intervention. Thus, a teacher must decide *where* to collect data, *when* to collect data, and *how often* to collect data so that she has *enough* information to make good judgments.

Deciding where to collect data involves selecting places in which the target behavior typically occurs. For example, if the target behavior either occurs (e.g., talking out), or should occur (e.g., staying on task), in the classroom, then the appropriate place to collect data is the classroom. A general guideline for selecting places to collect

data is to identify the most relevant setting(s) where the target behavior is either most necessary or most disruptive.

The guideline for deciding when to collect data is similar to the guidelines for deciding where to collect data. That is, data should be collected when the target behavior either is most likely to occur (e.g., task avoidance is worst during the first 10 minutes of class) or is most necessary (paying attention to the teacher during lecture time). One important thing to remember is that teachers should develop efficient data collection systems. A teacher does not need to collect data all day if the problem behavior is usually restricted to a particular time (e.g., immediately after lunch). A teacher needs to collect data at times when the target behavior is likely to occur. If the target behavior is evenly distributed across the day (e.g., teasing peers), then a teacher may need to collect data across the day. If the target behavior is associated with certain times and activities (e.g., noncompliance with academic task requests), then the teacher should collect data during those times.

Deciding how often to collect data is an important decision. One characteristic of applied behavior analysis is the consistent measurement (i.e., recording) of the target behavior. The underlying principle behind consistent measurement is that small daily changes in the target behavior add up to big changes over time, and unless there is proof of small daily changes, big changes cannot be expected and will not occur. Thus, a teacher needs to collect data frequently enough to identify the presence or absence of small changes so that there is enough information to determine whether to continue with the intervention or to make changes. This situation suggests that data need to be collected at least two or three times a week to be sensitive to small changes.

GRAPHING DATA AND MAKING INSTRUCTIONAL DECISIONS

Data enable teachers to evaluate and modify their instructional strategies based on the precise measurement of the target behavior. This is the instructional aspect of data collection. Another aspect of data collection is accountability. The accountability aspect of data collection means that teachers are able to determine whether their instructional or behavioral programs are effective and prove their efficacy by collecting, reacting to, and showing the data. As pointed out in chapters 2 and 8, progress monitoring and accountability have assumed a great deal of importance in special education because of the reauthorizations of IDEA in 1997 and 2004.

Teachers graph data so that they can have a visual representation of the occurrence of the target behavior over time. This visual representation provides a concise summary of the numerical occurrence and patterns of the target behavior. There are three steps for making instructional decisions: (1) accurately graphing the data,

(2) accurately analyzing the graphed data, and (3) using the analysis to guide instructional decisions. We now describe each step.

Graphing Data

Miltenberger (2004) stated that a complete graph has six components (see Figures 4-9 through 4-15):

1. *A y- axis and an x-axis.* The *y*-axis is the horizontal line and the *x*-axis is the vertical line that forms a right angle. The corner of the right angle is on the bottom left-hand side.

2. *The labels for the y-axis and x-axis.* The *y*-axis is labeled with the occurrences of the target behavior and the *x*-axis is labeled with a unit of time. The label for the *y*-axis is to its immediate left and the label for the *x*-axis is directly beneath it.

3. *The numbers for the y-axis and x-axis.* The numbers on the *y*-axis represent the occurrences of the target behavior and should directly correspond to the recording system. The numbers on the *x*-axis represent time and should directly correspond to the recording schedule.

4. *Data points.* A data point is placed on the graph to represent the numerical occurrence of the behavior (*y*-axis) for a particular unit of time (*x*-axis). A series of data points represents the occurrence of behavior over time.

Figure 4–9   Drawing the *X*- and *Y*-axes

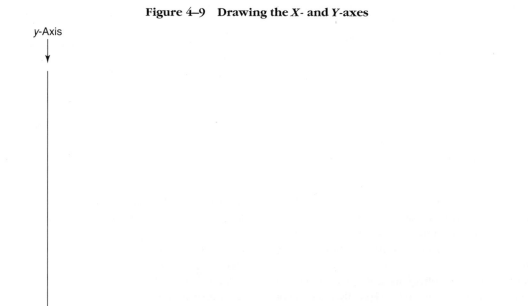

Figure 4–10   Labeling the *X*- and *Y*-axes

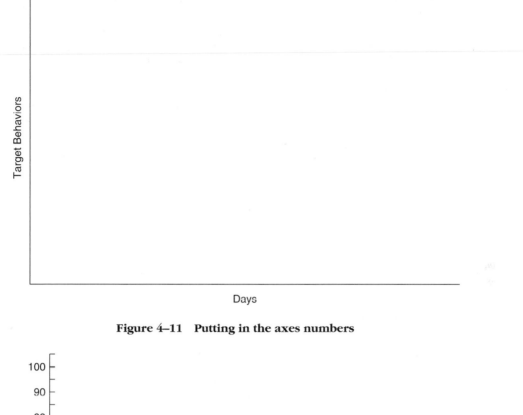

Figure 4–11   Putting in the axes numbers

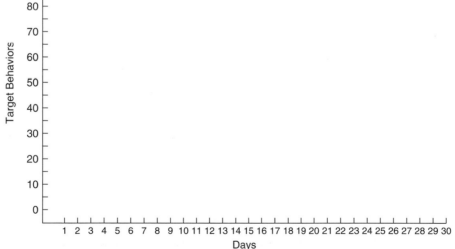

5. *Phase lines.* A phase line is vertical line on the graph that represents a change in conditions. Usually teachers will have at least two conditions on a graph. The first condition is baseline and the second condition is intervention. Data points *within each condition* are connected by lines so that it is easier to notice patterns. Data points are never connected across phase lines.

6. *Phase labels.* The phase labels describe the conditions in effect when the data were collected. Phase levels should be descriptive and brief.

It is important to remember that all graphed data, both within and across phases, must be collected under the same conditions. First, data should be collected during

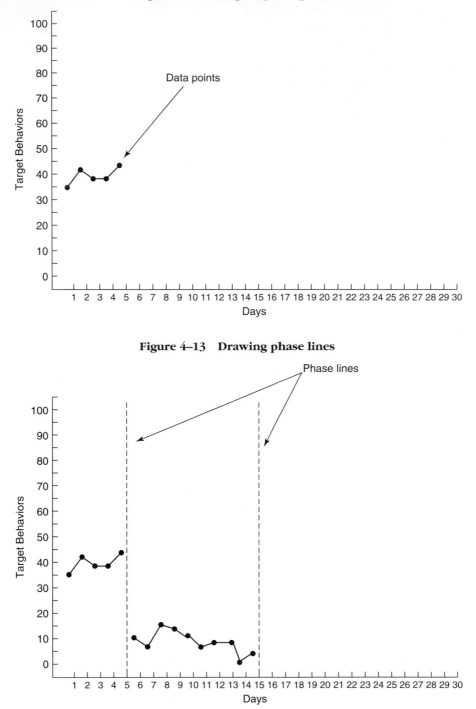

Figure 4–12   Graphing data points

Figure 4–13   Drawing phase lines

the same times each day or during the same activities each day. For example, if a student has talking-out behavior during academic times, then data should be collected during the same academic times each day. Second, graphed data should represent the occurrence of the target behavior either during the same time period, or if observation times differ, then data must be converted to a rate format. The reason for requiring the same conditions for all graphed data is to ensure that each data point can be compared to all other data points to assess the effectiveness of instruction. If conditions vary, then comparing data points to determine progress is like comparing apples to oranges.

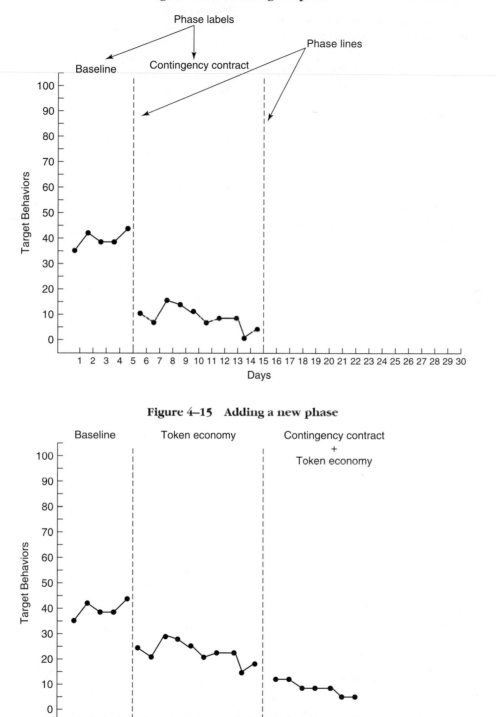

Figure 4–14 Labeling the phases

Figure 4–15 Adding a new phase

Graphing observation entails that information about the occurrence of the target behavior recorded on the data sheets is numerically summarized and represented on the graph. Usually, a day's worth of data is represented as a single point on the graph. Thus, a graph contains information about the target behavior's occurrence each day and across time.

Analyzing Graphed Data

A teacher analyzes graphed data by visually inspecting it. Visual inspection refers to making judgments about the effectiveness of intervention by visually examining the graphed observational data. Thus, to determine how effective instruction is, a teacher must collect, graph, and visually inspect data. There is no need for a teacher to analyze graphed data by using complicated statistical or mathematical formulae. Instead a teacher visually analyzes the graphed data by assessing trends, levels, and variability (Kazdin, 1982; Kennedy, 2005).

Trend Trend refers to the slope of the data. A trend is apparent when at least three consecutive data points are moving in the same direction. A trend can represent either an increase or a decrease in the target behavior. An increase in the occurrence of the target behavior is called an upward trend, and a decrease in the occurrence of the target behavior is called a downward trend. No trend is apparent when the data are horizontal. Figure 4-16 presents examples of upward, downward, and no trend data patterns.

Level Level refers to the difference between the occurrence of the target behavior at the end of one phase and the beginning of the next phase. Figure 4-17 presents data demonstrating different patterns in changes in levels.

Variability Variability refers to the fluctuation or stability in the day-to-day occurrence of the target behavior.

Figure 4-18 presents data that are highly variable and data with little variability.

It is hard to reach conclusions about the effectiveness of intervention when data are highly variable. When data are highly variable, it is important to identify the source of variability. Sources of variability can include factors associated with baseline and intervention conditions, or other factors. Factors associated with baseline and intervention observation conditions can include such things as introducing new material, changing presentation formats, or changing activity patterns from individual to group formats. Other factors may include events at home (e.g., parents divorce, student moves), changes in medication, or amount of sleep the night before. In any event, identifying trends and level changes becomes more difficult as variability increases.

Making Instructional Decisions

Student achievement is higher when teachers use data to make instructional decisions about progress than it is when teachers do not use data (Fuchs & Fuchs, 1986). Thus, teachers must use data to make decisions about instruction if they want to be effective. Making effective decisions begins with identifying relevant and meaningful target behaviors, creating efficient observation and recording systems, and accurately graphing data. When all this occurs, a teacher is well equipped to make instructional decisions.

Figure 4–16   Changes in trend

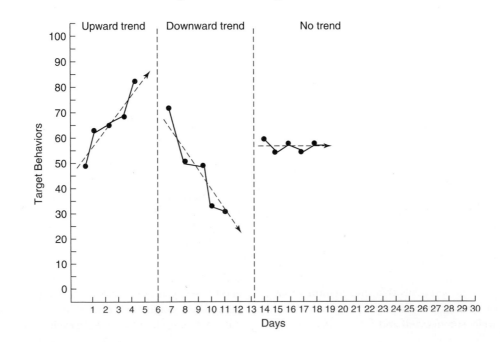

Figure 4–17 Changes in level

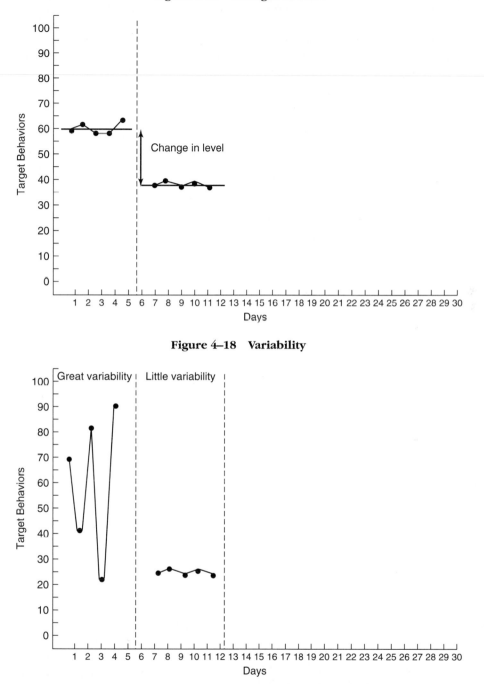

Figure 4–18 Variability

The analysis of data can lead to several different decisions (Wolery et al., 1988). First, if the data show that there is consistent improvement in the target behavior and that the pattern of improvement will result in attaining the desired outcome by the time specified in the behavioral goal or objective, then the decision is to continue. Second, if there is inadequate progress of the target behavior to reach the goal or objective, the teacher is faced with several decisions. These decisions can include (a) adjusting the timeframe necessary to reach the goal or objective, (b) beginning teaching prerequisite skills necessary to perform the target behavior, or (c) changing the instructional procedure. Whenever a teacher changes the instructional procedure, the graph needs to reflect this change by adding a new phase (see Figure 4-15). If a teacher is unclear as to which decision to make, it is often wise to continue collecting data under the current conditions until a pattern emerges. This pattern can then be used to guide instructional decisions. We also suggest that teachers refrain from making rapid and frequent instructional decisions. A general rule of thumb is that at least three data points are necessary to make any instructional decision, and that one data point is inadequate to make an instructional decision.

USING POSITIVE REINFORCEMENT TO CHANGE BEHAVIOR

The first part of this chapter provided information about the principles of behavior. We described positive reinforcement, negative reinforcement, extinction, and punishment, and also gave examples of their application to changing behavior. We now provide more information about positive reinforcement procedures that teachers can use to change the behavior of students with EBD. We emphasize these procedures for both empirical and philosophical reasons. First, they are highly effective at changing behavior (Maag, 2003), and second, they offer an alternative to punishment-based approaches. Teachers must pave the way for students to learn acceptable behavior, and to do this teachers need (a) to select alternative forms of desirable and acceptable behavior to teach, and (b) to provide consequences for desirable behavior that motivate students to master the alternative forms. This section is devoted to positive approaches to reducing undesirable behavior, and these approaches are offered as alternatives to punishment. All the approaches are characterized by (a) the selection of acceptable and desirable behavior, and (b) positive consequences for the new behavior.

Differential Reinforcement Strategies

Reinforcement is a contingent consequence that increases the future likelihood of a particular behavior. Differential reinforcement strategies are a set of effective procedures that rely on reinforcement for behavior change (Repp & Dietz, 1974, 1979). These procedures involve two steps: First, the undesirable behavior is identified and then a desirable alternative or replacement behavior is selected. For example, if the undesirable behavior is talking out, the alternative behavior may be remaining quiet, or raising one's hand to be called on before talking. The teacher provides reinforcement for the desirable behavior and withholds reinforcement for the undesirable behavior. Thus, the teacher would reinforce either being quiet or hand raising, but would not reinforce talking out. That is, talking out would be on extinction. When a student has several options for behaving, the teacher is in charge of determining which

option will occur by providing positive consequences for one (i.e., reinforcing it) and withholding consequences for the others.

Differential reinforcement strategies are based on the simple fact that a teacher gets better results when she "catches" students being good and rewards them than when she "catches" students being bad and punishes them. When a teacher moves away from a punishment-oriented perspective and toward this reinforcement-oriented perspective, many good things can happen to her and her students. First, her quality of relationships with students increases because now she is associated with pleasant and enjoyable consequences. Second, she reduces the potential for confrontations in which she "heaps on" more punishment as students try to avoid or escape the original punishment. Third, the quality of interactions among the students themselves may benefit as students copy the positive interaction style of the teacher. Finally, when students learn that certain behaviors result in positive and pleasant consequences, the students are more likely to try the new behaviors in other situations, other places, and with other people (i.e., the students are likely to generalize the new behaviors).

There are a number of differential reinforcement strategies, including differential reinforcement of low rates of behavior (DRL), differential reinforcement of other behavior (DRO), and differential reinforcement of alternative behavior (DRA). Although each of these strategies has a specific application, they all share a number of common steps that need to be followed if they are to be effective. Prior to describing each specific procedure and its application, we present the generic steps embodied in each differential reinforcement strategy (adapted from Miltenberger, 2004).

How to Use Differential Reinforcement

1. Define the desirable behavior. The behavior that you intend to increase first must be selected and then clearly defined. A clear and precise definition of the behavior is extremely important so that (a) the student knows exactly what is expected of him, (b) you can reinforce the new behavior, and (c) you can record its rate to determine whether the intervention is effective.

2. Define the undesirable behavior. The behavior that you intend to decrease must be defined so that you (a) do not reinforce its occurrence, and (b) can record its occurrence to determine whether it is decreasing.

3. Identify the reinforcer. All differential reinforcement procedures involve reinforcing a desirable behavior and withholding reinforcement for undesirable behaviors. Thus, the success of these procedures relies heavily on selecting powerful and motivating consequences to use as reinforcers. To start, reinforcers are different for different people, and it is important to determine specific reinforcers for your student. There are several ways to do this. First, you can use the reinforcer that is currently the consequence for the undesirable behavior. For example, if a student talks or acts out to get your attention, you can use your attention as the consequence for the desirable behavior you have identified. Second, you can observe the individual during free time and see what objects, activities, or interests the individual self-selects. For example, if a student has a favorite computer game or toy, either of these can be made available only for the occurrence of the desirable behavior. Third, you can directly ask the student what he likes best, or ask his parents to provide information about his favorite objects or activities.

4. *Reinforce the desirable behavior immediately and consistently.* When a student is acquiring a new behavior, it is imperative that its occurrence is reinforced immediately and consistently. Immediate reinforcement ensures that the student associates the desirable behavior with the consequence you are providing, and consistent reinforcement ensures that the student does not resort to the undesirable behavior because the new behavior does not always "pay off."

5. *Eliminate reinforcement for the undesirable behavior.* When undesirable behavior occurs, it is because there is some consequence that the student desires. The consequence may not happen every time, but it happens enough for the student to take a chance and see if the desired consequence can be obtained. For example, a student may act out because it results in getting the teacher's or peers' attention. Or a student simply may desire to "get the teacher's goat." Students also may act out because it is a fairly successful way to avoid schoolwork. Regardless of the exact consequence, students always get something out of undesirable behavior or they would not engage in it. Removing or eliminating the consequence reduces the likelihood that the student will continue the undesirable behavior. Sometimes it is impossible to eliminate the consequence. For example, if a student strikes a peer to get the teacher's attention, this type of behavior cannot be ignored. But the teacher can minimize the quality of her attention to the student by remaining calm, avoiding eye contact, and speaking quietly.

6. *Use intermittent reinforcement to maintain the desirable behavior.* When students are initially acquiring the new behavior, they need immediate and consistent consequences. After the desirable behavior is occurring at a high and steady rate, and the undesirable behaviors are rarely occurring, you don't need to provide consequences every time for the desirable behavior. But it is important to reinforce the desirable behavior every so often or the student is likely to revert to the undesirable behavior of the past. There always must be an occasional desired consequence available for the new behavior or it will "fade away and vanish" as reinforcement fades away and vanishes.

Specific Differential Reinforcement Procedures and Their Applications

Although each differential reinforcement procedure embodies the steps and principles presented previously, researchers have developed variations to adapt these principles to certain behaviors and situations. We now present the major variations and their applications.

Differential Reinforcement of Other Behavior (DRO)

Definition. In DRO, the teacher provides reinforcement following a specified interval of time in which the undesirable behavior does not occur. For this reason, DRO is often called the differential reinforcement of zero rates of behavior. In DRO, a teacher is reinforcing the *absence* of the undesirable behavior as well as reinforcing any other behavior that occurs during the interval.

Application. There are three important factors a teacher should consider before using DRO (Alberto & Troutman, 2006). First, DRO requires that the teacher reinforce the student whenever the undesirable behavior does not occur during the interval, *no matter what other behaviors occur.* For example, if the undesirable behavior is talking out and that doesn't occur during the interval, yet the student drops his pencil 30 times, technically speaking the student is entitled to the reinforcer. Second, because DRO reinforces the absence of an undesirable behavior, the teacher may be creating a "behavior vacuum" by eliminating the student's most prominent form of behavior. The student may invent other undesirable forms of behavior to fill this vacuum. Third, the effectiveness of DRO depends on the reinforcer selected. The reinforcer for not engaging in the undesirable behavior must be more *motivating* than the reinforcer for engaging in the behavior. For example, if the undesirable behavior of a student is to make odd sounds during class to get the attention of *all* his peers, and the reinforcer for making no sounds is 5 minutes of time alone at the computer, then most likely the student will opt for the attention of his peers. Thus, DRO is a good choice for students who engage in an undesirable behavior but have a wide variety of other acceptable behaviors in their repertoire and for whom a very powerful competing reinforcer is available.

Example. Mike is a student who asked the teacher every 4 or 5 minutes for permission to leave the classroom and go to the bathroom or get a drink. First, because the teacher knew that Mike really enjoys reading professional wrestling magazines, she decided to use these as Mike's reinforcers. Second, she explained to Mike that for every 5 minutes of class in which he did not ask to leave the classroom, he could earn a token. For every 5 tokens that he earned, Mike could spend them on 10 minutes of looking at the magazines. Finally, when Mike is earning tokens reliably, the teacher intends to increase the "cost" of time with the magazines from 5 tokens to 10 tokens.

Differential Reinforcement of Low Rates of Responding (DRL)

Definition. In DRL, the teacher provides reinforcement when the rate of the undesirable behavior is decreased to a predetermined level. In DRL the teacher reinforces a lower rate of behavior, whereas in DRO the teacher reinforces the absence of a specific undesirable behavior.

Application. DRL is used when a behavior becomes undesirable because it occurs too often or too rapidly, and when a lower rate of the same behavior is tolerable or even desirable. For example, it is desirable to have a student participate in a class discussion, but undesirable for the student to dominate it; it is desirable for a student to raise his hand when he has a question for the teacher, but undesirable for the student to constantly have his hand in the air. Thus, DRL is a good choice if the teacher's goal is to decrease the rate of an undesirable behavior but not to eliminate it.

Example. Laura constantly raises her hand and asks the teacher if she is doing her math seat work correctly. Laura asks if she has copied the problem correctly, if she has lined up the numbers in their columns correctly, if she has carried the numbers correctly, and if she has the correct answer. Laura asks these questions for every math problem. The teacher knows that Laura enjoys doing work around the classroom, such as watering the plants, feeding the hamster, or washing the blackboards and she has decided to use these "jobs" as Laura's reinforcers. The teacher has explained to Laura that if she raises her hand only three times during math seat work, Laura can "earn" one of the classroom jobs. The teacher plans to ultimately reduce Laura's hand raising to occurring only once or twice during math seat work.

Differential Reinforcement of Alternative Behavior (DRA)

Definition. In DRA, the teacher provides reinforcement for an alternative behavior that replaces the undesirable

behavior. That is, the alternative behavior gets the same consequence as the undesirable behavior. Whenever two or more behaviors result in the same consequence, or reinforcing outcome, they are called *functionally equivalent* (Carr, 1988). For example, waving to someone and saying "hi" are functionally equivalent behaviors.

In DRA, both the alternative behavior and the undesirable behavior can occur at the same time (e.g., shouting out during class and raising one's hand). There are two variations of DRA. One is the differential reinforcement of incompatible behavior (DRI), in which the alternative behavior and the undesirable behavior cannot occur simultaneously (e.g., shouting out and politely asking to be called on). The other is the differential reinforcement of communication (DRC), in which the alternative behavior serves a functionally equivalent communicative purpose (a student throws his book on the floor when he is tired of schoolwork; he is taught to say "I'll take a short break now" when he is tired of schoolwork).

Application. DRA is used when the purpose or function of a student's undesirable behavior is acceptable (e.g., getting the teacher's or a peer's attention) but the form is not (e.g., shouting, screaming, or hitting). Thus, when using DRA the new alternative behavior must result in the same consequence or reinforcing outcome as the student's undesirable behavior.

There are several criteria for selecting an alternative, or replacement, behavior. First, the alternative behavior must serve the same purpose for the student as the undesirable behavior serves (e.g., getting attention, asking for a break). Second, the alternative behavior must require less physical effort and result in both immediate and preferred consequences (Horner & Day, 1991). For example, if a student uses foul language to get attention from his peers, the new alternative behavior must be as quick and easy to "do" as swearing, as well as resulting in the same quantity and quality of attention from peers. Finally, the alternative behavior must be socially acceptable to those in the student's environment. In sum, a teacher should use DRA when the purpose of an undesirable behavior is acceptable but the current way of expressing it is not, when a new appropriate behavior to express it can be identified, and when the teacher or environment can provide the same or better consequences for using the new behavior.

Example. Every morning when Todd arrives at school, he punches or slaps several students in the back of the head. The students usually respond to this by yelling or shouting at Todd. The teacher has analyzed the situation and discovered that this is the way Todd announces his "arrival" and greets his fellow students. The teacher has concluded that the purpose of Todd's behavior, greeting other students, is acceptable, but the way he expresses it, punching or slapping other students, is not. She has decided that she will use DRA to teach Todd a new socially acceptable way to greet his peers. First, she selects a new behavior for Todd to announce his arrival. When he first arrives at school and enters the classroom, Todd will clap three times and say "I'm here." This will get everyone's attention. The teacher then will ask the students to say "good morning" to Todd. Over time, the teacher intends to teach Todd just to say "good morning" and not clap his hands, but for now she believes that it is a good idea for him to keep his hands busy first thing in the morning.

Differential Reinforcement and Punishment

Differential reinforcement strategies can be effective because they teach students desirable and acceptable forms of behavior by providing positive consequences that motivate students to respond with the new forms of behavior. We suggest that teachers always include differential reinforcement strategies in any approach to reducing problem behavior. Moreover, if a teacher decides to use punishment, it should always be used in combination with some differential reinforcement strategy. For example, if a teacher punishes a student by taking away tokens contingent on the occurrence of problem behavior (i.e., response cost), then the teacher ought to enable the student to earn back the tokens contingent on good behavior. Punishment by definition reduces behavior; therefore, every punishment procedure needs to be accompanied by a differential reinforcement procedure to increase alternative and desirable behavior.

PROGRAMMING FOR GENERALIZATION

Generalization refers to the "occurrence of relevant behavior under different, non-training conditions (i.e., across subjects, setting, people, behaviors, and/or time) without the scheduling of the same events in those conditions as had been scheduled in the training conditions" (Stokes & Baer, 1977, p. 350). According to this definition, there are at least three types of generalization. The first type of generalization happens when newly acquired behavior occurs in different places or with different people. This type of generalization is referred to as *stimulus generalization*. An example of stimulus generalization is when a student learns to be polite to the teacher, and then without any further training, is polite to peers and is polite to his parent at home. The second type of generalization happens

when a change in one behavior results in changes in other related behaviors. This type of generalization is referred to as *response generalization*. For example, if we teach a student to greet others by shaking hands, we might also see an increase in head nodding, waving, or saying "hi." The third type of generalization happens when a behavior continues to occur over time. This type of generalization is referred to as *maintenance*. For example, suppose a student learns to comply with teacher requests through reinforcement or other procedures. If compliance continues to occur after the program has ended, then maintenance has happened.

Generalization is remarkably important as an outcome of teaching because it means that a student uses newly learned skills in multiple relevant everyday situations. The purpose of school is to prepare a student for life outside school and, ultimately, for adult life after school ends. School can be conceived of as a preparation and training site for developing and practicing the skills necessary for a successful and productive life. From this perspective, generalization becomes central to every skill a teacher selects for a student; thus teachers need to incorporate strategies to enhance generalization throughout the teaching and learning process. We now present several strategies that teachers can use to enhance generalization (Stokes & Baer, 1977; Stokes & Osnes, 1989). We have grouped the strategies in an antecedent-behavior-consequence (A-B-C) sequence to emphasize the relationship of generalization to the behavioral sequence, and we use social skills training to demonstrate how multiple generalization strategies can be implemented for a behavior.

Antecedent Strategies

Antecedents are stimuli that set the occasion for a behavior to occur because they signify that reinforcement is available (Skinner, 1938). Therefore antecedents are important for generalization because they serve to cue the behavior. There are several antecedent strategies.

Train Loosely Train loosely refers to varying the conditions under which a behavior is learned so that the student does not attend to irrelevant but frequently present stimuli. For example, when teaching social skills, the teacher may want to teach skills at different times during the day, have different people teach (e.g., the school social worker or psychologist), and vary the order in which material is presented. Training loosely allows the students to attend to the social skills content, and not associate content with any one person or with any one way of presenting.

Train Sufficient Exemplars   Train sufficient exemplars refers to using lots of examples that represent the relevant aspects of antecedents. For example, when teaching social skills, a teacher must use lots of different examples that represent the range of situations in which the skills should be used. Training sufficient exemplars enables the student to respond to all relevant antecedents, rather than a small portion or subset of them.

Program Common Stimuli   Program common stimuli refers to using materials, people, settings, and situations that are the same as those in the generalization settings. If a student learns social skills by interacting only with a teacher, then the likelihood is reduced that the student will generalize the skills because there are very few teachers to interact with in the student's world outside school. Programming common stimuli replicates real-world conditions during teaching so that same antecedents present during teaching are present in other places.

Behavior Strategies

Behavior is the motor act that enables an individual to obtain reinforcement. One behavior strategy is to teach a student multiple responses (i.e., different motor acts) that will get the same outcome (i.e., obtain reinforcement). For example, if a teacher is teaching a student how to start a conversation, then she must provide the student with multiple "opening lines." That way, if one opening line does not start a conversation, the student would still have additional options for starting a conversation. Behavior strategies provide the student with multiple socially acceptable responses that result in the same outcome rather than making the student dependent on a single response that may or may not be successful.

Consequent Strategies

Consequent strategies emphasize the role of obtaining reinforcement in promoting generalization. The availability of reinforcement is signaled by the antecedent stimulus. The antecedent stimulus may initially evoke responding, but it is accessing reinforcement that maintains the response over time in the generalization setting. If reinforcement is not available in the generalization setting, responding may occur temporarily, but eventually responding will stop because the behavior is on extinction in the generalization setting. Thus, accessing reinforcement in the generalization setting is crucial for the durability of the new behavior.

Introduce to Natural Maintaining Contingencies
Introduce to natural maintaining strategies refers to identifying and teaching behavior that will access naturally existing reinforcement in the generalization settings. This procedure is also called trapping (Baer & Wolf, 1970). When reinforcement is naturally available in the generalization setting, the behavior is likely to occur because it results in accessing reinforcement. If a teacher teaches social skills that result in peer reinforcement, then it is likely that these skills will generalize to other settings where peer reinforcement is available. If a teacher teaches social skills, but the reinforcer is teacher attention, then it is likely that the skills will not generalize unless there are teachers in the students' everyday environment. Selecting skills that access natural communities of reinforcement may be the most important generalization strategy because reinforcement provides the motivation for the behavior to occur and to continue occurring over time.

Use Indiscriminable Contingencies   Using indiscriminable contingencies refers to the use of intermittent schedules of reinforcement during acquisition phases of learning that more closely replicate the intermittent schedules of reinforcement existing in most generalization settings. First, intermittent schedules of reinforcement during acquisition result in behaviors that are more resistant to extinction (Ferster & Skinner, 1957). Second, intermittent schedules of reinforcement maintain behavior with occasional reinforcement, and when a student is unsure which response will be reinforced, they are more likely to continue responding (e.g., Fowler & Baer, 1981). For example, if a teacher is teaching a student to start a conversation, she may want to start by reinforcing every initiation. She should, however, move quickly to an intermittent schedule of reinforcement to facilitate more response resilience and prepare the student for the intermittent schedule of reinforcement existing in the real world. Indiscriminable contingencies foster generalization by creating behaviors that can be maintained on thinner schedules of reinforcement.

Mediate and Reinforce Generalization   Mediate generalization refers to teaching students to monitor their own generalization and reinforce generalization refers to providing reinforcement for occurrences of generalization. Teaching students to monitor their own behavior should be a concomitant component of any skill development. A teacher could teach a student to mediate generalization by having the student describe how he or she could identify occurrences of generalization and report them back to the teacher. The teacher could then reinforce any occurrences of reported instances of generalization. Mediate generalization prepares a student to self-monitor generalization, and self-monitoring may become reinforcing in itself. Reinforcing generalization serves to promote generalization as a class of behavior in addition to reinforcing individual instances of it.

Promoting Generalization

Generalization does not occur automatically (Stokes & Baer, 1977; Stokes & Osnes, 1986). Rather, teachers must systematically program for it. In addition to the previously mentioned strategies, teachers can promote generalization in several other ways. First, teachers should select skills for students that will result in accessing reinforcement in multiple settings (e.g., school, home, community) contingent on the occurrence of the behavior. Second, teachers must analyze the antecedent conditions in these settings and then represent those conditions as nearly as possible during teaching. Third, teachers should select additional strategies as previously listed and embed them in teaching. Finally, teachers should never assume that generalization has occurred unless there is proof. Thus, teachers should collect data on the generalization of target behaviors, and alter their teaching approaches when the data warrant it.

Chapter Summary

Applied behavior analysis changes the behavior of students by using the principles of behavior. The principles of behavior are consequences that occur after a behavior and because of the behavior, and affect the likelihood that the behavior will occur in the future. Two principles, positive and negative behavior, either maintain or strengthen behavior. Two principles, extinction and punishment, weaken behavior.

Changing behavior begins by carefully selecting a target behavior that has relevance to improving a student's life. The target behavior is carefully monitored by collecting and graphing its occurrence to determine if instruction is effective at changing it. Any changes in the instructional program are based on a visual analysis of the data to support the need for a change. Generalization of the target behavior is an important goal and instructional programs need to include strategies that promote widespread use of the target behavior.

Functional Behavioral Assessments and Behavior Intervention Plans

Erik Drasgow, Christian A. Martin, Robert E. O'Neill, and Mitchell L. Yell

Focus Questions

- What is functional behavioral assessment (FBA)?

- What is a behavior intervention plan (BIP)?

- Why is it important that teachers of students with emotional and behavioral disorders be able to conduct an FBA and development BIPs?

- How can teachers conduct an FBA?

- What is the competing behavior model?

- How can teachers develop BIPs?

Functional behavioral assessment (FBA) refers to a process for gathering information about problem behavior to understand and describe the reasons why it occurs (Carr et al., 1994; Drasgow et al., 1999; Fox & Gable, 2004; Gable, Hendrickson, & Sasso, 1995; O'Neill et al., 1997). Behavior intervention plans (BIPs) consist of proactive and comprehensive interventions that are derived from the FBA information and are nonpunishment oriented (Drasgow & Yell, 2001; Dunlap & Koegel, 1999). We begin this chapter by presenting the conceptual, philosophical, and legal bases of FBAs and BIPs. Next, we describe the procedures for conducting FBAs. Finally, we describe the procedures for developing and implementing BIPs. We provide frequent application examples of FBA and BIP procedures for students with EBD throughout the chapter.

THE BASES OF FUNCTIONAL BEHAVIORAL ASSESSMENTS AND BEHAVIOR INTERVENTION PLANS

Knitzer et al. (1990) referred to the common practice of teachers in classrooms for students with EBD as the "curriculum of control." The authors used this terminology to signify that teachers typically tried to control their students' behavior, often through the use of punishment. Thus, the primary goal in these classrooms had been the control and reduction of problem behaviors, rather than systematically teaching prosocial behaviors to prevent and replace undesirable behaviors and then creating environments that foster and sustain these new behaviors. In a national survey of teacher intervention preferences, punitive and reactive methods continue to be the predominant model that teachers use in classrooms for students with EBD (Yell, 2006).

In the control curriculum, problem behaviors are seen as an interruption in the instructional process. The focus of intervention, therefore, is to reduce or eliminate the problem behavior so that instruction may continue. By intervening only to reduce or eliminate the behavior, however, we fail to provide supports and to teach alternative behaviors necessary for students to respond effectively to the situations that evoked the problem behavior in the first place (Neel & Cessna, 1993). The common practice of punishment and control has been abysmally unsuccessful in preparing students with EBD to function competently in society (Neel, Meadows, Levine, & Edgar, 1988; Walker et al., 1995; Walker, Stieber, & O'Neill, 1990; Walker & Sylwester, 1991).

Disillusionment with punishment for both ethical and empirical reasons began in the 1970s in the area of severe disabilities (e.g. Carr, 1977) and was motivated by the development of effective and more socially acceptable reinforcement procedures (e.g., DRO, DRA; see Chapter 4) that did not have the negative side effects of punishment (Kazdin, 1982b; Sidman, 1989). This disillusionment served as the impetus for the creation of a new approach to problem behavior (Drasgow, 1997; Maag, 2001) that began with students with severe disabilities (e.g., Carr & Durand, 1985) and since has spread to students with EBD (e.g., Dunlap et al., 1993; Kamps et al., 1995; Kern, Dunlap, Childs, & Clarke, 1994; Reed et al., 1997; Umbreit, 1995). We next examine the basis of positive behavior support and, in doing so, examine the bases of FBAs and BIPs.

Conceptual Basis

Positive behavior support grew out of applied behavior analysis (Carr, 1997; Carr et al., 2002; Gresham, Watson, & Skinner, 2001; Horner, Albin, Todd, & Sprague, 2006). Applied behavior analysts view behavior as a function of the interaction between the individual and the environment. That is, behavior is determined by how the environment sets the occasion for and responds to it (Sidman, 1960; Skinner, 1953). Environmental responses can be categorized as positive or negative reinforcement, extinction, or punishment (see Chapter 4). Those responses that are reinforced are more likely to occur in the future and those responses that are extinguished or punished are less likely to occur in the future. Thus, problem behavior is not a random occurrence, but rather it exists in a lawful relationship that is expressed by the three-term contingency relationship among behavior and its antecedent and consequent events.

Positive behavior support is based on the antecedent-behavior-consequent (A-B-C) relationship between behavior and the environment that is at the core of applied behavior analysis. By viewing behavior from this perspective, and by knowing what lawful and functional relationships exist between problem behavior and the environment, we have the tools to both predict and change problem behavior (Dunlap, Harrower, & Fox, 2005). Assessment is used to understand the relationship between the environment and problem behavior. Intervention is used to change existing relationships or to create new relationships that eliminate problem behavior. In sum, the two major characteristics of applied behavior analysis are its (a) focus on identifying behavior–environment relations and (b) emphasis on changing these relationships to improve a person's life. Thus, FBAs and BIPs are an elegant embodiment of applied behavior analysis.

Philosophical Basis

Applied behavior analysis in many ways provides the "how" for FBAs and BIPs. That is, ABA gives teachers and other professionals the tools both to understand and to change behavior. The philosophical basis of positive behavior support provides the "why" of positive behavior support. The "why" is driven by a number of philosophical principles and empirical facts:

1. Problem behavior usually serves a purpose for the person displaying it. Problem behavior is often a very predictable and effective way for a person to get a desired outcome (e.g., throwing books on the floor is an effective way to avoid schoolwork).

2. The goal of intervention is education, not simply behavior reduction. The main goal of intervention is to teach an individual new ways of influencing other people so that the problem behaviors are no longer necessary.

3. Problem behavior does not occur in a vacuum. It occurs in a dynamic and reciprocal social context. Thus, intervention involves changing social systems, not just individuals. Reducing problem behavior often involves change on everyone's part.

4. Complex problems require complex solutions. Problem behavior is most often the result of multiple factors and complicated situations. Thus, assessment and intervention must reflect strategies that take into account the complex nature of problem behavior.

5. Lifestyle change is the ultimate goal of intervention. The broader goal of intervention is to produce change that positively affects how people live their lives. Successful intervention enables a person to influence others without having to resort to problem behaviors. Most importantly, it permits a person to participate directly in the community, moves them toward independence, and allows them access to all the opportunities available in society (Carr et al., 1994).

Positive behavior support reflects the philosophy of inclusion and quality of life (Bambara, 2005; Carr et al., 2002). That is, simply reducing problem behavior does not provide a person with the adaptive skills necessary to be successful in school, at home, in the community, or in a work setting. Behavior reduction is "insufficient if it leaves the student compliant but in a socially, academically, and personally barren situation" (Horner, Albin, Sprague, & Todd, 2000, p. 208). Thus, behavior support is much more than behavior reduction. Behavior support is aimed at building skills that ultimately make a person successful in a wide variety of settings outside of the classroom. The major philosophical driving force underlying positive behavior support is its movement away from obedience and compliance as the desirable outcome and its movement toward skill development, inclusion in our society, and a good quality of life.

Legal Basis

The Individuals with Disabilities Education Act Amendments of 1997 (hereafter IDEA 1997) requires that when a student with a disability exhibits problem behavior that interferes with his or her learning or that of others, then the individualized education program (IEP) team shall "consider, when appropriate, strategies, including positive behavioral interventions, strategies, and supports to address that behavior" (IDEA Amendments, 20 U.S.C. § 1414(d)(3)(B)(I)). Thomas Hehir, former director of the U.S Department of Education's Office of Special Education Programs, stated that "the key provision in IDEA '97 is using positive behavioral interventions and supports" for students who exhibit significant problem behaviors (*Letter to Anonymous*, 1999). Failure to do so "would constitute a denial of the free appropriate public education (mandate of IDEA)" (IDEA Regulations, Appendix B, Question 38). Clearly, this statement seems to reflect support for a best practices position that positive behavior support should be used with all students with disabilities who exhibit problem behavior. The Individuals with Disabilities Education Improvement Act of 2004 (hereafter IDEA 2004) increased the support for the use of positive behavior support by (a) requiring that IEP teams base services for students with disabilities on evidence-based practices (e.g., positive behavior support); and (b) allowing school districts to spend a percentage of their IDEA funds on early intervening services for all students, such as positive behavior support.

Although the U.S. Department of Education has not defined either FBA or BIP, it is a reasonable assumption that Congress intended that those terms would be consistent with the existing professional consensus about the meaning of positive behavior support (Drasgow & Yell, 2001; Gorn, 1998). Thus, the legal term "functional behavioral assessment" is consistent with the existing term "functional assessment" and the legal term "behavior intervention plan" is consistent with the existing term "positive behavior support plan." It appears that by legally requiring FBAs and BIPS, the government has endorsed a new approach to problem behavior that compels teachers to move away from a reliance on punitive procedures and move toward a proactive, problem-solving approach that emphasizes skill building (Drasgow & Yell, 2001). If applied behavior analysis (ABA) provides the "how," and the philosophical basis provides the "why," then the legal basis provides the "you must do it this way."

Although neither IDEA '97 nor the regulations detail what problem behaviors are covered under the statute, Drasgow and colleagues (1999) infer from previous litigation that these behaviors include (a) disruptive behaviors that distract the teacher from teaching and other students from learning, (b) noncompliance, (c) abuse, of property, (d) verbal abuse, and (e) aggression toward students or staff (*Clyde K. v. Puyallup School District*, 1994; *Hartmann v. Loudoun County*, 1997). We suggest that most students with EBD engage in behavior that interferes with their learning and, thus, it is supported as problem behavior by previous litigation. Therefore, most students with EBD are candidates for FBAs and BIPs. In fact, as we explain in Chapter 3, an FBA should be completed as part of the assessment phase of IEP development, and the BIP should be incorporated into the IEP for all students with EBD.

A strict interpretation of the FBA requirements of IDEA requires that an FBA be conducted when students with disabilities are subject to disciplinary actions. We agree with Nelson, Roberts, and Smith (1998) and Nelson, Roberts, Mathur, & Rutherford (1999), that to use FBAs only in reaction to extreme or chronic problem behavior, however, is an inefficient use of this proactive technology. We endorse a broader interpretation of IDEA's behavior mandate that requires teachers to gather "functional" assessment information (see IDEA, § 614(b)(2)(A)) and develop positive behavioral interventions and supports whenever a student's problem behavior interferes with his or her learning or the learning of others (see IDEA, § 614(d)(3)(B)(i)). Thus, we believe that best practice and IDEA require that teachers of students with disabilities conduct FBAs with their students who exhibit problem behavior and include BIPs in the IEPs of these students.

SUMMARY

Applied behavior analysis provides the conceptual and technical basis of FBAs and BIPs. Skill development and quality of life, rather than simply behavior reduction, provide its philosophical basis. IDEA 1997 and IDEA 2004 provide its legal basis; thus teachers need to address problem behavior as the law mandates. It is important that teachers understand that the law has codified FBAs and BIPS as the expected standard in the field of special education. We believe that the seeds of successful behavior support are planted when teachers (a) are competent applied behavior analysts, and (b) embrace the values and philosophy driving positive behavior support. The rest of this chapter is devoted to explaining and illustrating FBA and BIP procedures.

FUNCTIONAL BEHAVIORAL ASSESSMENT

The purpose of FBA is to gather information about problem behavior to understand and describe the reasons *why* it occurs (Carr et al., 1994; O'Neill et al., 1997). The process of FBA includes gathering information about antecedents and consequences that are related to the occurrence of problem behavior (Miltenberger, 2004). This information improves the effectiveness and efficiency of the behavior intervention plan. An FBA should result in identifying the following types of information (Horner et al., 2006; Kern, O'Neill, & Starosta, 2005):

1. *A description of the problem behavior(s) and daily routines.* Assessment begins by accurately describing the problem behavior in observable and measurable terms. That is, assessment begins with an operational definition of the problem behavior. An operational definition allows for agreement on the actual occurrence, duration, and intensity of the problem behavior. Remember from Chapter 3 that operational definitions do not include subjective interpretations of underlying emotions (e.g., anger, frustration) but instead describe the actual observable behavior (e.g., hitting, throwing materials).

2. *Consequences maintaining the problem behavior.* Most behavior occurs because there are consequences maintaining it. Problem behavior is no different. Problem behavior generally occurs (e.g., swearing) because there is some consequence maintaining it (e.g., attention from peers in the form of laughing). Therefore, every FBA must contain information about the consequences that are maintaining the problem behavior. Functional behavioral assessment is driven by determining the *function* of the behavior. The function of behavior is determined by identifying its consequences. Consequences occur after the behavior, because of the behavior, and influence the future likelihood of the behavior. The functions, or consequences, of problem behavior consist of either positive reinforcement (i.e., the person *gets something*) or negative reinforcement (i.e., the person *avoids or escapes something*). The broad categories of positive and negative reinforcement can be divided into more specific categories that reflect the individualization of reinforcers. Table 5-1 includes examples of consequences maintaining problem behavior.

3. *Antecedent events that trigger problem behavior.* FBA information includes antecedents and antecedent conditions that are associated with problem behavior. Remember that antecedents set the occasion for behavior to occur because they signal that reinforcement is

Table 5–1 Examples of consequences maintaining problem behavior

Positive Reinforcement	Negative Reinforcement
Access to food	Avoid peer interaction
Access to activities	Avoid teacher interaction
Access to materials	Avoid peer teasing
Access to peer laughter	Avoid task demands
Access to peer conversation	Escape school (suspension)
Access to teacher assistance	
Access to teacher comments	

available (see Chapter 3). To prevent problem behavior from occurring by changing the environment, it is necessary to understand what antecedents are associated with both problem behavior and desirable behavior. Table 5–2 includes examples of antecedents associated with problem behavior and desirable behavior.

4. *Setting events that increase the likelihood of problem behavior.* Setting events affect states of deprivation or satiation and thus influence the value of reinforcers at any given time (Wahler & Fox, 1981). That is, setting events increase or decrease motivation. Setting events are different from antecedents in that they do not trigger behavior themselves, but instead they alter the probability that the antecedent will evoke the behavior. Some common setting events include being hungry, which increases the value of food as a reinforcer, and thus increases motivation to behave in ways that result in accessing food. Fatigue from lack of sleep increases the value of sleep as a reinforcer, and may also increase the aversiveness (i.e., motivation to escape) of task demands (e.g., schoolwork, paying attention). An FBA must identify powerful setting events because of their relationship to predicting and preventing problem behavior. Table 5–3 includes examples of setting events associated with problem behavior.

Table 5–2 Examples of antecedents associated with problem behavior and desirable behavior

Problem Behavior	Desirable Behavior
Error correction	Peer attention
Difficult tasks	Preferred activities
Boring activities	Adult assistance
Prompts	Fun activities
Requests	Easy activities
Task demands	Instructions
Teasing	
Lack of attention	
Down time	

Table 5–3 Examples of setting events associated with problem behavior

Setting Events		
Biological	**Environmental**	**Situational**
Medication	Noise/distractions	Personnel changes
Illness	Crowding	School breaks/ holidays
Fatigue	Activity sequence or structure	Routine changes
Hunger	Seating	Classroom transitions
Pain		Fighting with peers
		Arguing with adults

The purpose of conducting an FBA is to identify the factors that predict and maintain the problem behavior so that the function (e.g., getting attention, avoiding work) of the problem behavior can be determined (Carr et al., 1994; Gable, 1996; Horner, O'Neill, & Flannery, 1993; O'Neill et al., 1997). Focusing on the form of the behavior may not reveal its function, and similar forms (e.g., yelling, hitting) may serve different purposes for different students (Iwata, Vollmer, & Zarcone, 1990). An FBA is the first, and most critical, step toward developing a BIP because it guides the selection of intervention strategies that are related (a) to the purpose of the problem behavior and (b) to the daily routines of each particular student.

Horner and Carr (1997) state that an FBA has two important implications for developing interventions for problem behavior. First, it focuses on environmental events (i.e., setting events, antecedents, and consequences). Thus, problem behavior is viewed as the result of challenging social situations for which the problem behavior represents an attempted solution (e.g., yelling is one way to get attention), rather than viewing problem behavior as the result of invisible, dynamic forces residing within a person. Second, intervention is not focused on managing or controlling a person, but instead on redesigning the environment and on building new skills that make the problem behavior irrelevant, inefficient, and ineffective in that environment.

CONDUCTING THE FUNCTIONAL BEHAVIORAL ASSESSMENT

An FBA should achieve five outcomes (Horner, O'Neill, & Flannery, 1993; O'Neill et al., 1997):

1. Operational definition(s) of the problem behavior(s);

2. Description of the setting events and antecedents (e.g., times, places, activities) that predict the occurrence and nonoccurrence of the problem behaviors;

3. Description of the consequences responsible for the problem behavior;

4. Verification of the predictors and consequences through direct observation;

5. Summary hypothesis statements that serve as the basis for designing the positive behavior support plan.

There are three generic methods for completing an FBA and achieving these five outcomes: indirect methods, direct methods, and experimental methods (Miltenberger, 2004). These three methods are related and typically are conducted in the order in which they are listed here.

GENERIC METHODS FOR COMPLETING AN FBA

Indirect Methods

Indirect methods refer to gathering information about the student and the student's problem behavior from people who have direct contact with the student or know the student well. Indirect methods consist of referral information and school records, behavior rating scales and checklists, and interviews. The purpose of indirect methods is to collect a large amount of information in a short period of time by reviewing various sources of existing information. The accumulation of information gleaned from indirect methods is the starting point of an FBA and provides direction and focus for proceeding with the other methods.

Referral Information and School Records Collecting information from a student's teacher or teachers who have referred the student for special education or consultation is an initial step of an FBA. This information should include the student's age, grade, current placement(s) and teacher(s), and reason for referral. The reason for referral should describe the problem behavior in detail and what strategies have been used to address the problem behavior (Chandler & Dahlquist, 2006). Figure 5-1 provides a sample form that teachers can use to summarize referral information.

Figure 5-2 provides a completed form for the hypothetical student, Billy. Teachers can collect additional relevant information about problem behavior by conducting a systematic review of school records (Gresham et al., 2001). This review can provide such information as attendance records, grades and achievement test scores, retentions, previous narrative comments, suspensions, and records of parent conferences. School records can be helpful for collecting information about severe, low-frequency problem behaviors (e.g., fighting, property destruction) that are not amenable to other FBA methods (Witt, Daly, & Noell, 2000). Although useful, referral information and school records may not provide clear and specific information about setting events, antecedents, or consequences related to the occurrence of problem behavior.

Behavior Rating Scales and Checklists Teachers can use behavior rating scales and checklists as an initial method of collecting information that will guide later FBA methods. We suggest two useful checklists that teachers may want to consider using: the Problem Behavior Questionnaire (PBQ) (Lewis, Scott, & Sugai, 1994) and the Critical Events Index (CEI) (Walker & Severson, 1990). The PBQ has 15 items that evaluate setting events and maintaining consequences (i.e., positive or negative reinforcement). Informants are asked to rate the frequency observed for each item (e.g., never, 25% of the time, always). The CEI has 33 items and is especially useful for collecting information about low-frequency–high-intensity behavior. Behavior rating scales and checklists may provide some initial information about setting events, antecedents, and consequences related to the occurrence of problem behavior.

Interview Teachers may use an interview to get a beginning understanding of the problem behavior and its setting events, antecedents, and consequences. Teachers may interview themselves, other teachers, professionals who are most familiar with the individual's problem behavior, or family members. The teacher may interview the student if he or she believes that the student can provide reliable and valid information. In general, the interviewer asks people to describe three things: (a) the physical description of the problem behavior, (b) the circumstances that predict the occurrence and nonoccurrence of the problem behavior, and (c) the reaction that the problem behavior evokes from others (Carr et al., 1994; Durand, 1990; Lewis et al., 1994; O'Neill et al., 1997). The purpose of the interview is to gather information about the problem behavior and the setting events, antecedents, and consequences associated with its occurrence. Thus, interviews usually contain questions specific to setting events, antecedents, and consequences. Table 5-4 provides a list of sample questions for each variable.

The goal of the interviewer should be to get people to answer questions about environmental situations and events without inferences or interpretations (Miltenberger, 2004). For example, the interviewer may ask a teacher what happens immediately after she gives Harold, a student with a problem behavior, a task demand (e.g., "It's time to do your math worksheet"). The teacher may provide an

FIGURE 5–1

Referral information summary form

Student's name _____   School   _____

Age   _____   Teacher's name _____

Grade   _____   Phone   _____

Parents/guardians:

_____

Current educational placement:

_____

Special education services:

_____

Person responsible for initiating and implementing the plan:

_____

List any additional collaborating team members and their position:

_____

Team Members

Name	Role
1. _____	_____
2. _____	_____
3. _____	_____
4. _____	_____
5. _____	_____
6. _____	_____
7. _____	_____

Reason for referral: (List and describe behaviors that adversely affect the student's social or academic performance.)

1.

2.

3.

4.

Intervention strategies used before referral:

1.

2.

3.

4.

Describe the student's response to the strategies:

1.

2.

3.

4.

FIGURE 5-2

Referral information summary form for Billy

Student's name	Billy Smith	School	Andover Elementary
Date of birth	8/5/97	Teacher's name	Mrs. Quam
Grade	Fifth	Phone	999-999-9999

Parents/guardians:

Joe and Joan Smith

Current educational placement:

General education

Special education services:

Resource

Person responsible for initiating and implementing the plan:

Mrs. Quam

List any additional collaborating team members and their position:

Team Members

Name	Role
1. Mr. Edholm	Teacher
2. Dr. Yates	Behavior specialist
3. Dr. Rogers	LEA representative
4. Joe Smith	Parent or guardian
5. Joan Smith	Parent or guardian
6. Dr. DesRoches	School psychologist

Reason for referral: (List and describe behaviors that adversely affect the student's social or academic performance.)

1. *Noncompliance:* Not following teacher directions to work on a task within 10 seconds.
2. *Verbal aggression:* Audible talking not related to class work, using swear words, or using a voice that is significantly louder than other students.
3. *Physical aggression:* Making forceful contact on another person with any part of the hands, arms, legs, or feet or forcefully throwing items toward others.
4. *Running from class:* Leaving the classroom or building without permission.

Intervention strategies used before referral:

1. Sending him to the principal's office
2. Time-out in the hall

Describe the student's response to the strategies:

1. Billy is usually calm when he returns to the classroom from the principal's office or from time-out in the hall.
2. After 3 weeks of sending him to the office and placing him in time-out in the hall, Billy's problem behavior has started to occur more frequently.

Table 5–4   Interview topics and sample questions

Setting Events	Antecedents	Behaviors	Consequences
Is the student currently taking any medications?	What time of day is the behavior likely to occur?	How often does the behavior occur?	Does the student gain attention from the behavior?
Does the student have any medical or physical conditions that may affect his or her behavior?	What activities are associated with occurrences of behavior?	What does the behavior look like?	Does the student get out of doing something?
Does the student adapt well to changes in his or her routine?	Are particular people associated with occurrences of behavior?	How long does the behavior last?	What else might the student get or avoid?
Does the student have opportunities to make choices?			

answer that is interpretive:"Harold gets all upset when I ask him to do things he doesn't want to do"; or she may provide an answer that is objective and contains information about environmental events:"Harold starts swearing, crumbles up the worksheet, and throws it at a peer." The second response is the most useful one because it has information that accurately reflects observable environmental events. The purpose of these questions is to obtain enough information so that patterns of behavior begin to emerge. Teachers then analyze these patterns of behavior to develop hypotheses about the function of the problem behavior.

O'Neill et al. (1997) have developed a comprehensive functional assessment interview (FAI) format that is commonly used to interview adults familiar with the individual with problem behavior. The FAI is eight pages long and consists of 10 sections. Table 5-5 lists the topic of each section and provides sample questions.

In addition, O'Neill et al. (1997) have developed a shorter student-directed FAI that teachers can use when they determine that a student can verbally provide reliable and accurate information. Table 5-6 provides an overview of the content of the student-directed FAI.

Teachers of students with EBD may want to consider using both formats to interview adults familiar with the student and the student himself or herself. This approach will enable teachers both to get information and verify it by identifying consistency across interviewees.

Table 5–5   Content overview of the FAI

Topic	Questions
Description of behavior	Which of the behaviors described are likely to occur together in some way?
Setting events that predict or set the occasion for behavior	What medical or physical conditions does the person experience that may affect his or her behavior (e.g., asthma, allergies, rashes, sinus infections, seizures, problems related to menstruation)?
Antecedent events that predict occurrence and nonoccurrence of behavior	When (i.e., times of day) are the behaviors most and least likely to occur?
Consequences that maintain behavior	What are the specific consequences or outcomes the person gets when the behaviors occur in different situations?
Efficiency of behavior for accessing reinforcement	How quickly does the behavior result in consequences or outcomes?
Functional alternatives	What socially appropriate behaviors can the person already perform that may result in similar outcomes or reinforcers as problem behaviors?
Existing forms of communication	How does the person usually communicate? (e.g., vocal speech, signs/gestures, communication boards/books, electronic devices)? How consistently are the strategies used?
Interaction techniques	What things can you do to improve the likelihood that a teaching session or other activity will go well with this person?
Reinforcer inventory	What types of food items, toys and objects, activities, interactions, or routines at home or in the community does the person enjoy?
History of behavior	How long has the behavior been a problem?

Table 5–6 Overview of the content of the
student-directed FAI

Content Topics

1. Developing and introducing the interview
2. Defining problem behaviors
3. Identifying contexts where problem behaviors occur
4. Summarizing information from the interview
5. Diagramming and describing problem behavior
6. Developing a behavior support plan

The primary outcome and goals of the interview process are to develop an operational definition of the problem behavior; to allow a quick review of a large number of potential setting events, antecedents, and consequences; and to provide a good starting point to begin observational FBA methods. Based on this information, the interviewer can start to develop a tentative hypothesis, or summary statement, about the consequences that maintain the problem behavior. Figure 5–3 is an example of interview results concerning a hypothetical student, Billy.

Summary Hypothesis Statements The purpose of the indirect FBA methods already discussed is to gather information about the setting events, antecedents, and consequences associated with problem behavior. Thus, indirect FBA methods *do not prove* the function of problem behavior; rather, they lead to summary hypothesis statements about the *potential function* of the problem behavior. The summary statement is a testable hypothesis that serves as the connection between the FBA and the BIP because it (a) suggests which setting events, antecedents, and consequences should be manipulated in order to reduce the problem behavior, and (b) indicates which new behaviors should be taught to replace the problem behavior (Crone & Horner, 2003).

The purpose of subsequent FBA methods is to verify the accuracy of the indirect FBA information. Before the accuracy of the information can be verified, however, it needs to be organized so that it is concise and specific, and conforms to the principles of applied behavior analysis (see Chapter 4 on ABA). The format of each summary hypothesis statement begins with the structure depicted in Figure 5–4.

The information that is placed in each of the above boxes can be either very specific (e.g., missing breakfast as a setting event) or more general (e.g., any task demand as an antecedent). The way a teacher determines the content of each box is through a careful examination of the indirect FBA information. In general, the information must be specific enough to verify through observation; the more vague and ambiguous the information, the

---

FIGURE 5-3

Description of Billy's problem behaviors

Billy, a fifth-grade student, was referred to the school's child study team because he exhibited serious problem behaviors in a number of his classes. Dr. Yale, a behavior specialist for the school district, was assigned to observe Billy in these classes. He began by interviewing two of Billy's teachers to determine Billy's most significant problem behaviors.

Billy's language arts and social studies teacher, Mrs. Quam, was concerned with the intensity and type of problem behaviors that Billy engaged in during the class. For example, she reported that Billy's primary problem behavior was "throwing temper tantrums." Following a discussion of the tantrums, Mrs. Quam decided that Billy's specific problem behaviors during the temper tantrums consisted of not following directions, cursing, shouting, throwing books and materials at others, and running out of class. She also reported that the problem behaviors generally occurred during reading and writing activities, especially during independent work time. She stated that Billy seldom displayed problem behaviors during social studies class. Mrs. Quam also reported that Billy often comes to class in a bad mood when he seems tired. When she has questioned Billy about his behavior, he told her that sometimes he gets only a few hours of sleep and "that makes him mean." Mrs. Quam also said that the consequence for a temper tantrum is that Billy is sent to the principal or to a time-out in the hall.

Mr. Edholm, Billy's math teacher, reported that Billy's problem behavior consisted of "back talking," "talking out," "being off task," and "aggression toward others." Additionally, he said that there did not appear to be any pattern to Billy's problem behavior. When Mr. Edholm was asked when the behaviors occurred, he reported "all the time." He reported that he could never tell when Billy was about to exhibit problem behaviors, although he did note that often other students would tease him prior to his problem behavior. Mr. Edholm could not identify any likely outcome or consistent consequences associated with Billy's problem behavior, but that often students would stop antagonizing and laughing at Billy when he "acted out."

Following the interviews, Dr. Yale identified four problem behaviors. These behavioral categories and their operational definitions are listed as follows:

Noncompliance: Not following teacher directions to work on a task within 10 seconds or not staying on task until the task is completed.

Verbal aggression: Audible talking not related to class work, using swear words, or using a voice that is significantly louder than other students.

Physical aggression: Making forceful contact on another person with any part of the hands, arms, legs, or feet, or forcefully throwing items at others.

Running from class: Leaving the classroom or building without permission.

FIGURE 5-4

Summary statement

Setting Events	Antecedents	Behavior	Consequences

harder it will be to verify. Consider the following vague summary hypothesis statement in Figure 5.5.

This statement is very vague because most of the content is inferential and therefore would be almost impossible to verify. Figure 5–6 is a more precise way to summarize the indirect FBA information.

This summary hypothesis statement is more precise because it consists of observable information.

FIGURE 5-5

Example of a vague summary statement

Setting Events	Antecedents	Behavior	Consequences
When Billy is in a bad mood	and the teacher talks to him	he will get upset	to release pent-up emotions

FIGURE 5-6

Example of a precise summary statement

Setting Events	Antecedents	Behavior	Consequences
When Billy has had an argument with his best friend earlier in the day	and the teacher gives him an academic task demand	Billy will curse and shout	to avoid doing the task

Thus, it could be verified through subsequent FBA methods.

There are several other important characteristics about our well-formed summary hypothesis statement. First, the setting event and behavior are very specific. This is because the setting event and behavior are discrete and consistent, and do not represent variation that has to be condensed into a category. Second, the antecedent and consequence are more general. This is because the antecedent and consequence content has been summarized and categorized to represent consistency in factors associated with the occurrence of Billy's problem behavior. For example, the interviewees may have reported that Billy's cursing and shouting occurs when the teacher gives him worksheets in various academic areas (e.g., math, language arts, social studies). The variation in antecedent conditions can be summarized by the common condition of being some type of academic task demand. Consider the form of the consequence content. The consequence is also a category (i.e., negative reinforcement) that reflects a similar outcome of Billy's problem behavior even though interviewees report different observable outcomes. For example, one interviewee may report that when the teacher makes an academic task demand, and then Billy curses and shouts, the teacher "leaves him alone to cool down," or she "just walks away." Another interviewee may report that the teacher often says that "I can see Billy is not ready to work" or "Billy can time himself out at his desk until he is ready to

work." Taken together, the interview information suggests that the common outcome of Billy's behavior is that he postpones or escapes the academic task demands because, contingent on cursing and shouting, the teacher removes the task demand in various ways. This information is summed up by saying that the consequences of Billy's cursing and shouting is that he avoids doing the academic tasks. Figure 5-7 provides examples of summary hypothesis statements derived from an interview of the hypothetical student, Billy.

Indirect FBA Method Guidelines   Indirect FBA methods consist of referral information and school records, behavior rating scales and checklists, and interviews, and typically are the first step in the FBA. Teachers should be familiar with the appropriate procedures, interpretation, and application of indirect FBA methods information. We now provide some guidelines to help teachers make good decisions regarding their indirect FBA methods information. Table 5-7 summarizes these guidelines.

The purpose of indirect FBA methods is to accumulate substantial information quickly and efficiently about a student's problem behavior. This information is collected through methods that rely on informants' memories, and therefore this information may or may not be accurate. The information is then summarized in a way that is aimed at verifying its accuracy through future assessment. Thus, the information acquired during

FIGURE 5–7

Summary statement for Billy's problem behavior

Setting Events	Antecedents	Behavior	Consequences
When Billy has not had contact with his mother overnight and has slept less than 6 hours	and he is presented with a challenging academic demand or is antagonized by another student	he will refuse to do work, become verbally or physically aggressive, or run out of the classroom	to escape or avoid the academic demand or to escape being antagonized by other students

Table 5–7   Guidelines for evaluating indirect FBA information

Guidelines		
1. Does the informant frequently interact with the student?	Yes	No
2. Does the informant interact with the student in multiple environments?	Yes	No
3. Is the information factual (i.e., objective and measurable)?	Yes	No
4. Is the information consistent within or across informants?	Yes	No
5. Does the information provide a clear description of the problem behaviors?	Yes	No
6. Does the information lead to identifying specific contexts, environments, or times when the behavior is likely to occur?	Yes	No
7. Does the information lead to identifying specific consequences that maintain behavior?	Yes	No

indirect FBA methods should not be considered as the final or end product of an FBA; rather, it should be viewed as the first step in a multistep assessment process.

Drasgow and Yell (2001) examined 14 state-level due process hearings that involved a dispute over the FBA conducted by the school. Schools lost 94% (13 of 14) of the cases, often because their FBA methods were incomplete and consisted only of checklists, brief observations, or both. Thus, to be on solid legal ground, teachers must conduct comprehensive FBAs that *begin* with indirect methods and include additional procedures as well. Although teachers may be tempted to rely on indirect methods because of their brevity and efficiency (Gresham et al., 2001), we advise teachers to be aware that, in general, indirect FBA methods are inadequate to comprise a legally valid FBA.

One situation that teachers may face is conducting FBAs for students with low-frequency–high-intensity behavior (e.g., physically assaulting someone, bringing a weapon to school). These types of behavior often occur with such low frequency that they are not amenable to direct FBA methods. In this case, Gresham and colleagues (2001) suggest that school records, checklists, and interviews may be the only sources of FBA information for these students. We remind teachers that in this situation, teachers may want to use the Critical Events Index (CEI) (Walker & Severson, 1990) because of its specific focus on low-frequency–high-intensity problem behavior. Examples of low-frequency–high-intensity behaviors may include getting in a fight, bringing a weapon to school, or vandalizing school property. The main point is that if certain behaviors are serious and occur with low frequency such that they are not amenable to direct FBA methods, then teachers must use multiple indirect methods that consist of the most comprehensive, valid, and reliable procedures available.

There is emerging evidence that one way to predict low-frequency–high-intensity problem behavior is by identifying high-frequency–low-intensity behaviors that are similar in function (Rozalski, 2001; Sprague & Horner, 1999). For example, bringing a weapon to school may be preceded by increases in low-level noncompliance (e.g., not following teacher directions for homework submission). Moreover, setting events (e.g., fighting with a friend, ending a boyfriend–girlfriend relationship) may also increase the likelihood of a low-frequency–high-intensity problem behavior occurring. Thus, small problems may escalate into big problems if they are not resolved, and setting events may exacerbate the rate or intensity of the escalation.

Direct Observation Methods

The next step in the FBA process is to validate and clarify the summary hypothesis statement(s) by directly observing student behavior in relevant settings, including actual A-B-C relationships. There are two commonly used direct observation methods: scatter plot assessment and A-B-C observations of the target students.

Scatter Plot Assessment Problem behavior is not usually distributed evenly across the day. Instead it tends to occur more frequently at some times than at other times. A scatter plot assessment (SPA) can be used to determine when problem behavior is most likely and unlikely to occur (Touchette, MacDonald, & Langer, 1985), especially when the problem behavior occurs frequently and seemingly at random. The SPA can complement interview information and lead to more efficient and effective direct observation (Lennox & Miltenberger, 1998). Thus, the SPA may be useful after completing indirect FBA methods and before beginning A-B-C observation and direct student/peer observations.

A scatter plot is a grid that is divided into time intervals with corresponding spaces to code behavior across days. Each time interval on the grid can be filled in to represent whether the behavior occurred at a high, low, or zero rate. A teacher can analyze a completed grid to determine if problem behavior is associated with time of day, absence or presence of particular people, activities or events, physical or social settings, or any combination of factors. This information can then be used to refine or revise the summary hypothesis statement(s). Figure 5–8 provides an example of a completed scatter plot for the hypothetical student, Billy.

A-B-C Observation The major purpose of A-B-C observations is to get a reliable record of the antecedents and consequences that are typically associated with the problem behavior under normal conditions (e.g., Bijou, Peterson, & Ault, 1968; Gable, 1996; Quinn, Gable, Rutherford, Nelson, & Howell, 1998). A-B-C observation provides more reliable information about problem behavior than indirect methods because it relies less on memory or subjective interpretations. A-B-C observations consist of observing problem behavior and then immediately writing down the A-B-C sequence in observable and measurable terms. Direct observation documents the occurrences of problem behavior so that the information can be analyzed to determine antecedent or consequence patterns. We stress that direct observation information must conform to the principles of applied behavior analysis and that the information should not consist of inferring internal emotional states of the student. Although everyone would agree that emotions are an important part of life, they are not the type of information that results in an effective positive behavior support plan.

A-B-C observation consists of a person directly observing the problem behavior in the natural environment where the problem behavior typically takes place. The observer records the immediate antecedents and consequences each time the problem behavior occurs. This information is then structured by listing each problem behavior and the events that occur immediately before it (i.e., antecedents) and immediately after it (i.e., consequences) to identify any patterns that might indicate a functional relationship (Alberto & Troutman, 2006). Figure 5–9 provides an example of a simple but effective A-B-C recording form, and Figure 5–10 provides examples of A-B-C relationships.

Figure 5–11 shows one example of A-B-C information that confirms the indirect method summary hypothesis statement and shows one example that does not confirm the indirect method summary hypothesis statement. Teachers use direct observation information to infer which antecedent events trigger problem behavior and which consequence events maintain problem behavior. Direct observation does not usually provide information about setting events because setting events occur earlier in time. Information about setting events is typically collected through interviews, SPA, or logs. A-B-C observation is a crucial aspect of the FBA process because the accuracy of a summary hypothesis statement is extremely important for devising an effective and efficient intervention.

Direct observation paired with interviews can lead to appropriate summary hypotheses about antecedents and consequences that can be used to guide the development of behavior support plans (Horner et al., 2006). Thus,

FIGURE 5-8

Scatterplot for Billy

Billy's Scatterplot Data Sheet

Time	Noncompliance	Verbal Aggression	Physical Aggression	Running from Class	Total Occurrences for Time Period
7:30–7:45 a.m. arrival					
7:45–7:50 a.m. transition					
7:50–8:55 a.m. art					
8:55–9:00 a.m. transition					
9:00–10:00 a.m. language arts	///	////	/	/	9
10:00–10:05 a.m. transition					
10:05–11:00 a.m. social studies					
11:00–11:05 a.m. transition					
11:05–12:00 noon math		/////	//		7
12:00–1:00 p.m. lunch					
1:00–1:05 p.m. transition					
1:05–2:00 p.m. science					
2:00–2:05 p.m. transition					
2:05–3:00 p.m. PE					
Total number of occurrences per behavior	3	9	3	1	16

Operational Definitions

1. *Noncompliance:* Not following teacher directions to work on a task within 10 seconds or not staying on task until the task is completed.
2. *Verbal aggression:* Audible talking not related to class work, using swear words, or using a voice that is significantly louder than the other students' voices.
3. *Physical aggression:* Making forceful contact on another person with any part of the hands, arms, legs, or feet or forcefully throwing items at others.
4. *Running from class:* Leaving the classroom or building without permission.

Directions: Place a tally mark in the corresponding box each time a problem behavior occurs.

FIGURE 5-9

A-B-C recording form

A-B-C Recording Form

Student's name _____   Date _____

Observer's name _____   Location _____

Time	Antecedent	Behavior	Consequence

teachers who use indirect methods, develop summary hypothesis statements, and then validate or clarify these statements through direct observation are on strong educational and legal ground (Drasgow & Yell, 2001).

EXPERIMENTAL METHODS

Experimental methods systematically manipulate antecedents, consequences, or both to directly test their relationship to problem behavior. *Functional assessment* consists of collecting information to develop and validate summary *hypothesis* statements about the relationship between environmental events and problem behavior. Experimental methods demonstrate, or *prove*,

relationships between environmental events and problem behavior. Thus experimental methods are the most precise and rigorous category of FBA methods. We have several caveats about experimental methods before we describe them.

Experimental methods consist of creating conditions that may evoke problem behavior (e.g., Iwata, Dorsey, Slifer, Bauman, & Richman, 1982/1994; Wacker, Berg, Asmus, Harding, & Cooper, 1998). Experimental methods provide the most precise and rigorous information about problem behavior, but this precision comes at a cost. First, the technology of experimental methods is sophisticated and requires a high level of skill to conduct. Second, experimental methods can be dangerous

FIGURE 5–10

A-B-C recording form examples

A-B-C Recording Form

Student's name _____   Date _____

Observer's name _____   Location _____

Time	Antecedent	Behavior	Consequence
	Teacher asks students to get out their math books	Student does not comply with the teacher's request	Teacher ignores student behavior
	Teacher asks a student to complete a math problem on the board	Student curses	Teacher asks another student to complete the math problem
	Teacher asks a student to read a word problem from the math book	Student curses and throws book onto the floor	Teacher sends student to time-out in the hall
	Peer calls the student a derogatory name	Student curses at peer	Teacher reprimands peer
	Student has not interacted with peers for 10 minutes	Student begins to argue with the teacher	Teacher blushes and peers laugh
	Student works on a difficult academic task	Student complains about not feeling well	Teacher tells student he does not have to complete the assignment and to put his head on the desk
	Peers tease student	Student curses at peers	Teacher tells peers to stop teasing student
	Teacher asks student to read a paragraph from the reading book	Student curses and throws book onto the floor	Teacher sends student to time-out in the hall

because some conditions intentionally attempt to evoke problem behavior. Third, intentionally evoking problem behavior usually requires informed consent from parents and even human subjects' research approval from the school because they could present a safety risk to the student and any personnel involved in the analysis. Thus, experimental methods should be done only when (a) the benefits justify the risks, (b) the personnel conducting the experiment have appropriate knowledge and training, and (c) the school has adequate resources to ensure the safety of students and school personnel. We now briefly describe experimental methods to provide readers with a beginning understanding of their conceptual bases.

Functional Analysis

A *functional analysis* is an experimental method that tests hypotheses about behavioral function by systematically manipulating specific antecedent conditions and then by providing consequences for problem behavior to determine whether or not they influence the problem behavior. Thus, functional analyses test consequences that directly control problem behavior (Iwata et al., 1982/1994). The conceptual foundation of functional analysis can be traced back to Skinner (1953), and its methodological foundation can be traced back to Baer and colleagues (1968).

In general, conducting a functional analysis involves establishing that the purpose of the problem behavior is

FIGURE 5-11

A-B-C recording form confirming the indirect summary hypothesis statement

A-B-C Recording Form

Student's name   Billy Smith

Observer's name   Dr. Yale

Date: 4/5/2008

Location   Language Arts class

Time	Antecedent	Behavior	Consequence
9:10 a.m.	Teacher asks class for group answers	All students respond	Teacher says, "good"
9:20 a.m.	Teacher asks students to get in groups	Students get in groups	Teacher says, "thank you!"
9:23 a.m.	Teacher asks each group to complete a new activity	All groups begins working	Teacher walks around and talks with each group
9:30 a.m.	Teacher approaches Billy's group	Billy continues working	Teacher praises Billy for working
9:45 a.m.	Teacher tells students to independently work on their reading assignment	Billy yells, "boring."	Teacher ignores Billy
9:46 a.m.	Teacher walks around the room	Billy does not begin working	Billy avoids the assignment
9:47 a.m.	Teacher tells Billy to begin working on his assignment	Billy yells and curses at the teacher	Teacher begins to argue with Billy
9:49 a.m.	Teacher tells Billy he will need to do the assignment for homework	Billy curses, throws work materials at the teacher, and begins to leave the classroom	Teacher tells Billy to go to the principal's office

either to access something (e.g., teacher attention) or to avoid or postpone something (e.g., task demands). Functional analysis directly tests an association between environmental events, consequences, and problem behaviors. Functional analysis can be time and energy consuming, but in some cases, it may be the only way to ensure an accurate assessment of problem behaviors.

A functional analysis, however, always should be conducted by a person trained in the procedure because it involves creating situations that may provoke the problem behavior (O'Neill et al., 1997). For example, if interviews and descriptive observations suggest that a student engages in disruptive or aggressive behavior (e.g., name calling or throwing his chair) when a difficult task is introduced (e.g., spelling lists), then the systematic presentation and removal of the task may be carried out and data on the student's

behavior (i.e., number of times name calling occurs, number of times the student throws his chair) are collected during presentation and removal of spelling lists. The rates of behavior occurring during the presentation of the spelling list and its removal *contingent* on problem behavior are compared to rates of problem behavior that occur when the student is, for example, engaged in a preferred activity. Teachers should note that the functional analysis must have very precise procedures to be accurate, and that it may indeed evoke problem behavior (e.g., chair throwing).

Structural Analysis

A *structural analysis* is an experimental method that tests hypotheses about behavior by manipulating and assessing antecedent conditions that cue or trigger both problem and desirable behavior (Wacker et al., 1998). Structural analyses provide valuable information about antecedents that can be used to develop effective support plans. Researchers have developed structural analysis procedures because of their relevance in applied settings where practitioners may not have precise control over environments and where behavior is much more variable (Stichter, Sasso, & Jolivette, 2004). Structural analysis is conceptually and methodologically similar to functional analysis in that it relies on systematically manipulating variables to determine their effect on behavior. It is different from functional analysis in that its emphasis is on manipulating antecedents that may trigger problem behavior rather than on manipulating consequences that may maintain the behavior.

To demonstrate the use of structural analysis, we will use the same example of problem behavior that we used in the functional analysis section. Remember that in functional analysis, we determined the function of the student's behavior by comparing rates of problem behavior occurring under different conditions, and that the rate of behavior was highest when we would present the spelling list and then let the student escape the task contingent on problem behavior (i.e., name calling, chair throwing). To conduct a structural analysis with this same student, we would control antecedent conditions by, for example, giving him difficult words to spell versus easy words to spell, request that he complete his spelling list independently or with peer support, or let him do it at his desk or on the computer. In this situation, we could determine not only which antecedent conditions were associated with problem behavior, but also which conditions were associated with desirable behavior (e.g., competing work).

Conducting functional analyses, structural analyses, or both can be resource intensive, time consuming, and potentially risky. Moreover, functional or structural analyses should be conducted only when other assessment information does not lead to a clear hypothesis. There may be situations in which a hypothesis may not be clear, there are inadequate resources to conduct a functional or structural analysis, and it may take weeks to collect enough A-B-C observation information to clarify the hypothesis. In this scenario, teachers may want to conduct manipulations that are not as formal or rigorous as functional or structural analyses, but attempt to get at the same information. For instance, to continue with our previous example, a teacher could provide a more difficult spelling list on one day, and an easier one the next day. Or she could give the student a harder list and provide help one day, and provide an easier list with no help the next day. In other words, the teacher could use the same principles underlying functional and structural analysis to refine her hypothesis, but tailor the manipulations so that they are embedded into the daily schedule.

This section has presented information about indirect assessment, direct assessment, and functional analysis. Figure 5–12 shows an FBA report on our hypothetical student, Billy. Collecting assessment information is the first step of building a positive behavior support plan, or as the

---

FIGURE 5–12

Functional behavior report on Billy

Functional Behavioral Assessment

Student's name: Billy Smith

Dates of evaluation: 3/11/02, 4/5/02, & 4/22/02

School: Andover Elementary

Child's date of birth: 8/5/90

Source of referral: Mrs. Quam

Examiner's name: Mike Yale, PhD

Reason for Referral

Billy was referred to the behavior support team (BST) because of serious behavior problems in a number of his classes. Mrs. Quam, Billy's fifth-grade language arts and social studies teacher, referred him for problem behaviors that were described as "throwing temper tantrums." The BST decided to have a functional behavioral assessment (FBA) conducted to assess Billy's problem behaviors. In this report, I explain the procedures that I used to conduct the FBA and the results of the FBA. I also explain the hypothesis, or summary statement, generated from the FBA and my suggestions for interventions that the team may want to consider when developing the behavior intervention plan.

FIGURE  5–12

Procedures

I used three procedures to collect information about Billy's problem behavior. These procedures included a functional assessment interview (FAI), a scatter plot assessment, and direct observation procedures. The first procedure that I used was the FAI (O'Neill et al., 1997). The purpose for the FAI was to gather general information from Mrs. Quam, Billy's language arts and social studies teacher, and Mr. Edholm, Billy's mathematics teacher, about Billy's problem behavior. The second procedure that I used was a scatter plot assessment (Touchette et al., 1985). The purpose of the scatter plot assessment was to identify times that problem behavior was likely to occur. During this assessment process, I collected the scatter plot data for a week in early March. Third, I collected direct observation data. The observation procedure consisted of antecedent-behavior-consequences (A-B-C) recording (Kazdin, 2001). The purpose of this recording procedure is to identify environmental and contextual variables that occur prior to the problem behavior and those that follow the problem behavior. I collected three hours of direct observation data across Billy's reading, social studies, and mathematics classes. Each observation lasted for 1 hour.

Results

Interview

Results from the FAI show that Billy emits several behaviors that his teachers consider to be a problem. First, Mrs. Quam reported that Billy would throw temper tantrums in her language arts class during independent work time reading activities. She reported that temper tantrums consisted of not following directions, cursing, shouting, throwing books and materials at others, and running out of class. When Billy displayed temper tantrums she would send him to the principal or send him to time-out in the hall. She stated that Billy rarely emitted problem behavior during her social studies class. Mrs. Quam also reported that Billy often comes to class in a bad mood when he is left at home alone or gets less than 6 hours of sleep. Mr. Edholm reported that Billy's problem behavior consisted of "back talking," "talking out," "being off task," and "aggression toward others." Additionally, he said that there did not appear to be any pattern to Billy's problem behavior. When he was asked when the behaviors occurred, he reported "all the time" but that other students would often antagonize and laugh at Billy. He also suggested that often students would stop antagonizing and laughing at Billy when he "acted out."

Information provided by the two informants revealed that Billy emitted four categories of problem behavior. These behaviors and operational definitions are described as follows:

Problem Behavior	Operational Definition
Noncompliance	Not following teacher directions to work on a task within 10 seconds or not staying on task until the task is completed.
Verbal aggression	Audible talking not related to class work, using swear words, or using a voice that is significantly louder than other students.
Physical aggression	Making forceful contact on another person with any part of the hands, arms, legs, or feet or forcefully throwing items at others.
Running from class	Leaving the classroom or building without permission.

Scatter Plot Assessment

The data collected from the scatter plot assessment confirmed that Billy's problem behavior primarily occurs during his language arts class and his mathematics class. Billy rarely emitted problem behavior during any other times of the school day. Further analysis revealed that Billy's problem behavior occurs most frequently toward the end of the reading period during independent work time. In Mr. Edholm's math class, Billy's problem behavior is often distributed across the class period and across different activities.

A-B-C Analysis

Based on the data gathered from the scatter plot assessment, I observed Billy during the times when problem behavior was most likely to occur (i.e., language arts and mathematics class). During the observations, I recorded one instance in Mrs. Quam's reading class of "tantruming behavior" that consisted of verbal aggression, physical aggression, and leaving the classroom. These behaviors occurred shortly after Mrs. Quam assigned a new independent reading assignment. After Billy emitted several problem behaviors she sent Billy to the principal's office. Observations of Billy during Mr. Edholm's class revealed that verbal aggression occurred multiple times across several academic activities. However, Billy's behaviors typically occurred after being antagonized by

(cont.)

FIGURE 5–12

Functional behavior report on Billy (continued)

by peers. When Billy became verbally aggressive his peers would stop teasing him. Toward the end of class, Mr. Edholm sent Billy to time-out in the hall after he hit another student.

Functional Behavioral Assessment Summary

The FBA information leads to the hypothesis that Billy's "tantruming behavior" (i.e., noncompliance, verbal aggression, physical aggression, and leaving the classroom) in his language arts class functions to escape challenging academic tasks that he has to work on independently. When Billy is presented with a difficult academic task he will refuse to work, yell, curse, throw materials at others, and leave the classroom to escape or avoid the task demand. The FBA data also showed that antagonizing peer comments served as an antecedent that evoked Billy's verbal aggression and physical aggression in Mr. Edholm's mathematics class and were most likely maintained by escape from antagonizing peer comments. Based on the information gathered during the FBA process, the conditions that are associated with and maintain Billy's problem behaviors are described in the following summary statement.

Summary Statement from the FBA

Setting Events	Antecedents	Behavior	Consequences
When Billy has not had contact with his mother overnight and has slept less than 6 hours	and he is presented with a challenging academic demand or he is antagonized by another student	he will refuse to do work, become verbally or physically aggressive, or run out of the classroom	to escape or avoid the academic demand or to escape being antagonized by other students

Suggestions for the Behavior Intervention Plan

Based on information collected during the FBA on Billy's problem behavior, the behavior support team (BST) may want to consider several areas in which to intervene regarding his tantruming behavior. First, the team should generate strategies for addressing setting event conditions that influence occurrences of Billy's behaviors at school. Second, because Billy's tantruming behavior may be related to a mismatch between Billy's skills and the curriculum, the team may want to further assess Billy's skill levels in reading and make adjustments to the content, format, or level of assistance provided to Billy. Therefore, the BIP should address antecedent strategies (e.g., classroom modifications, curricular modifications) for changing environmental conditions that evoke his behavior. Next, the plan should address teaching strategies (e.g., teaching replacement behaviors that allow Billy to escape aversive academic tasks or antagonizing peer comments) for increasing socially appropriate behavior. Fourth, the intervention plan should address consequence strategies (e.g., positive reinforcement for socially appropriate behavior) for increasing and maintaining Billy's socially appropriate behavior. Finally, the intervention should include crisis management procedures (e.g., teacher–student interactions when Billy is having a temper tantrum, removal when his behavior becomes dangerous). The FBA data also indicated that Billy's off-task and talking-out behaviors were related to conditions in the classroom environment; therefore, the BST may want to consider environmental modifications that increase classroom structure and decrease free time.

---

law calls it, a BIP. The next section of this chapter describes procedures for using the assessment summary hypothesis statements to develop and implement effective BIPs.

POSITIVE BEHAVIOR SUPPORT AND BEHAVIOR INTERVENTION PLANS

Positive behavior support (PBS) refers to a comprehensive and noncoercive approach to teaching individuals adaptive and socially desirable skills that replace destructive and stigmatizing behavior (Koegel, Koegel, & Dunlap, 1996). *Comprehensive* means that positive behavior support consists of multiple interventions that are implemented across time in multiple settings by multiple people. *Noncoercive* means that PBS deemphasizes punishment-based procedures, especially those that harm or humiliate students. *Teaching adaptive and socially desirable skills* puts the focus of PBS on skill building instead of on behavior reduction. PBS replaces problem behavior that interferes with a person's quality of life with behavior that improves a person's quality of life. PBS is a technically sound and effective approach to behavior change (Carr et. al., 1999).

PBS is a term that has been used for almost 20 years in the fields of psychology and special education. It refers to a model or system for addressing problem behavior. A *positive behavior support plan* is the individualized application of the model or system to a specific person. When Congress reauthorized IDEA in 1997, it used the term *BIP* instead of *positive behavior support plan*. Apparently, Congress expected that "behavior intervention plan had a commonly understood meaning in special education" (Gorn, 1999) and we believe that the two terms are synonymous (Drasgow & Yell, 2001). The remainder of this chapter describes the characteristics and procedures of BIPs.

CHARACTERISTICS OF BEHAVIOR INTERVENTION PLANS

Positive behavior intervention plans (BIPs) have several defining characteristics that differentiate them from other approaches (Carr et al., 2002; Chandler & Dahlquist, 2006; Horner et al., 2006; Koegel et al., 1996; O'Neill et al., 1997).

1. BIPs are directly based on the results of the FBA. The purpose of an FBA is to understand *why* problem behavior occurs. The BIP is developed from the FBA information. Consider the following analogy: If we are ill, we go to see a doctor. The doctor takes our vital signs, asks questions about our symptoms, and then may make a diagnosis. If the doctor cannot make a diagnosis from his or her office examination, then he or she may send us for more tests. Once the doctor has enough information to make a diagnosis, then he or she can prescribe the appropriate treatment. Behavior intervention plans work the same way. We use the FBA to make a diagnosis (in the form of a summary hypothesis statement) and then the BIP is the "appropriate treatment" based on the diagnosis. Perhaps the core characteristic of the BIP is the relationship between the assessment of problem behavior and the treatment of problem behavior.

2. BIPs are technically sound. This means that both FBAs and BIPs are based on the principles of ABA. Functional behavioral assessment determines the relationship between the environment and problem behavior; BIPs change this relationship to foster socially acceptable behavior.

3. BIPs are a good fit with the values, resources, and skills of the people who will be implementing them. The purpose of the plan is not to design a perfect plan, but rather to design a plan that people will actually implement. Thus, the plan must fit current routines, be efficient in terms of time and resources, and be effective so that people continue to implement it. People will not implement plans that are cumbersome and effortful.

4. BIPs are comprehensive. They are a multidimensional approach to problem behavior that incorporates several procedures into one coherent plan that is implemented across all settings where problem behavior occurs. Positive behavior support plans will often include strategies that are related to setting events, antecedents, teaching, consequences, and so on. The goal of a BIP is to produce lasting and meaningful changes across all domains in a person's life; therefore, BIPs must be implemented in all the domains in which problem behavior occurs.

5. BIPs describe how everyone will change. The plan reflects the intricate relationship between problem behavior and the social context in which it occurs. Behavior intervention plans change behavior by changing the social context in which it occurs. Thus, a BIP specifies in great detail how teachers, parents, and staff will change their behavior. These characteristics serve as the foundation for building effective BIPs and should be reflected in each BIP.

BUILDING POSITIVE BEHAVIOR INTERVENTION PLANS

The *competing behavior model* (O'Neill et al., 1997) is an elegant approach for creating BIPs that are directly based on the functional assessment information.

The Competing Behavior Model

The competing behavior model consists of three steps. First, the FBA information is condensed into a concise summary hypothesis statement. This statement is organized according to the behavioral sequence of setting events, antecedents, behavior, and consequences that is central to applied behavior analysis. The summary statement serves as the backbone of the BIP and all interventions are logically related to it.

The second step of the competing behavior model is to select alternative or competing behaviors and the consequences associated with each. There are two types of alternative behaviors in this model. *Replacement* behaviors result in the same outcome, or consequence, as the problem behavior. For example, if a student throws academic work on the floor to escape the task demand, then a replacement behavior for that student may be to ask for a break from work, or to ask for help that reduces the aversiveness of the task. One way to think about replacement behaviors is to conceptualize them as empowering a student to influence their environment in socially acceptable ways so that they no longer have to resort to problem behavior to be "effective" communicators.

The other type of alternative behavior is the desired response that should occur, which has a different function than the problem behavior. In the previous example, the desired response would be that the student completes the academic task. Completing the task is not the same as escaping the task. Whereas replacement behaviors empower a student to communicate in more socially acceptable ways, desirable behaviors help the student meet important social and academic demands.

The third step of the competing behavior model is to identify changes that will make the problem behavior irrelevant, inefficient, and ineffective. We make the problem behavior irrelevant by changing the conditions that evoke it. Thus, if a student engages in problem behavior to escape academic demands, changing the characteristics of the academic demands so that they are no longer aversive makes escape irrelevant. We make problem behavior inefficient by providing the student with replacement behaviors that result in the same consequence as problem behavior (e.g., escape), but are easier to do, and work faster and more often than the problem behavior (Horner & Day, 1991). We make the problem behavior ineffective by eliminating or reducing the reinforcement for problem behavior and by providing reinforcement for replacement and desirable behaviors. The essence of the competing behavior model is its coordination of multiple intervention strategies that all address the causes and outcomes of problem behavior. Figure 5-13 provides a form for completing the competing behavior model approach to BIPs. Figure 5-14 is a completed competing behavior model for the hypothetical student, Billy. Note that the middle pathway represents Billy's problem behavior as it currently exists. The upper pathway represents what behavior (i.e., the desirable behavior) we would eventually like to see Billy exhibit. The bottom pathway represents the replacement behavior, which results in the same consequence as the problem behavior, but is acceptable to the teacher.

After a student's BIP or IEP team has completed the competing behavior model, they must generate the strategies to reduce the problem behavior and teach the new behavior. In addition to teaching the target student new behaviors or skills, the strategies must also change the student's environment by specifically focusing on the antecedents and consequences of behavior. The strategies that should be addressed include (a) setting event strategies, (b) antecedent strategies, (c) teaching strategies, and (d) consequence strategies.

Setting Event Strategies The purpose of setting event strategies is to prevent the problem behaviors from occurring by altering the events that have made it more likely that problem behaviors will occur in the first place. Remember that setting events are different from antecedents because they do not directly trigger problem behavior themselves, but instead alter the probability that the antecedent will evoke the problem behavior. We may think of setting events as those events that put a student in a "bad mood" even though they may be far removed in time from the antecedent. Thus, setting event strategies would attempt to remove the conditions that put the student in a bad mood. For example, if a student was more likely to exhibit problem behaviors when she came to school hungry, an appropriate setting event strategy would be to give the student breakfast at school, thus removing the event that put her in a bad mood and made it likely that an antecedent would trigger problem behavior. Similarly, if a student came to school tired because he had little sleep the prior night, an appropriate setting event strategy may be to allow the student to take a nap in the nurse's office before school begins.

Unfortunately, it is difficult to influence setting events that occur outside the school setting. For example, if the student is upset by a divorce or illness in the family, we cannot change the event. In such situations, however, it may be possible to reduce the negative impact of the setting event on the student's behavior (Chandler & Dahlquist, 2006). The impact may be reduced by interacting in a positive way with the student at the beginning of the school day or by changing certain variables in the school environment (Horner, Vaughn, Day, & Ard, 1996).

Antecedent Strategies Antecedent strategies prevent the problem behavior from occurring by altering or addressing the situations or events that trigger or set off the challenging behavior. Typically, such strategies will organize the environment so that the likelihood that the student will encounter the antecedent will be lessened. Examples of such environmental changes include (a) altering the physical setting, (b) enriching the environment, (c) improving the curriculum, and (d) increasing the student's choice of activity (O'Neill et al., 1997). Problem behavior will be irrelevant because the situations that set the occasion for problem behavior to occur are changed in ways that eliminate the need for problem behavior to occur. For example, if a student throws his worksheet on the floor to avoid doing work that is too

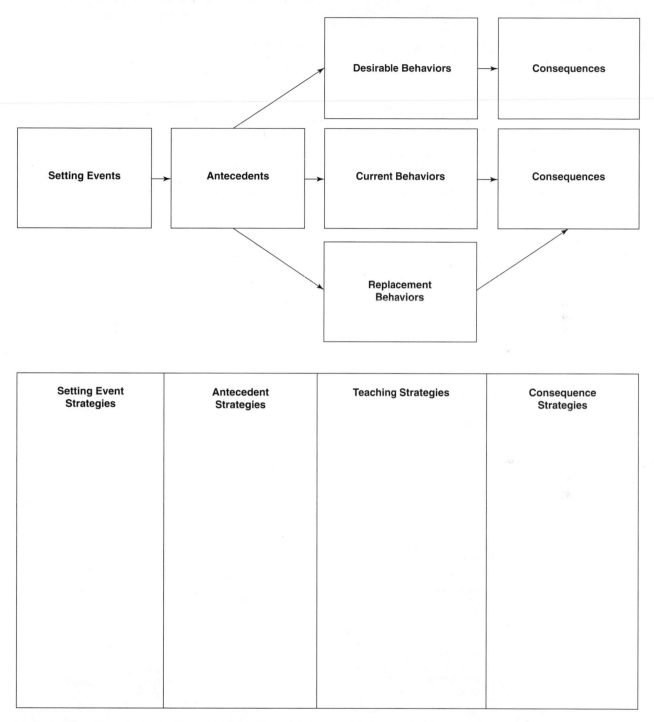

Figure 5–13   Example form for completing the Competing Behavior Model approach to BIPs

Source: Adapted from *Functional Assessment and Program Development for Problem Behavior: A Practical Handbook,* by R. E. O'Neill, R. H. Horner, R. W. Albin, J. R., Sprague, K. Storey, and J. S. Newton, 1997, Belmont, CA: Thompson/Wadsworth.

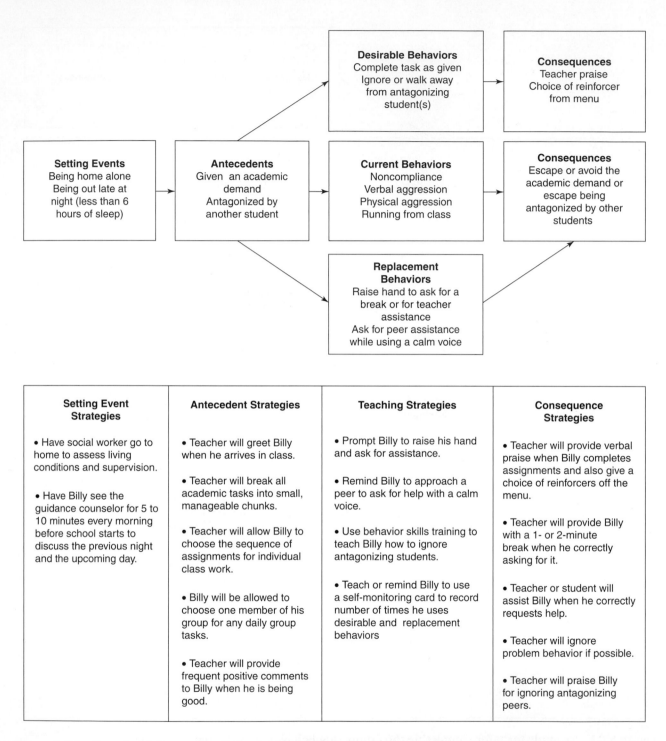

Figure 5–14   Completed Competing Behavior Model form for the hypothetical student, Billy

hard, a teacher can build the student's skills so that he is successful, change the characteristics of the worksheet so he can be successful, or do both.

Kern and Dunlap (1998) further examined evidence related to effective antecedent curricular interventions that reduce problem behavior. They identified three broad categories. The first category is modifying the task to reduce its aversiveness. Task modification consists of changing the task content to make it less difficult, changing the method by which the task is completed (e.g., use a computer instead of paper and pencil), or incorporating student preferences and interests into the task. The second category is to modify the instructional presentation format. Instructional modification consists of interspersing easy tasks or alternative and preferred tasks into challenging tasks, changing the pacing of task presentation, changing the task size by decreasing task duration by giving brief breaks, and presenting tasks in parts rather than presenting the entire task all at once. Teachers must select strategies for any particular student based on the functional assessment information and address the learning characteristics of the student.

Teaching Strategies   The purpose of teaching strategies is to enable students to learn new skills to influence their environment in alternative ways that are socially acceptable. Teaching strategies epitomize the skill development aspect of behavior support because students themselves learn new and alternative social, communicative, and academic skills. These new skills increase students' repertoires of socially acceptable behaviors and enable them to become adaptive across multiple environments. Halle, Barbara, and Reichle (2005) suggest that there are three types of alternative behaviors: replacement skills, general adaptive skills, and coping and tolerance skills. Replacement skills are behaviors that get the same outcome as the problem behavior, but are socially acceptable. For example, if a student makes silly noises to get the teacher's attention, a replacement skill may be for the student to raise his hand or to say "Excuse me, Mrs. Jones, but could I please talk to you for a minute?" Replacement skills occupy the lower box in the competing behavior model (see Figures 5-13 and 5-14).

General adaptive skills consist of students learning new skills that enable them to be successful in the situations that cause problem behavior. For example, if a student asks to go to the bathroom 30 times during math division seat work to escape doing the problems, then an adaptive skill would be learning to do division so that she can complete the problems. General adaptive skills occupy the upper box in the competing behavior model (Figures 5-13 and 5-14). Coping and tolerance skills

help students manage their behavior in situations that cause problem behavior but cannot be changed, or in which a replacement behavior cannot be honored. For example, if a student pushes or shoves other students out of the way in the cafeteria line because he sees ice cream, he cannot ask to go to the front of the line every day. Instead, he must learn to wait in line like everyone else. Coping and tolerance skills are embedded throughout the competing behavior model.

Teachers must make two major decisions when selecting teaching strategies. The first decision involves selecting the best alternative behavior or behaviors, and the second decision involves selecting the instructional method or format. Selecting an alternative behavior consists of identifying appropriate (a) replacement behaviors, (b) desirable and general adaptive skills, and (c) coping and tolerance skills. Replacement behaviors serve the same function as the problem behavior (i.e., get the same outcome). Teachers must be careful when selecting a replacement behavior because the student will continue to use problem behavior unless the replacement behavior is easier to do, gets the same outcome faster and more frequently, and gets an outcome that is just as good or better than the problem behavior gets (Halle & Drasgow, 2003; Horner & Day, 1991). For example, if a student shouts to get a teacher's attention, then a replacement behavior could be that the student raises his hand. But for a student to raise his hand instead of shouting, raising his hand must be easy to do, and the teacher must respond to hand raising more quickly and more often than she does to shouting, and respond to hand raising with the same intensity and duration of attention as she does to shouting.

When selecting desirable and general adaptive skills, the teacher should rely on the functional assessment information to identify problem situations, and then match meaningful skills that increase independence and quality of life in those situations. For example, if a student argues with the teacher to avoid getting started on her seat work, a general adaptive behavior may be for the student to develop a schedule of beginning her seatwork in a reasonable time (e.g., 1 minute after the request), when to take a short break, and how long it should take to complete the work. When selecting coping and tolerance skills, the teacher must target skills that increase the student's ability to wait (i.e., be patient) and to increase her self-control in situations that are challenging but important (Halle et al., 2005). Coping and tolerance strategies may include developing skills in the area of self-management, anger control, problem solving, and relaxation in unpleasant or stressful situations. To make the BIP as effective as possible, it is often a good idea to address all three areas in a support plan, as long as each strategy makes sense based on the FBA information and is individualized for the student.

The second decision that a teacher must make is to select the instructional method or format for teaching the skills that he or the IEP team have selected for the BIP. Instructional methods may consist of direct instruction, prompting and shaping, or behavioral skills training (BST; Miltenberger, 2004). A teacher may use a combination of teaching strategies to foster acquisition of the new behavior. Consider the following situation in which a teacher wants to teach a student to raise his hand for attention instead of shouting. First, the teacher begins with BST. The teacher starts by modeling, or showing, the student how the correct behavior looks. He then verbally describes the correct behavior to the student. Next, he has the student rehearse, or practice, the new skill. To help the student do the correct behavior, he may provide prompts. Finally, he gives the student feedback in the form of praise for correct responses. Throughout the teaching sessions, the teacher uses verbal prompts to help the student perform exactly the right behavior.

Consequence Strategies Consequence strategies refer to providing reinforcement to increase all socially acceptable behaviors, and withholding reinforcement (i.e., implementing extinction) for all unacceptable behaviors. These strategies mean that there must be frequent and immediate reinforcement for replacement skills, desirable and general adaptive skills, and coping and tolerance skills. Remember that problem behavior continues because it is being reinforced, and the purpose of the functional assessment is to identify the reinforcers responsible for the continued occurrence of problem behavior. The purpose of the BIP is to increase new socially acceptable behaviors identified in the BIP; thus the teacher must consistently reinforce these new behaviors at first on a continuous schedule that leads to their acquisition, and on an intermittent schedule after they are acquired, which causes them to be maintained. Conversely, the problem behaviors cannot be reinforced or they will continue to occur. If they are reinforced only occasionally, they are likely to reoccur because they are on an intermittent schedule and that is a powerful schedule for maintaining behavior (Ferster & Skinner, 1957). Sometimes it is impossible to not respond to problem behavior in ways that reinforce it. For example, if a student taunts peers through verbal or physical aggression to get his teacher's attention, it is impossible for the teacher to ignore the student or to not intervene in some way. If a BIP is properly developed, however, then it will contain a number of additional strategies that make the problem behavior irrelevant and thus less likely to occur.

IMPLEMENTATION FIDELITY

One of the greatest challenges for effective behavior support is getting all the components of the BIP implemented consistently. The FBA process can be complicated and the resulting BIP can be complex. The people who contributed to developing the BIP may not be the same people who will be implementing it. In any event, implementation of the BIP will be facilitated by creating a checklist that describes (a) who is responsible for implementing the BIP, and (b) what that person should do in simple and concrete language. In essence, a checklist can translate the complex BIP into an implementation task analysis that enables people to implement it successfully. Table 5-8 provides a checklist for Billy's BIP. Figure 5-15 is a completed BIP for Billy.

DATA COLLECTION

We would like to add one final component that is essential for a BIP to be effective: data collection. It is imperative that teachers collect numerical information to document a student's progress and to use for making instructional decisions. It is often the case that teachers collect data on the occurrence of problem behavior to determine if there is a reduction. But it is equally if not more important to collect information on the occurrence of alternative skills (i.e., replacement skills, desirable and adaptive skills, coping and tolerance skills) to determine if there is an *increase*. The essence of behavior support is its emphasis on skill development and thus increases in alternative skills represent skill development. Table 5-9 provides an example of Billy's BIP data sheet emphasizing data collection on skill development.

CRISIS MANAGEMENT

Positive behavior support (PBS) is a proactive and preventative approach to problem behavior that emphasizes skill development and does not rely on coercion or punishment to change behavior. PBS reduces the likelihood of problem behavior by developing a comprehensive multicomponent support plan. An additional component of behavior support is crisis management. The purpose of crisis management is to protect the safety of the student and others in the environment during an episode of aggressive or violent behavior. Crisis management reduces the likelihood that *someone will get hurt* during the occurrence of problem behavior.

PBS and crisis management are important aspects of behavior management. Together they comprise a seamless response to problem behavior that focuses mainly on skill development, but also includes a safety net to

Table 5–8   Checklist for Billy's BIP

BIP Checklist

Date _____   Student's name _____

Setting Event Strategies	Yes	No
1. I checked with the social worker at least once a week to get an update.		
2. I checked with Billy's counselor every day before Billy came to class.		
Antecedent Strategies		
1. I greeted Billy when he came to class.		
2. I broke Billy's academic tasks into small chunks.		
3. I let Billy choose the sequence of tasks.		
4. I let Billy choose at least one member for each group activity.		
5. I provided frequent positive comments whenever Billy was being good.		
Teaching Strategies		
1. I prompted Billy to raise his hand to ask for help.		
2. I prompted Billy to use a calm voice to ask a peer for help.		
3. I prompted Billy to ignore antagonizing students.		
4. I prompted Billy to use his self-monitoring card.		
Consequence Strategies		
1. I praised Billy when he completed his assignments.		
2. I gave Billy a choice of reinforcers when he completed his assignments.		
3. I gave Billy a 1- or 2-minute break when he asked for one.		
4. I or a student helped Billy when he appropriately requested it.		
5. I ignored problem behavior whenever possible.		
6. I praised Billy when he ignored antagonizing students.		

Directions: Place a check in the corresponding box for each strategy that you used before or during class.

FIGURE 5-15

Completed BIP for Billy

Behavior Intervention Plan

Student's name:	Billy Smith	Date of meeting:	5/4/03
Date of birth:	8/5/90	Teacher's name:	Mrs. Quam
Parents or guardians:	Joe and Joan Smith	Principal's name:	Dr. Rogers
Home address:	148 Mockingbird Lane	School:	Shangri-La Elementary School
	Toon Town, SC 22222	School address:	486 Mountain Retreat
Home phone:	999-999-8888		Toon Town, SC 22222
Phone:	999-999-9999		

(cont.)

FIGURE 5–15

Completed BIP for Billy (continued)

Team Members

Name	Role
1. Mrs. Quam	Teacher
2. Mr. Edholm	Teacher
3. Dr. Yale	Behavior specialist
4. Dr. Rogers	LEA representative
5. Joe Smith	Parent or guardian
6. Joan Smith	Parent or guardian
7. Dr. DesRoches	School psychologist

Student's Classification or Diagnosis

Billy Smith has an emotional disability in accordance with South Carolina's criteria for special education eligibility.

Description of the Problem Behavior(s)

Billy Smith was referred for problem behavior that was typically described as "throwing temper tantrums." Billy's problem behaviors consisted of the following:

1. *Noncompliance:* Not following teacher directions to work on a task within 10 seconds or not staying on task until the task is completed.
2. *Verbal aggression:* Audible talking not related to class work, using swear words, or using a voice that is significantly louder than other students.
3. *Physical aggression:* Making forceful contact on another person with any part of the hands, arms, legs, or feet or forcefully throwing items at others.
4. *Running from class:* Leaving the classroom or building without permission.

Based on information collected during the FBA, the behavior support team (BST) decided to generate strategies for reducing Billy's problem behaviors and increasing appropriate replacement behaviors. The data strongly indicated that Billy's tantrum behaviors were related to escaping academic demands and escaping antagonizing comments made by peers. The BST determined that Billy's problem behaviors were related to conditions in the classroom environment and therefore, the BST decided that environmental modifications would be made in his language arts and mathematics classrooms.

Functional Behavioral Assessment Summary

The following statement summarizes the conditions associated with Billy's problem behavior.

Summary Statement from the FBA

Setting Events	Antecedents	Behavior	Consequences
When Billy has not had contact with his mother overnight and has slept less than 6 hours	and he is presented with a challenging academic demand or he is antagonized by another student	he will refuse to do work, become verbally or physically aggressive, or run out of the classroom	to escape or avoid the academic demand or to escape being antagonized by other students

FIGURE 5-15

Competing Behavior Model

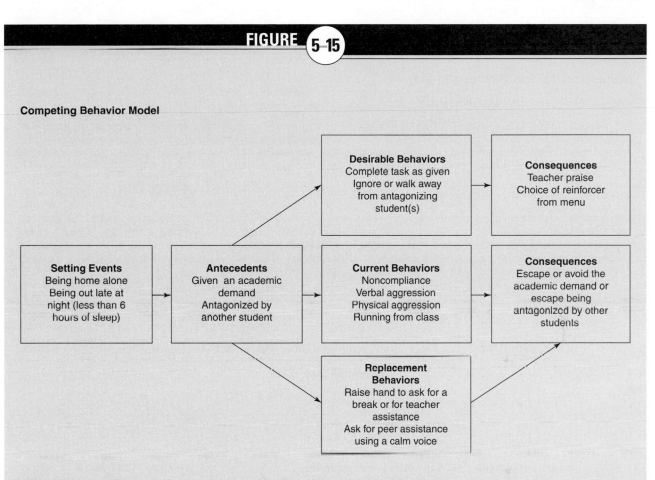

Behavior Change Plan

Setting Event Strategies

Two strategies were selected to address setting events that are likely to affect Billy's behavior. These strategies include (a) having a social worker go to his home to assess living conditions and supervision, and (b) having Billy see the guidance counselor for 5 to 10 minutes every morning before school starts to discuss the previous night and the upcoming day.

Antecedent Strategies

Five strategies were identified to address antecedents associated with Billy's problem behavior. The strategies include having teachers (a) greet Billy when he arrives in class, (b) break all academic tasks into small, manageable chunks, (c) allow Billy to choose the sequence of assignments for individual class work, (d) allow Billy to choose one member of his group for any independent tasks, and (e) provide frequent positive comments to Billy when he is being good.

Teaching Strategies and Replacement Behaviors

Several teaching strategies to increase replacement behaviors and reduce problem behavior include (a) teaching Billy to raise his hand and ask for assistance, (b) teaching Billy to approach a peer to ask for help with a calm voice, (c) using behavior skills training to teach Billy how to ignore antagonizing students, and (d) teaching Billy to use a self-monitoring card to record the number of times he uses desirable and replacement behaviors.

Consequence Strategies

Consequence strategies for reducing problem behavior and increasing socially appropriate behaviors include the teacher (a) providing praise when Billy completes assignments and a choice of reinforcers off the menu, (b) providing a 1- or 2-minute break when he correctly asks for it, (c) assisting Billy when he correctly requests help, (d) ignoring problem behavior if possible, and (e) providing praise when Billy ignores antagonizing peer comments.

(cont.)

FIGURE 5-15

Completed BIP for Billy (continued)

Crisis Management Strategies (If Needed)

If Billy begins cursing, talking loudly, and hitting or throwing materials at others, ask Billy to calm down in a matter of fact tone of voice. Guide Billy to the back of the classroom away from other students and call for additional assistance if necessary. Clear the classroom if Billy does not calm down or if his behaviors are likely to injure others or damage property. Currently, the severity or intensity of Billy's behaviors does not warrant frequent use of crisis management procedures.

Monitoring/Evaluation Plan

A data collection sheet will be used to monitor occurrences of Billy's problem behaviors (i.e., noncompliance, verbal aggression, physical aggression, and leaving the classroom) and replacement behaviors. Data will be collected daily by Billy's teachers and reviewed each week by his teachers and the behavior specialist. Weekly meetings will be scheduled to discuss Billy's progress and to determine if changes in his support plan are necessary. All members of the BST will meet monthly to discuss Billy's overall progress and the effectiveness of the behavior intervention plan.

Table 5–9   Example of Billy's BIP data sheet emphasizing data collection on skill development

Billy's BIP Data Sheet

Date_____

Time	Raised hand or used calm voice to ask for a break or for assistance?	Ignored antagonizing students during entire time period?	Completed all tasks as given during entire time period?	Noncompliance	Verbal aggression	Physical aggression	Running from class
Science 10:45– 11:40 a.m.		Yes No	Yes No				
Lunch 11:45– 12:20 p.m.		Yes No	Yes No				
Science 12:25– 1:20 p.m.		Yes No	Yes No				

Directions:
1. Place a tally mark (/) in the corresponding box for every occurrence of hand raising, noncompliance, verbal aggression, physical aggression, or running from classroom.
2. Circle either Yes or No for ignoring antagonizing students and completing all tasks during each corresponding time period. If there are no opportunities during a time period for these target behaviors, do not circle anything.

ensure that no one gets hurt while the skill development component is being refined. Crisis management plans need to be developed and individualized to reflect the unique characteristics and situations of each student. There is no "one size fits all" crisis management approach. Each crisis management plan must be implemented consistently according to a predetermined plan that reflects the best interests of the student. Crisis management does not work when people fail to effectively plan for an episode of problem behavior. In fact, responding without a plan may increase the severity of problem behavior during an episode and may even increase the severity and frequency of future episodes. In sum, crisis management works best when everyone has the training, resources, and administrative support to follow the predetermined plan.

Chapter Summary

Functional behavioral assessment is a systematic process for gathering information about environmental factors that influence the occurrence of problem behavior. In this chapter we describe three types of assessment methods for collecting information about problem behavior. Indirect assessment methods include procedures such as reviewing referral information and reviewing school records, using behavior rating scales and checklists, and interviewing people familiar with the student's problem behavior. Direct assessment methods include such procedures as collecting scatter plot data and observing student behavior using A-B-C recording. Experimental assessment methods include functional assessment and structural analysis procedures. Information gathered during the FBA process is used to (a) develop a clear description of problem behavior, (b) identify setting events and antecedents that predict the occurrence of problem behavior, (c) identify consequences that maintain problem behavior, (d) verify predictors and consequences through direct observation, and (e) develop summary statements that describe the relationship between environmental factors and problem behavior.

Behavior intervention plans represent a comprehensive approach for teaching students adaptive and socially acceptable behavior while making problem behavior irrelevant, ineffective, and inefficient. We have defined and described five fundamental characteristics associated with effective BIPs. First, FBA results provide the foundation for the development of intervention plans. Second, intervention strategies are based on the principles of ABA and reflect a competing behavior approach to skill development. Third, intervention plans reflect the values, resources, and skills of the people who implement the plan. Fourth, intervention strategies reflect multidimensional approaches to problem behavior. Fifth, intervention plans describe how everyone in the environment will change.

CHAPTER 6

Cognitive Behavioral Interventions

Mitchell L. Yell, T. Rowand Robinson, and Nancy B. Meadows

Focus Questions

- What are cognitive behavioral interventions and are they effective?
- How can teachers use cognitive behavioral interventions?
- How can students be taught to manage their own behavior?
- What is verbal mediation?
- What is self-instructional training?
- How can students with emotional and behavioral disorders (EBD) be taught to control their anger and use effective problem-solving strategies?
- What is rational emotive therapy?
- How can teachers of students with EBD use cognitive behavioral interventions in their behavior intervention plans?

When developing programs for students with emotional and behavioral disorders (EBD), the ultimate goal is to teach them more socially appropriate and adaptive forms of behavior that endure after they leave the school setting. Programs for students with EBD, therefore, should provide them with the skills and abilities to control their own behavior and function independent of teacher-mediated interventions and control. Thus, the primary aim of behavioral programs for students with EBD, regardless of a teacher's philosophical orientation and management methods, is to teach students to manage their own behavior.

Self-management or self-control refers to actions a person takes to change his or her own behavior. Procedures that teachers use to increase students' ability to manage their behavior often involve teaching students to engage in a specific behavior (e.g., self-instruction, self-monitoring) to change a target behavior (Shapiro & Cole, 1994). According to Shapiro and Cole, interventions that foster self-management abilities focus on skill building and teaching students to be more independent, self-reliant, and responsible for their own behavior.

In this chapter we examine a technology for teaching self-management that has a strong empirical base, 25 years of practical school-based intervention methods, and shows great promise for producing the long-term, permanent behavioral changes that teachers seek for their students. The general term for the procedures that we will explore is cognitive behavioral intervention (CBI). A CBI is not a single procedure or intervention; rather, CBI refers to a number of different, but related, interventions. Self-management, self-instruction, self-evaluation, and self-control training are all interventions that are included under the rubric of CBI. Cognitive behavioral interventions use the principles of behavior modification with cognitive approaches to give students the necessary tools to control their own behavior. These procedures show great promise because they involve students in the behavior change process and have the potential of being more likely to generalize to other settings beyond the school environment. By using CBIs, teachers can provide students with procedures to modify their thoughts and beliefs, thereby promoting self-regulation (Robinson, Smith, Miller, & Brownell, 1999).

In this chapter we introduce readers to the philosophy and interventions of CBI and provide a practical guide for educators so they may use these interventions in their programs.

COGNITIVE BEHAVIORAL INTERVENTIONS

Cognitive behavioral interventions share three basic assumptions (Hughes, 1988). First, all behavior is mediated by cognitive events. This means that thoughts and beliefs often guide people's actions. Second, changes in these cognitive mediating events can result in a change of behavior. Third, all persons are active participants in their learning. Thus, CBI is based on the reciprocal relationship between one's thoughts and behaviors. When teachers use CBI procedures, they are attempting to teach students how to control their behavior by teaching them how to regulate their thoughts and beliefs. The major goal of CBI, therefore, is to teach students to manage their own behavior through cognitive self-regulation (Yell, Busch, & Drasgow, 2005).

CBIs use the principles of ABA (e.g., antecedent control, reinforcement) and social learning theory (e.g., modeling, feedback) to modify underlying cognitions. These principles are combined with cognitive approaches to teach students strategies, such as anger control, to control their own behavior. The teacher then uses the principles of ABA to strengthen these new behaviors. Shapiro and Cole (1994) note that traditionally teacher-managed interventions have relied on punishing consequences to decrease behavior. In CBIs, teachers rely on reinforcement to strengthen the new target behaviors.

Proponents of CBI believe that sole reliance on externally controlled behavioral interventions makes a student overly dependent on a teacher. Such programs, however, do not provide students with the skills required for long-term behavior change. When a teacher uses the techniques and procedures of CBI to teach students self-management, the students become less dependent on the teacher and on external control and are more likely to learn to control their behavior.

Proponents advocate using CBI programs for many reasons. First, teaching self-management is a proactive approach rather than a reactive approach. Teaching students to control their behavior will *prevent* behavior problems from occurring. Second, students with self-management skills can learn and behave more appropriately without the constant supervision of the teacher. Third, self-management may enhance the generalization of behavior change. For example, when socially inappropriate behaviors are under external control by the teacher, the behaviors may occur in situations and settings where the teacher is absent. When students manage their own behaviors, however, these behaviors are more likely to endure and to carry over to different situations and settings. Finally, behavioral improvements established through self-management procedures may be more resistant to extinction than behavioral improvements established through external control procedures. When behavioral improvements are established through external control procedures, these improvements may disappear when the external reinforcers are removed. However, some researchers have suggested that this is less of a problem when behaviors are improved through self-management and reinforcement becomes internal (Kaplan & Carter, 1995; Shapiro & Cole, 1994). The many different procedures of CBI have been used in the

schools for about 25 years. In the next section we examine investigations into the efficacy of CBIs.

EFFECTIVENESS OF COGNITIVE BEHAVIORAL INTERVENTIONS

Many researchers have systematically examined the use of CBIs in schools. CBIs have been used for students with and without disabilities in a variety of settings. Table 6–1 lists examples of the successful use of CBI interventions across a wide range of disabilities. Additionally, CBIs have been used successfully with students who exhibit problem

Table 6–1   Selected studies using cognitive behavioral interventions (for full citations, see references)

Subject or Behavior	Studies
Students with autism	Callahan & Rademacher, 1999; Koegel, Harrower, & Koegel, 1999; Koegel & Frea, 1993; Koegel & Koegel, 1990; Morrison, Kamps, Garcia, & Parker, 2001; Newman, Buffington, O'Grady, Polson, & Hemmes, 1995; Strain, Kohler, Storey, & Danko, 1994
Students with behavioral disorders	Carr & Punzo, 1993; Clark & McKenzie, 1989; DiGangi & Maag, 1992; Dunlap, Clarke, Ramos, Wright, Jackson, & Brinson, 1995; Etscheidt, 1991; Fowler, 1986; Gregory, Kehle, & McLoughlin, 1997; Hogan, & Prater, 1993; Kern, Dunlap, Childs, & Clark, 1994; Kern, Ringdahl, Hilt, & Sterling-Turner, 2001; Kilburtz, Miller, & Morrow, 1985; Levendoski & Cartledge, 2000; McLaughlin, Krappman, Welsh, 1985; McLaughlin & Truhlicka, 1983; Minner, S., 1990; Moore, Cartledge, & Heckman, 1995; Nelson, Smith, & Colvin, 1995; Rhode, Morgan, & Young, 1983; Robinson, Smith, & Miller, 2002; Smith, Siegel, O'Conner, & Thomas, 1994; Smith, Young, West, Morgan, & Rhode, 1988; Young, Smith, West, & Morgan, 1987
Students with learning disabilities	De La Paz & Graham, 1997; Hallahan, Lloyd, Kneedler, & Marshall, 1982; Hallahan, Lloyd, Kosiewicz, Kauffman, & Graves, 1979; Hallahan, Marshall, & Lloyd, 1981; Lloyd, Bateman, Landrum, & Hallahan, 1989; Lloyd, Hallahan, Kosiewicz, & Kneedler, 1982; Lloyd & Landrum 1990; Maag, Reid, & DiGangi, 1993; Maag, Rutherford, & DiGangi, 1992; Prater, Joy, Chilman, Temple, & Miller, 1991; Reid & Harris, 1993; Rooney, Polloway, & Hallahan, 1985; Sexton, Harris, & Graham, 1998; Todd, Horner, & Sugai, 1999
Students with mental retardation	Hughes & Boyle, 1991; Hughes, Korinek, & Gorman, 1991; Osborne, Kosiewicz, Crumley, & Lee, 1987
Students with severe and multiple disabilities	Koegel, Harrower, & Koegel, 1999
Students with visual disabilities	Storey & Gaylord-Ross, 1987
Students without disabilities	Glynn, Thomas, & Shee, 1973; Olympia, Sheridan, Jenson, & Andrews, 1994
Students with ADHD	Barkley, Copeland, & Sivage, 1980; Kendall & Finch, 1979; Mathes & Bender, 1997; Shapiro, DuPaul, & Bradley-Klug, 1998
Students with aggressive behavior	Camp, Blom, Hebert, & Van Doorninck, 1977; Christie, Hiss, & Lozanoff, 1984; Feindler & Fremouw, 1983; Knapczyk, 1988; Lochman, Nelson, & Sims, 1981; Smith, Lochman, & Daunic, 2005; Smith, Siegel, O'Conner, & Thomas, 1994
Students with impulsive behavior	Meichenbaum & Goodman, 1971
Students who are angry	Christie, Hiss, & Lozanoff, 1984
Students who exhibit noncompliance	O'Brien, Riner, & Budd, 1983
Students with poor social skills	Kilburtz, Miller, & Morrow, 1985
Students who are depressed	Maag & Swearer, 2005; Reynolds & Coats, 1986
Students with academic deficits	Burkell, Schneider, & Pressley, 1990; Harris & Graham, 1992; Levendoski & Cartledge, 2000; Lloyd, Bateman, Landrum, & Hallahan, 1989; McDougall & Brady, 1998; Symons, Carigula-Bull, Snyder, & Pressley, 1999; Symons, McGoldrick, Snyder, & Pressley, 1989

behaviors and students who have been classified as having emotional or behavioral disorders (Robinson et al., 1999).

We have insights into the effects of CBIs on students with EBD in school settings provided by reviews of efficacy studies conducted by Hughes, Ruhl, and Misra (1989); Nelson, Smith, Young, and Dodd (1991); and a recent meta-analysis conducted by Robinson et al., (1999).

Hughes and colleagues (1989) reviewed data-based research articles published between 1970 and 1988 that used CBIs (i.e., self-monitoring, self-evaluation, self-reinforcement, or self-instruction) with students who were formally identified as behaviorally disordered or some variation of the label. Additionally, these students had to be served in a resource room, self-contained classroom, or mainstream classroom in a public school setting. The authors drew three major conclusions from their review of the literature. First, self-management procedures that are used in a package format show great promise for changing student behavior in the special education setting. This means that when one type of CBI (e.g., self-management) is used in combination with another type (e.g., self-instruction) and the teacher uses contingent reinforcement, the results will be more powerful. Second, with respect to generalization, self-instruction and self-evaluation seem to have greater support in the literature. When the authors examined studies that assessed generalization, they found positive effects. Third, additional research must be done regarding generalization of CBIs before claims of superiority over externally managed programs can be substantiated. From their review, Hughes et al. concluded that there is support for using CBIs in school programs for students with behavioral disorders. The authors also noted, however, that future research on CBIs and students with emotional or behavioral disorders should (a) include adolescent subjects; (b) study the efficacy of CBIs when applied to simple and complex social behaviors; (c) investigate maintenance and generalization across persons, settings, responses, and time; (d) compare CBIs to externally managed programs with respect to teacher time, generalization, student involvement, and superiority of effects; and (d) report all the important characteristics of subjects, settings, training, reliability, and validity.

Nelson and colleagues (1991) reviewed the results of studies that used CBIs in school settings with students who were classified as having behavioral disorders. They identified 16 studies conducted between 1976 and 1988. The authors concluded that when used in school settings, CBIs are powerful interventions that have positive effects on a variety of social and academic behaviors of students with behavioral disorders. Nelson et al. (1991)

also stated that generalization would not occur unless systematic programming for generalization was a part of the study.

Robinson and colleagues (1999) used meta-analysis to examine 23 CBI investigations, conducted between 1977 and 1993, that targeted the reduction of problem behaviors of children and youth with behavioral disorders in school settings. (For an explanation of meta-analysis see Figure 6-1.) The authors wanted to determine if CBIs were effective in decreasing hyperactivity/impulsivity and aggression in school settings, and if CBIs were successful in helping students maintain self-control following the removal of the intervention. They concluded that there was strong evidence for the efficacy of using CBIs with students with behavioral disorders. In fact, the mean effect size across all the studies was 0.74, and in 89% of the studies the students with whom CBIs were used experienced greater gains academically and behaviorally on posttreatment measures. Furthermore, behavior problems such as aggression and impulsivity, often viewed as being very resistant to change, were significantly reduced when teachers used CBIs. Additionally, Robinson et al. noted that their findings indicated that

FIGURE 6-1

What is meta-analysis?

Meta-analysis provides a strategy that researchers can use to examine results from numerous individual studies. In a meta-analysis, the results of many studies of a particular intervention or strategy are combined to yield a numerical indicator of the effectiveness of the intervention. This numerical indicator, called an *effect size (ES)*, is computed by subtracting the mean of untreated subjects in a study from the mean of treated subjects and dividing the difference by a measure of the variance (Forness, Kavale, Blum, & Lloyd, 1997). If there is no control group, an ES can be computed using pretest and posttest data. An ES of +1.00 represents an advantage of one standard deviation for the treatment group when compared to the comparison group, which indicates that 84% of the treated participants would be above the mean when compared to their comparison group counterparts (Hedges & Olkin, 1985).

The ESs from all the studies a researcher examines can be combined to yield a mean ES across all studies. Effect sizes of +.40 or greater are generally considered significant. Kavale, Mathur, Forness, Rutherford, and Quinn (1997) referred to meta-analyses of interventions with ESs of +.30 as "interventions that show promise," and interventions of +.60 and above as "interventions that work."

these interventions implemented in school settings resulted in treatment effects that were maintained following intervention.

These reviews indicate that CBIs are powerful procedures that can have positive results when used to teach students to manage their own academic and nonacademic behaviors. For an excellent review of cognitive behavioral interventions refer to Mayer, Lochman, and Van Acker (2005). Next, we review specific interventions. Our review of each intervention begins with a definition, followed by a summary of relevant research, and ends with guidelines for using the intervention.

PROCEDURES OF COGNITIVE BEHAVIORAL INTERVENTION

All CBIs share the common element of teaching students to manage their behavior. That is, teachers use behavioral principles with their students (e.g., reinforcement) to teach them cognitive strategies and to reinforce their use of appropriate behaviors. These strategies are varied and use some form of self-instruction or verbal mediation to control behavior. For example, some CBI procedures teach students to monitor and evaluate their behavior, whereas others teach students to solve academic or nonacademic problems, or to respond to provocation by following certain cognitive steps. Cognitive behavioral interventions are a heterogeneous group of procedures that overlap considerably with many cognitive and behavioral interventions. To facilitate our discussion, however, we will divide CBIs into two broad categories: (a) self-management-based interventions and (b) verbal mediation–based interventions. In each section we will define a specific intervention, discuss its theoretical and research base, and offer a generic instructional protocol to assist teachers to develop their own CBIs. We now examine the different interventions that fall under the rubric of CBI, starting with the self-management-based interventions.

Self-Management-Based Interventions

In self-management-based interventions, students are taught to (a) observe, (b) record, and (c) reinforce their own behavior. Shapiro and Cole (1994) assert that self-management-based interventions are very similar to teacher-controlled contingency-management procedures. In fact, they note that the use of self-management procedures is comparable to the ways in which a teacher may award points in a token economy. In a token economy, a teacher observes, records, evaluates, and reinforces appropriate student behavior. If the behavior meets a predetermined criterion, the teacher then reinforces the student. The primary difference in self-management-based interventions is that the student observes, records, evaluates, and reinforces his or her own behavior. This shift of control from the teacher to the student is an essential component of self-management-based interventions.

In this section we will discuss three procedures often used in self-management training: self-monitoring, self-evaluation, and self-reinforcement. Although each of these procedures is frequently discussed separately, in reality they are often combined and taught as self-management packages. We begin with a discussion of self-monitoring.

Self-Monitoring When students use self-monitoring or self-recording procedures, they observe and record the frequency of a particular behavior or behaviors. Self-monitoring has been used to improve students' social behaviors (DiGangi & Maag, 1992) and academic achievement (Webber, Scheuermann, McCall, & Coleman, 1994). Reid (1996) reviewed the research on self-monitoring and found that these procedures had been proven to be effective with diverse populations and behaviors. Moreover, Reid found that these procedures could easily be used in classroom settings.

There are two aspects to self-monitoring. First, a student must be aware of the behavior that he or she is counting. Second, he or she must record the behavior. For example, students may count the number of times they raise their hand to volunteer in class or talk out in class without permission by observing the behavior and then marking the occurrences on a piece of paper.

It has been demonstrated that having students collect self-monitoring data may often result in increases in desired behavior. This may be because the procedure forces students to monitor their own behavior. Baer (1984) stated that a reason for behavioral improvement may be that self-monitoring provides cues that increase a student's awareness of potential consequences for a particular behavior. Researchers have noted that behavior often improves simply because the student is collecting the behavioral data (Broden, Hall, & Mitts, 1971). This has been termed a *reactive effect*, which means that the behavior may change in the desired direction simply as a function of self-monitoring (Alberto & Troutman, 2006; Lloyd & Landrum, 1990). In an interesting elaboration of the reactive effect, DiGangi, Maag, and Rutherford (1991) found that self-graphing of on-task behavior actually enhanced the reactive effects of self-monitoring that behavior, and the academic performance of students with learning disabilities.

Research on Self-Monitoring. In a review of the self-monitoring research, Webber and colleagues (1994) concluded that self-monitoring could be used successfully with special education students of various ages in various settings to increase attention to tasks, positive classroom behaviors, and some social skills. Self-monitoring was also successful in decreasing inappropriate classroom behaviors. Additional benefits of self-monitoring included enhancing the likelihood of generalization, and the ease of teaching the procedures to students.

Teachers may be concerned with children's accuracy when self-monitoring. In a number of investigations, children have accurately recorded their behaviors; however, in other studies children have not been accurate. An important question is whether accuracy is a significant variable during self-monitoring. O'Leary and Dubay (1979) demonstrated that the accuracy of a child's self-collected data did not necessarily correlate with the child's behavior or academic performance. That is, when trying to increase appropriate behaviors, the act of self-monitoring alone may be more important than the accuracy of the child's data.

Some researchers believe that contingencies regarding the accuracy of the data should apply if a student is going to be reinforced on the basis of self-monitoring data (Gross & Wojnilower, 1984). Otherwise, students may rate their inappropriate behavior as appropriate to receive reinforcement. Thus, students may be reinforced for inaccurate self-monitoring. When accuracy is a concern, matching procedures may be used to check the student's data. When using matching procedures, a student's data are matched with the recorded data of an independent observer. The student is reinforced when his or her self-monitoring data closely match the data collected by the independent observer. For example, a student could be reinforced when his or her self-monitoring data matched the data recorded by a teacher or paraprofessional. The teacher could tell the student that he or she would give the student bonus points if the self-monitoring data were within one point of the teacher's recording. In addition to reinforcing the child for matching, the child should also be reinforced for appropriate behavior exhibited during the self-monitoring program.

Teaching Self-Monitoring. To teach self-monitoring, the teacher must train the student to collect data on his or her behavior. First, the student must be aware of the particular behavior that will be counted. To assist the student to identify the behavior of concern, the teacher must have a precise operational definition. Second, the student must be taught how to record occurrences or nonoccurrences of the behavior. The collected data

provide the child and the teacher with feedback regarding the frequency of the behavior. Teachers may find it useful to teach students how to chart and graph the behavior they count. Students often find this very motivating (Workman, 1998).

Students usually have to be taught self-monitoring by teachers. Self-monitoring systems can be used with event recording procedures and time sampling procedures. In event recording, the student counts the number of times a particular behavior occurs. An example of event recording would be if the teacher taught a student to record the number of times his or her hand was raised to ask a question or make a comment during class. Figure 6-2 depicts a self-monitoring form using event recording.

In time sampling recording, a student might count the number of occurrences of a particular behavior within a specified period of time. For example, a student may mark if he or she is seated when an audible beep on a tape is heard. This is a more sophisticated type of recording procedure (Rhode, Jenson, & Reavis, 1998). In addition to requiring that a student can observe his or her behavior accurately, the teacher must provide a tape with an audible tone. The tone serves as a cue for the student to record if the behavior occurred. Figure 6-3 is an example of self-monitoring using time sampling. Table 6-2 shows a generic instructional protocol for teaching self-monitoring.

Self-Evaluation In self-evaluation or self-assessment the child compares his or her behavior against a preset standard to determine whether the performance meets a particular criterion (Shapiro & Cole, 1994). For example, a teacher could have his or her students observe their behavior during a class period and then have them rate their behavior on a 4-point Likert scale (Shapiro & Cole, 1994). Maag (1999) referred to self-evaluation as self-monitoring followed by a covert evaluation of the behavior.

Research on Self-Evaluation. Empirical investigations have demonstrated that self-evaluation can be an effective intervention. For example, Smith, Young, West, Morgan, and Rhode (1988) trained four boys with behavior disorders in a self-evaluation procedure. The target behaviors were off-task and disruptive behaviors. Training was conducted in three phases. In the first phase the children were taught classroom rules. The students rated their behavior on a 5-point scale in accordance with how closely they followed the rules. The children filled out an evaluation card on their behavior every 10 minutes. The students was asked to record a "5" or "excellent" if they followed classroom rules and worked on assigned tasks for the entire interval; "4" or "very good"

Figure 6–2 Example of a self-monitoring form using event sampling

Name _____

Date _____

Class _____

Start time _____   Stop time _____

Record a "/" each time you talk without permission.

if they followed classroom rules and worked for the entire interval with the exception of one minor infraction; "3" or "average" if they followed the rules and worked without any serious offenses except for receiving two reminders to get to work; "2" or "below average" if they followed rules and worked for approximately half of the interval; "1" if they followed the rules and worked for half the interval but had to be separated from the group; and "0" or "unacceptable" if they did not follow classroom rules or do any work during the interval. The students were told to rank their behavior on the scale and that their teachers would do the same. The teacher would also mark each student's card to indicate her rating at the end of a certain period of time. The two scales then would be compared and the children would receive points for matching or nearly matching the teacher. Points could be exchanged for tangible reinforcers.

In the second phase the children continued to evaluate their behavior, but they matched evaluations with the teacher only every 15 minutes. During the third phase the children continued to evaluate themselves on the scale; however, they matched evaluations with the teacher only once every 30 minutes. Phase 3 was not as effective in reducing inappropriate behaviors as phases

1 and 2. Results indicated that the self-evaluation procedures paired with teacher matching were effective in reducing off-task and disruptive behavior in the special education classroom. The authors concluded that self-evaluation paired with teacher matching was an effective intervention, and that the procedures were effective even though the behaviors were not first brought under control by an external behavior management procedure. Data collected in regular classrooms did not show treatment generalization. According to the authors, this was anticipated because regular classroom teachers were unwilling or unable to implement the procedure. They suggested that peers in the regular classroom might be used in the program to match evaluations, thereby freeing the teachers from this responsibility.

Similarly, Nelson, Smith, and Colvin (1995) reported the results of an investigation of a self-evaluation procedure on the recess behavior of students with behavior problems. In this investigation, the authors also reported the effects of using peers to enhance the generalizability of the procedure. Target students were taught the guidelines for appropriate recess behavior using direct instruction and role-playing. Next, the students were taught to rate their actual recess behavior against the

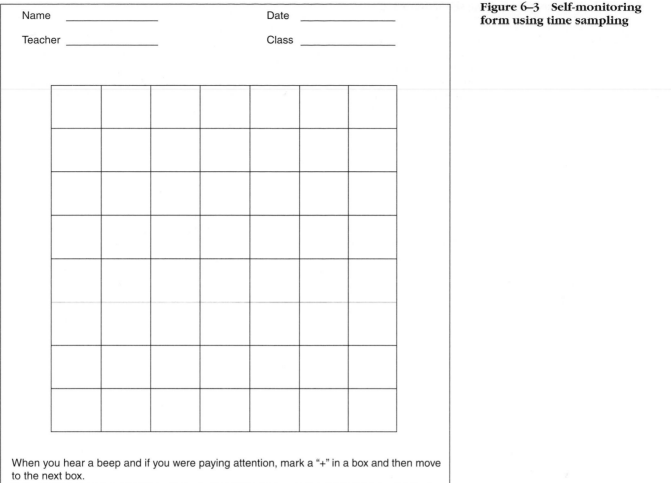

Name _____   Date _____

Teacher _____   Class _____

When you hear a beep and if you were paying attention, mark a "+" in a box and then move to the next box.
If you were not paying attention when you heard the beep, mark a "–" in the box and then move to the next box.

Figure 6–3   Self-monitoring form using time sampling

recess guidelines using a 4-point scale, with 3 as excellent and 0 as unacceptable. Students rated their behavior on point cards twice during the morning recess period. A peer matched to the target student also rated his or her behavior. Following recess, points were totaled and exchanged for backup reinforcers. Results indicated that the self-evaluation procedure produced clear improvements in the recess behaviors of the target students (e.g., positive social behavior toward peers, isolation, positive social behavior toward adults, appropriate equipment use, and game playing). The authors also reported that the improved recess behaviors generalized to the afternoon recess period.

Teaching Self-Evaluation. Teaching students to self-evaluate must begin with teaching the student to self-monitor. This is because self-monitoring is a prerequisite for self-evaluation; the student needs data to compare his or her performance against. Teaching students to use self-evaluation also requires that the teacher set a criterion or goal by which the student can compare his or her performance. Once such a criterion exists, the student will have information on which his or her performance can be evaluated. The end result of self-evaluation is that the student decides whether his or her behavior has reached the desired level or met the criterion.

Perhaps the simplest method of self-evaluation is to include a rating scale at the bottom of a self-monitoring sheet. The student first monitors and records the target behavior and then evaluates his or her behavior against the standard set by the teacher. For example, if the student is monitoring talking out during a 1-hour class period, after the monitoring is completed the student tallies the data and compares it to the criterion level. The student then evaluates the behavior monitored against a rating scale. A rating scale may have a range from 1 to 4

Table 6–2   Protocol for teaching self-monitoring

Step	Description
Step 1: Select a target behavior	Choose a behavior that interferes with your teaching, the student's or other students' learning, or the students' social development. Select both a maladaptive behavior and a fair-pair target behavior (see Chapter 7 for a description of the fair-pair rule). Collect baseline data on the target behavior.
Step 2: Provide a rationale for teaching self-monitoring	Tell students why it is important that they learn to monitor their own behavior. Students must understand why their behavior is maladaptive and why it must be changed.
Step 3: Define the target behavior operationally	Define the target behavior so both the student and the teacher agree when it occurs. The student must know precisely what behavior he or she is to monitor.
Step 4: Set a target goal	Set a reasonable target goal with the student. The student must be able to evaluate his or her progress against an expected standard. As the student succeeds, the difficulty level of the target goal should be increased.
Step 5: Develop and teach the self-monitoring system	Develop the monitoring system and teach the student to use it. The student should be involved during this phase. Break down the task into its component steps (i.e., task analysis). Teach and model each step. If you want to ensure student accuracy during self-monitoring, use a matching strategy (e.g., random student–teacher matches).
Step 6: Monitor the target behavior and evaluate student progress	Monitor the target behavior. Additionally, the student and the teacher should have frequent evaluation meetings so that the teacher can provide feedback and monitor progress.
Step 7: Reinforce the student	Reinforce students when they successfully achieve their target goal.
Step 8: Fade the self-monitoring system	Fade the self-monitoring system when the student's behavior reaches desired levels (e.g., increasing the intervals between self-monitoring periods, using self-monitoring less frequently).

with a definition for each point on the scale (e.g., 4 = excellent, 3 = good, 2 = fair, 1 = poor). An example of a self-monitoring sheet with an evaluation scale at the bottom of the page is depicted in Figure 6–4. Figure 6–5 shows an example of a self-evaluation rating scale that requires students to make evaluative judgments on their behavior following longer periods of time and without a formal self-monitoring system.

When using self-evaluation training to teach students to evaluate their own behavior, the following guidelines may be helpful. First, students must be able to accurately monitor their own behavior. To use a self-evaluation procedure students must be adept at monitoring behaviors; then they may (a) compare the behaviors they monitored to a preset criterion, and (b) evaluate their performance.

Second, the teacher and student should set a daily goal. This goal will then serve as a criterion by which the student can self-evaluate. The goal describes the level of performance toward which the student should work.

Third, the student should receive feedback from the teacher. If the student reaches the goal, he or she should receive systematic reinforcement. If the teacher is concerned about accuracy in ratings, he or she may want to include a matching procedure for additional reinforcement.

Finally, teachers should systematically fade their presence in the process. If self-evaluation training is to be effective, the student must be able to self-evaluate

independently of the teacher. Table 6–3 provides a generic instructional protocol for teaching students to self-evaluate.

Self-Reinforcement   In traditional behavior modification programs, the practitioner specifies the target behavior and delivers the reinforcers for performance of the behaviors. In many self-management packages the student chooses a reinforcer and delivers the reinforcer following appropriate behavior. This is referred to as self-reinforcement.

Research on Self-Reinforcement.   Empirical investigations on the efficacy of self-reinforcement are unclear. Some researchers have demonstrated that self-determined reinforcers can be as effective as or even more effective than teacher-controlled reinforcers (Hayes et al., 1985); whereas others contend that there is little empirical evidence to support the efficacy of self-reinforcement (Maag, 1999).

Self-reinforcement, like reinforcement delivered by teachers, must be delivered in a systematic and consistent manner. Research indicates that initially reinforcement should be teacher managed and delivered (Yell, Busch, et al., 2005). As the child progresses, teacher involvement should be decreased and the child's involvement increased. Wolery et al., (1988) offered the following guidelines for self-reinforcement: (a) the student

Name _____

Date _____

Class _____

Every time you hear the beep, record a "+" if you were paying attention or a "−" if you were not paying attention.

How did I do?

Poor	Fair	Good	Great!
1	2	3	4

Figure 6–4 Example of a self-monitoring form (event recording) with self-evaluation

should be fluent at self-monitoring; (b) the student should be involved in setting the criteria for receiving reinforcement and selecting reinforcers; (c) the teacher should provide reinforcement for target behaviors displayed by the student, accurate matches between the teacher's and the student's data, and accurate determination by the student of whether the criteria for reinforcement were met; (d) matching requirements and teacher evaluation should be faded over time; (e) opportunities for the students to evaluate their performance, determine criteria for reinforcement, select reinforcers, and administer reinforcement should be systematically increased; and (f) naturally occurring reinforcers should be used throughout the process. Other factors that contribute to the maintenance of desired behavior are (1) continuous teacher praise, (2) peer reinforcement for appropriate behavior, and (3) accurate self-evaluation (Drabman, Spitalnik, & O'Leary, 1973).

Whereas most self-management packages include self-reinforcement, some researchers have investigated the effectiveness of self-punishment. In self-punishment, the student is taught to punish rather than reinforce his or her own behaviors. In several investigations (Humphrey, Karoly, & Kirschenbaum, 1978; Kaufman & O'Leary, 1972) the self-punishment procedure used was response cost in conjunction with a token economy. Humphrey et al. (1978) compared self-punishment to self-reinforcement. The study took place in a chaotic elementary classroom in which a self-reinforcement system and a self-punishment system were compared. The students in the self-reinforcement condition reinforced themselves with tokens for accurate performance on reading assignments. The students in the self-punishment condition began each morning with tokens and removed them for inaccurate work or failure to complete work on time. The researchers found that under both conditions the rate of attempted reading assignments was accelerated and accuracy was maintained. The self-reinforcement condition, however, produced slightly better results.

Teaching Self-Reinforcement. When teaching students to use self-reinforcement, three important factors must be addressed. First, the student must be able to monitor and evaluate his or her behavior. Second, the teacher and

FIGURE 6-5

Example of a self-evaluation form

Name _____

Class _____

Date _____

First rating

Time _____

Poor	Fair	Good	Great
1	2	3	4

Points _____ + Bonus _____ = Total _____

Second rating

Time _____

Poor	Fair	Good	Great
1	2	3	4

Points _____ + Bonus _____ = Total _____

Table 6-3   Protocol for teaching self-evaluation

Step	Description
Step 1: Ensure that the student can self-monitor	Teach students to monitor their own behavior accurately. This is necessary before students can self-evaluate.
Step 2: Select a target behavior	Choose a behavior that interferes with your teaching, the student's, or other students' learning, or the student's social development. Select both a maladaptive behavior and a fair-pair target behavior (see Chapter 7 for a description of the fair-pair rule). Collect baseline data on the target behavior.
Step 3: Provide a rationale for teaching self-evaluation	Tell students why it is important that they learn to monitor and evaluate their own behavior. Students must understand why their behavior is maladaptive and why it must be changed.
Step 4: Set a target goal	Set a reasonable target goal with the student. The student must be able to evaluate his or her progress against an expected standard. As the student succeeds, the difficulty level of the target goal should be increased.
Step 5: Develop and teach the evaluation system	Develop the self-evaluation system and teach the student to use it. The student should be involved during this phase. Break down the task into its component steps (i.e., task analysis). Teach and model each step. If you want to ensure student accuracy during self-evaluation, use a matching strategy (e.g., random student–teacher matches).
Step 6: Monitor the target behavior and evaluate student progress	Monitor the target behavior. Additionally, the student and the teacher should have frequent evaluation meetings so that the teacher can provide feedback and monitor progress.
Step 7: Reinforce the student	Reinforce students when they successfully achieve their target goal.
Step 8: Fade the self-evaluation system	Fade the self-evaluation system when the student's behavior reaches desired levels.

Table 6–4 **Protocol for teaching self-reinforcement**

Step	Description
Step 1: Ensure that the student can self-monitor and self-evaluate	Teach students to monitor and evaluate their own behavior accurately. This is necessary before students can self-reinforce.
Step 2: Select a target behavior	Choose a behavior that interferes with your teaching, the student's, or other students' learning, or the student's social development. Select both a maladaptive behavior and a fair-pair target behavior (see chapter 7 for a description of the fair-pair rule). Collect baseline data on the target behavior.
Step 3: Choose the reinforcer(s)	Choose the reinforcer(s) that will be used. Use the same processes you would use when determining a teacher-administered reinforcer (e.g., interest inventory, reinforcer menu). Reinforcers should be readily available to the student.
Step 4: Determine the contingencies	Determine how often a student must engage in the target behavior, before he or she can administer self-reinforcement.
Step 5: Develop and teach the self-reinforcement system	Develop the self-evaluation system and teach the student to use it. The student should be involved during this phase. Break down the task into its component steps (i.e., task analysis). Teach and model each step. If you want to ensure student accuracy during self-evaluation, use a matching strategy (e.g., random student–teacher matches).
Step 6: Monitor the target behavior and evaluate student progress	Monitor the target behavior and self-reinforcement. A student should self-reinforce only when he or she has met the goal for the target behavior. Additionally, the student and the teacher should have frequent evaluation meetings so that the teacher can provide feedback and monitor progress.
Step 7: Fade the self-reinforcement system	Fade the self-evaluation system when the student's behavior reaches desired levels.

student must decide if the self-reinforcement will be external (e.g., tokens, tangibles, preferred activities) or internal (self-praise). Finally, the teacher and student should set a criterion level before the student can self-reinforce. Teachers should adhere to the principle of shaping successive approximations when having students use self-reinforcement. Table 6-4 provides a generic instructional protocol for teaching students to self-reinforce.

Teaching Self-Management Skills According to Sugai and Lewis (1990), when teaching self-management skills to students certain conditions must be maintained. During the preintervention phase of training, the student should be involved. Together, the teacher and student should develop the goals of the self-management program as well as the criteria and contingencies necessary to meet the goals. The recording instrument must be developed at this time and should be simple and easy to use. Furthermore, the student must be trained in the use of the recording procedure. The training should include direct instruction and numerous opportunities for practice. Prior to implementing the procedure, the student must be as fluent as possible in self-monitoring. If a self-reinforcement component will be used, the teacher should involve the child in selecting reinforcers. The student must then be trained in the use of the self-reinforcement procedure.

During the intervention phase of the procedure, Sugai and Lewis (1990) suggest using a matching strategy. This means that the student will be reinforced for accurate self-monitoring. Initially, prompts may be used to cue the child when to self-monitor and record (e.g., beeps on a recorder). The matching procedure, as well as the actual self-monitoring procedure, should be faded when the behavioral criteria are reached. Following the fading of the intervention, teachers should continue to collect data to ensure that behaviors continue at appropriate levels in all settings. If the target behaviors fall below the criteria, the procedure may have to be implemented again. Guidelines for increasing the effectiveness of self-management are included in Table 6–5.

Verbal Mediation–Based Interventions

In verbal mediation–based interventions, students are taught a generic set of statements that they say to themselves when confronted with various situations. Verbal mediation–based approaches include self-instructional training, problem-solving training, and anger-control training. These approaches assume that a student's problems are caused by deficient or maladaptive self-statements (Dush, Hirt, & Schroeder, 1989). These interventions, therefore, teach students to talk to themselves in appropriate and adaptive ways to control their own

Table 6–5   Guidelines for increasing the effectiveness of self-management

Suggestion	Description
External control	• Behaviors to be self-managed should first be brought under external control so the student associates the appropriate behavior with reinforcement. • Behavioral contracts for self-management can be used initially to provide structure.
Teaching and practicing	• Students must be taught the self-management procedure using direct instruction, modeling, guided and independent practice, and frequent feedback. • Students should have numerous opportunities to practice self-management with immediate feedback given.
Motivation	• Students must be motivated to participate because they actually run the procedure. • Student motivation can be increased by involving students in the procedure from the initial stages of the program. • Students and teachers should work together to set goals for the student when using a self-management system. • Student involvement and motivation can be increased by encouraging student involvement via recording and posting the student's behavioral performance.
Progress monitoring	• Teachers should monitor the procedure and provide "booster" sessions if necessary. If the procedure proves too difficult for the student to use, it should be modified • Student progress toward his or her goal should be monitored on an ongoing basis.
Reinforcement	• Reinforce students for successfully using self-management strategies.

behavior. In other words, the goal of these interventions is to help students think differently about situations before they act. In this section we review a number of interventions based on verbal mediation. We begin with an overview of the principles of self-instruction.

Self-Instructional Training   In self-instructional training, students are taught verbal prompts that will help them guide their nonverbal behavior. For example, when confronted with a mathematics assignment requiring long division, a student may be taught a series of strategy prompts to help him or her solve long division problems. Similarly, when confronted with a situation that may lead to anger, a student may be taught a series of prompts to keep himself or herself calm. When using self-instructional approaches, we assume that the student's problems are the result of deficits in his or her ability to respond in a nonimpulsive, reflective, and strategic manner. The verbal prompts that we teach are designed to initiate, direct, or redirect academic or social behaviors in ways that eliminate academic or behavioral problems (Meichenbaum, 1976). The ultimate goal of self-instructional training is for the student to internalize the verbal prompts so that he or she is able to use them in a variety of situations in everyday life (Maag, 1999; Robinson et al., 1999; Shapiro & Cole, 1994).

Theoretical Foundations and Research Basis.   Luria's (1961) developmental theory serves as the basis of self-instructional training. Luria proposed a three-stage developmental model of self-control. In the first stage, very young children's overt behavior is under the verbal

control of others in their environment (e.g., parents). In the second stage of development, children gain control over their behavior by using overt self-instructions. In the final stage, the overt self-instructions are internalized and children control their own behavior through the use of inner speech. Although most children follow a normal developmental sequence in which they acquire self-regulation in this manner, there are children for whom this does not occur or only partially occurs. These children are deficient in the ability to use *internal speech to control behavior*. Similarly, students who have not developed mediational skills will have difficulties in solving academic and social problems. Relying on the work of Luria, Meichenbaum and his colleagues investigated the relationship of impulsive behavior and deficits in self-instructional abilities.

Research on Self-Instructional Training and Problem Behavior.   Meichenbaum and Goodman (1971) investigated hyperactive and impulsive children. They found that many of the children in their studies had deficiencies in internal speech and verbal mediation abilities. Because of their verbal mediation problems, these children did not use self-talk to control their behavior. In a series of investigations, Meichenbaum and his colleagues (Meichenbaum, 1977; Meichenbaum & Asarnow, 1979; Meichenbaum & Goodman, 1971) used Luria's developmental sequence to teach these children to use self-instructions to control their behavior. In other words, the children were taught to talk to themselves as a method to learn to control their impulsive behaviors.

Meichenbaum and Goodman (1971) taught the impulsive children to ask themselves a series of questions when confronted with tasks that would typically lead to impulsive behavior. The four types of statements or questions the children were taught to say to themselves were:

1. *Problem definition:* For example, "What do I need to do?"

2. *Attention focusing and response guidance:* For example, "What should I do to solve this problem?"

3. *Self-reinforcement:* For example, "I did a good job."

4. *Self-evaluative, coping skills, and error correction:* For example, "I didn't do so well, but that's okay; I can start over again."

Meichenbaum and Goodman's (1971) study proved to be very successful. Based on their work with impulsive children, the researchers developed the following generic self-instructional training protocol.

Self-instructional training has also been used with aggressive children. Aggressive children tend to react to problem situations with anger, not taking time to "stop and think" or consider alternatives in responding to provocative situations.

Camp, Blom, Hebert, and Van Doorninck (1977) conducted some of the earliest studies examining the use of self-instructional training with aggressive children. The primary purpose of these research studies was to teach aggressive children to engage in coping self-instructions when responding to provocations. *Coping* refers to the child's ability to deal with perceived aversive events in a constructive rather than a negative manner (e.g., walking away from a perceived insult rather than starting a fight). Camp and colleagues developed the *Think Aloud* program to teach aggressive boys to use coping self-instructions. The self-instructional training methods were very similar to those developed by Meichenbaum and Goodman. The Think Aloud program attempted to train the aggressive boys in using self-instructions in a problem-solving sequence. The children were taught a generic format of instructional prompts to (a) identify a problem, (b) generate a solution, (c) monitor their use of the solution, and (d) evaluate their performance. The instructional prompts were questions the children would use when confronted with a provocative situation. The questions the children asked themselves were (a) What is my problem? (b) What is my plan? (c) Am I using my plan? and (d) How did I do? The researchers' goal was to teach these aggressive children to talk to themselves when confronted with situations that would often lead to aggression. The procedures were very successful in achieving the desired results.

Research on Self-Instructional Training and Academic Problems. Interventions using self-instructional procedures were originally devised to alter behavior problems in children. However, these procedures have also been extended to academic interventions, particularly in the area of academic strategy training (Lloyd, 1980). Self-instructional procedures, when applied to academic performance, are designed to help learners improve their academic problem-solving behaviors.

It has been theorized that in many instances, behavior problems actually stem from learning problems (Kauffman, 2005). Torgeson (1982) has stated that learning problems in children might be due to a failure to apply basic abilities efficiently by using effective task strategies. Students who manifest these failures have been referred to as inactive learners. To remediate these inefficient learning strategies, teachers should assess the cognitive task strategies needed for competence in a particular area. For example, if students are being taught long division, the teacher should teach the students the steps necessary to complete a long division problem. If these steps are taught to students, and they use them appropriately, they will become more active, self-regulating learners.

In designing CBI strategies, researchers conduct a cognitive task analysis of the processes involved and determine what processes academically successful students use. Researchers then develop a training procedure that will enhance the use of these processes (Wong, 1989). The purpose of these training procedures is to help learners improve their academic performance by using cognitive mediation strategies.

The basic procedures in many of these interventions are similar. The teacher models the processes while using self-instructions; students then follow the examples, first overtly, and then covertly (Meichenbaum, 1977). According to Meichenbaum, the teacher modeling provides a window on the thinking processes. Eventually by learning the strategies through modeling and self-instructions, the students take over their own learning.

A few examples will illustrate this process. Rinehart, Stahl, and Erickson (1986) taught summarization to grade school students using modeling and self-instructional training. The students were taught to produce summaries of reading material that included main and supporting ideas. The researchers found that the students trained in the procedure, when compared to students not trained, improved their recall of main ideas.

The teachers in this study used the self-instruction developed by Meichenbaum and Goodman (1971) to teach their students the verbal prompts that they should use when summarizing materials. There were three steps to this process:

Step 1: The teacher explained the purpose of summarization to the students.

Step 2: The teacher modeled writing summaries of sample paragraphs. The teacher used overt self-instructions while producing the summaries. The children did similar self-instructing. The teacher modeled monitoring of the summaries using the following instructions: "Have I found the overall idea that the paragraph or group of paragraphs is about? Have I found the most important information that tells more about the overall idea? Have I used information that is not directly about the overall idea? Have I used any information more than once?" Students then completed summaries while the teacher provided feedback.

Step 3: When the students become proficient in summarizing short paragraphs using this strategy, the teacher extends the summarization procedure to longer paragraphs.

Graham and Harris (1985) reported a self-instructional program to teach writing skills to students with learning disabilities. These researchers developed an instructional program based in part on Meichenbaum's (1977) self-instructional training. When teaching the writing program to students, the researchers assessed the student's level of performance, described the learning strategy, and modeled the strategy using self-instructions. When modeling the strategy the teacher used the self-instructions listed in Table 6-6.

After modeling the story, the teacher and student discussed the importance of using self-instructions. The student was asked to identify the self-instructions and to write examples of self-instructions in his or her own words. The self-control strategy training resulted in increases in student performance above baseline levels. The authors concluded that self-control strategy training improved and maintained composition skills among children with learning disabilities.

Teaching Self-Instruction. When using self-instructional training to teach academics or appropriate social behaviors, teachers do not need to adhere precisely to any formula. Instead they should follow the general procedure outlined by Meichenbaum and Goodman (1971) to teach the strategy. Whether teaching students to do long division or to respond in a nonimpulsive manner to provocations, a teacher should begin teaching these procedures by modeling the task and self-instructing while modeling. Through self-instructions students are taught to do a kind of thinking they could not, or would not, otherwise do (Meichenbaum & Asarnow, 1979). The students' internal dialogue, therefore, is used to facilitate performance.

The following guidelines based on Meichenbaum and Goodman's (1971) work when using self-instructions are useful when teaching students skills or strategies. First, the teacher should determine what the students need to know and what are their current performance levels. Second, the teacher must describe the strategy to be taught and model it to the students while using self-instructions. Third, the students should practice the strategy using self-instructions under the teacher's guidance. The self-instructions are spoken aloud. It is important at this stage that students have as many opportunities to practice as possible. Fourth, when students can successfully perform the strategy under controlled practice conditions using overt self-instructions, they should be allowed to independently practice using covert self-instructions. Students should be encouraged to monitor their use of strategies and to continue to use them. Explaining that the skills that are being taught will help decrease problem behaviors or increase performance in academic subjects can increase student motivation.

For example, if a teacher determines that a student cannot do long division, he or she should decide on a strategy for teaching the skill to the student. If the teacher decides to teach the student long division using the divide, multiply, subtract, bring down, check model (Burkell,

Table 6–6   Teaching students to use self-instructions to improve writing

Step	Self-Instruction
Step 1: Problem definition	What is it I have to do? I have to write a good story. Good stories make sense and use many action words.
Step 2: Planning	Look at the picture and write down good action words. Think of a good story. Write my story—make good sense and use good action words.
Step 3: Self-evaluation	Read my story and ask "Did I write a good story? Did I use action words?" Fix my story—can I use more good action words?
Step 4: Self-reinforcement	That was a great story.

Table 6–7   Protocol for teaching students to use self-instructions

Step	Description
Step 1: Cognitive modeling	The teacher models task performance while using self-instructions. This stage requires the teacher to model aloud. The child observes in this stage.
Step 2: Overt external guidance	The child performs the same task under the teacher's direction. The teacher says the self-instructions aloud while the student performs the task.
Step 3: Overt self-instructions	The child performs the same task, while saying the self-instructions aloud. The teacher observes and provides feedback.
Step 4: Faded self-instructions	The child performs the task while whispering the instructions to himself or herself. The teacher observes and provides feedback.
Step 5: Covert self-instructions	The child performs the task using covert self-instructions.

Schneider, & Pressley, 1990), he or she would explain the model and how it is used. The teacher would then model the strategy using self-instructions (first I divide, the next step is to multiply, etc.) while doing a long division problem to successful completion. The next step would involve having the child practice long division problems while the teacher gives the self-instructions. The student would then practice long division using self-instructions (still under the teacher's guidance) until he or she has mastered the strategy. When the teacher is satisfied that the self-instructional procedure has been mastered, the student should independently practice the skill using the self-instructional strategy covertly. Evaluation of the success of the self-instructional procedure must take place during training and on completion of training.

Whatever the purpose and content of training, the methods of training will be similar. There are five basic components that should be included. Table 6–7 provides a generic instructional protocol that can be used for self-instructional training in both behavior and academic strategies.

When using self-instructional training to teach students to be more reflective and deliberate in their responses to problems, the following guidelines may be helpful.

First, it is important that teachers model the self-instruction process. Teachers should perform the task and verbally self-instruct while the student is observing. It is important in modeling that teachers use the same self-instructional process as the child will be using.

Second, teachers must consider the ability of the student. It has been shown that if students need practice prior to performing a task or if they are unable to perform a task, self-instructions can actually interfere with their performance (Yell, Busch, et al., 2005). Self-instructions will not enable students to perform tasks that are not in their repertoires. Similarly students must be capable of understanding the statements to be used. Table 6–8 contains types of self-instructional statements.

Third, teachers should systematically fade their presence in the process. If self-instructional training is to be effective, the student must be able to self-instruct independently of the teacher. Fourth, teachers must systematically reinforce the student's accurate use of self-instructions and demonstrations of target behaviors.

Alternate Response Training   In alternate response training students are taught alternative or competing responses that interfere with opportunities for undesirable responses to be emitted (Wolery, et al., Sugai, 1988). If an alternative response already exists in a student's repertoire, it can be strengthened as he or she is taught to use the alternative behavior. When using alternate response training, a student must be able to self-monitor.

Table 6–8   Types of self-instructions

Type	Description
Problem definition instructions	The student defines the problem.
Problem approach instructions	The student verbalizes potential strategies to solve the problem.
Attention focusing instructions	The student focuses his or her attention on the problem by asking if he or she is using the strategy.
Coping statement instructions	The student uses statements to cope with errors and to encourage another attempt.
Self-reinforcement instructions	The student reinforces himself or herself for doing a good job.

Theoretical Foundation and Research Base. Robin, Schneider, and Dolnick (1976) developed an alternate response intervention called the turtle technique. The turtle technique is a procedure that was developed to teach aggressive students to manage their aggressive impulses. The procedure consists of teaching the students to pull their arms and legs close to their bodies, put their heads on their desks, and imagine that they are turtles withdrawing into their shells. The students were taught to do this when they perceived that a provocative situation was about to occur, they felt frustrated or angry, or a teacher or classmate called out "turtle." They were also taught a muscle relaxation procedure. Once students mastered this technique, they were taught to relax while doing the turtle. Eventually, the students learned to relax and imagine withdrawing from the situation rather than actually going into the turtle position. Robin and colleagues (1976) found that students who had been taught the procedure behaved less aggressively. Morgan and Jenson (1988) stated that the turtle technique and other similar approaches are worthy of consideration in selecting interventions.

Knapczyk (1988) reduced aggressive behaviors in regular and special class settings by teaching alternative social response training. Participants in the study were two male junior high school students in special education programs. Both had been referred because of aggressive behavior. The treatment involved training the students in social skills that could be used as alternatives to the aggressive behavior (see Chapter 7). The students learned alternate responses through modeling and rehearsal. Videotapes were prepared and shown to the students that provided examples of events that often led to aggressive behavior. The tapes had two male students (of high social status in the school) demonstrating alternative responses to the aggression. One of the actors played the part of the participant. In response to a particular event the student actor would first simulate aggressive behaviors. The student would then demonstrate an acceptable alternative response rather than the aggressive response. The other student actor represented the reactions of peers. The teacher and participant viewed the videotapes together. Following a discussion the participant was asked to demonstrate the appropriate behavior and provide additional alternatives. Results indicated that the treatments reduced the level of aggressive behaviors and led to an increase in peer-initiated interactions.

Teaching Alternate Responses. When teaching students to use alternate responses to anger or other maladaptive behaviors, three important factors must be addressed. First, the students must be able to monitor their behavior. Specifically they must be able to recognize when the behavior that the teacher hopes to eliminate is occurring. For example, students must recognize when they are becoming angry (e.g., stomach muscles tighten, fists clench). Teaching self-monitoring, therefore, is an essential prerequisite to alternate response training. Second, after the students have become adept at self-monitoring, they are taught a specific technique that will compete with the maladaptive behavior. It is important that these procedures are directly taught to students, that the teacher models the specific technique, and that students are given many opportunities to practice the procedure. When alternate responses are used appropriately, the teacher must reinforce the students. Table 6–9 provides a generic instructional protocol for teaching students to use alternate responses.

Problem-Solving Training Students are faced with conflicts, choices, and problems every day. Successful problem solving is necessary for effective coping and independence. The ability to confront and solve problems

Table 6–9   Protocol for teaching alternate responses

Step	Description
Step 1: Ensure that the student can self-monitor	Teach the student to recognize the target behavior through self-monitoring. Students must be able to recognize a target behavior before they can substitute an alternative response to that behavior.
Step 2: Select a target behavior	
Step 3: Provide a rationale for using an alternate response	Teach the student why it is important that he or she learn to monitor maladaptive behavior and use alternate responses.
Step 4: Choose an alternate response	
Step 5: Teach the alternate response	Teach the student how and when to use the alternate response. Break down the alternate response into its component steps (i.e., task analysis). Teach and model each step.
Step 6: Monitor the target behavior and evaluate student progress	Monitor the target behavior. Additionally, the student and the teacher should have frequent evaluation meetings so that the teacher can provide feedback and monitor progress.
Step 7: Reinforce the student	Reinforce students when they successfully achieve their target goal.

successfully is an important factor in social and emotional adjustment. The inability to solve problems in an effective manner can lead to future social and emotional difficulties. Researchers have attempted to remediate difficulties in problem solving through formal training. The training represents a form of self-instruction to teach procedures for systematically approaching, evaluating, and solving interpersonal problems (Braswell & Kendall, 1988). Training in problem solving has been effective in reducing behavior problems and aggression, controlling impulsivity, and increasing appropriate social interaction (Harris, 1982).

Theoretical Foundation and Research Base. Goldstein (1999) stated that problem solving typically involves a stepwise sequence of problem definition, identification of alternative solutions, choice of an optimal solution, implementation of the solution, and evaluation of the solution's effectiveness. Polsgrove and Smith (2004) presented five steps that could be used to teach students to problem solve:

> **Step 1:** *Recognizing that a problem exists.* Help the student learn to recognize problems and to realize that one can deal with problems in appropriate ways.
>
> **Step 2:** *Defining the problem in terms of goals.* Clearly define the problem and any factors related to it.
>
> **Step 3:** *Generating alternative solutions.* The teacher and student should think of as many solutions to a problem as possible.
>
> **Step 4:** *Evaluating solutions.* The teacher and student identify potential results or outcomes of the possible solutions.
>
> **Step 5:** *Implementing the plan.* The teacher and student should consider all alternatives generated in

the previous steps and devise a plan for implementing the chosen alternative.

> **Step 6:** *Monitoring the solution.* Implement the plan and monitor the results. If the problem is not solved, the teacher and student should start over at step 1.

The seminal work in problem solving was done by Spivak, Shure, and colleagues in the mid- to late 1970s. The training program developed by Spivak and Shure (1974) was called interpersonal cognitive problem solving (ICPS). The program was designed to teach students *how* to think, not *what* to think (Goldstein, 1999). Spivak and Shure believed that many teachers did not effectively teach problem solving. For example, when dealing with a student who hits another student, teachers might typically respond with one of the following actions: (a) they might demand that the behavior stop ("Stop because I said so"); (b) they might explain why an action is inappropriate ("You might hurt Johnny"); (c) they might try to help the student understand the effect of the situation ("That hurts Johnny's feelings"); and (4) they might isolate the student ("Go to time-out until you are ready to act appropriately"). Spivak and Shure believed that these responses have serious limitations if a teacher's goal was to help students develop effective ways of handling personal and interpersonal problems because the teacher did the thinking for the student. Therefore, in ICPS children were taught a problem-solving process rather than solutions to problems. The core of Spivak and Shure's program was six specific problem-solving skills that were taught to students. The goal of the ICPS program was to train students to be competent in six skill areas listed in Table 6–10.

Siegel and Spivak (1973) also developed an ICPS training program for older adolescents and adults. The program consisted of four problem-solving steps: (1)

Table 6–10   Problem-solving strategies

Strategy	Definition
Alternative solution thinking	The ability to generate different options or potential solutions to a problem was central to effective problem solving.
Consequential thinking	The ability to consider consequences that a behavior might lead to; this goes beyond the consideration of alternatives to the consideration of the consequences of potential solutions.
Causal thinking	The ability to relate one event to another over time with regard to why a particular event happened or will happen.
Interpersonal sensitivity	The ability to perceive that an interpersonal problem exists.
Means-ends thinking	The step-by-step planning done in order to reach a given goal. Means-ends thinking involves insight, forethought, and the ability to consider alternative goals.
Perspective taking	The ability of the individual to recognize and take into account the fact that different people have different motives and may take different actions.

recognition of the problem, (2) definition of the problem, (3) alternative ways of solving the problem, and (4) deciding which solution is the best way to solve the problem.

Goldstein (1999), drawing on the work done by Spivak and Shure, developed a problem-solving training program as part of the *Prepare Curriculum*. The Prepare Curriculum is a series of courses designed to teach adolescents and younger children prosocial competencies. It is specifically designed for students who exhibit prosocial deficiencies that fall toward either end of a continuum defined at one extreme by chronic aggressiveness, antisocial behavior, and juvenile delinquency, and at the other extreme by chronic withdrawal, asocial behavior, and social isolation. The problem-solving course is taught to groups of students over an 8-week period. Group structure is provided by a set of rules and procedures explained at the beginning of a session. During each session, a poster is displayed showing the problem-solving process being covered during that session. The program also uses a "problem log" that students fill out. The logs are intended to help students determine what their problem situations are, and to assist them to begin thinking about ways of handling the problems. An example of a problem diary similar to Goldstein's problem log is provided in Figure 6–6.

Problem logs are also used in role-plays. Skills taught in the program include:

Stop and think. Students in the program are taught that when a problem is encountered they must stop and think or they might decide too quickly. They are to use this time to think of alternate ways to handle the problem.

FIGURE 6-6

Problem diary

Problem Diary

What was the problem? Describe the problem.

What did you do to solve the problem?

Did your choice solve the problem?

How would you rate your solution? (circle)

Poor   Fair   Good   Great

How will you handle this problem if it happens again?

Problem identification. Once the students realize a problem exists and have stopped to think, they have to state the problem clearly and specifically.

Gathering information from their own perspective. Students have to decide how they see a problem and gather information about the problem before acting. If all the information is not available, trainees are taught to ask for it.

Gathering information from others' perspectives. Students learn the necessity of looking at situations from other people's points of view.

Alternatives. Students are taught that to make a good choice in any situation requires more than one way of acting.

Evaluating consequences and outcomes. Once trainees are taught to consider a number of alternatives, they are told they must consider the consequences of each. Once a decision is made it must be evaluated.

In a review of research on interpersonal problem-solving training, Coleman, Wheeler, and Webber (1993) found that although researchers were generally successful in demonstrating cognitive gains as a result of the training, they were far less successful in demonstrating generalization. The authors stated that the generalization problems called into question the basic premise of problem solving, which is that students will rely on the trained skills when faced with real-life problems. Based on their review, the authors offered recommendations for teachers in using problem-solving training. Their recommendations included (a) making efforts to individualize training by including only those students who demonstrate problem-solving deficits, (b) assessing the quality and quantity of alternative solutions that students generate as a result of the training, (c) pairing problem-solving training with social skills training and other behavioral interventions to remediate problem-solving deficits, and (d) evaluating the success of the program by choosing appropriate outcome measures such as problem-solving tasks, behavior ratings, and behavior observations.

Teaching Problem Solving. The work of D'Zurilla and Goldfried (1971), Spivak and Shure (1974), and Goldstein (1999) present useful models that teachers can use to teach problem solving to students. The following guidelines based on the work of these researchers should be followed when using CBIs to teach students problem-solving skills.

First, teachers should direct instruction to teach the fundamental concepts of problem solving. Teachers cannot assume the students will pick up these important skills by merely observing others. Important concepts should be presented using lecture, discussion, and examples and nonexamples. When appropriate, role-playing situations involving problem solving should be part of instruction. Additionally, students should be reinforced for appropriate participation in classroom activities.

Second, whenever possible, problem situations should be taken from students' real-life experiences. In this way the instruction is much more likely to be socially valid. This means that the situations will be more meaningful for the students because they are congruent with their social setting and age. A problem diary can be used as a springboard to class discussions (see Figure 6-6). Having students brainstorm during group discussions can also be used to generate lists of potential problems.

Third, problem-solving training should include the following components: (a) recognizing the problem, (b) defining the problem and the goal, (c) generating alternative solutions, (d) evaluating the solutions, and (e) making a plan to solve the problem. Training can be done individually or during group discussions. Teachers should also discuss the relevance of problem-solving training for students' lives.

Fourth, teachers should provide students with numerous opportunities to practice problem solving. This should be done both in and outside the classroom (e.g., home setting). Finally, teachers should be a model of effective problem solving. When problems arise, they must be able to deal with them in an effective manner and share with students their methods of arriving at solutions. Additionally, if teachers observe students using effective problem solving strategies outside the classroom, they should be reinforced. Table 6–11 provides a generic instructional protocol for teaching students to use problem-solving strategies.

Anger-Control Training In anger-control training, students are taught to inhibit or control anger and aggressive behavior through self-instructions. Three well-known anger-control training procedures are those developed by Novaco (1975), Feindler and colleagues (Feindler & Fremouw, 1983; Feindler, Marriott, & Iwata, 1984), and Goldstein (1999). These programs train children to respond to internal or external provocations with anger-control procedures rather than anger and aggression.

Theoretical Foundation and Research Base. Novaco (1979) defined anger arousal as an affective stress reaction. He stated that

–anger arousal is a response to perceived environmental demands—most commonly, aversive psychosocial events. Anger arousal results from particular appraisal of aversive events. External circumstances provoke anger only as mediated by their meaning to the individual. (pp. 252-253)

Table 6–11   Protocol for teaching problem-solving strategies

Step	Description
Step 1: Explain the importance of problem-solving training	The teacher tells students why it is important that they learn to solve problems. Students must understand why problem solving is an important skill for them to learn and commit to trying their best.
Step 2: Teach the students the steps of effective problem solving	The teacher describes the steps of the problem-solving process (e.g., defining the problem, generating alternatives, deciding on a course of action, implementing the potential solution, monitoring the results).
Step 3: Model problem solving	The teacher describes the situation in which the problem-solving strategies will be used, and the specifics of these strategies. The teacher then demonstrates the procedure with a co-trainer or another student.
Step 4: Role-play examples of problem solving	The participants take part in role-plays in which they demonstrate problem solving. Prepared situations or real-life examples can be used. All students should take part in the role-plays. Teachers give feedback following role-plays.
Step 5: Give homework	The students are assigned to practice the procedure in real-life situations. Personal anger diaries can be used in this phase.
Step 6: Provide feedback and reinforcement	The teacher gives the student feedback on his or her use of the problem-solving procedure. Students should be reinforced for using problem solving.

Novaco (1979) noted the importance of the individual's appraisal of events. Because Novaco believed that anger was created, influenced, and maintained by self-statements, he designed a program based on Meichenbaum's self-instructional training. The purpose of the training was to develop an individual's ability to respond appropriately to stressful events. The goals of the program were to (a) prevent maladaptive anger from occurring, (b) enable the individual to regulate arousal when provocation occurred, and (c) provide the person with the skills to manage the provocation.

Anger-control intervention consisted of three stages: (1) cognitive preparation, (2) skill acquisition, and (3) application training. In the cognitive preparation phase, trainees were educated about anger arousal and its determinants, the identification of circumstances that trigger anger, the positive and negative functions of anger, and anger-control techniques as coping strategies. In the skill acquisition phase, trainees learned cognitive and behavioral coping skills. Trainees were taught to recognize anger and to use alternative coping strategies. The self-instructional element of training was emphasized in this phase. In the final phase, application training, the trainee practiced the skills taught through role-playing and homework assignments.

The self-instructional component of this intervention consisted of self-statements in the four stages of the provocation sequence: (1) preparation for provocation, (2) impact and confrontation, (3) coping with arousal, and (4) reflecting on the provocation. Examples of self-instructions in an anger-control training program are listed in Table 6-12.

In the late 1970s and early 1980s, Feindler and colleagues researched and refined the techniques of anger-control training. In a series of investigations, support was provided for the cognitive preparation and skill acquisition phases and self-instructional training developed by Novaco. The investigations refined the three processes of Novaco's training (i.e., cognitive preparation, skill acquisition, and application training) to include five sequences to be taught to students:

1. *Cues:* The physical signals of anger arousal.
2. *Triggers:* The events and internal appraisals of those events that serve as provocations.
3. *Reminders:* Novaco's self-instructional statements that were used to reduce anger arousal.
4. *Reducers:* Techniques such as deep breathing and pleasant imagery that could be used along with reminders to reduce anger arousal.
5. *Self-evaluation:* The opportunity to self-reinforce or self-correct.

Goldstein and Glick (1987) added to the work of Meichenbaum, Novaco, and Feindler in developing an anger-control training program. The goals of anger-control training were to teach children and adolescents to understand what caused them to become angry and aggressive and to master anger reduction techniques. According to Goldstein (1999):

Many youngsters believe that in many situations they have no choice: The only way for them to respond is with aggression. Although they may perceive situations in this way, it is the goal of Anger Control Training to give them the skills necessary to

Table 6–12   Examples of self-instructions for an anger-control training program

Step	Description
Preparing for provocation	• This could be a rough situation, but I know how to handle it. I can work out a plan to deal with this problem. • Easy does it, stick to the issues, and don't take it personally. • There won't be any need for an argument. I know what to do.
Impact and confrontation	• As long as I keep my cool, I'm in control of the situation. • I don't need to prove myself. • Don't make more out of this than I have to. • There is no point in getting mad. Think of what I have to do. • Look for positives and don't jump to conclusions.
Coping with arousal	• My muscles are getting tight. Relax and slow things down. • Time to take a deep breath. • He probably wants me to get angry, but I'm going to deal with it constructively.
Subsequent reflection— conflict unresolved	• Forget about the aggravation. Thinking about it only makes me upset. Try to shake it off. • Remember relaxation. It's a lot better than anger. • Don't take it personally. It's probably not as serious as I think.
Subsequent reflection— conflict resolved	• I handled that one pretty well. That's doing a good job. • I could have gotten more upset than it was worth. • My pride can get me into trouble, but I'm doing better at this all the time. • I actually got through that without getting angry.

make a choice. By learning what causes them to be angry and by learning to use a series of anger reduction techniques, participating trainees will become more able to stop their almost "automatic" aggressive responses long enough to consider constructive alternatives. (p. 256)

Anger-control training consists of modeling, role-playing, and performance feedback. Group leaders describe and model the anger-control techniques and conflict situations in which they may be used. The students take part in role-plays in which they practice the just-modeled techniques. Role-plays are of actual provocative encounters provided by the students, with each session followed by a brief performance feedback period. In this phase the group leaders point out to the students involved in the role-play how well they used the technique. Group leaders also provide reinforcement following role-plays.

A unique aspect of the program used in the role-play situations is the "hassle log." The hassle log is a structured questionnaire that students fill out on actual provocative encounters. The trainees have to answer questions concerning where they were when the hassle occurred, what happened, who else was involved, what the trainees did, how they handled themselves, and how angry they were. The log is constructed so that even young children can fill it out; written responses are not required and children simply check off options on the form. The trainees complete a form for each provocative encounter, whether they handle it in an appropriate manner or not. The advantages of the hassle log are that it provides accurate pictures of actual provocative encounters that occur, it helps trainees learn about what makes them angry and how they handle themselves, and it provides role-playing material. An example of a similar anger diary is shown in Figure 6–7.

During the 10-week training period, the group leaders also teach (1) the A-B-Cs of aggressive behavior (A—What led up to the behavior? B—What did you do? C—What were the consequences?); (2) how to identify cues and triggers; (3) the use of reminders and anger reducers; (4) the importance of thinking ahead (the consequences of anger); and (5) the nature of the angry behavior cycle (identifying anger-provoking behavior and changing it).

A study by Etscheidt (1991) examined the effectiveness of the anger-control training program developed by Lochman, Nelson, and Sims (1981) in reducing aggressive behavior and increasing self-control in 30 adolescents with behavioral disorders. In the program students were taught to use a five-step sequential strategy in problem situations. The steps were as follows:

Step 1: Motor cue/impulse delay—stop and think before you act, cue yourself.

Step 2: Problem definition—say exactly what the problem is.

Step 3: Generation of alternatives—think of as many solutions as you can.

Step 4: Consideration of consequences—think ahead to what might happen.

Step 5: Implementation—when you have a solution, try it!

FIGURE 6–7

Anger diary

> **Anger Diary**
>
> Describe the problem that led to your anger.
>
>
>
> What did you do?
>
>
>
> Did your anger solve the problem?
>
>
>
> How would you rate your anger control? (circle)
>
> **Poor   Fair   Good   Great**
>
>
>
> How will you handle your anger next time?

Results indicated that students participating in the training had significantly fewer aggressive behaviors and were rated as having greater self-control than the control group. Although incentives were offered, they did not seem to enhance the effectiveness of the training program. The author concluded that the program did have a positive effect on the behavior of students, and that maintenance and generalization of behavior change should be a component of any anger-control training program.

Smith, Siegel, O'Conner, and Thomas (1994) investigated the effectiveness of an anger-control training program in reducing the angry and aggressive behaviors of students with behavior problems. Students were taught a cognitive behavioral strategy called ZIPPER. ZIPPER is a mnemonic for **Z**ip your mouth, **I**dentify the problem, **P**ause, **P**ut yourself in charge, **E**xplore choices, **R**eset. The strategy was directly taught to students, modeled,

role-played, and rehearsed. Additionally, the instructors gained the students' commitment to using the strategy outside the training. Results indicated that the students were able to learn the strategy and that the intervention resulted in a decreased level of the targeted behaviors. Data on maintenance indicated that the students were able to maintain the decreased levels of anger and aggression over time. The students enjoyed learning the strategy, and the teacher and paraprofessional in the classroom were very satisfied with the procedure. There was also some indication of generalization; a lunchroom monitor noted that the trained students seemed less angry and aggressive and were able to get along with other students. Additional investigations have indicated that CBIs offer efficacy for teaching students strategies to decrease hyperactivity/impulsivity and disruption/aggression, as well as to strengthen prosocial behavior (see Conduct

Problems Prevention Research Group [CPPRG], 1999a, 1999b; Robinson, Smith, & Miller, 2002)

Teaching Anger Control. Students with problem behavior often have difficulty controlling their anger. Teaching students to control anger will be extremely valuable to their long-term adjustment. The work of Novaco (1975), Feindler et al. (1984), and Goldstein (1999) present important models teachers can use to teach anger control to students. The following guidelines based on the work of these researchers should be followed when using cognitive behavior modification to teach students anger-control skills.

First, the teacher should direct instruction to teach the fundamental concepts of anger control. Important concepts in controlling anger should be presented using lecture, discussion, and role-playing situations. Additionally, students should be reinforced for appropriate participation in classroom activities.

Second, whenever possible, real-life situations involving students' anger should be taken from their experiences, making the instruction more socially valid. In other words, the situations will be more meaningful for the students because they are congruent with their social setting and age. An anger diary can be used to generate individual or class discussions (see Figure 6–7).

Third, anger-control training should include the following components: (a) recognizing anger (e.g., cues and triggers); (b) coping with anger (e.g., using reminders and reducers); (c) generating alternative solutions to anger; and (d) self-evaluating. This can be done individually or during group discussions. Teachers should also discuss the relevance of anger control for students' lives.

Fourth, teachers should provide students with numerous opportunities to discuss anger control.

Because anger control should be practiced in both school and home settings, students' parents or guardians should be aware of and participate in the anger-control program. Finally, teachers must model effective anger control. When a problem arises that could lead to an angry confrontation, manage the situation in an effective manner. Moreover, teachers should share their methods of arriving at a solution with the students. Additionally, if they observe students using effective anger-control strategies outside the classroom, they should reinforce and provide feedback for the appropriate behavior. Table 6–13 provides a generic instructional protocol for teaching students to use anger-control strategies.

Rational Emotive Behavior Therapy Zionts (1998) described rational emotive behavior therapy (REBT) as a cognitive behavioral intervention designed to help both students and teachers manage students' problem behavior. Zionts further noted that REBT was a combination of cognitive, emotive, and behavioral theory and methodology. Maag (2004) referred to REBT as a cognitive restructuring procedure, which he defined as an intervention that focuses on identifying and altering students' irrational beliefs and negative self-statements. According to Gonzales et al., (2004), REBT is one of a family of cognitive therapies under the umbrella of cognitive behavioral therapies. Furthermore, Gonzales and colleagues define REBT as an intervention in which children and adolescents use cognitive mediational strategies as a means of guiding their behavior.

Theoretical Foundation and Research Base. Albert Ellis introduced rational emotive therapy (RET) in 1955 as a comprehensive approach to psychological treatment. Ellis emphasized not only the emotional and

Table 6–13 Protocol for teaching anger control

Step	Description
Step 1: Explain the importance of anger-control training	The teacher tells students why it is important that they learn to monitor and control their anger. Students must understand why anger control is an important skill for them to learn and make a commitment to trying their best.
Step 2: Tell students what anger-control procedure will be taught	The teacher tells the students which anger-control technique or chain of techniques will be taught.
Step 3: Model the procedure	The teacher describes the situation in which the anger-control technique will be used, and the specifics of the technique. The teacher then demonstrates the procedure with a cotrainer or another student.
Step 4: Role-play examples of the procedure	The participants take part in role-plays in which they demonstrate the anger-control procedure. Prepared situations or real-life examples can be used. All students should take part in the role-plays.
Step 5: Provide feedback	The teacher provides feedback to students after each role-play is completed.
Step 6: Give homework	The students are assigned to practice the procedure in real-life situations. Personal anger diaries can be used in this phase.

behavioral aspects of human disturbance, but also stressed the "thinking" or cognitive component. According to Ellis, psychological problems arise from individuals' misperceptions and mistaken cognitions about what they perceive to be happening. Based on past experiences and "habitually dysfunctional behavior patterns," people either underreact or overreact to what should be normal and unusual stimuli (Ellis, 1994). In 1993, the term *behavioral* was added to *rational emotive therapy* to stress the importance of this procedure to modify and change behavior (Gonzales et al., 2004). The basic premise of REBT is that emotional and behavioral disturbances arise from faulty thinking about events rather than the events themselves.

Because of the increasing use of REBT in programs for students with EBD, a special issue of *Beyond Behavior*, edited by Paul Zionts (1998), was specifically devoted to REBT and students with problem behaviors. This special issue is available at the Council for Children with Behavioral Disorders Web site (http://www.CCBD.net).

REBT teaches students how to better understand their emotions and how to act "rationally" in situations that may often lead to problem behavior. By focusing on the present attitudes, feelings, and beliefs that can interfere with everyday functioning, REBT teaches individuals to recognize and change aspects of their thinking that are not sensible, accurate, or useful. It is sometimes described by educators as "remedial emotional education" because it focuses on methodologies designed to allow students to help themselves rather than relying solely on counselors or psychologists for personal problem solving (Zionts, 1998). According to Zionts, REBT is a practical, action-oriented approach that emphasizes proactive problem-solving strategies to teach people how to manage their feelings and emotions.

Rational emotive behavior therapy focuses on cognitive and affective domains and can be used as a curriculum to teach problem solving. It can also be an integral part of a preventive mental health curriculum (Zionts, 1998). In the classroom, REBT is typically implemented in small groups where peers help each other work through misperceptions. The concepts of REBT are reinforced through group participation and through the process of observing and helping a peer deal with a personal problem (Zionts, 1998). As a mental health curriculum, REBT concepts are taught through structured lessons and activities and may be integrated with health, language arts, or a vocational/transition class.

Principles of REBT. The following major principles underlie REBT.

Principle 1: Students are the sum total of their experiences including cultural, environmental, and family influences (Zionts, 1998). Students are taught through REBT that it is their interpretation of the present however, that is most important to their emotional health and well-being. Personal problems are the result of perceptions that have evolved from the thinking, feeling, and behaving that individuals have experienced throughout their lives.

Principle 2: Students are responsible for their own emotions and actions. A personal problem is defined as a negative emotional reaction to a negative event. The problem is not the event itself but rather how the individual *perceives* the event. Individuals cannot control events, but they can manage their perceptions of these events, and consequently how perceptions contribute to their feelings and emotions and, ultimately, their actions.

Principle 3: Harmful emotions and dysfunctional behaviors are the result of irrational thinking and cognitive distortions. Many emotional problems are due to errors in inferences. In most cases, these errors are the result of exaggerations (Zionts, 1998). For example, instead of looking at a tragic event as simply that—a tragic event—a student might infer that he or she has led a tragic life. In other words, a simple problem becomes a big problem that nobody can fix and one that has destroyed a life. It is important to note, however, that exaggeration errors are often exaggerations of correct thinking. It is appropriate to feel angry or hurt when being accused unjustly; it is an exaggeration, however, when anger or hurt leads to violent acts. REBT proposes that when negative emotions become too intense, an individual's ability to manage his or her life begins to deteriorate. REBT methods focus on restoring emotional balance and thinking more realistically about personal problems, other people, and the world.

Principle 4: Students have the capacity to recognize their irrational beliefs and change their thinking, and thus their behavior. Harmful emotions and dysfunctional behaviors are products of irrational thinking. The cause of irrational thinking is a set of rigid and absolute beliefs that students hold. Proponents of REBT maintain, however, that individuals can be taught to think rationally. Changes in thought processes result in different philosophies about life events. Through REBT, students develop more realistic views about themselves and others, leading to a deeper satisfaction in life.

Cognitive Distortions and Irrational Beliefs. Proponents of REBT assume that cognitive distortions are at the root of most emotional disturbances. Cognitive distortions result in absolute judgments about life events and people

(Newcomer, 1993). Absolute judgments are dominated by "should" and "must" beliefs and strongly influence and ultimately sustain emotional disturbance. Core "shoulds" and "musts" can be divided into three types:

1. Demands on self: "I must do well." "I should be happier."

2. Demands on others: "You must love me." "Everyone should like me."

3. Demands on situations: "Life must be fair always." "This should not happen to me."

Unrealistic demands on self typically result in anxiety, depression, and sometimes overassertiveness. When students have irrational or unrealistic expectations of others, they may feel resentment, hostility, and/or anger, and may also exhibit violent behaviors. Students who have irrational expectations in social situations may experience hopelessness, may procrastinate, and may have substance abuse problems.

Cognitive distortions common among students with EBD include:

- *Awfulizing*—"This event is catastrophic. My life has been (or will be) destroyed by this event."

- *Minimizing accomplishments*—"My successes are trivial and must be due to luck."

- *Maximizing mistakes*—"My mistakes are awful and always my fault."

- *Externalizing*—"My mistakes are never my fault."

- *Always and never*—"Life is always bad and will never be good again."

- *Lovable versus Unlovable*—"If I am not loved completely, then I am unlovable."

- *Overgeneralizing*—"I failed so I must be just like all the other losers in the world."

- *Focusing on the negative*—"Because something goes wrong, nothing good ever happens–or ever will happen to me."

- *Jumping to conclusions*—"Other people hate me; other people think I'm stupid; other people think everything is my fault."

- *Predicting the future*—"When people really get to know me, they will hate me for what I am."

- *Perfectionism*—"I should be able to do this perfectly. If I can't, I am totally incompetent."

- *Personalizing*—"People are talking about me and laughing at me behind my back. Nobody really likes me."

Cognitive distortions lead to certain core irrational ideas that are at the root of most behavioral and emotional disturbance (Ellis, 1994). Ellis has clinically observed and described 12 irrational beliefs that he believes sustain emotional problems. They are:

- *The idea that it is a dire necessity to be loved by significant others for almost everything they do*—instead of their concentrating on their own self-respect, on winning approval for practical purposes, and on loving rather than on being loved.

- *The idea that certain acts are awful or wicked, and that people who perform such acts should be severely damned*—instead of the idea that certain acts are self-defeating or antisocial, and that people who perform such acts are behaving stupidly, ignorantly, or neurotically, and would be better helped to change. People's poor behaviors do not make them rotten individuals.

- *The idea that it is horrible when things are not the way we like them to be*—instead of the idea that it is too bad, that we would better try to change or control bad conditions so that they become more satisfactory, and, if that is not possible, we had better temporarily accept and gracefully lump their existence.

- *The idea that human misery is invariably externally caused and is forced on us by outside people and events*—instead of the idea that neurosis is largely caused by the view that we take of unfortunate conditions.

- *The idea that if something is or may be dangerous or fearsome we should be terribly upset and endlessly obsess about it*—instead of the idea that one would better frankly face it and render it non-dangerous and, when that is not possible, accept the inevitable.

- *The idea that it is easier to avoid than to face life difficulties and self-responsibilities*—instead of the idea that the so-called easy way is usually much harder in the long run.

- *The idea that we absolutely need something other or stronger or greater than ourselves on which to rely*—instead of the idea that it is better to take the risk of thinking and acting less dependently.

- *The idea that we should be thoroughly competent, intelligent, and achieving in all possible respects*—instead of the idea that we would do better to accept ourselves as quite imperfect creatures, who have general human limitations and specific fallibilities.

- *The idea that because something once strongly affected our life, it should indefinitely affect it*—instead of the idea that we can learn from our past experiences but not be overly attached to or prejudiced by them.

- *The idea that we must have certain and perfect control over things*—instead of the idea that the world is full of probability and chance and that we can still enjoy life despite this.

- *The idea that human happiness can be achieved by inertia and inaction*—instead of the idea that we tend to be happiest when we are vitally absorbed in creative pursuits, or when we are devoting ourselves to people or projects outside ourselves.

- *The idea that we have virtually no control over our emotions and that we cannot help feeling disturbed about things*—instead of the idea that we have real control over our destructive emotions if we choose to work at changing the hypotheses which we often employ to create them." (pp. 2–3).

According to Zionts (1998), these 12 irrational beliefs can be generalized to the following four basic categories:

- "I need" occurs when students interpret events or actions as critical to their survival. Students who think in exaggerated terms "must" have their needs met and think they "need" everything. For example, a student "needs to have a new car so my friends will like me" or "must have a date for Saturday night so people won't think I am a loser." In reality, the world will not come to an end if the student does not get a new car or does not have a date for Saturday night. Life threatening consequences will not occur if an exaggerated need is not met. Students who exaggerate their needs often feel uncontrolled anger or frustration when their needs are not met. In REBT, "I prefer" is emphasized over "I need" statements, and "I would like" is practiced instead of "I have to."

- "It's awful" occurs when students interpret a problematic event or action as being catastrophic. "This is the worst thing that has ever happened to me" or "I would rather die than face this" are common "it's awful" statements. Although the event and resulting consequences may indeed be uncomfortable, they are not catastrophic. REBT teaches that when bad things do happen, they are a part of life and students must deal with them and move on. Students are taught to interpret problematic events in a rational way and given problem-solving strategies for dealing with their problems.

- "I am a . . ." or "You are a . . ." is the act of judging oneself or others in absolute terms. "I must be stupid because I can't read" or "He's a fool for acting that way" are examples of absolute judgments. Students who make absolute judgments about themselves or others do not practice the belief that all people are fallible. Instead, they assign pejorative labels that make it easy to be upset with themselves or the individual(s) they are judging. Rational emotive behavior therapy promotes self-acceptance and acceptance of others, and the belief that behaviors are not cause for automatic assumption or evaluation of an individual's worth.

- "I can't stand it" occurs when a student believes he or she cannot tolerate frustration and must have immediate gratification. "I'd rather stay home than go to school" and

"This shouldn't be so hard. I quit" are common "I can't stand it" beliefs. These types of exaggerations often result in avoidance, procrastination, and whining about current and upcoming events. REBT teaches students that performing unpleasant tasks can be tolerated and completed without life-threatening consequences.

Waters (1982) identified the following irrational beliefs as common to children with emotional disturbance:

1. It's awful if others don't like me.
2. I'm bad if I make a mistake
3. Everything should go my way; I should always get what I want.
4. Things should come easily to me.
5. The world should be fair; bad people must be punished.
6. I shouldn't show my feelings.
7. Adults should be perfect.
8. There's only one right answer.
9. I must win.
10. I shouldn't have to wait for anything (p. 3).

Waters also stated that irrational beliefs common to adolescents include:

1. It would be awful if peers didn't like me. It would be awful to be a social loser.
2. I shouldn't make mistakes, especially social mistakes.
3. It's my parents' fault I am so miserable.
4. I can't help it, that's just the way I am, and I guess I'll always be that way.
5. The world should be fair.
6. It's awful when things don't go my way.
7. It's better to avoid challenges than to risk failure.
8. I can't stand being criticized.
9. Others should always be responsible (p. 3).

Rational emotive behavior theorists have several explanations for how emotional disturbance is maintained. Ellis (1973) describes psychological problems in A-B-C terms: activating events, beliefs, and consequences. Individuals are emotionally disturbed when they do not understand the connection between their irrational beliefs/emotions (B) and consequences (C). Rather, they believe the activating events/situations (A) are the cause of the consequences incurred. For example, Natasha attributes her intense frustration to her teacher's unrealistic demands or the extreme difficulty of the task. She does not see the connection between her frustration and her belief that she should be able to do the work perfectly, or her need for total acceptance by her teacher.

According to Newcomer (1993), another reason that emotional problems are perpetuated is that "even when an individual recognizes the existence of irrational beliefs, she searches for the antecedents of the beliefs rather than concentrating on changing them" (p. 245). REBT focuses on present events rather than searching for underlying causal factors that may be hidden in the unconscious mind. Individuals are encouraged to use their energy to solve present-day problems, and strategies for exploring the unconscious mind are considered counterproductive to emotional health.

A third explanation has to do with the "I can't stand it" exaggeration. Individuals may not be willing to work hard enough to recognize and counter their irrational beliefs. Their low tolerance for frustration causes them to give up before they have learned the processes necessary to dispute irrational thoughts.

Research on REBT. The literature contains descriptions of the use of REBT with students with a number of emotional and behavioral problems. Gonzales and colleagues (Gonzales et al., 2004) conducted a meta-analysis of the research involving REBT when the procedures were used with children and adolescents. The purpose of the analysis was to evaluate the effects of REBT on treatment outcomes for this population. The following are the five major findings from the meta-analysis:

- REBT is an effective treatment for children and adolescents.
- REBT is useful in decreasing disruptive behavior in children and adolescents.
- Nonmental health professionals (e.g., teachers) can conduct REBT very effectively.
- The longer the duration of REBT the greater the effect.
- Children benefit from REBT more than adolescents do.

Gonzales and colleagues also noted that there were limitations in the studies that they reviewed. For example, most of the studies reviewed did not provide sufficient descriptions of the students who participated in the studies. Additionally, it was not possible to assess generalization and maintenance of treatment effects, and most of the studies did not report on fidelity of implementation. The authors noted that these and other limitations should be considered when assessing the benefits shown by the studies.

Teaching REBT The purpose of REBT is to teach students how to replace irrational beliefs with reality-based beliefs that help them achieve their social goals. The REBT process includes the following components:

- A: Activating events
- B: Beliefs
- C: Consequences
- D: Disputation
- E: Effect

Inaccurate interpretations or beliefs (Bs) regarding activating events (As) cause negative emotional reactions or consequences (Cs). When changes in perceptions are made through disputation (D), a cognitive and behavioral restructuring called the emotional or behavioral effect (E) may occur (Webber, Coleman, & Zionts, 1998).

Individuals learn to disprove their exaggerations through disputation processes. Disputation teaches that the world can be positive, negative, or neutral—that all human beings can make mistakes, and the world is not always consistent or fair (Zionts, 1998). During disputation, students begin to detect their unhealthy thinking and to discriminate between this thinking and their healthy thinking. Logical problem-solving processes are used to disprove unhealthy thinking. However, it is important to note that whether or not disputation is successful depends in large part on the ability of the teacher to utilize appropriate disputes and on students' cognitive and maturity levels (Zionts, 1998).

Rational emotive behavior therapy incorporates a wide range of strategies and methodologies to teach individuals to recognize, understand, and modify their irrational beliefs. Before implementing REBT, it is important to consider students' cognitive and reasoning abilities. Ellis refers to more advanced and sophisticated REBT as "elegant" therapy.

REBT can be implemented (a) informally using "curriculum of the moment" opportunities; (b) as in integral part of academic curricula such as language arts, social studies, and health; and (c) as structured lessons designed to directly teach REBT concepts. Additionally, REBT can be used as a group problem-solving process or as a preventive mental health curriculum (Zionts, 1998). In all cases, REBT should be part of a comprehensive and individualized program designed to meet students' needs.

IMPLEMENTING COGNITIVE BEHAVIORAL INTERVENTIONS

Developing and implementing CBIs requires (a) functional assessment of a student's problem behavior; (b) program planning and implementation, which involves choosing a CBI, teaching the procedures to the student, progress monitoring to ensure that the program is effective, and implementing the program with fidelity; and (c) programming for generalization. In the following sections, we briefly examine these components.

Assessment

A functional behavioral assessment (FBA) is an important crucial component in developing appropriate programming. This means that prior to developing the behavioral interventions that will be used, teachers should have a thorough understanding of the problem behavior, the function the behavior serves, and the consequences that strengthen and maintain it. As described in Chapter 4, the process of FBA includes (a) gathering information about the behavior, (b) generating hypotheses about the function the behavior serves, and (c) developing a behavior intervention plan (BIP). The hypotheses that we develop may lead us to include CBIs in a student's BIP. For example, when a student's problem behavior is maintained by positive reinforcement, such as peer attention, the BIP may include CBIs designed to teach and strengthen behaviors that serve as alternatives to the problem behaviors while producing similar consequences for the student. If the function the behavior serves is negative reinforcement, such as escape from work tasks, BIPs may include CBIs designed to teach appropriate alternatives to escape-motivated behavior or problem-solving strategies to minimize the effects of the aversive task demands (Shapiro & Cole, 1994). Similarly, if the hypothesis is that a student's inappropriate behaviors are the result of peer teasing or specific events that cause the student to lose their temper, teachers may use CBIs such as anger-control procedures to help the student deal with anger in a socially acceptable manner.

Professionals generally agree that BIPs based on functional behavioral assessments hold great promise for positively affecting the lives of students with EBD. Many researchers have identified a need, however, to create specific intervention procedures that reflect and capitalize on the cognitive and verbal skills of students with EBD (e.g., Drasgow et al., 1999; Gresham, Quinn, & Restori, 1999). Cognitive behavioral interventions seem to be ideally matched to the characteristics of students with EBD.

Program Planning and Implementation

When a teacher decides that a CBI may be an effective strategy to include in a student's BIP, he or she should first conduct a task and learner analysis. In a task analysis, a teacher should determine the cognitions and strategies necessary for successful performance in whatever is being taught. For example, the teacher might perform the task herself and note the strategies used, or observe students who do well on a task to determine necessary strategies that a student must use when using the CBI. In learner analysis the teacher examines a student's characteristics—such as his or her age, cognitive capabilities, language development, and learning ability—that may influence the choice of CBI to be used (Harris, 1982). It is very important that the CBI be matched to the learner's characteristics if the training is to be successful. Although some CBIs can be used with virtually all students (e.g., self-monitoring), others, such as self-instructional based interventions, require that students already possess skills (e.g., verbal and cognitive reasoning skills). Thus, such CBIs may not be as appropriate for students who are very young or who have more severe intellectual disabilities. Conducting a task and learner analysis will help ensure that the CBI procedure that is used in a program is appropriate for the students.

Including CBIs in Students' BIPs   When the teacher has determined that a CBI will be used with a particular student, the next step is to incorporate the CBI in the BIP. Chapter 5 explained the O'Neill et al. (1997) model for developing BIPs. In this model, the hypothesis generated from an FBA is used to develop the BIP. You will recall that in the O'Neill model, the BIP may include interventions in one or more of the following four areas: (a) setting events, (b) predictor strategies, (c) teaching strategies, and (d) consequence strategies. We next describe how teachers may add CBIs to the O'Neill et al. model.

Setting Event Strategies.   O'Neill et al. (1997) refer to setting events (e.g., medications, daily schedule) as "those aspects of a person's environment or daily routines that do not necessarily happen immediately before or after the undesirable behaviors but still affect whether these behaviors are performed" (p. 11). CBIs provide students with the ability to identify the factors (e.g., medication, noise level) that influence their behavior and with the skills to alter the environment so that they can interact appropriately. For example, students can ensure that they take their medication by reminding the teacher to let them go to the nurse's office or they may ask to be moved to a quieter part of the room to finish class work. The idea is that students are provided with the ability to identify a problem and then generate solutions to be implemented.

Predictor Strategies. O'Neill et al. (1997) refer to predictor strategies as techniques used to identify "specific situations in which the problem behaviors happen" (p. 12). Predictor strategies are used to identify such antecedents as time of day, physical setting, people, and specific activities related to problem behaviors. CBIs can provide students with skills to recognize antecedent events so that they can generate socially acceptable solutions to help them choose appropriate behavioral responses in a proactive manner. By identifying antecedent events, students will be able to plan their choices accordingly.

Teaching Strategies. The teaching strategies represent the techniques chosen to provide students with the knowledge base to behave in socially acceptable ways. When using CBIs in this section of the BIP, students may be taught strategies to self-manage their behavior through strategies such as self-instruction, problem solving, or anger control.

Consequence Strategies. O'Neill et al. (1997) refer to consequence strategies as those events that follow a behavior and increase the likelihood that it will occur again. Consequence strategies include providing environmental events (i.e., differential reinforcement) that increase the likelihood that socially acceptable replacement behavior (e.g., asking for help with class work as opposed to throwing it on the floor) and the desirable behavior (e.g., the student will complete class work as opposed to throwing it on the floor) will occur. The goal of all CBIs is to provide students with the tools to identify what they are trying to accomplish. Once the student identifies the problem, he or she can choose and implement a socially acceptable solution to achieve an outcome. The ultimate goal of CBI is for students to acquire skills to regulate their own behavior and achieve outcomes in socially acceptable ways. CBIs that can be used as consequence strategies include self-monitoring, self-evaluation, and self-reinforcement (Shapiro & Cole, 1994).

Teaching CBIs to Students   Once we have chosen the CBI that will be used, we can teach the student how to use the procedure. As explained earlier in this chapter, it is important that educators teach the procedures of CBI to their students. The goal should be to help students acquire the skills needed to implement the particular

CBI. Teaching CBIs to students should follow similar procedures used when teaching academic skills. Specifically, training should include four steps. First, teachers should provide direct instruction in the skill being taught. In addition to teaching the steps of the strategy, this phase should include teacher modeling of the CBI. It is crucial that students fully understand the strategy they are expected to apply. Second, students need opportunities to rehearse and practice the skill being taught. Behavioral rehearsal will help the student apply the strategy correctly in actual situations. Practice opportunities can be made more realistic, thereby helping transfer the newly acquired skill, if the teacher enlists help from others in a student's environment such as peers or parents (Shapiro & Cole, 1994). Third, the teacher must provide frequent reinforcement when a student performs the strategy successfully. Students with EBD often have a long learning history of exhibiting inappropriate behavior and being reinforced for this behavior. It will be difficult to replace the old inappropriate behavior with a new appropriate one, therefore, unless strong reinforcement (frequently and of high magnitude) follows occurrences of the new behavior (Walker et al., 1995). A mistake that teachers frequently make when using CBIs with their students is to assume that because the procedure involves self-management, external reinforcement is no longer necessary (Yell, Robinson, & Drasgow, 2001). This is a critical mistake that often leads to the failure of CBIs (Shapiro & Cole, 1994). Teaching CBIs must include environmental support and reinforcement as well as adequate training in the procedures. Finally, teachers need to develop and implement progress monitoring and evaluation procedures to ensure that the student is using the CBI correctly and that the interventions are working. This includes keeping accurate data to determine if the CBI is effective in reducing a student's problem behavior and increasing the expected behavior (Nelson, Roberts, et al., 1998; Walker et al., 1995). Monitoring will also indicate when further teaching or booster sessions may be required.

Generalization of Cognitive Behavioral Interactions

In this chapter we have discussed powerful strategies that have been used successfully by teachers to improve the behaviors of students. The effects of behavioral change programs, however, often do not generalize to other settings or maintain in settings when the intervention procedures are withdrawn (Kerr & Nelson, 2006). Morgan and Jenson (1988) referred to self-management strategies as being among the more promising strategies to facilitate generalization. When behaviors are under external control by the teacher the behaviors might not be controlled in situations and settings in which the teacher is not able to apply the external control procedures. When students are able to manage their behaviors, however, these behaviors will be more likely to last and to carry over to different situations and settings, even without external control by teachers. However, in a review of self-management strategies Nelson and colleagues (1991) found that treatment effects of self-management procedures do not automatically generalize. They suggest that treatment effects will generalize if we systematically program for generalization. (For discussion of generalization See chapter 4.)

Kaplan and Carter (1995) offered several suggestions that could be used by teachers to encourage students to use CBI strategies outside the training environment. These suggestions include:

Modeling the strategies. The teacher should model the strategies taught when appropriate. Students should be able to observe the strategies in action. Teachers should share how they are using the strategies to help modify their behavior.

Teaching the strategies to mastery. The teacher should teach the skills and subskills in the CBI strategy to mastery. Periodic assessments may be necessary to determine if a student has achieved mastery. When mastery is achieved a student is much more likely to use the strategy. According to Kaplan and Carter (1995), a student has achieved mastery of a strategy when he or she is both fast and accurate in its use.

Reinforcing appropriate use of strategies. Whenever we observe a student using a CBI strategy outside the training context, it is important that we reinforce him or her. We should also encourage the student's peers to reinforce appropriate behavior.

Programming for generalization by giving homework assignments. Giving homework assignments that will require the CBI strategies to be used in environments outside school may help promote generalization.

Discussing the relevance of each strategy when it is taught. Students should be taught how the particular strategy is relevant to them and their situations. An effective way to do this is to discuss the relevance of the strategy prior to training.

Chapter Summary

In this chapter we have examined a number of interventions that fall under the general category of CBI. The review was not exhaustive, but only meant to give the reader a flavor of the number of different strategies available to meet teachers' desired outcomes. Cognitive behavioral interventions refer to general approaches that combine traditional behavioral strategies (e.g., rewards, response cost) with cognitive approaches to provide problem-solving frameworks (Robinson et al., 1999; Yell, Busch, et al., 2005). Specifically, CBI uses the principles of behavior therapy (e.g., modeling, reinforcement) to modify underlying cognitions (e.g., self-instructions) that influence overt behavior.

The underlying assumption is that overt behavior is mediated by internal cognitive events that can be influenced to change behavior in purposeful ways.

Cognitive behavioral interventions have been used to modify behavior, facilitate academic performance, train problem-solving ability, and foster self-control. The major aim of CBI is to teach students to be their own agents of change, in control of their behavior and learning. When using CBIs, therefore, teachers help students become dependent on themselves as agents of change rather than becoming dependent on others in their environment for change.

CHAPTER 7

Social Skills Instruction

Nancy B. Meadows

Focus Questions

- How is social competence defined and assessed?
- What causes social skills deficits?
- What is social skills training and why is it done?
- What is the difference between formal and informal social skills training?
- How is the level of social competence in students assessed?
- Are there cultural and ethnic considerations in social skills training?
- How do teachers choose a particular social skills curriculum?
- What are social task curricula?
- What is a behavioral intent?

According to Gresham (1998b), social skills are "socially acceptable learned behaviors enabling individuals to interact effectively with others and avoid or escape socially unacceptable behaviors exhibited by others" (p. 20). The lack of social skills plays a significant role in the social, educational, and behavioral problems of students with EBD. In fact, the inability *to build or maintain satisfactory interpersonal relationships with peers and teachers* is a criterion included in the federal definition of emotional disturbance. The success of students with EBD in school, at home, and in the community depends on their acquisition of social skills.

Whereas most children seem to just "pick up" social skills, many children with EBD have difficulty learning those skills necessary to develop interpersonal relationships. They also have difficulty determining which social skills to use in different situations. Many researchers have assumed that students with EBD who display social skills deficits have not had the opportunity to learn and practice relevant social skills, which has led to the development of structured and explicit attempts to teach those skills needed for social success (Kavale, Mathur, & Mostert, 2004). According to Kavale and colleagues, the purpose of social skills training programs is to promote social acceptance by teaching these students socially acceptable behaviors and skills. In this chapter we examine formal and informal social skills instruction for students with EBD.

FORMAL SOCIAL SKILLS INSTRUCTION

Developing effective social skills curricula is important and teaching social skills should be an integral part of the daily curriculum, especially for students with EBD (Bain & Farris, 1991; Meadows, Neel, Parker, & Timo, 1991). However, social skills instruction has not been very successful at increasing overall social competence of children with behavior problems or improving their outcomes. Modest and less than dramatic effects have been reported in several meta-analyses of social skills interventions (Forness & Kavale, 1996; Kavale et al., 1997; Kavale & Forness, 1995; Mathur, Kavale, Quinn, Forness, & Rutherford, 1998). The general consensus is that formal social skills training programs have not produced behavioral changes that make students with EBD more socially acceptable (Kauffman, 2005). Several explanations can be drawn from these studies.

1. *The social skills targeted for instruction were not socially valid for students.* That is, they may be important social skills for the adults who wrote the curriculum, but the students do not perceive the skills as producing "valid" outcomes. As a result, socially incompetent students may not increase their levels of social acceptance even if specific skills are mastered (Gresham, 1986; Mathur & Rutherford, 1996; Winnett, Moore, & Anderson, 1991).

2. *Performance deficits are often confused with skill deficits.* Most social skills training systems assume that students need to learn appropriate social skills. These children have social problems because they have not learned social skills, so we often assume they have skill deficits. However, some students may have a performance deficit and, even though they have "mastered" a social skill, they may not "perform" the skill at appropriate times (Gresham, 1986).

3. *Social skills instruction, as it was typically implemented, lacked intensity.* Forness and Kavale (1996) found that, for students having learning disabilities, social skills training tended to be fewer than 3 hours per week for less than 10 weeks. Social skills were taught in much the same way as academic subjects—during scheduled time periods each day rather than throughout the day as an integral part of the curriculum.

4. *Most social skills training interventions were either published, preset curricula or were specifically designed for research purposes.* Many packaged social skills programs are based on models where best methods for working with *some* students have been established through research and then presented to *all* students with EBD (Forness & Kavale, 1996; Neel, Alexander, & Meadows, 1997; Peacock Hill Working Group, 1991).

5. *Social skills targeted for intervention were not appropriate "replacement behaviors" because they did not meet students' intended social goals (Neel & Cessna, 1993).* Problematic social behaviors serve a purpose for the child (e.g., gain attention, escape an unpleasant situation, avoid a task, etc.). New behaviors targeted for intervention were not ones that the student could substitute for problem ones and still reliably achieve his or her desired social outcome.

6. *Social skills were not taught within contexts that are relevant for students.* Social skills were too often taught out of context or within contexts that were relevant to adults rather than students which resulted in poor generalization to other settings and with individuals other than the teacher or trainer (Gable, Hendrickson, & Rutherford, 1991; Mathur & Rutherford, 1996; Neel, Meadows, & Scott, 1990).

In summary, to be most effective, social skills instruction must include skills that students feel meet their needs and therefore produce socially valid outcomes, be taught in relevant contexts, and be an integral part of students' total curriculum. In the first part of the chapter we discuss formal methods and curricula for increasing the social competence of children and youth with EBD. The seven main sections include (1) social skills assessments; (2) assumptions of social skills instruction; (3) structured learning approach; (4) teaching of presocial skills; (5) social skills strategy instruction; (6) published social skills curricula; and (7) how to choose and implement a social skills curriculum.

Social Skills Assessments

Effective instruction is based on accurate and ongoing assessment of students' social skill needs (Neel et al., 1997). Or, as Grant Wiggins has stated, "Good assessment is inseparable from good teaching" (Wiggins, 1993). One approach to providing instruction based on students' assessed needs has been termed *needs-based services* by Cessna and Skiba (1996). Providing needs-based services relies on the "identification of students' instructional needs as basic to making decisions about curriculum ('what' to teach) and instruction ('how' to teach it). Student needs, in turn, lead to designing systems ('who,' 'where,' and 'when') that facilitate meeting students' needs in the most integrated fashion possible" (Cessna & Adams, 1993, p. 16). Effective and individualized needs-based social skills curriculum is structured so that it is flexible and responsive to students' changing needs as well as any contextual changes that may occur in the environment (Cessna & Skiba, 1996).

Sugai and Lewis (1998) reported that social skills assessments, just as other classroom-based assessments, are conducted for several important purposes:

1. *Social skills assessments are used to screen the general social competence of individual students or groups of students.*

    Example: Use of a rating scale to determine if a student or group of students would benefit from social skills instruction

2. *Assessment strategies are used to collect information about the nature of a student's social skill problem.*

    Example: Direct observation of a student during recess to determine problematic situations or social tasks

3. *Social skills assessments are conducted to assist in selecting and modifying curriculum and design delivery of instruction.*

    Example: Use of direct observation and behavioral interviews prior to instruction to determine targeted social skills and their validity

4. *Assessment information is used to monitor and evaluate the progress students make in their social skills instruction.*

    Example: Role-play during instruction and direct observation in other settings to determine necessary modifications

A previous chapter discussed formal and informal assessment methods extensively. Consequently, our discussion here will be brief and related directly to the social skills interventions covered in this chapter. The three most commonly used assessments in planning and implementing informal social skills instruction are social skills ratings, behavioral interviews, and direct observations.

Social Skills Ratings Rating scales are useful because they provide information about appropriate and problematic social skills and are typically linked to outcomes such as peer acceptance or rejection and positive relationships with adults (Gresham, 1986; Sugai & Lewis, 1998). *Ratings by others* are usually completed by teachers, parents, or other significant adults in the student's life and contain lists of specific skills (e.g., follows directions, works independently, initiates social interactions with peers) that are rated on a Likert scale on frequency of use (e.g., 1 = never occurs, 3 = occasionally, 5 = frequently occurs) or on ability to perform the skill (e.g., 1 = unable to perform skill, 3 = performs skill well). Rating scales are often criticized, however, because they offer global rather than specific information about a child's social competence. Because rating scales are less sensitive to changes in actual behavior, they are more often used as screening devices (Zirpoli & Melloy, 1997).

Self-ratings involve asking students to rate their own social behaviors or their status with peers (Sugai & Lewis, 1998). They are not used as often by teachers or researchers because of their subjectivity and poor predictive validity with outcomes such as peer acceptance or rejection, teacher ratings of social skills, and direct observations in natural settings (Gresham, 1986). Their importance is also questioned because self-ratings only provide information about students' own perceptions of their social competence. However, it is important to remember that a student's self-perceptions can provide teachers with useful contextual information when planning informal social skills instruction.

Behavioral Interviews In behavioral interviews, students and their peers, teachers, or parents reconstruct social interactions and events. Behavioral interviews are indirect measures of social behavior in that they are removed in time from their actual occurrence. However, behavioral interviews can be very useful in developing contextual elements for informal social skills curricula (Gresham, 1992). Becker and Heimberg (1988) reported that behavioral interviews to assess social skills can be structured to assess

- settings where the behavior is problematic;
- the specific behavioral competencies necessary for effective performance in each target situation;
- whether or not the child possessed the necessary competencies;
- the antecedents and consequences for performance of the behavior in each setting;
- additional assessment procedures needed to complete the assessment of social skills.

Kerr and Nelson (2006) suggested that the following questions would provide useful information when teachers interview significant adults in students' lives:

- Who are this student's friends?
- What social situations are difficult for this student?
- What "social mistakes" does this student make?
- Does this student initiate social interactions?
- What social skills does this student have?
- What do others say about this student's social behavior?
- What skills does this student need to be more socially successful?
- Can this student maintain a social interaction?
- In what situations is this student socially successful?
- What behavior does this student exhibit in these situations (p. 244)?

Direct Observations Direct observations involve observing students in their natural settings (e.g., classrooms, cafeteria, playground, bus), noting contextual elements of the setting, watching students' interactions with others, and recording events as they happen. The observer is typically looking for characteristics of problematic behaviors such as frequency, duration, and/or latency as well as categories of behaviors (e.g., initiating conversations, entering a group, acting out physical aggression). Direct observations are probably the most

effective and useful measures of social competence, but they are also among the most time-consuming (Walker & Fabre, 1987).

Naturalistic functional assessment (NFA) utilizes direct observation and focuses on identifying naturally occurring environmental factors that may predict or maintain problematic behaviors (Repp & Horner, 1999; Sugai & Lewis, 1998). The purpose of conducting an NFA is to (a) collect baseline data without making any artificial manipulation in the classroom, and (b) identify the function of problem behavior from this naturalistic data. NFA assumes there are relationships between problematic social behaviors and environmental factors, and most important, gives indications of the conditions under which behaviors will reoccur and/or be sustained. When the information collected during the functional assessment is accurate and the hypothesis reliably describes the social interaction, valid and contextually relevant social skills interventions can be developed and implemented. According to Sugai and Lewis (1998), "because of its practical utility and technical adequacy, the functional assessment technology has been identified as a preferred practice when assessing social behaviors" (p. 147). (See Chapter 6, where functional assessment is explained in more detail.)

Outcome analysis is based on the assumption that all behavior is purposeful and serves a function for a student (Cessna & Borock, 1993; Neel & Cessna, 1993; Neel et al., 1990). The purpose of assessing behavioral intent is to determine the functions of behavior—that is, the relationship that exists between the students' behaviors and their desired outcomes. Students' behavioral intents are not always easy to determine and may require multiple observations and anecdotal records in order to hypothesize correctly. Behavioral intents common to most children include attention, escape, avoidance, power, control, protection, acceptance/affiliation, expression of self, gratification, and justice/revenge. According to Neel and Cessna (1993), it is important to correctly identify a student's behavioral intent in order to teach appropriate replacement behaviors that will generalize across time, settings, and individuals. For example, if the teacher has determined that a child is attempting to "escape" a math activity because it is the only way he knows how to deal with frustration, targeted replacement behaviors would focus on teaching new skills for escaping a frustrating activity (e.g., asking for help, taking a short break from the activity). In this same situation, if the teacher hypothesizes that the student is trying to "control" the activity or interaction, she might teach negotiating skills or offer the student a menu of other choices meeting the same academic objectives. In either situation, the teacher does not try to change the behavioral intent, but rather offers instruction of replacement behaviors that meet the desired behavioral intent. The outcome analysis worksheet developed by Cessna and Borock (1993) can be found in Figure 7-1.

When choosing a method to assess social skills, Scanlon (1996) recommended considering two factors: (1) determine which assessment measure can be used appropriately, and (2) select a method that assesses the social problem (or problems) the teacher feels is troublesome. In determining which assessment method is most appropriate, it is important to consider who will be conducting the assessment and under what conditions. For example, if the teacher believes that a social skills rating scale completed by a parent or family member is important, and the student has recently been placed in a foster home, then the person completing the assessment may not have known or been associated with the student for a long enough period of time. It is also important to consider which assessment best assesses which set of problem behaviors. For example, direct observation of a behavior in several settings would a better method for predicting future behavior patterns than if the teacher chose to use a rating scale (Scanlon, 1996).

FIGURE 7-1

Outcome analysis worksheet

Step 1: State the problems in your own words.

Step 2: Circle (underline) the specific behaviors that are identified in step 1.

Step 3: List the three behaviors that are of the most concern.

Step 4: Identify the situation that precedes each problem behavior.

Behavior   Antecedent

Step 5: Identify what happens following each problem behavior. Describe all major events that follow the problem behavior until the incident ends.

Behavior   Consequence Sequence

Step 6: List the hypothesized outcomes achieved for the student for each behavior.

Behavior   Hypothesized Student Outcomes

Step 7: Select the priority or predominant outcome from step 6. Write it below.

Theme:

Source: Cessna and Borock, 1993.

Cultural and Ethnic Considerations Classroom demographics continue to change, and as such, teachers who work with children with EBD need to be aware of the cultural and ethnic differences of the children they teach. Academic and social curricula need to be expanded to encompass these differences in ways that meet students' needs. It is important that children from culturally diverse backgrounds be able to maintain and "celebrate" their own cultural identity while learning about and accepting their mainstream cultural environment (Rivera & Rogers-Adkinson 1997).

To develop effective and appropriate social skills instruction for culturally and linguistically diverse students, the teacher must have an understanding of culturally influenced behaviors. This will enable the teacher to distinguish between social skill deficits and culturally based social skill differences. According to Rivera and Rogers-Adkinson (1997), prior to assessing students' social skills, the teacher must consider the following four factors:

• The influence of the child's culture on his or her behavior to determine difference rather than a deficit.

• Integration of traditional cultural values and beliefs into social skills curricula and instructional strategies (Cartledge & Milburn, 1995).

• Social skills curricula that promote understanding and acceptance of diverse cultures across students' peer groups.

• Multiple instructional strategies to allow students to process learning according to their individual learning styles and cultural perspectives.

Assumptions of Social Skills Instruction

There are several "assumptions" underlying social skills instruction that, if violated, may have an impact on the efficacy of informal social skills instruction (Mathur & Rutherford, 1996; Neel, Cheney, Meadows, & Gelhar, 1992; Sugai & Lewis, 1998). These assumptions, drawn from previous empirical studies and "theoretical" papers dealing with social skills instruction, serve as the basis for the classroom management strategies and social task curriculum to be discussed later in this chapter and include:

1. *Social skills are learned behaviors and can be taught.* Although there are many factors that influence and often serve as barriers to the acquisition of social skills, it is assumed that social skills are learned responses

that are acquired in much the same way as other skills. The learning may be planned (e.g., as in direct instruction of social skills) or unplanned (e.g., trial and error, observations) but the underlying assumption is that social skills can be taught (Sugai & Lewis, 1998).

2. *Social skills are prerequisite for academic success.* As Sugai and Lewis (1998) reported, many students are at a disadvantage academically because they lack appropriate presocial skills such as listening, following directions, asking for help, and working with peers. These are prerequisite skills for many teacher-directed learning situations, independent study, and cooperative learning activities (Melloy, Davis, Wehby, Murry, & Leiber, 1998; Sugai & Lewis, 1998).

3. *Behavior management problems are social skill problems.* When teachers deal with students with EBD in their classroom, control and containment tend to be their main goal (Knitzer et al., 1990; Muscott, Morgan, & Meadows, 1996; Peacock Hill Working Group, 1991). In an effort to run classes smoothly, teachers implement behavior management systems that overemphasize the consequences for misbehavior and underemphasize those for appropriate behavior (Knitzer et al., 1990). In such systems, responses to inappropriate behavior tend to be reactive and reductive in nature and occur only when the behavior problems have reached the high-intensity, chronic stage (Muscott et al., 1996). The aim of these behavior management systems is to decrease or eliminate the problematic behavioral patterns rather than to teach new and more appropriate social behaviors (Miller, 1998; Sugai, 1992).

4. *Targeted social skills must produce valid outcomes for students.* As discussed earlier, Gresham (1986) has pointed out that social skills must have significance for students. That is, some social skills are useful to students in some social contexts, but not in others. Valid social skills are those that predict important outcomes such as "peer acceptance, significant others' judgments of social skill, academic achievement, positive feelings of self-worth, and positive adaptation to school, home and community environments" (Gresham & Elliott, 1993, p. 139).

5. *Targeted social skills must meet students' social/behavioral intents.* Behavior is purposeful and achieves a desired result for the child (Neel & Cessna, 1993; Neel et al., 1992). In fact, it is the reinforcement received by reaching this social/behavioral goal that shapes the specific behavior used by the child. Persons who are perceived as socially competent achieve their desired social goals in a particular situation using social skills or behaviors judged as appropriate by others.

6. *Social skills are best taught in the context of social tasks and situations that are relevant to students.* Neel and colleagues (1992) stated that "the initial step, then, in altering the social outcomes of children who are behaviorally disordered is to identify a meaningful set of school related social tasks—tasks that are socially valid for the children teachers will be instructing" (p. 58). Mathur and Rutherford have also concluded that contextual factors must be considered when implementing social skills instruction (Mathur & Rutherford, 1996).

Structured Learning Approach

The structured learning approach for teaching social skills is based on the assumption that students need a well-designed curriculum that is systematic and skill specific. Skills are sequenced from easier to more complex. For example, students are taught the social skill of "listening" before they learn "following instructions." Structured learning curricula are developed using basic principles of direct instruction that include:

- Rapid pacing of presentation
- Cumulative instruction
- Practice of each skill step
- Presentation of minimally different examples and nonexamples
- Guided practice of skills
- Instant, specific feedback

Several published social skills instructional programs use the structured learning approach (e.g., Goldstein, 1988; McGinnis & Goldstein, 1984; Walker et al., 1993). Although these curricula may vary in the social skills they target and/or the identified skill steps for each social skill, most contain five common instructional components: modeling, role-playing, coaching, feedback, and generalization strategies.

Modeling occurs during the initial phases of structured learning when students learn by observing rather than engaging in responses. According to Bandura (1977), children learn new social behaviors by observing others and modeling, especially individuals they consider to be important in their lives (e.g., respected peers, friends, teachers, parents). Typically, the social skill is modeled by the teacher or a "socially competent" peer while other students observe the appropriate behavior(s). It is important that the students attend to the model and that the model be someone they identify with or look up to. It is also important that students are able to recognize specific responses and skill steps used by the model. In some instances, students may need help to understand the model's actions. Teachers may want to use different forms of modeling such as puppets or filmed examples of other students or fictional characters. In general, because modeling does not directly instruct a student in more appropriate social skills, it may be more appropriate for performance deficits rather than skill deficits. Modeling is not thought to be very effective when used in isolation, and is more effective when paired with other instructional components such as coaching and role-playing.

Role-playing often follows modeling in structured learning approaches. Role-plays involve students practicing in simulated settings the social skills they have previously learned. Role-plays give students the opportunity to practice their newly learned social skills in "safe" settings that are relatively free from ridicule and peer pressure. Once the students have learned how to role play, it is important to provide them opportunities to create and role-play their own realistic scenarios (Melloy et al., 1998). Role-plays serve several useful purposes in social skills instruction. First, they confirm that students actually know and can use the skill steps for each social skill they have been taught. Second, students build their confidence through practice and positive feedback following each role-play. Role-plays are also effective when used with students who have performance deficits due to fear and anxiety.

Coaching is a direct verbal instruction technique used to teach a specific social skill (e.g., accepting feedback). After the student has been "coached" in the skill, she is given opportunities to practice the skill either through role-playing or naturally occurring situations throughout the day. During these practice sessions, the coach offers clear prompts when necessary and gives feedback and suggestions for future performances. Kerr and Nelson (2006) suggested that using peers as coaches can be an effective strategy for teaching social skills to students who are withdrawn. Others (Ladd, 1981; Oden & Asher, 1977) have demonstrated through their research that coaching strategies are effective in increasing students' social acceptance by their peers.

Feedback is an integral component of structured learning. Verbal feedback immediately follows each role-play and should always be constructive, offering suggestions for improvement and praise for a good performance. Students with EBD often have a difficult time accepting feedback and, for that reason, Melloy and colleagues (1998) recommend that it be one of the first social skills targeted for instruction.

Generalization may be the most important component of structured learning because if students are unable to use new behaviors in environments other than the training environment, the new behaviors have little functional value. There are several generalization principles that are important to consider when using structured learning to teach social skills (Stokes & Osnes, 1986).

- *Teach behaviors that will be supported in the natural environment.* Inform others involved with the students which social skills are being taught. Targeted social skills should be supported by parents, teachers, and peers.

- *Provide instruction in the natural environment.* This is not always possible, but training settings should be as natural as possible. Role-plays using props and involving as many different people as possible are useful in simulating the natural environment.

- *Train sufficient exemplars.* Modeling and role-plays should involve multiple options to teach students to become responsive to variations and different expectations in different environments. Positive and negative examples should be part of the instructional process.

- *Train loosely.* Loosely structured environments are more like natural environments. After children demonstrate proficiency in scripted skills, encourage them to initiate and develop situations of their own.

- *Program indiscriminant contingencies.* This is a consequence of training loosely where teachers are recommended to maintain less rigid control over the consequences of students' behaviors. Examples include intermittent reinforcement, delayed reinforcement and vicarious reinforcement.

- *Program common contingencies.* Reinforcers in the natural environment should be consistent with those in the training setting. Social reinforcers involving teachers and peers that can be used in both settings are important.

- *Teach students to use mediators.* Mediators may be verbal and paired with behavioral rehearsal (What is my plan?); visual (close your eyes and imagine); or self-report (homework is assigned and student reports success or failure in using the social skill).

- *Train behaviors that trap natural reinforcers.* Students are taught behaviors that encourage peer acceptance and teacher approval.

When implementing a structured learning approach with students with EBD, Melloy (1990) recommends four phases: (1) discussion of the specific skill, the steps necessary for successful performance of the skill, and modeling of the skill by the instructor; (2) review of skill steps, followed by instructor modeling, student role-play activities, and instructor and peer feedback; (3) presentation of homework assignments, followed by reports of success in using the skill; and (4) a session in which students report the results of homework practice and discuss possible situations in which the skill might be necessary. In addition, she suggests that students keep a journal describing how and when they have used the targeted social skills, their perceptions of success or failure in using the skills, and any "missed opportunities" they may have had for using the skills. The journals are an excellent method of self-recording and self-reinforcement, as well as providing the teacher with opportunities to provide written feedback.

Elksnin and Elksnin (1998) developed a six-step instructional model for teaching social skills that incorporates many of the structured learning components. However, their model also teaches "body basic" skills such as facing the person, maintaining eye contact, using an appropriate tone of voice, and monitoring facial expressions (Hazel, Schumaker, Sherman, & Sheldon, 1995). Their model includes (1) providing students with a clear and concise definition of the social skill to be learned; (2) listing the verbal, cognitive, and body basic steps involved in performing the social skill; (3) providing students with a rationale as to why they are learning the skill; (4) describing settings and situations where the skill might be used; (5) teaching the social skill through modeling, role-playing, guided practice, and feedback; and (6) helping students identify the social rules that provide the framework for using the social skill.

Teaching of Presocial Skills

Through direct observations and sizing up assessments that occur at the beginning of each school year, teachers may conclude that some students lack presocial skills such as listening, working alone or in small groups quietly, or following directions (Melloy et al., 1998). Students with EBD, in particular, have a difficult time practicing these skills with their peers, especially ones they dislike or do not get along with. When teachers plan instructional activities that allow students to practice presocial skills, then support the new behaviors with reinforcement, students are more likely to add these cooperative behaviors to their behavioral repertoire (Melloy et al., 1998).

Melloy and colleagues suggest that the activities teachers develop to practice presocial skills should be based on (a) proximity and modeling, (b) parallel activity, (c) mutual activity, (d) group activity, and (e) cooperative activity. In the proximity and modeling phase, the teacher models an activity while the students are sitting in close proximity to the teacher and to each other. While the teacher is modeling, he is reviewing the targeted presocial skills of respecting body space, listening, and paying attention. During parallel activity, the students are asked to complete the same task as the teacher by following his directions and while working in proximity to their peers. During the mutual activities phase, students cooperate with each other to share materials while they are each completing an individual project. During interdependent group activity, students work together, following instructions, sharing materials, and helping each other produce a single product. The last phase, cooperative activity, is designed to enable students to practice the entire set of targeted presocial skills they have learned (Johnson, Agelson, Macierz, Minnick, & Merrell, 1995; Melloy et al., 1998).

Social Skills Strategy Instruction

Many students with learning problems are not good at recognizing appropriate social norms for a specific context and often lack the ability to choose appropriate social skills within a given context (Scanlon, 1996). They also often fail to monitor and control themselves in certain situations and fail to pick up cues that there is a problem. Schumaker, Pederson, Hazel, and Meyen (1983) make several recommendations for accommodating the learning characteristics of students with mild disabilities that teachers should consider when planning curriculum for students with behavior disorders:

- Assist students in identifying specific social cues.
- Teach students how to identify which situations call for a skill.
- Minimize failure while learning social skills.
- Make student aware of rationale for using a skill.
- Provide a strategy to facilitate skill learning and generalization.
- Promote motivation to set and achieve social goals after learning a skill.
- Provide many opportunities for student practice.
- Guide generalization of the skill to beyond the setting where it is learned.

Scanlon (1996) emphasizes teaching social skills through strategy instruction. He argues that not all published social skills curricula teach students how, when, and why to use a skill, nor do they teach students how to monitor their performance during social interactions. Strategy instruction enables students to perform specific social skills and to be a strategic user of the skills. According to Scanlon, "a strategic user of social skills is more likely to use appropriate skills across situations than one who has learned only a few isolated skills" (p. 394). He offers several methods for teaching social skills that are strategy based.

Promote student awareness by pointing out to them that a social skill problem exists. In a one-to-one conference or interview, the teacher and student discuss the problem behavior and its negative consequences. The goal is to make the student aware of the problem and to obtain his or her perspective. The teacher asks the student to (1) articulate the problem behavior and its consequences; (2) cite real examples and go into detail in explaining them; (3) relate insights into why he or she engages in the problem behavior; (4) think of alternative behaviors that would be appropriate in the situations previously described; and (5) develop a plan for learning and using the new behaviors.

Use journal keeping as another way of increasing students' awareness that there is a problem with their social skills. Journals are more effective when used along with other interventions. When writing in their journals, students (1) keep notes on their social interactions, (2) discuss their progress in using their new social skills, and (3) reflect on how they might improve or change behaviors in future interactions. Students may need prompts or questions to get them started (e.g., "Where were you?" "Who were you with?" "What social skills did you use?" "How did the others in the group respond?").

Encourage record keeping of one's own behaviors, similar to having students write in their journals. Record keeping involves using a tally sheet so that students can keep track of their performance when using the targeted social skills. This intervention would work best in classrooms where students were allowed to keep their tally sheet taped to their desk or in the front of their notebook. In addition to making a mark when they use the skill, students could be asked to rate how well they performed the skill (e.g., $+$, $-$, $=$).

Make contracts with students when certain social skills are targeted and students agree to use them. Before writing the contract, the teacher and student would conference (in a process similar to the one described previously) to determine the nature of the problem.

The purpose of the contract is to gain a commitment from the student to use the targeted social skill(s). When the teacher or other individuals involved with the student sign the contract, it signals a commitment to the student using the new social skill. One drawback to contracts is that they do not remind students to perform the skill when called for. As a partial solution to this problem, Scanlon recommends posting rules or expectations in the classroom where the student can see them and teachers can use them as prompts.

Use role-playing as a component of structured learning, as discussed earlier. Scanlon (1996) suggests, however, that role-plays be used to help students identify and become aware of their inappropriate behaviors. For example, a student may act the part of a peer while the teacher or a peer exhibits the inappropriate behavior during the role-play. Role reversal is often an effective strategy for increasing students' awareness of their own behaviors. Immediately following the role-play, students should be "debriefed" either individually or in the small group. According to Scanlon, guidelines for effective role-playing include (1) establishing clear objectives (e.g., learning two new ways to "avoid trouble" when being pressured by peers); (2) identifying specific roles and scripts for each role-player; and (3) establishing what the observers should be looking for and thinking about during the role-play. All students should have the chance to participate in role-plays because they learn more social skill strategies through participating than by merely observing.

Published Social Skills Curricula

It is important that social skills curricula include systematic data-based interventions and the continuous assessment and monitoring of student progress. Systematic data-based instruction (Kerr & Nelson, 2006) is instruction that is systematically and consistently applied while data are collected to review its effects. Continuous assessment and monitoring of progress implies that strategies are used to collect frequent, reliable, and valid information on all components (academic, behavioral, and social) of a student's program. Perhaps the best way to guarantee that students receive effective instruction is to systematically and continuously evaluate their performance and make instructional decisions based on an analysis of those data (Fuchs & Fuchs, 1986). In format, most formal social skills curricula are designed to closely resemble academic instruction (Neel & Cessna, 1993). In content, most address the interrelated issues of (a) affect or feelings, (b) overt behavior, and (c) cognition or thinking.

A number of commercially available programs have been developed to teach social skills. An ambitious project undertaken by the Center for Research in Education at the Research Triangle Institute in North Carolina has conducted a systematic investigation of approaches to developing social competence in students with disabilities. The purposes of this project were to (1) develop a framework to guide professionals in the selection of social skills training programs, and (2) carefully describe eight social skills programs that are generally representative of social skills instruction across age groups (Alberg & Petry, 1993). In response to the lack of clear guidelines for selecting social skills programs, this project has developed a resource guide that professionals can use to review programs that best meet the needs of their students. A checklist for reviewing and evaluating social skills programs has also been developed that addresses factors such as intended student outcomes, implementation requirements, staff training requirements, and evidence of effectiveness. In addition, the resource guide includes a comprehensive annotated bibliography of over 70 social skills programs available for use with students with disabilities including students with EBD. Of particular note are the eight social skills programs that were selected to represent the array of options available to educators. At the preschool level, *My Friends & Me* (Davis, 1988) was identified. For elementary settings, *Skillstreaming the Elementary Child* (McGinnis & Goldstein, 1984) and *Tribes* (Gibbs, 1987) were chosen. Middle school and junior high school programs selected included *The Prepare Curriculum* (Goldstein, 1988) and *ACCESS* (Walker, Todis, Holmes, & Horton, 1988). Programs for high school and adult settings were *Learning to Get Along* (Jackson, Jackson, Bennett, Bynum, & Faryna, 1991) and *LCCE: Life Centered Career Education* (Brolin, 1989).

Zirpoli and Melloy list five published social skills curricula that they determined to be "popular" among teachers of students with EBD: *Skillstreaming the Elementary Child* (McGinnis & Goldstein, 1984); *Skillstreaming the Adolescent* (Goldstein, Sprafkin, Gershaw, & Klein, 1980); *Learning the Skills of Peacemaking: An Activity Guide for Elementary-Age Children on Communicating/Cooperating/Resolving Conflict* (Drew, 1987); *The Walker Social Skills Curriculum: The ACCESS Program* (Walker et al., 1988); and *Teaching Social Skills: A Practical Instructional Approach* (Rutherford, 1992).

In addition to those listed, there are several social skills curricula that are appropriate for adolescents, which include *ASSET: A Social Skills Program for Adolescents* (Hazel, Schumaker, Sherman, & Sheldon-Wildgen, 1995);

Cooperation in the Classroom (Johnson, Johnson, & Holubec, 1988); and *Social Skills for Daily Living* (Schumaker, Hazel, & Pederson, 1988). Other noteworthy curricula at the elementary level include *I Can Problem Solve* (Shure, 1992); *Social Skills in the Classroom* (Stephens, 1992); and *Think Aloud Classroom Programs* (Camp & Bash, 1985).

How to Choose and Implement a Social Skills Curriculum

According to Carter and Sugai (1989), there are several questions teachers need to consider when choosing a social skills curriculum:

- *Is the curriculum data based and compatible with current research?* Curriculum authors should provide field test data, and lessons should be based on effective teaching practices and methodology.

- *What is the cost?* There are many curricula available for under $50. There are, however, complete programs available for much more.

- *Are the targeted social skills age-appropriate for students?* There are published curricula available for preschool through postsecondary-age students.

- *Are the targeted social skills socially valid and contextually relevant for students?* The targeted social skills must meet students' needs and be taught in contexts that are relevant for students.

- *Does the curriculum allow for individualization?* Lesson formats should be flexible enough to meet students' individual needs.

- *What assessment and monitoring procedures does the program use?* Assessments such as rating scales, role-plays, and observation procedures should be included in the teaching package.

- *Are generalization strategies an integral part of the curriculum?* Lessons should be written so teachers can "train loosely," and students should be given numerous opportunities for practicing new social skills in other settings.

- *Are the lessons easy to implement?* If lessons are difficult to implement or take too much preparation time, teachers will be less likely to use the curriculum.

Once a curriculum has been chosen, the teacher needs to consider (1) the physical setting where instruction will take place, (2) the size of the group, (3) the heterogeneity or makeup of the group, (4) materials students might need, (5) ongoing monitoring strategies, (6) if any-one other than the teacher will be instructing students, and (7) how parents and/or other significant individuals will be brought into the instruction. Social skills instruction, just as any other area of instruction, should be well planned.

INFORMAL SOCIAL SKILLS INSTRUCTION

Students who are socially competent get along well with peers and adults, have numerous friends, adapt well to different environments, are good problem solvers, and have more confidence in themselves, leading to a positive self-image. On the other hand, students who exhibit poor social skills in educational settings have less success academically, are more likely to be "rejected" by their peers, and as a result, have fewer friends, as well as difficulties with long-term relationships. Students with chronic disruptive and antisocial behaviors are demonstrating a lack of social competence, as are students who are painfully shy, withdrawn, and have a difficult time interacting with peers and/or adults. The long-term outcomes for students who are judged by others as socially incompetent are rather bleak (e.g., dropping out of high school, lack of employment opportunities and/or unsuccessful employment histories, few close friends, negative military records, depression) (Malmgren, Edgar, & Neel, 1997; Meadows et al., 1991; Neel et al., 1988).

Students with EBD are typically placed in classrooms where they engage in fewer positive social interactions with their peers (Kavale et al., 2004). By definition, EBD students have a difficult time interacting socially with their peers and teachers. Consequently, peer interactions are kept to a minimum, and teachers play a direct role in students' instruction and learning. This presents a problem for teachers and students in the area of social skills instruction. Students with EBD have fewer opportunities to learn social skills informally in unstructured settings; they do not engage in enough positive social interactions to reinforce appropriate behavior for increased social acceptance (Kavale et al., 2004). Teachers must then rely on formal social skills instruction to teach students with EBD skills that their peers learn naturally through informal social interactions. Teaching social skills requires formal and informal instructional methods as an integral part of the total curriculum. This highlights one of the problems teachers face in designing interventions for children who do not learn in the same way as their typically developing peers. How do teachers design informal instructional programs that replace skills normally learned naturally

and informally? The task is to develop an informal social skills curriculum that develops new skills without intruding into the social processes to such a degree that the instruction fundamentally alters the social interactions being promoted (Neel, Cheney, Meadows, & Gelhar, 1992).

The focus of this section of the chapter is on teaching students social skills through informal methods. There are five main topics: (1) social competence and social skills; (2) social competence and students with EBD; (3) classroom management encouraging prosocial behavior; (4) use of a social task model; and (5) cooperative learning and social skills.

Social Competence and Social Skills

Defining Social Competence Through the years, many authors and educators have offered various definitions of social competence. In 1982, McFall made a distinction between social competence and social skills. Social competence is a summative judgment of an individual by significant others; social skills are behaviors used to respond to specific social tasks in an individual's life. Sugai and Lewis (1998) conceptualized the different definitions of social competence on a continuum where at one end, definitions focus on general attributes of a person's character such as sensitivity, empathy, and cooperation. At the other end of the continuum are definitions that focus on specific behaviors such as saying "please" and "thank you," and compliance behaviors such as following directions, listening, asking for help in a polite manner, and waiting one's turn. In the middle of the continuum there are integrative definitions such as the one offered by Kerr and Nelson (2006) who defined social competence as "an individual's ability to use critical social skills at the right time and place, showing social judgment or perception about how to act" (p. 312). Three definitions of social competence are particularly relevant to the discussions of informal social skills curriculum in this chapter. These definitions are based on the concepts of (1) social validity, (2) social tasks, and (3) antisocial behaviors.

Social Validity. Gresham (1986) has provided us with one of the most widely accepted definitions of social competence. His definition highlighted the importance of social validity and included elements of social skills that most people feel are important (Melloy et al., 1998; Sugai & Lewis, 1998).

Social competence is an evaluative term based on judgments (given certain criteria) that a person has performed a task adequately. These judgments may be based on opinions of significant others (e.g., parents, teachers), comparisons to explicit criteria (e.g., number of social tasks correctly performed in relation to some criterion), or comparisons to some normative sample (Gresham, 1986, p. 146).

Social Tasks. Another conceptualization of social competence is based on the social task model originally developed by Dodge (1985) and subsequently expanded on by others (Neel et al., 1990, 1992, 1997). In this model, social interactions include a specific social context (person, setting, timeframe, general situation); a social goal or outcome (e.g., attention, escape, affiliation, power, control, acceptance, self-gratification); a social task (e.g., dealing with criticism, being provoked, being rejected); and a set of social behaviors or social skills. Using this framework, a socially competent person uses appropriate social skills that (a) deal with the different social tasks that occur within various social contexts, and (b) achieve their desired social goals or outcomes in ways judged appropriate by others.

Antisocial Behaviors. A third approach to understanding social competence, and one that is especially relevant in the field of behavior disorders, looks at antisocial behaviors of children and youth. Antisocial behaviors are considered to be "polar opposites of prosocial patterns, which are composed of cooperative, positive, and mutually reciprocal social behaviors" (Rutherford & Nelson, 1998, p. 72). Walker and colleagues (1995) stated that "antisocial behavior suggests hostility to others, aggression, a willingness to commit rule infractions, defiance of adult authority, and violation of the social norms and mores of society" (p. 2). Longitudinal studies have shown that boys who are considered antisocial are more likely to experience school failure, have negative interactions with peers and adults, and have a high rate of discipline referrals (Walker et al., 1990, 1991; Walker, Ramsey, & Gresham, 2004; Walker, Shinn, O'Neill, & Ramsey, 1987).

Important Social Skills in Educational Settings
Social skills, as they are related to school and school-related activities, have been described by Walker and colleagues (1995) as "a set of competencies that (1) allow an individual to initiate and maintain positive social relationships, (2) contribute to peer acceptance and to satisfactory school adjustment, and (3) allow an individual to cope and adapt effectively with the larger social environment" (p. 227). Epanchin (1991) identified seven categories of social skills that children need in order to be considered socially competent by their teacher and peers: (1) to read social rules and expectations, (2) to interpret social and interpersonal cues, (3) to

communicate effectively in social situations, (4) to initiate social interactions in an age-appropriate manner, (5) to establish and maintain friendships, (6) to solve problems when they arise, and (7) to negotiate tactfully and successfully with others.

There are certain "school survival" skills that are necessary for success in academic environments (Kerr & Nelson, 2006; Zigmond, Kerr, Schaeffer, Brown, & Farra, 1986). Skills such as following instructions, listening, asking questions appropriately, and completing assignments in a timely manner are considered by teachers to be "compliance" skills and aid in the smooth running of the classroom. Kerr and Nelson (2006) compiled definitions of school survival skills and deficits that fall into the following general categories of social behaviors: (1) on/off task, (2) preparation for work or activity, (3) use of manners, (4) positive statements about self and others, and (5) positive statements about present and future. These skills focus on compliance and academic productivity in the classroom—skills that have been shown to be very important for students in general education settings.

Another way to determine important social skills or behaviors in classrooms is to look at nonexemplars—that is, behaviors teachers find intolerable in the classroom. Table 7-1 shows a list of behaviors that were rated by teachers as intolerable. The list was compiled by Kauffman (2005) from behaviors identified by Kerr and Zigmond (1986) and Hersh and Walker (1983).

These represent behaviors, or classes of behaviors, that at least 75% of teachers agreed were intolerable in their classrooms. It is possible to look at a behavior that the majority of teachers considered intolerable, and then determine what acceptable social skills a student would need to replace the intolerable behaviors. For example, teachers identified "behaves inappropriately in class when corrected" as intolerable. Socially acceptable behaviors to teach students when accepting feedback from teachers might include "listening," "following directions," "asking questions," and "stating your point in a calm manner."

Table 7–1 Intolerable behaviors as rated by teachers

Engages in inappropriate sexual behavior
Steals
Behaves inappropriately in class when corrected
Damages others' property
Refuses to obey teacher-imposed classroom rules
Is self-abusive
Makes lewd or obscene gestures
Ignores teacher warnings or reprimands

Social Competence and Students with EBD

By definition, students with EBD are set apart by their lack of social competence. Lacking certain social skills and exhibiting inadequate social skills have contributed to the poor academic and social outcomes experienced by students with EBD (Gresham, 1986; Kauffman, 1997; Neel et al., 1990). When EBD teachers are asked to describe the social skills of their students, they often use descriptive phrases such as the following:

- Has poor interpersonal relationships with peers and adults;

- Seeks attention inappropriately;

- Is noncompliant with directions and instructions;

- Uses aggressive behavior with peers;

- Has very few friends;

- Frequently withdraws from the group (Kauffman, 2005; Meadows, 1999; Melloy et al., 1998).

Most children learn to recognize appropriate social behavior, identify their own needs and the needs of others, anticipate consequences, develop multiple solutions to social problems or social tasks, choose behaviors appropriate to their social interactions and situations, and evaluate the effectiveness of their behaviors. Most children learn these skills informally, through interactions with their peers and with significant adults in their lives. Students with EBD, for the most part, have difficulty picking up social skills informally or distinguishing which social skills to use when, where, and with whom. According to Scanlon (1996), when students not developed appropriate social skills, it may be related to (1) limited opportunities to learn, (2) negative academic and social self-concept, and (3) social isolation. Gresham and Elliott (1993) have hypothesized that social skill deficits may be a result of "(a) a lack of cues or opportunities to learn or perform prosocial behaviors, (b) the presence of interfering problem behaviors that either block acquisition or impede performance of prosocial behaviors, (c) lack of knowledge, (d) a lack of sufficient practice or feedback on prosocial behavioral performances, and (e) a lack of reinforcement for performance of socially skilled behaviors" (p. 141). Social skills deficits may result from one or a combination of these five factors (Gresham & Elliott, 1993).

Some students judged as socially incompetent might know how to perform the social skill in question but choose not to. Gresham has described this as a performance deficit (Gresham, 1986). He posited that a lack of motivation is one underlying cause for social skills performance deficits. Students do not judge the appropriate social skills as important enough to use, or the appropriate skill(s) may not meet their desired social goal. In a study conducted several years ago, students with EBD did not rate social skills such as "being of assistance to the teacher," "avoiding confrontations and problems with adults," and "disagreeing with adults in an acceptable way" as very important. They did, however, rate skills such as "standing up for your rights" and "looking good" as very important (Meadows et al., 1991; Neel et al., 1997).

Why did students with EBD indicate they placed less value on the skills that would enable them to get along with others? According to Gresham's conceptualization of social skills, students with EBD may not be motivated to perform these skills because the rewards are not great enough or because the skills do not meet their needs. When we look at important social skills in the classroom, students with EBD may find themselves in trouble with adults: They are not motivated to perform or use the social skills they have learned because the targeted skills are not a priority for them.

Challenges to the Development of Social Competence A number of environmental and personal variables may act as barriers to students with EBD developing the socially competent behaviors exhibited by most of their peers (Melloy et al., 1998). These barriers or "challenges" can be grouped into general categories consisting of (1) at-risk variables, (2) affective distortions, (3) cognitive distortions, (4) language disorders, and (5) educational environments (Gresham, 1986; Kauffman, 1997; Melloy et al., 1998). It is important to understand the challenges that students with EBD face because these challenges may have a direct impact on social skills instruction.

At-Risk Variables. Children are more likely to develop antisocial behaviors or be labeled as socially incompetent when they are exposed to certain high-risk factors such as abuse, neglect, poverty, dysfunctional family relationships, drug and/or alcohol use, unpredictable family situations, poor educational programming, and indifferent educators (Walker et al., 1987, 1996). Withdrawn children or those who avoid social contact with others may have had limited opportunities for social interaction due to overrestrictive and/or socially incompetent parents or a history of aversive social experiences such as peer rejection and teasing (Gresham & Kern, 2004; Kauffman, 2005.) In contrast, there are asset qualities that are associated with socially competent children and youth such as close parental monitoring, a consistent family structure, participation in planned or structured activities during free time, and a family supportive of education and academic success. Unfortunately, children and youth with EBD are typically exposed to more at-risk factors than asset qualities (Melloy et al., 1998).

Affective Distortions. Children with EBD often exhibit affective distortions, which means they have problems interpreting social cues, emotions, and feelings during social interactions (Giddan, Bade, Rickenberg, & Ryley, 1995). As a result, they respond with social behaviors that are judged by others as inappropriate for the situation (Cullinan, 2002; Kauffman, 2005). For example, a child might hit another child for seemingly no reason, and the teacher labels hitting as unprovoked aggression. It may be, however, that the aggressive child misinterpreted the other child's actions as threatening. Affective distortions also impact students' abilities to interpret their emotions, provide control over them, and integrate them into appropriate social behavior (Giddan et al., 1995). Kauffman (2005) asserted that effective social skills training requires that teachers alter the way that students (a) behave toward others, (b) interpret others' behavior, and (c) perceive and express their emotional arousal in social circumstances.

Cognitive Distortions. Researchers in the area of emotional intelligence have explained cognitive distortions as "misleading beliefs" that are the result of dysfunctional schemes developed during abusive and traumatic childhood experiences (Goleman, 1995). Cognitive distortions are similar to affective distortions in that children and youth who have these misleading beliefs often misread social interactions, making self-reflection and perspective-taking very difficult. Negative academic and social self-concept—blaming others and the inability to see that a person's behavior has a direct impact on consequences and outcomes—may also be the result of cognitive distortions and misbeliefs (Melloy et al., 1998). When students with EBD have cognitive distortions involving power, they often express themselves through violent and aggressive acts, the results of which give them power over others (Goleman, 1995).

Language Disorders. Being able to verbally and nonverbally communicate with others is essential to successful social interactions. Interestingly enough, a large percentage of students with EBD are reported to have language disorders (Rinaldi, 2003; Rogers-Adkinson & Griffith, 1999). The area of pragmatics, the everyday, practical, social use of language, is a particular problem for these students (Kauffman, 2005). Difficulty with the pragmatic use of language may seriously impact development and use of appropriate social skills (Kauffman, 2005; Sanger, Maag, & Shapera, 1994; Walker, Schwartz, Nippold, Irvin, & Noell, 1994). Students with EBD often find it easy to use words and gestures as a means of irritating or annoying others. They may not, however, be as skilled in using pragmatic language in socially appropriate or constructive ways or to identify, label, and express their needs, wants, and feelings (Kauffman, 2005). Socially withdrawn students may be less adept in their verbal and nonverbal communication skills simply because they have fewer interactions with their peers and with the adults who play significant roles in their lives.

Educational Environments. Creating an environment that fosters positive peer relationships is a critical component in the education of students with EBD. Typically, students with EBD spend more time interacting with adults in the classroom than with their peers. Their time in the classroom is structured rather than unstructured, therefore reducing the opportunity to learn social skills through informal social interactions. Quite often, students with EBD are taught in self-contained and/or structured classrooms where peer interactions are discouraged and teachers play a direct role in students' instruction and learning (Lloyd, Kauffman, & Kupersmidt, 1990; Neel et al., 1992). Consequently, they have limited opportunities to learn and practice social skills. This type of social isolation presents a problem especially when teachers rely more on formal social skills instruction to teach students with EBD skills that their peers are learning naturally through informal social interactions.

Classroom Management Encouraging Prosocial Behavior

Because poor social skills result in behavior problems in the classroom, effective classroom management is an important component of social skills instruction (Maag, 2001). In most management programs, too much emphasis is placed on controlling children in the classroom and not enough importance is given to creating positive learning environments for students and teachers. Behavior management is more than consistency and control. Teaching children new behaviors and teaching children to be good managers of their own behavior is an important part of classroom curricula (Cullinan, 2002; Meadows, Melloy, & Yell, 1996; Muscott et al., 1996; Neel, 1988). One approach to understanding the relationship between classroom management and social skills is to look at the social and behavioral expectations of students in school settings. Miller (1998) identified the following social expectations that teachers have of students in classroom settings. These social expectations include:

- negotiating
- making decisions
- asking questions
- listening carefully
- predicting the outcomes of behavior
- adapting actions to certain circumstances
- empathizing with others
- evaluating behavior
- answering questions
- making choices
- having fun (p. 147)

In their review of literature in prevention and intervention research in classroom management, Witt, VanDerHeyden, and Gilbertson (2004) found that research has remained "relatively stagnant over the past several years" (p. 426). Current "best practices" in classroom management are based on work primarily conducted in the 1980s (Brophy, 1983; Emmer, Evertson, & Anderson, 1982). Best practices in classroom management continue to include a mixture of proactive and reactive strategies. Proactive strategies include directly teaching rules, expectations, and procedures to students at the beginning of the school year, and periodically providing reinforcers to maintain appropriate behaviors. When behavior problems do occur, reactive strategies such as behavioral contracts and individualized behavior plans are indicated (Witt et al., 2004).

Witt and colleagues presented a pyramid model of classroom management that includes three integrated strands necessary for classroom management:

- Are academic skills taught appropriately?
- Are positive behavioral expectations taught appropriately?
- Are teacher responses to inappropriate behavior consistent and accurate?

The pyramid structure is foundational in that each level serves as a foundation for the next. Their recommendation is that teachers implement group-oriented strategies at these three levels almost simultaneously during the first several weeks of school. By definition, the needs of students with behavior disorders often go beyond these three levels. At the top of the pyramid are functional assessment and positive behavior support. Essentially, using the pyramid structure ensures that all students begin with classroom-based, group-oriented management strategies and gradually move up to interventions that are more individualized, prescribed, and data based (Witt et al., 2004).

Our approach to classroom management as a means of increasing social competence is this: It is a proactive curriculum based on a philosophy of teaching, not just managing behaviors in the classroom. Components of classroom management that we feel are closely related to the development of social competence and informal instruction of social skills include:

- Preventive strategies that emphasize classroom organization and structure;
- Positive teacher–student relationships based on clear and realistic expectations;
- Positive peer relationships and strategies that foster friendship development;
- Presocial skills that enhance academic success;
- Curriculum-of-the-moment situations that serve as contexts for teaching valid replacement behaviors.

Classroom Organization and Structure Classrooms should be organized to support the development of prosocial skills, with the lessons structured so that opportunities to practice social skills are an integral part of the day. Unfortunately, the physical and structural aspects of the classroom are often ignored or not very well thought out (Zionts, 1996). Kerr and Nelson (2006) stated that classroom organization and structure consists of "antecedent variables that the teacher may use to influence pupil behavior: the planning of physical space, daily schedule, rules, teacher movement patterns, and stimulus change" (p. 159). The following suggestions are related to classroom organization and structure, and are designed to facilitate the development of prosocial behaviors:

- Provide clear paths for teacher and student movement through the classroom.
- Physically arrange the room so that teachers can move freely to monitor students' behavior and work.
- Regulate students' movement in the classroom.
- Teach transition behaviors to students such as moving to and from different activities in the classroom, lining up to leave the room, and walking in hallways, to playgrounds, and to buses.

- Reinforce appropriate behaviors during transition times.

- Arrange students' work space to meet their behavioral patterns and needs. For example, active students need more space; provide more space during individual seat work to increase on-task behaviors (Kerr & Nelson, 2006).

- Arrange students' work space to meet instructional needs. For example, for in-group projects where peer interaction is necessary, close proximity is desirable.

- Provide separate areas for group and individual seat work. If space is limited, schedule noisy activities at separate times during the day (Kerr & Nelson, 2006).

- Provide study carrels or cubicles for students who need more privacy and a quiet place to complete their work. Isolated spaces should be used judiciously and no student should spend unnecessary portions of the day separated from their peers. As Kerr and Nelson (2006) noted, the strategy of "out of sight, out of mind" is never acceptable. As an alternative to study carrels, introduce students to the concept of "office time" (Kerr & Nelson, 2006; Zionts, 1996). "Portable offices" can be placed on top of students' desks during office time (Zionts, 1996). Teachers explain office space as places where work can get done more efficiently and on time. Office time can become a form of self-management where students actually choose to work in their offices to complete their work more quickly.

- Allow students opportunities to move about the classroom. Using a token or other type of reward system, students can "earn" the privilege of moving about the room or walking to other parts of the school (e.g., walking to the library to return books; turning in attendance sheets at the office) (Lewis & Doorlag, 1995).

- Use proximity control to monitor students' behaviors. For example, if a teacher is able to anticipate when a student is going to talk out, she can use her physical presence as a reminder to prevent inappropriate comments (Lewis & Doorlag, 1995).

Teacher–Student Relationships Relationships between students with EBD, especially those labeled as "acting out," and their teachers are often "negative, confrontational, and characterized by mutual hostility" (Walker, 1995, p. 39). When relationships such as this exist in the classroom, they disrupt learning for all students. More important, according to Walker (1995), aversive relationships can "condition teachers' instructional and management behavior toward acting-out children long after the specific behaviors in question have terminated" (pp. 39-40). In essence, teachers often expect to see inappropriate behaviors, and their expectations may actually precipitate the student's inappropriate behavior.

Effective classroom managers (a) consistently build and maintain positive teacher–student relationships, (b) function as role models for their students, and (c) reinforce appropriate behavior. To develop positive teacher–student relations teachers should be mindful of Ralph Waldo Emerson's advice that the heart of education lies in respecting the pupil. Teachers must listen to students, talk and act toward students in respectful and caring ways, and be willing to be honest and open with them (Meadows, Melloy, & Yell, 1996). Effective managers communicate clearly what is and is not acceptable in the classroom. When students behave in ways that are appropriate and show self-control, teachers need to acknowledge this and communicate approval. When students behave inappropriately, teachers must communicate disapproval and apply consequences consistently, but this should not be done by humiliating or belittling them. A positive teacher–student relationship implies respectful, supportive, fair, and consistent treatment of students.

Children learn behavior by watching others. As teachers, we are constantly modeling behavior to our students. The behaviors we model must reflect the values we hold and are trying to teach to our students. We cannot teach students to behave in a particular manner if we do not behave in that manner ourselves. Being a mature, responsible adult who exhibits self-discipline and deals with students in a fair and respectful manner is the best means by which we can foster growth in our students. Teachers must also be mindful of Walker's (1995) advice: "the emotional reactions of adults to child behaviors that they find highly irritating or aversive are slow to subside" (p. 39).

Classrooms must be positive places for students. To make their classroom positive, teachers need to watch for and consistently reinforce appropriate behavior. When appropriate student behavior is recognized and reinforced, students are motivated to choose appropriate behavior, thus creating a positive classroom atmosphere. This will not only reduce inappropriate behavior but it also will make classrooms a positive place to learn, and help improve relationships with students. Reinforcers may include positive notes and calls to parents, points, and privileges, and should always include teacher attention and meaningful praise.

Peer Relationships and Friendship Development As we discussed in the beginning of the chapter, students with EBD are often rejected or ignored by their peers. Consequently, peer acceptance is considered a valid outcome when programming for the needs of students with EBD (Gresham, 1986). When Miller (1998) examined the relationship of social skills to behavior management, she found "the most significant impact on management is student's relationship-oriented skills" (p. 147). For example, when the social expectation is to "work cooperatively with peers," socially competent students are "approved" by their peers and are typically invited in and included in peer groups. Socially incompetent students are usually excluded from groups and suffer peer disapproval and rejection (Miller, 1998).

There are numerous peer-related activities discussed in the literature that will promote positive peer relationships. More recently, educators have focused on friendship development strategies for students with EBD as a way of increasing peer acceptance (Salend, 1999; Searcy & Meadows, 1994). Strain and Smith (1996) concluded that there are peer social skills that distinguish students with disabilities who have friends from their peers with disabilities who do not have friends. Children with disabilities who have friends "tend to (a) engage in more 'shared exchanges' with their peers; (b) be children who suggest more play ideas, or who accept the suggestions of other children and follow along; (c) accept affection from others and occasionally display affection themselves; and (d) help other children" (Strain & Smith, 1996, p. 25).

Friendship development is affected by factors such as (1) how the environment is structured to encourage social interactions, (2) whether there is encouragement to interact with peers, and (3) whether different settings offer continuity of friendships over time and with the same people (Searcy, 1996; Searcy & Meadows, 1994). According to Searcy (1996), "our social and environmental structures may either enhance or limit the opportunities children have to develop and maintain relationships" (p. 131). The following suggestions fall within the domain of classroom management and will assist students with EBD in developing and maintaining friendships.

- Provide activities at the beginning of the year and periodically throughout the year to make sure that children know each other.

- Integrate "friendship" as an important part of classroom rules and procedures.

- Make sure that there are positive consequences for appropriate social behavior.

- Structure successful recess periods and social interactions at lunch.

- Prevent adult proximity or attention from interrupting and distancing children.

- Use activities with friends as a reinforcer.

- Set friendship goals with children and help them monitor their progress.

- Structure academic assignments that encourage students to interact with their classmates (Church, Gottschalk, & Leddy, 2003).

- Help students recognize nonverbal language in social situations (Cartledge & Kiarie, 2001).

- Help students read social cues in situations and recognize subtle, unwritten rules in social interactions (Church et al., 2003).

- Teach students cognitive problem strategies such as SLAM: Stop what you are doing; Look the person in the eye; Ask the person a question to clarify what he or she means; and Make an appropriate response to the person (Hallahan & Kauffman, 2003).

- Teach students to monitor and reflect on the success or failure of their social interactions and to generate alternative strategies.

- Encourage students to participate in after-school activities; involve parents in these plans.

Behavior Management Techniques Behavior management techniques have been discussed previously in the text. Here, however, we would like to emphasize behavior management strategies that teachers can use to help students become more socially competent. Using *social reinforcers* such as praise, attention, and approval is especially important when students are developing new social behaviors. Once a student has learned the new social skill and is using it consistently and appropriately, the teacher can begin an intermittent schedule of social reinforcers. Pairing social reinforcers with a *token economy* may be effective in increasing students' use of prosocial behaviors (Zirpoli & Melloy, 1997). Children earn a social reinforcer such as praise as well as a token when they act appropriately during social interactions.

Level systems are often used in conjunction with token economies to monitor students' increased use of appropriate skills (Cullinan, 2002). In a level system, targeted skills are arranged hierarchically from basic (e.g., listening, following directions) to more complex (e.g., negotiating, developing friendships). The hierarchy of skills is coordinated with a hierarchy of privileges, with students earning more privileges as they engage in more appropriate social behaviors. The Boys Town model originated by Father Flanagan's Boys' Home is an example of a published curriculum combining a level system with a token economy. The efficacy of level systems for students with EBD has been questioned (Scheuermann, Webber, Partin, & Knies, 1994). Level systems that are attached to students' gaining access to general education settings may violate court rulings on IDEA that link students' participation in general education settings to their behavior (Scheuermann et al., 1994). Level systems that link appropriate behavior to general education access also assume that students find moving into a less restrictive setting to be a reward. This is not always the case. Many students with EBD have chosen to "sabotage" their progress in order to remain in their special education setting.

Contingency contracting is another behavior management technique that may be effective in increasing prosocial behaviors (Zirpoli, 2005; Zirpoli & Melloy, 1997). It is important that (1) the student and teacher develop the contract together, (2) the appropriate social skill is clearly defined, (3) the "reward" is mutually agreed on, (4) data are collected to continually monitor the increased use of the targeted skill, and (5) the contract is rewritten when necessary.

Use of a Social Task Model

As we discussed earlier in the chapter, social tasks are a way of conceptualizing social competence (Meadows & Stevens, 2004). In the social task model, there are four major components of the social interaction process: the situation or context of the interaction, the individual's social goal or intended outcome, the presented social task, and specific skills or social behaviors.

The social task model for informally instructing social skills is just that—a model. It is loosely structured and based on the philosophy that replacement social skills must be taught within the context of relevant social tasks and must meet students' social goals. It is not a curriculum in and of itself; it is merely a foundation on which teachers can build their own informal social skills curriculum.

Social Situation or Context The contexts in which social interactions occur play an important role in deciding which social skills people choose to use. A major criticism of social skills instruction has been that it is not contextually relevant for students. That is, social skills curricula do not consider the skills that students will actually use with their peers or in the real-life situations or social tasks that students face each day. We know that students with EBD do not always "read" contexts correctly—nor are they good at picking up subtle social cues. Consequently, it is important that teachers not only teach social skills in contexts that are relevant for students; students must also be taught to scope out environments and read contexts correctly.

Accurately identifying the social context or situation typically involves descriptions of the participants, the setting, and the type of activity. Participants generally include peers (either one-on-one or in groups), teachers, or other adults such as instructional assistants, administrators, and counselors. Settings are described as structured or unstructured and may include classroom, the principal's office, hallways, the library, the playground, the gym, the cafeteria, and the school bus. Types of activities include those that are supervised or nonsupervised and instructional or non-instructional and may be either teacher- or peer-related activities.

Social or Behavioral Intent Most children seek similar social outcomes in their social interactions (Krasnor & Rubin, 1983; Neel, Jenkins, & Meadows, 1990). The following outcomes are considered common to most children (Neel & Cessna, 1993; Neel et al., 1990):

- attention
- escape/avoidance
- power
- control
- protection
- acceptance/affiliation
- expression of self and/or self-gratification
- justice/revenge

Neel and Cessna (1993) referred to these as behavioral intents described as "outcomes a student attempts to achieve through a series of social interactions, using a set of behaviors (skills) in a variety of settings" (p. 33). For example, the acting-out child with EBD who is seeking attention as a social goal may have an entire repertoire of inappropriate behaviors (e.g., talking out, getting out of his or her seat, talking back or arguing, hitting) that predictably gain attention (Walker, 1995). The more socially appropriate child typically chooses more appropriate behaviors (e.g., asking for help, offering to share) to meet the same need.

Escape is a frequently identified intent for both acting out and socially withdrawn students. A child may choose to "escape" a perceived unpleasant activity (e.g., doing a math worksheet, reading aloud, sitting still for a structured activity) by being verbally or physically aggressive to a teacher or peers. Depending on the situation, the child will choose a behavior with predictable results—that is, being asked to leave the classroom. In this same situation, a child judged as more socially competent might choose to "escape" the task by feigning sickness and being sent to the nurse. Although their behaviors may differ, the social/behavioral intent is the same in both situations.

Students with EBD who are socially withdrawn may escape by isolating themselves from people and activities. Kerr and Nelson (2006) referred to social withdrawal as "a cluster of behaviors that result in an individual escaping or avoiding social contact" (p. 243). It is sometimes difficult to determine whether the socially withdrawn child has a skill deficit or a performance deficit (Gresham, 1986). Some students withdraw because others have rejected them in the past or they associate social interactions with punishment or abuse (Kerr & Nelson, 2006). Others may have social skills deficits because of their long history of isolation and therefore lack of opportunity to learn the appropriate social skills. Socially withdrawn behaviors are often difficult to change because they are maintained through negative reinforcement (Kerr & Nelson, 2006). Students continue to isolate themselves because they are able to escape or avoid the aversive stimulus of social interaction. Social withdrawal is a serious problem because students who continue to isolate themselves limit their opportunities to learn social skills through naturally occurring social interactions.

Social Tasks Defined Social tasks are the problems a child faces or deals with when trying to achieve a social goal in a particular situation. The most important characteristic of social tasks is that they represent activities in students' daily lives. Dodge and colleagues have argued that identifying problematic social tasks is essential for planning social skills interventions (Dodge, 1985). Previously identified social tasks for adolescents with EBD include (Neel et al., 1992):

- Being provoked by a peer to fight or argue
- Dealing with the consequences of your behavior
- Being criticized or corrected by a teacher in class
- Being blamed for something you didn't do
- Being hit by others in school
- Being provoked or hassled by a teacher
- Being criticized by another student
- Being rejected by other students

- Being responsible for your own actions
- Dealing with tough kids
- Dealing with teachers who don't like you
- Dealing with peer pressure

Typically, when students with EBD are presented with these tasks, they react in inappropriate ways. For example, when provoked by a peer to fight, it is common for students with EBD to respond with verbally or physically aggressive behaviors.

Social Skills or Behaviors Social skills, according to Gresham (1986), are "those behaviors which, within a given situation, predict important social outcomes" (p. 5). As we discussed earlier in the chapter, teachers have indicated over and over again that compliance is an important social outcome for students. Consequently, instruction often focuses on social skills such as listening, following directions, asking questions appropriately, and accepting feedback. Kerr and Nelson (2006) noted that intervention efforts at the secondary level should first focus on teaching and increasing compliance skills such as

- meeting due dates
- arriving at school on time
- attending class every day
- exhibiting interest in academic work
- accepting consequences of behavior (p. 229)

Problem behaviors that should be decreased or extinguished include:

- Seldom completes assignments
- Cannot follow written directions
- Gives back talk to teacher
- Falls asleep in class
- Is quick to give up (Kerr & Nelson, 2006)

Social skills instruction is particularly difficult when students and teachers do not agree on what are valid social outcomes. For example, middle school students with EBD have reported self-expression skills such as "stand up for your rights" as an important social skill (Meadows et al., 1991). Students also reported social skills grouped around friendship issues as being important.

In this study, students did not value the same social skills as did the adults.

The social task model focuses on replacement social skills—new social behaviors or skills that are used in response to the social task presented and that meet the child's social/behavioral intent (Neel & Cessna, 1993; Neel et al., 1990). It is important for teachers to teach the skills that children will actually use, in language that is meaningful to them, and within the context of social tasks that are relevant to them. As discussed, it is also imperative that the new social skills be replacement skills that meet children's social or behavioral intents.

Implications for Teaching Social Skills In summary, the social task model has several implications for teaching social skills informally.

1. *Teach new social skills in the context of social tasks that are meaningful to students.* For example, if an elementary student has difficulty dealing with being teased by others, new social skills are taught to deal with the social task of being teased. Or, if accepting feedback is a problem for a student, it would be important to teach replacement skills the student would actually use when being given feedback.

2. *Teach new social skills that meet students' social/ behavioral intents.* For example, after analyzing a series of problem behaviors in several situations, the teacher determines that the student is frustrated, and the end result is that the student is somehow removed from the situation (e.g., taken to time-out, sent to the office). The teacher then hypothesizes that the student's intent is to escape, and escape becomes the instructional theme for informally instructing the student more appropriate ways to escape. The teacher's instructional plan for teaching replacement social behaviors focuses on the social task of dealing with frustration and the social/ behavioral intent to escape.

3. *Teach students to discriminate between settings or contexts.* For example, the social tasks in special education settings may differ from those that are presented to students in inclusive classrooms. In a general education classroom, a student with EBD may have to deal with the frustration of waiting to be called on by the teacher, whereas in a special education classroom the wait time may be of a much shorter duration. Also, dealing with being provoked by other students may be more of a problem in less structured settings such as bus rides, cafeterias, and in the hallways between classes.

4. *Teach students that social goals and social behaviors appropriate in some settings may not be appropriate in others.* For example, some behaviors are acceptable at home but may not be appropriate for school (e.g., arguing, fighting with siblings, negotiating deadlines, etc.). Also, some social/behavioral intents may have to be shifted to other settings or to other times during the day.

5. *The social tasks in special education settings differ from those in mainstream and inclusive classrooms.* Students with EBD seem to have an overabundance of adult-mediated experiences surrounded by a set of poor peer models. This may partially explain their difficulty in mainstreamed settings where teacher influence is less intrusive and the tasks presented are not similar to those that were practiced in special education.

Social Tasks as Curriculum-of-the-Moment Opportunities Children with EBD are unlike students with other disabilities: They often create their own curriculum through inappropriate behaviors and emotional outbursts (Neel & Cessna, 1993). Most often, teachers view these problem behaviors as interruptions of the teaching day, which disturb the normal school process and make them feel as if they are out of control of their classroom. However, these are the situations that become the curriculum of the moment regardless of whether the academic content is math, reading, or any other content area subject (Meadows, 1991, 1993). Consequently, teaching new behaviors becomes an integral part of informal instruction throughout the day, and is not always a scheduled part of daily instruction (Meadows & Cavin, 1996; Meadows et al., 1996; Neel & Cessna, 1993).

During curriculum-of-the-moment situations, teachers must ask themselves what other, more appropriate behaviors they can teach the child so that his or her needs are met (Meadows, 1993; Neel & Cessna, 1993). For example, the student with EBD who needs attention may have an entire repertoire of inappropriate behaviors (e.g., talking out, getting out of seat, talking back or arguing, hitting) that predictably gain attention. When a teacher plans an instructional intervention, the plan must be needs based. For example, if the teacher has determined that a child is attempting to escape a math activity because it is the only way he knows how to deal with frustration, intervention might focus on teaching new skills for escaping a frustrating activity (e.g., asking for help, taking a short time-out from the activity, implementing some problem-solving skills, etc.). In this same situation, if the teacher hypothesizes that the student is trying to control the activity, she might teach negotiating skills or offer the student a menu of other choices meeting the same academic objectives. In either situation, the teacher does not try to change the student's needs, but rather offers a plan for acquiring replacement behaviors that still meet the same need (Cessna & Skiba, 1996; Neel & Cessna, 1993).

Meadows and Cavin (1996) completed a school-based assignment designed to teach students social skills by creating an environment where social skills were necessary for successful completion of a class newspaper project. The instructional method was cooperative learning and the final product was a newspaper representing the interests of all the students in special education at the high school. Following the social task model, the identified behavioral intent was affiliation, the social task was dealing with others in a group setting, and the targeted social skills included listening, sharing, encouraging others, following instructions, and asking questions.

Cooperative Learning and Social Skills

Although cooperative learning groups may not be an appropriate setting for teaching social skills, groups do require students to use appropriate social skills (Scanlon, 1996). There are several key elements of cooperative learning that encourage positive social behaviors (Mcadows & Cavin, 1996). First, students experience positive interdependence as they work together (sink or swim) (Johnson & Johnson, 1987). This may be developed through mutual goals, joint rewards, shared resources, or assigned roles. Second, students promote each other's learning by helping, sharing, and encouraging one another. They explain, discuss, and teach their peers. Third, students develop and strengthen interpersonal and collaborative skills through leadership, decision making, trust building, communication, and conflict management. Fourth, students are engaged in group processing activities and skills. Groups are given time to complete their goals. Teachers direct groups to recognize actions that ensure success, and actions that could be changed or added for more successful completion of the task. Teachers monitor each group and give feedback on progress, success, and group skills. Finally, because students are placed in heterogeneous groups, students with different skill levels, abilities, and talents work collaboratively to complete a project or study a topic. Cooperative learning exposes students to others with different ideas and talents, often resulting in a deeper appreciation of others' viewpoints and more tolerant attitudes toward other types of people.

Chapter Summary

Strong social skills contribute to positive academic and social outcomes for children and youth. However, we can conclude from our discussions in this chapter that assessing and teaching the social skills that actually enhance social competence of students with EBD are not easy tasks. Teaching social skills is a complex process and one that has been fraught with difficulties, frustrations, and disappointments. Both formal and informal curricula are critical if students with EBD are to become more socially competent and more accepted by their peers.

Teaching students new social behaviors is a major component of any behavior management curriculum. Classroom management focuses on teaching and increasing new social behaviors through positive educative approaches rather than merely decreasing inappropriate social behaviors through reductive approaches. Typically, teaching behaviors depends on the curriculum of the moment and is part of informal teaching throughout the day.

When designing an informal social skills curriculum, it is important to identify the child's social goal in order to teach appropriate replacement behaviors. These replacement behaviors are new behaviors that meet the child's social goal. Children's social or behavioral intents are not always easy to determine and may require multiple observations, anecdotal records, and behavioral interviews in order to hypothesize correctly. But, learning new social skills that meet students' social goals are critical if these new skills are to generalize across time and settings.

When designing any type of social skills instruction, it is important for teachers to teach the skills that children will actually use, in language that is meaningful to them. It is also imperative that the new social skills meet children's social goals and are taught within the context of social tasks that are relevant to them. Cooperative learning requires students to use appropriate social skills and is an excellent instructional methodology to accompany informal social skills instruction.

CHAPTER 8

Meeting the Needs of Students with EBD Through Collaborative Teaming

K. Alisa Lowrey, Mitchell L. Yell, and D. Clark Cavin

Focus Questions

- What is collaborative teaming and why is it important when teaching children and youth with emotional and behavioral disorders?
- What are some different arrangements in teaming?
- Who should be involved in a collaborative team?
- What makes an effective collaborative team?
- How can educators and families collaborate effectively?

The purpose of this chapter is to provide a rationale and methods for using collaboration and teaming when developing and implementing educational programs for students with emotional and behavioral disorders (EBD). First, we define the concepts of collaboration and teaming in education. Second, we review the literature to provide a rationale for using collaborative teaming when working with students with EBD. Third, we describe three major components necessary to establishing effective collaborative teams. Fourth, we examine who should be involved in the collaborative process and give examples of interpersonal and interagency collaboration. Fifth, we discuss six themes that teachers should focus on when establishing collaborative relationships with families of students with EBD.

Throughout this chapter, we incorporate voices of parents and professionals currently working in the field. A survey on collaboration was mailed to former public school colleagues and parents of individuals with disabilities in order to get authentic voices from individuals required to collaborate every day. Each of these participants helped us better understand how collaborative teaming can be used successfully. Their comments are included in the figures throughout this chapter (see Figure 8-1).

COLLABORATION AND TEAMING DEFINED

The concepts of collaboration and teaming are fundamentally entwined. A team cannot operate effectively without good collaboration, nor can effective collaboration occur without having fellow team members with which to do so. In practice, therefore, collaboration and teaming are inseparable. We begin by defining each term.

Collaboration stems from the Latin phrase *collăbōro* meaning "to labor with or together" (Lewis & Short, 2006). This definition implies that collaboration is active and relational; it is something that is done with others. According to Friend and Cook (2000), "interpersonal collaboration is a style for direct interaction between at least two coequal parties voluntarily engaged in shared decision making as they work toward a common goal" (p. 6). This view of collaboration is certainly applicable when working in a school environment. Figure 8-2 shows the views of professionals on defining collaboration.

At the very core of collaboration is an understanding and acceptance by all parties that equality, engagement, shared decision making, and common goals are represented by the activity of collaboration. These concepts will be discussed later in the chapter. Collaboration, therefore, is both *what we do* and *how we do it*.

Fundamental to the concept of collaboration is the idea of a relational or a team approach and the idea of shared goals. With this in mind, we look at the concept of teaming. Teaming is an integral part of many aspects of our society. We establish teams for many purposes (e.g., sport teams, quiz teams, cooking teams, marching/drill teams, home repair teams). Team dynamics, however, are multifaceted. For example, teams can function independently as members (e.g., golf teams) to achieve a shared goal or teams may function with a level of interdependence (e.g., basketball team) to achieve a shared goal. In golf, team members' individual scores are added together to achieve the final overall score. In basketball, team members must assist one another in offensive and defensive efforts on the court to win the game. Thus, collaborative teams must have the same level of interdependence as a basketball team to achieve the shared goal. One of the first tasks of a collaborative team, therefore, is to establish a level of interdependence so that a shared goal can be defined. If collaboration is *what we do* and *how we do it*, collaborative teaming refers to *whom we do it with*. We will use the concept of collaborative teaming throughout this chapter.

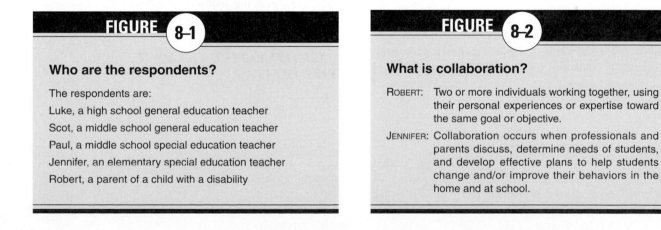

FIGURE 8-1

Who are the respondents?

The respondents are:
Luke, a high school general education teacher
Scot, a middle school general education teacher
Paul, a middle school special education teacher
Jennifer, an elementary special education teacher
Robert, a parent of a child with a disability

FIGURE 8-2

What is collaboration?

ROBERT: Two or more individuals working together, using their personal experiences or expertise toward the same goal or objective.

JENNIFER: Collaboration occurs when professionals and parents discuss, determine needs of students, and develop effective plans to help students change and/or improve their behaviors in the home and at school.

Rainforth, York-Barr, and MacDonald (1992) introduced the concept of collaborative teaming to create an approach to delivering services that transcended the role of a teacher working alone in his or her classroom with little or no interaction with other professionals. Although Rainforth et al. developed this approach working in programs for students with severe disabilities, the approach is certainly applicable to students with EBD. Gable, Quinn, Rutherford, Howell, and Hoffman (2000) summarized the need for using collaborative teams to address the needs of students with EBD as follows:

We want to stress the role that teamwork plays in addressing student behavior problems. When school personnel conduct functional behavioral assessments and develop behavior intervention plans, they should draw upon a range of communication and interpersonal skills. Like knowledge of assessment itself, IEP team members may need special training in the skills of successful collaboration, such as time management, group problem solving (including "brainstorming" strategies), active listening, and conflict resolution processes, to mention a few. . . . As with other collaborative efforts, building-level administrative and collegial support is essential to a successful outcome. The value and appropriateness of student and parent involvement in the process also should be carefully considered. Too often they are excluded from activities when they have much to offer. (p. 4)

TYPES OF COLLABORATIVE TEAMS

The literature on teaming contains descriptions of many different types of school-based teams (Friend & Cook, 2000). For example, a few of the different types of teams that currently operate in school systems include (a) multidisciplinary teams, (b) interdisciplinary teams, and (c) transdisciplinary teams. Knowing about these different models is important to understanding how teams may function collaboratively. Of course, the function of any team should be directly dependent on the individual student's needs and the purposes of the team (Downing, 1999). We next describe the operation of these three types of teams.

Multidisciplinary teams are composed of members representing different disciplines of expertise. Each team member independently contributes plans for addressing a student's needs based on his or her own professional expertise and assessment of the student. Members of multidisciplinary teams, therefore, work independently, although their goals are all the same—to develop an appropriate education program for a student. An example of an IEP team that functions as a multidisciplinary team occurs when members come with recommended goals and objectives specific to their own area of expertise and prepared without input from the other team members (e.g., the teacher writes his or her goals

without consulting the student's counselor about his or her intended goals).

Interdisciplinary teams are comprised of members representing different disciplines of expertise, yet working jointly to create programs that meet the student's need. Members of interdisciplinary teams work together to plan programs, but team members typically work separately to implement the programs. For example, if an IEP team functions as an interdisciplinary team, members would come together and discuss intended targets until shared goals were reached. Then team members would implement educational programs independently (e.g., teacher teaches content, social worker implements social skills training).

Transdisciplinary teams are teams comprised of members who represent different areas of expertise; however, each team member transcends those disciplinary boundaries to teach, work, and learn together new skills so that each team member can better serve the individual with disabilities. For example, a transdisciplinary IEP team would meet together to plan IEP goals and services across disciplines. Team members would then plan the implementation of the student's programs through integrated curriculum. For example, a teacher teaches academic content and the social worker trains the teacher to offer additional opportunities to develop specific social skills practice during lessons; a social worker learns what vocabulary words to focus on from the teacher while implementing social skills training; a speech therapist may come into the classroom during English language arts to work on speech with the student while the student is working on vocabulary.

In special education, the type of teaming used most frequently is the multidisciplinary team. A better approach would be to facilitate the development and function of transdisciplinary teams in order to enhance the ability of all team members to contribute their knowledge and skills to others on the team, thereby increasing the likelihood of embedding a variety of services into a student's educational program.

COLLABORATIVE TEAMING: WHY DO IT?

There are a number of reasons that professionals should take the time to engage in collaborative teamwork. First, collaborative teaming is a concept supported by law. The Individuals with Disabilities Education Improvement Act of 2004 (IDEA 2004) continues to require that multidisciplinary teams be involved in the following aspects of service delivery for students with disabilities: (1) the determination of eligibility; (2) the design, implementation, and evaluation of individualized education programs; and (3) the design, implementation, and evaluation of functional behavioral assessments (FBAs) and behavior intervention plans (BIPs). With each succeeding reauthorization, the Individuals with Disabilities Education Act (IDEA) has increased the emphasis on collaboration and teaming in developing programs and providing services to students with disabilities. Every reauthorization has clarified the role and membership of the team as well as stressed the importance of parental membership on that team. In addition, Section 504 of the Vocational Rehabilitation Act (1973) requires a team approach in developing and implementing accommodation plans. Furthermore, the Americans with Disabilities Act (ADA 1990) mandates accessibility for individuals with disabilities. This, in turn, has led to increased use of teaming approaches among employers and employees (Thomas, Correa, & Morsink, 2001). Thus, legislation requires that schools take a collaborative team approach when designing, implementing, and evaluating programs for students in special education programs.

A second reason to implement a collaborative teaming approach is that collaborative teaming facilitates a best practices approach. For example, the Center for Effective Collaboration and Practice (CECP) published guidelines titled *Improving Services for Children and Youth with Emotional and Behavioral Problems* (2000). Its mission statement embraces a dedication to a policy of collaboration at federal, state, and local levels that contributes to and facilitates the production, exchange, and use of knowledge about effective practices. Throughout CECP's suggested guidelines, a collaborative team approach is advanced as fundamental to the success of recommended interventions such as positive behavior supports, functional behavioral assessments, behavior intervention plans, and individualized education programs for students with, or at risk for, emotional and behavioral problems.

Research on teaching practices has identified strategies such as peer tutoring, cooperative learning, and an integrated curriculum approach as being best practices (Lewis et al., 2004). At the core of each strategy's implementation is collaborative teaming. Additionally, when mental health services are included in a student's educational program, school personnel will need to collaborate with other professions within and outside schools. When school-based teams involve all team members as equal partners in developing a student's program, thus ensuring that everyone understands the targeted outcomes, procedures for implementation, and evaluation, it is likely that the student's education will represent a best practices approach in delivering services to the student.

A third reason to implement a collaborative teaming approach is that effective collaborative teaming has the potential to change outcomes for students with EBD. Eber et al., (1997) asserted that effectively meeting the needs of students with EBD is an elusive goal. Koyangi and Gaines (1993) further stated that outcomes for students with EBD often include high dropout rates, academic failure, low achievement test scores, and increased risk of placement in institutionalized settings. According to Knitzer and colleagues (1990), one contributing factor to these dismal outcomes is the lack of coordination with appropriate service provider personnel, outside agencies, and families. Knitzner (1993) argued that failure by outside agencies and students' teachers to collaboratively plan programs and intervene with students with EBD seriously limits the likelihood of programs being successfully developed and implemented in multiple settings and across life domains. Using collaborative teaming to create a cohesive environment that applies seamless implementation of interventions and "wraps around" the child can directly affect the outcomes of students with EBD (Eber et al., 1997).

A fourth reason to implement a collaborative teaming approach when working with students with EBD is that it can help alleviate the critical shortage of qualified teachers in the area of EBD. Katsiyannis, Zhang, and Conroy (2003) stated that EDB is considered a critical needs area by the U.S. Department of Education and that there is a shortage of qualified teachers working in the field. One of the contributing factors is teachers who enter the profession only to leave a few years later. Often teachers who quickly leave the profession report that they experienced teacher burnout. Whatever the reasons for teacher attrition, steps must be taken to increase teacher retention in the field of special education and particularly in the field of EBD. Gersten, Keating, Yovanoff, and Harniss (2001) suggested that one method to increase teacher retention is meaningful collaboration with colleagues.

In *Bright Futures for Exceptional Learners: An Action Agenda to Achieve Quality Conditions for Teaching and Learning* (Council for Exceptional Children [CEC], 2000), it was reported that special education teachers frequently feel isolated in their schools. The report suggested that schools significantly increase opportunities for special educators to participate in and interact with both general and special education colleagues within their schools. A collaborative team approach is one of the ways that schools can address this need because collaborative teaming offers collegial support in decision making, implementation, evaluation, and communication with others about what the "team" is doing. This has the potential to remove the feelings of isolation and autonomy that plague individuals in their early teaching career (Johnson, 2000).

A final reason to implement a collaborative teaming approach is that effective collaborative teaming has the potential to improve the problem of disproportionate representation of students from minority backgrounds in programs for students with EBD. Data clearly show that minority students, particularly African American students, are overrepresented in programs for students labeled EBD (Landrum, 2000; Oswald, Coutinho, Best, & Singh, 1999). Additionally, this problem seems to be increasing (Landrum, 2000). Because of the negative outcomes that are frequently associated with the label of EBD, all attempts to be sure that the label is applied only when appropriate would seem to be a primary goal. According to Landrum (2000), deciding on or identifying the appropriateness of the label of EBD is challenging. Trent and Artiles (1994) asserted that a difference in cultural norms between majority and minority cultures is partially the reason for disproportionate representation of minority populations. To address this difference, Harry, Rueda, and Kalyanpur (1999) suggested professionals working with students and families adopt a posture of cultural reciprocity. Simply put, cultural reciprocity entails identifying, examining, and evaluating one's own cultural norms to recognize potential similarities to and differences from others' cultural norms. At its very core, cultural reciprocity embraces the concept of collaborative teaming. "Through explicit dialogue with families, we then compare our differing beliefs and work towards collaboration that builds on family beliefs and strengths rather than setting goals derived directly from a set of values that may be alien to the people we serve" (Harry et al., 1999, p. 126). By listening to families and learning about what is normal and appropriate for their ecoculture (e.g., a combination of ecology [activities, events, and routines] and culture [race, religion, and family mores]), we may identify differences in student behavior, teacher behavior, and expectations that may help us prevent some of the disproportionate representation of students from minority populations.

School-based teams, therefore, should use collaborative teamwork when developing and implementing special education programs because it (a) is legally mandated, (b) is a best practices approach, (c) affects student outcomes, (d) affects teacher retention, and (e) may improve disproportionate representation in programs for students with EBD. Figure 8-3 presents the views of professionals on why collaboration is important.

We have identified the *what* in collaborative teaming by defining collaboration, teaming, and collaborative

FIGURE 8-3

Why do collaboration?

JENNIFER: You cannot do it by yourself. I know that I may not be seeing all of what is going on with the child. I need information from all sources to have a full picture of the child. You need others to be a part of this process because it takes a united team approach when you are changing behaviors and implementing strategies. This will enable you to be consistent across settings, time, and people.

PAUL: Collaboration is vital for the student to see the multiplicity of individuals concerned with him or her. Collaboration allows for a variety of interaction techniques as well as concepts that enable everyone to be involved for the betterment of the student.

SCOT: Collaboration helps you see and understand different perspectives.

ROBERT: Collaboration is important when working with any child, professional, or friend. Little success can be expected without collaboration in some form.

teaming and the *why* of collaborative teaming by examining five rationales supporting a collaborative teaming framework in educational practice for students with EBD. Now, let's look at the core components required for collaborative teaming.

HOW DO YOU CREATE AN EFFECTIVE COLLABORATIVE TEAM?

An important question for special educators and administrators is how do you create an effective collaborative team? Several researchers have recommended important elements in creating effective collaborative teams (Fishbaugh, 1997; Harrison, Killion, & Mitchell, 1989; Phillips & McCullough, 1990; Thomas et al., 2001; Wangemann, Ingram, & Muse, 1989). Katzenbach and Smith (1999) emphasized three basic components: (a) commitment, (b) skills, and (c) accountability. Next we examine how to apply these three critical components to effective collaborative teamwork when working with students with EBD.

Core Component #1: Commitment

Commitment is critical to the effective functioning of a collaborative team. According to Katzenbach and Smith (1999), commitment is comprised of (a) specific goals,

(b) a common approach to the task or problem, and (c) a meaningful purpose. For example, in special education a specific goal is the development of an IEP that addresses the unique needs of a student with EBD. A common approach might be that *everyone* on the team is expected to bring at least three identified needs of the student to the IEP meeting and that all members have a voice in determining what priorities become the focus of the IEP goals and objectives. Finally, the team identifies a meaningful purpose (e.g., targeted outcome) for the IEP development such as the following: The purpose of the IEP is to help the student successfully transition from middle school to high school.

Thus, the fundamental goal of collaborative teaming when applied to students with EBD is to ensure appropriate educational decisions are made that directly impact a student's quality of life, both during school years and in adulthood.

Because a multidisciplinary approach is required by IDEA, the general purpose of the team is already identified. For example, the law requires that a special educator, general educator, LEA (local educational agency) representative, related services personnel, parent, and, when appropriate, the student serve on IEP teams. Furthermore, we know that the purpose of the IEP team is to design an individually appropriate educational program that includes appropriate goals, services, accommodations, modifications, and other necessary educational services (see Chapter 9 on IEPs). The process used to define the specific educational program, however, may vary by team. To ensure that everyone on the team has the same vision, it is important for teams to have a specific discussion clarifying the specific goals, meaningful purpose, and selected approach that they will take to develop an appropriate and meaningful IEP. This process is also important in the development of transition plans, functional behavioral assessments, behavior intervention plans, accommodation plans, and other educational plans. All members must be clear about the commitment of and to the team.

Core Component #2: Skills

A second core component recommended by Katzenbach and Smith (1999) is skills. Skills relate to many areas. Skills include (a) technical skills related to one's discipline and experience, (b) skills in problem solving, and (c) skills used when working with others. All three are required to function effectively on a collaborative team.

Technical Skills   Team members must be prepared to acknowledge what technical skills they do or do not bring to the team. This is part of the role identification and release process. Role release, as first defined by Lyon and Lyon (1980), directly affects one's impact to share skills collaboratively on a team. Role release consists of three components: (a) sharing general information about basic concepts, approaches, and practices; (b) sharing informational skills, which include detailed information about practices or methods; and (c) sharing performance competencies with other team members—this would include the actual teaching of intervention strategies or methods of teaching with team members. In practice, an example of sharing general information would be a teacher explaining to his principal the philosophy and principles of positive behavior support (PBS) and why a PBS approach is most appropriate for students with EBD (see Chapter 10 on schoolwide PBS). Sharing informational skills may consist of sharing information in a more specific area such as the use of precorrection or the ratio of positive to negative teacher comments. Sharing performance competencies with the team may consist of a teacher instructing paraprofessionals and parents how to implement the classroom expectations, and in using procedures for encouraging appropriate behavior and discouraging inappropriate behavior in the PBS model. Another way to think about role release is:

Sharing general information → Involves all

Sharing informational skills → Involves those that need to know

Sharing performance competencies → Involves teaching interventions to other team members

Problem-Solving Skills   In addition to technical skills, collaborative teams must develop problem-solving skills and operational procedures for the team as a whole (Katzenbach & Smith, 1999). Not all decisions of the team will be unanimous. According to Friend and Cook (2000), the time to establish problem-solving procedures is *before* a problem or disagreement actually occurs. They recommend several steps in collaborative team problem solving.

First, the team must *identify the problem*. Somewhat like conducting an FBA, identifying the problem is a critical part in the problem-solving procedure. If a problem is not identified accurately, the proposed solution will not correct the problem. Second, generate potential solutions. Team members should try to create a wide range of solutions. Friend and Cook (2000) suggested techniques such as brainstorming, brainwriting, and nominal group technique. We briefly describe these procedures in the following text.

Brainstorming consists of team members calling out solutions as they think of them, creating a wide list of possible solutions. Brainwriting consists of team members individually writing three to four possible solutions on a blank piece of paper and placing them in the center of a table. Members then pull from others' submissions, read them, and add additional suggestions to those on the sheet. When no new ideas are added, the solutions are ready for evaluation. Nominal group technique (Delbecq, Van de Ven, & Gustafson, 1986) consists of team members individually writing down as many possible solutions as they can generate independently. Then, one team member at a time shares one solution with the team. Others cross out that solution if it is on their paper. The next team member shares one solution and so on until all possible solutions have been shared. A list of all possible solutions is then made.

Third, after a number of potential solutions have been generated, the team must *evaluate the solutions*. To evaluate the potential solutions, a team must identify the positives and negatives to each potential solution. By weighing the advantages and drawbacks to each solution, a team can collaboratively decide which solutions are too risky, too harmful, or too uncertain. This should leave the team with several viable solutions. The team should then outline the tasks that would be necessary to implement the potential solutions. Outlining the tasks required allows the team to determine the feasibility of each solution. The team selects a solution based on its positive components and its feasibility of implementation.

After a solution has been selected, the team is ready for the fourth step in problem solving—to *implement the solution*. The details or plan of implementing the solution should have been determined in the previous step when discussing the feasibility. Now the team must (a) finalize implementation plans, (b) make detailed arrangements for implementation, (c) establish a criterion to measure success, and (d) schedule a time for future evaluation.

The fifth step is to *carry out the solution* to the problem. The final step in problem solving is to *evaluate the success* of the outcome. The timeline for doing this should have been established in the fourth step. Utilization of the problem-solving steps recommended by Friend and Cook (2000) can lead teams to collaboratively solve problems creatively and with the best interests of the student with EBD as a priority.

Interpersonal Skills Interpersonal skills are a critical component when working on a collaborative team. One's ability to interact with others directly impacts the success of the team. Role release is also a fundamental element of interpersonal skills when working with others. To work well with others, one has to be able to share what he or she does or does not know as well as be able to teach others required skills. Role release encourages working together toward mutual goals rather than protecting one's professional turf. Sharing skills in an educative manner creates an environment of trust (Thomas et al., 2001). In addition to role release, there must be an awareness of each member's individuality. Individuality consists of educational training and background, work and life experiences, interpersonal style, and cultural differences. Harry et al. (1999) identified practices in cultural reciprocity to prepare educators to identify their own ecoculture so that they could better understand others. Team members must be aware of their own interpersonal style in order to better relate to others. There are several formal and informal ways to assess your interpersonal skills. The DiSC Personality Assessment is an example of one formalized assessment used by schools and businesses to assess interpersonal skills of employees (see http://www.discprofile.com/ for more information). After you have established your own strengths and preferences as team members, you are better prepared to build on the interpersonal skills you already have and to seek new opportunities for challenging those areas in which you need to grow. Quality, interpersonal, collaborative teamwork contributes to the achievement of quality individualized outcomes for students with EBD.

Core Component #3: Accountability

Katzenbach and Smith (1999) identified accountability, both as an individual and as a team, as a core component of effective collaborative teams. Individually, team members are accountable for their identified responsibilities on the team. For example, the role of one IEP team member is to interpret the instructional implications of the evaluation results. This person must have a thorough understanding of the evaluation results, know how these results can inform the IEP development process, and be able to communicate this information to other members of the team. Role identification is also very important.

After roles have been identified and tasks have been assigned, individuals must exert adequate individual effort to fulfill their responsibilities to the team. Individual accountability is achieved by assessing each team members' quantity and quality of contributions to the team. These team assessments can be done formally through measures like the Team Management Systems (Margerison & McCann, 2006) or informally through team-developed self- and peer-evaluation rubrics, but it is important that accountability assessment be a standard part of collaborative teams. Friend and Cook (2000) asserted that "conducting such assessment serves many purposes, including clearly identifying contributions, reducing duplication of effort, reinforcing and clarifying responsibilities, articulating needs for assistance, and minimizing 'freeloading' by noncontributing members" (p. 42).

It is important that the team be accountable as well. Just as with problem solving, when developing a goal and a plan to reach that goal, collaborative teams must also develop a criterion by which the achievement of that goal can be measured. A timeline to evaluate the effectiveness of the team must be established. This directly impacts the team's ability to collaborate on future projects. Thomas et al. (2001) suggested that teams must be involved in ongoing analysis of team functioning. In addition, they must consistently monitor the performance or progress toward the program implementation. Figure 8-4 shows the views of professionals on how they participate in collaborative activities.

One way to increase the accountability of collaborative teams is to conduct effective team meetings. Figure 8-5 shows the view of professionals regarding how collaborative teams work.

Scholtes (1988) provided a framework for conducting effective team meetings. This five-step procedure provides a practical approach to conducting team meetings that allow for a framework in which accountability can be measured. The steps are as follows:

Step 1: *Premeeting preparation.* Information is collected by team members to present at the meeting. This information should directly relate to the problem being discussed and should be used to support the position of the team members as they present their ideas.

FIGURE 8-4

How do you collaborate?

Scot: I personally meet with the other three teachers on my team. We have team meetings 3–4 days a week. It helps.

Robert: Collaboration is achieved when doctors, therapists, teachers, caregivers, and parents place value and commitment into listening to each other's opinions and observations prior to making decisions, altering goals, and/or all things related to the needs of the child.

FIGURE 8-5

How do collaborative meetings work?

Robert: Most often, face-to-face meetings are set up; some verbal and some written communication is exchanged. Follow-up meetings are held to evaluate the success or limitations of what had been previously established in those meetings.

Jennifer: My team includes parents, speech therapist, staff in my room, autism consultant from the Department of Disabilities and Special Needs (DDSN), case worker from DDSN, and the principal. Sometimes it may involve the school psychologist or occupational therapist, but usually not. I meet with them to discuss my concerns, to get feedback about whether they are experiencing any of the problems that I may be having with the student. We meet as a team to discuss the problem and bring any data or observations to the table to use to help us make informed decisions.

Step 2: *Presentation or discussion.* Each team member who would like to contribute prepares a brief presentation to share the information.

Step 3: *Agenda development.* A meeting agenda should be disseminated to all members of the team in advance of the meeting.

Step 4: *Documentation procedures.* The meeting's agenda can function as a framework. Notes may be taken directly on the agenda during the meeting to detail how each item will be addressed. Each member's responsibilities should be clearly defined. Meeting minutes should be shared with all members of the team.

Step 5: *Evaluation procedures.* Participants should evaluate the meeting: Was it effective? Did it accomplish the task? What improvements would you suggest? and so on.

We have identified the *what* in collaborative teaming by defining collaboration, teaming, and collaborative teaming. We have identified the *why* of collaborative teaming by examining five rationales supporting a collaborative teaming framework in educational practice for students with EBD. We have identified the *how* in establishing effective collaborative teaming in educational practice for students with EBD. Now, let's look at *who* makes up collaborative teams. We will also examine the types of professionals who are most frequently asked to collaborate on teams that develop the educational programs of students with EBD.

COLLABORATIVE TEAMING: WHO IS INVOLVED?

As stated in the beginning of the chapter, collaborative teaming involves a "who" factor—it is done in relationship with others. The question becomes who is involved on collaborative teams? As we learned earlier, the purpose of the team must be established. If a team is an IEP team, the answer is found in IDEA. IDEA requires the following persons to be members of the IEP team:

- The parents or guardians of a student with EBD.

- At least one general education teacher if the student currently participates or may participate in the general education environment. This person must have knowledge of the student.

- At least one special education teacher or service provider of the student.

- LEA representative who is knowledgeable about the student and specially designed instruction that meets the needs of the student, supervision of that instruction, and knowledgeable about the availability of resources of the LEA.

- Someone who can interpret the instructional implications of the evaluation results.

- Other individuals who have special expertise regarding the student or who have knowledge of the student.

- The student, when appropriate. (IDEA, 20 U.S.C. § 614(d)(1)(B))

In addition to IEP teams, collaborative teams are also established for a number of other reasons. For example, functional behavioral assessments are frequently conducted using a team approach. Moreover, behavior intervention plans (BIPs) are created using a team approach. Intervention teams, discipline referral teams, and professional development teams are just a few examples of other types of teams that schools establish to incorporate the unique perspectives, ideas, and solutions of professionals working toward better outcomes for students with disabilities.

A general rule of thumb that schools can follow to determine who should be on teams is as follows: Anyone who has a contribution to make and information to share related to the task facing the team should be on the team. In general, representation from administration, general and special education teachers, paraprofessionals, related service personnel, parents, and students should be considered when forming collaborative teams.

There are two basic types of collaborative teams often used in program development. One type is the *interpersonal team*. Interpersonal teaming is essentially collaboration between persons. Teacher–teacher teaming is one type of interpersonal teaming. This and many other types of interpersonal teams will be discussed. The second type of collaborative team is *interagency teaming*. Interagency teaming occurs when school personnel work with professional agencies outside the school. For example, in delivering services for students with EBD, schools may work with outside counseling agencies, juvenile justice agencies, or adult service agencies. Specific examples of both types of collaborative teaming are presented in the following text.

Interpersonal Teaming

Teacher–Paraprofessional Collaboration Teachers and paraprofessionals working as collaborative team members can have a positive impact on the achievements and outcomes of students with EBD. Giangreco, Edelman, Broer, and Doyle (2001) reported that traditionally paraprofessionals have worked under the close supervision and direction of a special educator who is present in the classroom all or most of the time. This method for working with paraprofessionals is still used frequently; however, a trend is to send paraprofessionals into inclusive settings to work with students with disabilities without direct supervision of special educators. This trend intensifies the need for paraprofessionals and teachers to work collaboratively as a team to meet the needs of the students with whom they work. If teachers and paraprofessionals identify common goals, procedures, and responses in delivering educational programs to students with EBD, the students are the beneficiaries.

In a self-contained environment for students with EBD, the collaborative relationship between teacher and paraprofessionals creates a seamless environment for achievement of academic, social, and behavioral goals. Students and adults benefit when all adults in the room function on an equal basis and all are prepared to deliver the necessary programs. For example, positive behaviors and relationships can be modeled for students. Additionally, there are more opportunities for one-on-one time with students when necessary because other adults in the room are trained in program implementation. Moreover, tasks can be divided according to the strengths of each adult in the room. Working together may also lessen the sense of isolation often felt by teachers and

How can special education teachers and paraprofessionals collaborate effectively?

ROBERT: The educator must set clear guidelines as to how the assistant will address the children, what goals are expected, how the goals will be achieved. And the educator must always be in charge of the class and the students in attendance.

PAUL: Give assistants responsibility so they are not used or looked at like a "secretary," rather an integral part of the collaboration team.

LUKE: Provide detailed information about each student and what to expect from him or her.

paraprofessionals. Figure 8-6 shows the views of professionals on collaborating with paraprofessionals.

For further information on collaborating with paraprofessionals, refer to the National Resource Center for Paraprofessionals at http://www.nrcpara.org.

Teacher–Teacher Collaboration   Cook and Friend (1993) discussed four basic models of teacher–teacher collaboration: (a) one teach/one assist, (b) station teaching, (c) parallel teaching, and (d) team teaching. In the one teach/one assist model, both teachers are present, but one (often the general education teacher) takes the lead. The other teacher observes or roams around the classroom assisting (Cook & Friend, 1993). In the station teaching model, teachers divide the content to be delivered and present it in stations. The students may also work independently at some stations, but eventually all students rotate through the stations to learn the material at each location. The parallel teaching model is often used in elementary schools or when departmental planning is used. In this model, teachers jointly plan instruction, but each delivers it to a separate group or class. This model ensures the pace of instruction is the same for all classes. In the team teaching model, teachers share the instruction of the students. They may take turns leading a discussion or demonstrating concepts. They also can model appropriate questioning, problem solving, and conflict resolution. Some of these models as well as some variations on interpersonal collaboration are examined in the following text.

Teacher-Teacher Model in Special Education Settings.   When the two-teacher model is used within a special education classroom it is often a more powerful

extension of the teacher–paraprofessional model previously discussed. This is because all of the benefits created by having the strengths and abilities of the teacher and paraprofessional are enhanced when two teachers serve one classroom of students collaboratively. In the teacher–paraprofessional model, the teacher still has the primary role of designing and evaluating instructional programs. However, in the teacher–teacher model, the workload can be divided in numerous ways, each drawing on the strengths, weaknesses, and preferences of the two teachers involved.

Teacher–Teacher Model in Inclusive Settings.   Teacher-teacher models have been widely used in two different areas: team teaching across the curriculum (e.g., integrated curricula approach) and inclusion of students in special education in general education classrooms. An example of team teaching across the curriculum is when high school English and social studies teachers team up to teach multiple concepts. For example, at a local high school students take American literature while taking American Constitution. Literature created during the political context of the American Revolution will be examined in both classes. Figure 8-7 shows the views of professionals on collaboration between general and special education teachers.

In inclusive settings, the teacher–teacher collaboration model has been used in delivering services to students in both general education and special education. In this model, a general educator (i.e., the content-area expert) and a special educator work collaboratively to help students with special needs successfully participate in general education classes. For example, in the case of such a team working in a general education classroom with a student with EBD, the content-area expert teaches the subject while the behavior expert facilitates behavior intervention plans and helps to create an instructional environment in which the student can be successful. In addition, the special educator may make or suggest appropriate accommodations or modifications to the general education content and may assist in meeting the instructional and behavioral needs of other students in the class as necessary. The purpose of this co-teaching model is to allow general educators and special educators to combine their expertise to meet the needs of all students (Dieker & Barnett, 1996).

Teacher–Administrator Collaboration.   Collaborative teaming between classroom teachers and administrators, whether they are building-level or district-level administrators, can strengthen the teacher's effectiveness. According to Tindall (cited in Walther-Thomas, Korinek,

FIGURE 8-7

How can general education teachers and special education teachers collaborate effectively?

LUKE: Know your students' capabilities and exception-
            alities. Then, be well versed on the policies and
            regulations pertaining to your students.

PAUL: Allow the general education population to feel
            as involved as possible. Most general educators
            feel as if a burden is placed on them due to hav-
            ing a special needs student in their classroom.
            Provide positive information concerning this
            aspect.

JENNIFER: They (general and special education teachers)
            need to talk about the students because each
            brings experience and knowledge to the table.
            As a special educator, I offer assistance and
            education about the students' disabilities. This
            helps them understand better. I offer any help
            that they may need because it can be over-
            whelming for the regular education teacher to
            know what to do. Regular education teachers
            need to ask about what they do not know.

ROBERT: General educators should remember that while
            goals may change, the focus must remain on
            what is best for that child, and collaborating with
            special educators is simply seeking guidance to
            ensure that the child's needs are met.

FIGURE 8-8

How can teachers and administrators collaborate effectively?

PAUL: Teachers working with administrators?

SCOT: Be flexible.

JENNIFER: I talk with my administrator on a regular basis,
            not just when there is a problem. I keep her
            informed of any problems and what I am doing
            to manage the situation.

McLaughlin, & Williams, 2000), effective principals foster collaborative environments by (a) communicating a vision for collaboration, (b) demonstrating a value of collaboration, (c) leading faculty planning for collaborative approaches, (d) providing and participating in professional development opportunities, (e) committing resources toward the utilization of collaboration, and (f) recognizing student and teacher accomplishments. However, without this spirit of working together, teachers may feel frustrated and unsupported. Building-level support from principals and teachers has a tremendous effect, both directly and indirectly, on almost all critical aspects of teachers' working conditions (Gersten et al., 2001).

Several elements lead to the feeling of being supported by administration. First, teachers need to feel respected by the administrators. When administrators demonstrate an understanding of the complexity of skills demanded on a daily basis by teachers of students with EBD, and express an appreciation of his or her abilities, the groundwork is present for a successful collaborative

relationship. Second, the administrator should demonstrate a basic knowledge of the characteristics of students with EBD and the appropriate recommended practice for addressing their needs. Third, the administrator should demonstrate a belief that students with EBD are an important and valuable part of the school. Finally, the administrator must be available to teachers and willing to support or assist them as needed. Often teachers of students with EBD need help with a student, and it is critical that the administrator be supportive in that role. Figure 8-8 shows the views of professionals on collaboration between administrators and special education teachers.

Interagency Teaming

Teacher–Behavior Interventionist Collaboration

Occasionally teachers will collaborate with a professional from an outside agency. For example, one of the authors of this chapter worked in a day treatment program in a large urban district in North Central Texas, in which teachers employed by the district and behavior interventionists employed by a mental health agency both worked in a classroom for high school students with EBD. The teacher was responsible for delivering academic content and measuring progress across the curriculum. The interventionist was responsible for collecting and analyzing data for each student. They were both responsible for creating an appropriate learning environment through teaching acceptable replacement behaviors and correcting inappropriate behaviors. This model can prove highly effective for students with EBD. Problems can arise, however, when the expectations of the different organizations are at odds. Such problems can be avoided when clear definitions of roles of the teacher and outside agency personnel are clarified up front.

FAMILY AND SCHOOL COLLABORATION

One of the most complex collaborative teaming relationships is that established between home and school. Earlier in this chapter we discussed how working in collaborative teams could help positively affect the outcomes for students with EBD. Including families as members of the collaborative team is fundamental. Unlike other professional collaborative teaming relationships (e.g., teacher–teacher; teacher–administrator), the teacher–family relationship is established on different terms. Traditionally, the teacher functions as the expert on academic and behavioral interventions and progress whereas the family is seen as the expert on the child. Increasingly, the expertise of families is recognized by professionals in the field of EBD (Blue-Banning, Summers, Frankland, Nelson, & Beegle, 2004; Trivette, Dunst, Boyd, & Hamby, 1995).

Family members are aware of strategies that are successful or unsuccessful with their child, although they may not recognize them as specific strategies. Moreover, they are aware of behavioral triggers and preferences in structure, routine, or presentation. Families are also aware of social interaction patterns among peers, family members, former school personnel, and strangers. All of this information creates an expertise that is valuable to the development, implementation, and success of a student's educational program. Teachers are wise to tap into that source of expertise. The next sections discuss six themes of effective school–family collaboration. These themes promote a strong collaborative relationship between school and family. Figure 8–9 shows the views of professionals on collaboration between parents and special education teachers.

Blue-Banning et al. (2004) reported that there were six important areas to address when establishing collaborative partnerships with families. These themes were (a) communication, (b) commitment, (c) equality, (d) skill, (e) trust, and (f) respect. Suggestions for establishing an effective collaborative team with families will be discussed in the context of each theme.

Communication

Blue-Banning and colleagues' first theme was communication. Many types of communication can be used when establishing and maintaining relationships with families. Johnson, Pugach, and Hawkins (2004) suggested several practical ways to communicate with families. First, the most important foundation is to establish a relationship with the family before the school year begins. According

---

FIGURE 8–9

How can teachers and parents collaborate effectively?

PAUL: Do not send home information or contact parents concerning negative information only. Ensure you are discussing their students' positive aspects of their education . . . search hard . . . you can find SOMETHING!

LUKE: Communicate to parents what is expected of their child regarding behavior and academic requirements.

SCOT: Try to be proactive rather than reactive. Come up with a solution before the problem happens.

JENNIFER: Be honest and keep parents informed as much as possible, not just when things are going to explode because most of the time it can be handled before that point. Treat the parents with respect because they bring a lot of knowledge about their child to the table.

ROBERT: Teachers and administrators must remember that parents are not usually asking for their child to be treated better than others; they simply want their child to have the same opportunities and the same possibilities that all others have.

---

to Johnson et al. (2004) this can be accomplished by making a personal contact with all students' families before the beginning of the school year. This could be a phone call, a personal visit, or a personal letter or postcard. An additional suggestion for initial relationship building is to create a handbook for parents. This handbook would discuss the teacher's philosophy of education, classroom rules, major activities or curriculum foci, and a typical class day. After a teacher makes the initial contact, it is important to maintain contact. Johnson and colleagues suggested that teachers could maintain contact by (a) sending home announcements for special activities, describing the purpose of the activity and ways that families can participate; (b) mailing classroom newsletters home on a regular basis, which may include positive feedback for students and parents, information on upcoming events, and ways for parents to get involved in their child's classroom activities; (c) e-mailing personal notes to a student's parents'; (d) conducting teleconferences; and (e) holding face-to-face formal family conferences.

In teacher–family conferences it is important to plan for collaborative meetings. Turnbull and Turnbull (2001) recommended several steps in designing and completing a conference. First, teachers must engage in preconference planning. For example, teachers should (a) ask families and other team members for convenient times, locations, and important topics for discussion; and (b) establish an agenda that will be planned and shared with all participants in advance; and (c) set aside enough time to ensure adequate time for discussion of each agenda item.

Second, teachers should (a) begin the conference with broad statements, (b) use active listening throughout, and (c) summarize the discussion at the end of the conference. For example, teachers may want to begin the conference by making broad statements that set the tone and purpose of the meeting (e.g., "Today we are here to plan for Johnny's educational program. We look forward to everyone's input and encourage everyone to contribute any thoughts or ideas as we cover each area. I've provided an agenda to guide us as we work through our topics today"). After opening the meeting, teachers will want to use active listening throughout. It is important that families feel as though their perspectives and ideas are valued and included. As an active listener, you should be able to repeat the words of the speaker using your own words. This doesn't signify that you agree, simply that you understand. For example, you might restate what the person has said, summarize what the person has said, or ask additional questions for clarification (e.g., "I understand what you've said about your concern with Johnny's outbursts. Can you describe the specific things you're concerned about?"). All of these behaviors demonstrate active listening.

Third, postconference follow-ups are important to check for new information or to see if steps have been implemented. When conducting postconference follow-ups, teachers should contact team members (including family members) to follow up on the status of any action plan or team member assignments decided in the meeting. In addition to following up on team assignments, teachers should ask families if they remembered additional concerns or other information that might not have been discussed at the meeting. For example, teachers might call parents to find out the results from a doctor's appointment mentioned by the family at the meeting (e.g., "How did the Dr.'s meeting go? Did he recommend any change in medication?"). Teachers might also ask if family members were able to discuss everything they wanted to at the meeting or if there were other topics they had concerns about (e.g., "Did we cover everything you wanted to talk about in the meeting? Was there anything else you wanted to add?"). Preconference planning, active listening during a meeting, and postconference follow-ups all lead to stronger collaborative relationships with families. Finally, teachers should try to be ready for

unplanned conferences by having current and accurate data on student performance, and being prepared to listen to parental concerns while acknowledging when more time is needed to collect the appropriate information.

Commitment

The second theme presented by Blue-Banning and colleagues (2004) was commitment. They defined commitment of a professional to the family as valuing the relationship with the family. Examples of commitment are (a) being willing to meet at a convenient time or location for families, (b) making effective use of available resources and searching out new resources that will improve the student's outcomes, (c) remembering special days or events of the child, and (d) acknowledging families when the teacher meets them in the community. These small but important behaviors demonstrate a commitment to a student's family that goes above and beyond a professional's basic job description.

Equality

The third theme presented by Blue-Banning and colleagues (2004) was equality. Families define equality as a condition of reciprocity between families and professionals. Reciprocity refers to relationships that empower families to contribute and collaborate together in educational programming and implementation. An acknowledgement of the validity of parents' ideas, perceptions, and preferences is important when trying to establish a relationship based on equality. Informing parents of their rights, helping parents develop questions for medical professionals, helping them with wording or phrasing of their opinions, and sometimes going to meetings just for moral support is considered working toward a collaborative relationship based on equality.

Skill

The fourth theme presented by Blue-Banning and colleagues (2004) was skill. Families define skills as competence. It is crucial that parents believe that their child's teachers and other service providers are competent to work effectively and successfully to develop and implement meaningful programming. Professionals who (a) evaluate and adjust their instruction or interventions, (b) keep up-to-date with new technology and practices in their field, (c) acknowledge when they don't know something, and (d) seek out information or direct families to appropriate resources are exhibiting behaviors that the authors believed demonstrated skill.

Trust

The fifth theme presented by Blue-Banning and colleagues (2004) was trust. The authors defined trust as reliability, safety, and discretion. When parents believe that teachers are reliable, they have confidence that the teachers will do whatever they said they would do. When parents believe that their children are safe, they believe that their children are protected from peers or others who might try to take advantage of them. Finally, when parents believe that teachers are discrete, they know that the teachers can be trusted with confidential or personal information and will not violate that confidence. Being careful not to violate parents' confidence and to always honor commitments made to families are behaviors that teachers should practice if they want to establish trust when working with families of students with EBD.

Respect

The final theme presented by Blue-Banning and colleagues (2004) was respect. Like trust, respect seems somewhat subjective in that different people may have different ideas about what showing respect actually means in practice. Nevertheless, according to Blue-Banning et al. (2004), parents are clear about specific teacher behaviors that demonstrate respect. One behavior that shows that a teacher is respectful is being courteous toward parents. This could be shown by (a) using last names unless given permission to use first names, (b) acknowledging parental efforts and contributions toward the success of their child, and (c) being nonjudgmental about parental perceptions, beliefs, or practices. Demonstrating respect for others is important in interpersonal collaboration and is especially important in professional–family collaboration.

Special attention to each of these six themes can help professionals create collaborative partnerships with families that assist in the consistent application of educational and behavioral interventions. Harry et al. (1999) suggested that professionals adopt a posture of cultural reciprocity, and encouraged professionals to critically analyze their own practice in relation to these six themes and create a specific plan of action to improve or adjust practices as needed. Families are critical members of a collaborative team. All professionals should strive to ensure that they address these six areas effectively when working with parents.

Chapter Summary

The purpose of this chapter was to supply a framework for collaboration and teaming that teachers may use when developing and implementing programs for students with EBD. We began the chapter by defining the concepts of collaboration and teaming in education. Next, we provided a rationale based on five distinct reasons that the use of collaborative teaming is appropriate when working with individuals with EBD. Then, we described three major components necessary to establishing effective collaborative teams. We described who is involved in the collaborative process and gave examples of interpersonal and interagency collaboration. Finally, we discussed six themes to focus on when establishing collaborative relationships with families of students with EBD. Throughout, we have incorporated voices of parents and professionals from the field. Special thanks are offered to Luke, Scot, Paul, Robert, and Jennifer for their contribution. Collaborative teaming is a fundamental concept when working with students with EBD. Indeed, collaboration is a best practice for students with EBD.

CHAPTER 9

Developing Educationally Meaningful and Legally Sound Individualized Education Programs

Mitchell L. Yell

Focus Questions

- What are the procedural and substantive legal requirements educators must follow when developing IEPs?

- What are typical problems and errors that teams make when developing IEPs?

- How does the IEP planning process work?

- What are the required components of an IEP?

- How can educators develop educationally meaningful and legally correct IEPs?

When the Education for All Handicapped Children Act[1] (EAHCA) was enacted in 1975, the law (P.L. 94-142) mandated that participating states provide students with disabilities with a free appropriate public education (FAPE). To ensure that eligible students received an appropriate education, Congress required that all students have an individualized education program (IEP) developed to meet their unique educational needs. According to Zettel and Ballard (1982), Congress concluded that the requirement of a written IEP was crucial if the purposes of the EAHCA were to be achieved. In fact, one of the principal writers of the EAHCA, Senator Robert Stafford (1978), stated that the IEP was "the central part of this Act as we wrote it and intended it to be carried out" (p. 72).

When developing an IEP, a child's parents and all the persons involved in delivering educational services to the child were given an opportunity for input into a student's educational program. The IEP itself became the educational blueprint tailored to meet a student's unique needs. That is, all aspects of a student's special education program were directed by the IEP and monitored throughout the IEP process (Smith, 1990b). The IEP, therefore, formalizes and defines a student's FAPE (Bateman & Linden, 2006; Eyer, 1998; Huefner, 2005; Katsiyannis, Yell, & Bradley, 2001). In fact, the IEP is so crucial that the failure to develop and implement an IEP properly may render a student's entire special education program invalid in the eyes of the courts (Yell et al., 2004). Requirements regarding the IEP were altered in the IDEA reauthorizations of 1997 and 2004.

The purpose of this chapter is to present a method for developing educationally meaningful and legally sound IEPs. To do this, I first present an overview of the legal requirements of the IEP planning process. Second, I explain the required contents of the IEP. Third, I present requirements for developing, reviewing, and revising the IEP. Finally, I propose a framework for developing legally and educationally appropriate IEPs.

LEGAL REQUIREMENTS

An IEP is (a) a written document that records the essential components of an eligible student's educational program, and (b) a collaborative process between a child's parents and school personnel to design the child's special education program (Norlin & Gorn, 2005; Yell, 2006). During the IEP planning process the goals of a student's program, the special education and related services the student will receive, the evaluation and measurement

criteria by which the student's progress will be measured, and his or her educational placement are determined and written in the document. As the court in *Thorndock v. Boise Independent School District* (1988) stated, "The importance of the IEP [should not] be understated . . . [it is] the fundamental prerequisite of any FAPE" (p. 1246). Indeed, the IEP is the cornerstone of special education.

The IEP process includes procedural and substantive requirements that schools must follow. These requirements form the framework that guides the development and implementation of an individualized FAPE for a student (Drasgow, Yell, & Robinson, 2001).

Procedural Requirements

Procedural requirements refer to those aspects of IDEA that compel schools to follow the strictures of the law when developing an IEP. Adherence to these requirements is necessary, because major procedural errors on the part of a school district may render an IEP inappropriate in the eyes of a hearing officer or court (Bateman & Linden, 2006; Huefner, 2001; Yell & Drasgow, 2000). According to IDEA 2004, when school personnel make procedural errors when developing an IEP, hearing officers can find only that a school failed to provide a FAPE if the procedural errors are of such a nature that they (a) impeded a student's right to a FAPE, (b) significantly impeded the parents' opportunity to participate in the decision-making process, or (c) caused a deprivation of educational benefits (IDEA, 20 U.S.C. § 1415(f)(1)(B)(i)(3)(E)(ii)(I–III)). Nevertheless, it is very important that school district personnel understand their procedural responsibilities with respect to planning, developing, and reviewing the IEP.

Fortunately, procedural errors are easily avoided when IEP team members know the requirements of both IDEA and their state's special education laws. An effective way to develop IEPs that meet the procedural requirements of the law is for school officials to create an iron-clad system of checklists, procedures, and forms that IEP teams must follow to, in effect, legally "bulletproof" their IEPs (Drasgow et al., 2001).

Crafting an educationally meaningful and legally sound IEP is not just about following legal procedures; it is also about developing special education programs that lead to educational benefits for students. As the members of the President's Commission on Excellence in Special Education noted, educators often place "process above results, and bureaucratic compliance above student achievement, excellence, and outcomes" (President's Commission, 2002, p. 3). If procedural mistakes are made in the IEP process, but the parents are meaningfully involved in the process and a student achieves meaningful

---

[1] In 1990 the EAHCA was renamed the Individuals with Disabilities Education Act (IDEA).

benefit in his or her special education program, hearing officers will not rule that the procedural violations resulted in a school district failing to meet their requirements under the IDEA. On the other hand, *procedurally* *correct IEPs will not meet legal standards if the student's educational program does not result in his or her achieving meaningful educational benefit.* Table 9-1 is a checklist of procedural components that IEP teams may

Table 9–1   Procedural checklist

Conducting the Assessment

❏ The student's parents must give informed consent before the assessment can be conducted.

❏ An assessment for eligibility must be conducted within 60 days of receiving parental consent for the assessment (less if the state in which the student resides requires a shorter timeframe).

❏ The assessment team must use a variety of assessment tools and procedures to gather academic and functional information to determine (a) if the student has an IDEA-eligible disability, and (b) to determine the content of the IEP.

❏ Standardized tests must be validated for the purposes for which they are used and be administered by trained personnel in accordance with instructions provided by the test maker.

❏ School district personnel who conduct the assessment are qualified to do so.

❏ The student must be assessed in all areas related to the suspected disability.

❏ The assessment team must not use any single measure or assessment as the sole criterion to determine (a) a student's eligibility, or (b) his or her educational program.

❏ The assessment team must use technically sound instruments to assess relative contribution of cognitive, behavioral, physical, or developmental factors.

❏ Assessment procedures must be selected and administered to not be discriminatory and in the language and form most likely to yield accurate information.

❏ The IEP team must consider assessment data provided by the parents.

❏ Parents must be given an explanation of their right to seek an independent educational evaluation if they disagree with the school district's assessment.

❏ If existing assessment data exist, the assessment team must review that data, including classroom-based assessments or observations.

Preparing for the IEP Meeting: Parental Participation

❏ The parents must be notified of the IEP meeting early enough to ensure that they have an opportunity to attend.

❏ State timelines regarding IEP meetings must be met.

❏ The IEP meeting must be held at a mutually agreed on time and place.

❏ The parents must be informed of, and receive a copy of, their procedural rights under IDEA.

❏ In situations in which the parents cannot attend the IEP meeting, the team must keep documentation regarding its unsuccessful attempts to involve the parents in the meeting.

❏ The parents must be equal partners in the IEP process (from evaluation to placement).

❏ Any parental concerns or requests must be considered and discussed at the IEP meeting.

Conducting the IEP Meeting

❏ The IEP meeting must include all the required participants unless the parents agree in writing that a member may be excused and the excused team member submits written input into the development of the IEP prior to the meeting.

   ○ A student's parents or guardians

   ○ A representative of the local educational agency

   ○ A special education teacher

   ○ A general education teacher

   ○ A person who could interpret the instructional implications of the evaluation results (may be one of the previously listed team members)

   ○ The student, when appropriate

   ○ Transition services personnel (when transition services are required)

Preparing the IEP Document

❏ The IEP must include all of the required components.

   ○ A statement of the student's present levels of academic achievement and functional performance (including how the disability affects the student's involvement and progress in the general education curriculum)

○ Measurable annual goals (both academic and functional goals, if needed)

○ A statement of how the student's progress toward the annual goals will be measured

○ A schedule for reporting a student's progress to his or her parents

○ Short-term objectives (if required by the state or if the student is taking an alternative assessment)

○ A statement of the special education service, related services, and supplementary aids and services, based on peer-reviewed research, to be provided to the student, and a statement of program modification or supports provided to school personnel

○ An explanation of the extent, if any, to which the student will not participate with students without disabilities in general education

○ A statement of any accommodations necessary to measure the academic or functional performance of the student on statewide or districtwide assessment; if the student is participating in an alternate assessment, a statement of why the regular assessment could not be used and how an alternate assessment was selected

○ The projected date for beginning the services and modifications and the anticipated frequency, location, and duration of those services

○ A statement of appropriate measurable postsecondary goals based on age-appropriate transition assessments, and the transition services needed to assist the student in reaching those goals (when transition services are required)

❑ The IEP must be developed before the placement is determined.

❑ The IEP must be rewritten when an evaluation indicates the student's program needs revision.

❑ The student needs to receive all services and modifications listed in the IEP.

❑ An annual review of the IEP must be conducted to determine whether the annual goals are being achieved by the student.

❑ If the student is not progressing toward achieving the annual goals, the IEP must be revised.

Placing the Student

❑ The student's parents must be included in the placement decision-making process.

❑ The student's placement needs to be determined after the IEP is written.

❑ The continuum of placements must be used to determine the student's placement.

❑ The student must be placed in an appropriate setting, even if the school district has to contract for placement with another school district or private agency.

Evaluating the Student

❑ The evaluation must meet the federal and applicable state requirements.

❑ A reevaluation must be conducted when conditions warrant it or the parents or teacher request it.

❑ A reevaluation must be conducted every 3 years while the student is in special education.

❑ The IEP team may determine what assessments will be administered during the reevaluation unless the student's parents request a complete reevaluation.

❑ Prior to conducting a significant change in placement, a reevaluation must be conducted.

❑ School district evaluators must be qualified to conduct evaluations.

---

use to ensure that they meet the procedural requirements of the law.

Substantive Requirements

Substantive requirements refers to the content of a student's special education program, and compels schools to provide an education that confers meaningful educational benefit to a student. According to Drasgow et al. (2001), the crucial determinant in hearings or cases involving the substantive standard of IDEA is whether the student makes educational progress. This observation is reinforced by language in IDEA 2004 that requires hearing officers to base their decisions in special education cases on substantive grounds based on whether a student received a FAPE (IDEA, 20 U.S.C. § 1415(f)(1)(B)(i)(3)(E)(i)).

Regrettably, school-based teams often seem to have a difficult time with the substantive requirements in developing and implementing IEPs. In fact, there is probably less compliance with the mandate that students show educational progress than any other IDEA-related obligation (Bateman & Linden, 2006). To ensure that IEPs meet the substantive requirements of IDEA, school personnel must understand and correctly implement the three critical components of the IEP process: (a) assessment, (b) program development, and (c) progress monitoring. The substantive requirements refer to the educational benefit a student derives from his or her special education program. Table 9–2 shows a checklist of components

Table 9–2   Substantive checklist

Assessment

❏ The assessment process must include *both* assessment instruments and procedures to determine eligibility (e.g., standardized norm-referenced tests) and relevant assessment instruments and procedures to determine a student's educational programming (e.g., informal curriculum-based assessments, curriculum-based measurement, functional behavioral assessments).

IEP

❏ The statements of present levels of academic achievement and functional performance must be reflected directly in the annual goals, special education services, and progress monitoring procedures.

❏ The annual goals must be ambitious.

❏ The annual goals must be measurable.

❏ A progress monitoring system needs to be developed or adopted for measuring student progress.

❏ Special education services, related services, supplementary aids and services, and program modifications must be based on *peer-reviewed research*.

❏ Meaningful data must be collected on the student's progress toward achieving the annual goals at a minimum of every 9 weeks (i.e., progress toward goals is measured).

❏ If the data show that a student is not progressing toward his or her goals, the student's educational program must be altered in a meaningful way to improve student progress.

❏ The IEP must be reasonably calculated to confer *meaningful educational benefit* to the student.

❏ The school district must implement the IEP as written.

---

that may help IEP teams develop special education programs that meet the substantive requirements of IDEA.

PROBLEMS IN IEP DEVELOPMENT

Since their inception in 1975, IEPs have been fraught with problems and have, in many instances, failed to live up to their original promise (Huefner, 2001). Smith (1990b) identified a number of these problems in IEP development including (a) lack of adequate teacher training in developing IEPs, (b) poorly developed team processes, (c) mechanistic compliance with the paperwork requirements, and (d) excessive demands on teacher time. Additional problems the school-based teams often have with the IEP process are failing to

• involve general education (Gartner & Lipsky, 1992);

• address all of a student's unique educational needs (Bateman & Linden, 2006);

• include modifications to the general education classroom in the IEP (Bateman & Linden, 2006);

• link assessment data to instructional goals (Smith & Simpson, 1989);

• make placement decisions based on the IEP (Bateman & Linden, 2006; Yell, 2006);

• develop measurable goals (Bateman & Herr, 2003; Drasgow et al., 2001);

• base services on a student's needs rather than cost or availability (Bateman & Linden, 2006);

• monitor student progress (Bateman & Herr, 2003; Yell, 2006 Yell & Stecker, 2003).

Bateman and Linden (2006) and Smith (1990b) have also noted that often schools use the legally questionable practice of developing stock computer-generated IEPs.

After analyzing a survey of special education attorneys who have handled IEP disputes, Lake (2002) listed and described the 10 most common errors that IEP teams make when developing IEPs. These errors are as follows:

Error #1: The IEP team membership is incorrect or incomplete. According to Lake (2002), failing to ensure that the membership of a student's IEP team meets all federal requirements will often have serious consequences because a hearing officer or judge will likely conclude that any programming that came from a flawed IEP team will likewise often be flawed.

Error #2: The IEP lacks adequate parental input or consent. When parents have not been meaningfully involved in the IEP process, the IEP has often been determined to be defective and, thus, not met the requirements of the law.

Error #3: Key IEP components are missing. The IEP is the mechanism by which schools provide a

FAPE. IDEA contains several required components that must be included in every student's IEP. When any of these components are missing, the IEP will most likely not meet the requirements of the law.

Error #4: The IEP goals are incomplete, inadequate, or deficient. Perhaps the most difficult IEP challenge is to write measurable annual goals that address a student's unique educational needs. When IEP goals are not measurable, or not measured, the IEP will be inadequate. IEP teams, therefore, must ensure that all goals are measurable and measured. Lake (2002) noted that IEP teams must avoid "cookie-cutter" IEPs that contain predetermined goals that are associated with a student's age or disability group.

Error #5: The IEP's transition component is lacking or deficient. A common mistake is that IEP teams fail to include a transition component to the IEPs of students who are aged 16 or older. Another mistake that teams often make is failing to include transition service participants in the IEP meeting. Such IEPs often substantially deprive students of their right to a FAPE.

Error #6: The IEP fails to adequately address a student's LRE. IDEA requires that all students with disabilities be educated with students who are not disabled to the maximum extent appropriate. It is crucial that when determining a student's placement, the IEP team addresses the LRE (least restrictive environment) requirement. An IEP team should document its good-faith efforts to educate the student in the less restrictive setting before considering or proposing placement in a more restrictive setting.

Error #7: The placement offered in the IEP is inappropriate. An IEP team can make a placement decision only after the development of the IEP (IDEA Regulations, 34 C.F.R. § 300.552(b)(2)). This is because after the IEP is developed, the team has the basis for determining where a student's educational needs can most effectively be met. According to Lake (2002), preplacement decisions or making a final placement decision outside the IEP process is a serious mistake that will often lead to the denial of a FAPE.

Error #8: The district fails to provide or fully implement services under an existing IEP. After the IEP has been developed by the IEP team, the school district must ensure that the IEP is implemented as agreed on. Failing to provide services as required by an IEP is a very serious error.

Error #9: The IEP is not developed or revised in a timely manner. Serious errors that districts often make in this area are (a) failing to convene the IEP team in a timely manner, (b) failing to implement an IEP in a timely manner, or (c) failing to revise an IEP in the face of a student's lack of progress. Note that each state may prescribe specific timelines that school districts must follow when developing, implementing, or revising an IEP.

Error #10: The IEP fails to include positive behavioral interventions. One of the most frequently missing components in the IEPs of students with disabilities who exhibit problem behaviors are behavioral goals and positive behavioral interventions. When a student has problem behaviors that impede his or her learning or the learning of others, the IEP must include such interventions as required by the law.

Lake (2002) acknowledged that fulfilling these procedural requirements of IEPs has proven to be a daunting task for many school districts. He advised IEP teams to pay careful attention to both the federal requirements of IDEA and the requirements of individual state laws. He also asserted that when IEP teams make an error, the best practice is for them to admit the mistake, notify the parents, and take prompt and reasonable steps to correct the error. Lake further noted that failing to correct a known error can and often does lead to serious consequences for the district. To ensure that IEP teams do not make these errors and that they develop educationally meaningful and legally sound IEPs, administrators and special education teachers need to thoroughly understand both the procedural and substantive IEP requirements of IDEA. In the next section I describe the IEP planning process.

THE IEP PLANNING PROCESS

IDEA requires that school districts hold IEP planning meetings for students eligible for special education services. The purpose of the IEP planning process is to develop a student's special education program. To ensure that the parents and school personnel develop an appropriate educational program, IDEA mandates rigorous procedural requirements to be followed in the IEP process (see Table 9-1). Strict adherence to these procedural requirements (e.g., notice, consent, participants) is extremely important because major procedural errors on the part of a school district may render an IEP inappropriate (Bateman & Linden, 2006; Osborne, 1994). It is, therefore, extremely important that administrators and special education teachers understand their responsibilities with respect to planning, developing, and reviewing the IEP.

The IEP process is a set of procedures, set forth in IDEA, that govern how school districts determine the special education services that an eligible student with disabilities will receive (Gorn, 1998). This process leads to the development of the educational program that constitutes the FAPE for a student in special education. The following section examines the three major steps of the IEP process.

The starting point of the IEP process is the assessment for eligibility and instructional planning. The second stage is the development of the program based on the student's educational needs. The final step of the IEP process is determination of the student's placement based on the IEP. Bateman and Linden (2006) correctly stated that this sequence is a legally sound way to develop students' special education programs. These authors further noted that many school-based teams develop IEPs incorrectly by confusing the sequences as follows: First, they classify a student as disabled; second, they place the student; and finally, they develop the IEP. According to Bateman and Linden (2006), such a sequence is clearly erroneous and illegal.

Referral and Assessment

When a student is suspected of having a disability, he or she is referred to a school's multidisciplinary team (MDT). The referral process is generally initiated by school personnel, although if parents of a student with disabilities believe their child needs a special education program, they may refer their child (IDEA Regulations, 34 C.F.R. § Appendix C to Part 300, number 11). In fact, according to IDEA 2004, "either parents or the SEA [state educational agency], other state agency or LEA [local educational agency] may request an initial evaluation[2] (IDEA, 1414(a)(1)(B)).

If school personnel initiate the referral process, the parents of the referred student must be notified. Because IDEA provides no specific requirements regarding the referral process, states and local school districts are free to develop their own referral procedures. Typically school districts adopt formal referral processes in which the person referring the student assembles information such as observations, test scores, classroom difficulties, and interventions attempted prior to referral. This information is then presented to an MDT.

The MDT, which is typically composed of an administrator, special education teacher, regular education teacher, and school psychologist, has a function separate

from that of the IEP team (Yell, 2006). The task of the MDT is to review the referral to determine if an assessment for special education is warranted.

If the MDT determines that further assessment is needed, the school must seek informed consent from the student's parents. After written consent has been granted by the parents, the MDT appoints a person or persons to conduct the assessment. In situations in which a student's parents refuse to grant consent for the assessment, the school district may use mediation or due process procedures to obtain permission to conduct the assessment.

The time requirements for completing the assessment are often set by the state. For example, South Carolina requires that the assessment be completed within 45 days. IDEA, however, requires that the eligibility determination must be made within 60 days of receiving parental consent for evaluation. If the state has established a timeframe, as South Carolina has, that timeframe may be used. This timeframe does not apply in situations in which the parent repeatedly fails to produce the child for the assessment.

The purpose of the assessment is twofold. First, the assessment is conducted to determine a student's eligibility for special education services. Second, the information from the assessment is used by the IEP team to determine the student's educational needs in the program planning stage. (See Chapter 3 for elaboration on the legal requirements of the assessment process.)

To ensure that assessments are educationally meaningful and legally sound, the MDT must individualize the assessment to the student's specific needs. Furthermore, the student must be assessed in *all* areas related to the suspected disability. For example, if a student is referred because of problem behaviors, the MDT's assessment must address this problem. If the referral indicates that a student has additional problems (e.g., reading, speech), these areas must also be assessed. IDEA also requires that teams consider assistive technology when teachers request such an evaluation.

When the assessment results are gathered, the MDT must decide if the student is eligible for special education services. In making this decision, the MDT should rely on collective professional judgment based on all relevant information including test results rather than basing the decision solely on a formula or guideline. If the MDT determines that a student is eligible for special education and related services, the school must convene an IEP team within 30 calendar days to develop the IEP (IDEA Regulations, 34 C.F.R. § 300.343(c)).

The IEP Meeting During the IEP meeting, the team members usually begin by reviewing the student's referral

---

[2]*Note:* In IDEA, Congress used the term *evaluation* to refer to both the assessment and the evaluation process. For clarity I will use *assessment* and *evaluation* throughout this chapter.

and assessment and any other information that may be relevant (e.g., student's current records, including the current IEP if one exists, and heath-related information). The team must also consider the student's strengths; the parent's concerns; and the student's academic, developmental, and functional needs. Other areas that should be considered when they are pertinent to develop the IEP are (a) positive behavioral interventions and supports when the student exhibits problem behavior that impedes his or learning or the learning of others; (b) language needs when the student is limited English proficient; (c) the provision of instruction in Braille and the use of Braille, if appropriate, when a student is blind or visually impaired; (d) the provision of language or communication needs if the student is deaf or hard of hearing; and (e) assistive technology needs or services if appropriate (IDEA Regulations, 34 C.F.R. § 300.346(a)(2)).

The format, procedures, and forms used in IEP meetings are not dictated by federal law, but are the responsibility of the states or the schools. School districts, therefore, usually develop their own forms and procedures. A number of states have developed forms that are used by school districts. Shortly after the regulations implementing IDEA 2004 were released, the U.S. Department of Education's Office of Special Education Programs (OSEP) issued sample forms that may be used in the IEP process. These forms may be downloaded from OSEP's Web site: http://www.ed.gov/policy/speced/guid/idea/idea2004.html#tools http://www.ed.gov/policy/speced/guid/idea/idea2004 .html#tools.

When enacting IDEA 2004, Congress was mindful of the amount of time that the IEP process may take, and that the length of this process may be burdensome to administrators and teachers. The reauthorized law, therefore, includes six provisions intended to streamline the IEP planning process, especially during reviews and revisions of an initial IEP. First, a member of the IEP team won't be required to attend the IEP meeting or other meetings if the student's parents and the school personnel agree in writing that the person's attendance is not necessary because his or her area of curriculum or related services are not being modified or discussed at a meeting (§ 614(d)(1)(C)(i)). Second, a member of the IEP team may be excused from the IEP meeting if he or she submits a request in writing to the parents and the IEP team, and both the parents and IEP team agree with the excusal (§ 614(d)(1)(C)(ii)). These two provisions give IEP team members an opportunity to be excused from all or part of an IEP, thus releasing certain members, most likely general education teachers, from having to spend their time in meetings that do not directly concern them.

The third provision allows the IEP team to conduct IEP meetings by means other than face-to-face meetings.

For example, meetings can be held via conference calls, video conferencing, or other means. Additionally, placement meetings, mediation meetings, resolution sessions, and the administrative aspects of due process hearings may be held using alternative means if the parents and school personnel agree that this is acceptable. Fourth, if parents and school personnel agree, an existing IEP may be modified by writing a document to amend or modify the IEP rather than convening a meeting of the team to make the changes. Fifth, IDEA 2004 encouraged school districts to consolidate IEP meetings and reevaluation meetings whenever possible. Finally, IDEA 2004 allows the IEP team to make changes to the IEP by amending the IEP rather than redrafting the entire document (IDEA, 20 U.S.C. § 1414(d)(3)(F)). These provisions were added in IDEA 2004 to make the IEP planning process more flexible and convenient for parents and school personnel.

IDEA delineates the persons who are to compose the IEP team as well as persons who are permitted, but not required, to attend. In the following section I review the required participants in the IEP process.

IEP Team Participants

It is the responsibility of the school district to ensure that the required participants attend the IEP meeting. As Lake (2002) noted, school districts often run afoul of this requirement. Generally the number of participants in the IEP meeting should be kept to a minimum because the meeting will tend to be more open and allow for more active parent involvement. Moreover, smaller team meetings may be less costly, easier to arrange and conduct, and usually more productive. The school or the parents may invite other people to serve as members of the IEP team. According to IDEA the additional members must have knowledge or special expertise regarding the student.

The Student's Parents or Guardians IDEA specifies that parents are to be equal partners in IEP development. Equal partnership includes the right to actively participate in all discussions and decisions. This includes meaningful participation in all special education decision making, including IEP development and placement decisions. IEPs that have been developed without parental input have been uniformly invalidated by hearing officers and the courts (Gorn, 1998).

The school is required to follow specific procedures to ensure that parents attend and fully participate in the IEP meeting. These procedures include (a) notifying parents enough in advance to ensure that they will have an opportunity to attend the meeting, (b) scheduling meetings at a mutually agreeable time and place, and

(c) arranging other methods of including parents if they cannot attend the IEP meeting (e.g., conference calls).

If a student's parents cannot make the meeting, but still want to be involved, the school may hold the IEP meeting via telephone conference or video conferencing. If a student's parents refuse to attend the IEP meeting, the school district has no power to compel their attendance. Nonetheless, the school district may still hold the meeting and write the IEP. In such situations, school personnel should document their efforts to get the parents to attend. If the student's parents then refuse to sign the IEP or agree to a special education placement, the school district is *relieved of its obligation* to provide special education services to the student. In fact, according to IDEA 2004, school districts cannot use due process procedures to obtain consent for special education programming or placement when a student's parents refuse to consent to special education services (IDEA, 20 U.S.C. § 1414(a)(1)(D)(ii)(II)). Furthermore, a school district cannot later be held to have violated IDEA in such situations.

As previously mentioned, parents must be equal partners in the IEP meeting. Specifically, they must be allowed to participate in all the business of the IEP team including discussions of the (a) evaluation results and implications for the program; (b) nature, frequency, and location of special education services; (c) placement; and (d) related services. IEP team members must consider parental suggestions and, if appropriate, incorporate them into the IEP.

A Representative of the Local Educational Agency
A representative of the school or school district qualified to supervise the provision of special education and to ensure that the educational services specified in the IEP will be provided, must be in attendance. The representative of the agency must (a) be qualified to provide or supervise special education, (b) be knowledgeable about the general education curriculum, and (c) have the authority to commit school district resources (IDEA Regulations, 34 C.F.R. § Appendix C to Part 300, number 13). The school principal, special education administrator, or any member of the school staff designated by the principal or administrator may fill this position as long as they meet the previous qualifications.

The Student's General Education Teacher Prior to the passage of the IDEA Amendments of 1997, the "child's teacher" was required to participate in the IEP meeting. The law, however, did not specify if the teacher should be a student's regular education or special education teacher. The IDEA Amendments of 1997 added the student's general education teacher to the core IEP team

if the student is participating, or may participate in general education.

Because a general education teacher often plays a central role in the education of students with disabilities, Congress required that to the extent appropriate, a general education teacher should participate in the development of the IEP, including the determination of appropriate behavioral interventions and strategies, supplementary aids and services, program modifications, and support for school personnel. To ensure that the general education teacher on the IEP team is not given an excessive amount of additional duties or paperwork, the law indicates that they do not have to participate in all aspects of the IEP team's work, and should be involved only to the extent appropriate.

When a student (e.g., a middle school or high school student) has multiple general teachers, only one teacher is required to attend the IEP meeting. The school, however, may allow the other teachers to attend the meeting. Administrators may not take the place of teachers in IEP meetings (*OSEP Policy Letter*, 1992). The primary purpose of having a regular education teacher on the team is to ensure that someone who understands the general curricula is involved in program development, and also to ensure that general education teachers will be informed of their responsibilities.

The Student's Special Education Teacher At least one special education teacher or provider must be on the IEP team. Having the student's special education teacher or provider on the team ensures that the person who will implement the IEP will be involved in its development. If a teacher directly involved in educating the student is not a member of the IEP team, the IEP may not be valid (*Brimmer v. Traverse City*, 1994). According to OSEP, at least one member of the IEP team must be qualified in the area of the student's disability (*Letter to McIntire*, 1989). Because the student's special education will usually have expertise in the student's disability, that person will typically fill this role.

Often school districts appoint case managers to coordinate the IEP process, although having case managers on the team is not mandated by IDEA. The role of this person usually is to coordinate the evaluation process, collect and synthesize all reports and relevant information, communicate with parents, and participate in and conduct the IEP meeting (IDEA Regulations, 34 C.F.R. § 300 Appendix C:24). The case manager is usually the student's special education teacher.

A Person to Interpret the Instructional Implications of the Evaluation Results IDEA also requires that a person knowledgeable about the instructional implications of the evaluation be included on the team. Requiring someone with knowledge and expertise in evaluation at each IEP meeting provides a clearer link between evaluation results and instruction (Huefner, 2001). IDEA gives the school flexibility to choose who this person will be. Although this role has often been filled by school psychologists, someone who is already on the IEP team may fill this position (e.g., special education teacher).

The Student, Where Appropriate The school must inform the parents that the student may attend the meeting. The student, however, should be present only when appropriate. Additionally, if parents decide that their child's attendance will be helpful, the child must be allowed to attend. Whenever possible, the school and parents should discuss the appropriateness of having the student attend prior to making a decision. In cases where transition services are discussed, the student must be invited (IDEA Regulations, 34 C.F.R. § 300.344(c)(i)). If the student does not attend during transition planning, the school must take steps to ensure that the student's interests and preferences are considered in designing the transition plan (IDEA Regulations, 34 C.F.R. § 300.344((c)(i)(2)).

Other Individuals at the Discretion of the Parent(s) or School Either the school or the parents may invite other persons to the meeting. Weber (1992) contends that confidentiality rules may prevent the attendance of persons who are not employed by the school district unless the parents give consent in writing. This rule would not apply to attorneys working for the school district or related services personnel. It is inappropriate for representatives of teacher organizations or unions to attend an IEP meeting (IDEA Regulations, 34 C.F.R. § Appendix C to Part 300, number 20). When the school does invite additional persons, they must inform the parents who will attend. In contrast, parents are not similarly required to inform the school districts of additional persons they will bring to the IEP meeting. It would be appropriate, however, for the school to inquire if the parents intend to bring other participants. Parents may also request that school personnel who are not part of the core IEP team be present at the IEP meeting (Martin, 1996).

Parents may also bring anyone who is familiar with education laws or the student's needs. Such individuals may include independent professionals (e.g., psychologists, therapists). The school district is required to consider the additional participant's recommendations; however, the district is not required to accept their recommendations.

Related Services Personnel Related services personnel (e.g., school nurse, speech clinician, occupational therapist) should be invited to the IEP meeting if their participation is relevant to the education of the student. Related services personnel can be an important part of the IEP team. If related services personnel do not attend the IEP meeting, but will be involved in a student's educational program, they should provide a written recommendation to the IEP committee regarding the nature, frequency, and amount of related services to be provided to the student (IDEA Regulations, 34 C.F.R. § Appendix C to Part 300, number 23). In the IDEA reauthorization of 1997, Congress specifically noted that whenever possible a licensed registered school nurse should be a member of the IEP team to help define and make decisions about a student's educationally related health needs. If a student's primary disability is that he or she has a speech impairment, then a speech clinician must be on the IEP team and would serve in place of the special education teacher.

Transition Services Personnel If transition services are planned at the IEP meeting, the school must invite the student and a representative of the agency likely to provide or pay for the transition services. School personnel that may be involved in providing transition services (e.g., counselor, work-study coordinator) should also be invited. If a student does not attend his or her transition meeting, the IEP team must take steps to ensure that the student's preferences and interests are considered.

The IEP Document

The culmination of the IEP planning process is the IEP document. The IEP team, relying on data from a student's evaluation, professional judgment of the student's teachers and related service providers, and the parent's knowledge of their child, develops a program of special education and related services. The product of this process is the student's special education program, which is delineated in the IEP document.

Contents of the IEP Document IDEA regulations list eight categories of information that must be included in the IEP. It is crucial, therefore, that these components be discussed at the IEP meeting and included in the document.

A Statement of the Student's Present Level of Academic Achievement and Functional Performance. The first component in an IEP is a statement of the student's present level of academic achievement and functional performance (PLAAFP). This statement was formerly called the present level of educational performance. The name change emphasizes that this statement should include information on a student's functional performance as well as academic achievement when necessary.

The PLAAFP statement must include information on how a student's disabilities affect his or her involvement and progress in the general education curriculum. For preschool children this statement should specify how the disability affects the child's participation in age-appropriate activities.

The purpose of the PLAAFP statement is to describe the problems that interfere with the student's education so that (a) annual goals can be developed, (b) special education services can be determined, and (c) a student's progress can be measured. In effect, PLAAFPs are the starting points or baselines by which teams develop and measure the success of a student's program of special education.

The statement should contain information on the student's academic and functional performance. If the statement contains test scores, the statements must explain those scores. Additional information that an IEP team should consider when developing the PLAAFP statement may include (a) physical, health, and sensory status; (b) emotional, behavioral, and social development; (c) information from a student's parents, general education teachers, and special education teachers; (d) prevocational and vocational skills; and (e) the results of an independent educational evaluation (if one was conducted). Moreover, how these problems affect a student's performance in the general education curriculum should be specified. This is important because it will help provide information for determining what accommodations a student will need in the general education curriculum (Bateman & Linden, 2006). Labels (e.g., learning disabled, emotionally disturbed) are not appropriate substitutions for descriptions of educational performance.

The statement of needs should be written in objective terms using data from the MDT's evaluation. When test scores are included in this section, an explanation of the results should be provided. The results of these scores should be understandable to all parties involved. In a state-level due process hearing, *Pocatello School District* (1991), a school district's deficiencies in this present-levels statement were severe enough for the SEA to rule that the school district had denied a student a FAPE and thus violated IDEA. In this case the IEP was based on present-level information that included (a) numeric test scores with no explanation provided, and (b) descriptions of social and behavioral needs that were extremely vague, subjective, and "not suitable for use as a baseline to measure future progress" (Norlin & Gorn, 2005, p. 4:4).

The PLAAFP statements for students with EBD will need to include information regarding behavioral problems in addition to academic needs. The behavioral PLAAFP statements may include references to norm-referenced data, such as standardized behavior rating scales and checklists, or informal data from direct observations, and should provide explanations of these data. Moreover, there must be a direct relationship between the PLAAFP and the other components of the IEP (IDEA Regulations, Appendix C, Question 36). Each PLAAFP statement, therefore, must lead to a special education service, or an annual goal and a special education service. Not all needs require corresponding goals. For example, if the student needs an assistive technology device, the IEP must include the particular devices in the special education services section. However, a goal regarding the assistive technology device would not be required. If a student has either an academic or nonacademic need listed in the PLAAFP that will be addressed in the student's educational program, appropriate goals, benchmarks, and short-term objectives (STOs) should accompany these areas. For example, if the statement describes a reading skill deficit, this problem should be addressed in the measurable annual goals, special education services should be provided to the student, and student progress in this area must be monitored.

IDEA also requires that the PLP statement addresses how the student's disability affects his or her involvement and progress in general education. The purpose of this requirement is to infuse a general education perspective into the IEP planning process.

Clearly PLAAFP statements must be specific, objective, and measurable. Moreover, because everything in the IEP is related to the PLAAFP statement, every need must be clear and be linked to the other sections of the IEP.

Measurable Annual Goals. After the IEP team develops the PLAAFP statement, the team will develop a student's measurable annual goals, including academic and functional goals. The annual goals focus on remediating a student's academic or functional problems and are based on the student's PLAAFP statement. Annual goals are projections the team makes regarding the progress of the student in one school year. Annual goals indicate (a) if the anticipated outcomes for the student are being met and (b) whether the special education services and placement are effective (IDEA Regulations, 34 C.F.R., Appendix to Part 300–Notice of Interpretation, Question 38). Although annual goals have been an important component of IEPs since 1975, IDEA now emphasizes the development of *measurable* annual goals. Furthermore, the IEP must include a statement of how a student's progress will be measured and how a student's parents will be informed about his or her progress toward achieving the goals.

The purpose of goals and objectives is to help determine whether a student is making educational progress and if the special education program is appropriate for meeting educational needs. Correctly written goals enable the teachers and parents to monitor a student's progress in a special education program and make educational adjustments to the program when a student is not making adequate progress (Deno, 1992). In fact, when Congress reauthorized IDEA in 1997, it viewed the requirement of measurable annual goals "crucial to the success of the IEP" (Senate Report, 1997, p. 25).

When writing the annual goals, IEP teams should consider the student's past achievement, current level of performance in academic and nonacademic areas, practicality of goals, priority needs, and amount of instructional time devoted to reaching the goal (Strickland & Turnbull, 1990). Whereas goals should be written for a level that the student has a reasonable chance of reaching, courts have indicated that when goals are so unambitious that achieving them will not result in meaningful improvements in performance, the goals may render the IEP inappropriate (*Adams v. Hansen*, 1985; *Carter v. Florence*, 1991).

One of the primary problems that IEP teams have in writing goals is that often they are too broad, vague, and abstract. Table 9–3 contains examples of unmeasurable goals (which, unfortunately, were taken from actual IEPs!).

IDEA clearly requires that goals be specific and measurable. Goals must be written so the student's "teacher(s) and parents are able to track the child's progress in special education" (IDEA Regulations, 34 C.F.R. § Part 300, Appendix C, Question 37). The annual goals in an IEP, therefore, are for evaluative and communicative purposes. An IEP that lacks meaningful educational and properly written goals is legally and educationally flawed.

Benchmarks or Short-Term Objectives. In IDEA 2004 benchmarks or short-term objectives (STOs) were *eliminated* as a *federal* requirement, except for students who take alternate assessments (i.e., students with significant cognitive impairments). States, however, may retain their benchmark or STO requirement, in which case IEPs must develop either benchmarks or STOs for each annual goal.

The original reason for including STOs in IEPs was that they would describe expected student performance in measurable terms and would allow monitoring of student progress toward the annual goals on a short-term basis throughout the year. If a student achieves the benchmark or STOs, therefore, they should also achieve the annual goals (*Pocatello School District*, 1991). Thus, both benchmarks and STOs describe what a student is expected to accomplish in a given time period. They are "measurable intermediate steps between the present levels of educational performance . . . and the annual goals that are established for that student" (IDEA Regulations, 34 C.F.R. § Part 300, Appendix C, Question 39). Because IEPs now include *measurable* annual goals, statements of how the goals will be measured, and a schedule for informing a student's parents of his or her progress, Congress decided benchmarks or STOs were no longer necessary. In fact, in 1997 the U.S. Department of Education noted that

because of the requirement that the IEP contain STOs for every goal, teachers may spend significant time and energy developing a multiple of detailed and lengthy objectives that have little instructional utility. As a result, the IEP process often results in a paper exercise characterized by fragmented objectives, lower expectations, and instructional irrelevance. (p. 2)

Table 9–3 Vague, abstract goals

Goal	Problem
Caleb will develop a positive attitude toward schoolwork.	What is a positive attitude toward schoolwork and how will it be demonstrated?
Jeremy will improve his reading ability.	Very vague statement. How will Jeremy improve his reading ability? No criterion for acceptable performance.
Talia will demonstrate age-appropriate skills.	What are age-appropriate skills? How are they defined and measured?
Stacey will improve her spelling by the end of the year.	No criterion for acceptable performance.
Shan will become responsible for his own behavior.	Does this mean Shan will be responsible for both appropriate and inappropriate behavior? Does this mean if Shan takes responsibility for inappropriate behavior, he is meeting his goal?
When given the opportunity, Jerry will respect authority 80% of the time.	Misuse of percentages. How does one respect authority 80% of the time?
Melvin will use his time wisely.	Unclear.

When teachers work in states that still require that IEPs include STOs, the IEP team must remember that its purpose is to monitor a student's progress toward his or her goals. A benchmark or STO is used for formative evaluation of a student's progress toward his or her goal. Formative evaluation refers to ongoing evaluation conducted during the course of the educational program and benchmarks, and STOs are formative because measurement of them is ongoing during the school year. If measurement of a benchmark or STO indicates that the student's progress makes it unlikely that the annual goal will be met, the teacher must use this information to make an instructional or programmatic change.

Congress's purpose in retaining the STO requirement for students with severe disabilities may have been to ensure that IEP teams develop sequential intermediate steps that would allow a student to progress toward his or her annual goal. In this respect, the STOs would be a task analysis of the steps necessary for a student to progress from the PLAAFP to the annual goal.

How Student Progress Will Be Measured and Reported. The IEP must include a statement of how a student's progress toward the annual goals will be measured. This change relates to the requirement that goals be measurable. IDEA also requires that the parents of the child be informed of the child's progress toward annual goals through the use of quarterly or other reports that are issued at the same time as report cards. The purpose of this provision is to ensure that both teachers and parents know how student progress will be measured and how the student is progressing. Clearly, IDEA requires that goals be written that are measurable and that the goals are actually measured.

The Senate committee that drafted a report on the IDEA reauthorization of 1997 suggested a possible method of providing feedback to parents about their child's progress. IEP teams should develop an IEP report card with "checkboxes or equivalent options that . . . enable the parents and the special educator to review and judge . . . performance on a . . . multipoint continuum" (Senate Report, 1997, p. 25). Students' progress may be communicated on a scale ranging from "No Progress" to "Completed." In this way, the effects of the student's special education program can be evaluated and modified if necessary. (See Figure 9-1.)

Monitoring a student's progress toward meeting IEP goals is absolutely essential. Without such monitoring, the goals are meaningless because it will be impossible to determine success or failure. If the goals of the IEP cannot be measured or the student's progress evaluated, the IEP will not appropriately address his or her needs.

Statement of the Special Education and Related Services. Students' IEPs must include a statement of the specific educational services, related services, and supplementary aids and services to be provided by the school. The purpose of the statements is to clarify the services that the school will provide to help a student (a) progress toward his or her annual goals, and (b) be involved in and progress in the general education curriculum. The statement of services must be unambiguous so that the school's commitment of resources is clear to parents and other members of the team (IDEA Regulations, 34 C.F.R. § Appendix C to Part 300, number 51). Unfortunately, this crucial component of the IEP too often consists of only checkmarks on the face sheet of the IEP (Bateman & Linden, 2006). According to Bateman and Linden, a review

Figure 9–1 Progress monitoring form

Annual Goals	Progress Toward Goals				Evaluation Procedures	Is the progress sufficient for the student to achieve the goal by the end of the year?	
	Excellent	Good	Fair	Poor		Yes	No

of several hundred IEP rulings revealed that a much broader and detailed explanation of the services is required. Additionally, a statement of program modifications or supports for school personnel must be included in this section of the IEP. These modifications and supports are "aids, services, and other supports that are provided in regular education classes or other education-related settings to enable children with disabilities to be educated with nondisabled children to the maximum extent appropriate" (IDEA, 20 U.S.C. § 1401(25)).

In IDEA 2004, Congress added the requirement that these services must be based on *peer-reviewed research.* As mentioned in Chapter 2, IDEA 2004 does not provide a definition of peer-reviewed research. The No Child Left Behind (NCLB) Act, however, does provide a definition of scientifically based research: "Scientifically based research means research that involves the application of rigorous, systematic, and objective procedures to obtain reliable and valid knowledge relevant to education activities and programs" (NCLB, 20 U.S.C. § 7801(37)).

This language addition means that special education teachers need to know the research in the field of EBD. Moreover, teachers must be able to apply these research findings in their special education programs and be able to discuss these research-based practices in IEP meetings. If a parent inquires about the research base regarding the methods or practices that the teacher uses or if the parent disputes the special education services methods because he or she doesn't believe the research supports them, the teacher needs to know and be able to explain the peer-reviewed research behind his or her choice of educational practices and be able to defend the use of the particular practice. The U.S. Department of Education is investing in technical assistance centers and clearinghouses to help make peer-reviewed research knowledge readily available to educators. Table 9–4 lists Web sites sponsored by the U.S. Department of Education and a few other organizations where information on research-based strategies is available.

This requirement also gives school districts a framework for considering parental requests for particular methodologies, which means that if a parent requests that a teacher uses a particular methodology, an IEP team may determine if the methodology has support in the research before deciding if it will be used. If there is no empirical support for the parentally suggested methodology, the team could decide not to use the methodology on grounds that it is not supported by peer-reviewed research.

Statements of related services refer to the services and equipment provided to assist a student to benefit from special education. These services should assist a student to (a) advance toward attaining his or her annual goals, (b) be involved and progress in the general education curriculum, and (c) be educated with students without disabilities. This requirement commits the school district to providing these services at no charge to the parents. The team must determine the special education and related service needs of a student. This decision must be based on the student's needs, not on the availability of services. In addition to enumerating the types of services, the IEP should also include the amount, frequency, and duration of services. If the required services are not available in the district, but are determined by the IEP team to be necessary, they must be provided through contracts or arrangements with other agencies.

It is not necessary to include components of a student's educational program that are not part of the special education and related services required by the student. In fact, Gorn (1998) contends that nonmandatory educational services should not be included in the IEP. This is because adding particular nonmandated services to the IEP may create an obligation on the part of the school district to provide the services while the IEP is in effect.

Statement of the Extent to Which Student Will Not Participate with Nondisabled Children in the General Education Classroom. The IEP must also state the amount of time that the student will not participate in general education. Students with disabilities must be allowed to participate with their nondisabled peers to the maximum extent appropriate in both academic and nonacademic settings. Until IDEA 1997, the IEP required a statement regarding the amount of time in which a student with disabilities participated in regular education classes. The law now requires a statement of the extent to which a student with disabilities *will not* participate in regular education programs with nondisabled children. Huefner (2001) argues that this requirement is significant because it requires that the school bear the burden of proof in proposing a setting other than the regular education setting. Huefner also notes that the regular education setting is not necessarily the regular education classroom. For example, a regular education setting could be a regular education classroom along with special education services delivered in a resource room.

If modifications in the general education classroom are necessary to ensure that the student participates in general education, the modifications must be incorporated into the IEP. This applies to any general education programs in which a student participates (IDEA Regulations, 34 C.F.R. § Appendix C to Part 300, number 48).

Table 9–4 Web sites containing information on peer-reviewed research

Name	URL	Explanation
What Works Clearinghouse	http://www.whatworks.ed.gov	A clearinghouse established by the U.S. Department of Education (ED) that conducts systematic reviews of scientific evidence regarding what works in education.
National Technical Assistance Center on Positive Behavioral Interventions and Supports	http://www.pbis.org	A center established by the Office of Special Education Programs (OSEP) of the U.S. ED to give schools information and technical assistance for identifying, adapting, and sustaining effective schoolwide disciplinary practices.
National Center on Student Progress Monitoring	http://www.studentprogress.org	A center established by OSEP to provide technical assistance and disseminate information on scientifically based student progress monitoring.
National Dissemination Center for Children with Disabilities	http://www.nichcy.org/	A center established by OSEP to serve as a central source of information on disabilities in infants, toddlers, children, and youth, and research-based information on effective educational practices.
The Promising Practices Network	http://www.promisingpractices.net	The Promising Practices Network (PPN), operated by the RAND corporation, is dedicated to providing quality evidence-based information about what works to improve the lives of children, families, and communities.
The International Campbell Collaboration	http://www.campbellcollaboration.org/ECG/index.aspl	The International Campbell Collaboration is a nonprofit organization that prepares, updates, and rapidly disseminates systematic reviews of high-quality educational and training interventions conducted worldwide that are aimed at improving education and learning.
Blueprints for Violence Prevention	http://www.colorado.edu/cspv/blueprints/index.html	The Center for the Study and Prevention of Violence (CSPV), at the University of Colorado at Boulder, in a project called Blueprints for Violence Prevention, has identified 11 prevention and intervention programs that meet a strict scientific standard of program effectiveness. The 11 model programs, called Blueprints, have been effective in reducing adolescent violent crime, aggression, delinquency, and substance abuse. Another 18 programs were identified as promising programs.

Statement Regarding the Student's Participation in the Administration of State or Districtwide Assessments of Achievement. IDEA requires that all students with disabilities be included in statewide and districtwide assessments of student progress. The IEP team must determine how a student will participate in the statewide assessment. The team may determine that a student will take (a) the regular assessment based on grade-level achievement standards, which is given to all students; (b) the regular assessment with state-approved accommodations or modifications; (c) an alternate assessment based on alternate achievement standards; or (d) an alternate assessment based on modified achievement standards. Readers should note that the IEP team decides *how* the student will participate, *not whether* the student will participate.

Because students with disabilities may need individual modifications and accommodations to participate in these assessments, the IEP must include a statement detailing all such modifications. OSEP, however, has ruled that states may restrict the types of modifications or accommodations they allow to be used in statewide testing (Shriner, 2001). When considering the use of modifications in state testing programs, therefore, IEP teams should be familiar with state rules and regulations. If the IEP team determines that a student cannot be accurately assessed, even with modifications, the IEP must contain a statement why the assessment is not appropriate, and identifying an alternative assessment that will be used in place of the statewide or districtwide assessments.

For an excellent resource on testing accommodations for students with disabilities, refer to the following Web site maintained by the Council of Chief State School Officers (CCSSO): http://www.ccsso.org/projects/SCASS/Projects/Assessing_Special_Education_Students/. The CCSSO page contains excellent information on selecting, administering, and evaluating the use of accommodations for teaching and testing students with disabilities. The Web page also provides a link to all state education agencies. According to the CCSSO, there are four major types of accommodations:

- Presentation accommodations that allow students to access information in ways that do not require them to visually read standard print. These alternate modes of access are auditory, multisensory, tactile, and visual.

- Response accommodations that allow students to complete assignments, tests, and activities in different ways or to solve or organize problems using some type of assistive device or organizer.

- Setting accommodations that change the location in which a test or assignment is given or the conditions of the assessment setting.

- Timing or scheduling accommodations that increase the allowable length of time to complete a test or assignment and may also change the way the time is organized.

Table 9-5 contains examples of accommodations.

Projected Date for the Beginning of Services and their Anticipated Frequency, Location, and Duration. The IEP must be initiated as soon as possible after it is written. The only exceptions are if the IEP is written during a vacation period, the summer, or when circumstances require a short delay (such as working out transportation arrangements). When a student moves from another district, the delay should not be more than a week. A student must not be placed in a special education program prior to the initiation date in the IEP.

By requiring a statement regarding the frequency, location, and duration of services, Congress added clarity to the IEP. It is not permissible to include only a statement that a student will receive special education in a resource room or speech therapy. It is required that the frequency and location of these services be included. These requirements also include any modifications that will be made to the student's general education classes (e.g., behavior management plan, modification of assignments).

Statement of Needed Transition Services. A significant change made in IDEA 2004 was the requirement that transition services must be included in the IEP of a

Table 9–5 Testing accommodations

Category	Accommodation
Presentation	• Give brief and simple directions. • Have someone read the directions. • Use graphic organizers. • Highlight key words in directions.
Response	• Use a calculator. • Write in test booklet instead of on a scoring sheet. • Type of word processor. • Answer into a tape recorder. • Use spelling and grammar checkers.
Setting	• Change to a setting with fewer distractions. • Sit in front of the room. • Give test to a small group.
Timing/ Scheduling	• Give multiple or frequent breaks. • Cue student to begin working and to stay on task. • Allow extended time to take test.

student who turns 16 years of age. If state law requires transition services to be included in student's IEPs at an earlier age (e.g., 14), that requirement must be followed.

The transition section of the IEP must now include appropriate *measurable* postsecondary goals based on age-appropriate transition assessments related to training, education, employment, and independent living skills. These goals must be measurable and could be related to (a) job training, (b) continuing education, (c) postschool employment, and (d) independent living skills. This requirement was added to IDEA in the reauthorization of 2004.

The transition component of a student's IEP must also include the transition services, including courses of study, that will be provided to the student to assist him or her in reaching the goals. This section of the IEP must focus on all services that will be needed to assist the student's transition to postschool life.

IDEA now defines transition services as

a coordinated set of activities for a child with a disability that (A) is designed to be within a results-oriented process, that is focused on improving the academic and functional achievement of the child with a disability to facilitate the child's movement from school to post-school activities, including post-secondary, vocational education, integrated employment (including supported employment), continuing and adult education, adult services, independent living, or community participation; (B) is based on the individual child's needs, taking into account the child's strengths, preferences, and interests; and (C) includes instruction, related services, community experiences, the development of employment and other post school adult-living objectives, and, when appropriate, acquisition of daily living skills and functional vocational evaluation. (IDEA, 20 U.S.C. § 1402(34))

The purpose of including transition services in the IEP is to infuse a long-range perspective into the IEP process and to help students better reach their potential in postschool life (Bulen & Bullis, 1995; Bullis & Gaylord-Ross, 1991; Tucker & Goldstein, 1992). According to Maag and Katsiyannis (1998), the transition process must be outcome oriented and encompass a broad array of services and experiences that lead to employment, and it must promote movement from school to postschool outcomes. An IEP that includes transition services must include the areas that are listed in IDEA's definition (i.e., instruction, community services, and employment and other adult-living objectives). If any of these required services are not included in a student's transition plan, the IEP must include an explanatory note detailing the reasons they do not appear in the document (Goldstein, 1997).

Additionally, before a student graduates with a regular high school diploma or ages out of eligibility under IDEA (age 22 in most states), the IEP team must give the student a summary statement of his or her academic achievement and functional performance. This summary statement must include recommendations on how to assist a student in meeting his or her goals after high school.

Special Considerations in IEP Development

When IDEA was reauthorized in 1997, Congress added a section regarding special considerations in developing the IEP. These considerations must be part of the IEP planning process; however, unless a factor affects a student, it does not need to be included in the IEP. For example, one of the special considerations the IEP team must address is the student's need for assistive technology devices or services. If the team decides that a student does not require such services, they should not be included in the IEP. If, however, the team decides that assistive technology services are needed, this must be indicated in the student's IEP.

The first factor the IEP team must consider is if a student's behavior impedes his or her learning, or that of others, regardless of the student's disability category. If the team decides the behavior is a problem, then the team should consider appropriate strategies including positive behavioral interventions and supports to address that behavior (for elaboration on behavior intervention plans see Chapter 5). Second, when an IEP is developed for a student with limited English proficiency, the student's language needs that relate to the IEP must be considered. Third, in developing an IEP for a student who is blind or visually impaired, the IEP must provide for instruction in Braille and the use of Braille unless the team determines that instruction in Braille is not appropriate. The fourth factor must be considered when a student is deaf or hard of hearing. The student's language and communication needs, opportunities for direct communications with peers and professionals in the student's language and communication mode, academic level, and full range of needs must be considered. Additionally, the team must also consider opportunities for direct instruction in the student's language and communication mode. Finally, the IEP team should consider whether the student requires assistive technology devices and services. If the team determines that assistive technology services are required, they must be written into the IEP and provided to the student.

Placement Decisions

After the IEP team has completed a student's special education program, the team must determine a student's placement or where the student's IEP will be implemented.

In most cases the IEP team, including the parents, should make the placement decision. When determining placement, it is crucial that the placement is based on the IEP. Placement decisions, therefore, follow the planning of a student's educational program. School districts sometimes make the mistake of determining the placement prior to developing the IEP. This is not a legal practice, however, because IDEA requires that the placement must be based on the student's IEP (IDEA Regulations, 34 C.F.R. § 300.552(a)(2)). It is only after the IEP has been written that the team has the basis for determining the placement in which a student's particular needs can be met (Bateman & Linden, 1998; Gorn, 1998; Martin, 1996; Yell, 2006).

Placement decisions must be made in accordance with the least restrictive environment (LRE) principle of IDEA. This principle requires that students with disabilities must be educated with nondisabled students to the maximum extent appropriate. When the general education placement, even with the provision of supplementary aids and services, is not appropriate, the IEP team may decide to place a student in a more restrictive setting. Thus, IDEA expresses a preference for, but does not mandate, placing students with disabilities in general education (Bateman & Linden, 2006). (For elaborations on LRE, see Chapter 2.) Additionally, IDEA requires that unless the IEP specifies otherwise, students should be educated in the school that they would attend if they did not have a disability or educated as close to the home school as possible. This is also a preference, not a mandate.

IMPLEMENTING THE IEP

IDEA does not include specific time limits in which the IEP must be implemented following its development, although OSEP has indicated that generally no delay between the time the IEP is written and the provision of special education services is permissible (*OSEP Policy Letter*, 1991b). Regulations specify only that the IEP must be implemented as soon as possible after the IEP meeting. There are two situations in which a delay in implementation is permitted: (a) when the IEP meeting is held during the summer months or a vacation and (b) when circumstances, such as arranging transportation, require a short delay. In most situations, however, the school should provide services immediately following IEP finalization. Regulations require that the IEP be in place at the beginning of the school year (IDEA Regulations, 34 C.F.R. § 300.342(a)). To ensure that this requirement is met, the school may hold the IEP meeting at the end of the preceding school year or during the summer months.

REVIEWING AND REVISING THE IEP

IDEA mandates that the IEP be reviewed and, if necessary, revised annually. In the annual review, the IEP team must examine (a) any lack of progress toward the annual goals and in the general education curriculum where appropriate; (b) the results of any reevaluation; (c) information about the child provided by the parents; (d) the student's anticipated needs; and (e) other considerations as deemed appropriate.

The IEP team must review a student's IEP more frequently if needed. More frequent reviews should be conducted if (a) the progress monitoring data that the teacher has collected shows that a student is not going to meet his or her annual goals, (b) a student's teacher requests a review, or (c) the student's parents request a review. During this meeting the IEP team should review the instructional changes that a student's special education has made, and consider revising the student's special education program and placement if necessary. If a reevaluation or independent evaluation has been conducted, the IEP team should also review the results and determine if it should make changes to the special education program.

The timing of these reviews is left to the discretion of the school. The parent or the school, however, may initiate the IEP reviews as often as warranted. If either the school or parents decide that components of the IEP, such as the PLAAFP statements or measurable annual goals, need to be revised, a new IEP meeting must be called. A student's IEP remains in effect until it is revised or a new IEP is written. The IEP cannot be revised unless the parents are notified about the proposed change and the reasons for the change, prior to making the revision.

When a student moves from one district to another within the same state, the new school district shall provide the student a FAPE, including providing services that are comparable to the student's previous IEP, until the district adopts the previous IEP or develops and implements and a new IEP (IDEA, 20 U.S.C. § 1414 (d)(2)(C)). When a student from an IEP transfers from another state, the school district must provide the student a FAPE, including providing services that are comparable to the student's previous IEP, until the new school district conducts an evaluation, if necessary, and develops a new IEP (IDEA, 20 U.S.C. § 1414 (d)(2)(C)). In either case, the new school district must attempt to obtain a student's records as soon as possible and the old school district should reply promptly to any such requests.

If a school district proposes to change any aspect of the student's special education program, or refuses to change aspects of the student's program, it must issue prior notification to the parent. The notice must include a full explanation of proposed actions, justification for the changes, why alternatives were rejected, parental appeal rights, and other procedural safeguards. As long as the school provides adequate notice and conducts meetings in accordance with procedures set forth in IDEA, parental consent is not required for review and revisions of the IEP. If parents reject revisions, they have the option of calling a due process hearing.

DEVELOPING EDUCATIONALLY MEANINGFUL AND LEGALLY SOUND IEPS

Bateman and Linden (1998) stated:

Sadly, most IEPs are horrendously burdensome to teachers and nearly useless to parents and children. Far from being creative, flexible, data-based, and individualized application of the best of educational interventions to a child with unique needs, the typical IEP is empty, devoid of specific services to be provided. It says what the IEP team hopes to accomplish, but little if anything about the special education interventions and the related services or classroom modifications that will enable (the student) to reach those goals. . . . Many if not most goals and objectives couldn't be measured if one tried, and all too often no effort is made to actually assess the child's progress toward the goal. (p. 63)

The primary purpose in conducting the IEP planning process and writing the IEP document is to plan a program of special education and related services, including modifications and program supports, for educating the student in integrating settings. Furthermore, the IEP must be reasonably calculated to enable the child to receive educational benefits (*Board of Education of the Hendrick Hudson School District v. Rowley*, 1982).

It is legally sound and educationally useful to divide the IEP planning process into three distinct stages:

(a) writing the PLAAFP; (b) developing the special education program—which involves writing measurable annual goals, determining the special education services to be provided, and specifying the means for monitoring student progress; and (c) determining the student's placement. Figure 9–2 depicts this process.

Bateman and Linden (2006) suggested that IEP teams use what they refer to as an "IEP non-form" (p. 96) during the IEP meeting. A nonform would consist of several pages that each contain an IEP requirement(s) and then show the rest of the page blank so a team member can write in the information. This would avoid having team members searching through forms to locate and fill in the needed information. For example, one page of the document would consist of identifying information (e.g. student's name, age, IEP participants). Another page would have three columns that are labeled as follows: (a) the PLAAFP statement, (b) measurable annual goals, and (c) special education services. The rest of the page would be blank so a team member has space to write the PLAAFP statement, a goal, and a service or services. According to the authors, using the IEP nonform would facilitate the IEP process because it would require teams to focus on the primary purpose of the IEP, which is to answer the following three questions: (a) What are the student's unique educational needs? (b) What annual goals are appropriate for the student? (c) What will the school do in response to the student's needs? The IEP nonform is an excellent tool for developing an educationally meaningful and legally sound IEP. In the next section I describe the three major steps of developing an IEP.

Step 1: *Determine the present levels of academic achievement and functional performance.* The first task of the IEP team is to assemble the evaluation data and, using these data, determine the student's

Figure 9–2   The IEP process

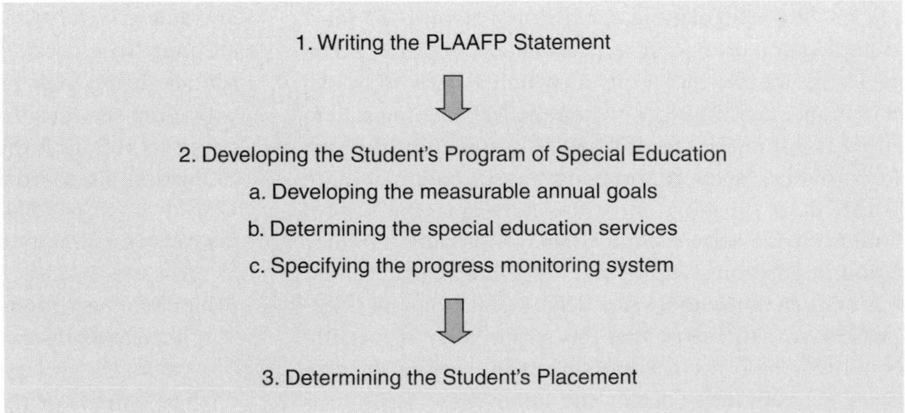

1. Writing the PLAAFP Statement

2. Developing the Student's Program of Special Education

   a. Developing the measurable annual goals

   b. Determining the special education services

   c. Specifying the progress monitoring system

3. Determining the Student's Placement

educational needs. These statements must describe the student's performance in any area that is adversely affected by the student's disability. This includes academic and nonacademic areas. The purpose of the present level of performance statements is to identify these areas of need so that an appropriate educational program can be devised. The statement does not need to address areas that don't require special education programming.

According to the Department of Education, when writing the PLAAFP statements, IEP teams must (a) describe the effect of the student's disability on his or her performance in any areas of education that are affected (e.g., reading, writing, behavior); (b) write the statement in objective and measurable terms that are easily understood by everyone on the team and are precise enough to allow progress to be measured; and (c) describe how the student's disability affects his or her involvement and progress in the general curriculum (IDEA Regulations, 34 C.F.R. § 300.347(1)). Additionally, if the student is aged 16 or older (or younger if required by the state) the PLAAFP must contain information regarding the transition assessment. Figure 9–3 provides examples of academic and behavioral PLAAFP statements that meet these

Table 9–6   Checklist for PLAAFP statements

✔ Is the PLAAFP statement individualized?

✔ Is the statement written in understandable language and clear to everyone on the team?

✔ Is the statement precise enough to lead to measurable annual goals?

✔ Does the statement describe how the student's disability affects educational performance?

✔ Does the statement explain how the student's disability affects his or her participation in general education?

✔ Does the PLAAFP statement describe *only* the unique needs that will be addressed in the IEP?

✔ Do all needs identified in PLAAFP statement lead to an annual goal, special education service, or both?

criteria. Table 9–6 is a checklist of important points to consider when writing the PLAAFP statement.

Step 2: *Develop the special education program.* After completing the PLAAFP statement the IEP team has the necessary information to develop the student's special education program. This consists of three subtasks that are all based on the PLAAFP statement. First, the IEP team must write measurable annual goals. Second, the IEP team must determine the special education services, and related services, supplementary aids, services, and program modifications that will help the student reach these goals. Third, the team must specify the means for monitoring student progress and ensure that the student's progress is actually monitored. Moreover, the IEP must detail how a student's progress will be measured and how progress will be reported to a student's parents.

Subtask 1: Develop the measurable annual goals. After the IEP team has written the PLAAFP statement and determined the special education services to be provided, the team develops the measurable annual goals. The question the team seeks to answer in writing the annual goals is, "If we provide a meaningful educational program, what improvements or gains can the student be reasonably expected to make in one year?" When developing the annual goals, teams must keep in mind the two major purposes of IDEA's emphasis on measurable annual goals, which are to provide (a) a focus for developing a student's special education program, and (b) a basis for monitoring a student's progress. It is crucial that the goals be ambitious enough so that by reaching them a student will have achieved meaningful educational progress.

FIGURE 9-3

PLAAFP statements—academic and behavioral

Reading PLAAFP

Billy is a fifth-grade student with a severe reading problem. He currently reads at an average rate of 42 words per minute (wpm) out of his grade-level reading textbook; his peers read at an average rate of 108 wpm in the same book. Billy's reading problems make it difficult for him to work successfully in general education classes that require him to learn by reading.

Behavior PLAAFP

Billy has difficulty staying on task during instruction. During three structured observation periods, he was on task an average of 54% of the time observed. Billy's peers were on task an average of 88% of the time observed. Billy's difficulty remaining on task results in low achievement in classes that require sustained attention to task. Additionally, his teachers report that he frequently talks in class, which also gets other students off task and disrupts the learning process.

Goals must be written in terms that are observable and quantifiable (Alberto & Troutman, 2006; Wolery et al., 1988). To communicate all the required information and provide a basis for evaluation, goals should contain four components: (1) the learner's name, (2) the target behavior or what the student is expected to do, (3) the conditions under which the behavior will be performed, and (4) the criteria for acceptable performance or how well the task is to be performed (Alberto & Troutman, 2006; Mager, 1997; Wolery et al., 1988). First, the student's name is included in the goal to promote individualization. According to Alberto and Troutman (2006), identifying the specific student in the goal reinforces the team's focus on the individual learner and communicates this focus to others. Second, the target behavior that the team seeks to change is clearly identified so the goal indicates what the student will do when the goal is reached. Furthermore, the target behavior must be described in terms that are observable, measurable, and repeatable so that the occurrence of the target behavior is verifiable (e.g., Jeremy will read 48 words aloud . . .). Third, the conditions of measurement are described—that is, the conditions that precede the occurrence of the target behavior to be measured. Conditions can include the materials the teacher will use in measuring the goal (e.g., Given a reading passage from Open Court reading book 4, Jeremy will . . .) and the environmental conditions (e.g., When playing with other children at recess, Jeremy will . . .). Fourth, the criteria for acceptable performance are listed. The IEP team sets the standard for minimally acceptable performance the student will achieve as the result of the program. Criteria are often specified in terms of accuracy (e.g., 90% of the time, 8 out of 10 days) and rate (e.g., 24 correct words per minute). Figure 9-4 provides examples of academic and behavioral goals that meet these criteria. Table 9-7 is a checklist of important points to consider when writing an annual goal.

Subtask 2: Determine the student's special education services. When the IEP team determines the special education and related services that will be part of a student's IEP, it is crucial that the team determines these services based on a student's needs rather than the services available. When determining services, the team must answer the question, "What services must be provided to ensure that the student will receive a meaningful education?" Merely checking off boxes to note the type of service the student will receive is not appropriate. The service must be

FIGURE 9-4

Annual goals—academic and behavioral

Reading Goal

In 32 weeks, when presented with a passage from the fourth-grade basal textbook, Billy will read aloud 90 wpm with fewer than 2 errors.

Behavior Goal

By the annual review on May 24, 2008, when observed on three separate occasions for 1/2 hour in each of his reading, math, and social studies classes, Billy will be on task 75% of the time observed as defined and measured by the pupil observation procedure.

Table 9–7 Checklist for measurable annual goals

✔ Are the goals linked to the assessment and the PLAAFP statements?

✔ Are goals specific, clear, and measurable?

✔ Do the goals contain the target behavior, the measurement conditions, and the criteria for acceptable performance?

✔ Do the goals provide a focus for a student's individualized program of special education?

✔ Does the goal section of the IEP contain information on how the student's progress will be measured?

✔ Does the goal section contain IEP information on how progress will be communicated to the student's parents?

✔ Can the goals be used to evaluate the effectiveness of the IEP?

✔ Is the student's progress toward achieving the goals actually measured?

fully described, including location, frequency, and duration, so that the exact nature of the services provided will be clear to all involved.

According to IDEA, the services that the IEP provides must allow the student to (a) "advance appropriately toward attaining the annual goals," (b) "be involved in and progress in the general curriculum and to participate in extracurricular and other nonacademic activities," and (c) "be educated and participate with other children with disabilities and nondisabled children" (IDEA Regulations, 34 C.F.R., Appendix to Part 300–Notice of Interpretation). IDEA repeatedly notes the importance of a student with disabilities accessing the general curriculum to the maximum extent appropriate.

The general curriculum refers to the curriculum in which students without disabilities participate. In passing the IDEA Amendments of 1997, Congress believed that the majority of students identified as eligible for special education were capable of participating in the general education curriculum to varying degrees with some adaptations and modifications (Senate Report, No. 105-17). It is important to note that IDEA does *not* require that all students in special education participate in the entire general education curriculum. Rather, it requires that, when appropriate, students with disabilities participate in the general education to the extent appropriate given the student's educational needs. Any adaptations and modifications that will allow a student in special education to participate in the general education classroom must be included in this section of the IEP.

With respect to participation in the general education classroom, it is not necessary that specific details of the general curriculum be included in the IEP. Furthermore, a specialized curriculum needed to provide an appropriate education *must not* be supplanted by the general curriculum. For instance, if a student needs to be taught in a reading curriculum other than the reading curriculum used in the general education classroom, it would be legally and educationally inappropriate to use the general education curriculum. Bateman and Linden (2006) made the important point that IEP teams must make the critical distinction between services that allow the student in special education to access the curriculum, which is appropriate (e.g., using a behavior management system to encourage a student to follow teacher directions), versus incorporating the general curriculum itself into the IEP, which is not appropriate (e.g., putting goals from a social studies class in the IEP). Bateman and Linden assert that it is special education services that allow access, not the general education curriculum itself, that is to be included in the IEP.

When determining the services that will be included in a student's IEP, the team must first determine the special education services that will be provided. For example:

- What services will be provided (e.g., reading programming, behavioral programming, transition services)?
- What is the nature of services (e.g., direct instruction in the five components of reading instruction, applied behavior analysis)?
- Where will the services be provided (e.g., resource room, self-contained classroom)?
- How many hours a day and how many days per week will the student receive these services (e.g., 1 hour per day, 5 days per week)?
- What peer-reviewed research supports these services (e.g., findings of the National Reading Panel)?

Additionally, the team must consider related services (e.g., counseling, transportation, inservice training for faculty), supplementary aids and services (e.g., one-on-one paraprofessional, check-in/check-out system, assistive technology aids or services), and program modifications (e.g., classroom behavior reports, additional time to complete assignments, special seating). Figure 9–5 provides examples of service statements. Table 9–8 is a checklist of

FIGURE 9–5

Service statements—academic and behavioral

Reading Service Statement

Billy will attend Mr. Korus's resource room for reading remediation 5 days a week for 1 hour each day. Programming will involve direct instruction on the five essential elements of reading as identified by the National Reading Panel (http://www.nationalreadingpanel.org/).

Behavior Special Education Service Statement

Billy will be put on a check-in–check-out program. He will meet with Mr. Cleveland each morning for the check-in phase. Billy will attend Mr. Cleveland's resource room for the final 20 minutes of each school day, 5 days a week. There he will go through the check-out phase of the program. Mr. Cleveland will develop a self-management program for Billy. Both the check-in–check-out program and a self-management program are well supported in the peer-reviewed literature.

Behavior Program Modification Statement

Billy will be on a behavioral contract to improve his on-task rates. He will bring a point chart to all his mainstream classes. Teachers will rank him on his on-task performance in each class. Billy will be reinforced by Mr. Cleveland when he earns enough mainstream points to fulfill the terms of his contract. Contracting and reinforcement are practices that are supported by peer-reviewed research.

Table 9–8   Checklist for service statements

✔ Are the service statements clearly based on the student's needs as described in the PLAAFP statements?

✔ Do the service statements clearly describe what the school will do in response to the student's unique educational needs?

✔ Do the service statements include the anticipated number of services and the frequency, location, and duration of these services?

✔ Are the services included in the student IEP based on peer-reviewed research?

✔ Did the IEP team consider services that would allow the student to be involved and progress in the general education curriculum?

✔ Are all the services included in the IEP being delivered exactly as specified in the IEP?

important points to consider when writing service statements.

Subtask 3: Specify a method for monitoring a student's progress. IDEA requires that all IEPs include statements of (a) how a student's progress toward his or her annual goals will be measured, and (b) how parents will be informed of their child's progress. This will require that the team determines or adopts an effective data-based method of monitoring a student's progress. An important decision that the IEP team must make concerns the nature of the data that the teacher must collect (Heflin & Simpson, 1998). Anecdotal data and subjective judgments are not appropriate for monitoring progress and should not be the basis of a teacher's data collection procedures. The most appropriate data collection systems are those that rely on quantitative data in which target behaviors can be measured, graphed, and visually inspected (e.g., curriculum-based measurement, direct observation) to monitor a student's progress toward achieving his or her goals. Additionally, data collection procedures should be easy to use, efficient, and effective. Figure 9–6 depicts examples of progress monitoring statements. Table 9–9 is a checklist of important points to consider when monitoring student progress.

Step 3: ***Determine placement.*** The final stage of the process is determining the student's placement. The IEP team makes the placement decision after the content of the student's program has been determined (IDEA Regulations, 34 C.F.R. § Part 300, Appendix C, Question 42). It is important that the placement decision is based on the content of the IEP. The IEP team, therefore, must first determine the content of the student's special education program

FIGURE 9-6

How progress toward the goal will be measured

Reading Goal

To measure Billy's progress toward his reading goal, Mr. Korus will measure Billy's oral reading fluency using curriculum-based measurement twice a week.

Behavior Goal

To measure Billy's progress toward meeting his on-task goal, Mr. Cleveland or his paraprofessional will conduct observations of Billy using the pupil observation procedure once every 2 weeks. Additionally, Mr. Cleveland and Billy's teacher will assess Billy's behavior by reviewing the point sheets once a week.

and then make the placement decision. The most common abuse at this stage is to base the IEP on the placement. Bateman and Linden (2006) concluded that to base the IEP on the placement would be to return to the days before P.L. 94-142 (EAHCA) when students were fit into programs rather than designing programs to fit students. Appropriateness of the student's educational program is the primary goal of IDEA; it takes precedence over placement decisions (Bateman & Linden, 2006; Yell, 2006). In fact, determining placement before finalizing IEP has been viewed by the courts as a serious procedural and substantive violation of IDEA (Gorn, 1998).

When determining a student's placement, IEP teams must consider the LRE. Champagne (1993) asserted that IDEA requires the maximum integration

Table 9–9   Checklist for monitoring student progress

✔ Was the student's progress toward each of his or her goals measured *at least* as often as students in general education get report cards?

✔ Was the student's progress toward the goals reported to his or her parents *at least* as often as students in general education get report cards?

✔ Was the schedule/format for reporting a student's progress to his or her parents included in the IEP?

✔ If the data showed that a student may not meet his or her goals, were needed instructional changes made to the student's program and did the teacher continue to monitor progress?

that will "work" for a student. An appropriate interpretation of IDEA is that students with disabilities belong in integrated settings and that schools must make good-faith efforts to make this possible. Such efforts may include supplementary aids and services and program modifications. If, however, an appropriate education cannot be achieved in the general education setting, a student may be moved to progressively more restrictive settings along the continuum until the appropriate setting is found. Moreover, schools must always integrate students with disabilities with their nondisabled peers, even in the most restrictive settings.

Champagne (1993) also asserted that school districts should adopt a sequential model in making placement decisions, which involves four steps after writing a student's IEP. Champagne's sequential model is as follows:

Step 1: Determine whether the special education services listed in the IEP could be delivered in the general education classroom in its current form. If yes, then the general education setting becomes the student's primary placement.

Step 2: If services could not be delivered in a general education classroom, the team would next determine if services could be delivered in the general education classroom if the setting is modified through the addition of supplementary aids and services. If yes, then the general education setting with supplementary aids and services becomes the student's primary placement.

Step 3: If the team determined that the general setting, even with supplementary aids and services, was not appropriate, the team should determine a student's placement by moving along the continuum of alternative placements one step at a time, from the least restrictive setting to more restrictive ones. At each step, ask whether the services called for in the IEP can be delivered in that setting with appropriate supplementary aids and services. If yes, then the setting becomes the student's primary placement.

Step 4: If a more restrictive setting is chosen, the team must determine if there are additional opportunities for integration with nondisabled students for some portion of a student's school day. If yes, include the student in the more restrictive setting for part of the school day and include the student in an integrated setting to the maximum extent appropriate

Champagne's sequential model is an organized way of applying the LRE requirement to whatever facts a particular student's situation requires. Thus, the model preserves the core statutory imperative that placements must be based on a student's individual educational needs. Figure 9–7 is a graphic depiction of the sequential method of determining a student's placement in accordance with the LRE requirements of IDEA. Table 9–10 is a checklist of important points to consider when determining a student's placement.

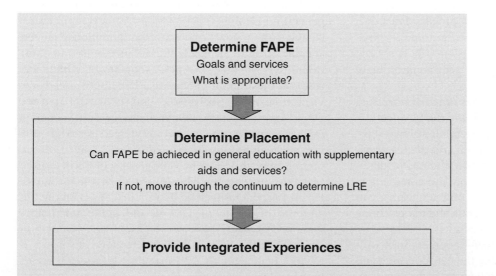

Figure 9–7 Determining placement

Determine FAPE

Goals and services
What is appropriate?

Determine Placement

Can FAPE be achieced in general education with supplementary
aids and services?
If not, move through the continuum to determine LRE

Provide Integrated Experiences

COMPLETING THE IEP

After the team has written the PLAAFP and annual goals, determined the special education services to be provided and the student's placement, and decided on a data collection procedure by which to monitor the student's progress, the heart of the IEP is completed. The team will then need to complete the IEP. As mentioned earlier, this will involve:

- Writing a statement as to the extent to which a student will not participate in general education. These statements are required only for students in settings that are primarily separate from students in the general education classroom, and do not include students who receive the majority of their instruction in general education classes.

- Determining how the student will participate in statewide assessments. That is, (a) will the student take the statewide assessment as his or her nondisabled peers do; (b) will the student be giving state-approved testing accommodations; and if so, describe the accommodations; or (c) will the student take an alternate assessment, and if so, describe how the student will be assessed.

Table 9–10   Checklist for determining placement

✔ Was the placement decision made by a knowledgeable group of persons, including the student's parents?

✔ If the student was removed from the regular class placement, were supplementary aids and services made available to try to maintain the student in the general education classroom?

✔ Was the placement determined individually for the student?

✔ Was the placement determined annually?

✔ Was program appropriateness the primary consideration in determining the placement?

✔ Were any harmful effects to the student or other students considered?

✔ Was the student placed in his or her home school, if appropriate?

- Providing information regarding the transfer of rights at the age of majority in their respective state (usually necessary when the student is 17 years of age).

- Completing other information required by the school district or state. For example, the South Carolina IEP developed by the Office of Exceptional Children in the State Department of Education has the IEP team answer questions regarding the provision of extended school year services.

Chapter Summary

In this chapter I have described IDEA's requirements for developing IEPs. The legally and educationally appropriate IEP is an individualized document, developed in accordance with the rules and regulations of IDEA, and is intended to serve as a blueprint for a student's special education program. The IEP is both a process and a document that determines and defines a student's free appropriate public education. That is, the IEP is reasonably calculated to allow the student to make meaningful educational progress.

The IEP process actually consists of two interrelated stages: the preplacement evaluation and the IEP meeting. These two processes are the responsibilities of two separate teams, the multidisciplinary team and the IEP team. The task of the former is to evaluate students to determine eligibility for special education and assess a student's educational needs. The tasks of the IEP team are to develop the special education program and to determine placement based on the IEP document.

When developing the IEP, team members start with the results of the evaluation. Using the data collected and relying on their professional judgment, team members must clearly specify the present-level of academic achievement and functional performance. The present-level statements are used to fashion a student's program of special education, related services, and modifications to allow the student access to and involvement in the general curriculum. This includes (a) developing measurable annual goals that represent ambitious, but reasonable, growth in academic achievement and functional performance, the achievements of which will result in meaningful educational benefit; (b) determining a program of special education services, related services, supplementary aids and services, and program modifications based on peer-reviewed research that confer meaningful educational benefit; and (c) determining how the student's progress will be measured and how parents will be informed of the progress. Finally, placement must be determined based on the IEP, and the principle of LRE should guide the team's decision regarding placement. The task of teachers of students with emotional and behavioral disorders is to assist in developing IEPs that are educationally meaningful and legally sound.

PART 2

Classroom and Behavior Management

CHAPTER 10

Schoolwide Positive Behavior Support

Mitchell L. Yell and M. Renee Bradley

Focus Questions

- What is schoolwide positive behavior support (PBS)?
- Why is it important that schools develop and implement schoolwide PBS systems?
- What are the major components of a schoolwide PBS system?
- How does schoolwide PBS fit in a response to intervention model?
- Why is it important that schoolwide systems also address student behavior in both classroom and nonclassroom settings and at the individual student level?
- How can a school develop and implement schoolwide PBS systems?

The basic requirement of schools is that they provide a safe and orderly environment in which students can learn. Nonetheless, the number of students who are exhibiting disruptive and dangerous behavior in schools has become an urgent concern for parents, educators, and politicians (Bullock, Reilly, & Donahue, 1983; Nelson, 2001; Sugai, Sprague, Horner, & Walker, 2001; Van Acker, 1996; Walker & Epstein, 2001; Yell & Rozalski, 2001). Fortunately, researchers have developed programs for preventing student misbehavior and teaching appropriate behavior on a schoolwide basis in an attempt to ameliorate these problems (Algozzine & White, 2002; Bradley, 2001; Eber, Sugai, Smith, & Scott, 2002; Lewis & Sugai, 1999; Nelson, 1996; Sugai & Horner, 2002). These programs have evolved out of a need for a more proactive approach to preventing problem behavior and improving school discipline (Sugai & Horner, 2002). Schools that adopt these proactive approaches systematically change the way in which they approach problem behavior by promoting and teaching prosocial behaviors, rather than merely reacting after problem behavior has occurred (Lewis, 2001; Skiba & Peterson, 1999). Such schools, therefore, are more likely to prevent problem behavior from occurring (Martella, Nelson, & Marchand-Martella, 2003; Scott & Barrett, 2004). Additionally, schoolwide systems are much more likely to result in an overall school environment that will be more supportive of students with EBD when they are included in general education settings (Brigham & Kauffman, 1998; Kamps & Tankersley, 1996).

In this chapter we examine schoolwide positive behavior support (PBS). First, we look at the need for PBS systems in schools. Second, we provide an overview of the components of schoolwide behavior support. Third, we discuss how to implement such a system in a school. Fourth, we examine schoolwide behavior support and academic achievement. Finally, we consider legal issues and schoolwide systems of positive behavior support.

THE NEED FOR SCHOOLWIDE POSITIVE BEHAVIOR SUPPORT

Parents, community leaders, and educators are concerned about safety in our schools. Issues of youth violence that we see in society seem to be spilling into our schools in unfortunate, but predictable ways (Leone et al., 2000; Scott & Nelson, 1999a; Walker & Epstein, 2001; Yell & Rozalski, 2001). When faced with challenging behavior, school administrators often resort to using practices that have not been proven to be effective, or in some cases have proven to be ineffective (Horner, Sugai, & Horner, 2000; Scott & Hunter, 2001).

An example of an ineffective practice is when schools respond by "getting tough." Typical get-tough practices include detention, suspension, expulsion, school resource officers, and metal detectors. The assumption of this approach is that by getting tough, schools can deter future occurrences of problem behavior (Gunter et al., 1993; Gunter, Jack, DePaepe, Reed, & Harrison, 1994; Skiba & Peterson, 2000; Sugai & Horner, 2002). Although the use of such practices may result in initial reductions of inappropriate behavior (most commonly due to the removal of a child from an environment), sustained improvement is not likely (Sugai & Horner, 2002; Walker et al., 1995, 2004).

Because these types of approaches are reactive responses (i.e., school personnel react to problems after they have occurred), they do little to promote appropriate skills and behaviors or contribute to the development of effective learning environments. Reactive responses are insufficient to meet the challenge of creating safe schools and positive school climates, and maximizing teaching time and learning opportunities (Sugai & Horner, 2002). Get-tough, reactive, punitive approaches, therefore, do not result in the creation or maintenance of safe learning environments, and may result in even more disruptive behavior (Horner, Sugai, Todd, & Lewis-Palmer, 2000; Nelson, 2001; Skiba, 2002). In fact, punitive environments actually promote antisocial behavior such as aggression, violence, vandalism, and escape (Mayer, 2002).

Another ineffective practice is to focus on a few especially challenging students. Horner, Sugai, et al. (2000) noted that because every school can identify a small number of disruptive and dangerous students, administrators assume that if the problem behaviors of those students can be contained, the school climate will improve. Research, however, indicates that focusing on a few students will not improve the overall climate of the school nor will it teach students appropriate behaviors (Horner, Sugai, et al., 2000).

A third example of an ineffective approach to addressing problem behavior is by providing professional development opportunities in accordance with a "train and hope" approach (Sugai, 2004). In a typical train and hope approach, an external consultant is hired to come into a school to provide staff training. The consultant trains the faculty in a particular approach to addressing problem behavior, and then leaves. Because there is no commitment to follow-up, coaching, monitoring, or sustained implementation, school administrators can only hope that the method will be sustained. Of course, such an approach will not be sustained and soon another expert is called in to fix the problem. Thus, the train and hope cycle begins again.

In this chapter, we examine an emerging proactive approach to addressing challenging behavior at the school level. This approach is referred to as schoolwide positive behavior support (PBS). Schoolwide PBS represents a proactive way to address the behavior of *all* students in a school. Positive behavior support refers to the use of positive behavioral interventions and systems to achieve socially important behavior change (Sugai & Horner, 2002). Recently, the concept of PBS has been applied as an intervention for entire schools (Lewis, Colvin, & Sugai, 1998; Sugai & Horner, 2002). When applied on a schoolwide basis, PBS is an approach that emphasizes designing environments to adopt and sustain the use of research-validated practices that improve learning and behavior for all students (Sugai & Horner, 2002). A schoolwide approach accomplishes this by emphasizing (a) preventing problem behavior, (b) teaching appropriate behavior, (c) reinforcing appropriate behavior, (d) developing a continuum of consequences for inappropriate behavior, (e) using evidence-based practices, and (f) collecting data to inform effective school practices.

Schoolwide PBS is not a quick fix. To properly implement PBS, school personnel must be committed to sustaining the effort. In fact, Sugai, and Horner (2002) estimate that it takes 3 to 5 years to design and implement a program of schoolwide PBS. Similarly, schoolwide PBS cannot be correctly implemented by adopting a single strategy (e.g., suspensions for inappropriate behavior); rather, PBS requires the implementation of multiple systems and strategies. To address problem behavior effectively, school administrators must adopt interventions for which there is empirical evidence of effectiveness. Such schools also emphasize the total system. Schoolwide PBS, therefore, affects all contexts within a school environment. Moreover, schoolwide PBS is based on empirical evidence and requires a commitment on the part of school staff to continued implementation. Schoolwide PBS relies on the building of capacity through the development of internal expertise (e.g., a behavioral expert on the school faculty). Next we examine the primary components of schoolwide PBS.

COMPONENTS OF SCHOOLWIDE PBS

Schoolwide PBS systems have been implemented in many schools, school districts, and states. When implemented correctly, these systems have produced excellent results. Results reported include (a) reduced number of office discipline referrals, suspensions, and expulsions; (b) improved school climates; (c) reduced absenteeism of teachers; (d) greater rates of teacher retention; (e) increased instructional time; and (f) improved academic achievement (Algozzine & White, 2002; Martella et al., 2003; Nelson, 1996; Scott, 2001; Sugai & Horner, 2002; Walker et al., 1996). In the following sections we examine the components typically used in schoolwide PBS models.

The Multitiered PBS Framework

Walker and colleagues introduced a multilevel system, adapted from a public health model, for use in education (Walker et al., 1996, 1998). This model has become increasingly accepted as a framework for multilevel prevention and intervention systems for both behavior and academics. This model is depicted in Figure 10–1. Schoolwide PBS uses this multitiered framework as a continuum of behavioral support in which the intensity of support increases as the behavioral needs of a student increase. This continuum of support consists of layers of intervention that respond to students' needs, with each layer providing more intensive interventions. The interventions vary in areas such as intensity, duration, setting, group size, and person delivering the intervention.

The benefits of this multitiered perspective are being demonstrated in schoolwide programs addressing both the academic and behavior domains. This approach is also being explored as a possible means for identifying children with certain disabilities such as learning disabilities. The primary goal of a proactive, preventive, schoolwide, multilevel intervention approach, however, is not to identify the few (approximately 5%) students who have the greatest needs and require the most intensive supports. The goal is to create a system that provides the research-based supports and interventions needed to make sure that the approximately 90% to 95% of the other students become proficient in academic and behavioral domains.

This framework has three levels: primary-level prevention, secondary-level interventions, and tertiary-level interventions. This continuum of behavior support allows educators to match the intensity of the intervention to the intensity of the problem behavior (Sugai, Sprague, et al., 2001). The first or primary prevention tier targets all students in a school and aims to prevent the occurrence of problem behavior by teaching and acknowledging appropriate behavior. Primary prevention provides behavior support to *every* student in a school and, thus, improves the levels of appropriate behavior of all students and prevents the occurrence of new cases of problem behavior. Secondary-level interventions refer to more specialized interventions that are needed by a small group of students who are at risk for developing problem behavior. The secondary-level

Figure 10–1 Multitiered system of PBS

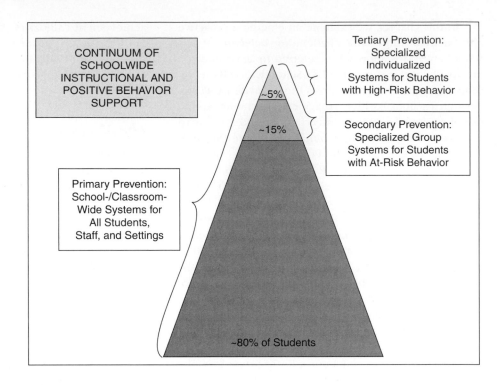

CONTINUUM OF SCHOOLWIDE INSTRUCTIONAL AND POSITIVE BEHAVIOR SUPPORT

Tertiary Prevention: Specialized Individualized Systems for Students with High-Risk Behavior

~5%

Secondary Prevention: Specialized Group Systems for Students with At-Risk Behavior

~15%

Primary Prevention: School-/Classroom-Wide Systems for All Students, Staff, and Settings

~80% of Students

increases the intensity of behavioral supports because these students need more specialized interventions than those that are provided at the primary level. Secondary-level interventions, therefore, reduce the number of current cases of problem behavior. The third level, or tertiary-level interventions, is needed for the few high-risk students who require the most individualized supports. These interventions are very intensive and are based on functional behavioral assessments. The goal of tertiary-level interventions is to reduce the intensity and complexity of current cases. The following sections explain these levels in greater detail.

Primary-Level Prevention According to Carr et al. (2002), "The PBS approach has helped give birth to what is, arguably, one of the greatest paradoxes in the field of developmental disabilities, namely, the notion that the best time to intervene on problem behavior is when the behavior is not occurring" (p. 50). The goal of the primary level of PBS, therefore, is to prevent problem behavior. At this level, school personnel (a) define schoolwide learning and behavior expectations, (b) teach students these expected behaviors, (c) acknowledge student behavior that adheres to these school rules, (d) develop procedures for addressing problem behavior, and (e) adopt record-keeping and data collection procedures. This prevention level includes practices and policies that need to be applied to all students, by

all staff, in all places within the school building. The goal of the primary prevention level is to actively teach, monitor, and reinforce appropriate behavior. Sugai and Horner (2002) estimated that approximately 80% to 85% of a school's students will respond to primary prevention efforts.

Secondary-Level Interventions The second level of intervention consists of continued access to primary intervention along with supplemental interventions for students who do not respond to primary intervention efforts or who are identified as at-risk students (Lane & Beebe-Frankenberger, 2004). Interventions at this level, which are designed to enhance primary intervention and reduce or extinguish behavioral problems, can be delivered to small groups of children with similar needs. Examples of secondary interventions may include social skills groups, anger management training, or similar interventions that can be implemented with various students and can address different individual needs (Lane & Wehby; 2002; Lewis, Colvin, & Sugai, 2000; Nelson, Martella, & Galand, 1998; Scott, 2001). According to Sugai and Horner (2002), approximately 10% to 15% of students will need the additional level of support provided at the secondary level.

Kamps and Greenwood (2003) identified the following variables that may increase implementation efforts at the secondary level: (a) a core group of committed teachers; (b) shared special and general education resources; (c) early screening and targeting of at-risk students; (d) creative and flexible scheduling to allocate additional time to instruction; (e) creative use of all school personnel; and (f) support in providing curriculum changes needed to focus on target areas for larger numbers of children. Schools that implement effective secondary-level interventions must be willing to be creative with their schedule, their curriculum, and their personnel when necessary. For example, schools that implement effective behavior programs may have all staff, including kitchen and custodial staff, trained in the behavioral system. In the case of schoolwide academic interventions, schools might train volunteers to be reading tutors. The focus at the secondary level is on providing as much additional time, instruction, and support as needed to get a student to the expected level of performance.

An example of a secondary-level intervention is the check-in, check-out system, also called the behavior education program (Crone, Horner, & Hawken, 2004; Hawken & Horner, 2003). In check-in, check-out, a student is required to check in with an adult (e.g., teacher, principal, counselor) before school. The adult greets the student and may inquire if he or she is ready for the new day, ask the student to identify daily goals, check on daily progress reports from the day before, and give encouragement for the upcoming day. Additionally, prior to each class period, a student brings a daily progress report to his or her teachers, so that each teacher can provide written feedback on the student's classroom behavior. Teachers also provide encouragement to the student. At the end of the day, when the student checks out, he or she takes the daily progress report to an educational assistant. This person tallies the points on the student's daily progress report and reinforces him or her if the goal is attained. If the student does not make the daily goal, the educational assistant encourages the student and discusses what he or she needs to work on the following day. The student then takes the daily progress form home to be signed by his or her parent or guardian and returns it when checking in the following morning. Hawken and Horner (2003) conducted a study of the check-in, check-out system in a middle school with four students who exhibited problem behavior but did not have individualized behavior intervention plans. They examined the effects of the system on the students' rates of problem behavior and academic engagement. Results of the study indicated that the school's faculty and staff were able to implement the system with high fidelity. Additionally, the overall levels of problem behavior were reduced and the students became more consistent in participating in class without exhibiting problem behavior.

Tertiary-Level Interventions Interventions at the tertiary level are highly individualized, intensive services based on a students' specific needs. In a schoolwide PBS system, students with the most challenging behaviors who do not respond to primary- and secondary-level interventions are provided with tertiary-level interventions. The interventions at this level may be the most difficult to implement due to the (a) intensity and individual nature of the child's problem; (b) lack of time, training, interagency collaboration, and current knowledge level; and (c) implementation capacity of schools. Implementing schoolwide behavioral models that effectively address this level is a tremendous challenge.

The focus at the tertiary level is on preventing long-term failure. Effective intervention plans typically involve multiple agencies, family components, and a broader array of needed skills to effect lifestyle changes. Functional behavioral assessments are critical to providing effective tertiary-level interventions because the interventions, supports, and services that are developed through these assessments are based on a student's specific individual needs (Crone & Horner, 2003; Dunlap, Foster-Johnson, Clark, Kerns, & Childs, 1995; Scott, Liaupsin, Nelson, & Jolivette, 2003). For elaborations on functional behavioral assessments and behavior intervention plans see Chapter 5.

Research demonstrates that in schools with effective, multitiered, schoolwide models in which interventions are implemented with high fidelity, fewer students will require tertiary-level interventions (Sugai & Horner, 2002). Moreover, in schools with effective primary and secondary prevention systems, the general education teachers will often be more skilled in addressing challenging behaviors and implementing interventions. Clearly, this will result in a school environment that provides more effective supports to students with EBD. Additionally, in such schools teachers and administrators have more time to address behaviorally challenging students because the majority of the students adhere to the schoolwide expectations.

PBS, Universal Screening, and Response to Intervention. Universal screening is also an important component of schoolwide PBS. According to O'Shaughnessy, Lane, Gresham, and Beebe-Frankenberger (2002), universal screening refers to assessment measures that schools use to screen all of a school's population on a measure of interest (e.g., reading difficulties, problem behaviors). The primary benefit of a universal screening system is that it can help ensure the early identification of those students who are at risk of serious problem behavior. This type of prevention strategy allows for the implementation of some easily administered preventative strategies prior to the development of more serious problems later.

Based on the findings of the universal assessment, curricular, instructional, and behavioral modifications can be identified for entire groups of students and the progress of students who are in trouble or at risk can be monitored. This process then allows for a systematic proactive identification of students who may develop problems. Access to, and participation in, a high-quality primary curriculum with a minimal amount of additional effort, either in instructional delivery or with whole-class behavioral interventions, will result in fewer children needing more intensive services at secondary and tertiary levels. Therefore, inappropriate referrals to special education services of children whose delays are primarily caused by lack of exposure to a high-quality curriculum addressing both academic and behavioral domains may be reduced.

Responsiveness to intervention refers to a change in behavior as a function of intervention (Gresham, 1991). In a response to intervention model a student with a behavior problem is exposed to an empirically validated intervention. If the intervention is implemented for a reasonable period of time and with integrity, and the student does not respond positively, then another intervention is implemented. In a schoolwide PBS model, all of a school's students are exposed to the primary prevention interventions (e.g., schoolwide rules, precorrection strategies). If the student fails to respond to this level of intervention, he or she may be exposed to secondary-level interventions (e.g., social skills interventions). If, after a reasonable amount of time, the student fails to respond to secondary-level interventions, tertiary-level interventions may be implemented (e.g., function-based interventions). Schoolwide PBS is a response to intervention model because the strength, intensity, and duration of interventions increase only after a student has failed to respond to previously used interventions. Next we discuss the four key features of a schoolwide PBS.

Four Key Features of Schoolwide PBS

There are many models of schoolwide PBS. Models that have been field-tested include the positive behavior support and intervention (PBIS) model (Sugai & Horner, 2002); unified discipline (Algozzine & White, 2002); the prevention, action, and resolution (PAR) model (Rosenberg & Jackman, 1997); and the schoolwide positive behavior support (SWPBS) model (Martella et al., 2003). In this chapter we will examine Sugai and Horner's PBIS model. It is important to note, however, that these models share many common components. In fact, Sugai and Horner (2002) have identified four key features that are common to all successful schoolwide models. These components, which are needed to implement and sustain a schoolwide PBS model, include (a) focusing on student outcomes, (b) using research-based practices, (c) developing and maintaining the systems needed to sustain practice, and (d) making decisions based on data. The purposes of these components are to improve social competence and academic achievement and to support student behavior, staff behavior, and decision making (Sugai, Colvin, Hagan-Burke, & Lewis-Palmer, 2001). (See Figure 10–2).

Improving Student Outcomes   The first feature is a focus on *improving student outcomes* such as teaching students more socially appropriate behaviors and improving academic achievement. These outcomes are socially valid and are valued by students, parents, teachers, and administrators. Moreover, school personnel must understand and be able to articulate these outcomes if they are going to be successful (Sugai & Horner, 2002).

Adopting and Sustaining Research-Based Practices
The second feature is *adopting and sustaining implementation of research-based practices* (Sugai & Horner, 2002). Schools have too many obligations and too few minutes to waste time and energy on programs or practices that do not have empirical evidence of their effectiveness. The use of evidenced-based practices is critical at every level of intervention. It is extremely important that research-based practices are implemented with high fidelity to ensure the desired result. Incorrect implementation of PBS at the primary or secondary level may have a dramatic effect on the numbers of children that require additional or more intensive assistance at subsequent levels.

Creating Effective Host Environments   The third feature focuses on *creating effective host environments* that support the sustained use of research-based practices (Sugai & Horner, 1999). Meaningful and sustained behavioral change will be possible only if systems are structured in a way that supports the practices and people charged with implementing the change (Carr et al., 2002). A critical variable of PBS, therefore, is how schools organize and operate the systems within their school (e.g., schoolwide routines, resources, and policies). Implementing a systematic approach to behavior provides a change of focus from "fixing" the child to an opportunity to focus on fixing the context (i.e., the school environment). Developing more comprehensive systems of

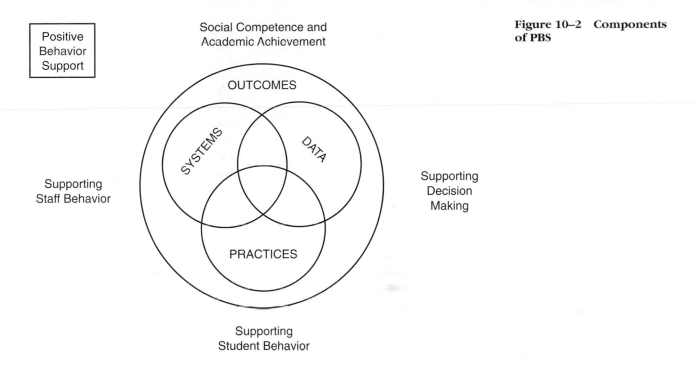

Positive Behavior Support

Social Competence and Academic Achievement

Figure 10–2   Components of PBS

OUTCOMES

SYSTEMS

DATA

Supporting Staff Behavior

Supporting Decision Making

PRACTICES

Supporting Student Behavior

support also provides for a more seamless process for addressing intensive needs of children through multiple service agencies.

Collecting and Using Data to Guide Decision Making   The fourth feature is *collecting and using data to guide decision making*. The collection and formative use of data is the most powerful means of ensuring that behavior change occurs. In an effective PBS model, data are continually collected on a school, classroom, and individual basis. The data serve as a primary tool for decision making and planning. There are numerous methods and systems for data collection, and schools need to determine which of these methods are most efficient and effective. According to Horner, Sugai, and Todd (2001), educators should follow four principles to ensure that a data system is useful. First, the data should be used for making decisions. The primary value of the data is that they can inform effective decision making. Therefore, before adopting a data system, school personnel should be clear about what decisions they will need to make and how data can be useful to them. Second, data systems should be easy to use and efficient because the amount of time needed to learn the system, gather the data, and use the information will determine if the data collection system will be used. Data systems that are cumbersome or burdensome will not be sustained. Third, the school personnel who collect the data should use the data. That is, if the data are collected and then sent

away for analysis, it may adversely affect the accuracy of the data as well as their practical value to the school. Fourth, schools should design repeating cycles of data use. Because most decisions in schools occur in regular cycles (e.g., decisions about curriculum), school personnel should use data systems that deliver the needed information at the right time. Thus, it is important that data are collected and reported in a manner that fits the school's decision-making timelines and needs.

PBS AND THE TOTAL SCHOOL SYSTEM

According to Sugai and Horner (2002), schools that adopt PBS should adopt a multisystem perspective. Such a perspective addresses all of the following: (a) the schoolwide systems, (b) the classroom setting systems, (c) the nonclassroom setting systems, and (d) the individual student systems. Figure 10–3 depicts these overlapping systems.

Schoolwide Systems

The focus at the schoolwide system is to create a supportive context or host environment that teaches and supports expected behavior. Developing the primary schoolwide PBS system requires that school personnel go through a few basic steps.

First, *school teams develop behavioral expectations or rules and a definition of these expectations*. School

Figure 10–3 Overlapping PBS systems

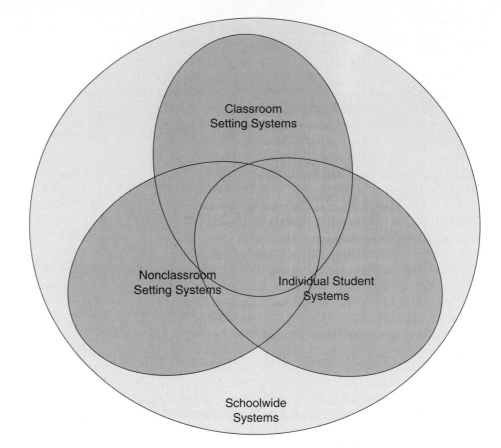

Classroom
Setting Systems

Nonclassroom
Setting Systems

Individual Student
Systems

Schoolwide
Systems

teams develop a few positively stated expectations that guide the behavioral curriculum and social standards of the school (Horner, Sugai, Todd, & Lewis-Palmer, 2000). Moreover, these expectations focus the students and teachers on appropriate behavior rather than inappropriate behavior. The expectations are posted in conspicuous locations throughout the school. Figure 10–4 lists examples of schoolwide expectations.

Second, *school personnel teach the behavioral expectations to students, who then practice them in a variety of settings within the school.* These expectations will become relevant to students when they are tied to very concrete behaviors (Sugai & Horner, 1999). A school's expectations are actively taught to students. Schools implementing PBS models dedicate substantial time at the beginning of each school year to teaching, reteaching, and reinforcing the expectations for every student. Moreover, time also has to be set aside for initial and follow-up opportunities for students to practice the expected behaviors in practical contexts (e.g., classroom, cafeteria, gym, hallway).

Horner, Sugai, Lewis-Palmer, and Todd (2001) suggested that an effective way to design a process for

teaching the behavioral expectations across a number of settings is to develop a teaching matrix. The matrix lists the behavioral expectations and the specific locations in which the expectations will be taught. In each cell, the school personnel identify and list a few specific appropriate behaviors that will demonstrate the behavior expectations for that setting. These examples then become the basis for lesson plans that are written to teach the appropriate behaviors in the various contexts. During these lessons students are then taken to each location and taught the expectations for that setting. Typically, a lesson follows a direct instruction format in which (a) students review the expectation, (b) teachers teach and model the expectation in the specific setting using both positive and negative examples, (c) students practice the correct behaviors, and (d) the teacher informally tests the students' knowledge. Figure 10–5 shows an example of a teaching matrix developed in an elementary school in South Carolina.

Third, *school personnel monitor and acknowledge correct performance of expected behaviors.* Teachers, staff, and administrators in the school monitor student behavior in all school settings and provide acknowledgments and

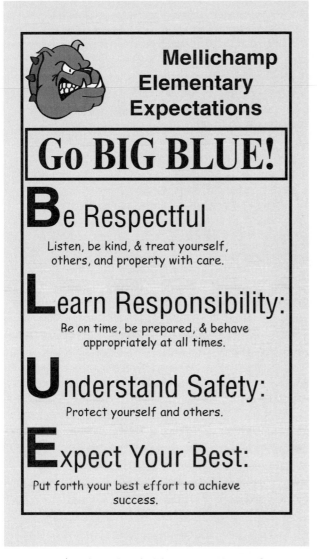

Figure 10–4   The schoolwide expectations of Mellichamp Elementary School, Orangeburg, SC

reinforcement when students exhibit appropriate behaviors. Acknowledgments may include social, token, or tangible reinforcers. The goal of the acknowledgment system is to create a positive school climate where students know that appropriate behavior is valued and appreciated, and where students have high rates of positive contacts with adults (Sugai & Horner, 2002). A school has a successful acknowledgment system in place, according to Horner, Sugai, Todd, and Lewis-Palmer (2004), if at any given time at least 80% of the school's students have been recognized for appropriate behavior within the previous 10 school days.

Fourth, *school teams develop clear and consistent procedures for preventing and discouraging problem behavior*. Although negative consequences are not the central point of a schoolwide PBS system, students need to understand that teachers and staff will deliver fair, consistent, and predictable consequences when they engage in problem behaviors. The purpose of a system to discourage inappropriate behavior is to (a) maintain safety and order, (b) prevent inappropriate behavior from escalating to severe problem behavior, and (c) provide a clear and unambiguous message to students who engage in problem behavior that such behaviors are unacceptable (Horner, Sugai, Todd, & Lewis-Palmer, 2004).

School personnel should provide clear definitions of problem behavior and divide such behaviors into minor and major offenses. The consequences vary in intensity with less intense, teacher-administered consequences for minor offenses and more intense, administrator-given consequences for major offenses.

Fifth, *school teams collect and use data to make decisions regarding the school's behavior system.* Data systems are used to provide feedback to school personnel about the status of their schoolwide system. The information that is collected provides information for program evaluation and refinement. Useful data collection systems also allow school staff to track individual students who may need more intensive interventions and to examine patterns across students, times, locations, and types of behavior challenges. The data are reviewed by school personnel on a regular basis and used in decision making. Figure 10–6 is a checklist of the required components of a schoolwide system.

Classroom Setting Systems

To ensure that classroom settings are effective, teachers must be as committed to teaching behavioral expectations, skills, and routines as they are to teaching academic skills. In other words, when they teach expectations and routines, effective teachers use the same empirically validated teaching strategies that they use for academic content (Colvin, Kame'enui, & Sugai, 1994; Sugai, 2002; De Pry & Langland, Lewis-Palmer, & Sugai, 1998; Lewis & Sugai, 1999). Teaching these skills provides students with a common language and understanding of what behaviors are expected of them. Additionally, teachers should focus on teaching and reinforcing appropriate behavior and discouraging inappropriate behavior.

Although PBS in the classroom shares many of the same features as a schoolwide PBS system, teachers must also organize their classrooms and manage student behavior in ways that support students' behavioral and academic needs (Sugai & Horner, 2002). For example, De Pry and Sugai (2002) examined the use of two proactive

FIGURE (10-5)

The teaching matrix of Mellichamp Elementary, Orangeburg, SC

	Classroom	Hallway	Lunchroom	Bus	Restroom	Playground	Media Center	Carpool	Bus Ramp
Be Respectful	1. Listen and follow directions. 2. Raise your hand and be recognized to speak.	1. Walk on the right side of the hall. 2. Keep hands to yourself and off the walls.	1. Use inside voices. 2. Chew when your mouth is closed and speak when your mouth is empty.	1. Stay in your assigned seat. 2. Use inside voices. 3. Follow the bus driver's directions.	1. Put all toilet paper and paper towels in the appropriate place. 2. Flush toilet 3. Deposit in the toilet.	1. Share and take turns. 2. Take care of habitat and equipment. 3. Listen to all adults.	1. Use inside voice. 2. Treat books and materials with care.	1. Remain seated in assigned area. 2. Keep hands, feet, and objects to yourself. 3. Listen to adults.	1. Wait in line with your teacher. 2. Listen to adults in charge. 3. Walk to the bus ramp.
Learn Responsibility	1. Be ready with materials and assignments. 2. Follow directions. 3. Be organized and stay on task. 4. Keep your areas clean.	1. Go directly and quietly to destination. 2. Carry a pass. 3. Use inside voices.	1. Clean up after yourself. 2. Stand in line in an orderly manner.	1. Be on time. 2. Stay in your assigned seat.	1. Go to restroom and return to class promptly. 2. Use good personal hygiene.	1. Stay with your group in designated areas. 2. Collect personal and classroom belongings before lining up. 3. Let adults know of any problems.	1. Return materials and books on time. 2. Use shelf markers appropriately. 3. Take care of books and equipment.	1. Keep your personal belongings together. 2. Watch for your ride.	1. Wait quietly in designated area. 2. Board bus in an orderly manner. 3. Go directly to the bus waiting area.

Understand Safety	1. Keep hands, feet, and objects to yourself. 2. Keep chairs flat on floor.	1. Walk on the right side of the hall. 2. Maintain appropriate distance.	1. Keep hands, feet, and objects to yourself. 2. Follow lunchroom safety rules. 3. Take trays in an orderly and quiet manner. 4. Report spills or food on the floor.	1. Keep hands and belongings inside the bus and out of the aisle. 2. Stay seated. 3. Use inside voices.	1. Report bathroom problems to an adult. 2. Enter and exit in an orderly manner. 3. Use equipment in an appropriate manner.	1. Use playground equipment appropriately. 2. Play in designated areas. 3. Keep shoes on.	1. Enter and exit in an appropriate manner. 2. Use side door unless it is raining.	1. Wait for an adult to walk you to your car. 2. Sit quietly in designated area.	1. Stay in assigned area until your bus arrives. 2. Keep hands, feet, and objects to yourself. 3. Listen to the adult in charge.
Expect Your Best	1. Do your best at all times. 2. Complete assignments on time. 3. Listen and follow directions the first time.	1. Be courteous in the hallway. 2. Walk in a quiet and orderly manner. 3. Show pride in Mellichamp	1. Use good table manners. 2. Clean up after yourself. 3. Always follow adult directions.	1. Set a good example by obeying the bus driver. 2. Get to the school safely and on time.	1. Leave the restroom better than you found it. 2. Help keep the restroom clean. 3. Go to the restroom and return promptly to class.	1. Be considerate of others at all times. 2. Be a good sport.	1. Challenge yourself with a variety of books. 2. Challenge yourself with more difficult books.	1. Model good behavior to maintain order. 2. Stay in assigned area. 3. Listen to the adult in charge.	1. Model good behavior to maintain order. 2. Walk with your teacher to the bus ramp. 3. Listen to the adult in charge.

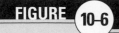

FIGURE 10-6

Checklist to ensure that required elements of schoolwide PBS are in place

Yes	No	Practice
☐	☐	A schoolwide leadership team is in place.
☐	☐	80% of the faculty agree to support schoolwide PBS.
☐	☐	Administration has agreed to a 3- to 4-year commitment to the plan.
☐	☐	The schoolwide plan is based on empirically validated practices.
☐	☐	The schoolwide plan includes five or six behavioral expectations.
☐	☐	Behavioral expectations are directly taught to students.
☐	☐	There is a system to acknowledge appropriate student behaviors.
☐	☐	There is a system to discourage inappropriate student behaviors.
☐	☐	There are procedures for collecting formative data.
☐	☐	Team decisions are informed by the data.

instructional strategies to manage minor student misbehavior, active supervision, and precorrections. The teacher was taught to actively supervise her classroom. The teacher would circulate around the classroom and interact with students. The teacher also used precorrections, which was defined as giving an instructional prompt to a student when he or she entered a context in which problem behavior was likely to occur. The purpose of the precorrection was to focus the student on the expected behavior. When the student engaged in the appropriate behavior, he or she was immediately reinforced by the teacher. The results of the study indicated that active supervision and precorrections were easily taught, and that their use reduced the number of minor behavioral incidents in the class.

It is important to note that, as is the case with a schoolwide system, in the classroom setting system teachers must adopt and sustain behavioral systems and curriculum that are supported by empirical research.

In Chapter 11 we will more fully discuss classroom management. Checklists of the required components of a classroom setting system are included in that chapter.

Nonclassroom Setting Systems

An often-neglected aspect of a schoolwide behavior plan is the articulation of clear routines in nonclassroom settings. These settings are challenging because in nonclassroom settings there are often large groups of students and a relatively low level of supervision. Examples of nonclassroom settings include school hallways, restrooms, and cafeterias. The large number of students and the smaller number of adults who supervise them is often a catalyst for nonclassroom settings becoming hot spots of student misbehavior.

A frequent problem in nonclassroom settings is that expectations for student behavior are not taught, monitored, or reinforced. Nelson and Colvin (1995) noted that routines minimize the likelihood of inappropriate behavior by explicitly identifying expectations and reducing barriers; therefore, it is important that students be taught explicit rules and routines in nonclassroom settings. In schoolwide PBS, expectations are developed, taught, and reinforced in these settings (see the expectations for nonclassroom settings in Figure 10–5).

Active supervision by educators is also critical in nonclassroom settings (Darch & Kame'enui, 2004; Sugai & Horner, 2002). Active supervision consists of having teachers (a) move about their classrooms, (b) scan the environment, (c) interact frequently with students, (d) reinforce students who exhibit appropriate behavior, and (e) stop inappropriate behavior when it occurs (De Pry & Sugai, 2002). Active supervision by teachers and paraprofessionals has been shown to be effective at reducing problem behavior in nonclassroom settings such as school cafeterias (Lewis et al., 2000) and playgrounds (Lewis et al., 1998).

Another procedure that can be very effective in reducing problem behavior in nonclassroom settings is precorrection (Colvin & Lazar, 1997; Colvin, Sugai, & Patching, 1993; De Pry & Sugai, 2002). Precorrections are verbal reminders that are delivered in situations where rule-violating behaviors are likely to occur or in situations where particular students may exhibit problem behaviors (Colvin & Lazar, 1997; Darch & Kame'enui, 2004; Sugai & Horner, 2002). The purpose of a precorrection is to prevent a problem behavior from occurring. For elaboration on precorrections see Chapter 11 on classroom management.

Two excellent examples of PBS in nonclassroom settings were provided by Leedy, Bates, and Safran (2004) and Kartub, Taylor-Greene, March, and Horner (2000). Both studies examined the effectiveness of PBS interventions in improving hallway behavior. Teachers (a) developed clear and consistent routines, (b) taught behavioral expectations, (c) supervised students in the hallway, (d) rewarded appropriate behaviors, and (e) corrected inappropriate behaviors. Data collection in both studies indicated substantial improvements in students' hallway behavior.

Sugai (2004) offered the following suggestions for supervising nonclassroom settings. First, supervisors should move continuously throughout the setting. Moreover, movements should be unpredictable and obvious. Second, supervisors should interact frequently with students, always making at least four or five positive contacts to every negative contact. Positive interactions should vary, include both social positives and the schoolwide acknowledgment system, and be noticeable. Third, supervisors should keep their heads up, make eye contact with students, and scan the entire area frequently. Fourth, minor rule violations should be handled quickly, privately, efficiently, and in a businesslike manner. Supervisors should always follow corrections of students with positive comments whenever appropriate. Fifth, when major rule violations occur, supervisors should also handle them quickly, in a businesslike manner, and disengage quickly. Figure 10–7 is a checklist of the required components of a nonclassroom setting system.

Individual Student Support Systems

Although schoolwide approaches are effective for 80% to 85% of a school's population, a small number of students, approximately 2% to 5%, with severe problem behaviors may not respond to primary or secondary interventions and will require more intensive and targeted interventions (Colvin et al., 1994; Hawken & Horner, 2003; Lewis et al., 1998; Sugai & Horner, 2002). In a schoolwide PBS system, an individualized approach to developing interventions may involve (a) using a team-based problem-solving approach, (b) adopting a person-centered approach to comprehensive interventions and service planning, (c) conducting functional behavioral assessments (FBAs), (d) using the results of the assessment to develop an individualized student behavior support plan, and (e) emphasizing individualized interventions that teach socially appropriate behaviors and self-management skills (Crone & Horner, 2003; Nelson, Roberts, et al., 1999; O'Neill, Horner, Albin, Story, & Sprague, 1997; Sugai & Horner, 2002; Sugai, Lewis-Palmer, & Hagan-Burke, 1998; Todd, Horner, Sugai, & Colvin, 1999).

FIGURE 10–7

Checklist to ensure that required elements of nonclassroom setting PBS are in place

Yes	No	Practice
☐	☐	The nonclassroom setting system is based on empirically validated practices.
☐	☐	Behavioral expectations in nonclassroom settings are directly taught to students.
☐	☐	All staff assume responsibility for supervising student behavior in nonclassroom settings.
☐	☐	Staff actively supervise in nonclassroom settings (e.g., scan, move, interact).
☐	☐	There is a system to acknowledge appropriate student behaviors in nonclassroom settings.
☐	☐	Staff maintain a 5:1 ratio of positive versus negative contacts with students.
☐	☐	There is a system to discourage inappropriate student behaviors in nonclassroom settings.
☐	☐	Staff deliver precorrections when necessary.

As we discussed in Chapter 5, an FBA is a process for identifying problem behaviors and the events that predict or maintain that behavior. Carr et al. (1999) conducted a research synthesis on PBS and determined that behavior support plans based on a functional behavioral assessment were twice as likely as those not based on a functional assessment to be successful. The Center on Positive Behavioral Interventions and Supports (2001) identified three key features of effective and efficient FBAs: (a) an operational definition of the behavior, including variables that predict and or maintain the behavior; (b) data based on direct observations that support the hypothesis; and 3) a behavior support plan. Support plans should include goals and procedures that bring about positive behavior changes improving a child's access to activities and services, and ensure that these changes endure. Behavioral support plans should include practical strategies that result in durable changes that will endure over time and result in overall improved quality of life for the student (Horner et al., 1990).

A primary goal of a PBS model is to prevent inappropriate behaviors from occurring in the first place. However, an effective PBS system does not negate the need for a well-developed crisis management plan that can be implemented in extreme situations to prevent anyone from being hurt. For most students in a well-implemented, systemic, schoolwide environment, the need for such interventions should be infrequent. In Chapter 12 we examine how school-based personnel can develop effective crisis management plans.

IMPLEMENTING A SCHOOLWIDE PBS SYSTEM

Sugai and Horner (2002) have identified five common steps needed to implement a schoolwide PBS system. They are as follows:

Step 1: *Establish a school-based leadership team* A school leadership team is an essential requirement in building and sustaining a PBS model. Colvin and Fernandez (2000), in describing an elementary school's success in developing and sustaining a schoolwide support system, found that "there was an overwhelming consensus that the single most important component of the effective behavior support model is the formation and productive operation of a leadership team" (p. 252). This team can oversee activities and strategies that have been identified as helpful in enhancing the effectiveness of the model such as pooling of special education and general education resources, early and universal screening, creative and flexible scheduling and use of personnel, and support for curriculum changes and enhancements to achieve desired results (Kamps & Greenwood, 2003). Moreover, by using a team-based process, schools can move from the outside expert consultation model to a system that builds in-school expertise (Lewis, 2001).

Sugai and Horner (2002) listed the following important roles of the school leadership team. First, the team should have a regular, effective, and efficient means of communicating with the entire school staff. Second, collectively the team should possess behavioral competence. This means that a member or members of the team should be competent in areas such as data-based decision making, functional behavioral assessment and behavior inter-vention planning, curriculum modifications, instructional delivery strategies, and family support and communication. Third, the team should meet regularly, preferably at least once a month. Fourth, the team's primary responsibility should be to (a) review school needs, (b) establish school action plans, and (c) determine staff development activities. Moreover, team meetings should focus on discussing schoolwide data and use this data to proactively solve problems.

The membership of the committee is extremely important. The school principal *must* be a member of the team because administrative support and active participation are critical to the success of schoolwide PBS. The administration must be committed to PBS, which includes committing to securing adequate resources, providing fiscal supports, and securing district- and state-level support. The rest of the team should be composed of respected members of the school's staff. Sugai and Horner (2002) also suggest that parents be tapped to serve as team members.

Step 2: *Secure schoolwide agreements and supports including a commitment to PBS* For a schoolwide PBS system to succeed, the leadership team must secure agreements that the staff and administration will make (a) a long-term commitment to implementing PBS for at least 4 years, (b) professional development in PBS a priority, and (c) a commitment to taking a preventive and instructional approach to schoolwide discipline and behavior management. Furthermore, schools must make addressing problem behavior a top priority (Lewis, 2001; Scott & Hunter, 2001; Sugai & Horner, 2002). In fact, Sugai and Horner (2002) recommended that PBS systems should not be put in place until 80% of the staff supports these agreements. Scott and Hunter (2001) noted that a typical school will not achieve 100% consensus, but if 80% commitment is achieved it is the principal's job to inform school personnel that because the majority of personnel made a decision to implement schoolwide PBS, the decision will be binding on all staff.

It is also important that adequate resources be put into the PBS system. This includes adequate funding, sufficient time, and effective ongoing professional development.

Step 3: *Develop a data-based action plan that focuses on all students, all staff, and all settings* The action plan includes a continuum of support systems, a focus on teaching and reinforcing behavioral expectations, and a system of data collection. Data is reviewed on a regular basis to formatively evaluate the schoolwide PBS system. By monitoring data collected in each of the four systems (i.e., schoolwide, classroom, nonclassroom, and individual), school personnel can determine which practices are working effectively and need to be maintained, and which are not effective and need to be improved or eliminated (Sugai & Horner, 2002).

The school leadership team uses the data to create an action plan, which is composed of measurable objectives and timelines to enhance the effectiveness of the schoolwide PBS system. Typically, action plans will focus on improving one objective at a time (Sugai & Horner, 2002). Scott and Hunter (2001) note that developing schoolwide action plans is a consensus-building process that can be time-consuming but is, nonetheless, very important. It is also crucial that school action plans focus on the identification, adoption, and sustained use of research-validated practices.

Step 4: *Arrange for high-fidelity implementation* After a school has adopted research-validated practices, the schoolwide PBS leadership team must be able to sustain the use of these practices. For these practices to be effective, of course, school personnel must implement them with a high degree of fidelity or accuracy. High fidelity implementation refers to the degree to which the plan or practice was implemented as originally designed (Gresham, 1998b; Lane & Beebe-Frankenberger, 2004). Prior to implementing new practices, therefore, school staff should be fluent in the use of these strategies. School leadership teams can help ensure fidelity of implementation by (a) assessing treatment integrity, often through the use of direct observation procedures; (b) arranging for high-quality professional development activities; (c) monitoring the degree of fidelity of implementation; and (d) scheduling booster sessions that include coaching. Scott and Hunter (2001) noted the importance of fidelity of implementation:

When schoolwide expectations, policy, and consequences are inconsistently applied across staff, they become ambiguous to students. And when students cannot predict the outcome of a given behavior, a significant number will act inappropriately. However, when the entire school staff is involved in determining and agreeing upon schoolwide expectations, policy, and consequences, staff consistency, and resulting student success are far more likely (p. 15).

Lewis (2001) asserted that a key to implementing a sustainable system of schoolwide PBS is to build capacity within schools through professional development and technical assistance. This means that to ensure high fidelity of implementation within a school, appropriate professional development opportunities, based on empirically validated practices, must be available to all school staff. Such professional development opportunities should (a) provide initial training on the essential attributes of a schoolwide system of PBS, (b) give regular feedback on outcomes, and (c) offer ongoing support and follow-up when needed (Lewis, 2001). Lewis suggests that training should include information on (a) proactive versus reactive management of problem behavior; (b) empirically validated management practices at the prevention, secondary, and tertiary levels; (c) academic accommodations; (d) parent training; and (e) individual interventions based on functional behavioral assessments.

Step 5: *Monitor performance using a formative data collection system* Schoolwide PBS requires that school leadership teams be committed to collecting data on the PBS system. Moreover, the data must be used to assess how the system is working, and guide the development of modification of the schoolwide system (Lewis-Palmer, Sugai, & Larson, 1999; Sugai & Horner, 2002). Data can be useful to assist with development of the system by indicating where problems are occurring and the effectiveness of any changes that have been put in place. There are many types of data that may be used (Lewis, 2001; Sugai & Horner, 2001; Tobin, Sugai, & Colvin, 2000). According to Lewis (2001), and Sugai and Horner (2001), two types of data that schools should collect and monitor are (a) data that indicate how the schoolwide system is working (e.g., attendance rates, number of suspensions and expulsions, and office disciplinary referrals); and (b) data that indicate how well the school is implementing the system (e.g., schoolwide climate assessment surveys, number of team meetings, implementation status surveys). Scott and Hunter (2001) note that schools should collect the simplest available source of data necessary to provide answers to their questions.

Sugai and Horner (2002) stated that one of the best naturally available data sources is the office disciplinary referral. An office disciplinary referral represents an event in which a staff member (a) observes a student engage in behavior that violates a school rule, and (b) refers the student to the school's administrative staff for the inappropriate behavior. Because the referral is written, it becomes a permanent record of the event. According to Sugai, Sprague et al., (2001), this record can serve as an index of student behavior and an index of the discipline system within the school. Office disciplinary referrals, therefore, are a convenient source of information for determining the effectiveness of a schoolwide PBS system as well as for indicating potential problem areas (Skiba, Peterson, & Williams, 1997; Sugai, Sprague et al., 2001, Tobin et al., 2000; Walker, Stieber, Ramsey, & O'Neill, 1991). Hirsch, Lewis-Palmer, Sugai, and Schnacker (2004) also suggest that bus disciplinary referrals can be a useful tool for identifying variables that are related to problem behaviors on the school bus. Moreover, the data from bus referrals can be used for developing effective interventions to improve bus behavior and to monitor the effectiveness of those interventions.

Sugai, Horner, and colleagues developed a very useful data collection tool called the School-Wide Information System (SWIS). SWIS is a Web-based data collection system that effectively and efficiently provides data charts that can be used for decision-making purposes and to determine a school's progress in supporting student behavior. This system can provide information on settings, classrooms, or nonclassrooms; on students or groups of students; types of behavior, time of day, location; and a host of other variables. These are examples of the types of data collection that should be ongoing and serve as the basis for decision making regarding the schoolwide behavior model. For further information on SWIS, go to the Web site http://www.swis.org.

SCHOOLWIDE PBS AND ACADEMIC ACHIEVEMENT

There is clearly a relationship between academics and behavior. Whether problem behavior affects academic achievement or poor achievement leads to inappropriate behavior, the relationship between the two has been demonstrated repeatedly (Bower, 1995; Hinshaw, 1992). The majority of children with behavioral problems also exhibit academic deficits (Coleman & Webber, 2002; Cullinan, 2002; Kamps et al., 2003; Kauffman, 2005; Kauffman et al., 1987; Landrum et al., 2003).

Chard and Kame'enui (2000) found that without appropriate intervention, children with poor reading skills in first grade had a 90% chance of poor reading skills at the end of third grade. Similarly, children who exhibit serious behavior problems early in elementary school and do not receive appropriate intervention are likely to continue a pattern toward being considered chronic offenders requiring tertiary-level interventions over a long period of time (Kazdin, Mazurick, & Bass, 1993; Lane, Gresham, & O'Shaughnessey, 2002).

Sutherland, Alder, and Gunter (2003) investigated the effects of increased opportunities to respond with students classified as having EBD. These authors determined that increased effective teaching practices lead to more appropriate classroom behavior of students with EBD. This is in line with an earlier review by Sutherland and Wehby (2001b) that concluded that increased opportunities to respond had a positive impact on both academic and behavioral outcomes. Unfortunately, teachers have fewer interactions with students who display problem behaviors and they may actually decrease the amount of instructional time provided when met with aversive or inappropriate student behavior (Wehby et al., 1998).

Effective implementation of schoolwide PBS models has contributed to improved academic achievement. This makes sense considering the reductions in inappropriate behaviors and the resulting gains in instructional time. Kellum, Mayer, Rebok, and Hawkins (1998) examined the connection between behavior and academics, specifically the effect of schoolwide behavior on early reading. They found that research-validated reading interventions implemented in classrooms that were not well managed did not result in improved reading performance. When those same interventions were implemented in combination with a schoolwide behavior model, significant academic gains were demonstrated. Kamps and Greenwood (2003) reported similar findings for schools that implemented a schoolwide reading and behavior model as compared to control schools without schoolwide models. In schools with such models, the researchers noted that more time was devoted to academic learning opportunities such as sustained silent reading. Additionally, students were more compliant with teachers' instructional demands, there were more opportunities to respond, higher levels of teacher praise, and slightly fewer reprimands. Although additional research is needed there does appear to be a positive correlation between implementation of PBS models and improved academic achievement.

A possible reason that schools may see an increase in academic achievement is because PBS leads to teachers and administrators spending less time addressing problem behavior and more time teaching and administering. Scott and Barrett (2004) discussed the amount of administrator and teacher time that was devoted to behavior problems in an elementary school in Maryland that had implemented a schoolwide PBS system. Making some assumptions regarding the amount of time needed to process office discipline referrals or suspensions/expulsions (10 minutes per referral, 45 minutes per suspension) and the amount of instructional time missed for the student (20 minutes per referral, 6 hours per suspension), the authors calculated the savings in administrative and teacher time over 2 years of implementation. From baseline to year 2 of implementation, Scott and Barrett found that reductions in office disciplinary referrals and suspensions resulted in a savings of 16.8 days for administrators and a reduction in instructional minutes lost. The gain in instructional time formerly lost because of inappropriate behaviors was 86.2 days for students. This example demonstrates the ability of school personnel to actually become more efficient with the additional time they have in the school day by focusing on teaching and learning. Schools with models of PBS systems see both improvements in student behavior and increased achievement levels.

SCHOOLWIDE PBS AND THE LAW

Drasgow and Yell (2002) examined laws and court cases that address schoolwide discipline policies and procedures and concluded that schoolwide PBS has legal support as well as empirical support. A principle that is well established in the law is that schools have a duty to maintain order by requiring students to obey reasonable rules and to respect the rights of others. This duty includes the power to regulate student conduct through the development of rules, procedures, and disciplinary sanctions.

When school personnel develop a schoolwide discipline plan, they should attend to the following three requirements. First, schoolwide discipline plans must be reasonable. This means they must have a carefully considered rationale and a school-related purpose. Second, school rules and consequences must be fair. Third, they must be communicated unambiguously to students so that they will have a clear understanding of what is acceptable and unacceptable behavior. Figure 10-8 lists and briefly describes Drasgow and Yell's legal guidelines that school districts should consider when they develop and implement schoolwide discipline programs.

Another important issue regarding schoolwide discipline policies is how they will affect students with disabilities. According to Yell and colleagues (2001), many school officials assume that because the Individuals with Disabilities Education Act (IDEA) places restrictions on school administrators' ability to unilaterally suspend and expel students with disabilities, regular schoolwide discipline policies do not apply to them. This is a mistaken

FIGURE 10-8

Schoolwide discipline plans: legal guidelines

Requirement	Explanation
1. Know the law.	• Administrators and teachers should understand federal and state laws and regulations regarding schoolwide discipline policies. • All administrators and teachers must understand their responsibilities under the schoolwide discipline policy and the disciplinary provisions of IDEA.
2. Include the entire school community when developing schoolwide discipline policies.	• Schoolwide discipline policies will be more meaningful if the entire school community is involved in developing them. • The community will help ensure involvement and understanding.
3. Conduct districtwide training of all staff in the schoolwide or districtwide discipline policy.	• All school personnel should receive ongoing and meaningful professional development in schoolwide discipline policies and procedures.
4. Collect meaningful data on program and student progress.	• The collection of meaningful data will allow educators to monitor the effectiveness of schoolwide discipline policies and make changes when needed.

assumption because students with disabilities who attend public school are subject to the same schoolwide discipline policies and procedures as other students. Schoolwide policies can run afoul of IDEA, however, if they (a) deprive students with disabilities of their special education and related services (i.e., long-term suspensions or expulsions without providing educational services); (b) trigger the procedural safeguards of IDEA (e.g., change a student's placement without a change in the individualized education program (IEP) or without prior notice); or (c) interfere with a student's IEP, behavior intervention plan (BIP), or Section 504 accommodation plan (Yell et al., 2001).

If a student's IEP team determines that (a) he or she will be subject to the school district's regular disciplinary policy, and (b) the policy *does not* violate the requirements of IDEA, the team may use the student's IEP or BIP to affirm that the student will be subject to the school's or district's schoolwide discipline policies and procedures (Gorn, 1999). Including a copy of the school's discipline policy along with the IEP or BIP will accomplish this. If a student's parents agreed to the IEP or BIP, then they are consenting to using the school's regular discipline policy. Students with disabilities should be subject to the same schoolwide discipline policy as other students in a school, and the policy should be included in the IEPs of students with disabilities who exhibit problem behavior.

Another area of the law that addresses schoolwide PBS is the Individuals with Disabilities Education Improvement Act (hereafter IDEA 2004). Amendments to IDEA in IDEA 2004 indicate the importance Congress attached to preventing students who may receive sufficient support from schoolwide systems, such as PBS, from being placed in special education prematurely. To encourage the use of schoolwide early intervening services, Congress allowed school districts to use up to 15% of their IDEA Part B funds to develop and coordinate early intervening services for students in Kindergarten through Grade 12 who have not been identified for special education services but who need additional academic and behavioral support to succeed in the general education environment.

Chapter Summary

Schools are being bombarded with new initiatives on a daily basis. Administrators, teachers, parents, and students are overwhelmed with the new fixes of the day. Positive behavior support not only provides a comprehensive way for schools to address behavioral needs of students, but when implemented systematically on a schoolwide basis, PBS also can provide an organizing framework or context for most school improvement initiatives. Creating a positive school context that supports learning for all children, providing a continuum of varying interventions based on individual needs, and embracing a decision-making model based on accurate and current data can serve as a foundation for sustained implementation of research-based practices that can lead to improvements. The national push to reach the goals set forth in No Child Left Behind (see Chapter 2) will not be realized without an equally comprehensive and intensive attention to creating school climates that support the behavioral and academic needs of all children.

CHAPTER 11

Classroom and Behavior Management I: Preventing Problem Behavior in the Classroom

Mitchell L. Yell

Focus Questions

- What is proactive or preventive classroom management?
- What is the difference between proactive and reactive classroom management?
- What are the primary components of a proactive classroom management system?
- How can teachers develop and implement proactive management systems in their classrooms?

One of the greatest challenges facing teachers of students with emotional and behavioral disorders (EBD) is classroom management. In fact, becoming skilled in classroom management is perhaps the major competency necessary for a teacher of EBD students to be successful (Bullock, Ellis, & Wilson, 1994; Gunter & Denny, 1996; Peck, Keenan, Cheney, & Neel, 2004). Moreover, teacher effectiveness research indicates that a teacher's classroom management skills are of crucial importance in determining teacher and student success (Evertson, Emmer, & Worsham, 2003; Rosenberg, O'Shea, & O'Shea, 2005; Simpson, Whelan, & Zabel, 1993; Wittrock, 1986). The purpose of the next three chapters is to examine classroom and behavior management. This chapter examines how teachers may develop management systems that prevent problem behavior in the classroom. First, I look at the seminal research in the area of prevention. Second, I examine the differences between a proactive and reactive classroom. Third, I discuss the important components of a proactive classroom. Fourth, I discuss how teachers can develop and implement an effective proactive classroom management system.

THE CLASSROOM MANAGEMENT PROBLEM

There are many adverse outcomes associated with ineffective classroom management. For example, in classrooms that are characterized by off-task and disruptive behavior, students do not learn as much as they would in successfully managed classrooms (Brigham & Kauffman, 1998; Kauffman, Mostert, Trent, & Hallahan, 2002; Levin & Nolan, 2004; Nelson, 2001). This is because disruptive behaviors take time away from teaching and learning. Ineffective classroom management is also a major cause of teacher burnout and dissatisfaction. In fact, stress related to inappropriate classroom management is one of the most frequently cited reasons that novice teachers leave the profession early (Brownell & Smith, 1992; Brownell, Smith, & McNellis, 1997; Kauffman, et al., 2002; Levin, 1980; Miller, Brownell, & Smith, 1999; Pullis, 1992; Zabel & Zabel, 1982). Additionally, principals and supervisors give low ratings to teachers who lack control of their classrooms (Good & Brophy, 2008). The bottom line is that to be successful, teachers must be competent and effective classroom managers (Bullock, et al., 1994; Gunter & Denny, 1996).

Many new teachers believe that the philosophies and techniques of classroom management are areas where they do not feel well prepared (Gable, Hendrickson, Young, & Shokoohi-Yekta, 1992; George, George, Gersten, & Grosenick, 1995; Jones & Jones, 2004). Even though courses in behavior management are typically included in teacher preparation programs in EBD (Katsiyannis, Landrum, Bullock, & Vinton, 1997; Maag & Katsiyannis, 1999), when preservice teachers of special education students are asked about concerns regarding student teaching assignments, typically they report anxiety and apprehension about their ability to manage a classroom and fears about losing control of their students (Rosenberg, et al., 2002). Moreover, special education teachers continue to report that neither their teacher training programs (Gable et al., 1992; George et al., 1995; Landrum, Tankersley, & Cook, 1997; Maag, 2004; Polsgrove, 2003) nor their school-based inservice training (Cheney & Sachs, 2000) prepare them to be skillful classroom managers. Because students with EBD may engage in higher rates of misbehavior than do nondisabled students or students with disabilities other than EBD, it is extremely important that prospective teachers of students with EBD are properly prepared to be effective classroom managers.

The major question then is, how can teachers become competent classroom managers? Unfortunately, often the advice that teachers receive regarding classroom management is based on untested theories or unsystematic personal testimonials about "what works best for me" (Good & Brophy, 2008, p. 127). Many of these testimonials are not based on empirical evidence but on idiosyncratic personal experience. Effective classroom management skills are not achieved through adherence to simplistic bromides, gimmicks, or a bag of tricks. There is no cookbook of techniques, special formulas, or management packages that fit all circumstances and situations. Rather, teachers become effective managers by understanding and developing personal management systems based on sound principles and guidelines supported by empirical evidence and information.

Fortunately, research on classroom management has grown considerably in the last quarter of a century, and has yielded a knowledge base that provides solid empirical evidence that can help teachers increase their effectiveness in this area (Evertson et al., 2003; Good & Brophy, 2008; Gunter & Denny, 1996; Jones & Jones, 2004; Walker, et al., 1995; Wittrock, 1986). For whatever reason, however, teachers do not seem to use research-based strategies to manage their classrooms. In fact, Gunter and Denny (1996) stated that an important area for future research is the classroom management practices of teachers of students with EBD. Specifically, Gunter and Denny noted that such research should examine the mismatch between empirically supported classroom management strategies and classroom strategies that are actually used in classrooms. If teachers of students with EBD are to become effective, they must have organized, efficient, and orderly classrooms. To accomplish this goal, teachers need to adopt those classroom management strategies that have empirical support (Bullock et al., 1994; Davis & Fox, 1999; Dunlap et al., 1993; Gunter & Denny, 1996; Kamps & Tankersley, 1996; Kauffman & Wong, 1991; Landrum & Tankersley, 1999; Whelan & Simpson, 1996).

The discussion is based on three dimensions that I believe, and research confirms, are important prerequisites needed to establish successful classroom management systems. These dimensions involve behaviors and skills that teachers must exhibit in classrooms to create classroom climates characterized by high rates of student engagement and low rates of student disruption. These dimensions are (a) preventing, (b) responding, and (c) intervening. The three dimensions are depicted in Figure 11–1.

The first dimension is preventing. This dimension involves prevention of problem behavior in the classroom. Teachers who are successful classroom managers prevent problem behaviors from occurring rather than merely reacting to problems that have already occurred. Preventing refers to those teacher behaviors and actions that prevent discipline problems and lead to higher rates of student engagement (Curwin & Mendler, 1998; Kamps, 2002; Meadows, et al., 1996). The purpose of this chapter is to discuss classroom-based antecedents and the influence they can have on behavior. As noted in Chapter 4, antecedents are conditions, events, or stimuli that set the occasion for behavior to occur. Most of the strategies in the preventing dimension involve arranging antecedent events to promote learning and reduce disruptive behavior. Some of the other strategies in the preventing dimension, such as praise and feedback, are reinforcing consequences that strengthen appropriate student behavior. In this chapter I will discuss the preventing dimension.

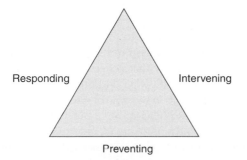

Figure 11–1   The dimensions of classroom management

The second dimension is responding. Teachers can create very efficient and effective classroom management systems, and students may still behave inappropriately. Teachers need to know how to respond in an appropriate manner to student misbehavior. It is especially crucial that when they respond to such behaviors they do so in ways that do not involve them in power struggles with students or escalate minor problems into major ones (Curwin & Mendler, 1998; Kauffman et al., 2002; Walker et al., 1995; Walker, Ramsey, & Gresham, 2004). This means that teachers' responses to problem behaviors must be efficient, effective, and appropriate to the level or degree of misbehavior exhibited by a student. I examine the responding dimension and offer recommendations to assist teachers in responding in an appropriate manner to student misbehavior in Chapter 12.

The third dimension is intervening. This dimension involves using research-based interventions in classrooms to encourage and teach appropriate behaviors and reduce inappropriate behaviors. Consequences that occur after a behavior, and are contingent on the particular behavior, will influence the probability of that behavior occurring in the future (see Chapter 4). The strategies in the intervening dimension involve manipulating consequences to either increase or decrease the likelihood that certain behaviors will occur in the future. Chapter 13 examines the intervening dimension, and offers recommendations to assist teachers in adopting research-based interventions in their classrooms.

PREVENTION AND CLASSROOM MANAGEMENT

Prior to the 1970s, approaches to teaching preservice teachers to manage classrooms were often based on procedures for disciplining students who misbehaved (Jones & Jones, 2004; Kaplan & Carter, 1995; Meadows et al., 1996). In other words, the emphasis of these programs was on what teachers should do after students exhibited problem behavior. Similarly, research on classroom management during this period also emphasized disciplining students following incidences of misbehavior. Teaching and discipline were often seen as separate aspects of education (Charles, 2002). Teaching was that aspect of education that helped students acquire information and skills, whereas discipline referred to actions that teachers took to stop students from misbehaving. This view began to change in the early 1970s. A major impetus to this change was a book written by Jacob Kounin (1970) titled *Discipline and Group Management in Classrooms*.

The Research of Jacob Kounin

Kounin's interest in classroom management began when he publicly reprimanded a college student during a psychology lecture he was giving. During his lecture, Kounin noticed a student reading a newspaper in the back row of his class. He reprimanded the student who immediately stopped reading the newspaper and began to attend to the lecture. Interestingly, Kounin also noticed an increase in attending behavior of students seated near the reprimanded student. Seemingly, the behavior of other students who had not been reprimanded changed as a result of the reprimand delivered to the newspaper-reading student.

As a result of this incident, Kounin became interested in discipline in schools and how teachers handled misbehavior. In one research project, he videotaped thousands of hours of instruction in over 100 elementary classrooms. For this research, Kounin and his colleagues focused on students who were "emotionally disturbed" and were taught in general education classrooms (Kounin, 1970, p. 60). Additionally, Kounin examined disciplinary interactions in classes where teachers were very successful in managing their classes, and in classes that were characterized by serious classroom management problems and where teachers were inept at classroom management. He hypothesized that differences in the disciplinary techniques used by teachers would account for differences in their ability to successfully manage and influence student behavior in their classrooms. Kounin was astonished by what he found: The disciplinary techniques that teachers used made no systematic differences in how students behaved in classes! Teachers who were successful classroom managers and those teachers who were inept managers whose classrooms were often out of control were responding to student problem behavior in very similar ways. Thus, the disciplinary procedures used were the same for good and poor managers.

Undeterred by the unexpected findings, Kounin and his colleagues reanalyzed the videotapes to find out if there were any systematic differences between the teaching methods and behaviors used by the successful and unsuccessful classroom managers. They were interested in finding "what it is that teacher's *do* that makes a difference in how children behave" (Kounin, 1970, p. 74). Their reanalysis showed that there were specific categories of teacher behavior that correlated with their success in classroom management. These teacher behaviors, however, did not occur after students misbehaved. Rather, the behaviors prevented misbehavior from occurring. Moreover, these same teacher behaviors prevented misbehavior in both general education students and students with emotional disabilities. As Kounin stated, "whatever the teachers did that was associated with high work involvement and low deviancy for the nondisturbed children was also associated with high work involvement and low deviancy (and deviancy contagion) for the disturbed children" (Kounin, 1970, p. 75). These unexpected findings changed Kounin's perception of the importance of discipline and prevention. He wrote:

That unexpected fact required unlearning on my part, in the sense of having to replace the original question by other questions. Questions about disciplinary techniques were eliminated and replaced by questions about classroom management; preventing misbehavior was given investigative priority in handling misbehavior. (p. 143)

Thus, as Kounin's pioneering research (Kounin, 1970; Kounin & Obradovic, 1968) clearly showed, teacher behaviors that prevented problem behaviors from occurring were a vital part of classroom management strategies. Subsequent research by other investigators confirmed Kounin's findings (Brophy & Good, 1986; Evertson & Emmer, 1982). Furthermore, Kounin's research showed that teachers who approach classroom management as a systematic process of establishing and maintaining an effective learning environment are more successful managers than those teachers who place more emphasis on their roles as disciplinarians.

The Curriculum of Control

In 1990 Knitzer and colleagues published their seminal examination of public school programs for student with EBD, *At the Schoolhouse Door: An Examination of Programs and Policies for Children with Behavioral and Emotional Problems.* One of their many interesting findings involved what the authors referred to as "the curriculum of control" (p. 25). According to Knitzer et al., a common variable underlying the overwhelming majority of classes for these students was an emphasis on control. That is, the structure of many classrooms was based on a point system that was used to control a variety of classroom and social behaviors (Webber & Scheuermann, 1997). Moreover, the classroom atmospheres were often rigid and controlling with teachers interacting with their students in negative ways. Additionally, the authors reported seeing little in the way of effective and engaging teaching in these classrooms, but rather observed classrooms in which students were required to do worksheet after worksheet and teachers used very limited and apparently ineffective teaching strategies. In other words, the classrooms examined in *At the Schoolhouse*

Door were characterized by the very behaviors that it is believed exacerbate student misbehavior: (a) boring and repetitive learning tasks, often at incorrect levels of difficulty; (b) excessive amounts of downtime; and (c) negative student–teacher interactions. Unfortunately, evidence indicates that the punitive and reactive curriculum of control is still the dominant model in many classrooms for students with EBD (Yell & Bradley, 2000; Zabel, 1992).

If teachers understand the importance of developing and maintaining a proactive environment in their classrooms and work diligently to do so, the result will be increased student learning and decreased student misbehavior. In the next section I will discuss the essential components of prevention-based classroom management system. I first describe the importance of developing and maintaining a proactive versus a reactive classroom environment. Second, I examine primary components of a successful classroom management system. Third, I discuss how teachers can implement such a system.

PROACTIVE VERSUS REACTIVE CLASSROOM MANAGEMENT

The key to an effective classroom management system is for teachers to adopt a proactive rather than a reactive approach to managing student behavior (Algozzine & White, 2002; Brownell & Smith, 1992; Colvin & Sugai, 1988; Heflin & Bullock, 1999; Kamps, 2002; White, Algozzine, Audette, Marr, Ellis, & 2004). In proactive management, teachers design their classroom environments and engage in behaviors that reduce the probability that disruptive behavior will occur. Moreover, "before an action or problem occurs, the teacher teaches carefully and strategically all that is required so that students have the information necessary to perform or behave appropriately" (Darch & Kame'enui, 2004, p. 3). In other words, teachers who adopt a proactive management style carry out actions either before or during a lesson to prevent problem behaviors from surfacing. In a reactive management system, on the other hand, teachers wait for problem behaviors to occur and then react to the occurrences.

Proactive classrooms are characterized by high levels of student engagement and low levels of disruptive and off-task behavior. In a proactive classroom, therefore, student learning is enhanced because the classroom environment is structured so that effective instruction can occur (Gunter & Denny, 1996; Shores, Gunter, & Jack, 1993). Such classrooms don't just happen, however; they are a result of well-prepared teachers using evidence-based procedures to organize their classrooms and interact with their students.

Unfortunately, general education and special education teachers have difficulty implementing proactive classroom management systems (Darch & Kame'enui, 2004; Zigmond & Baker, 1996). In fact, according to Zigmond and Baker (1996) teachers' attempts to use proactive management systems occur rarely and haphazardly at best. Fortunately, research has produced an impressive and consistent knowledge base regarding evidence-based practices that result in effective classroom management. To be effective, teachers must be committed to understanding and using these evidence-based practices. In the remainder of this chapter, I examine these proactive procedures.

PRIMARY COMPONENTS OF A PROACTIVE CLASSROOM MANAGEMENT SYSTEM

This section of the chapter examines four aspects of a proactive classroom management system: (a) teacher behaviors and attitudes, (b) teacher authority and credibility, (c) classroom structure, and (d) effective teaching.

Teacher Behaviors and Attitudes

Ryan (1986) discriminated between "frontstage" and "backstage" behaviors. Frontstage behaviors are those behaviors that teacher training programs concentrate on, such as the curricular and administrative functions of teaching. Backstage behaviors are those subtle behaviors that are often ignored in teacher-training programs but that, nonetheless, are important components of effective teaching. These are behaviors such as teacher-student interactions and teacher attitudes and beliefs. This section explores some of these backstage behaviors and highlights how teachers' beliefs and values impact the effectiveness of the classroom and the importance of teachers being aware of their own beliefs and how these beliefs can affect their daily actions and behaviors.

Researchers and theorists have noted that certain important teacher attitudes and behaviors are essential to managerial success in classrooms (Good & Brophy, 2008; Jones & Jones, 2004). According to Kauffman, Pullen, and Akers (1998), research based on the ecological principles of mutual influence and interdependence has clearly established that every person in a classroom, teachers and students alike, influence the behavior of every other person in the classroom. Classroom management strategies, therefore, must recognize the teacher's influence on students and students' influence on the teacher.

Student misbehavior can also be attributed to teacher behaviors. Kauffman (2005) notes that teachers may contribute to student misbehavior by (a) being inconsistent when applying rules and consequences, (b) reinforcing inappropriate student behaviors, (c) holding inappropriate expectations for students, (d) being insensitive to students' needs, and (e) demonstrating or encouraging undesirable models of behavior. This means that teachers must monitor their own behavior and the possible influences that this behavior may have on students.

According to Ginott (1971), teachers are a decisive and powerful force in their classrooms. They create and maintain the classroom environment. Their effectiveness depends on their ability to establish an educational climate that promotes learning and appropriate behavior. A number of key teacher attitudes and behaviors are important to establishing and maintaining such an environment, including (a) building a positive teacher–student relationship and maintaining a positive classroom structure, (b) communicating positive expectations, (c) praising students, and (d) enriching the classroom with incentives and reinforcers. Next I review these crucial attributes.

Building Positive Teacher–Student Relationships and Positive Classroom Climates

Building a positive relationship between a teacher and a student who exhibits problem behavior is an important way to positively affect students (Good & Brophy, 2008; Levin & Nolan, 2004; Rosenberg et al., 2002). Frequently students with EBD do not have positive relationships with their teachers. In fact, teachers often avoid interactions with students who exhibit problem behavior. Teachers should disregard any negative feelings they may have about students who are disruptive and work at building a positive teacher–student relationship (Levin & Nolan, 2004). Levin and Nolan suggest that teachers attempting to build positive relationships with such students need to be persistent, consistent, and predictable in their own behavior. Moreover, they must look for positive qualities in students that can be used as a foundation for building a positive relationship (Strachota, 1996). When students and teachers have a positive relationship and students know that their teacher likes and respects them, they are more likely to imitate the teacher's behavior, have better attitudes toward school, and have higher levels of academic achievement (Good & Brophy, 2008; Jones & Jones, 2004).

How do teachers build positive relationships with students? We know that students like teachers who are warm, friendly, and have a sense of humor. Noguera (1995) found that when asked to describe an ideal teacher, students consistently cited the following characteristics: firmness; compassion, and an interesting, engaging, and challenging teaching style. This does not mean that teachers should abandon their roles as authority figures in their classrooms to befriend their students; rather, they should strive to maintain a positive classroom climate while combining warmth and caring with realistic limits when dealing with students. A positive classroom climate is organized, warm, supportive, and pleasant (Charles, 2002; Rutherford, Quinn, & Mathur, 1996). Additionally, a positive classroom climate encourages learning, promotes good behavior, and rewards student accomplishments. In contrast, a poor classroom climate is disorganized and cold, and emphasizes obedience and duress. Such environments can depress learning and lead to misbehavior.

When a classroom has a positive climate, students look forward to being there. Furthermore, students expect to learn and receive assistance when they need it, and the teacher supports them in their efforts (Evertson et al., 2003; Good & Brophy, 2008).

Communicating Positive Expectations. Numerous studies have been conducted on the effect of teacher expectations on student achievement (Brophy, 1983; Good & Brophy, 2008; Jones & Jones, 2004; Rosenthal & Jacobson, 1968). In fact, Walker (1995) reported that during the past two decades there has been more research on teacher expectations than any other factor related to teacher effectiveness.

Good and Brophy (1997) discussed a consensus in the literature that "teachers' expectations can and sometimes do affect teacher–student interaction and student outcomes" (p. 81). Two types of teacher expectation effects have emerged from the literature (Cooper & Good, 1983). The first is the self-fulfilling prophecy effect and the second is the sustaining prophecy effect. Good and Brophy (2008) define these two expectations as follows. The self-fulfilling prophecy effect is a situation in which "an originally erroneous expectation leads to behavior that causes the expectation to come true" (p. 80). The sustaining expectation effect is when "teachers expect students to sustain previously developed patterns, to the point that teachers take these patterns for granted and fail to see and capitalize on change in students' potential" (p.80). They explain that the self-fulfilling expectations can be very powerful but the self-sustaining effects occur more often. Our expectations affect the way we behave and our interactions with others; therefore, it is important that teachers are aware of and monitor their expectations of students. "High teacher expectations for student behavior and academic performance have been consistently identified as a key correlate of effective schools" (Walker, 1995, p. 249).

According to Morgan and Jenson (1988), it is erroneous for teachers of children and youth with EBD not to expect a student to behave appropriately because he or she has the EBD label. Such thinking may result in an increase in a student's levels of inappropriate behavior and may lead to situations where inappropriate behaviors are excused or accepted (Morgan & Jenson, 1988).

Although it is sometimes difficult to avoid having negative expectations, and it is certainly unrealistic to expect teachers to have only positive expectations, they must always strive to maintain flexible expectations and emphasize the positive (Brophy, 1981; Good & Brophy, 2008). Keeping expectations flexible means that teachers must not assume that because students have performed or behaved a certain way in the past, they will always behave similarly in the future. A teacher's job is to change students' achievement and behavior for the better. They must always assume that they can make a difference and that negative expectations that they or other teachers hold "represent problems to be solved, not definitions of reality to which a teacher must adapt" (Good & Brophy, 2008, p. 107).

Teachers should form and project expectations that are as positive as possible while still being realistic (Brophy, 1981; Delpit, 1995, Good & Brophy, 2008). Brophy (1981) suggests that teachers should (a) emphasize positive achievements and behaviors, (b) keep expectations current by monitoring students' progress; (c) set goals for classes and individual students in terms of floors (e.g., acceptable standards) rather than ceilings (e.g., the highest possible standards), and let students' progress determine educational and behavioral programming; (d) stress students' continuous progress relative to their previous levels rather than comparing them with other students when giving feedback; (e) respond to student performance by providing feedback that will help students meet their academic and behavioral objectives; and (f) encourage students to achieve as much as they can and behave as well as they can.

Praising Students. Teachers should monitor and attempt to increase the number and quality of praise statements that they make to students. Teacher praise has been demonstrated to be an effective strategy in classroom management (Sutherland, 2000; Sutherland, Copeland, & Wehby, 2001; Sutherland, Wehby, & Copeland, 2000). For example, it has been demonstrated that when teachers praised appropriate behaviors, students' disruptive behaviors decreased (Madsen, Becker, & Thomas, 1968) and task engagement increased (Sutherland, Copeland, & Wehby, 2001; Sutherland & Wehby, 2001a). Furthermore,

the use of teacher praise can help establish and sustain a positive classroom environment and improve positive teacher–student relationships (Paine, Radicchi, Rosellini, Deutchman, & Darch, 1983; Sutherland, Copeland, & Wehby, 2001).

Darch and Kame'enui (2004) note that when teachers are primarily positive in their interactions with students, they set the stage for increased academic achievement and improved student conduct. Moreover, increases in the appropriate behavior of students result in more instructional time being available in the classroom and improved classroom climate. Positive teacher–student interactions can have a beneficial effect on students' academic achievement and appropriate behavior (Curwin & Mendler, 1998; Good & Brophy, 2008; Jones & Jones, 2004). For example, research indicates that teachers interact differently with students who are disruptive and violate classroom rules than they do with nondisruptive students who follow classroom rules (Coleman & Webber, 2002; Gunter & Denny, 1996; Lewis & Wehby, 1999; Van Acker et al., 1996; Walker, 1995; Walker et al., 1995, 2004). Unfortunately, when teachers interact with disruptive students they are more likely to reprimand inappropriate behavior than they are to praise appropriate behavior (Lewis & Wehby, 1999; Walker, 1995; Walker & Buckley, 1974). This differential treatment may actually result in the escalation of inappropriate behavior. Research has also shown that increases in teachers' positive interactions with students is often followed by decreases in students' inappropriate behaviors (Lewis & Wehby, 1999; Wehby, Symons & Shores, 1995). It is important, therefore, that teachers reinforce cooperative students frequently, and monitor their own interactions to ensure they interact in a positive manner with all students.

Knowing of the many positive benefits of a positive classroom climate, one would think that praise would be a frequent occurrence in classrooms. Unfortunately, research indicates that teachers of students with EBD rarely use praise in their classrooms (Gunter & Denny, 1996; Morgan & Jenson, 1988). For example, in studies by Shores, Jack, Gunter, Ellis, DeBriere, and Wehby (1993) and Wehby and colleagues (1995), rates of teacher praise with students with EBD were found to be as low as 1 time per hour. Walker et al., (1995) reported that teachers tend to deliver praise at very low rates of once every 15 to 30 minutes, whereas they tend to deliver criticism or reprimands at much higher rates of once every 2 minutes. Why are the rates of praise in classrooms so low if the benefits of praise are so noteworthy? Shores, Jack, et al., (1993) suggested that teachers may not be aware of the power of praise. Additionally, some students with EBD may be so aversive to teachers that they choose to ignore the student altogether (Shores, Gunter, et al., 1993).

According to Sutherland, Copeland, et al., (2001), teachers need to become more mindful of their use of praise. Sugai and Horner (2002) and Latham (1992) have asserted that in interactions with students, teachers should strive for a ratio of four to five positive interactions for every negative interaction. By attending to the positive aspects of behavior and to those children who are meeting behavioral expectations, the teacher shifts the focus of his or her attention to the behaviors that are valued and reinforced in his or her classroom and school.

Jones and Jones (2004) suggest four steps to monitor positive teacher communication. First, the teacher collects data about how he or she interacts with students (e.g., positive versus negative interactions). It is helpful to have another adult available to actually count the interactions and code them as positive, negative, or neutral. The second step suggested is to analyze the data. Third, the teacher determines whether he or she is responding differently to different students or different types of students. Fourth, the teacher attempts to alter his or her patterns of interaction if needed to increase positive interactions.

Sutherland and colleagues suggest that peer coaching and self-evaluation can be effective ways to increase a teacher's use of praise (Sutherland, Copeland, et al., 2001; Sutherland & Wehby, 2001a). In peer coaching, data are collected on the number of praise statements over a number of instructional sessions. Based on the data, a teacher sets a goal for increasing praise statements. The peer coach then (a) observes and records an instructional session, (b) provides feedback regarding the number of praise statements to the teacher, and (c) graphs the teacher's use of praise. When conducting a self-evaluation the teacher audiotapes a sample of his or her instructional sessions. The teacher then (a) makes a prediction regarding his or her use of praise, (b) counts the number of times he or she praised students, (c) compares the actual count to the prediction, and (d) sets a goal to increase praise statements. The teacher then continues to collect data, which are graphed. Such procedures have been shown to be effective ways to increase praise. Moreover, increased rates of praise have been shown to increase students' on-task time (Sutherland, et al., 2000).

Sutherland, Copeland, et al., (2001) also suggest that teachers use subtle reminders to increase their use of praise. Such reminders might include attaching Post-it notes to their desks that read "PRAISE" setting a personal praise statement goal and having the students evaluate the teacher; or labeling cups with each student's name and dropping a token in the cup each time he or she praises the student. Alderman (1997) suggests putting dried beans in a left pocket at the beginning of the day and each time the teacher makes a praise statement, transferring a bean to the right pocket. Teachers can evaluate their progress and reinforce themselves for increasing praise statements.

Teachers should increase not only the quantity but also the quality of their praise statements. Good and Brophy (2008) note that effective praise calls attention to a student's progress or accomplishments, and expresses appreciation for his or her efforts in ways that focus on these efforts or accomplishments rather than their role in pleasing the teacher. This means that effective praise attributes student performance to their abilities and efforts. Unfortunately, much teacher praise of students is directed more toward controlling behavior rather than expressing admiration for their efforts or accomplishments (Good & Brophy, 2008). Praise, however, is most likely to be effective when it is spontaneous and genuine rather than a calculated attempt to manipulate a student (Good & Brophy, 2008; Walker, 1995). Table 11-1 contains suggestions for using praise effectively.

Table 11–1   Guidelines for the effective use of praise

Do	Don't
Be sincere	Don't be overly effusive or exaggerate
Specify the behavior, performance, or accomplishment	Don't be general or ambiguous
Use a variety of praise statements	Don't repeatedly use the same praise statement
Praise contingently	Don't deliver praise unsystematically
Deliver praise immediately after target behavior occurs	Don't wait to deliver praise
Praise frequently	Don't be sparing in your use of praise
Praise prosocial behaviors	Don't ignore prosocial behaviors

Enriching the Classroom with Incentives and Reinforcers. According to Rhode, Jenson, and Reavis (1992), teachers should make their classrooms a positive place by using unique and interesting ways to provide recognition and motivation to their students. Incentives, rewards, and reinforcers add interest to the class while simultaneously reinforcing appropriate classroom behavior. When creating an incentive system, it is important that all students be able to access these incentives and rewards. It is also important that when developing such a system, the teacher takes into account students' preferences.

One of the most effective, but underused, potential positive reinforcers in classrooms is the teacher (Morgan & Jenson, 1988; Rhode et al., 1992). Teachers should move around their classrooms in a random manner and reinforce students. There are advantages to teachers moving around their classrooms, including (a) the teacher's proximity helps prevent problem behaviors from occurring, and (b) the teacher may provide positive social reinforcement to students who exhibit appropriate behaviors.

There are many types of incentives that teachers may use in their classrooms. A frequently used type of incentive involves recognition of students' work, good behavior, and accomplishments. Teachers can recognize students' accomplishments by creating classroom displays of student work and graphs of student progress in academics and behavior, writing notes or making calls to students' parents regarding their achievement or behavior, or simply verbally acknowledging students. Another type of incentive is allowing students to do a special activity as a reward (e.g., free reading, games, computer time, class party). In Chapter 6 we further discuss the use of reinforcers.

Summary of Teacher Behaviors and Attitudes Teacher behaviors and attitudes have a great influence on the students. It is important that teachers are aware of the importance of praise and strive to increase their rates of praise with students. Additionally, by communicating positive expectations of their students and enriching their classrooms with incentives and reinforcers they can help ensure that they build positive student–teacher relationships and maintain a positive classroom environment. Figure 11–2 is a checklist of important elements to consider regarding behaviors and attitudes.

Teacher Authority and Credibility

Teacher authority is an elusive, but extremely important, element that may make a crucial difference between success and failure in classroom management (Savage, 1999), especially in classes for students and youth with EBD (Wood, 1991; Yell, 1996a). According to Wood (1991), establishing authority and leadership in a classroom for students with EBD is a prerequisite for effective teaching. Therefore, teachers need to establish authority at the beginning of the school year. Authority is a student-recognized right to give commands, make decisions, and enforce standards of behavior. Authority must be earned; teachers cannot assume that students will come to school with an automatic respect for teachers' authority (Tauber, 1985). However, teachers who are liked, respected, and trusted by their students are more likely to have their authority recognized.

Attributes such as honesty, enthusiasm, a deep respect for others, and a sense of humor are important for establishing authority (Kouzes & Posner, 1987). French and Raven (1960) argued that the most effective ways to have students recognize teachers' authority was to ensure that their students know that their teacher (a) likes and respects them, (b) cares about them and their learning, (c) makes demands on them because it is in the student's own best interest, and (d) is knowledgeable and competent. The beginning point for developing authority and power in their classroom, therefore, is for a teacher to demonstrate expertise and concern for his or her students (Good & Brophy, 2008; Savage, 1999).

Establishing Credibility An essential behavior necessary for teachers to become an authority figure in the eyes of their students is to establish credibility. To establish credibility, it is important that teachers exhibit consistency between their words and their actions. This consistency provides the structure that students want and need (Good & Brophy, 2008). If students see that a teacher's behavior is not consistent with his or her word, it is likely that the teacher will lose credibility and respect in the students' eyes. On the other hand, if students know that they can depend on what their teacher says, they will be less likely to test his or her authority and be more likely to accept responsibility for their own behavior (Good & Brophy, 2008). Moreover, because special education classrooms for students with EBD often have two or more adults in the room, the teacher and the paraprofessional, it is extremely important that the adults work together to ensure consistency in their behavior and actions toward the students (Scott, Payne, & Jolivette, 2003).

An important aspect of consistency is rule enforcement. Classroom rules must be applied consistently on a day-to-day and student-to-student basis. This means that unacceptable behavior is always unacceptable regardless of the (a) mood of the teacher, (b) day it is exhibited, or (c) student who exhibits it (Levin & Nolan, 2004; Savage, 1999). To ensure that classroom rules and consequences

FIGURE 11–2

Teacher behaviors and attitudes checklist

Yes	No	Attribute
❏	❏	The teacher maintains positive attitudes toward his or her students.
❏	❏	The teacher is organized, consistent, and predictable in his or her behavior.
❏	❏	The teacher has an interesting, engaging, and challenging teaching style.
❏	❏	The teacher has a sense of humor.
❏	❏	The teacher maintains realistic limits when dealing with students.
❏	❏	The teacher communicates positive expectations to his or her students.
❏	❏	The teacher communicates an expectation that his or her students will behave.
❏	❏	The teacher maintains flexible expectations for his/her students.
❏	❏	The teacher emphasizes positive achievements and behaviors.
❏	❏	The teacher monitors student progress and responds to student performance.
❏	❏	The teacher monitors and attempts to increase his/her praise statements.
❏	❏	The teacher maintains a 5:1 ratio of positive to negative comments.
❏	❏	The teacher delivers effective praise statements.
❏	❏	The teacher acknowledges appropriate student behavior and achievement in interesting ways.
❏	❏	The teacher constantly moves about his/her classroom and maintains close proximity to students.

are applied consistently, it is important that teachers become good monitors of student behavior.

Monitoring Student Behavior Successful classroom managers have effective monitoring skills. This means that teachers need to constantly watch their students to ensure that students are (a) staying on task, (b) participating in learning activities, (c) behaving appropriately, and (d) complying with classroom rules and procedures. When teachers do not monitor student behavior, inattention and misbehavior among their students may increase and students may not get assistance on learning activities when they need it. Effective monitoring requires that teachers stand or sit where they can see all their students and that they scan the room frequently (Evertson et al.,

2003). Teachers who are successful classroom managers develop what Evertson and colleagues referred to as "active eyes" (p. 134).

Effective monitoring also requires that teachers circulate around the room frequently to check student progress. Successful classroom managers position themselves so they can see all their students. Moreover, teachers should never become so involved with an activity or one student that they forget to monitor all their students.

Withitness. Earlier in this chapter I briefly reviewed the research of Jacob Kounin. His research clearly showed that successful managers prevented problem behaviors from occurring in their classrooms. Kounin also found that there were specific categories of teacher behaviors that correlated with their success in classroom management. These behaviors are possible only when teachers effectively monitor their students. The most successful classroom managers displayed a trait that Kounin termed "withitness" (Kounin, 1970, p. 74). Withitness is exhibited when teachers communicate to their students that they are aware of all events going on within the classroom. Teachers demonstrate withitness when they deliver behavioral desists (i.e., when a teacher does something to stop student misbehavior). Four specific ways in which teachers can deliver desists in ways that communicate withitness to their students are to (a) choose the correct target or targets when delivering a desist, (b) stop the most serious misbehavior first when two misbehaviors are occurring simultaneously, (c) stop the misbehavior before it spreads to other students, and (d) stop the misbehavior before it becomes more serious. Kounin found that teachers who displayed withitness had higher rates of student involvement and lower rates of misbehavior in their classrooms.

Overlapping. Kounin found another teacher behavior that, when exhibited, also led to higher rates of involvement and lower rates of misbehavior. He called this teacher behavior "overlapping" (Kounin, 1970, p. 54). Overlapping occurs when a teacher has to deal with two or more matters at the same time. For example, a teacher is doing small-group work in reading and the other students in the classroom are working independently, when two students in the larger group begin talking loudly to each other. If the teacher notices the misbehavior he or she can (a) stop the group work while dealing with the behavior problem, (b) neglect the misbehavior and focus on the group work, or (c) attend to both the misbehavior and group work simultaneously. If the teacher attends to both misbehavior and group work at the same time, he or she might remain seated with the group and ask a student to read orally, while communicating to the misbehaving students that they must stop the problem behavior.

Kounin (1970) found in his research that there were many situations that occurred every day in which a teacher was confronted with situations that called for overlapping. He also found that teachers who frequently displayed overlapping behavior were more successful classroom managers. Thus, effective classroom managers could deal with more than one thing at a time. They were able to address misbehavior without disrupting ongoing activities.

Kounin summed up teachers who possess the attributes of withitness and overlapping when he said that successful classroom managers seem to have "eyes in the back of their head" (Kounin, 1970, p. 81). That is, effective classroom managers monitor their classrooms and are aware of what is going on at all times. Only when teachers effectively monitor student behavior are they able to display both withitness and overlapping. Students of such teachers know that their teachers are able to detect misbehavior quickly and identify the offending student accurately.

Modeling Self-Discipline and Self-Control Important aspects of teacher authority and credibility are self-discipline and self-control. Teachers must model appropriate behaviors, including self-discipline and self-control (Hallenbeck & Kauffman, 1995; Kauffman, 2005). This is especially true of teachers of students with EBD who spend a great deal of time working to help their students gain self-control. Teachers who cannot control their own anger and emotions can hardly expect their students to control theirs. Students learn much by observing the behaviors of others. Therefore, teachers must constantly exercise self-discipline and control, even in the face of severe student acting out. As Savage (1999) aptly stated, "In order for students to learn self-control, they must be involved with a responsible adult who demonstrates self-control" (p. 138). Students learn from the behavior that teachers model, whether it is appropriate or inappropriate. It is very important, therefore, that they are aware of the behavior that they display with students (Yell, 1996a). Savage (1999) asserted that teachers must be introspective regarding their behavior and constantly ask themselves questions such as: What messages are being sent by my behavior? How do I respond when things are not going well? Do I take responsibility for my own behavior?

Summary of Teacher Authority and Credibility Teacher authority and credibility make a crucial difference between success and failure in classroom management. Research shows that teachers who are (a) liked, respected, and trusted by their students; (b) consistent in their words and actions toward students; and (c) effective monitors of student behavior (e.g., possess withitness) are likely to be authority figures in their classrooms. Furthermore, teachers must model the personal characteristics (e.g., anger control, self-discipline) that they are trying to develop in their students. Figure 11–3 is a checklist of important elements to consider regarding teacher authority and credibility.

FIGURE 11–3

Teacher authority and credibility checklist

Yes	No	Attribute
☐	☐	The teacher establishes authority and leadership in his or her classroom.
☐	☐	The teacher communicates that he or she likes and respects his or her students.
☐	☐	The teacher has an interesting, engaging, and challenging teaching style.
☐	☐	The teacher demonstrates that he or she is knowledgeable and competent.
☐	☐	The teacher and classroom paraprofessional work together to ensure consistency in their behavior and actions.
☐	☐	Classroom rules and consequences are applied consistently to all students and at all times.
☐	☐	The teacher effectively and efficiently monitors student behavior.
☐	☐	The teacher circulates around the room and makes frequent checks on students' progress.
☐	☐	The teacher communicates to his or her students "withitness" by delivering desists accurately, effectively, and efficiently.
☐	☐	The teacher can attend to two or three events occurring simultaneously.
☐	☐	The teacher models self-discipline and self-control.

Classroom Structure

The third component of a proactive classroom management system involves the structure that a teacher creates in his or her classroom. By structure I mean the manner in which teachers organize their classrooms to ensure that teaching and learning are enhanced and problem behaviors are minimized. The primary goal when establishing classroom structure is to ensure that events in the classroom are as predictable as possible (Colvin & Lazar, 1997; Walker et al., 1995). When classrooms are structured and predictable, the likelihood of problem behavior is diminished and the likelihood of effective learning occurring is increased (Darch et al., 1998; Good & Brophy, 2008; Walker et al., 1995).

Effective classroom management begins with advanced planning by the teacher (Good & Brophy, 2008). This means that the structure of the learning environment and the classroom procedures are in place prior to the start of the school year. Investigations at both the elementary and secondary level conducted by Evertson, Emmer, and colleagues demonstrated the importance of advanced planning and how effective teachers manage the first day and first few weeks of school (Emmer, Evertson, & Anderson, 1982; Evertson & Emmer, 1982; Evertson, Emmer, Sanford, & Clemens, 1983). For example, in a study conducted in 28 third-grade classrooms, the researchers showed that the smooth and automatic functioning of classrooms of effective classroom managers were the result of careful planning, preparation, and organization at the beginning of the school year. The most effective managers spent a great deal of time teaching students about the operation of the classroom, including their expectations for behavior, routines, and rules. Furthermore, effective managers described the operation of the classroom, modeled correct procedures, answered questions, and had students practice and get feedback regarding procedures, rules, and consequences (Evertson & Emmer, 1982).

Comparable studies conducted in junior high schools revealed similar findings (Evertson & Emmer, 1982). In another series of studies, Evertson, Emmer, and colleagues trained teachers in these classroom management techniques (Evertson, 1989; Evertson et al., 1983). The studies clearly showed that teachers could learn these techniques and apply them in their classrooms. When the teachers correctly applied the techniques they had been taught, disruption in their classrooms decreased and rates of academic engagement increased.

In well-managed classrooms teachers have clear ideas of what types of classroom conditions and student behaviors a healthy learning environment requires (Evertson et al., 2003). Moreover, they work to establish and maintain these conditions. In this section we will examine specific strategies for maintaining such an environment.

Designing the Physical Environment Arranging the physical environment is a logical starting point for developing classroom structure because all teachers face this task before the school year begins (Evertson et al., 2003). Physical arrangement involves such items as furniture (e.g., teacher and student desks, bookcases, tables), computers, bulletin boards, overhead projectors, and personal objects that teachers may want in their classrooms (e.g., aquariums, plants). According to Paine et al. (1983), an appropriate classroom physical arrangement facilitates student performance in three important areas. First, careful arrangement of the classroom can decrease student noise and disruption. Moreover, when student disruptions are decreased, on-task behavior and academic achievement often increase. Second, proper organization of classroom space can improve the level and quality of student interactions. For example, often students with EBD spend time talking to other students when they should be working, especially when they are supposed to be involved in independent activities. An appropriate seating arrangement can decrease the amount of inappropriate student interactions and, thus, increase task engagement levels. Third, an efficient classroom physical environment can increase the amount of time that students are engaged in their academic tasks. When teachers are in close proximity to students they can ensure that students are doing what they are supposed to be doing.

The basic rules regarding the physical setup of the classroom are that the room should be arranged to (a) permit orderly movement, (b) keep distractions to a minimum, (c) make efficient use of available space, and (d) structure classroom space so that students can attend

to the teacher (Colvin & Lazar, 1997; Evertson et al., 2003; Paine et al., 1983). Efficient physical arrangements require that teachers carefully plan and attend to these elements.

According to Evertson and colleagues (2003) there are four keys to making decisions about classroom arrangement. First, high-traffic areas should be kept free of congestion. This is because areas that are used frequently, such as the pencil sharpener, water fountain, and computer stations, can become sites for distractions and disruptions. These areas should be widely separated from each other, have sufficient space, and be easy for students and the teacher to see and get to. Procedures should also be developed to regulate their use. Second, a teacher must be able to see all students at all times. Because monitoring of student behavior is an important task, clear lines of sight between instructional areas, the teacher's and students' desks, and student work areas must be maintained. Evertson and Harris (1992) suggest that when arranging their classrooms, teachers stand in different parts of the room and check for blind spots. Third, materials that are frequently used by teachers and students should be readily accessible. When such materials are accessible, neither teacher nor students will spend much time getting or returning the materials. This will help keep lessons flowing smoothly because breaks or slowdowns in lessons will be avoided with materials readily at hand. Additionally, if a teacher has to break a lesson to look for materials, students' attention may be lost and it is more likely that disruptions will occur. Fourth, the students' seating arrangement should allow them to see presentations without moving their desks or craning their necks. If students can see what is going on in the classroom it is more likely that they will be involved in the lesson.

Colvin and Lazar (1997) and Walker and colleagues (1995) suggested that prior to organizing the physical environment, a teacher should identify all functions and activities that will take place during the day and carefully arrange the room to accomplish these functions. They suggest the following functions and corresponding arrangements: (a) an independent work area consisting of individual student desks in low-traffic sections and away from materials, time-out areas, and free activity areas; (b) a small-group work area that minimizes distractions and where students can attend to each other and other students; (c) a free time or choice activity area in a quiet location for students who finish their work early or earn reinforcement; (d) a time-out or penalty area that isolates misbehaving students in a corner or the back of the classroom; (e) a quiet time area that can be used to calm an agitated student; and (f) the teacher's desk, which should be located in a very low-traffic area and out of the way so it receives as little use as possible during instruction. An appropriate placement for a teacher's desk is in a front corner of the room facing the students (Paine et al., 1983). If a paraprofessional is in the room, his or her desk could be placed in a back corner opposite the teacher's desk.

Walker et al. (1995) also suggested arranging the classroom with a notice board announcing activities, projects, and recognitions, placed in a highly visible area, and storage areas located in low-traffic areas to ensure easy access and avoid distractions. If a teacher uses different areas for various activities (e.g., free choice area, time-out area, computer area), he or she should identify the boundaries for each of these activity areas. Teachers may use bookcases and file cabinets to identify these boundaries.

Setting Up Classroom Seating Arrangements The seating arrangement in the classroom is another important element of the physical environment. Perhaps the most important consideration in arranging student seating is that keeping all students in the teacher's sight maximizes supervision. Furthermore, the teacher should be in close proximity to the students. Students have higher on-task rates and engage in less disruptive behavior when the teacher is physically closer to them (Morgan & Jenson, 1988; Savage, 1999).

A number of researchers have reported that the closer a teacher is in relation to his or her students, often referred to as proximity control, (a) the greater the control of a teacher's interactions with his or her students, (b) the higher the rates of academic engagement, and (c) the lower the rates of student disruption (Brown, Bryson-Brockman, & Fox, 1986; Gunter, Shores, Jack, Rasmussen, & Flowers, 1995; Hendrickson, Gable, & Shores, 1987; Shores, Gunter, et al., 1993). Additionally, Etsheidt, Stainback, and Stainback (1984) reported that for proximity control to be most effective, the teacher must be within about 3 feet of a student. The empirical research, therefore, shows that teachers should circulate around their rooms and make frequent individual contacts with their students.

Rhode and colleagues (1992) contended that students who tend to be off task and disruptive should be placed nearest the teacher because the teacher can more easily monitor these students and can immediately and easily reinforce them for appropriate behavior. The authors also warned against placing potentially disruptive students close to each other, and suggest the potentially troublesome students should be seated next to students who tend to behave appropriately.

When determining student seating, teachers should adopt a flexible approach to seating arrangements to accommodate the various learning activities that occur in the classroom (Levin & Nolan, 2004). For example, if the teacher frequently uses lecture or demonstration followed by independent practice, rows of desks facing toward the teacher and separated by aisles may be appropriate. Student desks should not face sources of distraction (e.g., windows). There should be enough room around each desk so that the teacher can circulate and work individually with students. In such arrangements, students can see and hear the presentation, independent seat work is facilitated, and teachers can easily monitor students. Moreover, the teacher can move freely around the class, thereby allowing him or her to monitor student behavior.

When teachers set up their classroom in the traditional row style for lectures, presentations, and demonstrations, they may find that this arrangement is less appropriate for small-group work. Teachers may want to use small tables for these activities. When a teacher is teaching in a small-group area, he or she should always face the rest of the class.

Teachers may also want to consider an important element that Savage (1999) refers to as the "action zone" for determining classroom seating arrangements. The action zone consists of the student desks across the front of the classroom and down the center of the room (Adams & Biddle, 1970). According to Savage, students seated in this zone have higher on-task rates, receive more feedback, and have higher achievement. Although the action zone concept may be of less importance in a resource room or self-contained setting with fewer students, general education teachers with larger numbers of students in their classes should consider placing students with academic and behavioral difficulties in the action zone.

Careful attention to the physical arrangement of the learning environment can make the classroom far easier to manage and may result in improved educational outcomes (Walker et al., 1995).

Summary of Classroom Structure The ways in which teachers organize their classrooms will help ensure that teaching and learning are enhanced and problem behaviors are minimized. In well-organized classrooms, teachers work to develop a structure that is predictable and a physical environment that is conducive to learning. Figure 11–4 is a checklist that will assist a teacher when considering the important elements of classroom structure.

FIGURE 11-4

Classroom structure checklist

Yes	No	Attribute
☐	☐	The teacher ensures that classroom events are as predictable as possible.
☐	☐	The teacher plans the structure of his or her classroom prior to the start of the school year (e.g., procedures, physical environment, rules, consequences).
☐	☐	The classroom is designed to permit orderly movement and keep high-traffic areas free of congestion.
☐	☐	The classroom is designed to minimize potential distractions.
☐	☐	All students can see the teacher.
☐	☐	The teacher can see all the students at all times.
☐	☐	Frequently used materials are readily accessible.
☐	☐	The teacher circulates around the room and makes frequent checks on students' progress.
☐	☐	The teacher is always in close proximity to the students.
☐	☐	The teacher maintains a pleasant but businesslike classroom atmosphere.

Effective Teaching

The fourth component of a proactive classroom management system is effective teaching. We know that effective classroom management and effective instruction are inextricably intertwined (Brophy, 1988; Curwin & Mendler, 1998; Emmer, Evertson, & Worsham, 2003; Evertson et al., 2003; Good & Brophy, 2008; Kauffman et al., 2002; Kounin, 1970; Wolery et al., 1988). Teachers who do not possess good classroom management skills are highly unlikely to use effective instructional practices that lead to high student achievement. Similarly, for effective teaching to occur, a classroom must be well managed. Moreover, research findings indicate that teachers who approach classroom management as a process of establishing and maintaining effective learning environments are more successful classroom managers than those who place more emphasis on their roles as authority figures and disciplinarians (Brophy, 1988). In his definition of classroom management, Brophy (1988) emphasized the importance of effective teaching.

Good classroom management implies not only that the teacher has elicited the cooperation of the students in minimizing misconduct and can intervene effectively when misconduct occurs, but also that worthwhile academic activities are occurring more or less continuously and that the classroom management system as a whole (which includes, but is not limited to the teacher's disciplinary interventions) is designed to maximize student engagement in those activities, not merely to minimize misconduct. (p. 3)

An essential component of effective classroom management, therefore, is the use of well-planned and motivating instructional strategies.

In Chapter 14, we examine the knowledge base regarding effective teaching. The principles in that chapter are extremely important ways to increase student achievement and decrease student off-task and disruptive behavior. Although I will not provide an in-depth discussion of these principles here, there are two areas that we will consider that have a profound effect on a teacher's success in classroom management (a) time management, and (b) lesson management.

Managing Classroom Time A proactive variable that is under teacher control, and is critical to academic achievement and appropriate classroom behavior, is the amount of time daily in which students are involved in academic tasks (Good & Brophy, 2008; Rhode et al., 1992; Savage, 1999). According to Good and Brophy (2008), student achievement is directly related to the amount of time students spend actively engaged in academic tasks. In fact,

Berliner and Biddle (1995) asserted that the "opportunity to learn is the single most important predictor of student achievement" (p. 55). Time management is also an important variable in preventing student misbehavior. This is because when students are not kept engaged and active, they are much more likely to become involved in disruptive behavior. Effective time management, therefore, is a key element in enhancing student achievement and minimizing student problem behavior. The following sections present aspects of time management that are particularly important in preventing student problem behavior.

Simply put, when students are actively involved in interesting and challenging activities, there is less time available for them to misbehave. When students have nothing to do, or they are engaged in boring activities, misbehavior becomes more likely. Increasing the amount of time that students are actively engaged, therefore, is an important part of managerial success. Four important ways in which teachers can ensure higher levels of student engagement are (a) planning learning activities that are at the correct level of difficulty, (b) providing clear directions prior to beginning activities, (c) monitoring student attention during lessons, and (d) holding students accountable for learning.

Determining the Correct Level of Difficulty. All instruction should be at the correct level of difficulty for students. When teachers plan instructional activities they should ensure that their lessons (a) will lead to student learning, and (b) will maintain student involvement (Evertson et al., 2003). Instructional content that is too easy for a student will not lead to student learning, nor will it keep students involved. Acting out and misbehavior become more likely when students become bored because their classroom work is too easy for them. Similarly, work that is too difficult will result in frustration, which, in turn may lead to acting out by students who are attempting to escape the task. Moreover, if the instruction is at too difficult a level for students, they will not learn. Chapter 4 on assessment contains strategies for determining the correct level of difficulty.

Providing Clear Directions. Students should be given clear directions prior to beginning an instructional activity. Unclear or poor teacher directions are a major contributor to loss of time in schools (Savage, 1999). When students do not understand directions, they may (a) need clarification, in which case the teacher has to stop the task to repeat the directions; (b) perform the task incorrectly; or (c) become frustrated and stop paying attention or act out. It is very important, therefore, that directions are clear and explicit.

Teachers should also give clear directions to students about what they should do if they finish their work before other students. When students complete their assignments and have to wait for others to finish they may become bored. Teachers have a number of options in such situations: They can instruct the student to read a book, complete unfinished work, or go to a free time area. Whatever a teacher chooses to do, he or she should have a routine developed to address this issue, and students should know what to do. When a teacher finds that many students are completing their work early, the assignments may be too easy or too much time may be assigned for the activity.

Monitoring Student Attention. Teachers should monitor student attention during lessons. Students are more likely to maintain attention if they know that their teacher watches students to see if they are attending or are having difficulty with learning activities (Good & Brophy, 2008). When teachers monitor student attention they can respond quickly when potential problems arise and they can attend to students who are having difficulty with the lesson. To ensure effective monitoring of student attention, teachers should scan and move around their classrooms. Additionally, when students are engaged in independent work, teachers should make brief contact with every student within the first few minutes of the lesson. The purpose is to monitor students' attention and to ensure that they are working. Teachers should limit contacts to making brief positive comments to students who are accurate in their work, and giving prompts and brief corrective feedback to students who are unsure of their work or are completing problems incorrectly. If the teacher notes that a student is having difficulty, the teacher can return to that student once he or she has made brief contacts with all of the students.

Holding Students Accountable. Students are more likely to remain engaged in learning activities when they know that they may be held accountable for attending to the lesson. Kounin (1970) found that teachers who had maintained high levels of student attention and involvement throughout the lesson were more successful classroom managers because their classes were characterized by high rates of student involvement and low rates of problem behavior. Effective managers accomplished this by involving all students in a learning task. One procedure that teachers can use to maintain student attention is group alerting (Kounin, 1970). When using this procedure, teachers alert students that someone will be called on to answer a question or perform a skill, and that it may be anyone in the class. Thus, the teacher keeps the students "on their toes" (Kounin, 1970, p. 117) through techniques such as asking a question and then calling on a student to answer and calling on students in a random rather than obvious manner (e.g., going down rows of the class). Teachers can maintain students' focus on a task by (a) asking questions of students, (b) requesting that students paraphrase information given, (c) having students signify agreement or disagreement with a statement, or (d) asking students to perform a skill (e.g., work a problem on the board). If students never know when their teacher may require them to respond to questions or perform a task related to the learning activity, they are much more likely to attend and remain engaged. On the other hand, if students know that during a lesson there is little likelihood that they will be held accountable for what is being taught, their attention may wander and rates of academic engagement will decrease.

Savage (1999) suggested that teachers always stay alert for opportunities to involve students and never expect students to sit passively during an activity. It is the teacher's responsibility, therefore, to work to maintain high rates of student engagement. By using time wisely and keeping students involved in classroom activities, teachers will keep rates of student engagement high and instances of student misbehavior low. To accomplish this, teachers need to plan their lessons well and do all they can to ensure high rates of academic engagement. Gunter, Hummel, and Venn (1998) developed a direct observation tool that teachers could easily use to collect data on their students' on-task time.

Managing Classroom Lessons Well-planned, interesting, and well-executed lessons not only keep students motivated and increase academic achievement, but they also prevent misbehavior (Evertson et al., 2003; Good & Brophy, 2008; Kounin, 1970; Levin & Nolan, 2004; Savage, 1999; Rutherford et al., 1996). In his seminal research, Kounin (1970) found that successful managers developed and implemented more effective lessons than did their counterparts who were less successful at classroom management. Kounin called these lesson design elements lesson movement and smoothness. He also noted that effective managers provided variety and programming to avoid satiation. In the following section, I will review some of Kounin's instructional management findings.

Maintaining Lesson Momentum and Smoothness. According to Kounin (1970), effective classroom managers keep their students engaged in their lessons by (a) starting their lesson quickly, (b) keeping the lesson moving along without interruptions, (c) bringing the lesson to a satisfactory end, and (d) transitioning to other activities efficiently and seamlessly. When teachers plan carefully to avoid slowing the momentum of a lesson

and, thus, maintain good lesson momentum, students are more likely to stay on task.

Additionally, teachers should plan their lessons to ensure that lessons are conducted at a brisk and smooth pace. That is, there should be a minimum of interruptions or abrupt changes during a lesson. This means that the teacher must stay with the lesson plan and avoid digressions that break the smoothness of the lesson.

Kounin (1970) also found that ineffective classroom managers frequently interrupted lesson momentum and smoothness by slowing down the lesson. Teacher interruptions of lessons may lead to problem behavior. Teachers need to be careful, therefore, to avoid any such interruptions. Table 11-2 lists and describes some teacher actions that Kounin found can negatively affect lesson momentum and smoothness and may lead to increases in off-task and problem behavior.

To ensure that teachers maintain lesson momentum and smoothness it is important that teachers are thoroughly prepared before teaching a lesson. Although this can be time-consuming, thorough preparation will pay off in higher rates of student learning and lower rates of disruptive behavior. In fact, a certain way to promote disruption is to be unprepared for a lesson or activity because it is far less likely that teachers will keep students engaged in meaningful activities (Rosenberg et al., 2002). To ensure that students are engaged in learning, teachers should have thoroughly planned and organized lessons and activities.

Providing Variety and Programming to Avoid Satiation. Effective managers have well-planned and interesting lessons in which a variety of activities are used to maintain students' interest. Kounin (1970) found that interesting lessons attract and hold students' attention, which results in more on-task behavior. On the other hand, if teachers tend to have students do the same thing over and over again, their students will become satiated. Satiation leads to decreased work quality and increased off-task and problem behavior.

It is important, therefore, for teachers to include a variety of interesting and challenging activities in each lesson. According to Savage (1999), a good rule of thumb is not to have students do any single activity for over 15 minutes. That means if a teacher has a 45-minute reading lesson, he or she may want to involve students in at least three different activities during the lesson (e.g., oral reading, skills practice, question answering, discussion, writing). If teachers have students do the same task over and over again (e.g., worksheets), they will become bored, which may lead to decreased work quality and increased errors, as well as off-task and problem behavior.

Table 11–2 Kounin's findings on teacher behaviors that negatively affect lesson momentum and smoothness.

General Behavior	Specific Behavior	Effects
Jerkiness		The teacher abruptly stops or interrupts the flow and pace of a lesson or activity.
	Dangles	The teacher suddenly stops an activity and leaves it hanging for an extended period of time.
	Truncations	The teacher abruptly stops an activity before it is finished and moves on to another activity.
	Flipflop	The teacher terminates an activity, begins a new activity, and then abruptly returns to the first activity.
	Stimulus Boundedness	The teacher has problems staying focused on the task at hand because he or she is distracted by something (e.g., storm outside, trash on the floor).
Slowdown		Teacher actions slow an activity down and result in students' attention wandering from the lesson or activity.
Overdwelling		The teacher goes on and on about a student's or all the students' behavior
Fragmentation		The teacher breaks down a lesson or activity into too many parts.

Summary of Effective Teaching Effective classroom management and effective instruction are inextricably intertwined. Thus, teachers who approach classroom management as a process of establishing and maintaining effective learning environments are more likely to be successful classroom managers. Effective classroom managers plan academic activities that are worthwhile, interesting, and motivating to students. Academic lessons and work must also be at the correct level of difficulty and should consist of various activities. Moreover, effective teachers monitor students' attention and hold them accountable for learning. Figure 11–5 is a checklist that will assist a teacher when considering the important elements of effective teaching.

DEVELOPING AND IMPLEMENTING A PROACTIVE CLASSROOM MANAGEMENT SYSTEM

Proactive classroom management systems do not just happen. Rather, teachers must spend a considerable amount of time organizing their classrooms in a positive and proactive manner. Teachers who organize their classrooms to prevent student misbehavior and then address student misbehavior quickly and effectively when it does occur will find that students learn more and misbehave less. Moreover, teaching becomes less trying and more personally satisfying when student problem behaviors are minimized and student engagement in worthwhile learning activities is maximized. In the following section,

I examine guidelines that teachers may follow when organizing their classrooms.

Step 1: Develop Classroom Procedures and Teach Them to Students

Classroom procedures are ways in which teachers may accomplish daily classroom routines and specific activities that recur frequently in classrooms (Emmer et al., 1982). Procedures are routines that are done at particular times or during particular activities and are directed at accomplishing something (Levin & Nolan, 2004). Thus, routines are established for *how* things will be done (Rutherford et al., 1996). In a well-managed classroom, teachers have taught their students how to adhere to the classroom routines.

Teachers need to consider what types of activities will be a part of the students' daily classroom life, and determine what methods are appropriate for implementing these activities when planning classroom procedures. Procedures are an integral part of classrooms because they address the behaviors that are necessary for smooth operation of the classroom (Levin & Nolan, 2004). When students are aware of and follow classroom procedures with minimum assistance from their teacher, on-task student behavior and engagement is maximized because students do not have to ask for directions and teachers do not have to give instructions for everyday activities. In other words, in a poorly managed classroom, much time is lost in handling routine chores (Savage, 1999). Thus,

FIGURE 11–5

Effective teaching checklist

Yes	No	Attribute
☐	☐	The teacher maximizes the amount of time that his or her students are actively engaged in learning activities.
☐	☐	The teacher plans interesting, varied, and challenging learning activities.
☐	☐	The teacher plans instruction at the correct level of difficulty.
☐	☐	The teacher monitors student attention and responds quickly when students need attention.
☐	☐	The teacher makes brief contacts with all of his or her students at the start of independent activities.
☐	☐	The teacher uses proximity control effectively.
☐	☐	The teacher can see all the students at all times.
☐	☐	The teacher holds his or her students accountable by asking questions, having students perform skills, etc.
☐	☐	The teacher's lessons proceed at a brisk and smooth pace without interruptions.
☐	☐	The teacher plans smooth transitions between lessons and activities.

procedures are extremely important components of efficient and effective classroom management systems.

Establishing Classroom Routines   There are a number of steps that teachers should follow when establishing classroom routines (Colvin & Lazar, 1997; Emmer et al., 2003; Evertson et al., 2003; Savage, 1999). First, teachers should identify those recurring and predictable events that occur every day. A teacher, therefore, must anticipate these routine events and then establish procedures for managing them. These events can be related to nonacademic activities (e.g., lining up to exit the classroom to another activity, sharpening pencils, transitioning from one activity to another); academic activities and lessons (e.g., asking for teacher assistance, beginning independent work, distributing materials); or interactions with and between students (e.g., contributing to class discussions, getting the attention of the class). The second important procedure when developing and implementing routines is to teach them to the students. When students are well aware of the classroom routines they will be able to follow them without wasting classroom time. Routines, like academic subjects, should be taught directly to students using

presentation, modeling, practice, feedback, and reinforcement (Darch et al., 1998; Evertson et al., 2003; Kamps, 2002; Savage, 1999). Rutherford and colleagues (1996) suggest making cue cards that list the steps to be followed in accomplishing routines, which can be used to help students learn these tasks. Third, because students may forget a particular routine or not perform it correctly, there may be a need for occasionally reteaching the routine. In summary, teachers should plan routines for recurring events, teach the routine to the class, require compliance, and monitor students as they perform the routines. Teachers who take such actions early in the school year can expect that their classroom management systems will run much more smoothly and efficiently. Figure 11–6 is a checklist of routines that teachers should consider when structuring their classrooms.

Three routines that are particularly important when teaching students with EBD are routines for (a) beginning a class period or the school day, (b) keeping students who have completed an assignment occupied while other students are still working, and (c) planning for transition times. These routines assist students to stay on target (Rutherford et al., 1996).

FIGURE 11–6

Developing routines checklist

Completed	Area	Routine
	General Procedures	
❑	Entering the classroom	
❑	Beginning the school day	
❑	Getting to work immediately	
❑	Daily schedule	
❑	Taking attendance and lunch tallies	
❑	Making announcements	
❑	Tardiness	
❑	Coming to class without materials	
❑	Hall passes	
❑	Movement in the classroom	
❑	Interruptions or delays	
❑	Leaving the classroom	
❑	Going to lunch	
❑	Bathroom breaks	
❑	Getting a drink	
❑	Recess	
❑	Fire and emergency drills	
❑	Assemblies and field trips	
❑	Distributing materials	
❑	Transitions between activities	
❑	Moving into small groups	
❑	Moving from one center to another	
❑	Getting materials, equipment, and supplies	
❑	Organizing and managing assignments	
❑	Using materials, equipment, and supplies	
❑	Assigning homework	
❑	Collecting homework	
❑	Speaking in class	
❑	Signaling for student attention	
❑	Quieting the class	
❑	Cleanup	
❑	End of class or end of period dismissal	
	Room Use	
❑	Teacher's desk and storage	
❑	Student desks and storage	
❑	Using computers	
❑	Books and materials storage	
❑	Small-group area	

FIGURE 11-6

Completed	Area	Routine
☐	Large-group area	
☐	Traffic patterns	
	Presentations and Student Work	
☐	Attention during presentations	
☐	Student participation	
☐	Working independently	
☐	Requesting help	
☐	Working in groups	
☐	Asking for help	
☐	Early finishers	
☐	Student behavior when seat work is done	
☐	Obtaining directions for assignments	
☐	Expected student behavior	
☐	Distributing materials and supplies	
☐	Collecting assignments and homework	
☐	Participating in discussions	
☐	Getting class attention	
☐	Quieting the class	
☐	Procedures following an absence	

Beginning the School Day Routines should be established and followed from the beginning of class when students first enter a teacher's room. Students must be engaged quickly and not allowed to mill about. Whenever students are allowed to wander, it is much more likely that misbehavior will occur. Moreover, if a teacher waits until the day or period starts before getting students in their seats and settled down, instructional time will be lost. A suggestion for beginning the day or class period is to have an opening activity waiting for students when they enter the room. For example, review questions for students to answer before the opening bell may be written on the board or a worksheet could be placed on students' desks. Opening activities do not have to be of an academic nature; they could consist of fun activities such as puzzles, riddles, or mazes.

Students should be taught the following routine: (a) enter the room, (b) go to their desk, and (c) begin working on the activity. Thus, students are engaged immediately and there is less opportunity for socialization, disruption, and loss of instructional time. Additionally, students could be taught to do administrative routines that often occur at the beginning of the day (e.g., recording attendance, counting students, taking lunch, sharpening pencils). If students perform these tasks, the teacher is free to monitor activities, get materials ready, and start the lesson. Moreover, the opening activity serves to focus students on educational activities and away from distractions or disruptions.

Keeping Early Finishers Busy Routines should also be established for times when students complete assignments early. When students have nothing to do, misbehavior and disruptions are more likely to occur. Rhode et al., (1992) referred to periods when students have nothing to do as downtime. Teachers must always strive to minimize downtime. Having materials ready for students who finish their work early will help accomplish this. Teachers can also have early finishers read a book or go quietly to a free time area after their work has been checked.

Planning Transition Times Transitions between lessons, classes, or activities, if not managed effectively, are opportunities for students to become disengaged from instructional activities and for disruptive behavior to occur (Good & Brophy, 2008). Additionally, once students become disengaged, it often takes time to get them reengaged. Teachers can minimize wasted time during transitions and lessen the likelihood of disruptive behavior if they develop routines to make transitions run smoothly. Managing routines, however, requires that teachers thoughtfully plan transitions in advance and constantly monitor students during transitions. There are three things that teachers can do to ensure that transitions are accomplished quickly and with a minimum of dead time occurring during the transition.

First, plan for the transition. This means that the steps of the transition process should be outlined and explained to the students. Additionally, students should practice the transition and be reinforced for following the procedures quickly and efficiently.

For example, a particularly difficult transition time occurs when students return from lunch. Often they enter the classroom individually and mill about until the next class begins. A good practice is to have a predetermined activity for the students to engage in immediately on returning from lunch. Before leaving for lunch, the teacher can provide instructions regarding the activity they will begin on return from lunch and have them prepare for that activity before leaving. "When we return from lunch we will begin our science lesson. Please put your science book and notebook on top of your desk and when you return from lunch open your books to page 27 and raise your hand. I will be looking for who is ready as soon as I walk into the room." When the teacher enters the room after lunch, he or she would immediately scan the room for students who have followed directions, and reinforce their appropriate behavior. "I see that Eric, Alex, and Nick have their books open to page 24. Excellent following directions!" This practice will be even more successful if the activity is the same every day—allowing for a consistent routine to be established. For example, every day after returning from lunch students could have 10 minutes to complete an activity such as writing in their journal, copying homework, or working with a partner. The teacher would follow a similar procedure as described, but the students would know that the same activity follows lunch most days. The important factor is to minimize unstructured time and prepare children in advance for completing transitions successfully.

Second, the teacher should have all materials ready before a lesson begins. When students transition from one activity to another, the teacher should have the materials for the second activity ready so he or she does not have to spend time locating them. Instead of having students wait, therefore, the teacher or students distribute materials to the class immediately after the first activity finishes. Implementing routines to assist with transitions is an extremely important part of classroom management.

Third, establishing routines that students know and follow makes for a more efficient classroom. Less instructional time is wasted and the opportunity for disruption is decreased. Moreover the amount of dead time—that is, the times when students are waiting for a change of activity and have nothing to do—is minimized. Management problems are often the result of students being idle, bored, or distracted (Good & Brophy, 2008). By developing and teaching classroom rules and procedures, teachers can minimize delays, downtime, and distractions, thus preventing problem behaviors.

Step 2: Develop Classroom Rules and Teach Them to Students

Classroom rules define the expectations for appropriate classroom conduct. They set the foundation for expected behavior in a classroom. Clearly stated rules describe what is and is not acceptable in the classroom. Rules provide students with guidelines for appropriate classroom behavior that, if followed, allow teaching and learning to take place in an efficient manner (Walker et al., 1995; White et al., 2004). Thus, rules are an extremely important part of a well-managed classroom.

According to Rademacher, Callahan, and Pederson-Seelye (1998), teachers should have procedures for planning and teaching classroom rules and for evaluating the effectiveness of the rules. Teachers should adhere to the following four guidelines when developing rules.

First, teachers should determine what student behaviors are most important for ensuring an environment conducive to learning. Due to the importance of rules in the overall functioning of the classroom, it is important that when teachers develop their classroom rules they should be mindful of their beliefs and values. Additionally, teachers should develop rules that are congruent with their values and belief system because then they are more apt to be able to be consistent with those rules.

Second, teachers should, individually or in conjunction with their students, develop a short list of rules that are fair, observable, and realistic. Moreover, students must understand that these rules are necessary for an appropriate classroom environment in which the teachers can teach, students can learn, and safety, property, and order

FIGURE 11-7

Examples of classroom rules

✔ Follow the teacher's directions (compliance rule).

✔ Have materials ready before class (procedure rule).

✔ When class ends, put away materials in 3 minutes (transition rule).

✔ Raise your hand for permission to talk (behavior rule).

✔ Keep hands, feet, and objects to self (behavior rule).

✔ Be in your seat when the bell rings (behavior rule).

✔ Be in class on time (procedure rule).

✔ Take care of your classroom (procedure rule).

✔ Hand in assignments on time (procedure rule).

✔ Listen quietly when others are talking (behavior rule).

FIGURE 11-8

A generic approach to teaching classroom rules, procedures, or consequences

1. Define the rules, procedures, or consequences.
2. Explain the purpose of the rules, procedures, or consequences.
3. Specify the expected behaviors.
4. Demonstrate the rules, procedures, or consequences.
5. Practice the rules, procedures, or consequences.
6. Post the rules, procedures, or consequences.
7. Monitor student performance.
8. Review the rules, procedures, or consequences.

are ensured. Figure 11-7 depicts examples of common classroom rules.

Third, rules should be written objectively so that compliance with them can be measured (Kamps, 2002). If rules are ambiguous students may be unsure if they are following them and teachers may be unsure when they are broken. Uncertainty or ambiguity will lead to problem behavior. Moreover, if a student is disciplined for breaking a rule that is so ambiguous that the student is unclear if it was broken, an argument or power struggle may ensue.

Fourth, rules should be taught, practiced, and posted. This will make it more likely that students will understand and remember the rules. The common assumption that posting the rules and reading them on the first day of school is sufficient is not only false, but can set the stage for uncertainty and lack of clarity about expected behaviors. Just as in academic instruction, a teacher would not hold a child responsible for content if he or she had not provided instruction. Such is the case with teaching rules and procedures. Direct instruction of classroom rules is one of the most important tasks a teacher needs to accomplish during the first few days and weeks of school. Students should have opportunities to discuss the rules, have examples of appropriate and inappropriate adherence to the rules, and have opportunities to practice following the rules. Figure 11-8 shows a general approach to teaching classroom rules, procedures, or consequences. Although each year should begin with time dedicated to teaching the rules, an effective teacher should use his or her professional judgment to determine the extent of time needed to teach rules. Effective teachers also realize that reviewing the rules is a process that continues throughout the year.

The rules should be posted in a prominent place within the classroom. The posting serves as a constant reminder of the rules to students. Moreover, posting allows other staff, substitute teachers, and visitors to see what is expected of students (Martella et al., 2003).

It is important to keep in mind that the end goal is not that students know the rules, but that they follow them (Paine, Radicchi, Rosellini, Deutchman, & Darch, 1983). It is extremely important, therefore, to monitor student adherence to the classroom rules. If teachers do not monitor rules, they will be less meaningful to students and it is likely that they will be violated more frequently. If students are consistently having difficulty following classroom rules, teachers should check to see if the rules are clearly understood by the students. Furthermore, teachers should also monitor their own consistency in applying and reinforcing the rules.

Step 3: Monitor and Acknowledge Correct Performance of Expected Behaviors

Teachers must closely monitor student behavior in their classrooms and provide acknowledgments and reinforcers when students exhibit appropriate behaviors. Acknowledgments may include social, token, or tangible reinforcers (see Chapter 9 for elaborations on the types of reinforcers). The goal of the acknowledgment system is to create a positive classroom climate where students know that appropriate behavior is valued and appreciated, and where students have high rates of positive contacts with adults (Sugai & Horner, 2002).

Just as students need to know what is expected of them in the classroom, they also need to know what the

FIGURE 11-9

Examples of Reinforcers

Extra free time

Lunch with a friend or teacher

Sitting by a friend

Playing a computer or video game

Pencils or pens

Puzzles and tricks

Use PE equipment

Drinking pop

Increased recess time

More reading time

Time with an adult

Playing games

Novelty items

Watching a Movie

Talking with a friend

Caring for class pets

Assisting the custodian

Going to the media center

No homework card

Art activities

Listening to music

Popcorn party

Helping the teacher

Computer time

Running an errand

Choosing a class activity

Marbles

Stickers

Positive home note

Eating a snack

Going to gym

negative consequences, especially with children who exhibit challenging behaviors. It is important to note that positive consequences or reinforcers should be something of value to the student, and not something the teacher thinks a student values. Figure 11–9 lists examples of reinforcers that teachers can use.

Teacher should deliver positive consequences frequently, consistently, and promptly after the behavior occurs. Moreover, teachers should vary the positive consequences or reinforcers used and always pair tangible reinforcers (if used) with social reinforcers such as verbal praise.

Step 4: Develop Clear and Consistent Procedures for Discouraging Problem Behavior

When classroom rules are developed, teachers must also develop a system of negative consequences to discourage inappropriate behaviors. The use of consequences can be as important as the implementation of a system of classroom rules.

Consequences refer to actions teachers take to reinforce rule-following behavior and punish rule-breaking behavior. Implementing clear and consistent consequences when students follow rules and when they break them is an important way to help them understand the association of behavior and consequences. Rules and consequences are a very important part of the overall classroom management strategy because they define the relationship between student behavior and consequences. Moreover, rules and consequences guide and direct both teacher and student behavior (Morgan & Jenson, 1988; White et al., 2004). In fact, Savage (1999) contends that teachers who complain that their students are constantly testing their authority often do not have a clear set of classroom rules or enforce them consistently.

Negative or reductive consequences should be implemented when students break classroom rules. The types of negative consequences that teachers use and the way in which the consequences are delivered can determine whether certain students will follow the classroom rules and whether they respect the teacher (Levin & Nolan, 2004). Colvin and Lazar (1997) noted that whereas positive consequences should be a teacher's primary response toward student behavior, negative consequences play an important role in effective classroom management. Negative consequences are procedures that teachers use to stop or suppress an inappropriate behavior (Morgan & Jenson, 1988; Rhode et al., 1992). When students choose to break classroom rules, teachers must have consequences

consequences are for following the class rules. This means that when a student follows classroom rules or procedures, teachers should deliver positive consequences to reinforce that behavior. When positive consequences or reinforcers are given for appropriate behavior, these behaviors will increase. Additionally, students should receive more positive consequences than negative. Teacher should strive to deliver five positive consequences for every one negative consequence (Latham, 1992; Sugai & Horner, 2002). Teachers need to be aware of this ratio, as it is often easy to fall into a cycle of that they can use to stop that behavior. Rademacher and colleagues (1998) note that students are more likely to accept negative consequences when teachers consistently apply logical consequences without publicly criticizing them.

Whenever possible, negative consequences should be logically related to the misbehavior. For example, for a student who fights with another student at recess, a logical consequence may be that recess privileges are removed for a certain amount of time.

Teachers often have difficulty identifying negative consequences. The result is often that teachers attempt to come up with negative consequences shortly after a student misbehaves. Such approaches may lead to the inconsistent and irrational use of consequences that students perceive as unfair and unreasonable (Levin & Nolan, 2004). This may undermine the teacher's authority and effectiveness as a classroom manager, leading to more disruptive behavior and less teaching and learning. Thus, it is important that negative consequences, like rules, be planned in advance. When teachers know what consequences they will use prior to serious problem behavior, and they know how they will use these consequences, they will become more confident and competent when addressing problem behavior (Algozzine & White, 2002). Consequences, like rules, should be clear and specific and, whenever possible, be logically related to the rule infraction. Examples of consequences include response cost, time-out, loss of privileges, removal from activities, staying after class, detention, and referral to the office.

Teaching Consequences As is the case with teaching classroom rules, direct instruction of classroom consequences is one of the most important tasks a teacher needs to accomplish during the first few days and weeks of school. The teacher should first explain the consequences. Students should have opportunities to discuss the consequences, be given examples of the consequences, and when and how they will be administered. The consequences should be posted in a prominent place within the classroom to serve as a constant reminder. Moreover, posting allows other staff, substitute teachers, and visitors to see what is expected of students (Martella et al., 2003).

Administering Consequences It is also important that teachers deliver consequences in an appropriate manner. In other words, deliver the consequence privately, in a calm manner, and in such a way as to preserve the student's dignity. Don't administer a consequence when you are angry, because the temptation is to use a consequence that is too severe for the behavior. Morgan and Jenson (1988) suggested that teachers use a preplanned

"What if?" chart in which they list the consequences on the right-hand side of the chart and how much or how long the consequence will be on the left-hand side. Also, consequences are listed in terms of severity. If teachers have preplanned their consequences in this way they will be less likely to deliver consequences that do not match the misbehavior in severity.

When administering a consequence it is very important that the teacher (a) remind the student of the rule being broken, (b) provide a warning that if the behavior does not stop the consequence will be administered, (c) state what the consequence will be in a matter-of-fact manner, (d) implement the consequence if the behavior does not stop, and (e) return to whatever he or she is doing (e.g., teaching a lesson). Canter and Canter (1992) suggest that, following administration of a consequence, teachers look for the first opportunity to recognize the student's positive behavior. Of course, it is crucial that consequences be delivered in a consistent manner.

Step 5: Collect Data on the Classroom Management System

If a teacher knows (a) where problem behavior is most likely to occur, (b) which students are most likely to misbehave, and (c) what problem behaviors are most likely to occur, he or she will be able to prevent problem behaviors from occurring by altering the classroom management system to address these issues. Teachers need to collect data to ensure that their classroom management system is working effectively. Scott, Payne, and Jolivette (2003) suggested that without the information from this data, teachers will have no reliable way of preventing problems and all efforts will be blind trials.

Teachers are unlikely to collect data, however, unless the data collection methods are easy to learn, easy to use, and don't take much time. Data collection systems that are too time-consuming or complex will often be abandoned because they become burdensome to teachers (Scott, Payne, et al., 2003). The challenge, therefore, is to develop efficient and effective data collection systems that will be used by teachers.

Scott, Payne, et al. (2003) suggested a three-part strategy to identify problems in a classroom management system. This process can lead directly to simple solutions to change a system to address the problems.

First, the teacher should involve the students in discussions regarding the types of problems they often experience in the classroom. Two advantages of this strategy are that (a) the perspective of students will be quite different from those of adults and may provide information that may not otherwise be available, and (b) the discussion with

FIGURE 11–10

Proactive classroom management checklist

Yes	No	Practice
☐	☐	The teacher directly teaches typical classroom procedures and routines.
☐	☐	The teacher directly teaches efficient transition routines.
☐	☐	The teacher directly teaches and posts classroom rules.
☐	☐	The teacher monitors student behavior and has a system for positively reinforcing students who follow classroom procedures, routines, and rules.
☐	☐	The teacher directly teaches and posts classroom consequences.
☐	☐	The teacher collects data on his or her classroom management system.

students will make it easier to provide a rationale for connecting changes in rules and routines to students' views.

Second, other adults (e.g., paraprofessionals, other teachers, parent volunteers) in the classroom can help determine predictability of problem behaviors in the classroom. When using this strategy the teacher first draws a map of the classroom setup, then the other adults are given stars to place on the map where problem behaviors occur. Additionally, stars should be placed on the map according to the students' input. By analyzing this classroom map, the teacher can determine where problem behaviors are most likely to occur.

Third, the teacher and paraprofessional (and other adults if possible) discuss when and why the problem behaviors occur. The teacher will then have information that he or she can use to improve the classroom management system. For example, if it was determined that problem behaviors frequently occur in a free reading area, it could be because student expectations are unclear, there are too many students in a small area, or

there is not enough supervision. Possible solutions could be to discuss expectations with the students, allow only a few students in the area at a time, or have the paraprofessional supervise the area when students are there. According to Scott and Hunter (2001), teachers should develop solutions that create the most logical link between where they are now and where they want to be. After the solution has been determined, the changes to the management system must be taught directly to the students using effective instructional processes (Scott, Payne, et al., 2003).

Summary of Setting Up a Classroom Management System Figure 11–10 is a checklist of important aspects to consider when setting up a proactive classroom management system. If these procedures, and others that we have discussed in this chapter, are considered when setting up a classroom management system, the teacher is much more likely to have an orderly, safe, and effective learning environment in his or her classroom.

Chapter Summary

Research clearly indicates that the key to effective classroom management is prevention. The attitudes and behaviors that teachers exhibit toward their students, the structure of their classroom (including procedures, rules, and consequences), and the effectiveness of their teaching all contribute positively to classroom environments. In such environments, academic engagement and

achievement are increased and disruptions are minimized. Teachers do not have to spend time correcting misbehavior that does not occur; therefore, there is more time available for teaching and learning. The second and third dimensions of classroom management—responding and intervening—are discussed in the next two chapters.

CHAPTER 12

Classroom and Behavior Management II: Responding to Problem Behavior

Mitchell L. Yell

Focus Questions

- Why do teachers need a systematic game plan for responding to problem behavior?
- What methods of responding to problem behavior are ineffective?
- What principles should teachers follow when they are responding to problem behavior?
- Should teachers respond differently to minor and serious problem behavior?
- What is noncompliance and how should teachers respond to it?
- What should a teacher do when faced with serious problem behavior?
- Why should teachers develop crisis management plans?
- How can teachers develop crisis management plans?

Preventive classroom management will help ensure that learning occurs and disruptions are minimized. Nonetheless, students will no doubt engage in problem behaviors and teachers must be prepared to respond effectively and efficiently to such behaviors (e.g., noncompliance, verbal abuse, physical aggression, property destruction, direct defiance, threats). The purpose of this chapter is to examine how teachers should respond to problem behavior in ways that will stop misbehavior before it gets out of control, and minimize threats to safety and classroom order.

First, I examine the nature of problem behavior, principles to follow in responding to problem behavior, and ineffective responding to problem behavior. Second, I discuss how teachers should respond to minor and major incidences of misbehavior. Third, I offer suggestions on developing crisis management plans and teaching students conflict resolution strategies.

THE NATURE OF PROBLEM BEHAVIOR

Students with EBD exhibit a wide variety of misbehaviors. Teachers are often exposed to a myriad of suggestions and advice in textbooks and workshops on how they should respond to particular incidences of student misbehavior (e.g., chewing gum, leaving their desk without permission, being off task, throwing objects, destroying property). Many of these suggestions may be useful; however, if teachers are to become skillful in responding to students' problem behavior, relying on a cookbook approach in which teachers attempt to match their response to particular forms of misbehavior will not suffice. Rather, teachers need a systematic game plan that they can consistently follow when responding to problem behavior. Thus, it is more useful for teachers to understand categories of misbehavior and how they may match their responses to these categories.

According to Evertson, Emmer, and Worsham (2006) there are four major categories of problem behavior: (a) nonproblems, which are problems that are brief and unnoticed by students (e.g., a student briefly looks out the classroom window while working on an assignment); (b) minor problems, which are violations of classroom rules or procedures but that do not disrupt classroom order or seriously interfere with learning (e.g., a student leaves his seat without permission); (c) major problems but limited in scope and effect, which are problem behaviors that disrupt classroom order and interfere with learning but whose occurrence is limited to one student or a few students who are not acting in concert (e.g., a student chronically disrupts the class); and (d) escalating or spreading problems, which are major problems that constitute a threat to classroom order and learning and that spread to other students in the class (e.g., a student hits another student and threatens the teacher when he or she tries to intervene). For this chapter, I will divide problem behaviors into two categories. The first category is minor behavior problems, which include Evertson et al.'s (2006) nonproblem and minor problem categories. The second category is major problems, which includes noncompliance and escalating or spreading problems, and verbal or physical aggression.

INEFFECTIVE RESPONDING TO PROBLEM BEHAVIOR

Unfortunately, when responding to problem behavior teachers sometimes resort to ineffective and obtrusive responses. At best, most of these procedures simply won't work; at worst, these procedures may escalate minor misbehavior to serious problem behavior. Moreover, the following procedures may positively reinforce students' misbehavior and may also cause a disruption in class activities.

Ignoring

Teachers may think that ignoring student misbehavior is an effective procedure for eliminating minor misbehavior. This is true if the teacher's attention is the sole source of reinforcement for the student's misbehavior. Unfortunately, this is rarely the case. The social attention provided by a student's peers for his or her misbehavior is much more likely than the teacher's attention to be the reinforcer for the student's misbehavior (Walker et al., 2004). In such a situation withholding teacher attention will not reduce the behavior. If, however, a teacher's attention is the sole reinforcement for a student's problem behavior, then ignoring can be an effective strategy. In such a situation, the teacher should (a) define the behavior to be ignored, (b) monitor the frequency of the behavior to determine if the ignoring is effective, and (c) use the ignoring strategy consistently each time the target behavior occurs (Darch & Kame'enui, 2004). Additionally, if the problem behavior meets the "nonproblem" criteria of Evertson et al. (2006) (i.e., the problem is brief and unnoticed by students), teachers may ignore the behavior.

A very serious problem with ignoring a student's obvious misbehavior is that the teacher inadvertently sends a message to the other students that he or she is not *withit* enough to notice the behavior, or that he or she chooses not to address the problem behavior. Moreover, Walker and colleagues (2004) noted that in many cases student misbehavior cannot be ignored for any length of time because of disruption to the school environment. Eventually the teacher will have to respond, which may provide intermittent reinforcement for the student, thus strengthening the very behavior that the teacher is attempting to ignore. Walker et al. (2004) also stated that if the student's misbehavior is maintained by negative reinforcement because it allows him or her to escape from task demands in the classroom, simply ignoring the student's problem behavior will be ineffective. Ignoring misbehavior also allows a student to continuing engaging in the misbehavior and hinders learning. For these reasons ignoring student misbehavior, especially in a special education classroom for students with EBD, will most likely not be an effective strategy.

Nattering

When it is clear that a student is misbehaving and the teacher wants to stop the misbehavior and quickly proceed with the normal classroom activities, it is ineffective to ask the student counterproductive or rhetorical questions such as "What is the matter with you?" "Why do you have to misbehave all the time?" and "How many times do I have to tell you to get busy?" (Good & Brophy, 2008). Such questions convey to the students that a teacher is not in control of the situation and may be interpreted by the misbehaving student as an attack or an attempt to humiliate, which may provoke a power struggle. Additionally, when teachers ask students why they are engaging in appropriate behavior, they are just asking for excuses.

Engaging in scolding in an effort to persuade a student to stop his or her misbehavior is an ineffective practice that Gerald Patterson (1982) called *nattering*. Nattering involves haphazard, ineffective, and irritating nagging or scolding that is repeated over and over. Additionally, there is often no consequence administered by the parson engaged in the nattering. In addition to being ineffective, nattering may also result in a student who exhibits problem behavior getting attention from the teacher and students, which may reinforce the inappropriate behavior. In fact, the student may learn that it is easier and usually more successful to obtain peer and teacher attention by engaging in problem behavior (Walker et al., 2004). Additionally, focusing on misbehavior and engaging in nattering often puts the teacher and student in conflict and may result in a power struggle.

In general, it is preferable to spend less than 5 seconds when interacting with a student regarding his or her misbehavior (Sprick, Borgmeier, & Nolet, 2002). Interactions that last longer than 5 seconds break the pace of instruction and provide attention from the teacher and his or her peers for the student's inappropriate behavior.

Yelling and Threatening

One of the most damaging ways in which teachers try to eliminate student misbehavior is through yelling, threatening, issuing increasingly harsh reprimands, or by making a public display of authority (e.g., "You will behave because I say so!"). Again, the student may interpret such behavior as an attack, thus leading to a power struggle. Other students in the classes may see such teacher behavior as an indication that the teacher is unsure if he or she can get the student to obey or that the teacher is acting unfairly (Good & Brophy, 2008). This type of teacher behavior may also serve as a prompt that begins a series of negative exchanges between the teacher and student that actually escalates the misbehavior.

Issuing Commands When a Student Is Agitated

Walker and Walker (1991) advised teachers not to make demands of a student when he or she appears to be agitated. This is because when a student is agitated, directions from the teacher, especially if delivered publicly, are likely to be perceived as an aversive, provocative event, which may serve as the trigger for an angry, escalating behavior episode (Walker et al., 2004).

Teachers need to be able to recognize the signs of student agitation. Students will usually have their own unique ways of showing when they are becoming agitated. For example, some students may become very sullen and quiet, whereas other students may become argumentative and noncompliant. By carefully observing their students' behaviors, teachers can often recognize when a student is becoming agitated. In such situations, teachers should attempt to calm the student and speak softly to him or her and attempt to determine the source of the problem. Teachers may also attempt individual problem solving with a student. For example, a teacher could quietly ask the student what the problem is and then assist the student in identifying solutions to the problem. Walker et al. (1995) suggested that these supportive procedures should be attempted at the earliest indication that the student is agitated and that the teacher should not issue a direction or command until the agitated mood has passed.

Engaging in Escalating Interactions with Students

Walker and colleagues (2004) referred to students with serious problem behavior as "grand masters of behavioral escalation" (p. 165). The authors pointed out that the students engage in behavioral escalation when a teacher issues a directive or command to which they do not want to comply. The student then escalates his or her level of noncompliance to ever-higher intensity levels until the teacher withdraws the directive, thus reinforcing the student for noncompliance. Patterson (1982) referred to this aversive behavioral escalation pattern as pain control or coercion. Figure 12–1 depicts an example of a coercive exchange between a teacher and student.

Colvin and Sugai (1988) warned that teachers cannot win this behavioral escalation game and should not get involved. Unfortunately, one of the most common mistakes that teachers make is attempting to control a student's problem behavior by using escalating interactions (Walker et al., 2004), thus becoming involved in a series of coercive interactions. Such interactions may involve arguing, shouting, grabbing, nattering, attempting to force the student to behave, and so on. The resulting behavioral escalation can be very frustrating to a teacher because the harder he or she tries to control the problem behavior, the less effect the teacher's efforts have on the student's behavior and the more likely that the student will be reinforced for his or her use of coercion (Walker et al., 2004).

Walker and colleagues (1995) and Colvin (2004) conceptualized this behavior cycle as an escalating behavior chain that begins with low-level misbehavior and eventually leads to serious acting-out behavior. For example, the chain may begin with talking out and end with physical assault. The chain consists of a series of interactions between a student and another person, usually the teacher, in which each ensuing behavior in the escalating behavior chain is more serious and disruptive than the preceding behavior. Colvin (2004) referred to these successive interactions between a student and teacher as a game of "my turn-your-turn." In the behavior chain, a teacher's response leads to a student's response; this in turn leads to another more assertive teacher

FIGURE 12–1

Example of a coercive power struggle

Teacher	Student
"Okay everyone, put away your art and take out your math books."	(Robbie ignores the teacher's direction.)
"Robbie, didn't you hear me? I said take out your math book."	"Just a minute; I'm busy." (Robbie makes an excuse.)
"The other students are busy too! Now get your book out!" (Teacher raises his voice.)	"No one else has to do such hard work!" (Robbie whines.)
"What do you mean? Everyone is doing the same assignment." (Teacher is exasperated.)	"I am sick of you always picking on me. I'm not going to do it!" (Robbie gets defiant and refuses to do work.)
"I've had it with you. Take your book and start working!" (Teacher opens Robbie's desk, grabs his math book, and slams it on Robbie's desk.)	"Don't you touch me or I'll sue. You can't make me do anything!" (Robbie starts to tantrum and pushes his book on the floor.)
"Fine, do whatever you want. Just sit there but be quiet. You're not going to pass any classes anyway. We'll see what the principal and your parents say about this." (Teacher withdraws the request, which may reinforce Robbie's coercion.)	(Robbie puts his head on the desk and mutters to himself. The reduction in Robbie's tantrum may reinforce the teacher for withdrawing the request.)
"What did you call me?" (Teacher grabs Robbie by the arm.)	"Get your hands off me you fat #*!@!"
"That's it; we're going down to the principal right now!" (Teacher tries to pull Robbie to a standing position.)	"F#*!@ you, you stupid #*!@!" (Robbie pulls away from the teacher and kicks over the desk.)

response; followed by a more coercive student response; and so on. That is, the adult gives a command when it is his or her turn. The student responds during his or her turn by questioning the teacher. It is then the teacher's turn and he or she threatens to send the student to the principal. On the student's turn, he or she reacts in a more aversive manner. In this chain, each response serves as a signal for the next response in the chain (Walker et al., 2004). When teachers engage in this sort of series of escalating interactions with a student, they often inadvertently set the stage for more serious student problem behavior and student–teacher power struggles (see Figure 12-1).

Teachers need to avoid such escalating interactions, and if they inadvertently get caught up in one, they should get out as quickly as possible (Walker et al., 2004). Walker and colleagues (Walker et al., 1995, 2004; Walker & Walker, 1991) suggest that the teacher should avoid responding to students in such situations whenever possible. This can be accomplished by (a) not making demands when a student is agitated; (b) not responding to a student's series of questions, comments about a situation, or attempts to argue; (c) not trying to force a student's hand if he or she doesn't comply through actions such as coercion or threats.

When a student who has a history of using behavioral coercion refuses to comply with an initial teacher request (e.g., a task assignment), the teacher should wait a reasonable amount of time for a student to respond to the request instead of directly confronting the student. When a student does not respond but instead intends to wait until the teacher withdraws the request, the teacher will have to address the situation. Rather than using direct confrontation in such instances, however, the teacher should speak in a low voice to the student so the situation is kept private. If the student begins to escalate his or her behavior by arguing, the teacher should disengage and tell the student that he or she can sit quietly and that they teacher will provide help if the student has any questions. The teacher should then leave the student alone and allow him or her to cope with the situation. The teacher, however, should make it clear to the student that he or she must comply with the request either now or later and that the lost time will have to be made up (Walker et al., 2004). It is important that the teacher do what is necessary to avoid a direct confrontation.

When teachers find themselves in an escalating behavior chain, they should escape the confrontation as quickly as possible by stopping their interactions and disengaging with the student (Walker & Walker, 1991). Continuing to argue or attempting to reason with a student in such a confrontation will make the situation worse. Again, it is important that the teacher make it clear to the student that he or she must comply with the request either now or later and that the lost time will have to be made up.

When addressing minor or serious misbehavior, teachers should avoid these ineffective practices. These teacher behaviors will most likely not be successful in eliminating the problem behaviors, and may actually result in an escalation of a student's problem behaviors.

PRINCIPLES TO FOLLOW IN RESPONDING TO PROBLEM BEHAVIOR

Too often teachers respond to problem behavior in a manner that seems intended to show a student who is boss, to enable the teacher to get revenge, or to embarrass a student (Savage, 1998). Responding in such a manner is certainly not ethically consistent with the educational role of the teacher and will not help move students to a greater ability to control their own behavior. A teacher's goal when responding to problem behavior should be to stop the inappropriate behavior while maintaining order in the classroom and reducing the likelihood that the problem behavior will reoccur. The following are a few important principles that teachers should follow when responding to problem behavior.

Principle #1: Emphasize Preventive Measures

Problem behaviors occur less frequently in classrooms that are managed in a proactive and structured manner (see Chapter 11). The following are steps that teachers can take to help prevent the occurrence of problem behavior.

Develop Classroom Rules Teachers should develop classroom rules that specify the expected student behavior. Chapter 11 addressed the importance of teachers developing classroom rules to communicate expectations regarding student behavior. When students clearly understand what behaviors are expected of them, it is more likely that these are the behaviors they will exhibit.

Minimize Student Downtime When students are not involved in classroom activities, the likelihood of problem behavior is increased (Good & Brophy, 2008; Paine et al., 1983; Rhode et al., 1992). Conversely, when students are actively and productively engaged in interesting learning activities, the likelihood of problem behaviors occurring is decreased (Colvin, 2004). To minimize student downtime, therefore, teachers should ensure that they (a) maximize the instructional time in which students are actively engaged in learning activities, (b) manage transition times so they are efficient and quick, and (c) plan learning activities that are varied and interesting so that students do not become bored. These activities, which are discussed in Chapter 11, are crucial to keeping students engaged, thus minimizing problem behavior.

Plan Lessons at the Appropriate Level of Difficulty

When teachers have a variety of lessons at the appropriate level of difficulty students will stay actively engaged and interested. When students are engaged in interesting activities, they are less likely to misbehave. Kounin (1970) found that the most effective classroom managers kept their students engaged in learning activities, whereas ineffective classroom managers tended to have boring and repetitive learning activities that did not keep students engaged.

Monitor Student Behavior   Kounin (1970) coined the term "withitness" to describe the importance of teachers being aware of what students were doing at all times. Teachers should regularly move about the classroom and monitor student behavior. In this way, teachers will be more aware of student misbehavior in the early stage and be able to "nip most of them in the bud" (Good & Brophy, 2008, p. 153). On the other hand, when teachers (a) deliberately or inadvertently ignore misbehavior, (b) target a minor misbehavior for correction when a more serious problem behavior is occurring, (c) fail to intervene until a problem behavior becomes more serious, or (d) target the incorrect student when addressing misbehavior, the teacher is communicating to the students that he or she does not know what is happening in the classroom (Good & Brophy, 2008; Kounin, 1970), or that he or she knows what is happening but will not address it.

Principle #2: Modify the Learning Environment

Darch and Kame'enui (1995) suggested that teachers should exhaust all instructional remedies when responding to persistent problem behavior. As a first step these authors recommended that teachers first conduct an assessment of their classroom organization and instructional procedures and, if necessary, make modifications to the learning environment and instruction to increase the effectiveness of their program to decrease problem behavior.

During the assessment phase, Darch and Kame'enui (1995) posited that teachers should ask themselves a number of questions, including the following:

- Are persistent behavior problems fostered by the organization of the classroom?

- Are the problem behaviors specific to a particular person or more than one person?

- Are the problem behaviors specific to a particular instructional task, response form, or problem type?

- Are the problem behaviors specific to a particular sequence of events?

- Are certain reinforcers or reinforcement schedules more effective than others in managing persistent problem behaviors?

These questions will help the teacher evaluate his or her learning environment.

Based on the assessment information, Darch and Kame'enui (1995) suggested that the teacher may want to modify the context and structure of the learning environment, modify the task dimensions, or modify the reinforcement. Modifying the context and structure of the learning environment may include (a) modifying seating assignments (e.g., having a disruptive student sit in front of the class); (b) modifying the sequence or type of learning assignment (e.g., selecting learning activities at the beginning of a lesson that help lower-performing students succeed, use change-up activities, such as games, to gain the attention and interest of students); or (c) modifying the physical arrangement of the classroom (e.g., changing the seating of students).

Student problem behavior often occurs during transition times between activities or during downtime (i.e., when a student is not involved in an activity during class periods). The remedy is to move through transition periods quickly and to keep students actively engaged to eliminate downtime (Evertson et al., 2006). This requires that teachers always have materials ready so they can move through transition times quickly and have activities prepared for students who finish classroom assignments early (Good & Brophy, 2008).

Because problem behavior can be caused by improper task structure and selection, Darch and Kame'enui (2004) also suggest modifying task structure and selection when needed. This may involve altering the learning task if it is too difficult for a student and he or she becomes frustrated. If a student is successful at the new task it is less likely that he or she will be disruptive. Similarly, teachers may often preempt problem behavior by allowing students to make choices in their activities because such activities heighten student engagement in the task selected (Dunlap et al., 1994; Jolivette, Wehby, Canale, & Massey, 2001). For example, during a reading class a student could be given a choice between various reading materials.

Darch and Kame'enui (2004) suggested modifying reinforcement procedures to keep a student academically engaged and to decrease the probability that problem behaviors will recur. For example, a teacher may use a more powerful reinforcer (e.g., using token reinforcers rather than social reinforcers) or increase the frequency of reinforcement if the current schedule seems inadequate.

Principle #3: Use Precorrection Strategies

According to Colvin (2004), many students who engage in serious acting-out behavior behave reasonably well until something in the classroom environment serves as a trigger for problem behavior. Triggers are specific events that occur at school that set the stage for problem behaviors. Thus, triggers may serve as antecedents for problem behaviors. One of the most effective ways for teachers to eliminate problem behaviors is to manage these triggering events by using a strategy called "precorrection" (Colvin, Sugai, & Patching, 1993). Precorrection is a useful technique for reducing the occurrence of problem behaviors (Darch & Kame'enui, 2004).

Precorrections are antecedent manipulations that are designed to prevent student problem behavior (Colvin, 2004; Colvin & Sugai, 1988), whereas corrections are consequent manipulations that are designed to stop misbehavior after it occurs (Colvin, 2004). To use a precorrection strategy, teachers must be able to identify the context or conditions that are likely to serve as triggers for problem behavior. When a teacher knows what these triggers are, he or she can act in a proactive manner to anticipate problem behaviors and take steps to foster the appropriate behavior before the student has the opportunity to misbehave (Colvin, 2004; Walker et al., 2004). Precorrection strategies are also instructional tools in which a teacher teaches a student appropriate ways of behaving in response to trigger situations.

Colvin (2004) stated that teachers should follow seven steps when using precorrection strategies. First, teachers must be able to identify the context or situation in which problem behavior is likely to occur. This context could be an event, task, condition, or environment that in the past has set the stage for problem behavior.

Triggers can be identified by directly observing a student or by conducting a functional behavioral assessment (FBA) to examine the antecedents for problem behavior. For example, Jeremy's teacher notices that when Jeremy has to work independently on a math worksheet, he often talks out to get assistance from the teacher, and if assistance from the teacher does not come shortly, he will throw his paper on the floor and shout at the teacher. Giving Jeremy an independent math worksheet, therefore, may serve as an antecedent or trigger for his problem behavior.

The second step in using precorrection strategies is for the teacher to clearly specify the behaviors that he or she wants the student to exhibit. The objective of this step is to eliminate the problem behavior while establishing the appropriate behavior that will replace the inappropriate behavior. For example, the replacement behavior that the teacher teaches Jeremy may be to raise his hand and ask for help. When possible, the replacement behavior should be incompatible with the problem behavior.

The third step is to modify the context to increase the likelihood that the appropriate behavior will occur by modifying the environment. For example, if an FBA of Jeremy's problem behavior shows that when Stacey is seated close to Jeremy he is more likely to have a temper tantrum when he doesn't get help on his independent math assignment, the teacher may move Stacey to another seat farther away from Jeremy. When a teacher changes the context, he or she should make the change before the student has an opportunity to exhibit problem behavior. Moreover, these changes should be minimal and unobtrusive.

The fourth step is to conduct behavioral rehearsals with the student. This will help the student learn and become fluent in the new skill. The teacher should conduct the behavioral rehearsal before students enter the environment where the problem behavior often occurs. In Jeremy's case, his teacher would practice having him raise his hand for help prior to going to math class.

The fifth step is to provide reinforcement when the student exhibits the replacement behavior in the particular context. In precorrection, the teacher instructs and rehearses the appropriate behavior and then provides reinforcement when the student behaves appropriately. Colvin (2004) stated that the reinforcers must be strong enough to overcome the reinforcement history that has maintained the student's inappropriate behavior.

The sixth step is to prompt the replacement behavior when the student is in the context in which the problem behaviors tend to occur. Colvin (2004) suggested that the teacher acknowledge the student immediately for the appropriate behavior and use gestures to prompt the correct behavior.

The seventh step for using precorrection strategies is to monitor the success of the precorrection plan by collecting data on the teacher's implementation of the plan and the student's behavior. The purpose of assessing the teacher's implementation of the plan is to ensure that it is carried out correctly. To ensure this, a checklist could be developed that describes each step of the precorrection plan and has the student's teacher check off each step as it is completed. Second, a data collection form could be developed in which either the occurrences of problem behavior or occurrences of appropriate behavior (or both) are recorded. As with any type of data collection, the system must be teacher-friendly and easy to complete. Figure 12-2 shows an example of a precorrection plan implementation checklist.

FIGURE 12–2

Precorrection plan checklist

Yes	No	Component
☐	☐	The teacher identifies the triggers for possible problem behavior.
☐	☐	The teacher specifies the behavior that he or she expects of the student.
☐	☐	The teacher modifies the environment to increase the likelihood of the appropriate behavior.
☐	☐	The teacher conducts behavioral rehearsals with the student.
☐	☐	The teacher reinforces the student for engaging in the appropriate behavior.
☐	☐	The teacher prompts the student to perform the appropriate behavior in situations where the inappropriate behavior may occur.
☐	☐	The teacher collects data to monitor the effectiveness of the precorrection plan.

Principle #4: Respond Privately Rather than Publicly If Possible

Privately responding to students who exhibit problem behavior is preferred for the following reasons. First, when teachers address a problem privately with a student it decreases the likelihood that the student will be reinforced by peer attention. Often students with EBD are reinforced by the attention they receive from their peers when they misbehave. When a teacher's response is private it lessens the chance that the classroom will become an audience for the student. Second, private responding does not disrupt classroom order and it allows learning activities to continue without interruption. This is especially true when a teacher displays overlapping behavior, and continues the class lesson or activity while simultaneously responding to a student. Third, private responding lessens the likelihood of a power struggle between the student and teacher. If a teacher publicly reprimands or attempts to correct a student, and the student becomes noncompliant, the teacher is put on the spot with the entire class watching. Because the teacher has been challenged and the class is waiting to see the teacher's response, the typical response is often for the teacher to escalate his or her behavior to force the student to comply (Savage, 2002). Thus, a power struggle ensues in front of an attentive audience. This situation is one to be avoided if at all possible.

Clearly, there are situations in which private correction is not possible (e.g., verbal or physical aggression), but teachers should always use private correction and attempt to respond to problem behavior unobtrusively. Use a soft voice and be in close proximity to the student when responding to a student's misbehavior (Curwin & Mendler, 2000). Additionally, when teachers have to deliver a direction to a student, the teacher should (a) use initiating commands rather than terminating commands (e.g., "John, take out your math book" as opposed to "John, stop goofing around and where is your math book?"); (b) give only one command; (c) give the student a few seconds to comply; and (d) do not engage in talk with the student.

Principle #5: Respond Consistently and Fairly

When a teacher responds in a consistent and fair manner, it means that he or she responds to all incidences of problem behavior whenever they occur and with the same measured response (e.g., a problem is not ignored one day and punished the next). Moreover, the teacher should respond to problem behavior regardless of who exhibits it. Students will perceive that a teacher is unfair if he or she ignores a behavior when it is exhibited by one student and punishes when it is exhibited by another. Classrooms that are characterized by students' constantly testing the rules are usually classrooms in which a teacher is inconsistent in responding to rule violations (Savage, 2002).

Principle #6: Use Alpha Commands

According to Walker and Walker (1991), short and clear directions, or *alpha commands*, are far more effective than wordy and unclear directions, which they call *beta commands*. Alpha commands give students specific information on what they need to do, whereas beta commands do little more than convey teacher frustration (Bateman & Golly, 2003). Thus, alpha commands are precise, direct, and to the point, giving students an opportunity to demonstrate compliance (Walker et al., 2004). In fact, alpha commands are associated with higher levels of compliance in both preschool and K–12 settings; in contrast, beta commands are associated with lower rates of compliance and therefore should be avoided (Walker et al., 2004). Figure 12–3 contains examples of alpha and beta commands.

Principle #7: Maintain a Student's Dignity When Responding

When students believe that their dignity is challenged, and that a teacher is attempting to humiliate them, the natural tendency is to strike back (Savage, 2002).

According to Colvin (2004), when students perceive that a teacher is trying to embarrass or ridicule them, they will often resort to more serious problem behavior in an attempt to maintain their dignity. Teachers, therefore, should never attempt to ridicule or embarrass a student. Rather, when they respond directly to a student's misbehavior, they should do so in a respectful and businesslike manner. When a teacher responds to problem behavior privately, the likelihood that a student will perceive that his or her dignity has been challenged is greatly diminished.

Principle #8: Maintain a Calm Attitude and Demeanor

When a student exhibits problem behavior to which a teacher must respond, it is important that the teacher maintain a calm and businesslike attitude. This can be difficult, especially in situations involving serious incidences of misbehavior. Nonetheless, teachers must respond in a calm and measured way or the likelihood of the student escalating the behavior may be increased (Colvin, 2004; Walker et al., 1995).

According to Colvin (2004), guidelines that teachers should follow when approaching a problem situation include (a) move slowly and deliberately; (b) speak calmly using a flat, controlled voice; (c) keep a reasonable distance and avoid crowding a student; (d) establish eye contact; (e) use brief, simple, and direct language; (f) stay with the agenda and do not get sidetracked; and (g) acknowledge cooperation if a student follows directions. The bottom line, according to Walker et al. (1995), is that the

---

FIGURE 12–3

Examples of alpha and beta commands

Alpha Command	Beta Command
"Take out your math book and turn to page 24."	"Jeremy, can't you hear me? I told everyone to take out their math book. Can't you follow directions?"
"Pick up the papers around your desk and throw them in the waste basket."	"Stacey, you are always so messy. Do you always expect people to clean up after you? You need to learn to clean up after yourself."
"Robbie, you need to stop talking."	"Robbie, you are always talking without permission. If I've told you once I've told you a thousand times to not talk so much. This is a warning."
"John, move your chair away from Jennie."	"Young man, teasing is disrespectful. Leave Jennie alone. How do you think she feels? I do not like your attitude. Unless I see an attitude adjustment you are going to be in trouble."

teacher must approach problem behavior in a calm, detached, unhurried, respectful, and step-by-step manner.

Principle #9: Develop a Game Plan for Responding to Student Problem Behavior

To respond to student problem behaviors in a calm, measured, and effective manner teachers should (a) have a consistent manner of responding when such situations arise, and (b) develop a hierarchy of consequences when students do not comply to teacher directions to stop misbehavior.

When teachers don't have a consistent way of responding, they are more likely to respond in an emotional and ineffective manner. Knowing how they will respond to problems will increase their confidence that they can address problem behaviors effectively. Moreover, when students know how teachers will consistently respond to misbehavior and that they cannot negotiate with or intimidate their teacher, they will be less likely to test the teacher's resolve. In later sections I discuss how teachers should respond to problem behavior.

The consequences that teachers use should be established before problem behavior occurs. Teachers should develop a hierarchy of reductive consequences that will be used if a student (a) breaks a classroom rule, (b) does not comply with the teacher's directions, and (c) exhibits serious or dangerous problem behavior. Obviously, the types of consequences that are used should be matched to the intensity of the student's problem behavior. That is, minor consequences should be used for minor misbehavior (reprimands, warnings); more serious consequences should be used for noncompliance (e.g., time-out, response cost); and the most serious consequences should be reserved for serious misbehavior (e.g., office referral, in-school suspension). Teachers, therefore, should determine a range of consequences to fit the intensity of problem behavior (Sprick et al., 2002). The worst time to select a consequence for misbehavior is during an argument or power struggle with a student (Rhode et al., 1992).

Principle #10: Provide Contingent Reinforcement for Appropriate Behavior

Teachers often ignore students with problem behaviors when they are calm and are on task, but provide attention when these same students are displaying problem behavior (Walker et al., 1995). If students receive more attention when they are acting out than when they are behaving appropriately, it is much more likely that they will continue exhibiting the problem behaviors (Colvin, 1997). In fact, Walker and colleagues (1995) asserted that contingent teacher attention for appropriate behavior will run counter to most of the prior experience of students with EBD.

Reductive consequences will only weaken inappropriate behavior. To increase students' appropriate behavior, teachers need to reinforce students when they follow school rules and comply with teacher directives. An intervention that applies consequences only for misbehavior will fail (Sprick et al., 2002).

Teachers need to catch students behaving appropriately and reinforce them. Curwin and Mendler (2000) suggest that teachers catch students being good every 15 to 20 minutes and then give the student positive feedback privately. Because many students with EBD may not have received attention for appropriate behavior often, teachers need to apply contingent attention consistently so that it will have the desired effect (Walker et al., 2004). Colvin (1997) asserts that frequently acknowledging and reinforcing appropriate student behavior is one of the most powerful strategies available to teachers. Such procedures call attention to appropriate behavior and provide a model for students. Colvin also suggests that teachers develop a system to remind themselves to frequently look for and reinforce students who are displaying appropriate behaviors.

When responding to minor or serious misbehavior, teachers should adhere to these suggested behaviors. These teacher behaviors often will be successful in eliminating the problem behaviors and may defuse potentially explosive problems.

RESPONDING TO PROBLEM BEHAVIOR

Savage (1999) asserted that teachers have difficulty responding to student problem behaviors because they are uncertain how to respond. They sometimes overreact to minor incidences of misbehavior and sometimes don't respond at all. When a teacher responds to student misbehavior it is important to keep the aforementioned principles of effective responding in mind while avoiding the ineffective responses to problem behavior. Figure 12–4 depicts the "do's and don'ts" of teacher responding.

Effective responding to student problem behaviors requires that teachers have a game plan for responding to both minor and major incidences of problem behavior. The other option, randomly choosing a response on the spot or following an impulse, will usually be ineffective (Savage, 1999). It is crucially important that when responding to problem behaviors, teachers do so in a

FIGURE 12–4

The do's and don'ts of teacher responding to student problem behavior

Do	Don't
Address the behavior privately	Ignore the misbehavior
Maintain the class' attention on the lesson	Provide attention to the misbehaving student
Use proximity control	Yell or threaten
Talk in a quiet, businesslike voice	Humiliate or be sarcastic
Give only one command at a time	Use beta commands
Deliver initiating commands	Make commands when the student is agitated
Be calm and respectful	Argue or verbally punish
Use a precision request	Engage in escalating prompts
Reinforce compliance	Ignore compliance

timely and effective manner (Colvin, 1997). Certainly, a prerequisite for responding in a timely and effective manner is that the teacher must be *withit* (Kounin, 1970). In the next section I address responding to (a) minor problem behaviors, (b) noncompliance, and (c) severe problem behaviors.

Responding to Minor Problem Behaviors

It is extremely important that teachers know how to effectively respond to minor misbehavior for four primary reasons. First, much of the student misbehavior that occurs in classrooms for students with EBD is of a minor nature (e.g., talking, leaving seat without permission, inattention). Second, minor misbehavior, if not addressed, will often lead to severe problem behavior (Rozalski, 2001). Third, effective teacher responding to minor misbehavior may stop misbehavior before it escalates into severe problem behavior. Fourth, ineffective responding to minor incidences of misbehavior can actually escalate minor misbehavior into a severe problem behavior.

When minor behavior problems occur, a teacher should focus on eliminating the problem behavior quickly and with a minimum amount of classroom disruption (Evertson et al., 2003; Good & Brophy, 2008; Savage, 1999). By eliminating the problem behavior quickly, a teacher ensures that the problem behavior

(a) does not spread to other students (see discussion on the ripple effect in Chapter 10); (b) does not escalate into more severe problem behavior; and (c) does not interfere with classroom learning.

Teachers should develop a game plan for responding to minor misbehavior. Certain unintentional misbehaviors that are not disruptive (e.g., a student failing to put materials in their proper place when finished using them) may be ignored and addressed at a later time. Misbehaviors that are repeated or sustained and may become disruptive, however, must be stopped quickly and efficiently. Again, in such instances, the teacher's goal is to stop the problem behavior quickly and with a minimum amount of classroom disruption. Therefore, when minor problems occur teachers should (a) respond immediately using unobtrusive methods, and (b) continue with instruction (see discussion of overlapping in Chapter 11).

Three strategies for responding to minor problem behaviors are (a) praise the appropriate behavior of a student or other students near the student who is engaged in the minor problem behavior, (b) use nonverbal responses, and (c) use unobtrusive verbal responding. The first strategy, praising student's appropriate behavior, has the following advantages: It lets the students who are behaving appropriately know that you recognize and appreciate their behaviors; it may alert the misbehaving student that he or she needs to stop the inappropriate behavior (and if the student stops the misbehavior, allows you to acknowledge him or her for appropriate behavior); and it allows classroom instruction to continue uninterrupted.

If that strategy is unsuccessful, the teacher should let the student know that he or she is misbehaving by using unobtrusive, nonverbal procedures. Such procedures, which Savage (1999) refers to as low-profile approaches, may include using proximity control, eye contact, and nonverbal gestures. For example, if students are talking in the back of the room, the teacher could move toward the offending students and make eye contact with the students accompanied by a nonverbal gesture (e.g., head nodding, pointing toward the students). A teacher could lightly touch the student's desk or perhaps his or her shoulder to gain attention and then point to what he or she should be doing. The advantages of this procedure are that it (a) alerts the misbehaving student that he or she must stop the inappropriate behavior in a direct manner that does not focus attention on the problem behavior, (b) communicates that the teacher is *withit* enough to recognize the inappropriate behavior that is occurring, and (c) does not disrupt the classroom activities. Moreover, unobtrusive, low-profile approaches allow students an opportunity to self-correct their behavior.

If neither of the first two procedures is successful, the teacher will need to let the student know that he or she is misbehaving by using slightly more intrusive, verbal procedures, such as reprimands. Again, it is extremely important that when using such procedures the teacher does this in an unobtrusive manner so as to not focus attention on the misbehavior or disrupt classroom activities. Thus, it is important that the verbal response be made privately and in an unemotional manner to a student who is misbehaving. The verbal command should be a brief and assertive command in which the student is told to stop the problem behavior and reminded of the appropriate behavior.

The advantage of reprimands is that they are easy to implement. Unfortunately, reprimands are ineffective with high-frequency or persistent problem behaviors and are ineffective as long-term management strategies (Darch & Kame'enui, 2004). When using verbal reprimands, teachers should move toward the offending student and use a quiet, businesslike, and unemotional voice to alert the student that he or she is misbehaving and must correct the behavior immediately. The teacher should (a) tell the student that the behavior is not acceptable, (b) tell the student why the behavior is not acceptable, (c) describe the acceptable behavior, (d) issue a warning regarding the consequences if the behavior continues, (e) give the student sufficient time to respond, and (f) not interact with the student while waiting for his or her response. If the student does not correct the behavior, the teacher must deliver the consequence. If the student corrects the behavior, the teacher should reinforce the student and move on. The teacher's objective is to be clear with the student while being unemotional but forceful. At the same time, the teacher should not disrupt the classroom activities.

Following any of these teacher responses, if the student complies or self-corrects his or her behavior it must be reinforced immediately. Acknowledging the student's good choice gives attention to his or her appropriate behavior.

In summary, many of the behaviors that students exhibit are minor forms of misbehavior. Nonetheless, it is important that teachers deal with these misbehaviors in an efficient and effective manner so they do not spread to others and do not escalate into serious problem behavior. Teachers must be able to deal with minor misbehavior in a relatively unobtrusive manner (which will communicate the teacher's *withitness* to his or her students) while maintaining the other students' attention to the task at hand. When addressing student misbehavior, teachers should follow a three-step procedure that begins with acknowledging the appropriate behavior of students who are near the offending student, proceeds to nonverbal contact when the acknowledgment does not eliminate the problem behavior, and ends with an unobtrusive verbal reminder and warning to stop the misbehavior.

Responding to Noncompliance

Noncompliance to teacher requests is a frequently occurring problem behavior among students with EBD. Persistent noncompliance is a problem that may lead to serious problems such as academic failure, social maladjustment, and more serious forms of disruptiveness and aggression, and may lead to more deviant forms of behavior (Morgan & Jenson, 1988; Walker & Walker, 1991). Moreover, persistent noncompliance can also have a negative effect on a student's postschool success in vocational, personal, and social areas (Walker & Walker, 1991).

Rhode and colleagues (1992) referred to noncompliance as a "king-pin" behavior (p. 3) around which a student's other behavioral excesses revolve. That means that many noxious behaviors such as arguing, tantruming, fighting, and rule breaking are secondary to a student's using noncompliance to escape teacher directions or particular tasks. That is, students are negatively reinforced for their noncompliance.

According to Walker and Walker (1991), students respond to commands and directions in one of three ways: The student (1) complies with the command within a reasonable amount of time; (2) fails to comply by delaying, ignoring, or actively refusing; or (3) changes the nature of the command through negotiation or influences the adult to withdraw it. Responses 2 and 3 represent noncompliance. It is very difficult and frustrating for teachers when students refuse to comply with teacher directions. When confronted with noncompliance, teachers frequently are unsure of how they should respond. In such situations, it is important that teachers have a systematic method of responding that they follow consistently.

Types of Noncompliance According to Walker and Walker (1991), there are four types of noncompliance: passive noncompliance, simple refusal, direct defiance, and negotiation. In passive noncompliance, a student chooses not to perform the behavior that the teacher requests, but he or she does not overtly refuse to do so (e.g., the student ignores the teacher's request to stop drawing). In simple refusal, the student acknowledges the request but does not comply (e.g., "No, I don't want to do that"). In direct defiance, a student's noncompliance is accompanied by hostility, anger, overt resistance to authority, and sometimes attempts at intimidating the teacher (e.g., "I'm not going to do this stupid math and you can't make me"). When students engage in direct defiance, they often do so in an angry, confrontational manner resulting in confrontation or power struggle between the teacher and the student. It is very important to avoid such hostile, confrontational interactions and to terminate them quickly if they develop. In negotiation, a student attempts to change the adult's command by negotiating the nature or the conditions of the command. For example, a student may attempt to (a) bargain with a teacher, (b) propose an alternative to the command, (c) redefine the teacher's command, (d) try to compromise, or (e) offer explanations and excuses (e.g., "Let me finish my art and then I'll do my math"). Teachers need to recognize that these four forms are all noncompliance.

Variables That Affect Compliance Researchers have shown that teachers can take a number of actions to increase the likelihood that students will comply with their directives (Morgan & Jenson, 1988; Rhode et al., 1992; Walker, 1995; Walker & Walker, 1991; Walker et al., 2004). These actions include:

- Issuing specific, direct, and unambiguous commands. Get the student's attention and then use a calm, firm, and matter-of-fact voice to issue an alpha command. When possible, commands should be initiating (e.g., "Doug, take out your homework") rather than terminating (e.g., "Doug, stop talking"). That is, commands should tell a student what to do, not tell the student to stop doing something. Additionally, teachers should use a quiet voice when issuing commands.

- Using a statement rather than a question when giving a command (e.g., "Robbie, please take out your math," not "Robbie, would you take out your math"). Rhode and colleagues (1992) asserted that teachers should phrase commands as questions only if they are willing to accept "no" for an answer. If "no" is not an acceptable response, then teachers should not use a question format.

- Issuing one command and repeating it once, if necessary. Giving the same request numerous times (e.g., "Robbie, take out your math now," "Robbie, didn't you hear me? I said now," "Robbie, you will get into big trouble if you don't get out your math,") or issuing many requests rapidly (e.g., "Jeremy, stop talking, get in your seat now, take out your homework, and stop looking at me like that") reduces the likelihood that the student will comply.

- Giving the student adequate time to comply. After a teacher issues a command, the student should be given between 5 and 10 seconds to comply. After the teacher has issued the command, he or she should not say anything, repeat the command, or issue another command, but rather wait silently.

- Standing close to the student and making eye contact. Commands are more likely to be followed when a teacher is standing close to a student when issuing them. Morgan and Jenson (1988) suggested that a teacher should issue a command from approximately 3 feet (1 meter), or the length of a desk, from a student to increase the likelihood of compliance. Moreover, making eye contact with the student can also increase compliance.

- Reinforcing student compliance. If a teacher wants behavior to be strengthened, immediate reinforcement should be delivered when a student complies with the teacher's command. Rhode et al. (1992) warned that it is easy to forget to reinforce a student when he or she has complied with the teacher's command, however, if teachers want compliance they need to reinforce students when they comply.

Precision Requests Morgan and Jenson (1988) advocated that teachers use a procedure called a "precision request" to increase the likelihood of students complying with their commands. By following the precision request format, depicted in Figure 12–5, a teacher would adhere to the important variables listed previously while avoiding the ineffective practices described earlier in this chapter. Morgan and Jenson (1988) reported that teachers who responded to student noncompliance by using this standardized approach in a consistent manner had higher rates of student compliance.

Following are the steps of the precision request:

Step 1: The teacher issues the request or command in a quiet, but firm, voice when standing close to a student (e.g., "John, return to your seat").

Step 2: After making the request, the teacher waits for 5 to 10 seconds. During this time the teachers does not interact with the student nor does he or she reissue the request.

Step 3: If the student complies, the teacher reinforces him or her.

OR

Step 3: If the student does not comply with the request, the teacher repeats the request using the word *need* (e.g., "John, you need to return to your seat"). Adding the word *need* to the initial statement is important because it signals the student that this is the last chance before an aversive consequence is delivered (Rhode et al., 1992).

Figure 12–5   The precision request

Adapted from Morgan & Jenson, 1998.

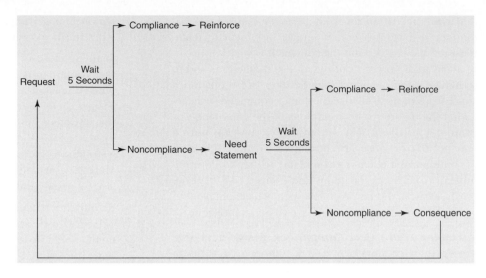

Step 4: After making the request, the teacher waits for 5 to 10 seconds. During this time the teacher does not interact with the student, nor does he or she reissue the request.

Step 5: If the student complies, the teacher reinforces him or her.

OR

Step 5: If the student does not comply with the second request, the teacher delivers a mild aversive consequence. Teachers must plan the consequence in advance. Morgan and Jenson (1988) suggested using time-out for the aversive consequence.

Step 6: After the student finishes the time-out, the teacher must reissue the request.

If teachers decide to use a precision request it is important that they follow the procedure consistently and reissue the request after the aversive consequence has been applied. If the request is not reissued, and the student thus escapes from the original command, the student's noncompliance will have been negatively reinforced. If the student does not comply, after the original aversive consequence another, more aversive, consequence should be used. Morgan and Jenson (1988), however, noted that if the procedure is applied consistently and correctly this will rarely happen.

Think Time   Nelson and Carr (2000) developed an intervention that teachers may use when a student misbehaves called "think time." The U.S. Department of Education's Expert Panel on Safe, Disciplined, and Drug-Free Schools designated think time as an exemplary program. Think time is based on the premise that problem behavior is a chain of interactions rather than an event, and that this

chain involves the teacher as well as the student. When this chain of interactions occurs between a teacher and student it often results in an escalation of minor misbehavior into major misbehavior that can develop into chronic misbehavior. The think time strategy breaks this chain of escalating problem behavior by (a) minimizing a teacher's verbal interactions with a student, (b) setting clear limits on a misbehaving student, and (c) removing a student from the environment where the problem behavior occurred (Martella et al., 2003; Nelson & Carr, 2000). Essentially, think time uses a variation of the precision request, time-out, and a debriefing strategy.

There are four steps necessary to implement think time (Nelson & Carr, 2000). First, a teacher must identify a cooperating teacher because the think strategy requires that teachers team together to use it. The cooperating teacher's classroom becomes the site where a student serves think time (i.e., the think time classroom). The teachers' classrooms should be close to each other so students do not have to walk far to enter think time. Second, an area within the classroom must be prepared for the intervention by placing a desk or two in an area that is designated for think time. This area should be free of distractions and located away from other students in the classroom. Third, the teacher must inform his or her students' parents about the think time intervention and when it will be used. Martella and colleagues (2003) suggested sending home a parent information letter regarding think time and discussing its use with them at conferences or other meetings. Fourth, the teacher must teach his or her students about the think time intervention and when and how the intervention will be used. The authors also stated that students should be taught (a) the overall goal of think time is to help students succeed in school and enjoy their classes, (b) what problem behaviors will lead to the use of think time, (c) how to move to and enter the think time classroom, (d) how to serve think time, (e) the debriefing process, and (f) how to rejoin the regular classroom.

To use the think time intervention appropriately teachers should adhere to the following guidelines:

- *Catching problem behavior early.* It is important that teachers catch problem behavior in its early stages and request appropriate behavior. If the student complies, the teacher reinforces him or her. If the student does not comply, the teacher directs him or her to the think time classroom. The teacher's interactions with the student should be simple, limited, and unemotional. Threats, warnings, and repeated requests must not be used.

- *Moving to and entering the designated think time classroom.* When a student is told to go to think time, he or she walks independently to the think time, classroom. To encourage students to go quickly to think time, teachers may track the amount of time a student takes to arrive at the classroom or send an escort with the student. The student then waits by the door until the cooperating teacher directs him or her to the think time desk.

- *Serving think time.* The student sits quietly in the think time desk for 3 to 5 minutes. During this time the student is supposed to think about the problem behavior and gain control of himself or herself.

- *Initiating the debriefing process.* After the student has sat quietly for 3 to 5 minutes, the cooperating teacher goes to the student and initiates the debriefing process. The teacher quietly asks the student to describe the behavior that led him or her to come to think time. The purpose of this question is to help the teacher determine if the student is ready to debrief. If the student gives an acceptable answer, the teacher gives him or her a short debriefing form to complete. (There are different forms for students of different age groups.) The form requires the student to fill out information about his or her problem behavior and the behavior that the student must display to get back into the classroom. If the student does not answer the initial question appropriately, the teacher simply says "I'll get back to you" in an unemotional tone and returns to the normal classroom duties. When this happens it is crucial that the cooperating teacher does not interact with the student.

- *Checking the debriefing form.* After the student completes the debriefing form, he or she waits for the cooperating teacher to check it to see if the form was completed correctly. If the form is filled

out appropriately, the teacher directs the student to return to his or her class. If the form is filled out incorrectly, the teacher says "I'll get back to you" and returns to the normal classroom duties. The debriefing process is then repeated until the student completes the form correctly.

- *Rejoining the class.* When the student reenters his or her classroom, he or she waits by the door until the teacher acknowledges the student. Then the teacher reads the debriefing form. If it is filed out correctly, the student is told to go to his or her seat. If the form is completed incorrectly, the student is told to return to the think time classroom.

Responding to Severe Misbehavior

Severe problem behaviors are characterized by behaviors such as defiance, intimidation, property destruction, physical aggression, and fighting. Responding to severe misbehavior is one of the most challenging, difficult, and stressful situations that teachers of students with EBD face. Such behavior may (a) destroy the learning environment, (b) threaten student and staff safety, (c) involve issues of liability, and (d) cause emotional distress for students and teachers. For these reasons it is crucial that teachers of students with EBD be knowledgeable about and fluent in managing crisis behaviors (Colvin, 2004).

Many, if not most, school districts have policies and procedures regarding crisis management (Rozalski & Yell, 2004), and teachers of students with EBD should become very familiar with their district's procedures. Additionally, there are many private companies that offer crisis management training programs to educators (e.g., Crisis Management Institute, Crises Prevention Institute, Mandt Training System). Specific procedures used in managing severe problem behavior (e.g., physical restraint) are taught, and practices in the training programs offered by these companies. Teachers of students with EBD are often involved in crisis situations; therefore, they should receive training in preventing and managing serious problem behavior. Such training should involve regular booster sessions and frequent practice. Additionally, one or more staff members in the school should also receive training.

When crisis situations occur, teachers should first assess the potential risks of the problem behavior. Clearly, if a behavior poses a physical threat to the student, his or her peers, or staff, that is an extremely serious situation and demands quick teacher action. According to Sprick, Sprick, and Garrison (1993), this category includes actions that threaten the physical safety of others (e.g., physical aggression, property destruction) and self-destructive behaviors (e.g., head banging, self-mutilation). It is extremely important that teachers develop a game plan for addressing serious behavior. Getting involved in a crisis incident is an extremely trying and stressful situation; teachers will be much more likely to respond in an appropriate manner if they have a plan. In these situations teachers should take the following actions:

Ensure the Safety of Students and Staff The teacher's first priority is to immediately remove other students who may be injured by the severe problem behavior. Removing the students from the classroom is important for three reasons: (a) it protects the other students from being involved in a situation in which they could be injured, (b) it deprives the student engaging in the problem behavior of an audience and possible reinforcement, and (c) it may make it easier for the teacher to calm down the student who is having the behavioral crisis. Sprick et al. (1993) referred to removing students from the area in which the incident is occurring as a "room clear."

When using room clears, teachers must determine where the class will go when an incident occurs (e.g., another classroom, the gymnasium). Moreover, because the teacher must remain in the classroom to supervise the student engaged in the problem behavior, an arrangement should be made with the administration, a paraprofessional, or another teacher to take charge of the students being removed. If the incident happens on a playground or in a hall, the teacher should disperse the students or move them away from the student who is engaging in the serious problem behavior. If it is not possible to remove the students, the teacher or teachers may have to physically restrain the out-of-control student.

Call or Send for Assistance When a student begins to engage in serious problem behavior, the teacher should have a prearranged procedure for summoning assistance. This procedure should include (a) who will respond (this person should also have been trained in crisis intervention); (b) the chain of command in case the first person is unavailable; and (c) a communication process to ensure that everyone involved will be kept informed (Sprick et al., 1993).

If the school has an intercom, the teacher should call for assistance. The responder should then come immediately to the classroom to provide assistance to the teacher. Additionally, this person also will be a witness to the incident. If the person who comes to assist is not an administrator, a school principal or assistant principal should be notified and apprised of the situation as soon as possible.

If the school doesn't have an intercom to call for assistance, Sprick and colleagues (1993) suggested that the teacher have a prearranged crisis signal, called a "red card," that a student messenger brings to the office where an immediate response is initiated by the school administration.

Attempt to Defuse the Situation In a serious behavioral incident the teacher needs to remain rational and calm. The teacher should attempt to calm the out-of-control student by speaking to the student in a calm, neutral voice. The teacher should stay about 3 feet away from the student and not make sudden movements, ignoring any screaming, yelling, or questioning by the student. Using the student's name, the teacher should give him or her simple, clear, and reasonable directions (e.g., "Robbie, you need to return to your desk") and not threaten, humiliate, or attempt to force the student to do anything.

Use Physical Restraint If Necessary If attempts to defuse the situation have not succeeded and the student remains a danger to himself or herself or others, physical intervention may be necessary. Physical restraint should be the last resort after all other efforts have failed. Of course to avoid concerns regarding the use of excessive force or allegations of abuse during the restraint, two adults should always be present before attempting the restraint. Because the use of physical restraint requires instruction, demonstration, and practice, teachers should contact their school district or state to see if such training is provided. Physical intervention training is beyond the scope of this, or any, textbook.

Keep Thorough Records of the Incident When an incident of severe problem behavior occurs, teachers should thoroughly document it. Documentation is important for a number of reasons. First, if liability issues arise from the incident—for example, if a student is injured—a record of the incident will exist. Second, if a student makes false accusations about the incident there is documentation to dispute the assertions. Third, the documentation of the incident provides information for administrators and teachers to evaluate the adequacy of their reaction to the incident.

The teacher should be responsible for completing the behavioral incident form. When teachers have paraprofessionals working with them, the paraprofessional may be assigned the duty of recording behavioral incidences. Figure 12–6 is an example of a behavioral incident form.

The following guidelines should be followed when completing the behavioral incident form:

- The form should be completed as soon as possible after the behavioral incidence occurs. This will ensure that the incident is fresh in everyone's mind and increases the likelihood of accuracy.

FIGURE 12–6

Behavior incident report

Behavior Incident Report

Student's name _____ Date _____ Grade _____

Teacher's name _____ Time of the incident _____

Location of the incident:

Description of the behavior incident (e.g., precipitating factors, students involved, incident description, etc.):

Did the student's behavior endanger the safety of the student or others? If so, how?

Description of interventions used to manage the problem:

Reason for actions taken:

Results of actions taken:

Reported to administrators and parents (incident must be reported to administrators and parents as soon as possible):

Signature of teachers   _____   _____

Signature of witness   _____   _____

                             _____   _____

Signature of parents   _____   _____

Signature of administrators _____   _____

- At the minimum, the documentation form must include certain information including (a) date of the report; (b) the names of all persons involved (e.g., teacher, paraprofessional, student, witnesses); (c) the date, time, and location of the incident; (d) an objective and truthful description of the incident; (e) a description of the action taken by the teacher and the results of the teacher actions; and (f) signatures of all persons involved.

- The school principal should be informed of the incident as soon as possible and should be involved in completing the documentation, including signing the completed behavioral incident form. Additionally, the student's parents should be informed immediately following the incidence and be given a copy of the report.

Notify the Student's Parents or Guardians Whenever there is a serious behavioral incident, a student's parents or guardians should be notified and asked to attend a conference in which (a) the teacher and administration communicate their willingness to work with the parents, (b) the severity of the problem is determined, and (c) a joint problem-solving process is begun (Sprick et al., 1993). Because parents of children with EBD have similar problems at home and do not know what to do about them, such a conference can be an excellent opportunity to build parent–school partnerships.

DEVELOPING CRISIS MANAGEMENT PLANS

In classrooms for students with EBD, behavioral crises will undoubtedly occur. Teachers should plan for these crisis situations. Indeed, a systematic and preplanned approach to crisis management is an important element of creating a safe classroom environment (Rock, 2000). During behavioral crises, students often exhibit behaviors that are serious, extremely disruptive, and can threaten the safety of students and staff (Colvin, 2004). Because these crisis situations can be dangerous, teachers should spend time preparing for them before they occur (Colvin, 2004; Johns & Carr, 1995; Myles & Simpson, 1994; Rock, 2000; Walker et al., 1995). This can be done by developing crisis management plans (Rock, 2000; Walker et al., 1995).

When teachers develop crisis management plans, there are some vital components that should be included (Gilliam, 1993; Rock, 2000). First, they should identify what constitutes a crisis episode (e.g., serious fights, property destruction, physical aggression) and when the teacher, teachers, or crisis management team will implement the plan's procedures. Second, they need to determine who will respond to the crisis situation. Scholars with expertise in crisis management usually suggest that a school should have a trained building team to respond to crisis situations (e.g., Colvin, 2004; Gilliam, 1993; Johns & Carr, 1995; Myles & Simpson, 1994; Rock, 2000; Walker et al., 1995). Rock (2000) advised that crisis team members must be able to respond immediately when a crisis occurs. Third, teachers must determine how team members will be summoned when a crisis occurs. Usually, a communication network will be established (Myles & Simpson, 1994). For example, cell phones, pagers, or the intercom may be used. Johns and Carr (1994) recommended developing a code for alerting and summoning the team quickly. Fourth, the plan should delineate what the roles of the team members will be during a crisis situation. That is, all team members should be clear on what their roles will be in the event of a crisis. For example, Meadows and et al. (1996) stated that the paraprofessional in a teacher's classroom could be responsible for taking the students in the classroom to a safe area. Moreover, the crisis management plan should specify the particular crisis intervention method in which the team has been trained. Fifth, the management plan should specify where the crisis intervention will occur. That is, the plan should state whether the student will be escorted to a particular area or if the other students in the classroom should be removed and the crisis intervention be conducted in the student's classroom. Sixth, following the crisis, the team members should meet to assess their performance and to determine why the crisis occurred.

Crisis management plans should be developed collaboratively with teachers, paraprofessionals, administrators, and parents (Colvin, 2004). Moreover, a crisis management plan should be written and disseminated to all team members. Walker et al. (1995) suggested that parent permission should be obtained in advance for using crisis management procedures that will be used in the plan. When teachers and teams develop plans, therefore, these plans should be explained to parents and the parents should discuss and sign them. There should be a record-keeping component to all crisis management plans. In fact, immediately following a crisis, the team should complete all documentation. These plans should then be included with the student's records. Teachers can ensure that they receive informed consent by discussing the crisis management plan during an IEP meeting and appending the plan to a student's IEP (Johns & Carr, 1995; Meadows et al., 1996; Rock, 2000; Walker et al., 1995). Figure 12-7 is an example of a crisis management plan.

FIGURE 12–7

Sample crisis management plan

Crisis Management Plan

Student's name _____ Date _____ Grade _____

Teacher's name _____ School _____

Persons on the crisis management team (must include a school administrator):

Circumstances in which the crisis management plan will be implemented:

How members will be summoned:

Actions to be taken in a crisis situation:

Description of interventions to be used in crisis situations:

Assessment of team's responses to the crisis, included methods to avoid similar situations in the future:

Signatures of the crisis management team:

Administrator _____

Team members _____   _____

_____   _____

_____   _____

Parents _____   _____

*The crisis must be reported to the student's parents as soon as possible. A behavior incident must be completed and the team members must convene a meeting to assess their response to the crisis.

AN ALGORITHM FOR RESPONDING TO PROBLEM BEHAVIOR

An algorithm is a step-by-step procedure for solving a problem. Although the term is most frequently used to refer to problem solving in mathematics, it is useful to consider a step-by-step procedure to responding to problem behavior. This particular algorithm is based on four assumptions: (a) that the teacher is using effective teaching techniques to keep the students involved and busy; (b) that the environment is predictable and is structured to encourage appropriate behavior and minimize downtime and transitions; (c) that the teacher is *withit* enough to catch the problem behavior early in its development; and (d) that the teacher contingently reinforces appropriate behavior. Additionally, *withit* teachers must be like good chess players who plan moves ahead; when the teacher sees a potential problem behavior about to occur, he or she should use a precorrection strategy. When problem behavior does occur, however, it is very important that a teacher has a game plan for responding to the misbehavior. The following algorithm represents a method that a teacher may use to respond to problem behavior.

Step 1: *Use Low-Profile Nonverbal Procedures* If the teacher's proximity or attempts at problem solving are unsuccessful, he or she should move on to low-profile responses to stop the misbehavior. The purpose of a low-profile response is to privately stop misbehavior without drawing attention to the student exhibiting the behavior and allow the class activities to continue uninterrupted. Examples of low-profile approaches include eye contact and nonverbal gestures that let the student know he or she is misbehaving and that it must stop.

Step 2: *Move In* If nonverbal procedures do not work, the teacher should quietly move to the student and redirect or remind him or her of the rules. When talking to the student, the teacher should speak privately to the student in a quiet and calm voice using a brief alpha command. For example, if the teacher is moving among the students during independent seat work and checking their work, he or she would walk over to check or assist the misbehaving student with his or her work or the work of students sitting close by. Additionally, the teacher would praise the appropriate behavior of a student or other students near the student engaged in the problem behavior. Proximity control is a powerful technique and may be enough to stop the problem. Moreover, if there is an easily correctable problem that may be a trigger for misbehavior, this gives the

teacher an opportunity to resolve the problem (e.g., if a student is frustrated with the academic task, the teacher may assist him or her).

Step 3: *Deliver a Precision Request* If the student continues with the misbehavior despite the teacher's use of low-profile approaches to stop the behavior, and the problem behavior threatens to disrupt the class, the teacher should deliver a precision request (see Figure 12–5). It is crucial that the teacher not become involved in escalating interactions with the student but deliver the precision request quietly and assuredly without becoming engaged in extra talk or discussion with the student.

Step 4: *Administer the Consequence* If the student complies with the precision request, the teacher should reinforce him or her and move on. If, however, the student doesn't comply, then the teacher must administer the prescribed negative consequence. Consequences should be planned by teachers before they have to administer them. Additionally, consequences should be approved by school administrators and explained to parents and students before they are used (Walker et al., 1995). Examples of negative consequences include time-out, response cost, overcorrection, in-school suspension, and an office referral. (For an examination of how teachers should plan and administer negative consequences see Chapter 11.)

Step 5: *Debrief the Student* Sugai and Colvin (1997) suggested that after teachers administer a negative consequence for problem behavior, they follow the consequence with a debriefing activity. Debriefing activities are short, proactive, preplanned interactions between a student and his or her teacher following the administration of the consequence. The purpose of debriefing is to (a) help the student identify the antecedent conditions that triggered the problem behavior; (b) provide feedback to remind or teach a student to identify and use socially appropriate behavior when confronted with similar conditions, thus increasing the likelihood that a student will display acceptable behavior in the future; and (c) prepare a student to successfully reenter normal classroom activities (Sugai & Colvin, 1997).

Debriefing is *not* an aversive consequence and should *not* include nagging, reprimanding, or threatening a student. Rather, the debriefing session should be a brief and positive encounter between a student and teacher. Sugai and Colvin (1997) and Colvin (2004) provided the following guidelines for conducting the debriefing session. First, the teacher explains the purpose of the debriefing session to the student (e.g., "Jeremy, you had to serve time-out for cursing at Staccy. Now let's put that behind us and talk about what we can do to prevent this behavior in the future so we can get you back to the class"). Second, the teacher asks the student a few questions regarding the incident to help him or her identify the antecedents of the problem behavior, including what, when, and why the incident occurred (e.g., "Jeremy, will you tell me what you did"). Third, the teacher asks the student what he or she can do next time instead of the problem behavior and get a commitment from the student (e.g., "Jeremy, tell me what can you do next time Stacey bothers you so that you will not get in trouble," "Good, you know what to do; now can you do it?"). Fourth, prepare the student to successfully reenter the normal classroom activity (e.g., "Good work Jeremy; remember what you will do the next time this occurs. Now let's go back to class"). Figure 12–8 shows an example of a format for debriefing a student.

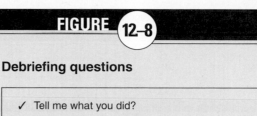

FIGURE 12–8

Debriefing questions

✓ Tell me what you did?

✓ What happened to you because of your actions?

✓ What could you have done instead that would not have caused this problem?

✓ The next time this happens what will you do?

✓ Will you do this?

✪ End the session on a positive note. Encourage the student and help him or her to transition to the next activity.

Chapter Summary

Students with EBD will engage in problem behaviors and teachers must be prepared to respond effectively and efficiently to such behaviors (e.g., noncompliance, verbal abuse, physical aggression, property destruction, direct defiance, and threats). Unfortunately, teachers often do not plan how to respond effectively and, therefore, resort to ineffective and intrusive responses to problem behavior such as ignoring, nattering, yelling, threatening, issuing commands when students are agitated, and engaging in escalating prompts. Proactive management strategies to prevent serious problem behaviors from occurring include modifying the learning environment and using precorrection strategies. Additionally, the following principles are important considerations in teacher responding:

- Emphasize preventive procedures.

- Respond privately rather than publicly.

- Maintain the student's dignity when responding.

- Respond fairly and consistently.

- Use alpha commands.

- Maintain a calm attitude when responding to problem behavior.

- Develop a game plan for responding to student problem behavior.

- Provide contingent reinforcement for appropriate behavior.

Moreover, teachers need to have preplanned and systematic ways to respond to (a) minor problem behavior, (b) noncompliance, and (c) severe misbehavior in ways that will stop misbehavior before it gets out of control and minimize threats to safety and classroom order.

Classroom and Behavior Management III: Intervening with Problem Behavior

Mitchell L. Yell

Focus Questions

- What are important considerations that teachers should adhere to when developing interventions to address problem behavior?
- How can teachers develop and implement behavior enhancement interventions?
- How can teachers develop and implement behavior reduction interventions?
- Are there legal guidelines teachers should follow when using behavior reduction interventions?

Chapters 10 and 11 addressed problem behavior on a schoolwide basis and in the classroom. The problem behaviors exhibited by many students with emotional or behavioral disorders (EBD), however, may be too frequent, intense, or persistent to be completely addressed by using the techniques in the preventing dimension (Brigham & Kauffman, 1998; Kauffman, 2005). Moreover, teaching students appropriate behavior, when they have long histories of being reinforced for using inappropriate behaviors, and reducing inappropriate behaviors will sometimes require specialized behavioral procedures. Teachers, therefore, will often need more powerful and direct interventions to teach appropriate behaviors and reduce or manage inappropriate behaviors of these students and the training to properly implement these interventions (Morgan & Jenson, 1988; Wolery et al., 1988; Zabel, 1987). I call this aspect of the classroom and behavior management the intervening dimension. The intervening dimension involves understanding and using research-based interventions to reinforce and teach appropriate behaviors or reduce the inappropriate behaviors of students with EBD.

This chapter examines a number of individual and group behavior management interventions. When teachers use interventions they are manipulating consequences to either increase desirable behaviors or decrease undesirable behaviors. The interventions that are used to increase or strengthen desirable behavior are referred to as behavior enhancement interventions. Interventions that are used to weaken or decrease undesirable behaviors are referred to as behavior reduction interventions. I begin the discussion with behavior enhancement interventions and conclude with behavior reduction interventions. Although I will discuss these interventions separately, often the interventions are combined as part of a total classroom and behavior management program.

CONSIDERATIONS WHEN INTERVENING TO ADDRESS STUDENT PROBLEM BEHAVIOR

When teachers decide to use behavior enhancement or reduction interventions, they should consider the five following factors.

First, teachers have a professional and ethical obligation to use behavior change procedures that have been shown to be effective in the research literature. Martella and colleagues (2003) aptly state that "students have a fundamental right to receive the most effective behavior management programs available" (p. 316). There is a large and impressive literature base regarding effective interventions with individual students and

groups of students with EBD. The knowledge of these practices must form the core of teachers' educational interventions if they are to effect meaningful changes in students and address students' special programming needs.

Second, the interventions that are used must be linked to assessment data. That is, the interventions that teachers use must be appropriate responses to students' problem behavior. For example, if a teacher's goal is to teach or increase behaviors, then he or she must use interventions, such as behavioral contracting or token economies, that positively reinforce, and therefore strengthen, appropriate behaviors. Similarly, if teachers seek to decrease inappropriate behaviors, then they must use behavior reduction interventions such as response cost or time-out.

Moreover, if interventions are used to reduce problem behavior, the interventions must match the function of the student's problem behavior as determined in a functional behavioral assessment (see Chapter 5 on functional behavioral assessments and behavior intervention plans). Not all interventions, even those that have been empirically proven, will be effective in every situation with every student. For example, if the function of a student's inappropriate behavior is to escape academic tasks, teachers should not use an intervention, such as time-out, in an attempt to reduce the problem behavior that allows the student to escape the task. On the other hand, time-out may be an appropriate intervention for a student whose problem behavior is maintained by attention. Using interventions that are based on the function of problem behavior will be more effective than using interventions that are not based on the behavior's function (Ingram, Lewis-Palmer, & Sugai, 2005).

Third, the behaviors that are selected to teach and strengthen or reduce, and the interventions that are used to achieve these goals, must be socially valid for the student. Social validity refers to the extent to which interventions are acceptable and socially meaningful to students. According to Lane and Beebe-Frankenberger (2004), socially valid interventions meet three criteria. First, the goals of the intervention must be socially significant. That is, the goals are important to the student because they will improve the quality of his or her life. Second, an intervention is socially acceptable when all parties involved (e.g., teacher, parents) believe that the intervention is reasonable and appropriate to use with a student. Third, social importance means that all parties involved believe the intervention will achieve the desired effects. Typically, social validity is assessed through indirect measures such as interviews, and direct measures such as observation.

Additionally, the primary criteria in choosing target behaviors should be what behaviors are socially valid and important to students. The target behaviors that are taught and strengthened should be those adaptive behaviors that are needed in less restrictive settings and that will continue to be reinforced in those settings (Allyon & Azrin, 1968; Wolery et al., 1988). In school settings, this means that target behaviors should include essential classroom expectations (e.g., talking only when given permission, raising hand for assistance, completing schoolwork). For example, teachers could use their classroom rule as the target behaviors to ensure that these important behaviors are reinforced. Additionally, if teachers post and frequently review these target behaviors, it is more likely that students will succeed in the reinforcement system (Rosenberg, 1986).

Fourth, interventions must be implemented with fidelity. When teachers use interventions they must ensure that the procedures are implemented as originally planned. There are many research-based interventions that have been shown to be very effective when used with students who exhibit serious problem behavior. However, if interventions are used as intended, they may not be effective. Additionally, if the intervention is not implemented correctly and a target behavior did change, we will not know why the change occurred.

When an intervention is implemented as originally intended, it has been implemented with integrity or fidelity (Gresham, 1989; Lane & Beebe-Frankenberger, 2004). To implement a treatment with integrity it is crucial that teachers (a) understand how the intervention is supposed to be used, and (b) implement the intervention in accordance with this understanding. When interventions are implemented with good treatment integrity, they are much more likely to be effective.

Unfortunately, teachers sometimes compromise the treatment integrity because they do not implement an intervention as it was originally intended. According to Lane and Beebe-Frankenberger (2004), teachers should monitor the degree to which each component of the intervention is implemented or designed. This can be done in a number of ways. First, a trained observer could watch the teacher as he or she implements the intervention and check for treatment integrity. Second, the teacher or paraprofessional could videotape the intervention being used, and then the teacher, the trained observer, or both could watch it at a later time and assess treatment integrity. Third, the teacher could prepare a checklist of treatment components to examine before or immediately after he or she implements the intervention.

Fifth, teachers must collect data to evaluate the effectiveness of the interventions that they use.

Guesses, feelings, and intuition are not effective ways to make instructional decisions. When important decisions about a student's program must be made, teachers need objective and reliable information to guide their decisions. To determine an intervention's effectiveness and to make accurate decisions regarding intervention changes after the target behavior has been determined, the teacher needs to collect baseline data on the target behavior so that student progress can be monitored (Deno, 2001). Then the teacher must collect data on a student's progress on a frequent and regular basis. When teachers frequently monitor student progress, the success or failure of intervention procedures becomes readily apparent (Wolery et al., 1988).

BEHAVIOR ENHANCEMENT INTERVENTIONS

Behavior enhancement interventions primarily use positive reinforcement to maintain, increase, or strengthen socially appropriate behaviors. Behavior enhancement procedures, like positive reinforcers, should be individualized. The following section describes a number of major behavior enhancement interventions. These interventions may be applied by themselves or in combination with other behavior enhancement procedures (e.g., using a token economy and a behavioral contract together). These interventions may also be used in combination with behavior reduction procedures (e.g., combining a token economy with a response-cost system). Prior to examining behavior enhancement procedures, however, we discuss how to identify reinforcers to use in interventions.

Identifying Reinforcers

In Chapter 4 we discussed the principles of behavior and defined reinforcement as the contingent presentation of a consequence that maintains or strengthens a behavior. To effectively use this principle of behavior, teachers must identify consequences that will increase the future likelihood of the occurrence of the behavior that they want a student to exhibit.

Teachers sometimes make the mistake of assuming that because a reinforcer has worked in the past it will work with all students in all situations. Similarly, sometimes teachers believe that because they tried a reinforcer in the past and it did not work, that the reinforcer (and sometimes reinforcement in general) does not work. Consequences that may be reinforcing to one student, however, may not be reinforcing to another student. Another mistake that teachers may make is in believing that what they *think* will be reinforcing to students will, in fact, be reinforcing to those students. Teachers must never confuse what they assume will be reinforcing for what can be demonstrated to be reinforcing. A consequence is reinforcing only when it can be *demonstrated that the behavior it follows is maintained or strengthened*. It is important, therefore, that teachers identify effective individual reinforcers for each of their students.

A number of methods can be used to identify consequences that are reinforcing to students. Two of the most common methods are to (a) watch them, and (b) ask them. Using the first method, teachers can give students an opportunity to engage in activities of their choice, then observe them and record their preferences. Premack (1959) demonstrated that the behaviors that people repeatedly engage in, which he termed high-probability behaviors, could be used to reinforce low-probability behaviors. The results of Premack's research indicated these preferred activities can then be used as reinforcers. Premack's formulation has been referred to as the *Premack principle*.

According to Wolery and colleagues (1988), teachers should ask the following questions when trying to identify possible reinforcers: (a) What do the students ask for? (b) What do the students do? (c) What are the objects, activities, and choices the students make when given an opportunity? After observing students choose reinforcers for themselves, teachers can assume that the activities students choose to do most frequently are reinforcing, and the things students choose to do less frequently are less reinforcing (Morgan & Jenson, 1988).

Teachers may also use a technique called *reinforcer sampling* to determine what will be reinforcing for individual students. In this procedure a number of reinforcers are made available to the student. The teacher then observes which reinforcers the student prefers. Reinforcer sampling can also increase the reinforcement value of a consequence by increasing a student's familiarity and experience with a reinforcer (Kazdin, 2001; Wolery et al., 1988).

The second method for identifying reinforcing consequences is to ask the student. Interviewing students about their preferences can provide useful information about potential reinforcers. When interviewing a student, Wolery and colleagues (1988) suggest that the teacher directly ask the student what he or she would like to earn. Similarly, interviewing students' parents, peers, or teachers can provide information about what is reinforcing to a student. If students do not provide useful information about what is reinforcing to them, the teacher may provide the students with a *reinforcer menu*. The menu is a list of possible reinforcers and students may choose what they would prefer from the list.

Types of Reinforcers

There are many types of reinforcers. Perhaps the most frequently used type is the *social reinforcer*. Social reinforcement refers to providing positive attention, feedback, and approval given by the teacher contingent on a student exhibiting a desired behavior. Social reinforcers should always be paired with previously established reinforcers. Table 13–1 depicts examples of social reinforcers. Unfortunately we know that teachers do not use social reinforcers, such as praise, very often (Good & Brophy, 2008; Walker et al., 2004).

A slightly more intrusive type of reinforcer is the *activity reinforcer*. An example is a teacher offering a student an opportunity to engage in an activity he or she likes doing, contingent on the student exhibiting a behavior that he or she is less likely to engage in. When teachers allow students to engage in high-probability activities after the students have completed a low-probability activity they are using the Premack principle (see Figure 13–1).

Activity reinforcers are more intrusive than social reinforcers because the teacher must identify the reinforcing activity and then make that activity contingent on a student completing a low-probability task. Table 13–2 depicts potential activity reinforcers.

Token reinforcement refers to the teacher giving a student a token (e.g., poker chips, points) when he or she exhibits the desired target behavior. The tokens, which have no inherent value, can be traded for backup reinforcers. These backup reinforcers must be reinforcing to the student for tokens to be successful. Tokens are the central aspect of a token economy, which will be explained later in this chapter. Table 13–3 lists examples of tokens.

When a teacher uses *tangible reinforcers*, he or she gives the student a tangible item (e.g., sticker, book) following the performance of a desired behavior. These may be used as immediate reinforcers or backup reinforcers.

Table 13–1   Social reinforcers

Verbal recognition	Verbal praise from teachers, administrators, other adults
Positive phone call home	Display of student work
Student for a day	First in line
Positive note to parents	Verbal praise from students

Table 13–2   Activity reinforcers

Playing on the computer	Playing basketball
Free time	Free reading
Extra recess	Listening to CDs
Watching a movie	Caring for a class pet
Choice of activities	Run errands

Example of the Premack principle

Although Nick could do his mathematics assignments, he seldom completed his daily assignment during the allotted class time. Because Mrs. Quam, his teacher, knew that Nick would not take the work home to complete, she decided to reinforce Nick for completing his work in class. In his free time Nick usually chose to play games on the computer. So Mrs. Quam told Nick that when he finished his math assignment with 100% accuracy he could play on the computer until class was over. Nick began finishing his assignments during class time and was given extra computer time by Mrs. Quam.

Table 13–3   Tokens

Points	Happy faces
Poker chips	Stamp marks
Gold stars	Check marks

Table 13–4   Tangible and edible reinforcers

Tangible Reinforcers	Edible Reinforcers
Trading cards	Fruit
Comic books	Fruit-flavored drinks
Rubber stamps	Candy
Magazines	Gum
Stickers	Pizza

Edible reinforcers, like tangible reinforcers, are relatively intrusive. As the name implies, contingent on a student performing a desired behavior, the teacher gives him or her an edible item to reinforce that behavior. Table 13–4 lists some examples of tangible and edible reinforcers.

Behavior enhancement interventions use social, activity, token, tangible, or edible reinforcers either by themselves or in combination. We next discuss four major types of behavior enhancement interventions: (a) token economies, (b) level systems, (c) behavioral contracting, and (d) group-oriented contingencies.

INTERVENTIONS

Token Economies

Token economies are comprehensive reinforcement systems that have been used successfully in a variety of settings, including resource rooms and self-contained

settings (Kerr & Nelson, 2006; Maag, 2004; Martella et al., 2003; Walker, 1995; Wolery et al., 1988; Zirpoli & Melloy, 2001). Many special education classrooms use some form of individualized or group token economy to manage the academic and social behaviors of students and to prepare them for entry into less restrictive settings (Wolery et al., 1988). In fact, token economies may be used by as many as 90% of teachers of students with EBD (Rosenberg, Wilson, Maheady, & Sindelar, 2004).

Token economies are reinforcement systems in which students earn tokens for appropriate behaviors and later exchange these tokens for backup reinforcers. Token economies are empirically supported practices that have been used to control problem behaviors (Allyon, Layman, & Kandel, 1975; Foxx, 1998; Hupp & Reitman, 1999; Kazdin, 1977, 1985; McLaughlin & Malaby, 1972; Robinson, Newby, & Ganzell, 1981). Table 13–5 lists some of the school-based research that has been conducted on token economies.

Advantages and Disadvantages of Token Economies

Token systems can be very effective for reinforcing appropriate behaviors and reducing inappropriate behaviors. A number of characteristics of token economies make them particularly effective in resource rooms and self-contained settings for students with EBD. First, the tokens can be given immediately to reinforce target behaviors, which may be especially important for young students and when teaching new behaviors. The time gap between target behavior and reinforcement is lessened or bridged when tokens are used. Second, teachers

Table 13–5   Research on token economies

Behaviors	Studies
Academic performance	• Birnbauer, Bijou, Wolf, & Kidder, 1965
	• Bushell, 1978
	• Fabry, Mayhew, & Hanson, 1984
	• McGinnis, Friman, & Carlyon, 1999
	• McLaughlin, 1981
	• Robinson, Newby, & Ganzell, 1981
	• Swain & McLaughlin, 1998
	• Trovato & Bucher, 1980
	• Wolf, Giles, & Hall, 1968
Classroom behaviors	• Barrish, Saunders, & Wolf, 1969
	• Birnbauer, Wolf, Kidder, & Tague, 1965
	• McLaughlin & Malaby, 1972
	• O'Leary, Becker, Evans, & Saudargas, 1969
	• Quay, Glavin, Annesley, & Werry, 1972
Self-management	• Goldstein, Shemansky, Cavalier, Ferreti, & Hodges, 1997
Aggressive behaviors	• Foxx, 1998

can give tokens or points quickly and discretely; thus the classroom environment will not be disrupted like it would be if the teacher were giving tangible reinforcers. Third, because tokens are generalized conditioned reinforcers, they can be given to students with different preferences in reinforcers.[1] Additionally, students are less likely to become satiated with them and tokens are less likely to lose reinforcing power. Fourth, tokens provide stimuli that control teacher behavior (Cooper et al., 1987). That is, tokens can serve as a cue to remind teachers to reinforce students. Cooper, Heron, and Heward (2006) give the example of a teacher keeping marbles in his pocket to dispense as tokens. They note that the weight of the marbles in his pocket functions as a discriminative stimulus, which leads to marble dispensing in the presence of target behaviors. Thus, tokens influence teachers to interact frequently with students.

Because token economies are based on the monetary system, they can also be used as instructional opportunities. For example, teachers can develop student savings accounts, in which the tokens they earn are deposited. Then when students spend their tokens they can withdraw them or write checks on their accounts. Students could also be required to balance their accounts monthly. Teachers can use the components of the token economy to teach basic concepts of consumer economics.

Another advantage of using a token economy in a resource room or self-contained setting is the system can easily be modified to reinforce students for behaving appropriately when they attend mainstream classes. Teachers can develop point sheets that students take with them to their mainstream classes. The point sheet can be used to reinforce the behavioral expectations of the student's mainstream teacher(s). Figure 13-2 depicts an example of a point sheet that could be used to monitor student behavior in general education classrooms.

The column headings are the target behaviors that will be reinforced by the mainstream teacher. The column on the far left indicates the class (e.g., social studies) or class time. The student brings the point sheet with him or her to the mainstream class. At the end of the class period, the mainstream teacher marks the appropriate box for each behavior. For example, the teacher could give the student a 4 for excellent, 3 for good, 2 for adequate, 1 for poor, and 0 for very poor. When the student

returns to the resource room or self-contained room, he or she gives the point sheet to the teacher, who dispenses the appropriate number of tokens (e.g., two tokens for a rating of 2). A similar system could be used at home. In this situation, the student would be reinforced for behaviors that his or her parents believe are most important. When a token economy is used in this way, teachers will need to develop procedures to fade its use.

The primary disadvantages of token systems are that they require a fair amount of time to set up and keep running efficiently and effectively, and can be complex and difficult for teachers, paraeducators, and parents to implement with fidelity. If the token economy will be used to reinforce behavior in the mainstream or home setting, the teacher and parents must understand the point system, use it consistently, and implement it correctly. If teachers or parents either will not cooperate in using the system or are inconsistent in giving points, the token economy will not work in these settings. For token economies to work effectively, teachers and others who implement the system must develop clear guidelines for operation and be committed to implementing the system with fidelity. Establishing and implementing token economies requires careful planning.

Setting Up a Token Economy Setting up a classroom token economy requires careful planning, consistent implementation, and constant monitoring (Alberto & Troutman, 2004; Martella et al., 2003; Wolery et al., 1988). When developing a token economy, teachers must develop rules and guidelines that clarify procedures for (a) identifying target behaviors, (b) specifying tokens, (c) choosing backup reinforcers, (d) delivering tokens, (e) exchanging tokens for backup reinforcers, (f) addressing problem behavior, (g) fading the use of a token economy, (h) fading the token economy, and (i) teaching the token economy to students. We next describe these essential steps. Figure 13-3 is a checklist to ensure that the token economy is implemented with fidelity.

Step 1: *Identify target behaviors.* Because the purpose of a token economy is to strengthen desirable behavior, the first step in setting up the token economy is to operationally define all target behaviors that will be reinforced in the token system (see Chapter 4 for a description and examples of operationally defined behaviors). When target behaviors are operationally defined, staff and students will clearly know what behaviors will be reinforced.

Step 2: *Select tokens.* Tokens are easily dispensed objects that can be given to students contingent on their performing specific target behaviors. Many

[1]A generalized conditioned reinforcer is a type of conditioned reinforcer that can be exchanged for a variety of item or activity reinforcers. Money is an example of a generalized conditioned reinforcer.

FIGURE 13–2

Example of a point sheet to use in general education classrooms

Student's name Billy_____ Date _____

Please rate Billy's behavior in each of the areas listed below. Use the following point system: 4 = outstanding, 3 = good, 2 = adequate, 1 = poor, and 0 = very poor. Place your initials in the last column. Please write comments on the back. Thank you.

Class	On-Time to Class	Behavior	Class Work	Other	Initials
Math					
Reading					
Social studies					
Science					
Special areas					

different objects can serve as tokens (e.g., points, poker chips, coupons, marbles). Objects that teachers choose to use as tokens should not be easily counterfeited (e.g., colored paper) or easily obtained from other sources (e.g., paper clips). Moreover, it is usually advisable for teachers to keep control of the tokens because of the potential problem of students losing their tokens or other students stealing them. Teachers should also choose tokens that are appropriate for age groups. For example,

young students may prefer tangible objects for tokens, whereas older students may prefer point cards. Cooper and colleagues (2007) also note that tokens should be safe. This means that for young children tokens should not be something they could swallow and for older students they should not be items that could be used as weapons.

The tokens themselves have no intrinsic reinforcing value. Their value is that they serve as a stimulus that bridges the delay between the target

FIGURE 13–3

Token economy checklist

Yes	No	Component
☐	☐	Target behaviors are identified. *-Are the target behaviors socially valid for the student?* *-Is the target behavior observable and measurable?* *-Have baseline measures been taken of the target behaviors?*
☐	☐	Tokens are selected. *-Are tokens convenient and easily managed and dispensed?* *-Are tokens controlled by the teacher?* *-Are tokens appropriate for the age group of the students?* *-Can tokens be easily counterfeited or obtained from other sources?*
☐	☐	Backup reinforcers are selected. *-Were backup reinforcers selected by observing students or asking them about their preferences?* *-Are backup reinforcers appropriate for the age of the students?* *-Are backup reinforcers assigned value in accordance with students' preferences?* *-Is the reinforcer menu publicly posted?*
☐	☐	Token delivery system is in place. *-Are the tokens delivered immediately after students engage in target behavior?*
☐	☐	Exchange method is in place. *-When will exchanges be made?* *-How will exchanges be made?* *-Where will the exchanges take place?*
☐	☐	Method for addressing problem behavior is selected. *-Is there a response-cost system in the token economy?*
☐	☐	Method to fade the use of the token economy is determined.
☐	☐	Data collection and record-keeping systems are developed. *-Has a data collection system to monitor student progress been developed?* *-Are records kept on the operation of the token economy?*
☐	☐	Students understand the token economy.

behavior and the delivery of the reinforcer (Kazdin, 1977; Wolery et al., 1988). Moreover, the tokens should be practical and convenient so that the teacher can dispense immediately after the target behavior occurs without disrupting the classroom environment. Often teachers use points or point cards rather than tokens to minimize disruptions when they are delivered to students.

Step 3: *Choose backup reinforcers.* Tokens become generalized conditioned reinforcers when they are paired with backup reinforcers. The effectiveness of a token economy depends on the backup reinforcers (Miltenberger, 2004); therefore, teachers

must take care in choosing them. The backup reinforcers can be selected using the methods previously described (e.g., observing students, interviewing students), and can include social, activity, tangible, or edible reinforcers. Backup reinforcers should be age appropriate for the students and should be as similar as possible to reinforcers that are available in less restrictive settings. Once the backup reinforcers are selected, a reinforcer menu should be developed and posted in the classroom.

Usually the backup reinforcers on the menu are assigned different values according to student preferences. A typical method for assigning point values to backup reinforcers is to assign higher token values to high-preference items and activities, and assign lower values to low-preference items and activities. For example, a student could trade a small number of tokens (e.g., 1 token) for early dismissal to recess, whereas a student would need a larger number of tokens (e.g., 10) to get a free homework card. When token economies have a sufficient number of items, privileges, or activities available as backup reinforcers, reinforcer satiation is less likely to be a problem because students will always have a number of options available to trade for their tokens.

Figure 13–4 depicts examples of backup reinforcers and their token values. Wolery et al., (1988) note that the smallest number of earned tokens should enable a student to access some level of backup reinforcers. Furthermore, backup reinforcers should not be available to students through means other than purchase with tokens a student has earned (Miltenberger, 2004).

Step 4: *Decide how you will deliver tokens.* Teachers need to determine how and when they will deliver tokens to students when they engage in the appropriate target behaviors. Methods of delivering tokens include giving the student a token (e. g., dropping a marble in a jar on his or her desk), punching a hole in a reinforcement card, writing the earned number of tokens in a "savings account," or making a tally on a bulletin board.

Teachers should deliver the tokens immediately after the students engage in the target behavior. This is especially important when teaching new behaviors and with young students. It is preferable to start a token system, therefore, by using a continuous reinforcement schedule. Later, when target behaviors occur more frequently, teachers may move to an intermittent schedule of reinforcement for delivering tokens (Miltenberger, 2004). Older students, however, may not require reinforcement as immediately as younger students. For example, with older students the teacher could deliver tokens at the end of every hour.

Step 5: *Determine how students will exchange tokens for backup reinforcers.* Teachers should develop guidelines about when, how, and where students can exchange their tokens for backup reinforcers. Specifically, the teacher must decide (a) when exchanges will be made (e.g., hourly, daily, or weekly); (b) how exchanges will be made (turning in point cards, trading actual tokens, writing checks); and (c) where the exchanges will take place (e.g., at the classroom store, at the teacher's desk). The goal is to gradually increase the time between when students earn tokens and when they purchase backup reinforcers.

FIGURE 13-4

Examples of backup reinforcers and token values (elementary level)

Reinforcer	Cost
5 minutes of free time	25 points
10 minutes of additional recess	35 points
10 minutes on a video or computer game	35 points
Snack from classroom store (e.g., ice cream)	40 points
Stickers from classroom store	40 points
Pens/Pencils from classroom store	40 points
Marbles from classroom store	50 points
Trading cards from classroom store	60 points
Posters from classroom store	60 points
Magic tricks from classroom store	60 points
Board games from classroom store	75 points
CDs from classroom store	100 points
MP3 player from school store	250 points

Step 6: *Decide how you will address problem behavior.* Another important decision that teachers must make is how they will address student problem behavior vis-à-vis the token economy. Tokens are excellent tools for immediately consequating inappropriate behaviors (Martella et al., 2003). A response-cost system works especially well with a token economy, although it is not necessary that a response-cost component be used in a token system. If, however, there are inappropriate behaviors that compete with the appropriate behaviors that a teacher is trying to strengthen with the token system, a response-cost component may be included with the system.

A response-cost system is frequently used in conjunction with a token economy. In response cost, the reinforcers that were previously earned (i.e., tokens) would be systematically removed contingent on inappropriate behavior (Zirpoli & Melloy, 2001). Later in this chapter I discuss response-cost systems and how they can be incorporated into a token economy.

Miltenberger (2004) suggests that if a response-cost component is used with a token economy, the response-cost system should be introduced only after the token economy has been in place for some time. This way the tokens will have been firmly established as conditioned reinforcers and the loss of them will be more likely to be an effective punisher. If a teacher is going to use response cost, it is important that he or she defines the behaviors that will result in a student losing tokens and lets students know the severity of the fine. Teachers never want to fine a student more tokens than they have because that would negate the positive reinforcement provided by the tokens (Maag, 2004; Miltenberger, 2004; Walker, 1995).

Step 7: *Determine how you will fade the use of the token economy.* Well-planned and implemented token economies are very effective. However, because they may not be used in less restrictive settings, teachers who use them must plan to fade the token economy. That is, teachers should establish procedures that gradually move students away from the token economy and toward conditions that are more like less restrictive settings (Wolery et al., 1988). If teachers fade the use of the token economy the behavior that has been strengthened more likely will be generalized to the regular school environment where natural reinforcers will maintain the desirable behavior (Kazdin, 1985; Miltenberger, 2004; Zirpoli, 2005). Similarly, if teachers do not fade the influence of the tokens and backup

reinforcers, maintenance and generalization will be less likely to occur.

The fading of the token system may be achieved by (a) delaying the delivery of tokens, (b) giving the tokens on an intermittent basis, (c) decreasing the amount of tokens earned for each behavior, (d) increasing the delay between delivering the token and allowing exchanges for backup reinforcers, (e) increasing the prices of backup reinforcers, and (f) providing the backup reinforcers on an intermittent basis (Cooper et al., 2007).

Teachers should always pair the delivery of tokens with praise. Praise will become a conditioned reinforcer if it is paired with the reinforcing tokens. After the token system is faded, teachers should continue to deliver praise to reinforce desirable behavior.

Step 8: *Develop a data collection and record-keeping system.* With all behavior management strategies, teachers should collect student performance data on a continuous basis to monitor student progress. Chapter 3 on assessment explains how teachers can collect data on student progress. When teachers use token economies, the tokens that students earn can be used as a rough indicator of student progress. However, merely counting tokens earned is not a true indicator of student behavior; only direct observation will provide accurate enough data for determining student progress.

Records should also be kept on the (a) number of tokens earned and lost, (b) types and numbers of backup reinforcers delivered, and (c) behavioral improvement from the progress monitoring data. This will help the teacher evaluate the effectiveness of the token economy. Having students or the teacher mark points on a card, rather than giving tangible tokens, will create a permanent product and facilitate record keeping. Wolery and colleagues (1988) suggest that students maintain graphs of the tokens that they earn. They further note that charting tokens earned and seeing their progress will be reinforcing to students.

Teachers should constantly assess the operation of the token economy. Student performance is, of course, the best indicator of how the system is working. Teachers should also note (a) which backup reinforcers are the most popular, (b) if there is a sufficient variety and amount of backup reinforcers, (c) if new backup reinforcers are needed, (d) how smoothly the delivery and exchange procedures work, (e) if response-cost procedures are being used appropriately, (f) if fading procedures are being implemented, and (g) if a record-keeping system is in place.

Step 9: *Teach the token economy.* After the teacher has planned the classroom token economy, he or she needs to teach the students about the system's operating guidelines. This includes (a) target behaviors, (b) earning tokens, (c) token value, (d) backup reinforcers, (e) exchanging tokens for reinforcers, and (f) consequences for inappropriate behavior. All aspects of the token economy should be explained and demonstrated until students clearly understand the procedure. Additionally, teachers should have all materials prepared prior to implementing the system (e.g., tokens, backup reinforcers, record-keeping forms).

Summary of Token Economies A token economy is a system for delivering reinforcement in which students earn tokens that can be exchanged for backup reinforcers. Many teachers of students with EBD, in both resource room and self-contained settings, use token economies. Establishing and using token economies is a time-consuming process that requires careful planning and accurate and consistent implementation. Using token economies in classrooms for students with EBD has empirical support and can be a powerful intervention to increase appropriate behaviors and reduce inappropriate behaviors.

Level Systems

Level systems were developed as comprehensive behavior management interventions. The basic idea of a level system is simple; students enter the system and are taught and reinforced for appropriate school-related behaviors. As the students master these behaviors, they progress to higher levels where they are taught and reinforced for performing more complex school-related behaviors. In this way, a level system shapes new behaviors, fades behavior management procedures, and programs for generalization of new skills (Morgan & Jenson, 1988). Level systems have been used in classrooms (Walker & Buckley, 1974), group homes (Phillips, Phillips, Fixsen, & Wolf, 1971), and in institutional settings (Bauer, Shea, & Keppler, 1986).

Teachers who use level systems develop a hierarchy of levels that increase standards for behavioral and academic improvement. When students enter the level system, the behavioral expectations are simple, fundamental, and are often directed toward decreasing behavioral excesses. The entry level may involve following basic classroom rules (e.g., keep hands, feet, and objects to yourself) and basic academic behaviors (e.g., bringing materials to class).

When a student has met the behavioral expectations of the initial level for a predetermined amount of time or to a predetermined level of accuracy, he or she moves to a higher level. Student advancement through the levels, therefore, is based on an assessment of student progress toward meeting the behavioral and academic expectations of each level. When a student reaches higher levels, the behavioral and academic expectations increase in complexity (e.g., completing assignments on time, self-monitoring). Moreover, with each new level more natural reinforcers are used and behavioral structure decreases.

Often a level system is operated in conjunction with a token economy, and the behavior expectations at each level are reinforced using tokens or points. These tokens or points can then be exchanged for backup reinforcers. As the student moves to higher levels, new and preferred types of backup reinforcers are available. At the most advanced levels, reinforcement systems are faded. The students at these levels learn to monitor and evaluate their own behavior. Behavior management systems at the highest levels are the same as those systems typically used in general education classrooms. As students progress through the levels, they must exhibit the set of behaviors required on the new level, as well as continuing to demonstrate mastery of the behaviors required in the lower levels.

Morgan and Jenson (1988) and Bauer and Shea (1988) asserted that the initial levels of the system should be designed to control behavioral excesses and feature external control systems, such as points or tokens. Middle levels are designed to teach replacement behaviors of academic and social skills. The upper levels are designed to teach self-management skills. As students become accurate in self-management, the use of an external management system is faded. Figure 13–5 shows an example of a level system.

Although level systems are widely used in classrooms for students with EBD, there has been little empirical validation of their effectiveness with this population (Scheuermann & Webber, 1996). Table 13–6 lists some of the school-based research that has been conducted on level systems.

Table 13–6   Research on level systems

Behaviors	Studies
Classroom behavior	• Gable & Strain, 1981
	• Mastropieri, Jenne, & Scruggs, 1988
	• Schloss, Alper, & Green, 1984
	• Schloss, Holt, Mulvaney, & Green, 1988

FIGURE 13–5

Level system

Level	Behaviors	Incentives
Level 1—entry	-Keep hands, feet, and objects to self -Talk only when given permission -Leave seat only when given permission -Follow teacher directions	Token economy reinforcers
Level 2—intermediate	-Exhibit entry-level behaviors -Get to class on time -Bring materials -Participate in class activities	Token economy reinforcers and behavioral contracts
Level 3—intermediate	-Exhibit entry-level and level 2 behaviors -Complete 75% of assignments -Complete 75% of homework -Maintain excellent attendance rate	Behavioral contracts
Level 4—advanced	-Exhibit entry-level, level 2, and level 3 behaviors -Complete 95% of assignments -Complete 95% of homework -Participate actively in class activities	Total school privileges

Advantages and Disadvantages of Level Systems
According to Morgan and Jenson (1988), there are four basic advantages to using level systems. First, classroom rules are made explicit because the description of the level system—including levels, rules, and privileges—is posted in the classroom. Second, the public posting gives students visual feedback about their performance. Third, classroom privileges are contingent on explicit and well-defined performance. Finally, the level system serves as a program for shaping, fading, and generalizing behaviors. Additionally, student's progress through the level system serves as a rough type of progress monitoring. If a student in the level system continues to exhibit problem behavior, it is an indication that the program needs modification.

As previously mentioned, although level systems are widely used in classrooms for students with EBD, there is little empirical validation of their effectiveness (Scheuermann et al., 1994; Scheuermann & Webber, 1996; Smith & Farrell, 1993). Most of the literature on level systems merely describes their use, with no accompanying data (Scheuermann & Webber, 1996). Research is needed to determine if level systems are effective interventions to use in programs for students with EBD. Additionally, some researchers raised legal concerns about level systems (Scheuermann & Webber, 1996; Scheuermann, Webber, Partin, & Knies, 1994). Although there is nothing inherent in level systems that are illegal, if they are used in ways that remove students from less restrictive settings without notice being provided to parents, or they restrict students' access to less restrictive environments, they certainly violate the spirit and the letter of IDEA.

Setting Up a Level System Like establishing a token economy, setting up a classroom level system requires careful planning, consistent implementation, and constant monitoring. Teachers should consider the following steps when setting up a level system. Figure 13–6 is a checklist to ensure that the level system is implemented with fidelity.

Step 1: *Define the levels in the system.* Every level in the system has specific behavioral expectations, reinforcers, and consequences. The entry levels typically provide greater structure, fewer choices for reinforcement, and focus on the student's behavioral excesses and deficits, including social skill and academic deficits. The middle levels usually have less structure, more choices for reinforcers, and emphasize teaching replacement behaviors and desirable behaviors. At the upper levels, the structure

FIGURE 13-6

Level system checklist

Yes	No	Component
☐	☐	Levels are defined. -*Do the entry levels typically provide greater structure, fewer choices for reinforcement, and focus on the student's behavioral excesses and deficits?* -*Do the middle levels have less structure, more choices for reinforcers, and emphasize teaching desirable behaviors?* -*Do the upper levels have minimal structure and emphasis behaviors that are required in general education settings?*
☐	☐	Privileges and rewards at each level are defined. -*Do entry levels reinforce students with external reinforcement systems?* -*Do teachers use reinforcers that are available in the less restrictive settings as the students' progress through the level system?*
☐	☐	Behavioral criteria for moving among levels are determined. -*What behavioral and academic skills will students need to demonstrate as they move up the level system?* -*Will a minimum stay be required at each level?* -*How frequently will a student's status be reviewed?* -*Who will review a student's status?* -*What level of appropriate behavior will be required to remain at a level?*
☐	☐	Consequences for inappropriate behavior are identified. -*Will behavior reduction procedures be used if students engage in inappropriate behaviors?* -*Will inappropriate behaviors cause a student to regress to a lower level?*
☐	☐	How students will be moved through the level system is determined. -*Will students be required to reach specific behavioral goals on a level and maintain that behavior for a specified period of time before they move to the next level?*
☐	☐	Data collection and record-keeping systems are developed. -*Has a data collection system to monitor student progress been developed?* -*Are records kept on the operation of the level system?*
☐	☐	Students understand the level system.

decreases and behaviors that are expected include self-management skills and other behaviors that are required in general education settings.

Step 2: ***Choose the privileges and reinforcers that will be available at each level.*** The teacher needs to decide how students will be reinforced at each level. Typically, students in the entry levels are reinforced using external reinforcement systems such as token economies. As students progress through the level system, teachers should use reinforcers that are available in the less restrictive settings. At these stages some form of reinforcement

may be necessary, but teachers still should fade the use of these external reinforcement systems.

Step 3: ***Determine the behavioral criteria necessary for students to move from one level to another.*** Teachers must choose the behavioral and academic skills that students need to demonstrate as they move up the level system. After the behavioral criteria are chosen, the teacher must clearly explain these criteria to the students. Students must demonstrate the required levels of the specified behaviors for a specified amount of time before they are moved to a higher level.

Although the level system is for the entire group of students with whom the teacher works, it should be individualized for the unique needs of each student. That is, teachers should target increasing the appropriate behaviors, and reducing the inappropriate behaviors that the student exhibits.

Additionally, the teacher should decide (a) if a minimum stay will be required at each level, (b) how frequently a student's status will be reviewed, (c) who will review a student's status, (d) what level of appropriate behavior will be required to remain at a level, and (e) what student self-monitoring and teacher monitoring will be needed (Walker & Shea, 1999). Teachers determine how they will communicate with parents, students, and other involved staff members.

Step 4: *Clarify inappropriate behaviors and their consequences.* Many level systems include punishers if students engage in inappropriate behaviors. Teachers should be clear about what constitutes inappropriate behavior that will be punished. These punishers may include response cost or time out.

Additionally, because a student's progress to higher levels is contingent on him or her exhibiting the new behaviors *and* continuing to demonstrate mastery of the behaviors at the previous levels, the teacher must decide if inappropriate behaviors will cause a student to regress to a lower level. Moreover, the teacher must decide when students may be demoted to lower levels contingent on inappropriate behaviors (e.g., what amounts or types of inappropriate behaviors will result in a student losing a level). Schloss and Smith (1998) suggest that demotion to a lower level may serve as a type of probation. The student would stay at the lower level for a short period and if he or she earns a predetermined number of points, he or she may be moved back to the original level.

Step 5: *Establish how students will move through the level system.* Teachers must decide on the criteria that will enable students to move to a higher level. Often students will be required to reach specific behavioral goals on a level, and maintain that behavior for a specified period to move to the next level. In addition, on higher levels students must continue to achieve all of the goals on the lower levels.

Step 6: *Develop a data collection and record-keeping system.* As previously mentioned, teachers should collect student performance data on a continuous basis to monitor student progress. Student progress through the levels can be used both as a rough indicator of student progress, as well

as a measure of the effectiveness of the system. However, progress through the levels is not a true indicator of student behavior; only direct observation will provide accurate enough data for actually determining student progress.

Step 7: *Teach the level system.* After the teacher has planned the classroom level system, he or she needs to teach the students about the system's operating guidelines. This includes (a) behavioral expectations on each level, (b) privileges and reinforcers associated with each level, (c) inappropriate behaviors and consequences associated with these behaviors, and (d) student movement through the levels.

Summary of Level Systems Level systems are frequently used in classrooms for students with EBD. In a level system students are placed in an entry behavior level. They are then taught and reinforced for appropriate school-related behaviors. As students master these behaviors, they progress to higher levels where they are taught and reinforced for performing more complex school-related behaviors. In this way, a level system shapes new behaviors, fades behavior management procedures, and programs for generalization of new skills. More research on level systems is needed to determine if they are effective interventions to use in programs for students with EBD.

Behavioral Contracting

Behavioral contracting is a procedure used to teach and reward appropriate behavior.[2] A behavioral contract is a verbal or written arrangement between two or more people that specifies how a person's behavior will change and what rewards will be available to him or her when the behavior changes. Contracts are most often an arrangement between a teacher and a student, parents and their children, or a teacher, a student's parents, and the student, and are useful when working with students who can understand and enter into the agreement. A behavioral contract outlines what each participant must do to satisfy the contract's terms.

The contract is based on the principles of positive reinforcement, but may also involve behavior reduction procedures. Behavioral contracts include an accountability mechanism, because rewards and behavior measurement methods are clearly specified. Additionally, Cooper et al., (2007) state that contracts must be fair, clear, and honest. First, the reward specified in the contract must be fair considering the amount and difficulty of the task

---

[2]Note that a contract specifies a reward, rather than a reinforcer. If, in fact, the reward results in an increase or strengthening of the target behavior, then, and only then, will it be a reinforcer.

to be completed by the student. Second, expectations for each of the parties (e.g., parents, teachers, students) must be clearly specified. Third, the reward delivered must be exactly as described in the terms of the contract. Additionally, the reward must be delivered in accordance with the provisions of the contract (e.g., time, amount).

Although reports of the effective use of behavioral contracts appear frequently in the literature, there has not been much research conducted on the components of a contract that may make them more or less effective (Kazdin, 2001). Therefore, there is little guidance to help teachers make their behavioral contract maximally effective. Table 13-7 lists some of the school-based research that has been conducted on behavioral contracts.

Advantages and Disadvantages of Behavioral Contracting There are a number of characteristics of behavioral contracts that make them particularly effective in resource rooms and self-contained settings for students with EBD. One significant advantage of behavioral contracts is that they can be written to reward students for behaving appropriately when they attend mainstream classes. For example, a teacher could develop a point sheet that students take with them to their mainstream classes. Contingent on a student's behavior, the points earned in the mainstream class could be counted toward fulfilling the contract. Thus, the contract could be used to reinforce the behavioral expectations of the student's mainstream teacher(s).

Similarly, if contracts are written to improve behaviors both at home and at school, parents and teachers will be working together to support a child's learning and behavior (Cooper et at., 2007). Moreover, indirect benefits of home–school cooperation may include (a) more positive parent–child relations as parents recognize their child's efforts, and (b) more parental involvement in the child's school program (Heward & Dardig, 1978). Stuart (1971) reported that using behavioral contracts could serve as a catalyst for more positive parent–child interactions.

Another advantage is that because students and their parents are involved in writing the contract, the performance of the students may be improved because they had input in designing the program. This input may increase the students' personal investment in the intervention. Having parents involved also creates opportunities for school–home involvement. For example, the parents could supply the reward for the students' performance in school or vice versa.

Gelfand and Hartmann (1984) also note that an advantage of behavioral contracts is that they can be used to facilitate a student's transition from a highly structured program to a less structured self-management program by systematically allowing a student to assume greater responsibility for selecting behaviors and reinforcers that are included in the contract. Thus, the contract can be a useful means to facilitate generalization of behavior change.

A further advantage, according to Wolery and colleagues (1988), is that contracts can also function to develop personal relationships between teachers and students and between teachers and parents. In addition, they can be helpful when working with families—especially those who may need some guidance in managing their children—because the contract makes the target behaviors and the contingencies for delivering the reward very explicit and thus easier to implement.

Contracts may be less effective with very young children and children with developmental disabilities who may be less capable of entering into agreements and understanding the consequences associated with their behavior (Wolery et al., 1988). Additionally, Gelfman and Hartmann (1984) reported that contracts may be less effective with some antisocial students.

Setting Up a Behavioral Contract Behavioral contracts consist of six major elements: (1) the behaviors to be achieved, (2) the rewards that the student will receive for achieving the behavioral outcomes, (3) a means of record keeping, (4) the written contract, (5) the signatures of the parties involved in the contract, and (6) a means of progress monitoring. Figure 13-7 is a checklist to ensure that the behavioral contract is implemented with fidelity.

Table 13–7   Research on behavioral contracts

Behaviors	Studies
Academic productivity and performance	• Bristol & Sloan, 1974 • Kelley & Stokes, 1982 • Trovato & Bucher, 1980
Classroom behavior	• Allen, Howard, Sweeney, & McLaughlin, 1993 • Miller & Kelley, 1994 • Roberts, White, & McLaughlin, 1997 • Ruth, 1996
Self-control	• Brisman & Siegel, 1985 • Kabler, 1976 • MacKinnon-Slaney, 1993 • Raubolt, 1983 • White & Greenwood, 1992
Disruptive and aggressive behavior	• Bagarozzi, 1984
Homework performance and accuracy	• Miller & Kelley, 1994

FIGURE 13-7

Behavioral contract checklist

Yes	No	Component
☐	☐	Target behaviors are selected. -*Is the target behavior socially valid for the student?* -*Is the target behavior observable and measurable?* -*Have baseline measures been taken of the target behaviors?*
☐	☐	Reward for fulfilling the terms of the contract is specified. -*Was the student involved in choosing the reward?* -*Are the specifics about the reward clear (i.e., what, how, and when)?*
☐	☐	Bonus clause is determined. -*Does the contract include a bonus clause if a student does a particularly good job in completing the contract?*
☐	☐	Penalty clause is determined. -*Does the contract include a penalty clause?*
☐	☐	Behavioral contract is negotiated, written, and signed. -*Is the contract written in positive language?* -*Do the parties agree on the requirements and conditions of the contract?* -*Has the contract been signed by all involved parties?*
☐	☐	Data collection and record-keeping systems are developed. -*Has a data collection system to monitor student progress been developed?* -*Are records kept on the operation of the behavioral contract?*
☐	☐	Monitoring system is developed. -*Does the teacher continuously monitor how well the contract is working?*

Step 1: *Select the target behaviors.* When setting up a behavioral contract, teachers must (a) select the target behaviors that will be reinforced, and then (b) define them in observable and measurable terms. All parties involved in the contract must agree on the definition of the behavior so that everyone is clear about what the contract requires. Jenson and Reavis (1996) cited behaviors such as "hand in work at the end of the class period" as being preferable to a less precise behavior such as "improve classroom responsibility."

The behaviors required in the contracts should be realistic and not overly ambitious. For example, if a student never turns in his or her homework, writing a contract that requires the student to complete 100% of the homework assignments in a month would probably be too ambitious. A more realistic goal may involve a shorter time period (e.g., 1 week), a smaller percentage (e.g., 70%), or a combination of a shorter time period and smaller percentage. When deciding on the behaviors, the parties must be careful not to make the terms on the contract too difficult for the student to achieve.

Step 2: *Identify the reward for fulfilling the terms of the contract.* The reward the parties agree to must be defined in the contract. Thus, the contract specifies what the student will earn if he or she fulfills the terms of the contract.

When developing contracts, teachers assume that the rewards or privileges will have strong reinforcing qualities; therefore, the student should be involved in choosing the reward. The specifics of the reward should be made clear in the contract. How and when the reward will be delivered should also be specified in the contract. The reward should be delivered immediately on successful completion of the contract. Any special requirements or supports provided to assist the student to meet the goals of the contract should also be included.

Step 3: *Include a bonus clause for students who do an excellent job completing the terms of the contract, a penalty clause for students who fail to fulfill the contract, or both (optional).* Including a bonus clause if a student does a particularly good job in completing the contract can be a useful extra incentive, especially for unmotivated students (Rhode, Jenson, & Reavis, 1992). For example, if a contract specifies that homework must be completed with a specified degree of accuracy 7 times within 2 school weeks, and the student turns in homework 10 times in the following 2 school weeks, the student would receive an additional reinforcer.

The parties involved in the contract may also decide if there will be a penalty clause if the student fails to fulfill the terms of the contract. Penalty clauses must be specified in the contract. Thus, the consequences will be systematic, planned in advance, and agreed to by all parties. As is the case with other elements in a behavioral contract, the parties involved must understand and agree to all provisions of the contract. This will minimize future controversies that can result from vaguely worded provisions of the contract (Schloss & Smith, 1998).

Step 4: *Negotiate, write, and sign the behavioral contract.* After all the involved parties have agreed to a contract, it should be written in language that is clear to everyone (Homme, Csanyi, Gonzales, & Rechs 1970). Clarizo (1980) recommended that the contract be stated positively and any punitive overtones be minimized. After writing the first draft of the contract, the parties should review all its requirements and conditions (Wolery et al., 1988). If everyone agrees on the terms of the contract, it should be signed by all involved parties. Figure 13–8 is an example of a behavioral contract.

Step 5: *Establish a record-keeping system.* For record-keeping purposes Martella et al., (2003) suggest that a recording sheet be developed and attached to the contract. The teacher can record data on the form. These authors also suggest that teachers integrate self-recording or self-monitoring into the recording sheet. Students can then fill out the record indicating whether they met the behavioral expectations for the day. This may help increase student involvement in the contract.

Step 6: *Continuously monitor the contract.* After the contract is implemented, teachers need to continuously monitor how well it is working. If a student meets the terms of the contract, he or she should be given the reward immediately (Homme et al., 1970). If it is working and the target behavior is being exhibited at agreed-on levels, then new behaviors may be added or a teacher could begin including self-monitoring components in the contract. If the contract is not working, it must be revised until the behavior improves.

Summary of Behavioral Contracting Behavioral contracts are used frequently in classrooms for students with EBD. The behavioral contract is an agreement between a teacher and a student, and sometimes other parties, that specifies each party's responsibilities in fulfilling the terms of the contract. The contract includes a description of the target behaviors, and the reward for fulfilling the terms of the contract. Contracts rely primarily on positive reinforcement to increase appropriate behaviors, although they may include consequences for failing to fulfill the terms of the contract. Contracts are very effective behavior enhancement procedures that can be used to teach a variety of behavioral skills.

Group-Oriented Contingencies

Token economies, level systems, and behavioral contracting are teacher-directed interventions for changing an individual student's behavior. Reinforcement systems, however, can also reinforce the behavior of groups of students. Such systems are referred to as group-oriented contingencies. The primary characteristic of these interventions is that a reinforcer, aversive consequence, or both are applied to an entire group based on the performance of individuals in that group. Like the previously discussed interventions, group-oriented systems are used to establish appropriate behaviors and reduce inappropriate behaviors. The interventions differ in that they exert control over student behavior by using peers to influence the behavior of other students in the group (Gresham & Gresham, 1982; Schloss & Smith, 1994; Wolery et al., 1988). Group-oriented contingencies, therefore, are well suited to situations in which there is a student peer group and in which the teacher is interested in reinforcing similar behaviors of all the students in the group (Kauffman et al., 1998; Kazdin, 2001; Smith & Misra, 1994; Tankersley, 1995).

The effects of group-oriented contingencies on student behavior have been empirically examined for more than 25 years. This research has produced a substantial body of literature that supports the effectiveness of group contingencies in a number of settings, such as special education classrooms (Brigham, Bakken, Scruggs, & Mastropieri, 1992; Gresham & Gresham, 1982; Hopps & Walker, 1988; Kohler et al., 1995), general education

FIGURE 13-8

Behavioral contract

Contract

Contract between _____(Student's name)_____ , _____(Teacher's name)_____ ,

and _____(Parent's or guardian's name)_____ Date _____

Dates of the Contract: From _____(Beginning date)_____ to _____(Ending date)_____

Terms of the Contract

_____(Student's name)_____ agrees to the following terms:

_____

_____

If _____(Student's name)_____ fulfills the terms of this contract, _____(Teacher's name)_____ agrees to provide the

following reward:

_____

_____

If_____(Student's name)_____ fulfills the terms of this contract, _____(Parent's or guardian's name)

_____ agrees to provide the following reward: _____

_____

Bonus clause _____

_____

Penalty clause _____

_____

Signatures

_____ (Student's signature)   _____ (Teacher's signature)

_____ (Parent's or guardian's signature)   _____ (Parent's or guardian's signature)

_____ (Others' signature)   _____ (Others' signature)

Table 13–8   Research on group-oriented contingencies

Behaviors	Studies
Academic and social behaviors	• Speltz, Shimamura, & McReynolds, 1982
	• Kern, Dunlap, Childs, & Clarke, 1994
	• Lloyd, Eberhardt, & Drake, 1996
	• West, Young, Callahan, Fister, Kemp, Freston, et al., 1995
Academic achievement	• Hamblin, Hathaway, & Wodarski, 1974
Academic productivity	• Wolf, Fantuzzo, & Wolter, 1984
	• Darveauz, 1984
Aggressive behaviors in the classroom	• Brown, Reschly, & Saber, 1974
	• Gresham & Gresham, 1982
Disruptive behaviors in the classroom	• Allen, Gottselig, & Boylan, 1982
	• Barrish, Saunders, & Wolf, 1969
	• Darveauz, 1984
Disruptive behavior on school buses	• Greene, Bailey, & Barber, 1981
Disruptive behavior in school libraries	• Fishbein & Wasik, 1981
Cursing and obscene language	• Salend & Meddaugh, 1985
	• White & Koorland, 1996
On-task behavior in the classroom	• Henderson, Jenson, & Erken, 1986
Social interactions in the classroom	• Kohler, Strain, Hoyson, Davis, Donina, & Rapp, 1995
Noise levels in the classroom	• Schmidt & Ulrich, 1969
Noise levels in the school cafeteria	• Michaelson, Dilorenzo, Calpin, & Williamson, 1981
Stealing	• Switzer, Deal, & Bailey, 1977
Vandalism	• Gresham, 1983

classrooms (Brantley & Webster, 1993), and at home (Darveauz, 1984; Gresham, 1983; Salend, Whittaker, & Reeder, 1992). Additionally, group-oriented contingencies have been used to improve a wide variety of behaviors. Table 13-8 is a partial list of the behaviors that have been improved and the corresponding studies that have shown group-oriented contingencies to improve these behaviors.

Types of Group-Oriented Contingencies There are three primary categories of group-oriented contingencies: dependent, independent, and interdependent (Litow & Pumroy, 1975). The primary differences among the three types is in how students earn reinforcement (Schloss & Smith, 1998; Wolery et al., 1988). We next describe these categories of group-oriented contingencies and the advantages and disadvantages of each.

Dependent Group-Oriented Contingencies. In a dependent group-oriented contingency, the performance of one student, or a small group of students, determines the reinforcement that the entire group receives. For the group to receive reinforcement, the student or small group of students must reach a criteria level set by a teacher. For example, if a teacher uses this particular contingency, he or she would determine a reinforcing consequence for the entire classroom. Whether the group receives their reinforcing consequence, however, will depend on the behavior of one student or a few students in the classroom. According

to Kerr and Nelson (2002), this type of group contingency tends to work best if the behavior of the entire group is better than that of the target student or students.

In a dependent group system, the teacher sets a behavioral criteria level that the target student (or students) must reach (e.g., the target student must earn 35 out of a possible 40 points in 1 week). If the target student meets or exceeds this level, then the entire group receives the reinforcement. Thus, the group is dependent on a student or students for reinforcement. If teachers want to work on the behavior of a number of students or they don't believe a student should be singled out, they may randomly select students to base the group reward on and not tell the group whose behavior will be used to determine the group reward. If the group earns the reward the teacher could identify the student whose behavior was counted. If the group does not earn the reward, the teacher should keep the student's name confidential. Figure 13-9 is an example of a dependent group-oriented contingency.

Independent Group-Oriented Contingencies. In an independent group-oriented contingency, the same consequence is in effect for the entire group. In order to participate in the group reinforcer, each individual student must meet the criteria that the teacher sets for participation. The contingency that is in effect for all group members, therefore, is applied to individual students. Sulzer-Azeroff and Mayer (1991) pointed out that in an independent

FIGURE 13-9

Dependent group-oriented contingency

Mr. Cleveland wanted to increase the homework completion rates of students in his class. He decided to use a dependent group contingency in which students were to turn in their daily homework completed with 90% accuracy. He explained the system to his students and asked them to pick a group reward. The class chose to have 5 extra minutes of afternoon recess time.

Every afternoon before dismissal, Mr. Cleveland assigned homework for the following day. Additionally, he randomly picked a student's name. Mr. Cleveland did not reveal the student's name to the class; rather, he wrote the name on a piece of paper and put it in an envelope, which he taped to a bulletin board.

After lunch the next day, the students would correct their homework and pass it to Mr. Cleveland. In the afternoon, before recess, he would reveal the student's name. He would then check to see if the student's homework had been turned in and was 90% correct. If the student had completed his or her homework to criterion, the entire class would receive the extra 5 minutes of recess.

FIGURE 13-10

Independent group-oriented contingency

Mr. Cleveland wanted to increase the homework completion rates of students in his class. He decided to use an independent group contingency in which students were to turn in their daily homework completed with 90% accuracy. He explained the system to his students and asked them to pick a group reward. The class chose to have 5 extra minutes of afternoon recess time.

Every afternoon before dismissal, Mr. Cleveland assigned homework for the following day. After lunch the next day, the students would correct their homework and pass it to Mr. Cleveland. He would then check to see if each student's homework had been turned in and was 90% correct. If a student had completed the homework to criterion, he or she could participate in the extra 5 minutes of recess.

In a lottery contingency, every student that meets the predetermined criteria for acceptable behavioral performance has his or her name entered in the lottery. A winner or winners are then drawn, and awarded the predetermined reinforcer. For example, if the target behavior is completing homework, the teacher could award students a lottery ticket each day that they completed their homework. Then on a certain day, perhaps the end of the week, the teacher would draw a winner or winners.

Interdependent Group-Oriented Contingencies. In an interdependent group-oriented contingency, the group is treated as a single individual. Whether the group receives the reinforcer is dependent on the group reaching a predetermined behavioral criterion. The teacher, therefore, determines the contingency for the entire group and the final evaluation is based on the level of group performance that the teacher specifies.

For example, if a teacher uses an interdependent group-oriented contingency, he or she determines the behavioral criteria and the reinforcing consequence for the entire class. When the entire group has reached the behavioral criteria, the group receives the reinforcement. Thus, the students in the group are interdependent for reinforcement. Figure 13-11 shows an example of an interdependent group-oriented contingency.

A type of interdependent group-oriented contingency in which a class of students is divided into teams is a called a team-based contingency (Kazdin, 2001). In a team-based contingency, students are divided in two or more teams, with each team functioning as its own group. The teams often compete against each other for

group-oriented contingency there is no incentive for group members to attempt to influence the behavior of other students. An independent contingency, therefore, may not be a true group-oriented contingency (Schloss & Smith, 1994) because students do not depend on each other to earn a reward.

If a teacher uses this particular contingency, he or she would determine a reinforcing consequence for the entire classroom and the behavioral criteria necessary for a student to receive the reinforcement. When the group receives reinforcement, every student who reached the behavioral criteria could participate. Thus, each student must earn the group reinforcer independently. Figure 13-10 shows an example of an independent group-oriented contingency.

A variation of an independent group-oriented contingency is a lottery. A lottery is an especially useful way to arrange contingencies to develop specific behavior in a group of students (Kazdin, 2001; Morgan & Jenson, 1988). In a lottery contingency, like any group-oriented contingency, the teacher determines the reinforcer that will be available to the group. Usually the reinforcer that can be won in the lottery is a larger or more desirable reinforcer than is usually available to students. Unlike other group-oriented contingencies, however, not everyone in a group will earn the reinforcer—only the winner or winners of the lottery.

FIGURE 13–11

Interdependent group-oriented contingency

Mr. Cleveland wanted to increase the homework completion rates of students in his class. He decided to use an interdependent group contingency in which students were to turn in their daily homework completed with 90% accuracy. He explained the system to his students and asked them to pick a group reward. The class chose to have 5 extra minutes of afternoon free time. Additionally, he told the students that each day 95% percent of the entire class had to turn in their homework and meet the criterion for accuracy for the students to receive the additional recess time.

Every afternoon before dismissal, Mr. Cleveland assigned homework for the following day. After lunch the next day, the students would correct their homework and pass it to Mr. Cleveland. He would then check to see if the students' homework had been turned in and was 90% correct. He would also calculate the class average to see if 95% of the students had completed their homework with 90% accuracy. If the students achieved the required percentage completing their homework to criterion, the entire class was given the extra 5 minutes of recess.

points. Although teachers often set up such competitions so that all groups that achieve their goal are reinforced if they meet or exceed a desired level of performance, the team that wins the competition often receives an additional reinforcer (Kazdin, 2001). Kazdin notes that dividing a group of students into teams appears to enhance the effectiveness of a group contingency system.

A commonly used team contingency is the "good behavior game" (Tankersley, 1995). Research has shown that the good behavior game can be a powerful group-oriented contingency program (Kamps, 2002). In the good behavior game, a class is divided into two or more teams. A group target is set and the teacher keeps a count of the behavior. For example, if the target behavior is talkouts, the teacher would set the target behavior criteria (e.g., fewer than five group talkouts per day). The teacher would then reward the team with the fewest talkouts; if both teams received fewer than the group talkout total of five, both groups would be rewarded.

In Darveauz's (1984) "good behavior game plus merit" game, rewards are given for increasing appropriate behavior. For example, teams can earn points if team members complete their assignments with 75% accuracy and participate in class. Darveauz showed that the good behavior game plus merit when used in a general education setting increased on-task behavior, number of assignments

completed, and reduced disruptive behavior of students with EBD and their peers.

Brigham et al. (1992) developed a variation of the good behavior game called "cooperative behavior management." The system added a few enhancements to the good behavior game. First, both teams could earn the rewards if they met the target criteria. Second, individual students could earn rewards by exhibiting self-control over their own behavior, even if the team did not earn a reward. Third, the teacher could grant accommodations to students who had particular behavioral difficulties by issuing a warning and reminder to the student prior to deducting a team point.

Advantages and Disadvantages of Group-Oriented Contingencies Group-oriented contingencies have a number of advantages. One advantage is that these systems allow students opportunities to learn appropriate behaviors within a social context. Thus, the opportunities to learn from watching other students are enhanced. Students can learn behavior modeled by their peers and see the peers receive reinforcement. Because students have to function successfully with other students in the general education classroom, group systems can help further these goals by ensuring that students work together in the resource room or self-contained classroom. Second, peers often actively support each other for doing well so the group can earn reinforcers. Third, teachers can manage a large group of students using a single reinforcement system. Wolery and colleagues (1988) point out that classroom resources and personnel are limited, so a reinforcement system that uses an entire group to change behavior can be an efficient use of time.

A potential disadvantage of most group-oriented contingency programs, but especially of dependent and interdependent group-oriented contingencies, is that students who do poorly and cause the team to fail to meet the group criteria may be the targets of excessive peer pressure, including threats and bullying. Teachers must monitor group-oriented interventions closely to ensure that this does not occur.

Another problem that may occur is when a student or group of students attempt to subvert the system by deliberately causing their group to fail to meet behavioral criteria or when a student has very high rates of misbehavior and thus loses points and the opportunity to gain reinforcement. In such situations, a teacher should remove the student from the group contingency intervention. The student could, in effect, be his or her own team with private goal setting and rewards (Kamps, 2002). A similar situation is the fairness problem. This happens when the behavior of one student causes a well-behaved group of students to lose their opportunity for reinforcement. Teachers can reduce the likelihood of either of these problems by carefully planning group membership. Schloss and Smith (1998) suggest that teachers may want to deal with the fairness issue up front by discussing the purpose of the intervention with parents and students.

Teachers should arrange groups with students who have similar behavioral and academic characteristics. Additionally, Wolery et al. (1988) suggest that some students in groups should be more fluent at behavior and academic skills so they can serve as positive examples to others. Similarly, teachers should arrange group membership so that all members of a group are capable of performing the prerequisite behaviors that are needed for individual and group success. This is an extremely important consideration, and if not followed could result in the failure of the group-oriented contingency and the potential abuse of some students by their peers.

Setting Up a Group-Oriented Contingency System

Implementing a group contingency consists of six major steps: (a) determining the type of group-oriented contingency system that will be used, (b) determining the target behaviors, (c) choosing the rewards/reinforcers, (d) defining the criteria for reinforcement, (e) developing a means of data collection and record keeping, and (f) teaching students the system. Figure 13–12 is a checklist to ensure that the group contingency is implemented with fidelity.

Step 1: *Determine the type of group-oriented contingency that will be used and assign students to groups.* The teacher must determine which procedure will be used; the dependent group contingency, independent group contingency, or interdependent group contingency. Additionally the teacher should decide if he or she will use a lottery or team-based component with the contingency. After determining the type of reinforcer, the teacher should assign students to groups. Whenever possible, the teacher should arrange groups with students who have similar characteristics. Additionally, it is important that all students within a group be capable of performing the target behavior.

Step 2: *Identify target behaviors.* Because the purpose of the group contingency is to strengthen desirable behavior, an important step in setting up a

FIGURE 13–12

Group-oriented contingencies checklist

Yes	No	Component
☐	☐	Type of group-oriented contingency is chosen. - *Will a dependent, independent, or interdependent group-oriented contingency be used?* - *Will a lottery or team-based component be used with the contingency?*
☐	☐	Target behaviors are selected. - *Are the target behaviors socially valid for the students?* - *Are the target behaviors observable and measurable?* - *Have baseline measures been taken of the target behaviors?*
☐	☐	Group rewards are chosen. - *Have group rewards been chosen using reinforcer menu and sampling procedures?* - *Was the group involved in choosing the group reward?*
☐	☐	Criteria for reinforcement are defined. - *What criteria must students reach to earn the group reinforcer?*
☐	☐	Data collection and record-keeping systems are developed. - *Has a data collection system to monitor student progress been developed?* - *Are records kept on the operation of the level system?*
☐	☐	Students understand the group-oriented contingency.

group contingency is to operationally define all target behaviors that will be reinforced in the system (see Chapter 4 for a description and examples of operationally defined behaviors). When target behaviors are operationally defined, staff and students will clearly know what behaviors will be reinforced. After the target behavior has been determined, the teacher will need to collect baseline data on the target behavior so that a reasonable criterion can be set and student progress can be monitored.

Step 3: *Choose group rewards.* Teachers should select rewards that they believe will have reinforcing value for each member of the group. The teacher must be sure that the items or activities will actually be reinforcing to the group. This is important because if group members work together to achieve the reinforcer, individual involvement will be increased and the common goal will increase group cohesion (Wolery et al., 1988). To identify reinforcers, the teacher may want to use the reinforcer menu and sampling procedures discussed earlier in this chapter.

Step 4: *Define the criteria for reinforcement.* The teacher must decide what criteria students must reach to earn the group reinforcer. For example, teachers could use average numbers (75% of behavior points earned daily) or total numbers (40 behavior points earned daily). The teacher should use the baseline information, collected in step 2, to determine the starting criteria for earning reinforcement. The teacher must not set the criteria too high, or the group contingency may not work. As the behavior improves, the teacher should make the criteria for group reinforcement more stringent (Schloss & Smith, 1998).

Step 5: *Develop data collection and record-keeping procedures.* Teachers should collect data on the target behaviors of their students to see if the group-oriented contingency is effective. If the teacher is unsure of which group-oriented contingency to use, he or she could try each one and then determine the respective effectiveness by looking at the data. Additionally, teachers should use the data to inform the students how they are doing.

Step 6: *Teach the group-oriented contingency system.* Prior to implementing the group-oriented contingency, the teacher must explain the system to his or her students. This includes explaining the purpose of the intervention, the behaviors that are targeted for improvement, and the specifics of the system that will be used (e.g., the reinforcer, how students earn points, the criteria for acceptable performance). Moreover, these points should be publicly posted.

Summary of Group-Oriented Systems Group-oriented contingencies are powerful systems designed to increase appropriate behaviors and reduce inappropriate behaviors in students. The distinguishing feature of group contingencies is that reinforcers are delivered to a group of students contingent on their behaviors. The behavior of one student, a group of students, or all the students in a classroom determines the consequences received by the classroom as a whole. A basic idea behind the use of group-oriented contingencies is that they exert control over student behavior by using peers to influence the behavior of other students in the group.

There are three types of group-oriented contingencies: (a) independent group-oriented contingencies, in which the contingencies are in effect for the entire group but rewards are earned by each student independently; (b) dependent group-oriented contingencies, in which the contingencies are in effect for the entire group but the reward for the group is dependent on the performance of one student or a small number of students within the larger group; and (c) interdependent group-oriented contingencies, in which the contingencies are in effect for the entire group and the reward for the group is based on the performance of all the group members. A substantial body of empirical literature supports the effectiveness of these interventions.

BEHAVIOR REDUCTION PROCEDURES

Behavior reduction interventions use punishment procedures, such as time-out and response cost, to decrease socially inappropriate behaviors. These interventions may be applied by themselves or in combination with a specific behavior enhancement procedure (e.g., using a token economy with a response-cost component). This section of the chapter examines (a) important implementation guidelines that teachers should follow to ensure that behavior reduction procedures are used appropriately and effectively, (b) the major types of behavior reduction procedures, and (c) how to ensure that behavior reduction procedures are implemented in a legally correct manner.

Implementation Guidelines

The following section describes six implementation guidelines that teachers should follow when they use behavior reduction procedures.

First, behavior enhancement strategies should form the core of teachers' interventions when working with students with EBD. The first priority in working with students with EBD is skill development. Behavior reduction procedures do not teach students appropriate behavior. Moreover, the excessive use of punishment may create a negative classroom environment (Darch & Kame'enui, 2004). It is crucial, therefore, that prior to using behavior reduction procedure we identify the inappropriate behavior that we want to reduce *and* identify the appropriate behavior that we want to take its place. We must develop behavior enhancement programs that teach and reinforce the desirable behaviors. In this way we strengthen the appropriate behavior and also reduce the likelihood of the inappropriate behavior occurring (Kerr & Nelson, 2002; Maag, 2004; Wolery et al., 1988; Zirpoli & Melloy, 2001).

A number of researchers, however, have noted that often behavior enhancement procedures alone may not be effective when working with students with EBD (Kerr & Nelson, 2006; Morgan & Jenson, 1988; Walker, 1995). Shores, Gunter, et al. (1993), for example, found that interventions that combined positive reinforcement procedures and punishment procedures were superior to either reinforcement or punishment alone in reducing the problem behaviors of students with severe problem behavior. Teachers, therefore, may need to combine behavior reduction interventions with behavior enhancement interventions when working with students with EBD.

Second, use only behavior reduction interventions that have empirical support of their effectiveness. Kaplan & Carter (1995) emphatically stated, "It is unethical to use a behavior reduction procedure for which there is no demonstrated efficacy" (p. 187). When teachers use ineffective procedures they waste their time and, more important, they waste their students' time. When there are not enough data to prove efficacy of an intervention, yet the teacher decides to use the intervention, the teacher should adhere to the principle of the least dangerous assumption (Wolery et al., 1988). According to this principle, the behavior reduction intervention that the teacher uses should produce the least amount of harm if the procedure is ineffective.

Third, when using behavior reduction procedures teachers must identify the reinforcer that is maintaining the inappropriate behavior and prevent student access to it. Students with EBD often have very long histories of problem behaviors working successfully for them. As long as the problem behaviors continue to be effective for a student, even on an intermittent basis, the behaviors will continue to be exhibited. Teachers, therefore, must systematically prevent a student from being reinforced for exhibiting the problem behavior.

Fourth, when interventions to decrease inappropriate behavior are used, teachers should always simultaneously use interventions to teach or increase appropriate behaviors. As we discussed in Chapter 4, behavior reduction or punishment procedures do not teach new behavior. Unfortunately, teachers of students with EBD have a tendency to focus on reducing behaviors without simultaneously increasing appropriate behaviors. It is our duty when educating students to teach them skills, both behavioral and academic, that will enable them to lead successful lives. Merely reducing problem behavior will not accomplish this, unless we also teach students appropriate and adaptive behaviors. This is referred to as the fair-pair rule (White & Haring, 1980). According to this rule, behavior reduction interventions should always be accompanied by interventions designed to teach an appropriate skill, which will replace the behavior we are targeting for reduction (Wolery et al., 1988). This replacement behavior should serve the same function for the student as the problem behavior did (i.e., positive or negative reinforcement). This intervention is differential reinforcement of incompatible behavior, if the appropriate behavior is incompatible with the inappropriate behavior; or differential reinforcement of alternative behavior, if the appropriate behavior is not topographically incompatible. A teacher's first choice in reducing undesirable behavior should always be differential reinforcement. Refer to Chapter 4 for a discussion of differential reinforcement.

Fifth, teachers must implement the behavior reduction interventions calmly and consistently. Once a teacher decides to use a behavior reduction strategy to reduce an inappropriate behavior, the intervention must be applied in the same way every time a student exhibits the inappropriate behavior (Darch & Kame'enui, 2004; Morgan & Jenson, 1988; Wolery et al., 1988). If the intervention is not used consistently, it will not be effective. Additionally, behavior reduction procedures will be more effective if they are implemented in a calm and matter-of-fact manner (Darch & Kame'enui, 2004; Rhode et al., 1996).

Sixth, teachers should use a data collection system to monitor and evaluate the intervention. There are two reasons for teachers to adopt a data collection system to track student behavior. First, by collecting student performance data on a continuous basis, teachers can monitor student progress. Thus, the data will help teachers determine if the intervention is effective. If the data show that the intervention is not working, the teacher can make modifications or changes. Unfortunately, teachers sometimes use the same behavior reduction procedures over and over again (e.g., response cost, time-out) regardless of whether they are effective. This is unethical and unprofessional (Kaplan & Carter, 1995). Second, the data can be used to provide feedback to parents, students, and others about how well he or she is doing in the program.

TYPES OF INTERVENTIONS

The following section examines a number of major behavior reduction interventions. Behavior reduction interventions are used to manage and reduce behavioral excesses. Two behavior reduction interventions, differential reinforcement and extinction, were examined in Chapter 4 and will not be discussed here.

Response Cost

Response cost is a procedure in which a previously earned reinforcer is removed following the emission of a previously defined target behavior in an attempt to reduce the future probability of that behavior. In essence, the student's inappropriate behavior results in a fine or cost to him or her. The basic idea behind response cost is the student loses something of value as a consequence of engaging in inappropriate behavior. Response cost is a negative punishment procedure when the procedure results in a decrease in the target behavior.

There are three basic types of response-cost approaches. They are to remove (a) a tangible item, (b) a preferred activity, or (c) tokens that represent items or activities when a student exhibits an inappropriate target behavior. Response cost has been used in a variety of settings to decrease inappropriate behaviors (see Table 13–9).

Advantages and Disadvantages of Response Cost

According to Kazdin (1977), a primary advantage of response cost is that it is effective while avoiding many of the undesirable features and side effects of punishment (see Chapter 4 for an explanation of the side effects of punishment). Another advantage is that response cost is easy to implement, especially when a token economy is already in place (Kazdin, 2001). Response cost, used in conjunction with a token economy, is very convenient because as soon as an undesirable behavior occurs, a token can be removed quietly and effortlessly and without disrupting ongoing activities (Sulzer-Azeroff & Mayer, 1991). Moreover, response-cost systems can be used with individuals or with groups of students. Additionally, teachers seem to regard response cost as a socially acceptable form of punishment (Elliott, Witt, Peterson, & Galvin, 1984).

According to Sulzer-Azeroff and Mayer (1991), another advantage of response cost is that the intervention usually results in strong and rapid behavioral reduction with few

Table 13–9   Research on response cost

Behaviors	Studies
Off-task behaviors	• Iwata & Bailey, 1974 • Rapport, Murphy, & Bailey, 1982 • Sullivan & O'Leary, 1990 • Witt & Elliott, 1982
Disruptive and inappropriate talkouts	• Salend & Kovalich, 1986 • Yell, 1988
Aggressive behaviors	• Dougherty, Fowler, & Paine, 1985 • Foreman, 1980 • Phillips, Phillips, Fixsen, & Wolf, 1971 • Reynolds & Kelley, 1997
Overactivity	• DuPaul, Guevremont, & Bakley, 1992 • Rapport, Murphy, & Bailey, 1982
Vandalism and stealing	• Switzer, Deal, & Bailey, 1977
Disruptive behaviors	• Kelley & McCain, 1995 • Proctor & Morgan, 1991 • Rapport, Murphy, & Bailey, 1982 • Salend, Tintle, and Barber, 1988
Obscene language	• Trice & Parker, 1983

negative effects. Kazdin (1977) further points out that behavior change with response cost and a token economy will be more rapid if the tokens lost for inappropriate behaviors are incompatible with the tokens earned for appropriate behavior.

The primary disadvantages are the same disadvantages as exist with all punishment procedures. First, teachers may use it too often and in an overly harsh manner. That is, the teacher may give excessively large fines or use it constantly. This may be because of the ease of use and rapid effects of the intervention (Sulzer-Azeroff & Mayer, 1991; Wolery et al., 1988). Because punishment procedures can negatively reinforce teachers, they may begin to focus exclusively on the reduction of inappropriate behaviors rather than reinforcing appropriate behaviors (Maag, 2004).

Additionally, when teachers overuse response cost and fine students an excessive number of tokens or points, students may give up because regaining lost points may seem too difficult. Similarly, students may be in the hole and wind up owing tokens or points. When this occurs, a response-cost system will not work. Teachers must plan and supervise the system carefully to ensure this does not occur.

A similar problem may occur when teachers allow students to earn back lost tokens or points when they get upset or begin to become coercive in an attempt to regain the lost points. According to Schloss and Smith (1998), allowing the student to regain the lost points may actually negatively reinforce the inappropriate behavior and should be avoided. This is not to be confused with rewarding a student's appropriate behavior. Schloss and Smith suggest that teachers be prepared to sustain the response-cost contingency regardless of a student's reaction.

Another disadvantage, as the case with all punishment procedures, is that response cost alone does not teach appropriate behavior. Response cost, therefore, should always be paired with behavior enhancement procedures. As we have previously discussed, response cost should be a component of a token economy. In fact, research indicates that using a token economy with a response-cost system may be more effective than using either intervention by itself (Sulzer-Azeroff & Mayer, 1991).

Setting Up a Response Cost System Response cost can be an effective intervention when it is implemented with accuracy, consistency, and fidelity (Walker, 1983). Response cost is most effective when used in conjunction with a token economy (Sulzer-Azeroff & Mayer, 1991). After students have earned reinforcers in the token economy, and have established a reinforcer reserve, the response-cost intervention can be implemented (Wolery, et al., 1988). Figure 13–13 is a checklist to ensure that the response-cost system is implemented with fidelity. Teachers should adhere to the following steps when developing response cost.

Step 1: ***Identify target behaviors.*** Because the purpose of the response-cost intervention is to reduce undesirable behaviors, an important step when developing the intervention is to operationally define all the target behaviors to be reduced (see Chapter 4 for a description and examples of operationally defined behaviors). When target behaviors are operationally defined, staff and students will clearly know what behaviors will be penalized. After the target behavior has been determined, the teacher needs to collect baseline data on the target behavior so that a reasonable criterion for reduction can be set and student progress can be monitored. Each time a target behavior occurs, the teacher should immediately impose the response-cost fine. As is the case with all behavioral interventions, consistency is crucial.

Step 2: ***Ensure that students have a reserve of reinforcers prior to implementing response cost.*** Sulzer-Azeroff and Mayer (1991) point out that a response-cost system is most effective after students have had an opportunity to earn, sample, and build up a reserve of reinforcers because they know what they will be missing and will work to avoid the loss of the reinforcers. Moreover, a response-cost system will not work if students lose all of their reinforcers (Walker, 1983); it is unlikely that students will

FIGURE 13–13

Response cost checklist

Yes	No	Component
❏	❏	Target behaviors are selected. -Is the target behavior socially valid for the student? -Is the target behavior observable and measurable? -Have baseline measures been taken of the target behaviors?
❏	❏	Students have a reserve of reinforcers so they will not go in the hole.
❏	❏	Size of fines is determined.
❏	❏	Method for collecting fines is developed.
❏	❏	Data collection and record-keeping systems are developed. -Has a data collection system to monitor student progress been developed? -Are records kept on the operation of the level system?
❏	❏	Students understand the response-cost system.

be motivated to control their behavior to avoid losing reinforcers that they don't have. A similar problem may occur if students have so many reinforcers that the response-cost system becomes meaningless. For example, students will probably not be motivated to control their behavior to avoid losing a token or two if they already have a hundred tokens. Teachers can ensure that these potential problems do not occur by carefully keeping track of the number of reinforcers students can earn and lose, and then systematically adjusting token delivery to ensure that students always have a reserve of reinforcers, but that this reserve does not become too large. Maag (2004) suggested that as a general rule students should earn 3 to 5 points for appropriate behavior for every 1 point they lose for inappropriate behavior.

Step 3: *Determine the size of the fines.* The intensity of a punisher is related to the effectiveness of the procedure to reduce a target behavior (Cooper, Heron, & Hewitt, 2007; Maag, 2004; Sulzer-Azeroff & Mayer, 1991). The more intense the punishment, the more effective it is in reducing behaviors. In a response-cost system, the intensity of the procedure is in the size of the fine. It is important, therefore, that teachers adjust the size of the fines for maximum effectiveness. Additionally, the magnitude of the fine should be commensurate with the severity of the misbehavior (Cooper et al., 1987). That is, the more serious the infraction, the greater the fine should be. The fine must be of sufficient size that it reduces a target behavior, but it must not be so large that it depletes the reinforcer reserve. The most effective way for teachers to ensure that fines are of an appropriate size and result in reduction of the target behavior is to carefully monitor the target behavior when various fines are imposed and see if the behavior is reduced. Teachers should begin with fines that they expect will be effective. If the size of the fine does not reduce the target behavior, it should be increased until effects are noted. Sulzer-Azeroff and Mayer (1991) noted, however, that fines should not be increased in small increments or the student may adapt to the gradual increase.

Step 4: *Determine how fines will be collected.* How fines will be collected depends on the manner in which tokens are given to students. If actual tokens are given to the students they will have to be physically taken back. This could result in students resisting the teacher. If tokens are controlled by the teacher or points are used, removing them will be easier.

Fines should be administered with a calm and businesslike attitude. Additionally, teachers should avoid personalizing the removal of points. It is appropriate, however, to deliver a quiet and personal, but not public, reprimand to the student. When delivering the reprimand, the teacher should (a) say the student's name, (b) tell the student that he or she must stop the undesirable behavior, (c) give the student a very brief rationale for stopping the behavior, and (d) identify an appropriate alternative to the behavior (Schloss & Smith, 1998).

Teachers must also plan how they will respond if students get aggressive, have a disruptive outburst, or refuse to give up their tokens or points when the teacher imposes a fine. The likelihood of such an outburst is lessened if the students clearly understand the response-cost system, the target behaviors, and the magnitude of fines in advance (see step 6 on teaching the system). Nonetheless, teachers have to be prepared for the student who does become aggressive, and should never negotiate with students or get involved in a power struggle with them over the fine. Rather, teachers should have a standard response to student noncompliance (Wolery et al., 1988). For example, when teachers explain the system to their students they may announce that a fine will be increased if a student becomes aggressive or disruptive when the fine is imposed. If the fine for a particular behavior is two tokens, the teacher could double the penalty if a student becomes disruptive when the penalty is imposed. If the tokens are actually reinforcing, and the teacher is consistent in doubling the fine when students become disruptive, this tactic may be very effective. Teachers, however, should avoid continually raising the fine if the disruption continues because they may inadvertently put students in a situation in which they have lost all their points or owe points and, therefore, have nothing to lose. Additionally, getting attention from the teacher and other students may be more reinforcing than the point loss is punishing. Instead of further removal of points for continued disruption, the teacher should consider using of an alternate punisher, such as time-out.

Another option that may be effective is to return part of the fine if the student acts appropriately when he or she is penalized. In this way the teacher may avoid aggressive or disruptive behavior while simultaneously reinforcing behavior that is incompatible with aggression (Sulzer-Azeroff & Mayer, 1991). If teachers decide to do this they should explain this policy when they teach the response-cost system.

Step 5: *Develop a data collection and record-keeping system.* With all behavior management strategies, teachers should always collect student performance data on a continuous basis to monitor student progress. Chapter 3 on assessment explains how teachers can collect data on student progress. When teachers use response-cost systems, the tokens or points that students earn can be used as a rough indicator of student progress. However, as stated earlier, this is not a true indicator of student behavior; only direct observation will provide accurate enough data for determining student progress.

Records should also be kept on the number of tokens or points that student lose so they can assess how the intervention is working. Moreover, data on the target behaviors should be collected and interpreted so the effectiveness of the response-cost intervention can be determined.

Step 6: *Teach students the response-cost system.* Prior to implementing the response-cost intervention, teachers should teach their students how the system works. When students clearly understand the intervention, the likelihood of response cost being successful and avoiding potential problems is greatly enhanced. All aspects of the response-cost intervention should be explained and demonstrated until students clearly understand the procedure. Additionally, teachers should have all materials prepared prior to implementing the system (e.g., chart of response-cost penalties, record-keeping forms).

Summary of Response Cost Response cost is a behavior reduction intervention in which a student loses a designated number of tokens or points, which he or she already has earned, contingent on the occurrence of a target problem behavior. Thus, the student is fined for inappropriate or undesirable behavior. Response cost is especially effective when used in conjunction with a token economy. Response-cost systems are easy to implement and use. Moreover, a substantial research base shows that response cost can be an effective intervention if implemented correctly and consistently. To implement the intervention properly requires careful planning.

Time-Out

Time-out from positive reinforcement is a behavior reduction procedure that is frequently used by teachers of students with EBD (Ryan, Saunders, Katsiyannis, & Yell, 2007; Zabel, 1986). The intervention generally involves placing a student in a less reinforcing environment for a period of time contingent on inappropriate behavior (Nelson & Rutherford, 1983; Twyman, Johnson, Buie, & Nelson, 1993). Time-out is based on the assumption that if a behavior is followed by a period in less reinforcing conditions, the behavior will decrease in frequency (Johns et al., 1996; Nelson & Rutherford, 1983; Noll & Simpson, 1979; Ryan et al., 2007; Wolery et al., 1988). Thus, behavior is reduced by withdrawing the opportunity for reinforcement for a period following the occurrence of a behavior (Rutherford & Nelson, 1982).

There is a large research base that demonstrates the effectiveness of the different types of time-out in decreasing inappropriate behaviors. Table 13–10 shows a partial list of studies of time-out in school settings.

Advantages and Disadvantages of Time-Out Time-out, when used correctly, is a powerful procedure for reducing problem behavior. Furthermore, research indicates that time-out can be used effectively with students of various ages and abilities, and in a variety of settings. The primary benefit of time-out is that it can be very effective, especially combined with procedures to teach appropriate behavior.

Table 13–10   Research on time-out

Behaviors	Studies
Aggressive behaviors	• Adams & Kelley, 1992
	• Bostow & Bailey, 1969
	• Foxx & Shapiro, 1978
	• Murphy, Hutchinson, & Bailey, 1983
	• Noll & Simpson, 1979
	• Pease & Tyler, 1979
	• Porterfield, Herbert-Jackson, & Risley, 1976
	• Roberts & Powers, 1990
	• Webster, 1976
	• Wilson, Robertson, Herlong, & Haynes, 1979
Disruptive behaviors	• Ramp, Ulrich, & Dulaney, 1971
	• Sachs, 1973
	• Safer, Heaton, & Parker, 1981
	• Salend & Gordon, 1987
	• Spencer & Gray, 1973
	• Tyroler & Lahey, 1980
Noncompliance	• Bean & Roberts, 1981
	• Handen, Parrish, McClung, Kerwin, & Evans, 1992
	• Hobbs, Forehand, & Murray, 1978
	• Roberts, 1984
	• Roberts, Hatzenbuehler, & Bean, 1981

There are four primary disadvantages to using time-out. First, when a student is in time-out he or she loses valuable instructional time. This is a serious concern with low-performing students. Thus, it is important that teachers keep track of the amount of instructional time that students lose when they are in time-out. If this amount appears excessive, teachers should use another behavior reduction intervention. Second, time-out may actually be reinforcing to students if they are allowed to escape from aversive academic activities. Teachers must never let students escape or avoid academic or nonacademic activities by engaging time-out. Thus, if time-out is used, teachers should always require students to make up any activities that were missed. Third, time-out is a procedure that is often overused because of its ease of use and effectiveness. Because teachers are negatively reinforced for using time-out (i.e., they escape from an aversive situation), they may implement time-out much more frequently than necessary. Time-out may become the teacher's intervention of choice, and they may use it for minor and major misbehaviors. Teachers must plan and supervise the system carefully to ensure this does not occur. Fourth, as is the case with all punishment procedures, time-out alone does not

teach appropriate behavior. Therefore, it should always be paired with behavior enhancement procedures and differential reinforcement.

Setting Up a Time-Out System   Time-out is a complex procedure involving much more than merely removing a student from activities and returning him or her to the environment following a brief period. Time-out requires careful planning and teachers should make decisions concerning time-out prior to implementing the procedure (Harris, 1985; Johns et al., 1996; Wolery et al., 1988). When developing and implementing a time-out intervention, careful consideration of these factors will help increase the effectiveness of time-out and decrease the possibility of abuses of the procedure. Figure 13–14 is a checklist that teachers may follow when setting up a time-out system.

Step 1: Enrich the Time-In Environment. Time-out is based on the assumption that because a student is moved from a reinforcing environment to a less reinforcing environment, the behavior that results in time-out will decrease in frequency (Wolery et al., 1988). Time-out will work only if a meaningful difference exists between time-in (the time during which the student is in the classroom)

FIGURE 13-14

Time-out checklist

Yes	No	Component
❏	❏	The time-in environment is enriched.
❏	❏	Target behaviors are selected. -*Is the target behavior socially valid for the student?* -*Is the target behavior observable and measurable?* -*Have baseline measures been taken of the target behaviors?*
❏	❏	Type of time-out that will be used is selected.
❏	❏	Implementation guidelines are selected.
❏	❏	Warnings and explanations are given.
❏	❏	Duration of time-out is determined.
❏	❏	Release criteria are defined.
❏	❏	Data collection and record-keeping systems are developed. -*Has a data collection system to monitor student progress been developed?* -*Are records kept on the operation of the level system?*
❏	❏	Students understand the time-out intervention.

and time-out (the time during which the student is removed from the classroom environment). To the teacher using time-out, this means that the time-in environment must be rich in reinforcers. Time-in can be enriched in a number of ways such as making the classroom a stimulating and interesting environment or providing activity and token reinforcement for appropriate behavior.

It is also crucial that all sources of reinforcement are removed when a student is in time-out. If all sources of reinforcement are not removed, the procedure that is being used is not time-out (Martella et al., 2003).

Step 2: Identify Target Behaviors That Will Result in Time-Out. Because the purpose of a time-out intervention is to reduce undesirable behaviors, an important step when developing the intervention is to operationally define all the target behaviors to be reduced (see Chapter 4 for a description and examples of operationally defined behaviors). When target behaviors are operationally defined, staff and students will clearly know what behaviors will be penalized. After the target behavior has been determined, the teacher needs to collect baseline data on the target behavior so that a reasonable criterion for reduction can be set and student progress can be monitored.

Step 3: Select Type of Time Out and Choose the Location. Several different time-out procedures have been identified that teachers can use in the classroom. In each procedure, emission of the target behavior results in a period of time during which the teacher reduces access to reinforcers. The primary decision that teachers must make is whether the student should be removed from the time-in or the reinforcing conditions present in time-in be removed from the student. When reinforcers are removed from the student contingent on inappropriate behavior, the type of time-out is referred to as nonexclusionary. Examples of *nonexclusionary time-out* include planned ignoring, removal of reinforcing objects, and the time-out ribbon. In planned ignoring the teacher removes his or her attention from students for a brief period when they engage in an undesirable behavior. Planned ignoring is based on the premise that a teacher's attention during time-in is reinforcing and that when this attention is removed the behavior will be suppressed (Rutherford & Nelson, 1982). In the removal of tangible objects time-out, the teacher removes materials that the student is interacting with for a brief period when they engage in problem behavior. Foxx and Shapiro (1978) developed a type of nonexclusionary time-out called the time-out ribbon. This procedure has been used with groups of students (Salend & Gordon, 1987) and with

individual students (Salend & Maragulia, 1983). Typically, in a time-out ribbon procedure, students are given a ribbon to wear. When they are engaged in appropriate behavior they continue to wear the ribbon. The ribbon serves as a cue to teachers and staff to reinforce a student. However, if the student engages in an inappropriate behavior, the ribbon is removed. When the ribbon is removed, the teacher does not reinforce the student and the student does not engage in reinforcing activities. A number of different types of time-out ribbons have been used, including ribbons worn around the neck and Velcro wrist bands. The difficulty with nonexclusionary time-out is that before teachers can remove reinforcing conditions, they must know what is reinforcing the student and then be able to remove the reinforcers. In the complex environment of the classroom this can be very difficult.

Time-out procedures that remove students from the time-in environment are referred to as *exclusionary time-out*. These procedures are more intrusive than nonexclusionary because a change in the student's location is required. There are three major types of exclusionary time-out: contingent observation, exclusion, and isolation/seclusion. In *contingent observation time-out*, contingent on misbehavior, the student is removed to another location in the classroom where he or she is instructed to watch but cannot participate in activities. In *exclusion time-out*, contingent on misbehavior, a student is temporarily removed from instructional activities and is not able to watch these activities. The student, however, is not removed to an isolation area. In *isolation/seclusion time-out* the student, contingent on misbehavior, is required to leave the classroom and enter a separate time-out room for a brief duration. Isolation/seclusion is the most restrictive form of time-out and is perhaps the most frequently abused. Because of the potential for abuse, a number of states restrict the use of isolation/seclusion time-out (Rozalski, Yell, & Boreson, 2006).

Research has shown that the previously discussed types of time-out are effective in reducing behavior. In determining the type of time-out that will be used, it is important that the teacher consider all these different types and choose the least intrusive time-out procedure that is effective in producing behavioral change.

Step 4: Determine Implementation Guidelines. A number of researchers have addressed ways in which time-out can be made more effective when used in classroom settings (Brantner & Dougherty, 1973; Harris, 1985; Johns & Carr, 1995; Nelson & Rutherford, 1983; Wolery et al., 1988). Three decisions teachers should make prior to using the procedure are (a) if warnings and explanation will be used, (b) what duration of time-out will be used, and (c) how students will be released from time-out.

Using Warnings and Explanations Prior to Using Time-Out. Teachers must decide if they will give students a warning prior to sending them to time-out. A warning is a brief statement given to a misbehaving student indicating that if the inappropriate behavior continues, the time-out procedure will be administered. Although it is unclear if warnings actually are effective, they may serve a useful purpose because they give a student an opportunity to escape the intervention by improving his or her behavior.

In a study in which warnings were used prior to implementing time-out, Yell (1990) found that time-out with warnings and time-out without warnings were equally effective in reducing target behaviors. When warnings were delivered prior to using time-out, however, students received fewer time-outs and spent less time in time-out and away from classroom activities. Using a warning before administering time-out, therefore, may result in a less intrusive intervention without reducing its effectiveness in reducing target behaviors. It appears that using a warning prior to time-out, therefore, might be the method of choice over using time-out without a warning (Yell, 1994).

Closely related to using warnings is the practice of giving explanations prior to using a behavior reduction procedure. Teachers should also determine if they will use verbal explanations when administering time-out. A verbalized explanation to the student indicates why he or she is being timed out. When used, verbal explanations should be businesslike, brief, and specify the behaviors leading to time-out (Wolery et al., 1988). In fact, Martella and colleagues (2003) suggest that to minimize the possibly reinforcing attention that a student receives, the teacher's explanation to a student should be kept to fewer than 10 words. Research that has investigated the use of verbal explanations with time-out appears to indicate that they neither hinder nor facilitate the effectiveness of time-out (Harris, 1985; Yell, 1990).

Selecting the duration of time-out. Another important decision that teachers have to make involves the duration or length of the time-out. Duration is the intensity of the time-out procedure (Wolery et al., 1988). With any punishment procedure intensity is a very important consideration. A minimum level of intensity is often ineffective and too high a level of intensity can be unnecessarily intrusive without producing additional benefits. According to Harris (1985), a variety of durations from

10 seconds to 1 hour have produced reductions in target behaviors. Durations that are too long, however, are both practically, legally, and ethically difficult. Long durations can interfere with a student's opportunity to learn, suppress behavior in general as well as suppressing target behavior, and may increase the rate of undesired behavior (Harris, 1985). Additionally, longer time-outs do not appear to provide any further reductive effects on behavior than do shorter periods (Sulzer-Azeroff & Mayer, 1991). Cooper and colleagues (1987) suggested that 5 minutes is a reasonable rule of thumb for initial implementation. The teacher should determine and use durations that are as short as possible while still resulting in the desired behavior change.

Setting release criteria. How a teacher chooses to release students from time-out is an important decision that must be made. Several possible criteria for releasing students from time-out are as follows:

• *Fixed duration.* The student is released from time-out after he or she has served the complete duration. Release is not contingent on behavior when in time-out. For example, if the time-out duration is 3 minutes, the student would be released after 3 minutes regardless of his or her behavior while in time-out. The problem with using a fixed duration is that disruption during time-out may be greater, and that inappropriate behaviors occurring near the end of the time-out period may be negatively reinforced by release (Harris, 1985).

• *Minimum duration plus extension until appropriate behavior occurs.* The teacher assigns a minimum duration that the student is required to serve. To be released at the end of the time-out period, the student must be behaving appropriately. If the student is not behaving appropriately, time-out is extended until appropriate behavior is displayed.

• *Minimum duration plus extension for a fixed interval.* The teacher assigns a minimum duration that the student is required to serve. To be released at the end of the time-out period, the student must behave appropriately for this predetermined interval. If the student behaves inappropriately during this interval, the student is required to stay in time-out for an additional interval of the same length. For example, if the teacher decides on an interval of 25 seconds, and the time-out duration is 3 minutes, the student has to serve the duration of 3 minutes. Additionally, the student must behave appropriately for the final 25 seconds of the 3 minutes. Inappropriate behavior during this interval will extend time-out for another 25 seconds before the student is released.

• *Release contingent on appropriate behavior.* Release from time-out is contingent on the student displaying appropriate behavior for a specific interval. For example, if the teacher determines that the time-out interval will be 3 minutes the student has to behave appropriately for 3 minutes. Following 3 minutes of appropriate behavior, the student will be released from time-out.

Step 5: Develop a Data Collection and Record-Keeping System. When teachers use time-out they should collect behavioral data on the students' target behaviors to assess student progress. Records should also be kept on the number of time-outs given so that they can assess how the intervention is working. Additionally, because exclusion and seclusion time-out are intrusive interventions, teachers should keep thorough records of incidences that lead to either type of time-out (see Figure 12–6 in Chapter 12 for an example of a behavior incident report).

Step 6: Teach Students the Time-Out System. Before the time-out intervention is used teachers should explain to their students why, how, and when time-out will be administered. When students clearly understand the intervention, the likelihood of time-out being successful, and potential problems being avoided, are greatly enhanced. All aspects of the time-out intervention should be explained and demonstrated until students clearly understand the procedure.

Summary of Time-Out Time-out is a behavior reduction procedure that involves the temporary removal of reinforcement contingent on an inappropriate target behavior. There are two major types of time-out: (a) nonexclusionary time-out, where the source of reinforcement is removed from the student, and (b) exclusionary time-out, where the student is temporarily removed from the source of reinforcement. There is a large body of research that has demonstrated time-out to be effective when used appropriately and consistently. Nonetheless, time-out is a complex intervention and a teacher who uses it must make several important decisions before implementing a time-out system.

Overcorrection

Overcorrection is a behavior reduction procedure in which a teacher requires a student who has engaged in problem behavior to repeat the behavior in the correct way numerous times. There are two types of overcorrection: restitution and positive practice. In *restitutional overcorrection* a student who has disrupted the environment is required to restore the environment to a better state than it was before the disruption. For example, if a student

has colored on his or her desk, the teacher would require the student to clean all the desks in the classroom. Compare this to simple restitution where the student would be required to clean his or her own desk (Zirpoli & Melloy, 2001). In restitution, the student experiences the effort that is required to correct the results of his or her misbehavior.

In *positive practice overcorrection*, a student who exhibits inappropriate behavior is required to perform an appropriate form of the behavior numerous times. For example, if a student runs from his or her classroom to the buses after school is dismissed, a teacher may require the student to walk from the classroom to the buses a number of times. Compare this to simple positive practice procedure where the student may be required to stop running and walk to the buses.

The two purposes for using overcorrection are to (a) reduce the inappropriate behavior and (b) require the student to practice an appropriate alternative behavior. Moreover, by using overcorrection teachers require students to take responsibility for their own actions (Maag, 2004; Wolery et al., 1988). Thus, there is an educational component to overcorrection because correct behaviors are taught through an exaggeration of those behaviors (Alberto & Troutman, 2004).

Overcorrection has been successfully applied in many settings and with a variety of behaviors. The majority of these studies have been conducted in residential settings. Table 13–11 is a partial list of studies of overcorrection in school settings.

Advantages and Disadvantages of Overcorrection An advantage of overcorrection is that it uses consequences that are directly related to the inappropriate behavior (Maag, 2004; Schloss & Smith, 1994; Wolery et al., 1988), whereas interventions such as time-out and response cost lack this logical connection (Foxx & Bechtel, 1983). According to Foxx and Bechtel, this relatedness will reduce the likelihood of using the procedure in a punitive or arbitrary manner. Moreover, a differential reinforcement procedure can be used to increase the appropriate behavior whenever the student engages in the correct alternative behavior.

Overcorrection, unlike the other behavior reduction procedures, has been used successfully to improve various academic behaviors such as oral reading (Singh & Singh, 1986), spelling (Matson, Esveldt-Dawson, & Kazdin, 1982), mathematics (Skinner, Turco, Beatty, & Rasavage, 1989), and cursive writing (Mabee, 1988). Lenz, Singh, and Hewett (1991) referred to the use of overcorrection procedures when used to correct academic errors as directed rehearsal.

Table 13-11   Research on overcorrection

Behaviors	Studies
Academic behaviors	• Lenz, Singh, & Hewett, 1991
	• Mabee, 1988
	• Matson, Esveldt-Dawson, & Kazdin, 1982
	• Ollendick, Matson, Esveldt-Dawson, & Shapiro, 1980
	• Singh, 1987
	• Singh, Singh, & Winton, 1984
	• Stewart & Singh, 1986
	• Skinner, Turco, Beatty, & Rasavage, 1989
	• Trap, Milner-Davis, Joseph, & Cooper, 1978
Aggressive behaviors	• Adams & Kelley, 1992
	• Bierly & Billingsley, 1983
	• Luiselli & Rice, 1983
	• Ollendick, & Matson, 1976
Disruptive behaviors	• Azrin & Powers, 1975
	• Bornstein, Hamilton, & Quevillon, 1977

The primary disadvantage of overcorrection is that it can be a time-consuming process that requires the full attention of the teacher (Alberto & Troutman, 2006). When teachers use overcorrection procedures they must be prepared to direct the student in the overcorrection activity for between 5 to 15 minutes if needed. In fact, long durations of overcorrection have been shown to be more effective than short durations (Wolery et al., 1988). Moreover, the teacher must be prepared for the student to attempt to escape or avoid the overcorrection intervention.

Setting Up an Overcorrection System Overcorrection has been shown to be a very effective intervention when it is implemented with accuracy, consistency, and fidelity (Alberto & Troutman, 2006). It does not require as much time to organize as the other interventions reviewed in this chapter because the intervention is chosen according to the student's misbehavior. Figure 13–15 is a checklist that teachers may follow when setting up an overcorrection system.

Step 1: *Choose the type of overcorrection.* The type of the overcorrection that a teacher uses should be dictated by the type of student misbehavior. If there is an environmental disruption (e.g., a student writes on a hallway wall), then restitution should be used. If a student engages in an inappropriate behavior, but there is no environmental disruption (e.g., running in a school hall), then positive practice should be used. The two procedures can also be used in combination. Additionally, a minimally intrusive procedure should be tried first.

If it doesn't work, then a more intrusive procedure may be used.

Step 2: *Identify target behaviors that will result in overcorrection.* Because the purpose of overcorrection is to reduce undesirable behaviors, an important step when developing the intervention is to define all the target behaviors to be reduced in observable and measurable terms. When target behaviors are defined in this way, staff and students will clearly know what behaviors will be penalized.

Step 3: *Determine implementation guidelines.* Wolery et al., (1988) suggest that teachers administer overcorrection in the following manner. First, they should tell the student that he or she is behaving inappropriately. Second, they should stop the student from engaging in the activity. Third, they should instruct the student to begin the overcorrection procedure immediately. When students are engaged in the overcorrection, the teacher should be careful not to reinforce them in any way because that could result in an increase of the inappropriate behavior that led to the overcorrection procedure (Martin & Pear, 1996). Fourth, the student should return to the ongoing activity. Additionally, if it appears that the student enjoys the activity or gets attention from engaging in overcorrection, the intervention should not be used (Maag, 2004).

The teacher must determine how to get students to engage in the overcorrection procedure (Maag, 2004). According to Azrin and Powers (1975), verbal instructions and gestural prompts should be attempted first. If these directions are not successful, then a minimal amount of physical guidance may be used. If this doesn't work, the teacher may need to use another behavior reduction procedure (e.g., time-out).

Step 4: *Develop a data collection and record-keeping system.* When teachers use behavior reduction interventions they should collect behavioral data on the students' target behaviors to assess student progress. Additionally, because overcorrection is an intrusive intervention that may require physical guidance, teachers should keep thorough records of incidences that lead to either type of overcorrection.

Step 5: *Teach students the overcorrection procedure.* Teachers should explain the overcorrection procedure to the students. Specifically, they should address the purpose of the procedure and when it will be used. In addition to discussion, students should be given an opportunity to role-play and

FIGURE 13–15

Overcorrection checklist

Yes	No	Component
☐	☐	Type of overcorrection that will be used is selected. -*Will restitution, positive practice, or both procedures be used?*
☐	☐	Target behaviors are selected. -*Is the target behavior socially valid for the student?* -*Is the target behavior observable and measurable?* -*Have baseline measures been taken of the target behaviors?*
☐	☐	Implementation guidelines are determined. -*Does the teacher have a procedure to engage a student in overcorrection?*
☐	☐	Data collection and record-keeping systems are developed. -*Has a data collection system to monitor student progress been developed?* -*Are records kept on the operation of the level system?*
☐	☐	Students understand the overcorrection intervention.

practice the procedure. Students should also be told of backup procedures that will be used in case they do not voluntarily engage in the overcorrection (e.g., response cost, time-out).

Summary of Overcorrection Overcorrection is a behavior reduction procedure in which a teacher requires a student who has engaged in problem behavior to repeat the behavior in the correct way numerous times. There are two types of overcorrection: restitution and positive practice. In restitutional overcorrection a student who has disrupted the environment is required to restore the environment to a better state than it was before the disruption. In positive practice overcorrection, a student who exhibits inappropriate behavior is required to perform an appropriate form of the behavior numerous times. Overcorrection has been shown to be a very effective intervention when it is implemented with accuracy, consistency, and fidelity.

ADMINISTRATIVE AND LEGAL GUIDELINES WHEN USING BEHAVIOR REDUCTION INTERVENTIONS

To ensure that behavior reduction procedures are administered in a legally correct manner, teachers should adhere to the specific guidelines (Braaten, Simpson, Rosell, &

Reilly, 1988; Darch & Kame'enui, 2004; Yell, 1996b, 2006). It should be noted that informing a parent about all aspects of a student's program is important.

Teachers and administrators should also understand that the more intrusive behavior reduction procedures may be used, even in the absence of parental consent, if such procedures are necessary to protect the safety of the student, other students, or staff. In such situations it is crucial that the incident be documented and used in a reasonable manner.

Principle 1: Teachers need to be aware of, and act in accordance with, local school district or state policies. Prior to implementing behavior reduction procedures, teachers must determine if their school districts have policies that restrict or prohibit the use of certain interventions. Additionally, if states have regulations or guidelines on using behavior reduction interventions, they must be understood and followed. Typically, if such rules or regulations exist at the local, district, or state level, they will cover the more restrictive forms of behavior reduction interventions (e.g., seclusion time-out). Nonetheless, from a legal standpoint it is important that behavior reduction procedures be used according to research-based best practices (e.g., collect data on the effectiveness of behavior reduction procedures).

Principle 2: Teachers should have written procedures on the more intrusive behavior reduction procedures that they may use in their program. Teachers should inform a student's parents about how, when, and under what conditions the procedures will be used. It is important that teachers have written procedures that explain the rationale and methods for using the more intrusive behavior reduction procedures (e.g., time-out). These guidelines must be followed when implementing the procedures.

Principle 3: Teachers should obtain informed consent from a student's parents or guardians prior to using the more intrusive behavior reduction procedures. When a student's parents understand the intrusive behavior reduction intervention and how it will be used, the teacher should obtain their consent to use it. Parental consent should be documented by having them sign a form that stipulates that they understand and agree to the procedure. Section 504 plans and IEPs can be used for this purpose by attaching a crisis management plan to the document (see Chapter 10).

Principle 4: Teachers should always adhere to the principle of hierarchical application when using behavior reduction procedures. According to this principle, more intrusive (i.e., inhibits student's personal rights) and restrictive (i.e., inhibits student's freedom) behavior reduction procedures should only be used when less intrusive and restrictive procedures have been tried and found to be ineffective (Braaten et al., 1988). This means that when teachers plan interventions to reduce a student's problem behavior, they should begin by implementing less intrusive interventions (e.g., response cost) and move to the more restrictive interventions (e.g., time-out) only when the less intrusive procedures have not been successful.

Principle 5: Teachers should use behavior reduction procedures only when the procedures serve a legitimate educational function. Teachers should use intrusive behavior reduction procedures for legitimate educational reasons. For example, seclusion time-out may be used to (a) protect the education environment from serious disruption; (b) reduce problem behaviors that deny a student or his or her peers the opportunity to learn; or (c) protect a student, other students, or staff. However, using seclusion time-out because a teacher was angry with a student or the student was engaged in a trivial misbehavior (e.g., chewing gum) would not serve a legitimate educational function. Using an intervention for a legitimate educational reason requires that teachers use good judgment.

Principle 6: Teachers should give one warning prior to implementing intrusive behavior reduction interventions. When teachers use intrusive behavior reduction, they should warn the student that unless the behavior changes the procedure will be implemented. The warning should be one brief and businesslike statement. The advantage of using a warning prior to any behavior reduction procedure is that the teacher gives the student an opportunity to change the behavior and thus avoid the procedure.

Principle 7: Teachers must use intrusive behavior reduction procedures in a reasonable manner. When intrusive behavior reduction procedures are used, teachers must use them reasonably. When courts examine if such procedures were used reasonably, they do not have specific guidelines to make the determination. Rather, the standard is whether a reasonable person used the intervention in this manner. This means that the intrusive behavior reduction procedures should not be used in a harsh or severe manner. For example, if time-out is used, the length of time-out should be proportionate to a student's age. If a 6-year-old student was put in an unsupervised seclusion time-out room for 2 hours, a court would probably view this as unreasonable. If that same 6-year-old were put in supervised seclusion time-out room for 10 minutes, a court would probably view that as reasonable. It is a standard that requires good judgment on the part of the teacher.

To ensure that intrusive procedures are administered reasonably, teachers should (a) receive training in the appropriate use of a procedure, and use the procedure in accordance with the training; (b) inform the students' parents of guidelines for using the procedure, and then follow these guidelines; (c) administer the behavior reduction procedure in proportion to the gravity of the offense and the age of the student; and (d) never act out of anger or malice when administering the behavior reduction procedure. Courts would probably view a behavior reduction procedure used in accordance with these guidelines as reasonable.

Principle 8: Teachers should keep thorough records whenever intrusive behavior reduction procedures are used. When an intrusive behavior reduction procedure is used, teachers must thoroughly record the incident. Elements that should be recorded include (a) the names of the student, teacher, and any witnesses; (b) the date, time, and location of the incident; (c) the behavior that led to the use of the procedure; (d) specific information about the use of the procedure (e.g., length of time-out); and (e) the results of the procedure (including effectiveness data).

Principle 9: Teachers must continuously monitor student progress when using behavior reduction procedures. To monitor student progress, a teacher must collect data on the target behavior to determine if the behavior is being reduced. Teacher decisions must be made on the basis of data, rather than on the basis of subjective judgment. In Chapter 6, we discussed methods by which teachers may collect this data. If the data show that the procedures are not effective in changing student behavior, then the teacher must adjust the intervention plan. On the other hand, if the data show that a student has responded and the inappropriate behavior is under control, behavior reduction procedures may be gradually withdrawn.

Chapter Summary

Students with EBD exhibit behaviors that negatively affect the quality of their lives. Teachers often need to use powerful interventions to teach these students appropriate behavior and to reduce the problem behaviors exhibited by them. In this chapter several interventions were discussed that can be used to increase appropriate behaviors and decrease inappropriate behaviors.

The interventions presented have been found to be effective in research conducted with children and youth in a variety of settings. There are, however, no interventions that will be successful with all students across all settings. Although these are evidence-based procedures, interventions must always be (a) linked to assessment data; (b) implemented in accordance with intended guidelines (i.e., implementation fidelity); and (c) evaluated by collecting data on student progress.

PART

3

Teaching Students with EBD

CHAPTER 14

Teaching Students with EBD I: Effective Teaching

Mitchell L. Yell

Focus Questions

- What are the principles of effective instruction?
- Do teachers of students with EBD use the principles of effective instruction?
- How can teachers of students with EBD become more effective teachers?
- How can effective teachers ensure that they maintain their effectiveness?

Low academic achievement and school failure are primary characteristics exhibited by students with emotional and behavioral disorders (EBD; Coleman & Webber, 2002; Foley & Epstein, 1992; Kauffman, 2005; Lane; 2004). According to Mastropieri et. al., (1985), research findings support the notion that students with EBD are deficient in all areas of academic functioning, and that with respect to academic performance there are few differences between students with EBD and students with learning difficulties. Students with EBD experience high rates of academic failure, low grades, grade retention, school avoidance, and school dropout, which lead to major adjustment problems later in life (Bullock, Gable, & Melloy, 2006; Lane & Beebe-Frankenberger, 2004; U.S. Department of Education, 1994).

Indeed, failure to achieve is a defining characteristic of EBD. According to IDEA and its regulations an emotional disturbance is a "condition exhibiting one or more of the following characteristics over a long period of time and to a marked degree *that adversely affects a child's educational performance*" (IDEA Regulations, 34 C.F.R. § 300.7(b)(9); emphasis added). Moreover, the first of the characteristics listed in the federal regulations is "an *inability to learn* that cannot be explained by intellectual, sensory, or health factors" (IDEA Regulations, 34 C.F.R. § 300.7(b)(9); emphasis added). Most states also require that academic deficits be one of the criteria for determining eligibility in the category of EBD (Coleman & Webber, 2002). Clearly, academic underachievement is a significant problem for students with EBD.

In the next three chapters, we will examine this research based on effective instruction and teaching students with EBD. In this chapter I discuss the principles of effective instruction and how teachers can maintain their effectiveness. In Chapter 15, we look at research-based strategies for teaching reading, writing, mathematics, and study skills. In Chapter 16, we conclude with an examination of procedures for planning and evaluating instruction.

DO TEACHERS OF STUDENTS WITH EBD USE EFFECTIVE INSTRUCTIONAL STRATEGIES?

The seminal work of Knitzer and colleagues (1990) revealed that many classrooms of students with EBD are characterized by (a) boring repetitive academic lessons consisting primarily of worksheets; (b) irrelevant instructional programs that are not matched to students' abilities; (c) low rates of active academic responding and engagement; and (d) very little, if any, thought given to instructional planning. In fact, Knitzer et al. characterized classrooms as being focused on a curriculum of control that emphasized keeping kids quiet, and as failing to teach students the kinds of skills they need to successfully participate and become involved in general education.

Too often, teachers of students with EBD neglect academics in an attempt to get the students' behaviors under control (Scheuermann, 1998). The research of Wehby and colleagues (Sutherland & Wehby, 2001b; Wehby, Falk, et al., Wehby 2003; Wehby et al., 1995; Wehby, Lane, et al., 2003) have documented the often poor instruction found in classrooms of students with EBD. In fact, Wehby, Lane, et al. (2003) argued that the limited attention given to the academic needs of students with EBD has contributed to the extremely poor outcomes for these students such as high rates of absenteeism, low grade point averages, academic failure, and high rates of school dropout.

Moreover, research suggests that there is often (a) little systematic instructional programming in classrooms for students with EBD (Wehby et al., 1998); (b) few positive interactions between students with EBD and their teachers (Shores, Jack, et al., 1993; Van Acker et al., 1996; Wehby et al., 1995); (c) low rates of instructional interactions (Shores, Jack, et al., 1993; Wehby et al., 1995); (d) attention to misbehavior while ignoring appropriate behavior (Walker & Buckley, 1974); and (e) high rates of teacher reprimands (Wehby et al., 1993, 1995). In fact, many classrooms for students with EBD lack several of the basic components that are necessary for effective instruction (Gagnon, Wehby, Strong, Falk, 2006; Wehby, Lane, & Falk, 2003).

Without a doubt, teaching students with EBD is a challenging task, made even more difficult by these students' complex behavioral needs (Scheuermann, 1998). Nonetheless, the research is clear that students with EBD have moderate to severe academic difficulties and desperately need quality academic instruction; unfortunately they frequently do not get it. Some reasons this occurs may include (a) little emphasis on effective instructional methods in teacher preparation programs because of the focus on behaviors (Lane & Beebe-Frankenberger, 2004; Rosenberg et. al., 2008; Wehby, Lane, et al., 2003; Whelan & Simpson, 1996); (b) the lack of research on academic interventions and students with EBD (Coleman & Vaughn, 2000; Gunter & Denny, 1998; Gunter, Hummel, et al., 1998; Moore, Epstein, Reid, & Nelson, 2003; Ruhl & Berlinghoff, 1992); and (c) inadequate coverage of academic issues in EBD textbooks (Lane, Gresham, & O'Shaughnessy, 2002). It may be, as Levy & Chard (2001) asserted, that because so much attention has been devoted to managing disruptive behavior, the questions regarding what and how students with EBD should be taught are not afforded careful consideration.

Whatever the reason may be, it is clear that teachers of students with EBD do not systematically engage in those instructional practices most associated with effective instruction or those practices that have strong empirical support (Gunter, Hummel, et al., 1998). Wehby, Lane, et al. (2003) stated that teachers in self-contained classrooms of students with EBD devote only approximately 30% of their school day in actual academic instruction. When they do, Walker et al. (1998) noted "substantial numbers of educators seem to ignore the concept of best practices and rely upon a hodgepodge of activities, unplanned curricula, and conceptually incompatible interventions to accomplish teaching, learning, and management goals" (p. 8). The bottom line is, many teachers of students with EBD do not use effective teaching practices. Why this is the case is a question that has long puzzled researchers. If research-based teaching practices would lead to increased academic achievement and lowered rates of problem behavior, why don't teachers use these practices? Furthermore, there is evidence that when teachers of EBD demonstrate effective instructional behaviors, the results are significant improvements in their students' academic and social behavior (Sutherland & Wehby, 2001b; Sutherland, Wehby, & Yoder, 2001). An emphasis on effective teacher behaviors and instructional procedures that leads to improved academic performance of students with EBD may also result in decreases in challenging and disruptive behaviors (Wehby, Lane, et al., 2003).

A large body of research exists on effective instruction with general education students, low-achieving students, and students with learning disabilities from which teachers can develop their instructional programs (Ellis, Worthington, & Larkin, 1994; Good & Brophy, 2008). Researchers are now conducting important investigations of effective interventions that can be used successfully with students with EBD (see especially the work of researchers such as Drs. Denny, Gunter, Lane, Sutherland, and Wehby).

Moreover, federal laws such as No Child Left Behind (hereafter NCLB) and the Individuals with Disabilities Education Improvement Act (hereafter IDEA 2004) demand that teachers use research-based instruction in their educational programs. Specifically, IDEA 2004 requires that the IEP include a "a statement of the special education and related services and supplementary aids and services, based on *peer-reviewed research* to the extent practicable, to be provided to the child" (IDEA, 20 U.S.C. § 1414 (d)(1)(A)(i)(IV); emphasis added). It is crucial that teachers become consumers and users of effective practices with their students to ensure higher academic achievement, lower rates of problem behavior, and to meet the mandates of federal law.

PRINCIPLES OF EFFECTIVE INSTRUCTION

There is a large body of research, often referred to as the teacher effectiveness or teacher effects research, in which teacher behaviors and student achievement have been examined. The purpose of the teacher effectiveness research has been to identify the characteristics of teachers who elicit strong achievement gains among their students (Good & Brophy, 2008). This research, which consists of over 100 correlational and experimental studies, has important implications about the role of the teacher in presenting information to students and engaging them in active learning activities and assignments (Good & Brophy, 2008; Rosenshine, 1997). The teacher effectiveness research is important because it addresses what teachers can do to maximize student learning (Mastropieri & Scruggs, 2005).

Research findings have consistently shown that teachers who are the most effective teachers of students with disabilities exhibit the same characteristics as do general classroom teachers (Mastropieri & Scruggs, 2005; Rosenshine, 1997). If teachers understand and practice these skills they will become more effective teachers. I next examine some of the principles from this research.

Principle #1: Maximize Academic Engaged Time

The greater the amount of time that a student devotes to a particular subject or skill, the more likely that student is to master the subject or skill (Good & Brophy, 2008; Mastropieri & Scruggs, 2005). In classrooms of the most effective teachers, students spend most of their available time in instructional activities, rather than nonacademic activities or games (Good & Brophy, 2008). The amount of time that students spend on instructional activities is often referred to as *time on task*, and the greater the amount of time that a student is actively engaged in learning, the more he or she will learn. Clearly, increasing the amount of time that a student spends meaningfully engaged in a task is an important principle of effective teaching.

Teachers therefore must strive to increase the amount of time that students spend engaged in a task. Time on task is an important principle; however, there is a difference between the amount of time a teacher sets aside for an activity, called *allocated time*, and the actual time in which a student is actively involved in an instructional activity, called *academic engaged time*.

To illustrate allocated time, a resource room teacher may decide that 45 minutes a day will be allocated to teaching mathematics. This does not mean that the teacher's students will be engaged in mathematics learning or activities (i.e., engaged time) for 45 minutes. Much of the allocated time could be taken up by time wasters such as transition time, student misbehavior, teacher digressions, downtime, and student inattention. In fact, Christenson and Ysseldyke (1986) reported that in special education classrooms, students were actively engaged in relevant learning activities in only 20% to 30% of allocated time devoted to that activity. Haynes and Jenkins (1986) conducted research on allocated and engaged time in elementary schools. They found that in only 44% of the allocated time were students actively engaged in learning activities.

Academic engaged time includes student behaviors such as attending to the teacher, attending to instructional materials, answering teacher questions, reading aloud, asking questions, taking notes, and completing independent work. The greater the amount of time that a student is actively engaged in instructional activities, the greater the amount of learning. Mastropieri and Scruggs (2005) assert that teachers may actually double the amount of classroom learning simply by increasing student engagement in learning activities throughout the allocated time period. Teachers therefore should ensure that students are actively engaged in learning to the maximum extent possible during allocated time (Marchand-Martella, Slocum, & Martella, 2004; Mastropieri & Scruggs, 2005).

Increasing Academic Engaged Time An effective way that teachers can increase the academic achievement of their students is to increase the amount of academic engaged time. An additional benefit of increased academic engaged time is that it decreases downtime in the classroom, which makes it more likely that students will be on task and less likely to misbehave (Martella et al., 2003). The following are a number of actions teachers can take to increase the time in which students are actively engaged in learning activities.

Plan Lessons That Maximize Academic Engagement. When teachers plan their lessons they need to ensure that students will be actively engaged during as much of the allocated time as possible. For example, if a teacher plans a 60-minute reading period, he or she should incorporate activities that require students to be engaged and respond to instruction for at least 80% of the 60-minute period (i.e., 48 minutes). Although some time will be taken up with transition activities and other classroom tasks, to ensure that these tasks take a minimum amount of time teachers should prepare lesson materials and supplies before class, have any needed equipment ready for the lesson, store materials in readily accessible areas, and have an efficient plan for collecting and correcting homework (Hofmeister & Lubke, 1990).

Use Time Efficiently. Paine et al. (1983) compared instructional time to money: It can be managed, but it also can slip through a teacher's hands. These authors also stated that it is very important for teachers to manage time—a basic resource in education—wisely and efficiently. In classrooms there are many time killers, caused by teachers and students, that teachers need to avoid. Table 14–1 shows examples of how teachers and students waste time.

Teachers can ensure that they use time effectively by (a) establishing classroom routines for identifiable and recurring classroom events, (b) providing a brisk pace for learning activities, (c) providing clear directions to students, (d) questioning students frequently, (e) managing transition times efficiently, and (f) praising and reinforcing students for on-task behavior.

Improve Classroom Management Skills. Teachers with poor classroom management skills spend excessive amounts of time disciplining students (e.g., reprimanding students, referring students to administrators); as a result the amount of academic engaged time is decreased. In fact, research has demonstrated that the least effective teachers spend a considerable amount of classroom time attempting to manage student behavior (Mastropieri & Scruggs, 2002). The quality and quantity of student engagement depends on the teacher's ability to organize and manage the classroom as an efficient learning environment where academic activities run smoothly and little time is spent dealing with problem behavior (Brophy & Good, 1986). Chapter 11 addresses proactive classroom management.

Reinforce Students for Increasing Academic Engaged Time. An effective way to increase academic engaged time is to reinforce students. For example, a teacher could verbally praise students who exhibit on-task behavior. If a student is off task, his or her teacher could praise students who are on task. If praise is not reinforcing to a student, the teacher could provide social or token

Table 14–1 Time wasters

Teacher	Student
Digressions (e.g., teacher talks about an irrelevant subject during lecture)	Inattention (e.g., student stares out window)
Classroom management (e.g., stopping instruction to manage student behavior)	Acting out (e.g., student pokes his or her neighbor with a pencil)
Downtime (e.g., students who finish assignments early are given nothing to keep themselves occupied while others finish)	Procrastination (e.g., student mills around in back of classroom after bell rings; student does not begin work when rest of class does)
Interruptions (e.g., teacher takes a telephone call during class)	Inappropriate behavior (e.g., student passes a note to his or her neighbor)
Disruptions (e.g., teacher loudly reprimands a student)	Off-task behavior (e.g., student draws pictures during math class)
Lack of organization (e.g., teacher misplaces worksheets; teacher does not begin class immediately after bell rings)	Inappropriate talkouts (e.g., student talks loudly during a lecture)
Unclear directions (e.g., teacher gives an assignment but does not tell students how to do it)	
Inappropriate assignments (e.g., teacher gives students assignments that are not at the correct level of difficulty)	
Transitions that are too long (e.g., students wait as the teacher attempts to locate materials for the next lesson)	

reinforcers for on-task behavior or for accurately completing academic tasks within a designated time period. Additionally, a teacher could use a group contingency to increase on-task behavior or completion of academic work. Mastropieri and Scruggs (2002) gave the example of a teacher setting a timer to ring at random intervals and then reinforcing the entire group if all the students are on task when the bell rings (e.g., allowing the class an additional minute of recess when all the students are on task). Increasing on-task time will result in improved academic achievement as well as decreased rates of problem behavior.

Monitoring Rates of Student Academic Engaged Time. To improve students' academic achievement, teachers should increase the amount of time that their students spend actively engaged in academic activities. To accomplish this, teachers will need to monitor the rates of active academic engagement in their classes. Walker et al. (1995) suggested an effective method for monitoring students' academic engaged time. The steps of this method are as follows:

Step 1: *Define academic engaged time.* Academic engaged time means that a student is actively engaged in working on assigned learning materials or activities (Walker et al., 1995). Students should be considered to be academically engaged when they

(a) attend to the material or task; (b) make appropriate motor responses (e.g., writing, computing); (c) ask for assistance (when appropriate) in an acceptable manner; (d) interact with the teacher or classmates about academic matters; and (e) listen to the teacher's instructions, lectures, and directions.

Step 2: *Have an observer monitor the student(s) engaged time.* If the teacher has a paraeducator or colleague who can serve as an observer, have this person use a stopwatch to record engaged time for an individual student or for the entire class. The observer should be seated where he or she has an unobstructed view of the student or class and record the hour and minute when the recording session begins.

Step 3: *Record the academic engaged time.* The observer should start the stopwatch as soon as he or she begins the recording session, and keep it running when the student engages in behavior consistent with the definition in step 1. When the student is off task (i.e., engaging in behaviors that are not consistent with the definition, such as not attending, or engaging in disruptive behavior), the observer should turn off the stopwatch, then restart it when the student becomes academically engaged again. The observer repeats this procedure throughout the observation session, recording the hour and minute when the session stops.

Step 4: *Calculate the percentage of academic engaged time.* The observer can compute the percentage of academic engaged time by dividing the time on the stopwatch by the total time observed and multiplying this figure by 100. This procedure should be conducted for a couple of observation sessions to ensure accuracy.

The percentage of academic engaged time should approach 80% to 85% of the allocated time (Algozzine, Ysseldyke, & Elliot, 1997; Walker et al., 1995). If the percentages from the observation sessions are not close to 80%, the teacher is losing valuable instructional time and should take steps to increase the percentage of academic engaged time. Teachers can maximize academic engaged time by also focusing on the following principles.

Principle #2: Ensure High Rates of Correct Academic Responding

According to Greenwood, Delquadri, and Hall (1983), an important variable in a student's learning is the number of response opportunities he or she has during an instructional activity. The researchers referred to this concept as *opportunity to respond*. By increasing the number of students' active responses, teachers can increase students' academic achievement. Sutherland and colleagues (2003) investigated opportunity to respond in nine elementary students with EBD. The researchers found that when the teachers increased the opportunities for students to actively respond to academic requests, the students had fewer disruptions, increased on-task rates, and had more correct responses. The importance of increasing students' opportunities to respond was further highlighted by the Council for Exceptional Children (CEC) in 1987, when it cited opportunities to respond as an effective teaching practice for special education teachers (CEC, 1987).

Berliner (1991), however, noted that in addition to academic engaged time and opportunities to respond, students must also experience a high rate of success in the academic tasks that they are assigned. Gunter and colleagues (Gunter & Denny, 1998; Gunter, Hummel, et al., 1998; Gunter, Hummel, & Conroy, 1998) have noted the importance of students with EBD making correct academic responses. In fact, Gunter, Hummel, et al. (1998) considered correct academic responding to be the primary measure of success in academic instruction of students with EBD.

According to the CEC (1987), during instruction teachers should elicit from four to six responses per minute from their students, and during independent

practice students should make from eight to nine responses per minute. Moreover, students should respond correctly to instruction of new information at an accuracy level of 80% and should demonstrate correct academic responding to drill and independent practice activities at an accuracy level of 90%. These high levels of accuracy are very important to academic achievement. Additionally, a number of studies have shown that high rates of student success are positively correlated to student learning outcomes, and low rates of success are negatively correlated with student learning outcomes (Fisher et al., 1980; Reith & Evertson, 1988). Thus, there is a considerable positive relationship between high success rates and academic achievement (Ellis et al., 1994). When teachers plan instruction, therefore, the rate of success at which a student completes a task should be considered a critical instructional variable (Ellis et al., 1994).

Correct academic responding is an extremely important classroom behavior that is correlated with many other behaviors of effective teachers (Gunter & Denny, 1998). For example, students receive three times more attention from teachers when they engage in undesirable behaviors than when they engage in desirable behaviors (Sprick et al., 1993); however, when students respond correctly they are much more likely to receive positive teacher attention. In fact, Van Acker and colleagues (1996) found that correct academic responses were the only student behavior that reliably predicted teacher praise, which is a teacher behavior associated with academic success (Good & Brophy, 2008; Gunter, Hummel, et al., 1998).

Van Acker et al. (1996) reported that young students at risk for aggressive behavior make very few correct academic responses during a school day. In fact, the researchers found that the average rate of correct academic responding for these students was between .014 and .021 per minute, or about five to eight correct academic responses per day. Gunter, Hummel, et al. (1998) asserted that such low rates mean that these students are not receiving effective instruction. The researchers further noted that in this study the probability of teacher praise following correct academic responding was .43, which means that these students were probably receiving only 3.5 teacher praise statements per school day.

When teachers engage in effective teaching behaviors, such as modeling, giving positive statements and attention, and providing corrective feedback, their students produce more correct academic responses (Gunter, Hummel, et al., 1998). Additionally, correct academic responding relates not only to increased academic achievement, but also to internalized attributions of success (Ellis et al., 1994). Unfortunately, students with disabilities tend to make few correct academic responses, which may indicate that teachers of these students do not engage in effective teaching behaviors (Gunter, Hummel, et al., 1998). Additionally, Gunter, Shores, Jack, Denny, and DePaepe (1994) found that when teachers of students with EBD requested student responses without providing sufficient information for the student to respond correctly, the students were more likely to engage in higher rates of problem behavior. When teachers provided sufficient information for the students to respond correctly, students engaged in lower rates of problem behavior. The conclusion of Gunter and colleagues was that when teachers attempt to teach students with EBD using ineffective methods, it is likely that the students will learn to use problem behaviors to escape the interactions.

Increasing Correct Academic Responding To increase correct academic responding teachers need to (a) increase the opportunities in which students have to respond, and (b) ensure that students are engaged in activities that are at an appropriate level of difficulty.

Increase Opportunities to Respond. To increase student response opportunities teachers should strive to use instructional formats that will increase student responding. Examples of ways to increase response opportunities include (a) asking many questions, (b) requiring choral or unison responding, (c) planning active practice activities, and (d) using response cards (Berliner, 1991; Christle & Schuster, 2003; Paine & Anderson-Inman, 1988). Figure 14-1 describes how response cards may be used to increase academic responding.

Ensure That Student's Responses are Correct. It is important that teachers monitor students' responses to ensure that they are responding correctly at least 80% to 90% of the time. Additionally, teachers should reinforce students for responding correctly. When students respond incorrectly the teacher should correct them immediately to remediate errors (Paine & Anderson-Inman, 1988).

Monitoring Rates of Student Correct Academic Responding To improve students' academic achievement, teachers should increase the numbers of correct academic responses made by their students. To accomplish this, teachers will need to monitor the correct academic responses of a student or students in their classes. Gunter, Hummel, et al. (1998) suggested an effective

FIGURE 14-1

Using response cards

Directions for Using Response Cards

Materials:

- The response cards consist of plastic sheet protectors and recycled manila folders. Each manila folder is cut in half in order to fit inside a plastic sheet protector and provide stiffness to the response card.
- Each student is given a dry-erase marker to write responses directly on the plastic sheet protector.
- Each student is given an eraser, which can either be a piece of felt or a used dryer sheet.

Steps:

- The teacher explains and demonstrates how students will use the materials before handing them out.
- Explanations should include examples and nonexamples (e.g., "You write your answer only on the response card with the marker. You do not write on anything else with the marker. You do not draw or write anything but your answer to the question").
- This includes what the students will do when the teacher gives the following cues:
  - Write your answer means write on the response card and keep it face down on the desk until the next cue.
  - Cards up means to hold the response card with both hands above heads with the answer facing the teacher until the next cue.
  - Cards down means to put the response card down on the desk and erase the answer to get ready for the next question.
- After handing out the materials the teacher asks a question that requires a short answer, number, or letter. The teacher may have the choices displayed on the board or overhead projector.
- The teacher says, "Write your answer."
- Next the teacher says, "Cards up."
- The teacher scans the cards and verbally states the correct answer (e.g., "Good. 4/5 is the correct answer") and also may show the correct answer from a model.
- The teacher says, "Cards down."

Source: Developed by Dr. Christine Christle of the University of South Carolina based on the following article: Christle, C. A., & Schuster, J. W. (2003). The effects of using response cards on student participation, academic achievement, and on-task behavior during whole-class, math instruction. Journal of Behavioral Education, 12, 147–165.

method for monitoring students' academic engaged time. The steps of this method are as follows:

Step 1: *Define correct academic responding.* Correct academic responding occurs anytime a student gives a correct response in an academic task. Students should be considered to be responding correctly when they (a) answer an academic question posed by the teacher, (b) make correct motor responses (e.g., writing a correct answer), (c) answer correctly during choral responding, and (d) answer the question by showing the correct response card answer.

Step 2: *Have an observer monitor the frequency of student correct academic responses.* If the teacher has a paraeducator or colleague who can serve as an observer, the teacher could have this person do simple frequency counts of correct academic responses for an individual student or for the entire class. The observer should be seated where he or she has an unobstructed view of the student or class, and record the hour and minute when the recording session begins. Additionally, the observer should record if the teacher is presenting new information, or if the primary purpose of the lesson is to practice using information that has already been presented.

Step 3: *Count the correct academic responses.* The observer should start counting correct academic responses as he or she begins the recording session. The observation session should last 20 minutes or more. The observer should note that correct academic responses can include oral answers and motoric responses.

Step 4: *Calculate the rate of correct academic responding.* The observer can compute the rate of correct academic responding by dividing the number of correct responses by the time the student was observed. The frequency of correct academic responding is presented in rate per minute. Gunter, Hummel, et al. (1998) suggested that appropriate rates of correct academic responses for new material should be three per minute, and for drill and practice should be eight per minute. This calculation should be conducted over a couple of observation sessions to ensure accuracy.

Teachers should attempt to increase their students' rate of correct academic responding. Because high rates of correct academic responding may be considered important indicators of effective teaching, teachers may be confident that good instruction

is occurring when these rates are high (Gunter, Hummel, et al. (1998).

Principle #3: Maximize the Amount of Content Covered

Mastropieri and Scruggs (2005) defined content coverage as the amount of academic content to which students are exposed throughout the school year. The amount of content that teachers cover during a year is determined by a number of factors such as (a) state standards, (b) curriculum guides, and (c) the length of the school year. Nonetheless, these factors only reflect opportunities to cover content; teachers determine the actual amount of content covered in their classrooms (Mastropieri & Scruggs, 2005).

Increased opportunities to learn content are correlated positively with increased student achievement and viewed by some as the single most important instructional principle derived from the teacher effectiveness research (Ellis et al., 1994). Thus, it is important that teachers attempt to increase the amount of content they cover in specific academic areas. Content coverage, therefore, should be an important part of a teacher's long-range planning. (Chapter 16 addresses teacher planning in greater detail.)

Because of the federal directives in the Improving America's Schools Act and the No Child Left Behind Act (NCLB), all states have academic content standards at each grade level. These content standards specify what students should know and be able to do and when. Moreover, NCLB requires states to develop or adopt statewide achievement tests that are given every year to all public school students between Grades 3 and 8. These tests assess students' knowledge and skills as defined in the state academic content standards. Teachers must teach content to their students with these standards in mind. (To see the standards of all 50 states go to "Academic Benchmarks" at www.academicbenchmarks .com/search or StateStandards.com, the definitive source for state standards, at www.statestandards.com.)

Increasing Content Coverage In planning to maximize content coverage for an academic school year, teachers should determine the scope and sequence of the content standards of the curriculum from which they will be teaching. The *scope* refers to the amount of content that will be covered and the *sequence* refers to the order in which the content will be covered. By using the state standards, therefore, teachers can set their goals for the amount of content they need to cover in a year. In areas such as mathematics and social studies this can be an effective method for maximizing content coverage. In areas where it may not be appropriate to use a state's academic content standards (i.e., a special reading program) a teacher may use the scope and sequence that is usually found in a teacher's manual to plan for maximum content coverage during the school year. If curricula guides are not available, teachers should plan their own scope and sequence based on the IEP goals.

Monitoring Content Coverage According to Mastropieri and Scruggs (2002), teachers can ensure that content will be maximized if they carefully plan and monitor the pace at which their students are moving through the academic content. This can be accomplished by listing the scope of the content (e.g., all of the state or curricular content standards in mathematics for the year) in the proper sequence in a table. The teacher then needs to determine when to finish each objective or standard to ensure that all the objectives will be completed by the end of the school year and include the dates in the table. As the school year progresses, the teacher checks off the completed objectives. If the pace is too slow to finish the content by the year's end, the teacher must accelerate the pace of content coverage by (a) increasing time on task, (b) allocating additional time to instruction, or (c) eliminating less important aspects of the content to be covered (Mastropieri & Scruggs, 2005).

Principle #4: Match Assignments to Student Ability

In 1982 Center, Dietz, and Kaufman reported that students were more likely to exhibit inappropriate behaviors when there was a mismatch between academic task demands and students' ability levels—that is, when the assignments that teachers gave to students were too difficult for them, they misbehaved. DePaepe, Shores, Jack, and Denny (1996) similarly found that increased levels of problem behaviors and lower levels of on-task behaviors were observed when students with EBD were presented with difficult tasks versus easy tasks. These researchers hypothesized that because the difficult academic tasks may have been aversive to the students in their study, their disruptive behavior might have functioned as one means by which the students could escape the difficult activities. Similarly, Lee, Sugai, and Horner (1999) conducted a study that revealed a functional relationship between the presentation of difficult tasks and occurrences of problem behaviors among students with EBD. The authors' study also showed that effective academic instruction reduced escape-motivated problem behaviors.

To increase academic achievement, it is crucial that teachers be able to match learning tasks and assignments to their students' ability levels (Good & Brophy, 2008). To avoid problem behaviors, Gunter and colleagues (1993) suggested that teachers systematically plan activities that are appropriate to students' levels, and that teachers then monitor correct responses and error rates to ensure that instructional tasks are appropriate. DePaepe et al. (1996) further noted that precisely matching instructional tasks and materials to students' performance levels may represent a means of decreasing disruptive behavior in classrooms while promoting gains in academic performance. By knowing what skills students will need to perform and clearly understanding what those skills "look like" when performed expertly, teachers are better prepared to teach students the necessary steps of a complex task. If the teacher is able to accurately identify a student's abilities and present level of performance on the required academic task, the teacher is likely to overcome the difficulty of balancing time and schedule when attempting to teach the student precisely what he or she needs to know within that skill set (Hosp & Hosp, 2003). Although some researchers (e.g., Fuchs, Fuchs, & Hamlett, 1993, 1994) have suggested that technology can help overcome the logistical problems associated with actual implementation, the importance of completing a thorough task analysis and carefully assessing a student's abilities cannot be overstated.

Completing a Task Analysis Assessing a task requires that the teacher understand how to break a larger task into smaller components; that is, a teacher must know how to complete a task analysis. To begin a task analysis, the teacher must first identify the sequence of behaviors that make up the task. There are many ways to determine the tasks required and the order in which they should be taught. For example, Miltenberger (1997) suggested that a teacher could either observe a competent student actually engaging in the task, or ask an expert to review the instruction. It is essential that teachers perform the task themselves and then try to determine if the suggested approach is efficient or if there is a need to revise the task analysis. Because many students with EBD have difficulty completing their homework, a simple task analysis is provided in Figure 14–2.

Assessing Student Abilities Understanding a student's abilities requires that the teacher carefully pinpoint what the student can and cannot do. Although standardized achievement and norm-referenced tests can be useful tools, they often do not provide the level of detailed assessment information necessary to match

FIGURE 14-2

Homework completion checklist

❑ Find a distraction-free place to work (e.g., avoid areas with a phone or TV).

❑ Ensure that you have the material you need (e.g., homework pad and folder, books, notebooks, a writing utensil).

❑ Referring to your homework pad, attempt to complete the first assignment on the list.

❑ If you cannot complete a portion of the assignment, make a note in your homework pad and continue with that assignment.

❑ Check the assignment for errors.

❑ If there is a portion that you have not yet completed, check your notes or call your homework buddy.

❑ After completing the assignment, check off the assignment in your homework pad.

❑ Attempt the next assignment in your homework pad.

❑ If you cannot complete a portion of the assignment, make a note in your homework pad and continue with that assignment.

❑ Check the assignment for errors.

❑ If there is a portion that you have not yet completed, check your notes or call your homework buddy.

❑ After completing the assignment, check off the assignment in your homework pad.

❑ Repeat the previous five steps until all assignments are completed.

❑ Place the homework assignments with your homework pad and folder.

❑ Collect your materials and homework pad and folder and put them in your book bag.

❑ Place your book bag next to the shoes you plan to wear to school in the morning.

assignments to student ability or monitor student progress (Deno, 1985, 1992). Curriculum-based assessments (CBAs), using teacher-made tests that have been structured to assess the varying components of a larger knowledge set or skill, are frequently used by teachers to determine the specific "level of mastery within a skill sequence" (Deno, 1992, p. 6). This information about a student's specific ability allows a teacher to initially match instruction to ability. It is, however, only the first step; the teacher must then monitor the student's progress using a more rigorous and research-validated approach, such as curriculum-based measurement (CBM; Deno, 1985, 1992, 1998; Deno, Marston, & Tindal, 1986; see also Chapter 15).

Principle #5: Teach Academic Content Explicitly

Effective teachers actively instruct their students by demonstrating skills, explaining concepts, conducting numerous and effective opportunities to practice, and reviewing frequently. Effective teachers are active teachers. Rosenshine (1978, 1987) referred to this type of instruction as explicit teaching. Explicit teaching is "a systematic method of teaching with emphasis on proceeding in small steps, checking for student understanding,

and achieving active and successful participation by all students" (Rosenshine, 1987, p. 34). Rosenshine and Stevens (1986) summarized the teacher effectiveness research and concluded that effective teachers use the following procedures:

- Begin a lesson with a short review of previous learning.

- Begin a lesson with a short statement of goals.

- Present new material in small steps, providing for student practice after each step.

- Give clear and detailed instructions and explanations.

- Provide a high level of active practice for all students.

- Ask a large number of questions, check for student understanding, and obtain responses from all students.

- Give corrective feedback to students during initial practice.

- Provide systematic feedback and corrections.

- Provide explicit instruction and practice for seatwork exercises and monitor students during seatwork.

Rosenshine (1978) further grouped these instructional procedures under six teaching functions, which he suggested are most appropriate when the goal is to teach skilled performance or specific content. These six steps are identified with their general aim in Table 14-2, and described in detail in the following text.

Using Teaching Functions Rosenshine and Stevens (1986) noted that "results have consistently shown that when teachers teach more systematically, student achievement improves—frequently with gains in students' attitudes toward themselves and school" (p. 69). Gage (1978) referred to this model of explicit instruction as "the scientific basis of the art of teaching" (p. 10).

Teaching Function #1: Daily Review. The goal of the daily review of previous material is to make certain that the students are firm in their knowledge of previously taught skills. Furthermore, daily practice provides the additional practice in and overlearning of the previous material (Rosenshine & Stevens, 1986). Additionally, a daily practice

session allows the teacher to see if additional practice activities and reteaching may be needed when students are having difficulty (Rosenshine, 1997).

When conducting daily practice activities, teachers should begin each lesson with a 5- to 8-minute review of content or skills covered in the last lesson. Depending on the previous lesson, this review may include (a) correcting homework, (b) questioning students, (c) providing additional practice, (d) reexamining recently acquired vocabulary or skills, or (e) giving a short quiz.

Teaching Function #2: Presentation. The goal of the presentation is to teach novel skills and/or new knowledge. Presentation is an efficient way to expose students to content or a skill while allowing the teacher to control the material that he or she teaches (Good & Brophy, 2008). To accomplish this, teachers must focus on the learner and teach one point at a time. Furthermore, teachers should present materials in short steps interspersed with questions or activities (Good & Brophy, 2008; Rosenshine, 1997). Brophy and Evertson (1976)

Table 14–2   The six teaching functions

Teaching Function	Principle Aim	Activities
Daily review	To ensure that students have learned the previously presented materials and are ready for new knowledge or skills to be taught	• Review homework • Ask questions
Presentation	To teach new materials or skills	• State goals of lesson • Present new material in small steps • Demonstrate and model new material • Provide examples • Check for student understanding • Provide corrective feedback
Guided practice	To provide closely monitored practice activities for students	• Practice activities with additional help • Ask frequent questions • Provide corrective feedback • Do choral responding • Continue practice until students are fluent • Ensure that all students participate and receive feedback
Corrective feedback	To respond to students' answers	• If the student is correct: Praise • If a student is correct but hesitant: Praise and give process feedback • If a student is incorrect: Praise, give process feedback, and reteach if necessary
Independent practice	To provide the additional practice needed to move students toward fluency	• Students work independently on same work as given in guided practice • Shorter teacher–student contacts • Independent seat work (e.g., worksheets) • Computer work or peer-assisted learning • Homework
Weekly and monthly reviews	Ensure that student is learning and practicing the skills being taught	• Review previous week's work each Monday • Review previous month's work every fourth Monday

found that low-ability or low-achieving students learn more by having less material taught to them in small steps that they can master without becoming frustrated. The researchers also concluded that teachers of low-achieving students should err on the side of overteaching rather than moving too quickly for students to master material. Next we review six important factors to consider when presenting new material.

Advance Organizers The teacher should begin by establishing the "why" by discussing the importance of the content being covered and the lesson objective, including a specific rationale and context for the lesson. Ausubel (1960) developed the concept of advance organizers, the purpose of which is to tell students what they will be learning before the instruction begins. Good and Brophy (2008) noted that advance organizers give students a structure within which they can relate to the specific information presented by the teacher. The advantage of using advance organizers with low-achieving students is that it helps them focus on the main ideas and ensures that they will understand what they can expect to learn and why it is important that they learn it.

Brisk Pacing The presentation should be briskly paced to maintain student attention and lesson momentum. Brisk pacing facilitates the efficient use of instructional time, maintains student interest, and decreases off-task behavior (Rosenberg, O'Shea, & O'Shea, 2008). Additionally brisk pacing often results in fewer student errors (Colvin, 1997). On the other hand, slow pacing increases off-task behavior, boredom, and student misbehavior (Savage, 1999). Carnine, Silbert, Kame'enui, and Tarver (2004) noted that brisk pacing means that teachers present their material in a lively, animated manner without hesitations. Carnine et al. (2004) also stated that providing a briskly paced lesson does not mean that the teacher rushes the students through the lesson, but that there is no downtime after the students make a response. After the student makes a response (remember the importance of giving students many opportunities to respond), the teacher immediately moves on to the next step of the presentation (e.g., presents more material, asks another question, corrects a response).

Clarity The teacher's presentation must be clear so the students can understand the concepts and skills being taught. To ensure that lessons are clear, effective teachers often (a) present new material in small steps, (b) give clear and detailed instructions and explanations, and (c) provide practice activities for students after each step. Presentations that are confusing, unclear, or ambiguous will result in student misunderstanding. Additionally, teacher digressions during presentations may be confusing to students.

According to McCaleb and White (1980), if teachers follow these four guidelines, they will present with greater clarity. First, the material must be organized to promote a clear presentation by (a) stating the purpose of the presentation, (b) previewing the organization, (c) reviewing the main ideas, and (d) providing transitions between sections. Second, the information to be presented should be sequenced by gradually increasing its difficulty or complexity. Third, the teacher should define major concepts or skills and use examples to illustrate these concepts or skills. Finally, the teacher should pace the presentation at a rate that is conducive to learning. Additionally, clarity will be enhanced if the teacher speaks clearly and uses visual aids.

Demonstration Research regarding teachers' presentation styles has shown that effective teachers spent more time demonstrating new material than less effective teachers did (Evertson, Emmer, & Brophy, 1980; Good & Grouws, 1979; Rosenshine & Stevens, 1986). According to Evertson et al. (1980), more effective mathematics teachers spent about 23 minutes per period in lecture, demonstration, and discussion, whereas less effective teachers spent only 11 minutes per period in similar activities.

Rosenshine and Stevens (1986) noted that when teachers spend additional time on demonstration, they provide numerous explanations, redundant explanations, and sufficient instruction, which results in greater student learning. The authors also reviewed the literature on effective demonstrations and found that the most effective teachers (a) clearly state the primary goals and main points to be learned, (b) present material in small steps while providing practice activities, (c) model the skill or process while giving many detailed and concrete explanations during the modeling, and (d) check for student understanding of the skill by asking questions.

Enthusiasm Students learn more when teachers display enthusiasm (Mastopieri & Scruggs, 2005). An effective lesson is presented enthusiastically. According to Patrick, Hisley, and Kempler (2000), when the teacher is enthusiastic students are likely to be interested, develop enthusiasm, and achieve at higher levels. Additionally, when teachers are enthusiastic their students become more engaged with the lesson, thus increasing academic engaged time (Brigham, Scruggs, and Mastropieri, 1992).

Good and Brophy (2008) noted that teacher enthusiasm includes at least two major aspects. First, enthusiastic teachers convey a sincere interest in the subject. Second, the teacher exudes "dynamic vigor" (Good & Brophy, 2008). This means that the teacher is lively and expresses his or her enthusiasm in voice and action. The teacher also relates material to personal experiences and shows that he or she is interested in the subject.

Feedback During a presentation, teachers frequently check for student understanding so that they can provide feedback and corrections. Teachers can accomplish this by (a) asking frequent questions, (b) requiring students to summarize materials, and (c) prompting student responses and then monitoring student answers. Procedures such as these are important because they maintain student involvement in the lesson, provide students with practice opportunities, and give teachers immediate information to help them determine if students are learning the material.

It is also important that teachers give all students a chance to respond on many occasions. To ensure that all students respond, teachers should be aware of who responds and how often. Teachers should randomly call on students to respond, and not choose students who volunteer to respond. If students are not responding correctly 80% to 90% of the time, the teacher will have to provide feedback and corrections or even reteach the skill if necessary.

Teaching Function #3: Guided Practice. Guided teacher practice activities are used by the teacher after he or she is convinced that students have mastered the material (e.g., students evince a high rate of correct academic responding to questions). The goal of the guided practice is to provide the active practice, enhancement, and elaboration that are needed to move to a new level of learning. Additionally, during guided practice the teacher can correct errors, reteach, and provide sufficient practice activities so that students can move on to independent practice. To accomplish this, teachers must continue to offer guidance and appropriately model accurate performance of the skills. The teacher effectiveness research demonstrated that the least effective teachers—those with the lowest achievement gains by their students—would present an entire lesson and then pass out worksheets for the students to complete (Rosenshine, 1997). Often researchers noted that students would become confused and make errors.

An example of guided practice after a skills lesson in mathematics would be to provide a few math problems on a worksheet, the board, or projected on a screen. The teacher would prompt the students to complete the problems and then go from student to student to (a) supervise the students' work; (b) provide appropriate feedback; and (c) provide process feedback (i.e., the teacher restates the steps of the problem as the student proceeds). In addition to supervising his or her students, the teacher should question the students to check for understanding. Thus, the teacher can determine if the students are ready to move on to independent practice or if they need additional practice or reteaching.

Most teachers spend some time doing guided practice activities. Rosenshine (1986) stated that the more effective teachers devote more time to it. That is, effective teachers spend more time asking questions, correcting errors, repeating the new material, and helping students work out problems than less effective teachers do. Both correlational and experimental studies have shown that a high frequency of teacher questioning and student answers are important for instruction in basic skills areas (Rosenshine & Stevens, 1986). In fact, research by Stallings and Kaskowitz (1974) identified the pattern of a teacher questioning a student, followed by a student response, and then by the teacher providing appropriate corrective feedback as being extremely important for increasing student achievement. A number of other researchers have noted that although all teachers ask questions, the most effective teachers ask many more questions, and the less effective teachers ask few questions (Coker, Lorentz, & Coker, 1980; Evertson, Anderson, Anderson, & Brophy, 1980; Rosenshine & Stevens, 1986). Clearly teachers should ask many questions during guided practice activities, and provide feedback when students respond.

Additionally, teachers should have interactions with all of their students as quickly as possible when beginning a guided practice activity. Contacts with individual students, however, should be brief so the teacher can get to all of his or her students within a few minutes.

Teaching Function #4: Feedback and Corrections. The fourth teaching function involves providing feedback to student answers and corrections to student errors. The goal of providing feedback and corrections is to ensure that students are practicing the new skill correctly. To accomplish this, teachers must carefully assess their students' understanding of the skills or content being taught, and then provide specific feedback, adjusting instruction and reteaching lessons if necessary.

A teacher should differentiate between positive feedback that is contingent on student performance, and corrective feedback that should be coupled with constructive comments. For example, if an answer is correct, the teacher can move on or give a short statement of praise; if the answer is incorrect, the teacher should provide hints, re-ask the question in a different way, or re-explain the steps to be followed (a less effective teacher will simply call on another student and move on without providing specific corrective feedback).

According to Rosenshine and Stevens (1986), there are four types of student responses to teacher questions. First, students may respond with a quick and firm answer that is correct. In most cases, a teacher should respond with a praise statement ("excellent job") and move on. Second, the student may make a hesitant but correct response. The hesitancy may indicate that the student is unsure of himself or herself. The teacher should provide a praise statement followed by process feedback, in which he or she reviews the steps used to arrive at the correct answer (Anderson, Evertson, & Brophy, 1979); Evertson, Emmer, & Worsham (2006). This type of response will help the student overlearn the correct steps in the process. Third, if the student makes an incorrect response due to carelessness, the teacher should correct the student and move on. Fourth, if the student makes an incorrect response because he or she lacks knowledge of the skill or concept, the teacher should first try to prompt the correct answer by giving process feedback and encouraging the student to keep trying, and by letting the student know that he or she will be right back. The teacher should leave, make brief contacts with the other students, and then return to the student who does not have the skill and reteach the material.

In large classrooms, reteaching can be a problem. How do you reteach one student when there are many other students in the class? Three options are to (a) reteach the skill or concept to the student when the other students are engaged in independent activities, (b) have peer tutors reteach, or (c) provide reteaching to a group of students having difficulty, but at a later time.

Jones (1987) developed a procedure for providing student assistance that he called praise-prompt-leave. The strategy consisted of (a) arranging student seating so that the teacher could easily see all of his or her students and get to them quickly, (b) displaying charts of the directions and the assignment so students can seek clarification by looking at the charts and (c) providing for a signal system for students when they need assistance. After a student signals that he or she needs assistance, the teacher should go to the student's desk as soon as possible. First, the teacher praises the student for something that he or she has done correctly. Second, the teacher prompts the student about the next step or gives a quick correction. Third, the teacher leaves the student and moves on to assist another student. Fourth,

in a few minutes, the teacher checks back with the student who needed help to check on his or her progress and reteach if necessary. Jones also stated that teachers should attempt to keep student contacts to between 60 and 90 seconds.

Rosenshine (1997) and Good and Brophy (2008) stated that it is crucial that teachers check for all students' understanding, and if a student or students are making errors, correct the errors as soon as possible. Rosenshine (1997) also notes that it is inappropriate to give only the student making the error the correct answer and then move on. He also noted that if student errors go uncorrected, they can become extremely difficult to correct later, and that they may lead to interference with subsequent learning. The point is that students learn more effectively when teachers check for understanding and give corrective feedback immediately.

Teaching Function #5: Independent Practice. After students have shown proficiency in the content or skill areas in the guided practice sessions, the teacher should move to independent practice. The goals of independent practice are to (a) provide the additional practice that students need to become fluent at a skill (i.e., automaticity); and (b) integrate the new information or skills with previous knowledge or skills (Rosenshine, 1997).

In independent practice, teachers provide students with work in the same material covered during guided practice; however, the students work without the extensive assistance provided by the teacher. During independent practice, the teacher should circulate around the room, ensuring that there is consistent but short student-teacher contact (e.g., 30 seconds), and that students are achieving high rates of success (i.e., at least 85% to 90%). The teacher should make a brief contact with each student in the first few minutes of independent practice. Because one of the purposes of independent practice is to help students perform smoothly and confidently, independent practice should occur only after sufficient guided practice, and recently acquired skills should be carefully monitored by the teacher before being assigned as homework (Mims, 1991).

According to Good and Brophy (2008), independent assignments should be basic parts of the curriculum, not merely time fillers. Therefore, teachers should (a) plan their independent assignments carefully so they provide their students with meaningful opportunities to practice at the correct level of difficulty (i.e., not too difficult nor too easy); (b) make the importance of the independent practice activities clear to the students; and (c) monitor student progress on the assignments and provide feedback to students who experience problems.

It is extremely important that teachers maintain high rates of student engagement during independent practice. Rosenshine and Stevens (1986) stated that a student's level of engagement is affected by how adequately prepared he or she is to do the seat-work activities, and how effectively the teacher keeps the student on task during seat-work activities. To increase student engagement during independent seat work teachers should:

- circulate around the classroom;

- make brief contacts with all students;

- check for understanding and giving short explanations if needed;

- ensure that students are ready for independent work by achieving 85% to 90% accuracy during guided practice;

- connect the independent activities closely to the presentation and guided practice.

Additionally, teachers should establish a set routine that students are instructed to follow during seat work activities. Such routines should prescribe how students should conduct themselves during seat work, what activities they should engage in, how they can get assistance from the teacher if they need it, and what they should do if they complete the work early.

Teaching Function #6: Weekly and Monthly Reviews. The goal of the weekly and monthly reviews is to make certain that the child is learning and practicing the skills that are being taught. To accomplish this, teachers could review the previous week's work every Monday and the previous month's work every fourth Monday. The teacher should ensure that the reviews provide the additional, successful practice that students need to become smooth performers, capable of applying their skills to new areas. If reviews indicate that a student's skills are breaking down, then the teacher should reteach the skill. Frequent reviews are especially important for low-achieving students to determine if they have attained mastery of a skill or lesson (Rosenshine & Stevens, 1986).

Teaching Functions and the Missouri Mathematics Effectiveness Project. Good and Grouws (1979) conducted a treatment study using a lesson format that used similar teaching functions in fourth-grade mathematics classes. Twenty-one teachers were in the treatment group and 19 teachers were in the control group. The treatment group teachers taught their math classes using a whole-class instruction model that involved frequent practice and reviews. The teachers in the treatment group used the following instructional format:

- Daily Review (first 8 minutes of class except on Monday)
  - Review the concepts and skills associated with the previous day's homework
  - Collect homework assignments

- Presentation (approximately 20 minutes)
  - Focus on prerequisite skills and concepts
  - Use explanations, demonstrations, and modeling to teach
  - Assess student progress
  - Repeat and elaborate as necessary

- Guided Practice (approximately 15 minutes)
  - Provide uninterrupted successful practice
  - Maintain momentum
  - Let students know work will be checked
  - Check work and give feedback

- Independent Practice (including a homework assignment)
  - Have students work independently and then assign every day at the end of math class (except Friday)
  - Assign approximately 15 minutes of work at home

- Weekly Review
  - Conduct review for the first 20 minutes each Monday
  - Focus the review on the previous week's skills

- Monthly Review
  - Conduct review every fourth Monday
  - Focus the review on skills taught since the last monthly review

The treatment classes substantially outperformed the control classes on a standardized mathematics achievement test and a criterion-referenced test covering that content taught during the investigation. Additionally, the students of the teachers in the treatment group who had the highest implementation scores during observations produced the best results. Furthermore, the low-achieving students in the treatment groups made greater achievement gains than did the normal- and high-achieving students. The results of this study clearly indicated the positive effects of using a teaching model based on the teaching functions.

Principle #6: Scaffold Student Instruction

A scaffold is a temporary platform that construction workers sit or stand on when they are building a structure. It provides support to the workers until they finish the permanent structure, whereupon the scaffold is removed. Similarly, *scaffolding* is an instructional strategy in which a teacher provides students with support while they are learning skills or concepts. After the student learns the skill or concept, the support can be withdrawn. Wilen, Ishler, Hutchison, and Kindsvatter (2000) stated that scaffolding is metaphorically comparable to instructional training wheels.

Instructional scaffolds are strategies that allow teachers to teach effectively while increasing the opportunities for students to learn and at the same time decreasing the chance of students making errors (Martella et al., 2003; Rosenshine, 1997). According to Ellis et al. (1994), students can become independent, self-regulated learners when teachers deliberately and carefully scaffold their instruction. Moreover, Good and Brophy (2008) noted that a key finding of the teacher effectiveness literature is that teachers who elicit strong achievement test scores actively scaffold their students' learning rather than expecting the students to learn primarily from the curriculum materials. These authors also asserted that scaffolding is especially important for low-achieving students who often do not effectively learn on their own. Such students can acquire new skills and concepts through explicit instruction, demonstration, and modeling.

Using Scaffolds in Instruction Teachers can scaffold their instruction by using prompting strategies. According to Rosenshine (1997), procedural prompts are useful in scaffolding instruction because a teacher can use prompts to supply a student with specific procedures or suggestions that facilitate the completion of a task. Students rely on these prompts until they develop their own "structures." Martella and colleagues (2003) provided the following examples of response prompting strategies: (a) antecedent prompt and test procedure (i.e., prompting students during instruction and then providing practice or testing activities after removing the prompts similar to a model-lead-test format); (b) most-to-least prompting (i.e., decreasing assistance to a student in a progressive manner and creating a prompt hierarchy); (c) least-to-most prompting (i.e., increasing assistance when a student does not perform a behavior); and (d) antecedent prompt and fade procedure (i.e., providing more intrusive prompts initially and then fading out the prompt in a systematic manner).

Teachers can scaffold instruction by demonstrating a new concept or skill. The presentation of a new concept or skill should be broken into a sequence of steps, which could be modeled to the students by using a think-aloud procedure. For example, the teacher could demonstrate a procedure, such as a math problem, and then model solving the problem while talking through the steps of the process. When thinking aloud, therefore, a teacher vocalizes the internal thought processes one goes through when using the strategy.

Another effective way to scaffold instruction is to ask frequent questions of students to check for understanding during demonstration and practice. Teachers then provide reinforcement to students when they are correct, reinforcement and explanation when they are correct but hesitant or unsure, and reinforcement and further demonstration when they are incorrect. Another scaffolding strategy is to provide visual prompts, such as flow charts, concept maps, or graphic organizers, and task orders, which assist students to use the skill being taught (Wilen, Ishler, Hutchison, & Kindsvatter, 2003). For example, when teaching students the process for solving long division problems, a teacher could display a chart that explains and gives an example of the process on the classroom wall.

Teachers should also ensure that there are opportunities for guided practice activities in which the teacher closely monitors the students and provides help when needed. To provide help, teachers could give students feedback and additional instruction or arrange for students to get assistance from their peers (Good & Brophy, 2008).

Finally, teachers could scaffold instruction by providing study guides, outlines, or task organizers to help students follow presentations, understand reading assignments, and pay attention to key ideas. The purpose of such guides and organizers is to focus a student's attention on main ideas, steps in completing a problem, or the steps involved in a process, and the strategy that he or she should use to complete these steps (Good & Brophy, 2008).

Principle #7: Use Direct Instruction

The previous six principles address how teachers can most effectively deliver instruction. The principles do not, however, address matters of instructional design. If a systematic, research-based instructional program is not used along with these effective teaching principles, students will not achieve as much as they could if an effective instructional procedure were used. As Adams and Engelmann (1996) aptly stated:

Installation of these "effective practices" without a systematic instructional sequence will not necessarily lead to highly effective teaching. It may result in an improvement over what had been achieved but it will not cause superior performance. The reason is that the curricular sequence is solely responsible for the various concepts and skills that are [taught] to the student. If the instructional sequence is weak, the [effectiveness principles] will not make it strong. (pp. 31–32)

Teachers need to ensure that they teach their students by using the effectiveness principles in a research-based curriculum. It is indeed fortunate that there are effective instructional curricula that use these principles. One such procedure is *direct instruction (DI)*. DI is a research-based practice that is associated with strong achievement gains (Good & Brophy, 2008; Marchand-Martella et al., 2004; Tarver, 1999). Moreover, DI procedures have been shown to be effective with a wide variety of students, including minority students, students with learning disabilities (Swanson, Carson, & Sachse-Lee, 1996); students with EBD (Yell, 1992); students with traumatic brain injury (Glang, Singer, Cooley, & Tish, 1992); and typically achieving students (Adams & Engelmann, 1996; Vaughn, Gersten, & Chard, 2000).

Over 30 years of research strongly supports the effectiveness of DI procedures (Adams & Engelmann, 1996; Tarver, 1999). One of the earliest efforts that dramatically supported the effectiveness of DI was Project Follow Through (Adams & Engelmann, 1996; Stallings & Kaskowitz, 1974). Project Follow Through was a 5-year federally funded study (over $1 billion) in which a number of different educational models were compared. The goal of the investigation was to show which educational approach produced the best results among disadvantaged students in kindergarten through Grade 3 (Adams & Engelmann, 1996). The following educational methods were investigated: direct instruction, behavior analysis, parent education, cognitive curriculum, responsive education, open education, and a constructivist approach called the Bank Street model. In addition to comparing the results of the educational methods on basic skills (i.e., reading, mathematics, language, and spelling), Project Follow Through also compared the educational methods in improving cognitive (i.e., higher-order thinking skills) and affective skills (i.e., self-esteem). The results clearly demonstrated the superiority of DI in teaching basic skills, and it also showed that DI was the most effective method in improving the cognitive and affective skills of students.

In 1996, Adams and Englemann reported on the results of a meta-analysis of DI. Thirty-seven research studies were included in their meta-analysis, and their findings were equally impressive. The average effect size per study for students in special education was .90. For students in regular education the effect size was .82.

DI is one specific model of teacher-directed explicit instruction (Tarver, 1999). The practices described in the effective teaching research, and in this chapter, are integrated into DI; however, Tarver noted that DI differs from other methods of explicit instruction because it focuses not only on how students are taught but what they are taught. Similarly, Marchand-Martella and colleagues (2004) asserted that although DI uses the principles of effective instruction, it contains organizational elements beyond those described in the effective teaching literature.

The central philosophy of DI is that teachers are responsible for student learning and that curriculum design is a critical variable in student achievement. Tarver (1999) also noted that the goal of DI is to accelerate student learning by maximizing efficiency in the design and delivery of instruction. The primary way in which DI extends the effective teaching literature is its emphasis on program design (Marchand-Martella et al., 2004; Tarver, 1999). Whereas the teacher effectiveness research stresses methods for delivering content, DI emphasizes instructional programming that uses efficient strategies and structured methods to teach content.

There are four primary organizational components in DI (Marchand-Martella et al., 2004).

- *Instructional grouping.* Students are placed in groups in which instruction is appropriate for all students in the group because they have the necessary prerequisite skills and need to master the same objectives. Most published DI programs have instructional placement tests to ensure that students are placed in appropriate groups.

- *Academic engaged time.* This refers to the amount of time that students are directly engaged with the learning materials. That is, teachers must allocate sufficient time for instruction and ensure that their students are actively engaged during the allocated time. Moreover, students must experience high rates of success during instruction.

- *Scripted presentation.* Because the teaching of reading, mathematics, and writing requires careful planning and precise implementation, DI programs have detailed scripts with clear explanations, carefully selected and sequenced examples, and carefully structured demonstrations (Marchand-Martella et al., 2004; Tarver, 1999). The scripts in DI programs are carefully designed and developed and extensively field-tested plans that allow teachers to deliver lessons that use the principles of effective instruction.

- *Continuous assessment.* It is extremely important that teachers continuously and systematically monitor their students' progress toward meeting their program objectives. DI programs all have some type of ongoing assessment monitoring component. The continuous assessment procedures provide teachers with feedback on how students are learning, and allow them to make informed instructional decisions.

Direct instruction also clearly defines the teacher's role in delivering instruction. Because the scripted programs relieve teachers of their instructional design roles, their role is to deliver instruction in an effective manner and to make instructional decisions based on the continuous assessment data (Marchand-Martella et al., 2004). The ways that teachers are to deliver instruction is usually described in DI materials. These delivery features include rapid pacing, signaling, choral responding, individual responding, corrective feedback, reteaching, reinforcement, guided practice, and independent practice.

According to Marchand-Martella et al., (2004) there are over 60 published DI materials in areas including reading, mathematics, language, writing, spelling, and science. Included are materials designed for typically achieving students and remedial programs for low-achieving students. Teachers can also design their own DI programs, including content-area programs. For information on DI programs, refer to the publications listed in Figure 14–3.

FIGURE 14-3

Books on direct instruction

Carnine, D. W., Silbert, J., Kame'enui, E. J., & Tarver, S. J. (2003). *Direct instruction reading* (4th ed.). Upper Saddle River, NJ: Merrill/Pearson.

Carnine, D. W., Silbert, J., Kame'enui, E. J., Tarver, S. J., & Jongjohann, K. (2005). *Teaching struggling and at-risk readers: A direct instruction approach.* Upper Saddle River, NJ: Merrill/Pearson.

Kame'enui, E. J., & Simmons, D. C. (1990). *Designing instructional strategies: The prevention of academic learning problems.* Upper Saddle River, NJ: Merrill/Pearson.

Marchand-Martella, N. E., Slocum, T. A., & Martella, R. C. (2004). *Introduction to direct instruction.* Boston: Allyn & Bacon/Pearson.

Stein, M., Silbert, J., & Carnine, D. W. (1997). *Designing effective mathematics instruction: A direct instruction math* (3rd ed.). Upper Saddle River, NJ: Merrill/Pearson.

Principle #8: Monitor Student Progress

Effective teaching requires the ongoing evaluation of student performance (Deno, Espin, & Fuchs, 2002). Effective teachers, therefore, monitor their students' progress frequently and regularly. Progress monitoring is formative evaluation, as opposed to summative evaluation. Summative evaluation refers to evaluation data that is collected after program implementation or instruction (e.g., at the end of a grading period or at the end of a school year). When evaluation data are collected after instruction the data can be useful for a program evaluation, but it is too late to benefit students who have not learned the material (Deno, Espin, & Fuchs, 2002). Formative evaluation, on the other hand, occurs when teachers gather information on student learning and development on a frequent and regular basis throughout the school year. This information is used to make instructional decisions. Because the teacher knows how students are responding to instruction they can review, reteach, or they can make instructional changes to the student's program when necessary. That is, formative evaluation makes it possible for the teacher to alter instruction based on student performance.

There are two general approaches to formative evaluation, each of which provides a teacher with different types of information: (a) mastery measurement and (b) general outcome measurement (Espin, Shin, & Busch, 2000). Mastery measurement is a task-analytic approach to evaluation of student progress in which the teacher breaks down the particular skill being taught into subskills. For example, if a teacher is working with a student in reading and decides to teach decoding, he or she might break the area of decoding into a number of subskills such as segmenting and blending sounds, matching letters with sounds, and sounding out words. The teacher would teach each subskill and then assess student mastery of each of the subskills as it was being taught. Generally, teachers develop the tests for the different subskills that are being taught and use these tests to determine mastery (see Chapter 3 on assessment). When the student reaches the preselected mastery criterion on a subskill assessment (e.g., 80%), then the teacher begins teaching the next subskill. This cycle of (a) breaking a large skill into subskills, (b) teaching a subskill, (c) assessing a student's mastery of the subskill, and (d) teaching the next subskill if the student reaches mastery (or reteaching if the student doesn't master the subskill) represents teaching by using a mastery measurement type of formative evaluation. According to Espin et al. (2000), mastery monitoring answers the question, "Has the student learned the skill that I taught?" Curriculum-based assessment (CBA) is a type of mastery measurement.

General outcome measurement is an approach to monitoring student progress that focuses on the desired long-term outcomes. When a teacher uses general outcome measurement he or she repeatedly samples the student's performance on probes that represent the desired long-term outcome (Deno, 1998). For example, if a teacher is working with a student in reading, he or she would assess a child's progress in general reading proficiency by using a general outcome measure such as reading aloud from text. According to Espin et al. (2000), general outcome measurement answers the question, "Has learning this skill led to growth and improvement in the general academic area?" A progress monitoring system that is a general outcome measurement is curriculum-based measurement (CBM).

In both types of formative evaluation, teachers frequently and systematically collect data on student performance. These data are then used to determine if the student is progressing in the instruction and whether instructional changes are needed (if the student is not progressing). Often the data are graphed. Graphing facilitates more accurate and frequent analysis by teachers and also provides more useful feedback to students and their parents (Espin et al., 2000). According to Fuchs and Fuchs (1986), formative evaluation leads to greater student achievement. Chapter 16 addresses formative evaluation in greater detail.

MAINTAINING EFFECTIVESS

The most effective teachers keep abreast of new research and developments in their field and constantly reflect on and evaluate their teaching (Good & Brophy, 2008). With the tremendous demands placed on teachers of students with EBD, it sometimes seems difficult to find the time for reflection and to stay current on the literature. Nonetheless, if teachers are to improve the quality of their students' lives, it is crucial that they do so. Because IDEA mandates that teachers base their students' special education programs on peer-reviewed research (IDEA 20, U.S.C. § 614(d)(1)(A)(i)(IV)), it becomes more than best practice that teachers stay current on research in special education; it has now become the law.

Two ways in which teachers can continue to grow in their profession are (a) to keep abreast of the research in the field, and (b) to self-evaluate their abilities and techniques. I next examine these two important areas.

Keep Up with Field Research

Researchers in special education continuously conduct investigations and develop instructional strategies and procedures that improve educational opportunities for students with disabilities. A particularly exciting and growing area of research is the academic instruction of students with EBD. Moreover, there is an extensive body of knowledge regarding effective instruction of low-achieving students. This knowledge base and the ever-expanding information about educating students with EBD make it imperative that teachers of students with EBD have a working knowledge of the principles of effective instruction, and that they continue to keep abreast of developments in their field. Unfortunately, many teachers do not even attempt to keep current. For example, data show that over 80% of teachers have not been to a professional conference for an average of 10 years, and 40% have not been to a professional conference in 16 years (Wong & Wong, 2001). Additionally, there is the well-known research/practice gap in education. As Wong and Wong stated, "the great majority of teachers refuse to learn and grow, yet they expect their students to do so" (p. 306). Three ways in which teachers can keep abreast of developments in their field are (a) read the professional literature, (b) join a professional organization, and (c) take advantage of professional development activities.

Read the Professional Literature Perhaps the easiest way for teachers to keep current in their field is to read the professional literature. In the area of EBD, two of the most important journals—*Behavioral Disorders* and *Beyond Behavior*—are published by the Council for Children with Behavioral Disorders (CCBD). *Behavioral Disorders* is a peer-reviewed journal that publishes research. *Beyond Behavior* is a practitioner-oriented journal in which the essential findings from research are written in an easy to read manner that is free of the statistics and research jargon that teachers sometimes find difficult to read. A third highly respected peer-reviewed research journal is the *Journal of Emotional and Behavioral Disorders,* published by Pro-Ed. Figure 14–4 is a list of journals in special education that address the needs of students with EBD.

Another source of potentially valuable information is the Internet. For example, past issues of both *Behavioral Disorders* and *Beyond Behavior* are available on the CCBD Web site (www.ccbd.net). The Web site contains a wealth of information important to teachers of students with EBD. Additionally, a great deal of information on education is available on the U.S.

FIGURE 14-4

Professional journals

Journal	Website
Behavioral Disorders	www.ccbd.net
Beyond Behavior	www.ccbd.net
Exceptional Children	www.cec.sped.org
Journal of Emotional and Behavioral Disorders	www.proedinc.com/Scripts/prodView.asp?idProduct=572
Journal of Special Education	www.proedinc.com/Scripts/prodView.asp?idProduct=2122
Preventing School Failure	www.heldref.org/psf.php
Remedial and Special Education	www.proedinc.com/scripts/prodView.asp?idProduct=2133
Teaching Exceptional Children	www.cec.sped.org

Department of Education Web site (www.ed.gov). The Internet, however, must be approached with caution because there is no peer review of the contents.

Join a Professional Organization New and veteran teachers can maintain knowledge of current evidence-based practices by participating in a professional organization. The primary professional organization for special education is the International Council for Exceptional Children (www.cec.sped.org). In addition to the national organization, many states have their own CEC, and often the state CEC will have local chapters. There are many advantages to being in CEC. For example, the national organization holds an annual conference and professional development opportunities throughout the year. Additionally, many states hold their own annual conferences. CEC also publishes two journals—*Exceptional Children*, a peer-reviewed research journal published four times a year, and *Teaching Exceptional Children*, a practitioner-oriented journal that is published four times a year—and a newsletter. Additionally, CEC maintains a Web site with extremely useful information for teachers and members (www.cec.sped.org).

CCBD is a subdivision of CEC. The purpose of CCBD is to promote and facilitate the education and general welfare of students with EBD. CCBD holds a biannual conference and conducts many professional development workshops throughout the year. Additionally, many states have their own CCBD, and many state organizations also hold an annual conference. CCBD publishes the aforementioned peer-reviewed research journal *Behavioral Disorders* four times a year, the practitioner-oriented journal *Beyond Behavior* four times a year, and a newsletter. CCBD also maintains a Web site for teachers and members, as already stated.

Participate in Professional Development Opportunities Professional development should be an expectation for and obligation of all educators. A teacher's development should not end when he or she is first certified and takes the first teaching job. Rather, teachers should continue their professional development throughout their careers. It is doubtful that many people would knowingly go to a doctor who stops keeping abreast of medical developments when he or she graduates from medical school, or would hire a lawyer who didn't think it was important to keep up with case law. Why should it be any different for teachers?

Fortunately, teachers often can receive state and local assistance in finding appropriate professional development opportunities. State departments of education have continuing education requirements that teachers must meet to renew their teaching licenses, and local school districts hold professional development activities for new and experienced teachers. The purpose of these activities is to support teachers' continued expertise by providing ongoing professional growth opportunities (Rosenberg, O'Shea, & O'Shea, 2002). Staff development programs often comprise a good-sized percentage of a school district's discretionary budget, both for supporting teachers in attending conferences and by sponsoring their own professional development opportunities. In fact, many school districts now involve groups of teachers, supervisors, and administrators in planning staff development activities (Good & Brophy, 2008). Congress believed that providing teachers with professional development activities was so important that in No Child Left Behind, it required that school districts work with state departments of education to develop professional development activities for teachers that are grounded in scientifically-based research. This means that teachers must be taught research-based interventions and strategies that have a proven track record of improving student achievement. Moreover, states must ensure that the school districts are using scientifically-based professional development strategies (Yell & Drasgow, 2005). To maintain personal effectiveness, it is important that teachers take advantage of these opportunities.

Unfortunately, staff development programs are often one-time events in which a speaker comes to a school and holds a presentation or workshop, but afterward there is little or no follow-up and no attempt to assess the program's effectiveness (Good & Brophy, 2008). Stokes and Baer (1977) referred to this type of professional development as "Train and Hope" (p. 24). According to the U.S. Department of Education (1998), such professional development efforts often have little impact on student learning, are disjointed and unfocused, and offer teachers few opportunities to learn by doing and reflecting on practice with their colleagues.

Teachers of students with EBD work in complex environments that involve laws, regulations, policies, and a rapidly changing field. The research is constantly showing new and improved ways to educate students. It is the teachers' professional and ethical obligation to improve their teaching, and thus the lives of their students, by becoming lifelong learners. Taking advantage of the growth opportunities presented by professional development opportunities is one way to continue to grow in the profession.

Self-Evaluate

Teaching students with EBD is a complex and taxing job. Because few teachers excel in all areas for successfully working with these students it is important that they continue to strive for improvement. As Good and Brophy (2008) stated, "Teaching is challenging and exciting

work, but it takes time to develop and refine teaching skills" (p. 475). The authors suggested that teachers should study the effects of their behavior and teaching on the classroom behavior and learning of their students. One way teachers can do this is through self-evaluation.

In this textbook we have discussed the skills and attributes necessary for being a successful teacher of students with EBD. By comparing their skills and abilities to those required as shown in the research, and by keeping track of growth in these areas, teachers can become more effective. One way to do this, according to Good and Brophy (2008), is to list the skills and abilities that the literature says are important, and then list these behaviors in accordance with the following categories: (a) perform capably, (b) need improvement, and (c) not sure. The authors stated that if teachers have a difficult time self-assessing their skills and abilities, they should have a teacher or supervisor observe them and help them complete the lists. Finally, teachers must make explicit plans on how to improve their teaching. Good and Brophy asserted that these plans must be specific and concrete; otherwise, like the halfhearted New Year's resolutions that are made annually, they will be quickly forgotten. Making goals that are observable and measurable are much more likely to be accomplished (e.g., "I will increase praise statements to 10 every half hour"). It is also important that teachers choose a few goals at a time, and work on accomplishing them. After the goals are accomplished, the teacher may choose new goals. Working on too many goals at once will make it less likely that any will be accomplished.

Gunter, Denny, and colleagues (Gunter et al., Gunter & Reed, 1996; Shores, Gunter, Denny, & Jack, 1993) suggested that if teachers were to remediate skill deficits they would need to acquire the skills to objectively and observationally self-evaluate their instructional behaviors. The authors also suggested that teachers make and review videotapes of their teaching.

Gunter and Reed (1996) suggested behaviors that teachers should monitor, and provided a protocol for coding and analyzing the videotapes of teaching, which they referred to as functional assessment of teaching behavior. Furthermore, the authors provided the following guidelines for making videotapes:

1. Set up the video camera so that the light source is behind the recorder.

2. Place the video camera close to the selected group that will be recorded to improve the video and audio quality.

3. Conduct two or three videotaping sessions to find the best camera settings and classroom setting for

video and audio recording. These sessions allow students time to desensitize to the videotaping process.

4. When recording for self-evaluation, tape for a minimum of 5 minutes at a time.

5. Note the subject taught, date, and length of the videotaped segment.

6. View the tape and score the target behaviors.

Teachers could watch for the presence or absence of effective teacher behaviors and note the frequency with which they exhibit these behaviors (e.g., is there a 5:1 ratio of positive comments to negative reprimands?). Additionally, teachers view the videotapes and score certain behaviors using existing protocols. Two examples of such protocols were developed by Gunter and Reed (1996) and Espin and Yell (1994). Refer to these sources for further information.

Chapter Summary

Low academic achievement and school failure are primary characteristics exhibited by students with EBD. In fact, there are few differences between students with EBD and students with learning difficulties with respect to academic achievement. Teachers of students with EBD, therefore, can expect that they will often be remediating students' weaknesses in basic skill areas. Although little research has been done on teaching students with EBD, a larger amount of research is available on effective teaching in the learning disabilities and general education literature. The purpose of this chapter was to review the principles from the effective teaching literature. These principles included:

1. Maximize academic engaged time.

2. Ensure high rates of correct academic responding.

3. Maximize the amount of content covered.

4. Match assignments to student ability.

5. Teach academic content explicitly.

6. Scaffold student instruction.

7. Use direct instruction.

8. Monitor student progress.

Teachers of students with EBD should pay as much attention to improving their students' academic performance as they do to improving their behaviors. One way that teachers can improve their instruction is to use these principles in their teaching. Additionally, in a field such as special education of students with EBD it is crucial that teachers keep up with research developments by (a) reading the professional literature, (b) joining a professional organization, and (c) taking advantage of professional development opportunities. We also discussed the importance of teachers evaluating their own teaching by using procedures such as videotaping.

CHAPTER 15

Teaching Students with EBD II: Evidence-Based Instructional Procedures

Michael E. Rozalski, Paul J. Riccomini, and Mitchell L. Yell

Focus Questions

- What research-based strategies can be used to teach reading to students with EBD?
- What research-based strategies can be used to teach writing to students with EBD?
- What research-based strategies can be used to teach mathematics to students with EBD?
- What research-based strategies can be used to teach study skills to students with EBD?

Meaningful instruction is a critical component of successful programs for students with emotional and behavioral disorders (EBD); however, teachers of students with EBD spend less time on active academic instruction and their students engage in lower rates of academic behavior than do teachers and students in general education (Gunter, Hummel, & Venn, 1998; Scheuermann, 1998; Stein & Davis, 2000). In their seminal study titled *At the Schoolhouse Door*, Knitzer and colleagues (1990) clearly described the bleakness of classrooms for students with EBD, which too often consisted of a "very limited and . . . ineffective set of teaching strategies" (p. 27) and a typically "impoverished" (p. 65) academic program.

Wehby, Lane, et al. (2003) stated that a major reason there is such a limited focus on academics in the field of educating students with EBD is the limited research on academic instruction of these students. Recent reviews of the literature on academic interventions for students with EBD confirm this problem (Coleman & Vaughn, 2000; Lane, 2004; Mooney et al., 2003; Trout, Nordness, Pierce, & Epstein, 2003). Wehby, Lane, et al. (2003) asserted this problem has contributed to the absence of an empirically valid knowledge base with which to guide future research and the subsequent preparation of teachers. Nonetheless, there is small but growing literature on academic interventions and students with EBD. The purpose of this chapter is to describe these research-based instructional procedures and strategies in reading, mathematics, and written expression. We first examine research-based strategies for teaching reading. Second, we address the teaching of writing. Third, we look at research-based strategies for teaching mathematics. Finally, we examine strategies to teach study skills.

An examination of evidence-based instructional procedures can help teachers design and deliver effective lessons for students with EBD. Moreover, an increased focus on academic instruction and evidence-based programming for students with EBD, in addition to promoting the academic progress of students with EBD, is likely to produce important reductions in the interfering behaviors these students so often exhibit (Deno, 1998). That is because academic progress is incompatible with the behaviors that are viewed as disturbed and disturbing. Deno (2000) asserted that "by making academic progress the primary focus, . . . [teachers] will help to create EBD programs that encourage behavioral development and prevention rather than behavior reduction and correction" (p. 16).

TEACHING READING

Components of Effective Reading Instruction

How to effectively teach students to read has been a matter of some debate (e.g., Atkinson, Wilhite, Frey, & Williams, 2002; Carnine et al., 2004; Din, 2000; Harp & Brewer, 2005; Hyter, 2003; National Institute of Child Health and Human Development [NICHD], 2000; Torgesen, 2004). On extreme ends of the continuum lie top-down (meaning-based) or bottom-up (code-based) approaches to teaching reading; theorists and researchers argue for the merits of the extremes of this continuum or argue for combining elements from both approaches. Considerable scientific evidence (Baber & Bacon, 1995; Carnine et al., 2004; Foorman, Francis, Fletcher, Schatschneider, & Mehta, 1998; Fuchs & Fuchs, 2005; Gaskins, Gaskins, Anderson, & Schommer, 1995; NICHD, 2000; Wehby, Falk, Barton-Arwood, Lane, & Cooley, 2003) suggests that there are common components of effective reading instruction: phonemic awareness, phonics, fluency, vocabulary, and comprehension. In this section, we will review each component, keeping in mind that good instruction is always individualized to the student (Atkinson et al., 2002; Gibb & Wilder, 2002).

Phonemic Awareness Although phonemic awareness is often confused with phonics instruction, the two terms are not synonymous. Phonemic awareness refers to an understanding of how sounds are used to form words in spoken language. Understanding how to identify and manipulate individual sounds within words is a crucial first step for many beginning readers. In fact, phonemic awareness and letter knowledge are the two best predictors of how well children will learn to read in the first 2 years of instruction (NICHD, 2000). Students who have been unresponsive to early reading interventions have frequently lacked appropriate phonemic awareness skills (Al-Otaiba & Fuchs, 2002).

Phonemic awareness can be taught, particularly to students who are traditionally underserved, such as low-income, inner-city students (Blachman, Ball, Black, & Tangel, 1994) Hispanic students (Gunn, Biglan, Smolkowski, & Ary, 2000), and students with emotional and behavioral problems (Nelson, Benner, & Gonzalez, 2005). Goldsworthy (2003) argued that students must increase phonemic awareness by being explicitly taught at three levels: word, syllable, and sound. The levels, goal, and several sample strategies are outlined in Table 15-1. See Goldsworthy (2003) for additional instructional activities and a list of resources appropriate for use in phonological awareness training.

Table 15–1   Explicitly teaching phonemic awareness: Level, goal, and sample strategies

Level	Goal	Sample Strategies
Word	Recognize that sentences are composed of a word or words	Students can count the number of words seen in written sentences or heard in orally presented sentences.
		Using magnetic poetry, students can creatively rearrange words to make sentences and stories. Some resources (e.g., Funky Fridge Refrigerator Magnets at www.funkyfridge.com/magnetic-poetry.html?adwords_magnetic-poetry) have sets available by theme so that students can write a targeted story (e.g., about a visit to the zoo or using Spanish vocabulary only); large-print magnets are also available for students with visual impairments.
		Students can use the Cloze procedure, which takes a passage and systematically blanks words (e.g., every fourth word), to practice completing meaningful sentences with appropriate words. For example, to review this section, students could complete the following Cloze sentence: "To practice word-level _____ awareness skills, students could _____ the words in a _____, creatively rearrange words using _____ poetry, or use the _____ procedure to compose meaningful _____."
Syllable	Recognize that words are made of a syllable or syllables.	Students can count or tap the number of syllables in each word.
		Using compound words, students can rearrange the component words to make and illustrate funny nonsense words (e.g., *pigtail* becomes *tailpig*).
		Given two possible components, students can determine which of the three possible compound words are not real (e.g., *pig* _____: *tail, pen, nose*; Brett (2005) maintains sample activity sheets at www.janbrett.com/piggybacks/compound.htm.
Sound	Recognize that syllables have onset and rime and can be divided into a phoneme or phonemes.	Students can play Alphabet Words, identifying a word ending such as *are* and moving through the alphabet (e.g., *bare, care, dare* . . .) to categorize which words are viable, nonsense, or simply just too hard to pronounce.
		Using a book like Dr. Seuss's *ABC: An Amazing Alphabet Book* (1963), students can see similarities in onset (e.g., extensive alliteration for each letter of the alphabet).
		Students can create activity sheets for their peers, asking the question, "Does *this* rhyme with *that?*" Encourage students to challenge their peers with tough queries, using words such as *cough, dough,* and *plough*.

Phonics   Phonics is an understanding of "the system by which symbols represent those sounds in the alphabetic writing system" (Carnine et al., 2004, p. 51). According to the bottom-up view of reading (Harp & Brewer, 2005), readers must understand sound–symbol relationships (grapheme–phoneme) before understanding words, sentences, and stories. To understand the sound–symbol relationship, readers must move from (a) recognizing the grapheme; (b) producing the phoneme; (c) blending sounds in words; and (d) reading words, sentences, and stories. Research indicates that systematic phonics instruction improves decoding and word recognition skills, and improves students' ability to read words, particularly for students with learning disabilities (LDs), from lower socioeconomic status, and who were not disabled but were low achievers (NICHD, 2000).

As such, NICHD has suggested that one of the most important elements of systematic reading instruction is that students are explicitly taught sound-letter relationship (Grossen, 2005). Although authors disagree on the exact number (Carnine et al., 2004; Gaskins et al., 1995), Grossen (2005) identified 48 letter–sound relationships that represent the sound that occurs at least 75% of the time with the respective letter or letter group (see Table 15-2).

Fluency   Fluency is the ability to read with speed, accuracy, and, when reading aloud, using appropriate expression. Fluency is generally measured in either the number of words correctly read per minute or the percentage of words read correctly from a passage of a given length. For words per minute, fluency is expected to improve as students become more capable readers, though research indicates that students who have been unresponsive to early reading interventions lack fluency skills (Fuchs, Fuchs, McMaster, Yen, & Svenson, 2004). Table 15-3 outlines the minimum number of words that students should read correctly in 1 minute in the elementary grades (Good, Simmons, Kame'enui, Kaminski, & Wallin, 2002).

For the percentage of words read correctly from a passage, fluency is generally divided into three levels: independent, instructional, and frustration (Leslie & Caldwell, 2001):

- Independent—when the student can read without assistance, with 98% to 100% of the words correctly identified;

Table 15–2   The 48 most regular sound–letter relationships

a as in fat	g as in goat	v
m	l	e
t	h	u-e as in use
s	u	p
I as in sit	c as in cat	w "woo" as in well
f	b	j
a-e as in cake	n	I-e as in pipe
d	k	y "yee" as in yuk
r	o-e as in pole	z
ch as in chip	ou as in cloud	kn as in know
ea beat	oy toy	oa boat
ee need	ph phone	oi boil
er fern	qu quick	ai maid
ay hay	sh shop	ar car
igh high	th thank	au haul
ew shrewd	ir first	aw lawn

Source: Grossen, 2005.

- Instructional—when the student can read with assistance, with 90% to 97% of the words correctly identified;

Table 15–3   Expected fluency in beginning grades (words correctly read per minute)

At End of Grade	Minimum Expected Fluency
1st	40
2nd	90
3rd	110
4th	118
5th	124

- Frustration—when the student struggles to read or comprehend the material, with less than 90% of the words correctly identified.

Several strategies are commonly used to help students improve the fluency with which they read: (a) sight vocabulary instruction (Fry, 1980); (b) repeated readings of oral text (Fuchs & Fuchs, 2005); and (c) silent independent reading (Harp & Brewer, 2005). The first two strategies have research and practical support. Frantantoni (1999) found that direct instruction of sight vocabulary increased students' reading rate, and Fry's (1980) *New Instant Word List* (see Table 15-4) is often cited as an important list of sight words for direct instruction. Repeated guided oral

Table 15–4   Fry's New Instant Word List: The first 300 words

the	or	will	number	over	say	set	try	high	saw	important	miss
of	one	up	no	new	great	put	kind	every	left	until	idea
and	had	other	way	sound	where	end	hand	near	don't	children	enough
a	by	about	could	take	help	does	picture	add	few	side	eat
to	words	out	people	only	through	another	again	food	while	feet	face
in	but	many	my	little	much	well	change	between	along	car	watch
is	not	then	than	work	before	large	off	own	might	mile	far
you	what	them	first	know	line	must	play	below	close	night	Indian
that	all	these	water	place	right	big	spell	country	something	walk	real
it	were	so	been	years	too	even	air	plant	seen	white	almost
he	we	some	called	live	means	such	away	last	next	sea	let
was	when	her	who	me	old	because	animal	school	hard	began	above
for	your	would	oil	back	any	turn	house	father	open	grow	girl
on	can	make	sit	give	same	here	point	keep	example	took	sometimes
are	said	like	now	most	tell	why	page	tree	begin	river	mountains
as	there	him	find	very	boy	ask	letter	never	life	four	cut
with	use	into	long	after	follow	went	mother	start	always	carry	young
his	an	time	down	things	came	men	answer	city	those	state	talk
they	each	has	day	our	want	read	found	earth	both	once	soon
I	which	look	did	just	show	need	study	eyes	paper	book	list
at	she	two	get	name	also	land	still	light	together	hear	song
be	do	more	come	good	around	different	learn	thought	got	stop	being
this	how	write	made	sentence	form	home	should	head	group	without	leave
have	their	go	may	man	three	us	American	under	often	second	family
from	if	see	part	think	small	move	world	story	run	late	it's

Note: Counting from top to bottom, left to right, the first 10 words make up approximately 24% of all written material contained in newspaper articles, magazines, textbooks, children's stories, and novels. The first 100 words make up about 50%, and the first 300 about 65%.
Source: Fry, 1980.

reading has been shown to increase word recognition, fluency, and comprehension (NICHD, 2000), and has been recently popularized in elementary schools. Although commonly used, the third strategy of silent independent reading (e.g., strategies like Drop Everything and Read or DEAR; Harp & Brewer, 2005) has little research backing to suggest that silent independent reading of approximately 20 minutes per day improves reading skills, including fluency, or increases how much students read. Because of its continued widespread use, additional systematic research is needed (Carnine et al., 2004; NICHD, 2000).

Vocabulary Most words that appear in primary-grade reading books are in the average speaker's vocabulary. However, from about 4th grade on, students are challenged by language that is less familiar to them (Carnine et al., 2004). Although students learn a great deal of vocabulary indirectly (e.g., hearing new words from peers, adults, and TV characters; reading materials outside school) and from narratives (Graesser, Golding, & Long, 1991), it is estimated that students remember only 5 to 15 of every 100 unfamiliar words to which they are exposed (Nagy, Herman, & Anderson, 1985; Swanborn & de Glopper, 1999). Systematic vocabulary instruction can

help students overcome these challenges and allow them to learn some of the estimated 50,000 words that they will know by 12th grade. Additionally, because vocabulary instruction leads to increased student comprehension, particularly when the instruction includes repeated and varied exposure (NICHD, 2000), systematic teaching of word pronunciation, meaning, and usage is critical.

Explicit instruction of vocabulary can include formal presentation of new vocabulary or reference skills (e.g., defining new words and providing synonyms, teaching a student to use a dictionary; Carnine et al., 2004), or be informal and creative (e.g., engaging students with games and puzzles; Harp & Brewer, 2005). Table 15–5 outlines various instructional strategies and examples for systematically teaching new vocabulary.

Comprehension We read to comprehend. As students progress through school and life, they will be presented with increasingly complex reading materials from more varied sources. Instructional strategies that develop students' comprehension and critical reading skills are essential, though often not allotted significant instructional time in the classroom (Durkin, 1981). Fortunately, explicit teaching of cognitive reading strategies greatly

Table 15–5   Explicit instructional strategies: Vocabulary

Type of Instruction	Activity	Description and Examples
Formal presentation	Modeling	When introducing new vocabulary, provide students with clear examples and nonexamples of the target word. For example, when teaching "tastes" like bitter, sweet, sour, salty, and spicy, cover students' eyes and have them taste and categorize foods that represent each new word they are experiencing.
	Definitions and synonyms	When introducing new vocabulary, provide clear definition and synonyms for each word. Identifying an engaging and meaningful application of the word (e.g., showing students where the word appears in the latest *Harry Potter* installment) helps students remember the definition and synonyms.
Reference skills	Thesaurus and dictionary	Teach students to use print and electronic versions of dictionaries and thesauruses. Creative Web sites can encourage students to use these reference tools (e.g., www.visualthesaurus.com).
Games and puzzles	Concentration	Have students create a pair of cards with the new vocabulary and the word's definition. Shuffle all the cards together and place them in columns and rows on a table (or tape to a chalk- or whiteboard). In teams, have the students match the vocabulary they uncover with the definition of the word. Variation: Use pairs of cards with vocabulary and synonyms (rather than definitions).
	Bingo	Give students a list of vocabulary words and blank Bingo cards (so each student can make his or her own card). Call either the definition or synonym of each vocabulary word and have students mark their cards until someone has Bingo. Variation: Use antonyms to "clear" the cards—first to have an empty card wins.
	Word of the day	Have students select interesting or challenging words from material that they encounter and have them place the vocabulary and definition on an index card in a "Word of the Day" box. Draw a card daily. If the student whose word is drawn can provide a definition and use the word in a sentence (remember, students recall only a small percentage of the words they encounter), then the student is able to draw the next day's card.

Table 15–6   Strategies for improving reading comprehension

Strategy	What Good Readers Do	Examples
Comprehension monitoring	Good readers actively examine what they are reading.	Students may use a strategy such as K-W-L (Ogle, 1986) to monitor their understanding before ("What do I **K**now?" and "What do I **W**ant to Learn?") and after ("What did I **L**earn?").
Cooperative learning	Good readers learn strategies with their peers.	Students can work in cooperative groups (DuPaul, Ervin, Hook, & McGoey, 1998; Falk & Wehby, 2001; Gillies & Ashman, 2000; Martella, Marchand-Martella, Young, & MacFarlane, 1995) and cross-age tutoring (Elbaum, Vaughn, Hughes, & Moody, 1999) to practice the question generation and answering strategies.
Use of graphic and semantic organizers (including story maps)	Good readers make visual representations of the material they are reading.	Students who make story maps or visual representations to help organize what they are reading (Anderson & Pearson, 1984) have better comprehension (Babyak, Koorland, & Mathes, 2000). See Figure 15-7 for a sample semantic map.
Question answering	Good readers respond to teacher-presented questions; teachers provide immediate feedback to students.	Students should ask a range of questions from Bloom's Taxonomy (Harp & Brewer, 2005) and immediately provide positive feedback for correct answers and corrective feedback for incorrect answers.
Question generation	Good readers ask themselves questions about the material they are reading.	Students should ask questions that carefully measure their understanding (Pearson & Fielding, 1991): (1) Is there any vocabulary I didn't understand? (2) What was the take-home message?, (3) What was the author's tone and purpose?
Story structure	Good readers use the organization of the material to help them recall specific content.	Younger students can practice recalling story structure and sequence by ordering illustrated cutouts (e.g., life cycle of plant, comic strips). Older students should answer: "What was the main point and did the supporting details flow?" Story and text structure instruction can improve comprehension (Brennan, Bridge, & Winograd, 1986; Williams, 2005).
Summarization	Good readers synthesize information and make generalizations.	Students should be able to able to verbally and visually summarize a story, while making connections to other curricular materials or personal experiences (Pearson & Fielding, 1991).

improves comprehension (NICHD, 2000). In the National Reading Panel's review of 481 studies that were published over 30 years, seven strategies that "appear to have a solid scientific basis" for teaching comprehension (NICHD, 2000, p. 15) were identified (see Table 15-6 for examples).

In addition to the strategies outlined previously, there are additional strategies that should be explicitly taught at various grade levels. For example, in the early primary grades, students should be taught sequencing (Carnine et al., 2004). Without the ability to understand how a story progresses (i.e., there is a beginning, middle, and end), students will be unable to determine cause and effect or make inferences and inductions. In the late primary and intermediate grades, students must become more astute critical readers. These older students must be able to (a) discriminate between literal and inferred or induced meaning; (b) determine the trustworthiness of an author or source, particularly in the age of electronic publishing and the Internet (Carnine et al., 2004); and (c) read and comprehend within increasingly challenging content areas, like science (NICHD, 2000). Although some authors (e.g., Alverman, Smith, & Readence, 1985; Anderson,

Reynolds, Schallert & Goetz, 1977; Johnston, 1984) warn that activating prior knowledge can interfere with comprehension, some research suggests that this activation allows students to perform better on measures of comprehension (Recht & Leslie, 1988). Additional research is needed to determine if activating prior knowledge is an effective instructional strategy.

Teaching Procedures

The Individuals with Disabilities Education Improvement Act of 2004 (IDEA 2004) and the implementing regulations of 2006 require that teachers of students with disabilities base their special education programs on peer-reviewed research (IDEA, 20 U.S.C. § 1414(d)(1)(A)(i)(IV)). Refer to the reviews by Lane (2004); Riveria, Al-Otaiba, and Koorland (2006); and Coleman and Vaughn (2000) for analysis of the small literature base on effective reading interventions and students with EBD. Table 15-7 lists several empirical studies that have been conducted in reading interventions and students with EBD.

Next we examine two reading programs that have support in the empirical literature.

Table 15–7 Research-based reading interventions and students with EBD

Authors	Subjects	Intervention	Setting	Results
Babyak, Koorland, & Mathes, 2000	4 males with EBD, LD, and ADHD, Grades 4–5	Story mapping instruction and reinforcement system	Public summer school program for students with EBD	Improved percentages of correct responses on story retells and measures of story elements
Falk & Wehby, 2001	6 males and 1 female in EBD resource, Grade K	K-PALS peer tutoring and a reinforcement system	Self-contained classroom for students with EBD	Increases in letter-sounding and blending skills scores
Lane, O'Shaughnessy, Lambros, Gresham, & Beebe-Frankenberger, 2001;	7 students (5 males, 2 females), Grade 1	Phonological awareness training and reinforcement for participation	At-risk students in a general education classroom	Improvements in word attack skills, words read correctly in 1 minute; decreases in disruptive behavior and negative social interactions
Lane & Menzies, 2003	210 at-risk students	Multilevel reading and behavioral intervention program	General education classrooms in an elementary school for at-risk students	Improved reading skills as measured by district-level tests and curriculum-based measurement
Lane, Wehby, Menzies, Gregg, Doukas, & Munton, 2002	7 students (4 males, 3 females), Grade 1	Supplemental phonics instruction	At-risk students in a general education classroom; the students were unresponsive to a schoolwide literacy intervention	Improvements in nonsense word fluency and oral reading fluency; decreases in disruptive behavior and negative social interactions
McCurdy, Cundari, & Lentz, 1990	2 male students, ages 8–9	Direct teaching strategies (time-delay and trial and error) and observational learning	Private laboratory schools for students with EBD	Few differences between the strategies, although direct teaching yielded slightly better results; students maintained high levels of words read correctly in both phases
Scott & Shearer-Lingo, 2002	3 males with EBD, Grade 7	Repeated readings	Self-contained middle school classrooms	Improvements in oral reading fluency and on-task behaviors
Resnick, 1987	9 males with EBD (3 in Grades 5–6 were tutors; 6 in Grades 2–3 were tutees)	Cross-age peer tutoring	Resource rooms in a public school	Both tutors and tutees showed gains on standardized reading tests (Woodcock-Johnson Reading); tutees also showed increased satisfaction with reading
Shisler, Top, & Osguthorpe, 1986	23 students with EBD, Grades 5–6	Peer tutoring	General education classroom	Tutors increased reading scores on 2 of 3 reading tests; tutees increased reading scores on 2 of 5 measures
Wehby, Falk, Barton-Arwood, Lane, & Cooley, 2003	8 students with EBD, ages 5–6	Decoding lessons and peer tutoring sessions	Self-contained classrooms	Increased performance on measures of letter–sound identification and blending skills
Yell, 1992	16 students with EBD, Grades 5–6	Direct instruction on sight words	Self-contained classrooms	Direct instruction was more effective than other procedures used (language master, individually prescribed instruction) on increasing sight words learned, measures, improving on-task behaviors, and decreasing interfering behaviors

Direct Reading Instruction The knowledge base for teaching reading to students with EBD, a group of students with significant difficulties with reading, is surprisingly limited but emerging (e.g., Fleming, Harachi, Cortes, Abbott, & Catalano, 2004; Hooper, Roberts, Zeisel, & Poe, 2003; Hyter, 2003; Nelson, Benner, & Rogers-Adkinson, 2003; Rinaldi, 2003; Rogers-Adkinson, 2003; Rogers-Adkinson & Hooper, 2003; Vaughn, Levy, Coleman, & Bos, 2002; Wehby, Falk, et al., 2003); only eight published studies were conducted between 1975 and 2000, and no specific instructional procedures were identified as effective, even though a focus group and the existing research suggested that direct instruction and cross-age peer tutoring may be effective (Coleman & Vaughn, 2000). Direct instruction (DI) has repeatedly been shown to help students make efficient academic gains in reading (e.g., Din, 2000), particularly for young students considered at risk for academic failure (e.g., students receiving Title I services were shown by Foorman et al., [1998] to make marked progress).

DI involves teaching students essential skills, grounding both the methods of providing instruction and the skills taught in scientifically based research (Carnine et al., 2004). As such, teachers use research-supported strategies to directly teach students the research-identified skills essential for beginning readers (e.g., how to decode and comprehend various texts). Although the pedagogy, or "how" students are taught using DI has been discussed in Chapter 13, and the essential skills, or "what" students are taught is outlined in the "Components of Effective Reading Instruction" section of this chapter, we will highlight some of the critical features of DI, along with some additional teaching techniques.

Critical Features of Direct Reading Instruction.
According to Carnine and colleagues (2004), there are six components of a DI program that are essential to selecting, implementing, and modifying a reading program:

1. Specifying objectives

2. Devising instructional strategies

3. Developing teaching procedures

4. Selecting examples

5. Sequencing skills

6. Providing practice and review

These components exemplify the importance of task analysis, modeling, and feedback. In a task analysis, tasks are broken down into smaller teachable subunits. Task analysis serves a diagnostic purpose by allowing teachers to pinpoint specific student functioning levels with respect to the targeted skills, and also provides a basis for sequential instructional programming. Teachers must then instruct and assess students on the subunits and larger skills (i.e., the combination of the smaller subunits) in an established sequence. While conducting a task analysis, a teacher should (a) limit the scope of the task, (b) write the subtasks to be performed in observable and measurable terms, (c) carefully select examples and model how to successfully complete the subunits and larger skill when teaching, and (d) provide students an opportunity to perform the task while being evaluated.

Monitoring Progress in Direct Instruction Programs.
The importance of monitoring progress and providing immediate and constructive feedback cannot be overstated. Without continual evaluation, students may make and practice errors that go uncorrected. When first learning to add two two-digit numbers—for example, 77 + 33—a common error is 1010 (7 + 3 is added in the ones column to get 10 and then 7 + 3 is added in the tens column to get 10 and the two answers are put side by side). Although a student who has made this mistake has clearly neglected to "carry" to the tens column, what if the student has completed an entire worksheet of problems like this while making the same error? This student will have to unlearn the mistake before being taught the correct procedure for adding and carrying. Similar mistakes can occur with reading instruction; according to Carnine et al., (2004), three types of errors are common: (a) confusing letters or words (e.g., mistaking *d* for *b*), (b) mispronouncing a letter or word; and (c) misunderstanding a signal to start or end when the teacher indicates that a choral response is appropriate. Being aware of the potential pitfalls allows teachers to help students avoid them.

Monitoring progress must be done systematically by following a predictable daily, weekly, and monthly routine (Deno, 2000; Fuchs, 1989; Langdon, 2004). Using a research-validated technique such as curriculum-based measurement (CBM) is perhaps the most effective means to evaluate the effectiveness of the reading program (Deno, 1985, 1992, 1998; Deno et al., 1986; Green, 2001; Shinn, 1989). For a discussion of CBM's technical merits, including reliability and validity, see Marston (1989) and Bain and Garlock (1992). Refer to Chapter 3 in this textbook for further information on CBM.

Peer-Assisted Learning Strategies (PALS) Peer tutoring refers to instructional strategies in which students are taught by their teachers to tutor their fellow students. Greenwood, Delquadri, Carta, Hall, and colleagues conducted systematic investigations of a peer tutoring strategy that they referred to as Classwide Peer-Tutoring (Delquadri, Greenwood, Whorton, Carta, & Hall, 1986; Greenwood, Carta, & Hall, 1988; Greenwood, Delquadri, & Hall, 1989; Greenwood, Maheady, & Delquadri, 2002).

In classwide peer tutoring systems the students tutor each other using a highly structured tutoring procedure. Classwide peer tutoring has been used successfully with a wide variety of students in a number of different settings to teach many different skills (Maheady, Harper, & Mallette, 2003). Spencer (2006) conducted a research synthesis of 38 studies in which students with EBD served as tutors or tutees in peer tutoring investigations. She reported that peer tutoring is an effective instructional strategy for elementary, middle, and high school students with EBD in academic, social, and behavioral realms.

In 1996, Fuchs and Fuchs and colleagues developed a specific peer tutoring intervention, which was called peer-assisted learning strategies, or PALS, for supplementing instruction in reading and mathematics programs (Fuchs, Fuchs, Mathes, & Simmons, 1996). This strategy has over 10 years of scientific evidence supporting its efficacy in improving reading and math scores across a wide variety of students, including students with LD and EBD, as well as low-achieving students without disabilities, average-achieving students, and high-achieving students (Fuchs, Fuchs, & Burish, 2000; Barton-Arwood, Wehby, & Falk, 2005). In fact, the U.S Department of Education's Program Effectiveness Panel included PALS reading and math in the National Diffusion Networks' list of effective educational practices. Originally PALS was designed to be used in classrooms of students in Grades 2 through 6. Recent research and program development, however, has extended PALS to kindergarten (i.e., K-PALS), first grade, and high school.

Typically, teachers use PALS reading 3 days a week for about 16 weeks. Students are trained by their teachers to conduct the tutoring sessions and then are closely monitored by their teachers during the sessions. To set up a PALS reading program in a classroom the teacher must pair each student with a peer partner. This is accomplished by rank ordering the students by their reading skill. The students are then split into a higher performing half and a lower performing half. The top-ranked higher performing student is then paired with the top-ranked lower performing student; the second-ranked higher performing student is then paired with the second-ranked lower performing student, and so on until all students have a partner. After the students are paired, the teacher divides them into two teams. The purpose of the teams is to provide motivation for students to work hard and get good daily scores, which are added to the overall team scores. Students remain with the same partner for about 4 weeks.

The PALS reading session consists of three different activities:

- Partner reading: In partner reading the higher functioning reader in the peer tutoring pair begins reading first. He or she reads aloud from the chosen text for 5 minutes. The lower performing reader then reads the same text for 5 minutes. The lower performing reader in the pair sequences the major events from what has been read.

- Paragraph shrinking: In paragraph shrinking the higher performing reader continues to read the new text in the story. He or she stops after each paragraph to summarize that paragraph. The lower performing student then continues to read the story for the next 5 minutes, stopping after each paragraph to summarize.

- Prediction relay: In prediction relay the higher performing reader makes a prediction, reads a half page or full page of text aloud, and then stops to check the accuracy of the prediction. He or she then predicts what will happen on the next half page and continues reading. This takes 5 minutes. The lower performing student repeats this sequence.

The PALS peer tutoring procedure is an evidence-based procedure that should be used to supplement students' reading programs. For more information, go to the PALS Web site, (http://kc.vanderbilt.edu/pals). The site contains summaries of research on PALS reading and math, and ordering information.

Summary

Though considerable, and at times heated, debate about the best approach to teaching reading has come to characterize the field, a large body of scientific evidence suggests that there are common components to effective reading instruction (Baber & Bacon, 1995; Carnine et al., 2004; Foorman et al., 1998; Fuchs & Fuchs, 2005; Gaskins et al., 1995; NICHD, 2000; Wehby, Falk, et al., 2003). These major components—phonemic awareness, phonics, fluency, vocabulary, and comprehension—have been investigated for years, and specific strategies designed to improve reading skills and abilities have emerged from this research (Atkinson et al., 2002; Gibb & Wilder, 2002). Next, we address strategies for teaching writing.

TEACHING WRITING

Written expression, which refers to text that a student composes (Kame'enui & Simmons, 1990), is one of the many skill deficiencies of students with disabilities (Graham & Harris, 1988; Mastropieri & Scruggs, 2002; Tindal & Crawford, 2002). According to Tindal and Crawford, writing is especially difficult for students with EBD. For example, Nelson, Benner, Lane, and Smith (2004) found that students with EBD, from kindergarten to Grade 12, scored well below average on standardized tests of writing ability. Teaching students with EBD to write well at an early age is important for several reasons. First, writing has the potential to serve as an expressive outlet for students with EBD, which they can use to obtain recognition and express their thoughts (Tindal & Crawford, 2002). Second, written expression skills are especially important to a student's academic success in high school and post-secondary education. As students progress through school more and more writing is required on tests and papers (Bradley-Johnson & Lesiak, 1989). Third, Lane, Graham, Harris, and Weisenback (2006) asserted that it is extremely important that young students with EBD receive good instruction in writing before their writing problems become intractable because waiting until later grades to correct these deficiencies will not be successful. Clearly the ability to write is an important life skill.

Unfortunately, written expression has been given insufficient attention in remedial programs and the empirical literature (Isaacson, 1987). A review of the literature on teaching academic skills to students with EBD by Lane (2004) reported no empirical studies that addressed written expression. Lane reviewed 25 empirical studies published between 1990 and 2004 and found no studies on written expression that met the inclusion criteria for her review, although one included study did address spelling. Lane concluded that "academic interventions targeting written expression of students with or at risk for EBD represent, by far, the least developed instructional area of [reading, mathematics, and writing]" (p. 475).

In addition to the dearth of research in this area, it would seem that teachers of students with disabilities do not spend time directly teaching writing (Graham & Harris, 1988, 1997). This may be because teachers often assume that writing cannot be taught because it develops naturally (Graham & Harris, 1997 Kame'enui & Simmons, 1990;). However, this assumption is false; written expression is a set of skills that can be taught and learned like other academic skills (Graham & Harris, 1997 Kame'enui & Simmons, 1990;). In the following section we address models for teaching written expression and instructional recommendations.

In their chapter on designing instructional strategies for teaching expressive writing, Kame'enui and Simmons (1990) related a worse-case scenario of writing instruction. On the first day of school, a teacher gives her students a 30-minute assignment in which they are to write a three-page paper on how they spent their summer vacation. A few students begin to write; others sit idly. The teacher later evaluates the students' work by noting punctuation and spelling errors. The students in this scenario were asked to perform a complex task without receiving any instruction and no useful feedback. Unfortunately, this scenario seems to represent the method of teaching writing in too many classrooms for students with disabilities. Kame'enui and Simmons (1990), however, pointed out that researchers are learning more about how to teach writing skills. This section briefly reviews recent findings in teaching written expression and highlights instructional recommendations for instructing students with disabilities to be better writers.

Models for Teaching Written Expression

Traditionally there have been two models of teaching written expression: product-based instruction and process-based instruction. The goal of both models is to produce students who are skilled writers; however, the teaching methods and procedures in these two models are very different. Kame'enui and Simmons (1990) proposed a third model for teaching written expression, which they referred to as a skills approach.

Product Approach The product approach to writing focuses on students using good grammar, spelling, capitalization, and punctuation. According to Newcomer, Nodine, and Barenbaum (1988), adherents of the product approach posited that students learn to write based on reading and analyzing the writings of experts. Supposedly, the students' exposure to good writing will allow them to apply the important features of the expert's writing to their own composition. After being exposed to these writings, students are given writing assignments that are similar to those they had read. The teacher then evaluates the students' compositions by marking errors in mechanics (e.g., punctuation, capitalization, spelling). Typically, that ends the process and there is no opportunity for revising the writing. Typically, the teacher provides minimal instruction during this process. Kame'enui and Simmons (1990) noted that merely exposing students with disabilities to examples of good writing and assuming that they will be able to extract the critical features and apply them to their own writing is incorrect. These researchers also asserted that the fundamental flaw of the product approach was that adherents failed to teach students to write in a systematic and explicit manner. The product approach, which was popular in the 1970s and 1980s, is no longer considered an adequate method for teaching writing. Unfortunately, it is still used in many classrooms.

Process Approach The process approach to teaching writing was a reaction to the nonteaching method of the product approach (Hume, 1983). This approach is based largely on the procedures skilled writers use to produce written products. The process approach consists of four overlapping and interactive stages of writing: (a) planning or prewriting, (b) writing a first draft, (c) revising or editing, and (d) publication or sharing (Bos, 1988). Some researchers define these stages in a slightly different manner, but most agree on the basics of the four-step model. During the planning stage the students generate ideas for their writing. They organize their ideas and generate a framework for their composition (Bos, 1988; Kame'enui & Simmons, 1990). Sometimes teachers have their students write outlines of their proposed composition. They also give students time to plan. In the second stage, in which students write their first draft, the teacher assists students to put their ideas into language (Flower & Hayes, 1981), although students may continue to plan and revise their plans. In this stage teachers allow students time to continue to plan, but they also encourage their students to get their ideas down on paper. It is important that students understand that this first attempt at composition may be modified and changed before the final product is produced. The third stage is revising or editing. Students are encouraged to modify and edit their first draft until the composition is ready to share with an audience. This includes editing for mechanics. The teacher may assist in correcting grammar, spelling, and punctuation errors within the context of the students' writing; however, this is only a small part of the entire process. According to Bos (1988), the fourth stage is sharing and publication[1]. She noted that this gives value and worth to the process because students get feedback and perceive themselves as authors responding to an audience.

In the process approach the teacher becomes the facilitator of students writing by conferring with them, making suggestions, and responding to their writing. Graham and Harris (1988) asserted that teachers may help students with disabilities develop these processes central to writing by dividing the composition process into these relatively discrete stages. Teachers can also help students with disabilities gain competence in these processes by teaching them self-regulatory and metacognitive strategies (Harris & Graham, 1992).[2]

Kame'enui and Simmons (1990) stated that the process approach is far superior to the practice of giving students a topic and letting them write, but the process approach does not teach students how to write, a process that is crucial if low-achieving students are going to learn this important skill. They also noted that even when teachers instruct students in planning, drafting, revising, and editing, the process approach rests on the assumption that students already possess fundamental writing skills. If students do not possess such skills, when engaged in the writing process they will consciously attend to these low-level skill deficiencies, which may interfere with the higher order cognitive process that is required in using a process approach (Graham & Harris, 1988). Kame'enui and Simmons (1990) noted that because low-achieving students need to be taught basic writing skills a third model was needed: a skills approach to expressive writing.

Skills Approach   The skills-based approach to teaching writing uses specific instructional design principles to teach basic skills and systematically develop these skills through exercises and applications (Kame'enui & Simmons, 1990). Englemann and Silbert (1985) provided a rationale for a skills-based approach to teaching writing:

Teachers understand that teaching reading to beginners involves a careful sequence of steps. No teacher would expect the beginning reader to tackle fifth-grade material because this material requires too many reading skills. Paradoxically, teachers often fail to recognize that expressive writing is like reading. Writing involves a series of skills and implies a sequence of activities, starting with those that are basic to all expressive writing. (p. 1)

According to Kame'enui and Simmons (1990) a skills-based approach to teaching writing requires a scope and sequence. Moreover, they asserted that a teaching approach that requires low-achieving students to use their imagination to develop a story and then write the story places an unfair burden on students by requiring them to use many advanced skills in their writing (e.g., good grammar, acceptable sentences, appropriate punctuation and capitalization, use of consistent tenses, organization of paragraphs). These advanced skills must be taught to students; they cannot write using such skills without first receiving direct instruction, clear demonstrations, and extensive practice.

Kame'enui & Simmons (1990) proposed a scope and sequence of skills for teaching beginning expressive writing skills. Their scope and sequence does not address more complex skills such as descriptive writing, but rather consists of four basic strands and the component skills within each strand (see Table 15–8). An example of

---

[1]Some researchers do not consider sharing and publication a separate stage in the process approach to teaching writing.
[2]For an excellent introduction to self-instruction and self-regulation in the writing process, refer to this source: Harris, K. R., & Graham, S. (1992). *Helping young writers master their craft: Strategy instruction and self-regulation in the writing process.* Cambridge, MA: Brookline Books.

Table 15–8 Scope and sequence for teaching beginning writing skills

Strand	Component
Learning the mechanics of writing	a. Copying sentences accurately. b. Capitalizing the first word in a sentence. c. Ending a telling sentence with a period. d. Ending an asking sentence with a question mark. e. Indenting the first word of a paragraph.
Writing simple sentences	a. Identifying a sentence as naming somebody or something and telling more about the person or thing. b. Selecting sentences that name somebody or something and tell more about the person or thing depicted in a picture. c. Completing sentences that name somebody or something and tell more about the person or thing depicted in a picture or series of pictures. d. Generating sentences that tell the main thing that happened in a picture or a series of pictures. e. Generating sentences that name somebody or something and tell more about the person or thing without the use of pictures. f. Combining simple sentences to create more complex sentences.
Writing paragraphs	a. Identifying a paragraph as naming a topic and telling more about the topic depicted in a picture. b. Identifying the topic of a paragraph as the main thing that the paragraph tells about as depicted in a picture or a series of pictures. c. Completing paragraphs that refer to pictures. d. Generating paragraphs that report on an individual in an illustration. e. Generating paragraphs that tell about a series of things that an individual did in a sequence of pictures. f. Generating paragraphs that interpret what must have happened between pictures in a sequence. g. Generating paragraphs without reference to pictures.
Editing	a. Identifying sentences that do not report on what a picture shows. b. Correcting mistakes in capitalization and punctuation. c. Identifying sentences in a paragraph that do not tell about a specified topic. d. Correcting run-on sentences. e. Correcting sentences with present-tense verbs by changing them to past-tense and writing all sentences in past tense. f. Correcting inappropriate noun–verb relationships and inappropriate pronouns.

a writing curriculum that uses a skills approach to expressive writing is that of Englemann and Silbert (1985).

Teaching Procedures

A number of researchers have offered instructional recommendations to teach writing to students with disabilities (Graham & Harris, 1988, 1997; Isaacson, 1987; Kame'enui & Simmons, 1990). We review some of these strategies in the following text.

Avoid Instructional Practices That Do Not Improve Students' Writing Performance According to Graham and Harris (1988) and Isaacson (1987), one of the most persistent myths associated with teaching writing is that the systematic teaching of grammar, usage, and punctuation must be an essential component of writing instruction. Research conducted over the last 80 years, however, has provided evidence that such methods are ineffective (Graham & Harris, 1988, 1997). Knowledge of grammatical concepts is not necessary for skillful writing and traditional grammar instruction does not improve students' writing performance (Graham & Harris, 1988). In fact, Hillocks (1984) found that students who were taught to write in

programs that emphasize mechanics and grammar have been shown to achieve lower gains in writing than students who receive writing instruction in which mechanics and grammar are considered irrelevant. Hillocks (1984, 1987) reviewed over 2,000 research studies that examined six instructional procedures for teaching writing. His findings are briefly reviewed in Table 15–9.

Isaacson (1987) suggested that teachers should teach mechanics, grammar, and punctuation because they influence judgments of others regarding the quality of writing; however, these skills should be taught separately so they don't interfere with students' attempts to write. As students become more fluent at writing, mechanics and conventions should be introduced as an editing task (Graham & Harris, 1988; Isaacson, 1987).

Another common practice that should be avoided is overemphasizing errors that students make in their writing (Graham & Harris, 1988). Hillocks (1984) asserted that intensive evaluation of a student's errors may make the student more aware of his or her limitations and more likely to avoid tasks that involve writing. Graham and Harris (1988) suggested that when teachers correct student compositions, they focus on only one or two

Table 15–9   Hillock's findings

Instructional Practice	Finding
Grammar	The study of traditional school grammar (e.g., the definition of parts of speech) has no effect on raising the quality of student writing.
Models	The presentation of good pieces of writing is more useful than studying grammar; however, the use of models alone will not raise the quality of student writing
Sentence combining	The practice of building complex sentences from simple ones has been shown to be effective in many experimental studies. An excellent book on using sentence combining in teaching writing is Strong, W. (1986). *Creative approaches to sentence combining.* Urbana, IL: National Council of Teachers of English.
Criteria scales	Scales, criteria for evaluation, and specific questions that students use when judging their writing or the writing of others can have a powerful effect on improving the quality of students' writing.
Strategies	Focusing students' attention on strategies to use when writing is very effective in improving the quality of students' writing.
Free writing	Although free writing is more effective than teaching grammar, it is less effective than the other techniques reviewed.

types of errors—those that occur frequently and those that interfere with the readers' understanding of the text. In addition, students should be given feedback that is specific and includes suggestions for making corrections.

Allocate Time for Writing Instruction   To help students learn to write in a clear and effective manner students need to be encouraged to write frequently and for extended periods of time (Graham & Harris, 1987). Unfortunately, teachers seldom devote sufficient time to writing activities (Kame'enui & Simmons, 1990). Leinhart, Zigmond, and Cooley (1980) found that students with LD spend than less than 10 minutes a day in writing. If teachers fail to allocate sufficient time to writing, students with disabilities will not learn to write. According to Graham and Harris (1997, 1988), students should spend 45 minutes a day in writing activities.

Create an Atmosphere Conducive to Writing   Writing activities should be interesting and engaging and the classroom climate should be conducive to writing (Graham & Harris, 1988; Kame'enui & Simmons, 1990). Teachers should (a) be accepting and encouraging of students' writing efforts; (b) develop a supportive, pleasant, and nonthreatening writing environment; (c) emphasize students' successes with charts, graphs, and bulletin boards devoted to students' writing; (d) promote sharing of writing with an audience; (e) allow students to work on writing projects of their own choosing whenever possible; and (f) provide positive reinforcement for writing. Providing such an environment can have a positive effect on the behavior and performance of students (Graham & Harris, 1985). Bos (1988) said that teachers should develop classrooms that are writing communities through support, acceptance, and collaboration.

Teach Writing Directly   Creating an atmosphere that is conducive to writing and providing students with opportunities to write are important to improving students' writing. By themselves, however, these strategies are not sufficient to teach writing to students with disabilities. Writing does not development naturally; it must be taught (Graham & Harris, 1997; Kame'enui & Simmons, 1990). Teachers need to provide direct instruction aimed at providing students with the skills necessary to the writing process so they become fluent in writing (Graham & Harris, 1988). In addition to directly teaching sentence and paragraph structure, and vocabulary and word usage, such instruction should include handwriting and spelling (Bradley-Johnson & Lesiak, 1989; Graham & Harris, 1997; Mastropieri & Scruggs, 2002). Teachers also should provide direct instruction aimed at increasing their students' knowledge of the characteristics of the different types of writing tasks that may be required of them (e.g., narrative writing, expository writing). Graham and Harris (1997) noted one way this can be accomplished is by exposing students to examples of the different types of writing through teacher modeling, practice, and corrective feedback. Additionally, teachers may assist their students to become better writers by acting as collaborators with their students and helping them through conferencing with them on how to improve their writing.

Teaching students with disabilities to use self-instructional strategies when they are writing can also help them in their development (Harris & Graham, 1992). Harris and Graham (1996) proposed a model for teaching students writing strategies, called the Self-Regulated Strategy Development (SRSD) approach, which required teachers to play an active, facilitative role in the development of a student's writing abilities. In addition to directly teaching strategies, teachers also conference, model, prompt, and dialogue with students. To use this strategy successfully teachers must understand the writing process and be able to provide their students with direction and support by providing the level of structured guidance appropriate for the student's ability level (Harris & Graham, 1996). In this procedure students are taught a number of strategies that help them understand writing tasks, regulate their writing behavior, and enhance their motivation.

In the SRSD approach, there are seven basic stages of instruction that are used to introduce and teach the strategy. Harris and Graham's (1996) seven phases are as follows:

1. *Preskill development.* In this stage, the teacher assesses a student's level of skill development. Preskills, such as vocabulary concept, that are not developed but are necessary for more advanced learning, are assessed and taught.

2. *Initial conference: Instructional goals and significance.* The teacher and student collaboratively decide the strategy that will be developed. A conference is held in which the teacher and student discuss the significance, benefits, and goals of the strategy.

3. *Discussion of the composition strategy.* The teacher discusses the composition strategy, explains each step of the strategy, and, if a mnemonic is used, describes the mnemonic strategy.

4. *Modeling of the composition strategy and self-instructions.* In this stage, the teacher models the composition strategy and the self-instructions that will be used while the student writes an actual composition. If the strategy involves the use of prompts or a mnemonic, the teacher should model those too. The student then is asked to develop and record his or her self-instructions.

5. *Mastery of the strategy.* The student memorizes the steps in the composition strategy and mnemonics that are used to remember the strategy. The student should also memorize the steps of the strategy he or she developed in stage 4.

6. *Collaborative practice.* In this stage, additional self-regulation procedures are discussed and initiated (e.g., goal setting, self-monitoring, self-reinforcement). Students use the strategies they have developed while writing. Teachers and students also develop individual goals regarding the students' writing.

7. *Independent use.* The students use the self-regulation strategy independently. The teacher and student evaluate the effectiveness of the strategy and the student's performance.

Empirical investigations have shown that SRSD has been successful in improving the writing performances of struggling writers (Graham & Perrin, 2006), students with learning disabilities (Graham & Harris, 2003), students with ADHD (Leinemann, & Reid, 2006), and students with EBD (Lane et al., 2006).

Summary

Students with disabilities will not learn to write by merely providing them with free writing opportunities or by the so-called natural writing method. It must be taught. Teaching students to write is a difficult and complex process that requires that teachers directly instruct their students in the skills and processes of writing. The ability to write is an important life skill for all students and will become especially important to students' academic success in high school and postsecondary education.

TEACHING MATHEMATICS

Success in mathematics is becoming increasingly important for today's students. Improving the mathematics achievement of *all* students is a national priority (Goals 2000: Educate America Act of 1994). The mathematical performance of students is important because other curricular areas rely on arithmetic skills (e.g., vocational education, algebra, business, science courses), and proficiency with basic computation is necessary for everyday living situations. According to the National Research Council (2003):

Success in tomorrow's job market will require more than computation competence. It will require the ability to apply mathematical knowledge to solve problems. If today's students are to compete successfully in the world of tomorrow, they must be able to learn new concepts and skills. They need to view mathematics as a tool they can use every day. (p. 3)

Math education has seen much reform over the last several years. In 2000, the National Council of Teachers of Mathematics (NCTM, 2000) produced a revised set of mathematics standards called *Principles and Standards for School Mathematics.* The revised six principals of high-quality mathematics education include the areas of equity, curriculum, teaching, learning, assessment, and technology (Table 15–10).

Table 15–10 Six principles of high-quality mathematics education

Principle	Description
Equity principle	• Excellence in mathematics education requires equity—high expectations and strong support for all students.
Curriculum principle	• A curriculum is more than a collection of activities: it must be coherent, focused on important mathematics, and well articulated across the grades.
Teaching principle	• Effective mathematics teaching requires understanding what students know and need to learn and then challenging and supporting them to learn it well.
Learning principle	• Students must learn mathematics with understanding, actively building new knowledge from experience and prior knowledge.
Assessment principle	• Assessment should support the learning of important mathematics and furnish information to both teachers and students.
Technology principle	• Technology is essential in teaching and learning mathematics; it influences the mathematics that is taught and enhances students' learning.

Source: NCTM, 2000.

In addition to the six principles, NCTM (2000) also established 10 standards for school mathematics to describe the mathematical understanding, knowledge, and skills that all students should acquire as they progress through school (see Table 15-11). The standards are described as either content standards or process standards. A content standard has two to four specific goals and each goal includes as many as seven specific expectations. A process standard has goals described through examples that demonstrate how the standard should look and the teacher's role in achieving the standard (NCTM, 2000). For individuals responsible for teaching mathematics to students with EBD, it is important to become familiar with the principles and standards delineated by NCTM (2000).

Teaching Mathematics to Students with EBD

Students with EBD also need to gain proficiency in mathematics. Many students with EBD fail to master basic skills, and the lack of basic math skills often leads to school failure and may lead to failure later in life (Reid, Gonzalez, Nordness, Trout, & Epstein, 2004). Researchers have soundly established the depth of academic performance problems of students with EBD; however, researchers have not fully addressed the analysis of

Table 15–11 Standards of school mathematics

Content Standards	Process Standards
Number and Operations	Problem Solving
Algebra	Reasoning and Proof
Geometry	Communication
Measurement	Connections
Data Analysis and Probability	

Source: NCTM 2000.

effective academic interventions for students with EBD (Hodge, Riccomini, Buford, & Herbst, 2006; Reid et al., 2004; Ruhl & Berlinghoff, 1992; Ryan, Reid, & Epstein, 2004), especially in the area of math (Hodge et al., 2006). Although important, researchers have primarily focused their efforts on interventions to improve student behaviors, even though a clear relationship exists between academic achievement and problem behaviors (Barriga et al., 2001).

Whereas previous chapters have focused on classroom management techniques and characteristics of students with EBD, this chapter focuses on teaching procedures with the assumption that the classroom management methods from previous chapters are used in combination with the instructional procedures and strategies discussed in this chapter. Students with EBD experience difficulties learning math, with problems surfacing early and continuing throughout a student's education (Nelson et al., 2004; Wehby, Lane, et al., 2003). Moreover, increasing numbers of students with EBD are receiving their education within general education classrooms; both special and general education teachers must work to improve their students' mathematical skills. The purpose of this chapter is to describe effective instructional procedures and strategies to help you design and deliver more effective math lessons for students with EBD. The chapter concludes with a brief review of promising practices from the research for teaching mathematics to students with EBD. The following section is designed to provide a framework to help teachers provide more effective math instruction to students with EBD.

Classroom Scenario 1

Friday is fraction review day in Mrs. Smart's class. Every Friday, the students complete a worksheet that contains 10-15 problems on previously learned math concepts—equivalent fractions. When students have completed the worksheet, it is reviewed by Mrs. Smart for accuracy. If the students have correctly answered 90% of the problems, they are able to select a reward (e.g., candy, stickers, pencil, computer time). As several of the students finish their fraction worksheet and selected rewards, Mario is becoming more and more frustrated and disruptive. He begins to disrupt the students sitting beside him. After about 5 minutes, Mario says, "I hate fractions and I'm not doing anymore!" and crumbles up his worksheet and throws it at his teacher.

Mario is an 11-year-old student in a fourth-grade regular education classroom. He was identified in third grade as having severe behavior problems. In addition to his behavior problems, he displays significant academic deficits in both reading and math, but is considerably weaker in math. The classroom scenario occurs quite frequently when Mario is asked to complete math problems independently. The question for Mrs. Smart now becomes, is this pattern of behavior an issue of CAN'T DO or WON'T DO?

After reading this chapter on effective mathematics instruction, discuss how Mrs. Smart might design instruction to better help Mario succeed in her math class.

Designing an Effective Math Lesson

Because similar levels of academic performance are observed across students with LD and students with EBD (Anderson, Kutash, & Duchnowski, 2001), it is logical to conclude that instructional practices effective for students with LD may also be effective for students with EBD (Bauer, Keefe, & Shea, 2001). In math, where minimal research has been conducted investigating effective instructional practices for students with EBD (Hodge et al., 2006), a brief review of generally effective instructional practices and math specific instructional practices from the literature of students with LD is prudent and will help form the framework needed to design and deliver effective math lessons to students with EBD.

General Review of Research on Effective Instruction
Many students with EBD may receive minimal instructional opportunities because of their behavioral problems (see classroom scenario 1). It is clear from the research on students' mathematical performance that the instruction they obtain is not effective (e.g., poor student outcomes). Inadequate instruction is a contributing factor in children failing to learn basic academic skills. Clearly, instruction that is more effective should produce better math achievement.

A number of empirically validated instructional techniques have been identified for general instruction and specifically for mathematics. Rosenshine and Stevens (1986) promote five teaching behaviors necessary for effective instruction. Their general lesson model includes (a) review and check previous day's work; (b) present new content; (c) guide student practice and check for understanding; (d) provide feedback, correctives, and reteach if necessary; and (e) provide weekly and monthly reviews (see Tables 15–12 and 15–13.)

These teaching behaviors are reflected in the model of explicit instruction advocated by Gersten and associates, who articulated six instructional variables (Gersten, 1985; Gersten, Carnine, & Woodward, 1987). The instructional variables include (a) explicit step-by-step problem-solving strategies, (b) emphasis on small-group instruction as opposed to students working alone, (c) systematic correction process for student errors, (d) highly structured practice faded to a level of independent practice, (e) a range of well-conceived examples with adequate practice, and (f) cumulative review of concepts (Gersten, 1985; Gersten et al., 1987).

Math-Specific Instructional Components
The general teaching behaviors and instructional variables advocated by researchers apply to all instruction and are similar to those advocated specifically for mathematics instruction by several researchers (e.g., Bottge & Hasselbring, 1993; Jitendra & Xin, 1997; Miller & Mercer, 1993). For example, Jitendra and Xin (1997) conducted an extensive review of the literature on problem-solving instruction and concluded that instructional methodologies emphasizing explicit instruction for teaching problem-solving skills were most successful. Similarly, Maccini

Table 15–12   Characteristics of effective teachers

1. Lessons begin with a short review of previous learning
2. A statement of goals is included in the beginning of the lesson.
3. New material is presented in small steps with practice opportunities provided after each step.
4. Instructions and explanations are clear and detailed.
5. A high level of active practice is provided for all students.
6. A large number of questions are asked, understanding is checked frequently, and responses are obtained from all students.
7. Students are guided during initial practice.
8. Systematic feedback and corrections are provided.
9. Explicit instruction and practice seat-work activities are provided and monitored.

Table 15–13 The general lesson model

Lesson Structure	Components
Review	• Review homework—reteach if necessary. • Review relevant previous learning. • Review prerequisite skills and knowledge for the lesson.
Presentation	• State lesson goals or provide outline. • Present new material in small steps. • Model Procedures and give 3–5 examples. • Provide examples and nonexamples. • Use clear and consistent age- appropriate mathematically correct language. • Check for student understanding. • Avoid digressions.
Guided practice	• Spend more time on guided practice. • Provide a high frequency of questions. • Ensure that all students respond and receive feedback. • Earn a high success rate (80% or higher). • Continue practice until students are fluent.
Corrections and feedback	• Provide process feedback when answers are correct but students are hesitant. • Provide sustaining feedback, clues, or reteaching when answers are incorrect. • Reteach material when necessary.
Independent practice	• Provide students an overview and/or help during initial steps. • Continue practice until students are fluent. • Provide active supervision. • Use routines to provide help for slower students.
Weekly and monthly reviews	• Review critical math concepts. • Conduct distributed review.

Source: Adapted from "Teaching Functions." by B. Rosenshine and R. Stevens, in *Handbook of Research on Teaching* (3rd ed., pp. 745-799), by M. C. Wittrock (Ed.), 1986, New York: Macmillan.

and Hughes (1997) conducted a literature review of research on mathematics instruction and concluded that teacher-directed instruction, strategic instruction, and certain instructional design variables appear to have a positive effect in teaching mathematics to students with LD.

Mercer and Miller (1992) compiled a list of 10 components of effective math instruction. These components are consistent with the literature disseminated in the last decade, which indicates that both curriculum design and teacher behavior directly influence the mathematics achievement of students with learning problems. These 10 effective instructional components are (a) selecting appropriate math content, (b) establishing goals and expectations, (c) providing systematic and explicit instruction, (d) strategically teaching math concepts, (e) monitoring student progress, (f) providing corrective feedback, (g) teaching to mastery, (h) teaching problem solving, (i) teaching generalization, and (j) promoting positive attitudes toward math. An instructional program, Strategic Math Series (Mercer & Miller, 1991), was developed using the 10 components and then field-tested. The field-test results indicated that students with learning problems were able to substantially improve their

mathematics skills when instruction followed the instructional components used in the Strategic Math Series.

Both general as well as math-specific instructional principles share common procedures. Mathematics lessons incorporating the instructional components identified by Gersten (1985), Rosenshine and Stevens (1986), and Mercer and Miller (1992) should be more effective for students with EBD. Thus, mathematics instruction for students with EBD should include the following 11 instructional components: (a) appropriate math content, (b) concept and application instruction, (c) problem-solving instruction, (d) systematic and explicit instruction, (e) instruction for the general case, (f) progress monitoring, (g) corrective feedback, (h) high success rate, (i) guided practice, (j) independent practice, and (k) cumulative review. Refer to Table 15-14 for a brief description of each component.

Teaching math to struggling students with EBD requires skillful planning and deep understanding of mathematical concepts. Teachers who combine effective classroom management methods and design mathematics lessons based on the previously described components of effective instruction will increase the likelihood of their students' success in mathematics. Math educators

Table 15–14 Components of effective mathematics instruction

Component	Description
Appropriate math content	Students have the necessary preskills and prior knowledge.
Concept and application instruction	Instruction beyond the rote memorization of basic facts.
Problem-solving instruction	Story problems, word problems, and/or problems related to real-world situations.
Systematic and explicit instruction	Model-prompt sequences, monitoring, highly organized and sequential, and clear and concise directions.
Generalization instruction	Promoted through the inclusion of numerous and varied examples, and real-life problems, discussing rationale for learning.
Progress monitoring	Frequent checks of student's academic work and progress.
Corrective feedback	Regular correctives provided to students.
Success rate	At least 80% or higher for instructional purposes.
Guided practice	Mediated scaffolding, monitoring and checking for student understanding, initial prompts provided and then faded.
Independent work	Student directed, prompts removed, practice problems, review games, worksheets, and homework.
Cumulative reviews	Systematic and frequent practice and/or reteaching of previously covered skills.

must remember that it is their responsibility to design and deliver mathematics instruction based on the considerable research available specific to effective instructional practices. Teachers must realize that the delivery of inadequate instruction is at least partially responsible for the many students, especially students with EBD, who struggle with mathematics. Instruction that is validated and more effective should produce better student mathematical achievement. Therefore, teachers must incorporate these 11 instructional components to maximize instructional effort and outcomes with students of all abilities.

Preventing students with EBD from failing mathematics and promoting mathematical proficiency is an enormous challenge. Instruction is the essential element in the classroom completely within the control of the teacher. Teachers cannot change what students learned or did not learn in previous years; however, teachers can focus on designing and delivering instruction that is more effective. The principles of effective instruction described are a set of tools already available to increase positive educational outcomes for students struggling to learn math and should be considered when designing instructional lessons for math.

Basic Fact Fluency Few individuals would disagree with the notion that the ultimate goal of mathematics education is for students to have the ability to apply mathematical knowledge to solve real-world problems. However, for mathematics to be useful to an individual, one must have the ability to easily and accurately use basic mathematics skills. Arduous application of basic math facts and computation not only is frustrating to the individual trying to solve a problem, but it does little to aid students' overall mathematical comprehension and

motivation. Mathematical proficiency is a functional skill important for adult competence in today's society.

Many students with EBD fail to master basic math skills, struggling with both accuracy and fluency (Greenbaum et al., 1996; Reid et al., 2004). When students lack the skills to compute basic number combinations quickly and accurately (e.g., $4+3, 16-8, 8\times6, 9\div3$), they cannot effectively use them to solve more complex math problems. This can cause students to become easily frustrated and unmotivated. If this type of frustration and lack of motivation occurs early in a student's educational experiences, he or she is likely to develop a lifelong dislike for mathematics. Mastery of basic facts is very important for students to accomplish early and helps form the basis for mathematical thinking (Wu, 1999).

To help students attain fluency with basic facts, teachers may have to supplement their current math curriculum with additional structured practice opportunities for students. The most critical aspect for students to develop mastery of facts is adequate practice opportunities that include a systematic cumulative review of previously learned facts. Most math curricula do not provide sufficient practice opportunities, and fact fluency instruction is often overlooked (Stein, Kinder, Silbert, & Carnine, 2006). When developing a program to promote fact fluency acquisition, Stein and colleagues recommended that teachers consider the following five components:

1. Set the student criterion level for the introduction of new facts (e.g., >85%).

2. Develop practice activities with heavy emphasis on newly introduced facts and systematic practice on previously learned facts.

3. Schedule regular and adequate time for fluency building (e.g., 20 minutes two to three days per week).

4. Develop data management of student's progress.

5. Implement a motivation system for students who reach the criterion.

It is important to find a balance of time to provide sufficient instruction and practice for students struggling with their facts and to move forward with more advanced important math concepts and procedures. Instruction in more complex mathematical concepts and procedures should not be withheld from students still struggling with basic facts. Although very important to students overall, mathematics proficiency, fact instruction, and fluency-building activities should not use all of the instructional time allotted to mathematics.

As stated, because many mathematics curricula do not include adequate fluency instruction and practice opportunities, many students with EBD may struggle to master basic facts. NCTM (2000) includes Numbers and Operations as one of the five content standards in *Principles and Standards for School Mathematics* because basic number computations are essential for other content standards such as algebra, geometry, measurement, data analysis and probability, and problem solving. Students who do not develop fluency and accuracy with basic facts and computation will struggle in all areas of mathematics.

Mathematics Vocabulary

Mathematics Vocabulary The importance of learning vocabulary is well recognized in the area of reading and identified as a "big idea" by the National Reading Panel. Unfortunately, the significance of students learning mathematical vocabulary is often underestimated and overlooked during math instruction. Vocabulary development is crucial and central to the mathematical proficiency of students. Mathematics should be thought of as a language, and if students are to communicate and apply mathematics proficiently, the language of mathematics must be meaningful for students (National Council of Teachers of Mathematics, 2000).

Many mathematical terms are easily confused (e.g., numerator, denominator) and difficult to learn for students struggling in math. Additionally, mathematical terminology is rarely used in real-life conversations, further adding to the unfamiliarity of mathematics language. For some students vocabulary must be directly taught and purposefully connected to meaningful contexts. There are many different methods to teach vocabulary to students, but one especially effective method for teaching vocabulary is through verbal elaboration. Verbal elaboration is a broadly defined set of strategies by which students are taught specific steps to help them connect new and unfamiliar information with previously learned and familiar information.

One especially effective type of verbal elaboration is the keyword strategy. The keyword strategy helps students learn a new and often unfamiliar vocabulary term by directly associating the new vocabulary term with a word familiar to the student. In addition to linking the new vocabulary word to the familiar word, a picture is used to represent the meaning (i.e., definition) of the new vocabulary term. Scruggs and Mastropieri (2002) list the following steps in developing a keyword strategy for new vocabulary terms: (a) *recode* the unfamiliar word to an acoustically similar but familiar word (i.e., keyword); (b) *relate* the keyword in an interactive picture that represents the meaning of the new vocabulary term; and (c) *retrieve* the new definition by thinking of the keyword and what is represented in the picture. Figure 15–1 illustrates the keyword strategy.

Recode the New Vocabulary Term. Choose a word that is important for the students to learn. For illustration purposes, we will select the term *intercept*—the place where a line, curve, or surface crosses an axis. Now, have the students think of an acoustically similar sounding word, the keyword. The most important aspect of this step is that the keyword selected is a word that the students already know and are familiar with. In the instance of *intercept,* we selected *intersection.* This application is completely reference related. If the students can't relate to this keyword, the strategy won't work because the students do not know either word. For example, selecting *Central Park* for a keyword might work for students in New York City, but probably not for students in Tempe, Arizona. Teachers must use their professional judgment in determining if the selected word is an appropriate keyword for their particular students.

Relate Keywords to Symbols. Next, use an interactive picture to represent the definition of the vocabulary term and relate to the keyword. Recent technological advances in easily accessible computer graphics and clip art offer infinite possibilities for students and teachers when determining an appropriate picture. But remember, the pictures can also be sketched by the students. For our example, we selected a clip art picture of an intersection and then superimposed the *x-* and *y-* axis to show where the intercept is located. We highlight the intersection of the axis using a white circle. This picture will help the student link the meaning of *intercept* with the keyword *intersection.* To reinforce the definition of

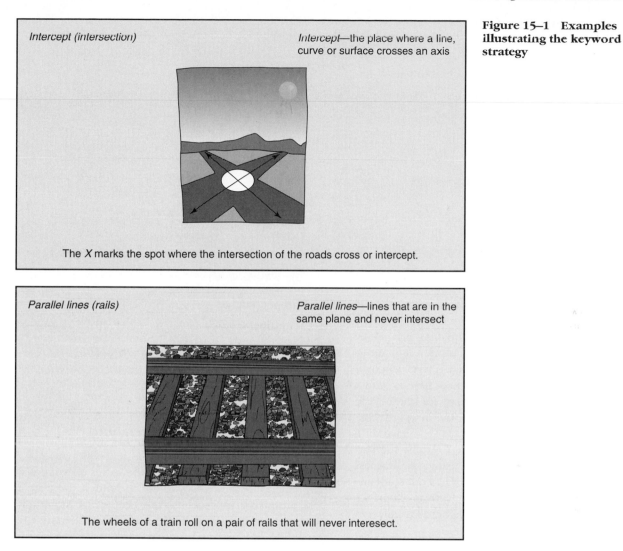

Intercept (intersection)

Intercept—the place where a line, curve or surface crosses an axis

The *X* marks the spot where the intersection of the roads cross or intercept.

Parallel lines (rails)

Parallel lines—lines that are in the same plane and never intersect

The wheels of a train roll on a pair of rails that will never interesect.

Figure 15–1   Examples illustrating the keyword strategy

intercept and further connect the keyword with the new vocabulary term, a sentence is created that represents the important information from the picture.

Retrieve New Definitions. The students practice retrieving the new information visualizing the information represented in the picture with the keyword linking the picture to the new vocabulary word. For our example, the students visualize the two roads forming an intersection, and the intercept is located in the center of the intersection. After the students have studied their keyword representation (i.e., intercept-intersection-picture), when asked later to define or describe the meaning of *intercept,* students retrieve its definition by thinking of the keyword and the interactive illustration and its corresponding sentence, leading them to the correct definition.

Another illustration is provided with the term *parallel lines.*

Notice the structured keyword worksheet that prompts the three steps in the keyword strategy. This is a scaffold or support to help students learn the components of the keyword strategy. Providing students this scaffold or support during initial instruction helps students remember the required steps. The structured keyword worksheet also offers students a permanent record of their new vocabulary words that can then be used as a cumulative review of important mathematical terminology later in the year. Some students may need the structured keyword worksheet when developing a strategy; however, it is important to encourage students to develop their own system for using the keyword strategy (see Figure 15–2). This may lead to students using the keyword strategy in other classes.

Figure 15–2   Example of scaffolded keyword strategy

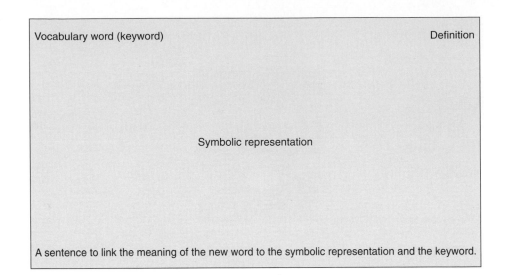

Vocabulary word (keyword)	Definition

Symbolic representation

A sentence to link the meaning of the new word to the symbolic representation and the keyword.

The keyword strategy is used in many vocabulary-intense subjects, but has not been used specifically for mathematics vocabulary and concepts. As previously mentioned, mathematics vocabulary is often difficult to learn because much of this vocabulary is rarely encountered in everyday life, and students do not have a context or the background knowledge necessary for learning the vocabulary (Monroe & Orme, 2002). The keyword strategy is a very valuable tool for students who have difficulty with vocabulary. Teaching students to use the keyword strategy helps make sense of sometimes meaningless words and directly connects the word to the students' current construct. Helping students learn mathematics vocabulary can mean the difference between success and failure.

Classroom Scenario 2

Mr. Smith is planning a unit on fractions for his fifth-grade class. He realizes there are many new and challenging vocabulary words that students must learn in order to have a conceptual understanding of fractions. For students to become proficient with fractions, he recognizes that students need to know more than just the numerator is the top number and the denominator is the bottom number. Although important, simply knowing that information is necessary, but insufficient for students to gain a solid conceptual understanding of fractions. Help Mr. Smith design a keyword strategy for the following fraction-related terms:

1. fraction
2. denominator
3. numerator
4. fraction bar
5. proper fraction
6. improper fraction

Remember that Mr. Smith is teaching fifth-grade students, so design the keyword strategies that are appropriate for students in fifth grade.

Considering New Instructional Practices in Mathematics

Even though the research on mathematics instructional approaches for students with EBD is limited, there are a few promising approaches emerging in the literature. Recently, Hodge and colleagues (2006) systematically reviewed and analyzed the experimental research on mathematics instructional approaches designed to improve the performance of students with EBD. Instructional approaches were defined by Hodge and colleagues as specific instruction, or instruction in a strategy or skill that promotes students' mathematical performance. After a comprehensive search, the researchers located only 13 studies that met the criteria for inclusion in the review. (Refer to Table 15–15 for a listing of the studies.) The studies reviewed by Hodge and colleagues fell into four categories: (a) student-directed strategies, (b) teacher-directed strategies, (c) peer tutoring strategies, and (d) computer-assisted instruction. The following section contains detailed description of each area.

Student-Directed Strategies In the area of student-directed strategies, Hodge and colleagues (2006) identified two categories of instructional approaches: (a) self-monitoring interventions and (b) strategy instruction.

Table 15–15   Research-based mathematics interventions and students with EBD

Authors	Subjects	Intervention	Setting	Results
Cade & Gunter, 2002	3 males with EBD 2 AA; 1 Cau Ages: 11, 12, 14 years	Mnemonic strategy to solve basic division facts	Special day school	Mnemonic strategy increased students' accuracy on division by 7 math facts
Carr & Punzo, 1993	3 AA males with EBD Ages: 13–15 years	Self-monitoring during independent work	Middle school self-contained class	Increased accuracy and productivity across subjects and settings
Davis & Hajicek, 1985	7 students with EBD Ages: 9–15 years	Strategy training and self-instructional training for problem solving	Psycho-educational center	Self-instruction condition led to greater improvements in accuracy and attention compared to strategy training alone
Franca, Kerr, Reitz, & Lambert, 1990	8 males with EBD Ages: 13–16 years	Four-step peer tutoring	Self-contained classroom in a private school	Both tutor and tutee improved social interactions and math performance
Jolivette, Wehby, & Hirsch, 1999;	3 males with EBD Ages: 9, 10, 11 years, 4th grade	Preassessment, strategy instruction, preferred strategy replication	Summer school program	All students demonstrated increased accuracy
Landeen & Adams, 1988	10 males with EBD, Ages: 8–10 years	Paper-and-pencil and computer-assisted drill and practice	Self-contained special education class	Both conditions resulted in increased ratio of correct to incorrect
Lazarus, 1993	18 students with EBD: 14 males; 4 females Ages: 11–13 years	Teacher directed instruction and self-management	Middle school self-contained special education class	Increased math performance
Lee, Sugai, & Horner, 1999	2 males with EBD Age: 9 years 3rd grade	Individualized direct instruction	Self-contained special education classroom	Increased accuracy on math skills assessment and decreased off-task behavior
Levendoski & Cartledge, 2000	4 males with EBD 3 Cau; 1 AA Ages: 9–11	Self-monitoring with visual and auditory cues	Self-contained classroom	Increase in on-task behavior and math productivity
Scruggs, Mastropieri, & Tolfa-Veit, 1986	85 total: 63 males; 22 females 11 EBD 44 LD 4–6th grades	Test-taking strategies	Self-contained classroom	Significant effects for word study skills and math concepts; no difference between groups
Skinner, Bamberg, Smith, & Powell, 1993;	3 males with EBD Ages: 9, 12, 12 years	Cover, copy, and compare practice strategy	Private school self-contained elementary class	Increased rate of accurate responses
Skinner, Turco, Beatty, & Rasavage, 1989;	4 students with EBD: 3 males; 1 female two 4th grade and two 10th grade	Look, cover, write answer, evaluate	Special school for students with EBD	Increased rates and accuracy; maintained over time
Skinner, Ford & Yunker, 1991	2 males with EBD Ages: 9, 11	Verbal and written cover, copy, and compare	Residential school	Verbal cover, copy, and compare was more effective than written, cover, copy, and compare

Source: From "A Review of Instructional Interventions in Mathematics for Students with Emotional and Behavioral Disorders," by J. Hodge, P.J. Riccomini, R. Buford, and M. Herbst, 2006, *Behavioral Disorders, 31*(3), pp. 297–311. Adapted with permission of the authors.

Note: EBD = emotional or behavioral disorders; AA = African American; Cau = Caucasian.

Classroom Scenario 3

Darius is a 12-year-old sixth-grade student with EBD who is having difficulty both behaviorally and academically in school. He is currently receiving his math instruction in the general education classroom. Mr. Smith, his math teacher, describes Darius as a student with the capabilities to succeed in his math class, but he rarely completes any of his assignments whether homework or class work. He also performs poorly on his math tests. He often works problems only partially or leaves questions blank. During instructional time, Mr. Smith frequently has to redirect him to the task. As a result of not paying attention during instructional times and not completing independent activities, Darius is falling behind his peers and in danger of failing.

To try and help Darius, Mr. Smith and Mr. Jones, the special education teacher, decided to systematically observe Darius during instructional time and independent activities using a behavior checklist. After 2 weeks of observation, Darius was always the last student to open his book and get ready to take notes. He also spent more time at the pencil sharpener and asking to go the restroom or get a drink of water. When he did take notes, his notes were often filled with doodles and pictures. When Mr. Smith and Mr. Jones reviewed the behavior checklists, they discovered that Darius was working on his math assignments for only 10 minutes of the 45-minute class. Clearly, if Darius is to improve his math performance, Mr. Smith and Mr. Jones must help Darius increase his on-task behavior.

How can Mr. Smith and Mr. Jones help Darius monitor his on-task behavior during math class using a self-monitoring strategy?

Both approaches resulted in a positive effect on the accuracy and fluency of basic computation. Self-monitoring approaches require students to regulate their own behavior during an instructional activity. Self-monitoring interventions are broadly defined and used to improve both behavior and academic performance of students with EBD across many different settings. Teachers wishing to implement a self-monitoring strategy should follow these five general procedures:

1. Create instructional materials (e.g., recording sheets).

2. Instruct the student how to use the self-recording sheet.

3. Provide the student opportunities to practice using the self-recording sheet.

4. Implement the self-monitoring procedure during instructional activities.

5. Keep data on academic improvement and share them with students.

For example, a teacher might teach students a self-monitoring strategy to evaluate and record the number of math problems answered correctly and incorrectly on an independent math activity. This information can then help the students set new academic goals. The number correct and incorrect is compiled on a self-recording sheet (see Figure 15–3). The student then tries to improve the number correct and decrease the number incorrect on subsequent independent math activities. As the data are collected and compiled, teachers can determine which students require further instruction or more practice on specific sets of skills.

Self-monitoring strategies are also beneficial to help students monitor their on-task behavior during instructional episodes. Increasing students' on-task attention levels also increases levels of academic engagement, a very important component of effective instruction. Students who are more actively engaged in relevant instructional tasks are likely to learn more (Mastropieri & Scruggs, 2004). Teaching students to monitor their attention during instructional time is very important. Increasing students' attention during instructional time is done by teaching a self-monitoring strategy that focuses on their attention. The same general procedures described previously are used, but instead of monitoring correct and incorrect problems, the student monitors his or her attention levels. This type of self-monitoring is generally achieved by having students check their attention at set intervals (e.g., every 3 minutes) and using a self-recording sheet to record their attending behavior (see Figure 15–4). Once collected, the data are reviewed and discussed with the student and a plan is formulated to increase attention during instructional time.

Hodge and colleagues reviewed seven studies that incorporated strategy instruction to improve mathematical performance of students with disabilities. Although the strategies implemented varied across studies, results from six of the studies indicated that strategy instruction was an effective approach to increase students' accuracy with basic math facts. Strategy instruction is an approach that teaches students "how to learn" versus what to learn (Lenz, Ellis, & Scanlon, 1996). Teachers can help students become better learners through strategy instruction.

For example, one effective strategy for students with EBD was the cover, copy, and compare (CCC) strategy (Skinner, Bamberg, Smith & Powell, 1993; Skinner et al., 1989; Skinner, Ford, & Yunker, 1991). For the CCC strategy, students are taught to (a) look at the problem and the answer, (b) cover the problem and answer, (c) write the problem and answer, and (d) uncover the answer and evaluate what was written. Students can use the strategy to solve simple computation problems. Results indicate that students using the CCC strategy were able to increase their accuracy rates of solving simple computation problems.

A strategy is a systematic approach used by students to solve a problem. Students with disabilities often lack effective and efficient strategies (Carnine et al., 2004) and require systematic and explicit instruction to learn a strategy. It is very important that teachers directly teach students "how to learn" strategies before, during, and

FIGURE 15–3

Example of self-monitoring worksheet for basic facts

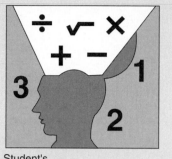

Do I

Know my

math facts?

Student's
name   Goal

Math Fact Sheet	Number Correct	Number Incorrect	Which Problems Did I Miss?	Did I Reach My Goal?

Note: The table can be modified to fit specific math objectives or activities.

FIGURE 15-4

Example of a self-monitoring recording sheet for attention during instructional time

Was I

paying

attention?

	Yes	No
1.		
2.		
3.		
4.		
5.		
6.		
7.		
8.		
9.		
10.		
11.		
12.		
13.		
14.		
15.		
16.		
17.		
18.		
19.		
20.		
Total:		
Goal:		

	Yes	No
1.		
2.		
3.		
4.		
5.		
6.		
7.		
8.		
9.		
10.		
11.		
12.		
13.		
14.		
15.		
16.		
17.		
18.		
19.		
20.		
Total:		
Goal:		

after content instruction. Some students may experience difficulty learning the steps to a strategy especially if the strategy is taught at the same time as the content. Students may also require additional support and encouragement to continuously use the strategy. Students who are taught strategies that can be applied across various settings and situations have a greater likelihood of succeeding.

Teacher-Directed Instruction Consistent with the rather extensive literature base on direct instruction (DI) and students with LD, Hodge and colleagues found teacher-directed instruction as a promising practice for students with EBD. Unfortunately, only one study (see Lee et al., 1999) using a DI approach to teach math was identified. The consistent demonstration of the effectiveness of teachers who design lessons following DI principles warrants more experimental studies that include students with EBD.

Many educators equate traditional teacher-directed instruction with DI. DI is a more involved process than traditional teacher-directed instruction. A main assumption of DI is that all children can learn if provided with appropriate instruction and practice. There are six critical features of DI:

1. Explicit step-by-step strategy instruction;
2. Mastery attained at each step;
3. Systematic correction process for student errors;
4. Highly structured practice faded to independent practice;
5. Range of examples provided with adequate practice;
6. Cumulative reviews of concepts.

The one study that Hodge and colleagues reviewed on DI (Lee et al., 1999) is significant for two reasons. Not only did the mathematical performance of students with EBD greatly improve, but students' behavior also improved. Given that students with EBD by definition have severe behavioral problems, instructional interventions that improve both academic performance and overall behavior provides teachers with a more efficient method for teaching students with EBD. Notice the overlap between the Lee et al. (1999) study and the 11 components of effective instruction—further evidence for the use of the previously described components of effective instruction.

Peer-Mediated Interventions Another promising practice for improving academic performance in mathematics for students with EBD identified by Hodge and

colleagues is peer-mediated interventions. Peer-mediated interventions include a set of instructional procedures whereby students are taught by peers (Maheady et al., 2003). Generally, students work together through a series of structured activities to practice important skills during peer-mediated instructional time (McMaster, Fuchs, & Fuchs, 2006). Many varied approaches have been developed in which students work in pairs or small cooperative learning groups (i.e., Peer-Assisted Learning Strategies [PALS] in Reading and Mathematics). Peer-mediated interventions offer a promising approach for improving academic performance in mathematics for students with EBD (Ryan et al., 2004).

Peer-mediated interventions have been extensively examined with other student populations and in other areas such as reading for students with EBD (Elbaum, Vaughn, Hughes, & Moody, 1999; Falk & Wehby, 2001; Mathes & Fuchs, 1994). Unfortunately, only six studies in the literature investigated the effects of a peer tutoring intervention on the mathematical performance of students with EBD. In one study reviewed by Hodge and colleagues, researchers investigated the effects of a peer tutoring procedure on the basic computation skills of middle school students with EBD (Franca, Kerr, Reitz, & Lambert, 1990). The peer tutoring intervention consisted of four steps: (a) problem presentation, (b) instructions, (c) error corrections, and (d) social reinforcement. The authors reported increased accuracy and fluency by both tutor and tutee math worksheets during the course of the study.

Peer-mediated intervention procedures vary across students, grades, and content areas. Ryan et al. (2004) identified eight different types of peer-mediated interventions. Teachers designing and implementing a peer-mediated intervention must plan procedures for the following seven general components:

1. Create tutoring pairs.
2. Develop structured instructional procedures.
3. Develop specific error correction procedures.
4. Develop a scoring system for correct responses and following procedures.
5. Develop a scoring system for appropriate behaviors.
6. Develop an organizational system for materials.
7. Develop a data management system.

Another important consideration is the organizational system for handling the materials for each pair of students. Because pairs are formed by ability levels, teachers can individualize the content to each student's skill level. Creating folders for each pair allows peer-mediated activities to flow smoothly and minimizes instructional disruptions. Each folder should contain the instructional procedures, rules, error correction procedures, and team point sheets. Students also enjoy creating names for their teams and decorating their folders. Refer to Figure 15–5 for examples of peer-mediated materials for teaching basic facts.

We have been focusing on designing a generic peer-mediated intervention based on the seven general components described; however, there are peer-mediated intervention-based programs for mathematics available commercially. One especially effective commercially available program is Peer-Assisted Learning Strategies (PALS) in Math (Fuchs et al., 1997; Fuchs, Fuchs, & Karns, 2001; Fuchs, Fuchs, Yazdian, & Powell, 2002). PALS Math is a classwide peer tutoring program that provides different practice activities on important math skills critical for academic success. There are PALS math materials for (a) kindergarten, (b) first grade, and (c) second through sixth grade students (Figure 15–6).

FIGURE 15–5

Example of peer-mediated intervention materials for practicing basic multiplication facts

Instructional Procedures for Coach

1. The "coach" holds up fact set number one and says each fact AND the answer.
2. The "player" repeats the SAME set of facts and answers.
3. Check each answer.
4. If your partner misses a fact or pauses for more than 3 seconds, follow the procedure on the "If someone misses a fact" sheet.
5. Repeat with the second fact set.
6. Give your team member 1 point for each correct fact.

Error Correction Procedures

If someone misses a fact or pauses for more than 3 seconds, SAY . . .

1. STOP . . . you missed this fact. Can you figure it out? (Player says fact within 3 seconds.)
2. Good! _____X_____ is _____
3. Let's start at the beginning of that fact set.

   OR

If someone misses a fact or pauses for more than 3 seconds, SAY . . .

1. STOP . . . you missed this fact. Can you figure it out? (Player waits longer than 3 seconds.)
2. _____X_____=_____
3. What does _____X_____ equal?
4. Good! Let's go back to the beginning of that set.

Team Points:

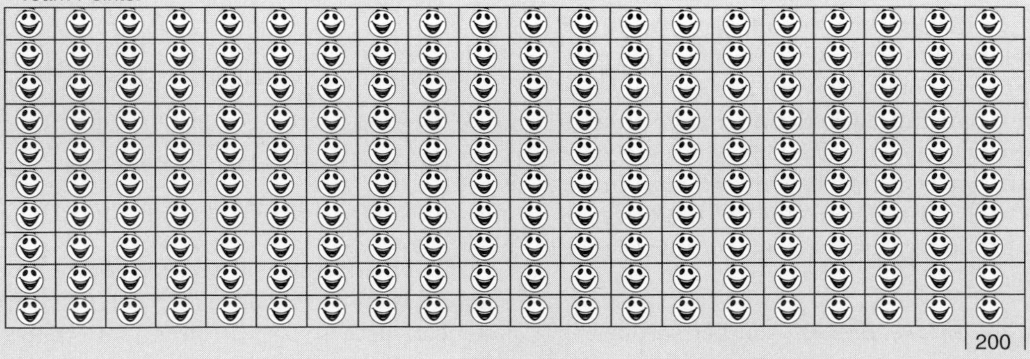

200

FIGURE 15-6

Research highlight: Peer-assisted learning strategies (PALS) in math

PALS-Math Activities

PALS-Math incorporates different activities at different grade levels reflecting an appropriate set of developmental skills critical to academic success. PALS-Math is designed to supplement a teacher's existing math program. PALS-Math can be used with any instructional program and takes only several 30-minute sessions per week depending on grade level.

PALS-Math Kindergarten

The focus of PALS-Math is on number recognition, number concepts, and the development of a mental number line representation. Accordingly, children practice associating numerals with numerical value, play games involving "more" and "less," and work with number lines to compare the placement and value of numbers. Early concepts of addition and subtraction are also introduced with an emphasis on "number stories."

PALS-Math Grade 1

PALS-Math becomes more challenging. In addition to a strong focus on number recognition and the development of a mental number line representation, emphasis is on place value within numeration, number concepts, and addition and subtraction concepts. The first-grade PALS curriculum also address missing addends and mathematical operations, and the number values extend to the hundreds.

PALS-Math Grades 2–6

The PALS-Math program covers the comprehensive math curriculum including numeration, number concepts, computation of whole numbers, fractions, and decimals, measurement, geometry, figures/graphs, and word problems. The specific skills addressed at each grade level correspond to the standards most frequently represented at each level of the curriculum.

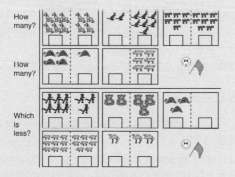

Sample Kindergarten PALS-Math gameboard for story problems

Sample Kindergarten PALS-Math lesson focusing on addition and subtraction

Source: From "PALS: Peer-Assisted Learning Strategies for Accelerating Achievement in Reading and Math," by L. Fuchs and D. Fuchs, 2003. Available from http://kc.vanderbilt.edu/pals. Copyright © 2003 by John F. Kennedy Center for Communication Services.

Computer-Assisted Strategies Technology is one possible remedy for the poor mathematical performance of students with EBD. Instructional technology has the potential to assist and improve teachers' ability to individualize instruction, provide immediate and continuous feedback, maximize functional practice, better motivate students to learn, and ultimately improve students' mathematics performance. Computer-assisted instruction (CAI) has emerged as an alternative delivery system for learning (Fuchs & Allinder, 1993). Computers, computer software, and videodisc technology offer a promising medium through which mathematics instruction and practice opportunities can improve. Teachers of students with EBD should exercise caution in the use of CAI, however.

Hodge and colleagues found one study that compared the effects of a CAI program and a paper-and-pencil practice session to help students learn basic computation skills

(Landeen & Adams, 1988). Interestingly, the students using the CAI program to practice basic facts required three times as many sessions to reach criterion compared to the students using paper and pencil. Additionally, students using the CAI program preferred to use paper and pencil. One plausible explanation for the lack of student progress was the CAI program was limited to drill and practice and included no motivational components. When academic tasks are uninteresting, students with EBD are more likely to become restless and act out. These findings, however, stand in stark contrast to the literature on students with LD using CAI programs to increase mathematical performance.

Based on an extensive literature review on CAI and mathematics, Hughes and Maccini (1997) reported that the use of CAI can increase students' mathematical performance. Their review focused on students with LD. However, the review can provide guidance to teachers of students with EBD. Consider the following aspects when selecting CAI programs for students with EBD: (a) computer-based programs utilizing specific design features more effectively increased students' mathematics achievement than traditional basal instruction, (b) CAI and teacher-directed instruction with effective design principles were equally effective, and (c) instruction delivered via videodisc increased students' problem-solving skills. Logically, CAI programs used to teach mathematics skills based on effective instructional principles should increase students' mathematics achievement, even students with EBD.

Summary

The current emphasis on the use of practices based on scientific evidence highlights the need to identify effective mathematical interventions for students with EBD. The review by Hodge and colleagues clearly indicates a critical need for research on improving the mathematical performance of students with EBD. Teachers charged with the responsibility of delivering scientifically based instruction to students with EBD should be concerned regarding the paucity of research on instructional methods focusing on mathematical concepts and skills.

Even though the research on mathematics instructional approaches for students with EBD is limited, examining the specific instructional approaches used may provide helpful information for teachers responsible for teaching mathematics to students with EBD.

TEACHING STUDY SKILLS

Students with EBD often do not have study skills such as the ability to (a) listen to lectures, (b) take tests, (c) conduct reference and research work, (d) remember academic content, and (e) take notes (Bos & Vaughn, 2002; Mastropieri & Scruggs, 2000; Schloss, Smith, & Schloss, 2001; Scruggs & Mastropieri, 1992). The development of these skills, however, is very important if students are to succeed academically (Ellett, 1993; Wood, Woloshyn, & Willoughby, 1999). Fortunately, instruction in these skills has been effective with students with disabilities (Mastropieri & Scruggs, 2000), and elementary (Mastropieri & Scruggs, 2000), high school (Gall, Gall, Jacobsen, & Bullock, 1990), and college-age students (Gall et al., 1990; Tuckman, 2003). Teachers should integrate study skill instruction into their classroom curriculum (Marshak, 1984; Mastropieri & Scruggs, 2000; Scruggs & Mastropieri, 1992). When teachers do integrate study skills into their teaching, they should be aware that not all strategies work for all students (Wood, Willoughby, & Woloshyn, 1999) and that careful monitoring of students' progress toward gaining and effectively practicing these skills is essential (Scruggs & Mastropieri, 2000).

Listening Skills

"Despite decades of advice to the contrary, teachers at all levels still lecture" (Devine, 1987, p. 19). Putnam, Deshler, and Schumaker (1993) found that teachers in secondary settings spend at least half of their class time presenting information through lectures. To be successful, students with EBD need to listen, a skill not generally identified as a characteristic of these students. Fortunately, students can be taught (Devine, 1987) listening skills in a variety of engaging ways (see Table 15–16). Teachers can have students:

☐ Play games like Simon Says.

☐ Give an "oral test" with funny questions (Custer et al., 1990).

☐ Listen to songs or audio books, and require students to retell the story or explain the main point.

☐ Complete Sound Stories, an activity where the students listen to four to six distinct sounds on tape, and then are required to write a story recalling the order of the sounds (Devine, 1987).

☐ Identify the "choke," the one factual error in a lecture that is incongruent with the reading the students completed on the same topic.

In addition to playing games, teachers can also prepare students for the lecture by prompting them with guiding questions, reviewing vocabulary, providing guided notes, completing K-W-Ls, making the lesson personal by connect the topic to students' life experiences, encouraging active participation, presenting an agenda, using visuals

Table 15–16 **Example of oral test with answers**

Questions That Require Students to Listen	Answers
1. A plane crashes on the border of North and South Carolina. Where do they bury the survivors?	You don't bury survivors.
2. A farmer had 17 sheep. All but 9 broke through a hole in the fence and wandered away. How many were left?	Nine sheep.
3. A snail is at the bottom of a 30-foot well. If he climbs up 2 feet every day and slips back 1 foot every night, how many days will it take the snail to climb out of the well?	Twenty-nine days.
4. Which weighs more, a pound of bricks or a pound of feathers?	They both weigh a pound.
5. Is there a 4th of July in Russia?	Yes (Russians don't celebrate our Independence Day, though).
6. How much dirt is in a hole that is 2 feet deep, 3 feet wide, and 4 feet long?	None; it's a hole.
7. How many Ping-Pong balls can you put into an empty size 10 shoebox?	None, because it wouldn't be empty then.

aids, assessing and reteaching portions of the lesson if necessary, and allowing time for questions at the end (Bos & Vaughn, 2002; Custer et al., 1990; Schloss et al., 2001).

Test-Taking Skills

Students with EBD struggle with many academic tasks, including taking tests (Bos & Vaughn, 2002; Schloss et al., 2001). These students often lack appropriate test-taking skills and are more likely than their peers to perform poorly. Fortunately, there is evidence that students can be taught good test-taking skills, which in turn will promote increased academic success.

Often students with EBD perform poorly on tests because they are overwhelmed by anxiety. Anxiety, as measured by student's self-report and actual pulse rates, can be reduced when students use anxiety controls (Beidel, Turner, & Taylor-Ferreira, 1999) such as (a) positive self-talk, (b) deep breathing, and (c) test preparation forms (Basso & McCoy, 1996; Wood & Willoughby, 1999). Table 15–17 outlines these anxiety-reducing strategies along with when the strategies should be used.

Table 15–17 **Test-taking strategies and when to use them**

When to Use It	Strategy
Before the test	1. Use a calendar to keep track of when tests are scheduled.
	2. Schedule study sessions, including place and time (Hughes, 1996).
	3. Ask yourself the following (adapted from Basso & McCoy, 1996):
	☐ I know what kinds of questions will be on the test. Circle all that apply:
	T/F multiple choice matching short answer essay open book other: _____
	☐ I know how many points the exam is worth: _____ points out of _____ points for the _____ (semester, grading period, year).
	☐ I know what material will be covered: _____ (information, books/chapters).
	☐ I know what to study. Circle all that apply:
	old tests notes textbook worksheets homework handouts videos other: _____
	☐ I know what materials I need to bring to the test. Circle all that apply:
	#2 pencil pen notes other: _____
	☐ I know that I have prepared for this test and can pass it.
During the test	4. Before starting the test, reduce anxiety by using deep breathing and positive self-talk.
	5. Write your name on the test.
	6. Survey the test, estimating how long it will take to complete it (Bos & Vaughn, 2002).
	7. Write down any mnemonics that you have memorized for the test (Bos & Vaughn, 2002).
	8. Read the instructions carefully, underlining what is important (Hughes, 1996).
	9. Read over the entire test before turning it in (Custer et al., 1990).
After the test	10. After receiving the graded test, carefully check where you have erred. Be sure to determine how you can avoid making those same mistakes in the future (Custer et al., 1990).

Table 15–18   Types of tests

Recognition	Integration
True/false	Fill in the blank
Multiple choice	Short answer
Matching	Essays

Although these general strategies can help students with EBD develop a successful routine for taking tests, there are additional methods that can assist students depending on the type of tests. There are two broad categories of tests: those that require recognition of knowledge because the correct answer is included in the question prompts, and those that require students to remember and integrate information. Table 15–18 details the types of tests students typically encounter.

When taking a recognition test, students should remember the mnemonic *DREAMS*:

☐ *D*irections must be read carefully. Students should look for keywords to determine what the teacher is attempting to evaluate (e.g., *incorrect, wrong, right, worst, best, none, never, less, least, more, most, all, always*).

☐ *R*ead all answers before committing to one (Custer et al., 1990).

☐ *E*asy questions must be answered first. Skip the hard ones initially.

☐ *A*bsolute qualifiers (e.g., *no, none, never, only, every, all, always*) are usually false.

☐ *M*ark questions as you read them (i.e., cross out the ones you have completed and place a star next to more difficult ones you need to revisit).

☐ *S*imilar and absurd options can usually be eliminated (Hughes, 1996).

When taking tests that require students to remember and integrate information, students with learning and behavioral problems often interpret test questions incorrectly (Bos & Vaughn, 2002; Schloss et al., 2001). Teaching students the importance of reading instructions carefully and what tasks are required by common keywords can greatly improve their test-taking skills. Table 15–19 details some keywords and what they are likely signaling students to do.

Regardless of the type of tests students take, they must be taught the importance of carefully managing their time; creating study aids in advance; using error-avoidance, deductive reasoning, and guessing strategies; and knowing as much as they can about the test (e.g., predict questions if samples are not provided) before the day of the test (Bos & Vaughn, 2002; Scruggs & Mastropieri, 1992). Without this preparation, test-taking strategies are unlikely to help students succeed. These strategies are directly taught to students using guided and independent practice. Descriptions of these strategies follow:

✔ Time-using strategies: Teaching students techniques to allow them to work quickly and efficiently on the test and when they study for a test.

✔ Study aids strategies: Students who, prior to quizzes or tests, rearrange their notes, develop strategies (e.g., storytelling or mnemonics), or otherwise organize their material are more likely to remember information when tested.

✔ Error-avoidance strategies: Teaching students to (a) pay careful attention to directions, (b) mark their answers carefully, and (c) check their answers.

✔ Deductive reasoning strategies: Teaching students to apply a variety of strategies, such as eliminating incorrect options and using content information, to determine the correct answers.

✔ Guessing strategies: Teaching students to guess efficiently when they do not know the answer.

✔ Test preparation strategies: Students should know something about the test before they take it. For example, students who have reviewed the format of the test (e.g., numbers and types of questions) are more likely to have productive levels of excitement when the test is given, instead of being overwhelmed by it.

Table 15–19   Keywords and what task is signaled

Likely Keywords	What You Need to Do
• *Draw, illustrate, diagram, graph*	Draw a picture.
• *Compare, contrast, analyze, evaluate, relate, criticize*	Compare at least two concepts or terms.
• *Describe, list, outline, define, state*	Briefly describe.
• *Discuss, explain, summarize, interpret, justify*	Requires longer answer/explanation.

Scruggs and Mastropieri (1992) pointed out that teaching students test-taking strategies improves the validity of tests because students' scores will more accurately reflect what they actually know; when students do lose points it will be because they don't know the information rather than because of mistakes such as marking a test answer incorrectly. These researchers distinguish teaching test-taking skills, which involves directly teaching format and other conditions of testing, from teaching to the test, which involves teaching specific items that may appear on a test. Scruggs and Mastropieri (1986) found that by teaching test-taking skills to students with behavioral disabilities and LD, the students gained between 10 to 15 percentile points on standardized tests. Two years later, Scruggs and Mastropieri (1988) found that adolescents with behavioral disorders who were trained in test-taking skills scored significantly higher (almost 50%) on content-area tests than controls who were not trained. In this era of statewide testing to the requirements of No Child Left Behind, such skills are extremely important.[3]

Reference and Research Skills

Traditional reference and research skill instruction has included teaching students how to use encyclopedias, dictionaries, biographical sources (e.g., *Who's Who in America*), almanacs, and card catalogs (Devine, 1987). The arrival of the electronic age and conversion of many library resources to computer or Web-based systems makes these skills no less critical. How we encourage students to access these resources, however, has changed considerably. Teachers can still share some fundamental reference and research strategies and provide the means to practice those skills.

Because students with EBD often lack elemental reference and research skill (Bos & Vaughn, 2002; Hamilton, Seibert, Gardner, & Talbert-Johnson, 2000; Schloss et al., 2001), teachers should start by introducing students to the library (Devine, 1987). Arrange to meet with a librarian who can provide a tour and overview of the resources and, at a later time, teach them how to use the library's electronic database, search tools, and interlibrary loan system. Without this as a starting point, students given an assignment like a research paper will be overwhelmed with the prospect.

After introducing the students to the library and its resources but before asking them to complete a major research assignment, teach them to enjoy research. Playing Scavenger Hunt with a wide variety of requests that might intrigue students can encourage them to find satisfaction in the hunt (Devine, 1987). The following are a few suggestions from Feldman's *When Do Fish Sleep? And Other Imponderables of Everyday Life* (1990):

- ☐ Why do we park on driveways and drive on parkways?
- ☐ Who was the first person who decided to squeeze a cow's udder and drink what came out?
- ☐ Why do we pay tolls at a turnpike?
- ☐ Why is there a light in the fridge and not in the freezer?
- ☐ Why does Goofy stand erect while Pluto remains on all fours? Aren't they both dogs?

After students have completed the Scavenger Hunt, have them brainstorm and select an imponderable. Allow them to research and write a short paper that summarizes and documents their answer. Be sure to monitor their progress at each stage (e.g., development of the question, location of sources and how they confirm their validity, writing, and citing).

At that point, students can be explicitly taught the formal steps for completing a research paper (adapted from Devine, 1987, and Petercsak, 1986), including:

1. Know the library and its resources.
2. Select a topic and know the purpose of the paper.
3. Narrow the topic.
4. Caution students about plagiarism and teach them how to avoid it (Liles & Rozalski, 2004).
5. Begin the search, taking careful notes, particularly for the references/sources.
6. Evaluate the sources, especially what's available electronically.
7. Identify gaps in the references/resources.
8. Construct a reference list.

One of the most difficult steps is to evaluate the source. To practice analyzing different opinions from a wide range of sources (e.g., newspapers, books, magazines, Web, etc.), teams of students may research and debate points and counterpoints using an analysis and remembering strategy like the *SQ3R* (see Table 15–20; Robinson, 1946). Allow a panel of student "experts" to deem one of the teams as "masters of the source."

---

[3]For an excellent guide on teaching students test-taking skills, refer to this source: Scruggs, T. E., & Mastropieri, M.A. (1992). *Teaching tests-taking skills: Helping students show what they know.* Cambridge, MA: Brookline Books.

Table 15–20   SQ3R method

Step	Purpose	Details
1. Surveying	Understand the big picture	☐ Survey the entire book, including preface and table of contents. ☐ Survey the chapters, summaries or conclusions, and subheadings. ☐ Find the pages of your assignment. ☐ Estimate the time you need to complete the assignment.
2. Questioning	Understand the purpose	☐ Ask what you expect to learn, jotting down the question you want answered. ☐ Turn the subheadings into questions. ☐ Be prepared to answer any questions that appear at the beginning or end of the chapter.
3. Reading effectively	Monitor what you are reading	☐ Read actively, checking predictions and unknown vocabulary. ☐ Read and summarize tables, figures, and other visual material. ☐ Skim the less important parts.
4. Reciting	Repeat important points	☐ Repeat and record important concepts. ☐ Retell "stories" or the main points to another student in your own words.
5. Reviewing	Review the big picture, purpose, and details about what you learned	☐ Resurvey the summaries and subheadings. ☐ Reread and answer chapter questions. ☐ Go back to any section that you cannot remember.

Thinking Skills

For students to succeed in school, they must be taught thinking skills (Algozzine et al., 1997; Algozzine, Ysseldyke, & Campbell, 1994; Devine, 1987). Teachers should (a) model thinking skills, (b) teach fact-finding skills, and (c) teach divergent thinking (Algozzine et al., 1997). See Figures 15–7 and 15–8 for two examples of methods to teach thinking skills.

Table 15–21 outlines strategies and tactics for teaching thinking skills. Algozzine and colleagues (1997) suggest a fourth strategy (i.e., teaching learning skills) that will be covered in the next section.

Memory Skills

Teachers of students with disabilities frequently have to assist their students with academic tasks from the general education classes. Often these tasks will involve memorization. Unfortunately, students with EBD may have difficulty recalling academic information (Scruggs & Mastropieri, 2000), which often leads to school failure on academic tests (Scruggs & Mastropieri, 1986). If teachers can teach their students simple ways to remember information and concepts, these skills will certainly allow them to perform better academically (Bos & Vaughn, 2002; Scruggs & Mastropieri, 1986, 2000). The method for teaching students

Figure 15–7   Semantic map of the components of effective reading instruction

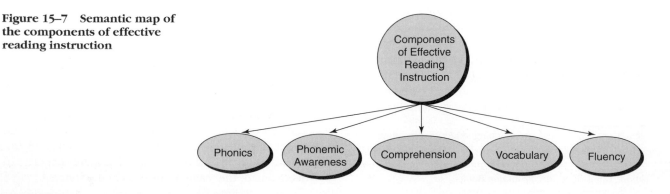

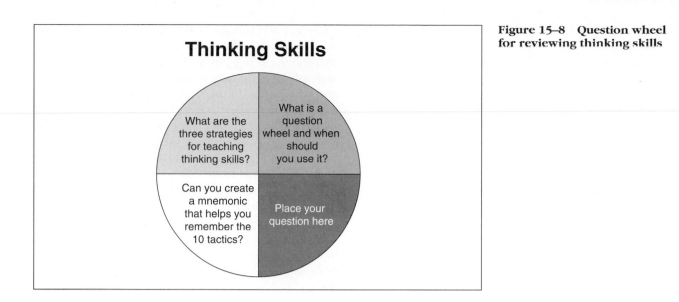

Figure 15–8 Question wheel for reviewing thinking skills

Thinking Skills

What are the three strategies for teaching thinking skills?

What is a question wheel and when should you use it?

Can you create a mnemonic that helps you remember the 10 tactics?

Place your question here

Table 15–21 Thinking skills

Strategy	Tactic	Description
Model thinking skills	1. Teach think-aloud strategies	Teach students how to use think aloud strategies by talking as you solve a problem. For instance, when deciding how to respond to a question about the cause of the U.S. Civil War, start by stating, "Okay, I know that economic and social differences including slavery, were points of contention between the North and South. What else should I consider before responding?"
	2. Use HDYKT	Teach students to critically evaluate statements that other students make by encouraging them to ask "How do you know that?" (HDYKT) whenever they are presented with facts. Eventually, students will grow accustomed to providing evidence for their assertions.
	3. Teach predicting and correction procedures	Before reading Frank Stockton's *The Lady or the Tiger?* have students predict what the short story is about. Before reading the last page, have them predict, based on the story, whether it is the lady or the tiger behind the door. After reading the ending, students must check their predictions against what happened. Most important, to teach students to actively monitor what they know, have them answer, "Were your predictions right or wrong; why?"
Teach fact-finding skills	1. Use story maps, webs, and other visual representations	Teach students to make story maps, webs, or other visual representations to help organize what they are reading. For instance, picture a triangle with each side represented by (a) model thinking skills, (b) teach fact-finding skills, and (c) teach divergent thinking). Write the statement "How to Teach Thinking Skills" in the center of the triangle. See figure 15–7 for an example of a semantic map.
	2. Use question wheels	Given a topic, have students brainstorm questions that assess their knowledge. Check students' understanding by playing this game: Place all questions on the wheel and have a student or team spin the wheel and answer the question. Ensure that all students can answer the questions. See Figure 15-8 for a wheel summarizing some of the thinking skills you need to know.
Teach Divergent Thinking	1. Use K-W-L (Ogle, 1986)	Teach students how to use K-W-L to monitor their understanding before ("What do I *K*now?" and "What do I *W*ant to Learn?") and after ("What did I *L*earn?"). Encourage them to share their K-W-Ls with other students and to develop additional questions that they should research.
	2. Use think-pair-share (Kagan, 1994)	After assigning students to groups of four, teach students to follow a three-step process: (a) *Think*—given a problem or questions, students are to silently "think" of responses, (b) *pair*—ask students to "pair" with another student in the group and discuss their answer; and (c) *share*—the pairs "share" their answers, determining the most important points the foursome should share with the class.

Source: Adapted from Algozzine, Ysseldyke, and Elliot, 1997.

memory skills that has the greatest support in the empirical literature is the use of mnemonics.

Mnemonics are memory-enhancing strategies that have been highly successful in improving memory for specific content (Mastropieri & Scruggs, 1998). In a meta-analysis of the effects of mnemonics, Mastropieri and Scruggs (1989) found an overall effect size of 1.62 standard deviation, which is an overwhelmingly positive effect size (Forness, Kavale, Blum, & Lloyd, 1997; Lloyd, Forness, & Kavale, 1998; Scruggs & Mastropieri, 2000). In an updated meta-analysis, Scruggs and Mastropieri (2000) found an identical effect size of 1.62. Moreover, the potential effects of mnemonics instruction were positive for all groups and the particular academic content area taught (e.g., science, social studies, vocabulary) made no difference. Scruggs and Mastropieri (2000) noted that mnemonic strategies are most effective on one aspect of education—the recall of academic content— and that teachers of students with disabilities should strongly consider the use of these strategies.

The seminal research on the use of mnemonics in teaching students with disabilities has been conducted by Mastropieri and Scruggs of George Mason University.[4] These researchers and others have investigated mnemonic strategies such as acronyms, acrostics, keywords, pegwords, methods of place, and rhymes or songs to help students remember information (Algozzine et al., 1997; Brigham, Scruggs, & Mastropieri, 1995; Bulgren & Lenz, 1996; Bulgren, Schumaker, & Deschler, 1994; Condus, Marshall, & Miller, 1986; Custer et al., 1990; Devine, 1987; Fulk, Lohman, & Belfiore, 1997; Graves & Levin, 1989; Hughes, 1996; King-Sears, Mercer, & Sindelar, 1992; Mastropieri & Scruggs, 1989, 1991, 1998; Petercsak, 1986; Rafoth, Leal, & DeFabo, 1993; Scruggs & Mastropieri, 2000; Willoughby & Wood, 1999).

Table 15–22 provides a summary and examples of various mnemonic devices.

Note-Taking Skills

Teachers in secondary settings spend at least half of their class time presenting information through lectures (Putnam et al., 1993). Because many "students who have trouble taking notes usually try to write too much, thereby missing many of the important points" (Schloss et al., 2001, p. 215), it is essential to teach students how to take notes. To take effective notes, students must learn to write down fewer words without sacrificing understanding

(Devine, 1987; Suritsky & Hughes, 1996). Teachers can help students learn to use abbreviations (i.e., *abbr.*), modified shorthand (e.g., *bx* for *behavior*), a simple strategy such as recording only subject and verb, or organizing notes visually (e.g., the herringbone technique; Custer et al., 1990). Another note-taking strategy commonly taught to students with learning and behavioral problems is the three-column system (Bos & Vaughn, 2002). This system (see Figure 15–9) is designed to allow students to follow up their classroom lecture with (a) additional notes from reading about the same topic, and (b) a short summary, without allowing students to rely on passive strategies (i.e., underlining or highlighting) that often have little value (Custer et al., 1990; Devine, 1987). Although these strategies are particularly effective because they are active processes and students can generalize their use to other classes, another effective means of helping students is to provide completed notes or a summary of the material to students in advance (Suritsky & Hughes, 1996).

For any given class presentation, teachers often assume that this "summary" should include an entire set of notes. Research, however, indicates that completed notes may not be the most effective way to assist students. Researchers (e.g., Hamilton et al., 2000; Kiewra, Benton, Kim, Risch, & Christensen, 1995; Kiewra, DuBois, et al., 1991; Kiewra, Mayer, Christensen, Kim, & Risch, 1991; Kiewra et al., 1997; Robinson & Kiewra, 1995) have found strikingly similar results. These studies found that students who took no notes performed poorly and students who did not review their notes performed as poorly as those who took no notes. Moreover, students who reviewed other students' notes performed better than those who took no notes. When given the option of reviewing notes after the session and note-taking choices ranging from (a) none—no notes could be taken; (b) blank page—blank pages were provided for note taking; (c) outline—an outline of major points and subtopics was provided; and (d) matrix—a visual display of major points/subtopics was provided, students' performance was affected by how the students took and reviewed their notes. When students took and reviewed their own notes, they scored higher on recall and relational tests than any other condition. Outline or matrix notes were the most effective note-taking strategies, vastly superior to other means of recalling (e.g., contrary to popular opinion, essay writing in not a generally effective means to help students synthesize information for later recall and relational testing). When teachers use advance organizers such as outline and matrix notes, therefore, and encourage active note reviewing (without a reliance on essays), they are providing essential tools to students who struggle with note taking.

---

[4]For an excellent guide on using mnemonic strategies, refer to this source: Mastropieri, M.A., & Scruggs, T. E (1991). *Teaching students ways to remember: Strategies for learning mneumonically*. Cambridge, MA: Brookline Books.

Table 15–22   Memory devices: strategies, definitions, and examples

Mnemonics	An elaboration (Rafoth, Leal, & DeFabo, 1993) strategy (e.g., analogy) that allows students to remember a concept(s) by creating a unique or meaningful relationship. Mnemonic strategies are enjoyable, engaging, and highly successful (Scruggs & Mastropieri, 2000).	A mnemonic for remembering the theory of plate tectonics and Wegener's continental drift is the idea that paper plates floating in a tub of water will behave similarly (e.g., when they collide, one will ride on top of another—this is why earthquakes happen and mountains form).
Acronyms and acrostics	A chunking strategy that allows students to remember a concept(s) by providing a word or sentence that summarizes components of the concept(s).	An acrostic for remembering the order of algebraic operations is "**P**lease **E**xcuse **M**y **D**ear **A**unt **S**ally," which stands for **P**arentheses, **E**xponents, **M**ultiplication-**D**ivision, **A**ddition-**S**ubtraction.
Keyword method	A visualization strategy that allows students to remember a concept(s) by creating a picture that summarizes the concept(s). The keyword method is an effective and versatile mnemonic that enhances concreteness and meaningfulness of new information because it closely ties new information to students' prior knowledge (Scruggs & Mastropieri, 2000).	A keyword for remembering the classification system in biology (i.e., kingdom, phylum, class, order, family, genus, and species) is picturing **K**ing **P**hillip standing on a **C**an **O**f **F**ried **G**reen **S**pam.
Pegword method	This method uses a system of rhyming pegwords to enhance memory for numbered or ordered information (Scruggs & Mastropieri, 2000). Examples of pegwords include *one = sun; two = shoe; three = tree; four = door; five = hive; six = sticks, seven = heaven, eight = gate; nine = vine; ten = hen.*	To help students remember that spiders have eight legs, display a picture of a spider spinning a web on a gate (Scruggs & Mastropieri, 2000).
Method of Place	A visualization and association strategy that allows students to remember a concept(s) by having them associate a portion of the concepts with a series of places	A method of place for remembering memory devices is to visualize a baseball infield, "seeing" acronym pitching to acrostics, with mnemonic on first, keyword on second, place at shortstop, and rhyme on third base.
Rhymes or songs	An auditory strategy that allows students to remember a concept(s) by providing a catchy little ditty.	A rhyme for remembering the number of days in the months of the year is "Thirty days hath September, April, June, and November. All the rest have thirty-one except February alone, which has eight and a score, until leap year gives it one day more."

FIGURE 15-9

Sample three-column system

Student's name _____   Topic _____   Class _____

Key Concepts Source: _____ (Complete before class)	Class Notes Date: _____ (Complete during class)	Reading Notes Source: _____ (Complete after class)
One-sentence summary:	One-paragraph summary:	Two-paragraph summary:

Summary

Many teachers assume that students know how to memorize, listen, take notes and tests, conduct research, and cite references. For students with EBD, however, these study skills are often underdeveloped or missing (Bos & Vaughn, 2002; Schloss et al., 2001). If students are to succeed academically, they must develop these skills (Ellett, 1993; Wood, Woloshyn, et al., 1999). Instruction in these skills has been shown effective with a variety of students (Fremouw & Feindler, 1978; Gall et al., 1990; Tuckman, 2003), and specific strategies can and should be integrated into the regular classroom curriculum (Marshak, 1984).

Chapter Summary

Meaningful instruction is a critical component of successful programs for students with EBD; however, teachers of students with EBD spend less time on active academic instruction and their students engage in lower rates of academic behavior than do teachers and students in general education. In fact, classrooms for students with EBD have been described as consisting of an impoverished academic program with a limited and ineffective set of teaching strategies. A major reason there is such a limited focus on academics in the field of educating students with EBD is the inadequate research on academic instruction of these students. The purpose of this chapter was to examine the research base in teaching reading, writing, mathematics, and study skills.

CHAPTER 16

Teaching Students with EBD III: Planning Instruction and Monitoring Student Performance

Mitchell L. Yell, Todd W. Busch, and David C. Rogers

Focus Questions

- Why is planning instruction important?
- How can teachers plan instruction in an effective manner?
- What is the systematic teaching and recording tactic?
- How can teachers write effective lesson plans?
- Why is it important to monitor student progress?
- How can teachers monitor their students' progress?
- What is curriculum-based measurement?

Planning instruction is one of a teacher's most important responsibilities (Mager, 1997; Price & Nelson, 2007; Rosenberg et al., 2008). This is because when teachers systematically plan their instruction they increase the probability of effective teaching, which results in greater student achievement (Wilen, Ishler, Hutchinson, & Kindsvatter, 2004). Thus, the most effective teachers spend time planning their lessons. In fact, researchers have found that teachers who set specific objectives and develop detailed lesson plans are more effective than teachers who do not plan their instruction (Algozzine et al., 1997; Mager, 1997, Orlich, Harder, Callahan, Trevisian, & Brown, 2007; Rosenberg, O'Shea, & O'Shea, 2008). Additionally, Good and Brophy (2008) reported that teachers who plan and organize teacher-controlled and structured lessons with a strong academic focus and high rates of engaged time and hold students accountable for their learning tend to have higher student achievement. Careful and thorough instructional planning is especially important with students with EBD because often these students are behind their nondisabled peers, and if teachers are to close this achievement gap they will need to teach systematically using evidence-based procedures. The purpose of this chapter is to examine how teachers can plan their instruction, which includes planning what to teach, how to teach, and how to evaluate the results of instruction.

First, we examine the nature of planning, focusing on what teacher planning is and why it is important that teachers engage in planning. Second, we discuss prerequisites for effective planning. Third, we discuss ideas on planning what to teach and how to teach—for example, we review the Systematic Teaching and Recording Tactic (START), developed by Deno and his colleagues, for both short- and long-range instructional planning. Fourth, we address a procedure that can be used to monitor student progress.

THE NATURE OF INSTRUCTIONAL PLANNING

A systematic and focused approach to planning instruction is a characteristic of effective instruction. Clark and Yinger (1980) reported that teachers spend about 12 hours per week engaged in instructional planning. Additionally, research on teacher planning shows that most teachers begin the planning process with general ideas about the subject matter and then think through issues such as classroom management and instructional time as they continue to modify and elaborate their plans. Most planning is in the teacher's mind, with little written down (Earle, 1992). According to Wilen et al. (2004), teachers who develop or adopt routines for planning instruction tend to become more systematic in their planning activities. Unfortunately, teachers often do not plan their instructional systematically; rather, they tend to make decisions about instructional content and then ignore objectives and evaluation (Wilen et al., 2004). Teachers need to systematically plan their objectives, lesson content, methods, and evaluation procedures.

PLANNING WHAT TO TEACH

According to Wilen et al. (2004), the planning process should begin with determining learning content, move to developing objectives, choosing methods and strategies to teach the content, and then deciding how to evaluate if the students achieve the lesson objectives.

Using IEP Goals to Guide Instruction

Educational programming for students with disabilities is developed on the basis of the goals written in a student's IEP. Thus, the IEP becomes the foundation for a teacher's planning for his or her students, in both academic and functional areas. Moreover, because correctly written IEP annual goals must be measurable, and the IEP must include a description of the methods to measure student progress, the criteria that specify acceptable performance toward meeting the annual goal should be available to the teacher. The teacher's task is then to plan a program of instruction that enables a student to reach his or her long-term goals.

For example, if one of Billy's IEP goals is in reading (e.g., In 32 weeks when given a reading passage from the second-grade basal reader *Sunburst* from the Houghton Mifflin reading series and 1 minute in which to read, Billy will correctly read aloud 48 words) and he is placed in a resource room for 2 hours per day, one of the areas in which Billy's teacher will plan instruction will be in reading. Additionally, the assessments that were completed prior to IEP development may be useful for the teacher in planning instruction if the assessments were designed to analyze a student's academic problems (e.g., criterion-referenced tests, curriculum-based measurement). If, however, the assessment was solely designed to determine edibility and the assessments used were primarily norm-referenced tests, the teacher will need to do additional testing to determine what the student should be taught. As Salvia and Hughes (1990) stated, "information from a careful assessment of achievement is a necessary but insufficient condition for planning instruction" (p. 26). Nonetheless, knowing what the student needs to learn is the starting point of instructional planning.

Using Assessment to Guide Instruction

After a teacher knows a student's needs, as reflected in the present levels of academic achievement and functional performance (PLAAFP) statement of the IEP, and the goal of a student's program of instruction, as reflected in the measurable annual goals, he or she may begin the instructional planning process. Often a teacher will have limited choices regarding the specific curriculum because his or her school district uses a particular curriculum with all students at specific grade levels. For example, a school district may use the *Open Court* reading series published by Science Research Associates/McGraw-Hill. In this situation, the teacher will need to determine (a) where to place a student in the curriculum, or (b) how to supplement the curriculum to meet the student's needs.

Often published curriculum will contain a scope and sequence. This refers to a plan for teaching the particular curriculum according to the scope, the instructional objectives of the curricula, and the sequence, the order in which the objectives are taught. Such curricula will often include placement tests that can be given to students. The purpose of these tests is to assess a student's skills and mastery of content in the curriculum and to provide guidance as to where a student's knowledge ends or mastery is emerging. The teacher then can place the student at the appropriate level in terms of scope and sequence, where instruction should begin (Salvia & Hughes, 1990).

Unfortunately, not all published curricula present skills in such an organized fashion, nor do they have placement tests. It is up to the teachers to evaluate the components required to successfully complete complex tasks. Teachers could develop their own scope and sequence and develop informal assessments. Because teachers need to be able to use these assessments to gain an understanding of the student's mastery of the skills or content to be taught, the tests must contain enough questions per content area (e.g., sight words, long division problems) to allow them to make a reasonably accurate decision about where in a curriculum to begin instruction (Hosp & Ardoin, 2007; Salvia & Hughes, 1990). This is extremely important in planning instruction because if teachers' decisions are not accurate and they plan and implement instruction at an inappropriate place in the curriculum sequence, it is likely that valuable instructional time will be lost presenting instruction

that does not address the students' needs (Hosp & Ardoin, 2007).

Informal teacher-made tests can be developed in any academic area. When developing such tests, teachers should (a) determine prerequisite skills that are needed to access the curriculum, (b) outline the scope and sequence of the curriculum, and (c) develop a test to determine the student's level of performance in the scope and sequence of the curriculum. (For elaboration on assessment see Chapter 3. For greater in-depth information on conducting and understanding assessments of students with disabilities, refer to Layton and Lock (2008) and Venn (2007).

Using State Standards to Guide Instruction

The No Child Left Behind Act of 2001 requires that all states develop academic content standards to in order to guide the instruction of students in the general curriculum. Academic content standards are goals that were meant to standardize the learning experiences of all students in the content areas by providing guides for teachers. No Child Left Behind requires goals in reading and mathematics; however, states have developed standards in other areas as well (e.g., science, social studies). Because state standards determine what teachers are expected to teach at specific grade levels, general education teachers will often use state standards to plan instruction.

IDEA requires that eligible students with disabilities have access to the general education curriculum. Thus, special education teachers must determine what this means for each of their students. According to Nolet and McLaughlin (2000), special educators must ensure that their students have an opportunity to learn the important content reflected in state standards. Special education teachers, therefore, should know the standards in their states and use them in planning instruction. Moreover, IEP teams should know the standards when planning a student's supplementary services and program modification to enable him or her to participate in general education.

Most states publish their academic content standards and make them available through their Web sites. Table 16–1 contains the URLs of two Web sites that link to all the states' academic content standards.

PLANNING HOW TO TEACH

After a teacher has determined what to teach a particular student, he or she must determine how they will teach the student. Teachers make the how-to-teach decisions in

Table 16–1 Web sites on state curriculum standards

Website	Description	URL
National Education Association	Contains links to curriculum standards for all states and many professional organizations	www.nea.org/classroom/curr-standards.html
Education World	Contains links to all state standards by topic and grade level (also has good information on lesson planning)	www.education-world.com/standards/state/toc/index.shtml#arts

order to identify types of strategies and instruction that they will be providing to a student. How-to-teach decisions should be based on the principles of effective instruction (see Chapter 14). That is, teachers should instruct their students using evidence-based procedures. For example, when teaching a curriculum that includes specific skills to be mastered, teachers should instruct students in accordance with the six teaching functions of (a) daily review, (b) presentation, (c) guided practice, (d) feedback and corrections, (e) independent practice, and (f) weekly and monthly reviews (Rosenshine & Stevens, 1986).

Ultimately, how-to-teach decisions are made based on progress monitoring data that the teacher collects. If the data show that a student is learning new skills or content is mastered, new objectives are selected as the student moves through the scope and sequence of the curriculum. If, however, the data show that the student is not making adequate progress toward meeting his or her annual goals, the teacher should modify or supplement the curriculum. We will discuss how progress monitoring data can be collected and instructional programs can be modified in a systematic manner later in this chapter.

Teachers generally develop both long-range plans and short-range or daily lesson plans. The long-range plans usually involve course or program goals and are developed for a semester or a year (Wilen et al., 2004). The daily lesson plan typically is written in greater detail because it is the organizational blueprint of the lesson that will be taught. Next we discuss a method for organizing long-range and short-range plans.

USING THE SYSTEMATIC TEACHING AND RECORDING TACTIC (START) FOR LONG-RANGE PLANNING

After teachers have determined what they are going to teach and how they are going to teach, they must begin the long-range planning process. Long-range planning begins with the student's present abilities, as listed in the current level of educational performance, and ends with what the teacher and IEP team believes are the student's present and future skill needs, as listed in the student's measurable annual goal contained in his or her IEP. Thus, the long-range plan is a teacher's strategy for bringing the student from where he or she is in an area of need to where the teacher wants the student to be. It is the path that will be followed in determining a student's instructional program (Wolery et al., 1988).

Additionally, IDEA requires that annual goals include a method for monitoring student progress and a procedure for informing a student's parents of their child's progress toward meeting his or her goals. Therefore, long-range planning must also include a progress monitoring component. A procedure that teachers may use to systematically develop long-range plans that include a progress monitoring component is to adopt the Systematic Teaching and Recording Tactic (START) developed by Dr. Stanley Deno and colleagues at the University of Minnesota.

In 1981, Deno and colleagues developed a systematic instructional planning procedure they called the basic instructional plan (BIP). BIPs were initially designed to provide teachers of students with special needs a systematic format or procedure for long-range planning of instruction. Moreover, when BIPs were used in conjunction with progress monitoring procedures, the plans would allow teachers to evaluate the effectiveness of their instruction and make systematic changes in the important variable of instruction listed in the BIP.

In 2001, Rogers, Deno, and Markell began referring to the BIP as the Systematic Teaching and Recording Tactic (START). This was done for two reasons: (a) After the passage of the Individuals with Disabilities Education Act Amendments of 1997 the acronym *BIP* was used to refer to "behavior intervention plan"; and (b) the plan represented a good place for teachers to "start" developing effective instruction for their new students. The acronym served as a helpful reminder. The START is depicted in Figure 16–1.

START specifies an outline of an instructional plan that consists of alterable variables of instruction (columns) and

FIGURE 16–1

START form

Systematic Teaching and Recording Tactic (START)

Student's name	Subject	Date	Teacher's name

IEP goal

Instructional Activities	Arrangement	Time	Materials	Motivation	Evaluation Criteria

Source: Adapted from D. C. Rogers, S. L. Deno, and M. Markell, 2001. "The systematic teaching and recording tactic (S.T.A.R.T.): A generic reading strategy." *Intervention in School and Clinic, 37*(2), 96–100.

the specific classroom instructional activities throughout the course of a lesson (rows). The variables represented by the columns are aspects of the teaching situation that can be modified with appropriate changes or combination of changes that hopefully will lead to student growth or performance improvements. These include (a) instructional activities; (b) arrangement (i.e., teacher–student ratio); (c) amount of time to complete a task; (d) materials and motivational strategies; and (e) evaluation strategies. (The column for evaluation activities was added in 2001 by Rogers, Deno, & Markell.) We discuss these variables in the following text.

First, START specifies the instructional activities that the teacher will use. A careful assessment of the students' strengths and weaknesses is needed to understand what type of instruction should be provided. As a starting point, teachers should used research-based strategies for all instructional procedures listed in START. For example, if a reading assessment showed that a student had a

problem in fluency and his or her teacher decided to begin reading instruction with repeated readings to develop fluency, the teacher writes "Repeated readings" in START under "Instructional Activities" (column 1). Second, START specifies the terms of the student–teacher ratio. For example, if the teacher worked with two students in this activity, he or she writes "2:1" under "Arrangement" (column 2). Third, the teacher lists the number of minutes spent in the repeated readings activity. This is recorded in START under "Time" (column 3). Fourth, the teacher specifies the motivational strategies. For example, if the teacher awards points to the student for completing the activity, he or she may write "point reinforcers" under "Motivational Strategies" (column 4). Finally, the teacher specifies the method of evaluation. For example, if the teacher is graphing student results and comparing current efforts with previous efforts, he or she may write "Graphing and comparing current to previous efforts" under "Evaluation Criteria" (column 6). This is

FIGURE 16–2

START reading form

Systematic Teaching and Recording Tactic (START)

Student's name Billy   Subject Reading   Date   Teacher's name

IEP goal: In 32 weeks when given a reading passage from the basal reading series, level 4, and 1 minute in which to read, Billy will correctly read aloud 48 words.

Instructional Activities	Arrangement	Time	Materials	Motivation	Evaluation Criteria
Phonics exercises	4:1	10 min.	*Crack the Code*	Praise	90% correct from phonics questions from lesson
Repeated readings	1:1 (alternate students)	2 min.	Reading passage of student's choice	Graphing progress	Graphing to track student improvement toward goal
Direct instruction	4:1	10 min.	*Corrective Reading* series	Praise	Teacher questioning
Comprehensive activities	4:1	20 min.	Reading passage of teacher's choice	Points	90% correct student responding to questions on passage content
CBM and word practice (alternate students)	1:1	15 min.	Basal textbook and monitoring materials	Graphing progress	Graph comparing trend line to goal line

depicted in Figure 16–2. Figures 16–2, 16–3, and 16–4 show STARTs for Billy in reading, writing, and mathematics. These figures represent examples of a teacher's long-range plans for Billy's instruction.

WRITING DAILY LESSON PLANS USING START

After the long-range plans have been developed, the teacher can then plan the student's instructional program on a short-term or daily basis. These short-term plans represent smaller steps that will be taken to reach the goals of the long-range plan and the IEP. For example, the long-range plan may end with the goal of a student reading 84 words aloud in 1 minute. The daily lesson plans are intended to prescribe the instruction that will enable the student to reach that goal.

Daily lesson plans that are developed in a systematic manner and contain detailed instructional information are useful because they provide a teacher with the (a) objectives of the lesson, (b) schedule of learning activities, and (c) method for monitoring or evaluating student progress. There are many different forms for daily lesson plans and no single way to write them. Whatever form is used by a teacher should be user-friendly and well organized. We suggest a modified START to develop and write daily lesson plans.

The START daily lesson plan specifies an outline of an instructional plan for either a single class, as is typically the case in a resource room setting, or a number of classes, as typically will be the case in a self-contained setting. The class or classes are listed along with the instructional objective. Columns include the subheadings "Instructional Activities," "Materials," "Time," and "Evaluation." The START daily lesson plan form is depicted in Figure 16–5.

Instructional Objectives

The purpose of instructional objectives is to specify what students should know and be able to do as a result of instruction (Bigge et al., 1999; Mager, 1997; Wolery et al.,

FIGURE 16-3

START written expression form

Systematic Teaching and Recording Tactic (START)

Student's Name Billy   Subject Language   Date   Teacher's name

IEP goal: In 32 weeks when given a story starter and 3 minutes in which to write a story, Billy will write 42 correct word sequences.

Instructional Activities	Arrangement	Time	Materials	Motivation	Evaluation Criteria
Curriculum-based	4:1	10 min.	Story starter and monitoring materials	Graph	Graph comparing data to goal line
Presentation on writing strategy	4:1	20 min.	Expressive writing lesson	Graph	Teacher questions
Guided practice	4:1	20 min.	Teacher-made activities	Praise	Expressive writing exercises
Independent practice	4:1	10 min.	Worksheet	Points	90% correct on worksheet

FIGURE 16-4

START mathematics form

Systematic Teaching and Recording Tactic (START)

Student's name Billy   Subject Math   Date   Teacher's name

IEP goal: By the time of the annual IEP review in 32 weeks, when given a mixed single-digit addition and subtraction probe and 2 minutes in which to work, Billy will compute 48 correct digits.

Instructional Activities	Arrangement	Time	Materials	Motivation	Evaluation Criteria
Daily review	4:1	10 min.	Overhead	Praise	Teacher questioning
Presentation	4:1	20 min.	Connecting math concepts	Graphs	Connecting math probes
Guided practice	4:1	10 min.	Overhead	Praise	90% correct on practice problems
Independent practice	4:1	15 min.	Worksheet (math curriculum)	Points	90% correct on worksheet
Math probes of daily activity	4:1	5 min.	Teacher-made probes	Graphs	Graph formative evaluation

FIGURE 16–5

START daily lesson plan

Systematic Teaching and Recording Tactic (START) Daily Lesson Plan

Student's name	Subject	Date	Teacher's name

Instructional objective

Instructional Activities	Materials	Time	Evaluation

1988). A lesson plan is a written description of how students will progress toward a specific objective; therefore, the objective or objectives are the basis of the lesson activities and should be the first step in lesson planning (Price & Nelson, 2007). Unfortunately, when teachers develop objectives they tend to do so after the rest of the lesson is planned, if they do it at all (Wilen et al., 2004). The reason for beginning lesson planning with a clear lesson objective is that it will help him or her select the instructional content and procedures and the method of finding out if the intended outcome was actually accomplished (Mager, 1997).

Characteristics of an Instructional Objective In his seminal work on writing instructional objectives, Mager (1970) asserted that a well-stated instructional objective lets the teacher and others know what the teacher intends for his or her students to achieve. Mager also stated that an instructional objective has three characteristics. First, an objective must describe an intended outcome, rather than the process for achieving those outcomes. For example, providing guided practice on long division problems is part of the instructional process (i.e., what the teacher does to help the student learn long division), so to write an objective such as "the teacher will provide guided practice on long division" or "the teacher will lecture on civil war history" is incorrect because it does not describe the intended outcome of instruction. Second, an objective is specific and measurable, rather than broad and intangible. Objectives that are broad, general, or intangible do not help teachers make good instructional decisions. For example, "will develop a positive attitude" or "will picture in her head" cannot be measured. Third, an objective is concerned with students, not teachers. This means that objectives should describe a student's performance, not that of the teacher. Instruction is successful only when it succeeds in changing student behavior in the intended manner. If instruction is going to accomplish the desired outcomes, the teacher must have a clear picture of the desired outcome. Wolery and colleagues (1988) also noted that an instructional objective (a) provides teachers with a focus for their instruction, (b) becomes a standard or a marker by which a student's progress can be evaluated, and (c) is a useful tool for communicating accurate information about students.

Components of an Instructional Objective A well-written instructional objective has three components: (a) behavior, (b) conditions, and (c) criterion for acceptable performance (Mager, 1997; Wolery et al., 1988). The first part of the objective identifies the expected behavior that the student will perform to demonstrate that the objective has been accomplished. It is very important that this behavior be specified in observable and measurable terms. That is, the behavior must be something that the teacher can see, hear, and count. Examples of words describing observable and measurable behaviors include *prints*, *writes*, *reads aloud*, *describes*, *solves*, and *names*. Examples of words describing behaviors that are neither observable nor measurable include *understand*, *appreciate*, *know*, *believe*, and *discovers*. It is extremely important that the precise target behavior that the student is to perform be specified in the objective; without it neither the teacher nor the student will know if the skill has been acquired because it will be impossible to evaluate the effectiveness of the instruction (Wolery et al., 1988).

The second part of an objective specifies the condition under which the target behavior will occur. In other words, the objective must describe what the student will be doing when he or she has demonstrated mastery of the objective (Mager, 1997). The conditions of the student's performance of the behavior should include measurement conditions (e.g., amount of time), environmental conditions (e.g., the setting), materials (instructional materials provided to the student), and amount of teacher assistance (e.g., verbal cues from the teacher). According to Mager (1997), the conditions component of the objective must add enough description to make it clear to everyone concerned what the teacher expects from the learner. Examples of phrases describing conditions under which the behavior will occur include *computing long division problems when given worksheet*, *correctly reading sight words when shown flashcards*, and *correctly writing words when given a story starter*. Nonexamples include *when given instruction, as the result of teaching*, and *after thinking about*.

The third component of an objective describes the criterion of acceptable performance or how well the student will need to perform the task or behavior to show that he or she has demonstrated mastery of the objective. The criterion is needed to enable the teacher to have a definitive marker of when a student has met his or her

objective (Mager, 1997; Wolery et al., 1988). When the objective has been met, a teacher can move on to teaching skills.

There are a number of ways that teachers may write the criterion for acceptable performance. According to Wolery et al., (1988), the most basic and frequently used form is to specify an accuracy criterion, such as percentage correct (e.g., *90% of double-digit multiplication problems requiring carrying*). Speed, accuracy, and fluency may also be used as criteria for acceptable performance (e.g., *reads aloud 124 words in 1 minute with less than two errors*). Examples of appropriately written criterion statements include *24 per minute with 100% accuracy*, *answer 9 out of 10 factual questions*, and *48 correct digits within 5 minutes*. Examples of inappropriate criterion statements include *as measured by teacher observation*, *write a story with 100% accuracy*, *complete problems at his own pace*. According to Price and Nelson (2007), the criterion statement of an objective must pass the stranger test. That is, the statement communicates the criterion for acceptable performance so clearly and specifically that a stranger (e.g., another teacher, a substitute teacher) will interpret the statement just as the writer does. There is no room for interpretation.

Instructional Activities

The second component of the START daily lesson plan is the instructional activity. In the instructional activities part of the lesson, the teacher specifies what he or she will be using and what the students will be doing. The activities the teacher uses during this section of the lesson typically begin with the lesson opening, which includes focusing the students and briefly reviewing previous learning. The lesson activity continues with teacher instruction, which includes frequent teacher checks for student understanding. This section of the lesson usually ends with guided and independent practice activities, with the teacher offering feedback and corrections to the students. The instructional activities, therefore, encompass five of the six teaching functions listed by Rosenshine (1983). These five teaching functions are (a) daily review, (b) presentation, (c) guided practice, (d) corrections and feedback, and (e) independent practice. (For elaborations on Rosenshine's teaching functions see Chapter 14.)

When beginning the daily instructional activity, the teacher should prepare his or her students for the upcoming activity. This can be accomplished by getting the students' attention, and telling the students what they will be doing during the lesson and why they will be doing it. Price and Nelson (2007) suggested that the teacher open with a statement that describes the objective and purpose of the lesson and why the skill or knowledge being taught is important. Once the students are attentive, the teacher may begin by conducting a brief daily review. The purpose of the daily review is to (a) make certain that the students are firm in their knowledge of previously taught skills or material, (b) provide the additional practice in the previous skill area or material, and (c) connect the previous learning with the new information or skill to be taught (Rosenshine & Stevens, 1986).

The instruction that is directly related to the lesson objective occurs in this phase of the daily lesson plan (Price & Nelson, 2007). Typically, the instruction phase will consist of (a) teacher presentation, (b) corrections and feedback, (c) guided practice, and (d) independent practice. For further elaboration of teacher presentation, guided practice, corrections and feedback, and independent practice see Chapter 14.

One of the most important tasks of the teacher during this phase is to get his or her students actively engaged in learning. This can be done by planning activities that require student responding (e.g., asking frequent questions and calling on students to provide answers, using response cards, asking for choral responding, asking for written responses).

Because practice activities are a key to student success in learning, the instruction component of the lesson should include opportunities for guided or supervised practice and independent practice (Price & Nelson, 2007; Rosenshine & Stevens, 1986). Practice activities help build student fluency and provide information regarding student progress in the skill or activity. For example, if students are making numerous errors during the practice activities, they likely have not achieved mastery of the skill and need reteaching. If students are responding correctly during the practice activities, the teacher may move to another activity or skill after conducting the guided and independent practice.

Materials and Time

The second and third columns in the daily START lesson plan are the materials and time for the lesson. Under the materials column the teacher should list the lesson materials that will be used for each instructional activity. Under the time column the teacher should list the amount of time that will be devoted to each instructional activity.

Evaluation

The lesson is followed by an evaluation of the students' learning as described in the lesson objective (Price & Nelson, 2007). Effective teachers constantly check for student understanding during the lesson and practice activities so they can adjust their instruction if necessary. The evaluation phase of the lesson, however, involves more formal evaluation activities. Typically, such evaluation will occur at the end of the lesson and provide the information needed for the teacher to determine whether his or her students have mastered the lesson objective. Price and Nelson (2007) asserted that a well-written lesson objective describes what a student will do to demonstrate mastery of the learning objective, so this part of the daily lesson plan describes the formal plan for determining student mastery.

Figure 16-6 depicts a daily lesson plan using the START procedure.

MONITORING STUDENT PROGRESS

In Chapter 4 we discussed the importance of monitoring students' progress. IDEA requires that all IEPs include statements of (a) how a student's progress toward his or her annual goals will be measured and (b) how parents will be informed of their child's progress. This means that IEP teams must determine or adopt effective data-based methods for monitoring students' progress. An important decision that the IEP team must make concerns the nature of the data that the teacher must collect (Heflin & Simpson, 1998). Anecdotal data and subjective judgments are not appropriate for monitoring progress and should not be the basis of a teacher's data collection procedures. The most appropriate data collection systems are those that rely on quantitative data in which target behaviors can be measured, graphed, and visually inspected (e.g., curriculum-based measurement, direct observation) to monitor a student's progress toward achieving his or her goals.

Because students with EBD frequently have deficits in basic skills areas (Kauffman & Landrum, 2008), having a system for monitoring their progress in the areas of reading, mathematics, and written expression is extremely important. Progress monitoring allows teachers to frequently and systematically collect data in order to determine if their instruction is helping their students master the basic skills. Moreover, when teachers know how their students are performing in learning important skills they may quickly change their instruction if students are not progressing as expected.

FIGURE 16-6

START daily lesson plan example

Systematic Teaching and Recording Tactic (START) Daily Lesson Plan

Student's name Billy   Subject Reading   Date Monday, March 11   Teacher's name

Instructional objective

1. Given 24 words with short vowel sounds, Billy will correctly pronounce 22 words.
2. Given a set of flashcards with words missed in the previous lesson, Billy will correctly read 90% of the words.
3. Given 10 teacher-made comprehensive questions from today's reading, Billy will correctly answer 9 questions.

Instructional Activities	Materials	Time	Evaluation
Repeated reading	2 copies of attached reading passage (student's choice), stopwatch	5 min.	Enter the number of words read in this session on Billy's graph
Phonics practice (short vowel sounds) 1. Teacher and student read words chorally 2. Student reads words independently 3. Teacher corrects errors	2 copies of page 36 of phonics workbook (24 words with short vowel sounds)	10 min.	90% of sounds correct
Sight word practice 1. Student reads error words from previous lesson 2. Student practices reading 10 new words from today's lesson	Flashcards with errors from previous lesson Flashcards with difficult words from lesson	10 min.	90% of words correct from previous lesson and new words
Story reading 1. Teacher reads beginning of story (model) 2. Teacher and student read together (lead) 3. Student reads independently (teacher notes errors)	Story 4 from student anthology reading book (Grade 5)	25 min.	90% of words correct from Story 4
Comprehensive activity 1. During each section, teacher asks question 2. Student retells story	Ten teacher-generated comprehensive questions from story (factual and inferential questions)	Same	90% answered correctly; accurate story retell

What Is Progress Monitoring?

Progress monitoring is a generic term that refers to a simple procedure for repeated measurement of student growth toward long-range instructional goals (Deno, 1985). Simply stated, progress monitoring is the frequent collection of student data to determine how students are progressing in a specific academic area. Two of the systems that are frequently used for monitoring student progress in the basic skills areas are curriculum-based measurement (CBM; Deno, 1985) and general outcome measures (Fuchs & Deno, 1994). Teachers who use curriculum-based measurement develop the measures that are used to monitor their students' progress from the same curriculum in which students are working. In contrast, teachers who use general-outcome measures to monitor their students develop the measures from a curriculum that is different from the curriculum that their students are using.

Regardless of which monitoring system is implemented, the goal for each is the same. Teachers take repeated measures in a basic skill area such as reading, written expression, or mathematics. The data are graphed and compared to a long-range instructional goal. Instructional decisions based on students' progress toward the long-range goal are then made by the teacher. If the student is not progressing at an adequate rate, an instructional change is made in an attempt to increase the student's rate of progress toward the long-range goal. By using progress monitoring to collect frequent student data, teachers can determine the effectiveness of their instruction based on the progress of their students. Figure 16–7 shows an example of a progress monitoring graph.

Characteristics of Progress Monitoring Measures

The measures used for progress monitoring are designed to make them simple to design and efficient to administer. The measures administered to students can be created with materials readily available in most classrooms and they take little time to construct. More important, the measures have been shown to be reliable and valid for indicators of student performance (Deno, Mirkin et al., 1982; Deno, Mirkin, & Marston, 1980; Skiba, Magnusson, Marston, & Erickson, 1986). The measures are highly related to other measures of performance in basic skills areas (such as standardized tests) but can be given frequently in order to track student performance. Although different measures are used in each basic skill area, they all share a common set of characteristics. Following is a list of the common characteristics for the measures used in progress monitoring:

1. Multiple forms. To reduce practice effects, multiple forms of the measures are administered across time to the students.

2. Inexpensive. The measures are inexpensive to produce. Because multiple forms are required for progress monitoring, the cost of developing the forms is minimal.

3. Easy to understand. Becuase graphs are used to illustrate student performance, parents, teachers, and administrators can easily understand the results of the progress monitoring.

4. Time efficient. Administering and scoring the measures requires little classroom time.

5. Sensitive to small changes in growth. The progress monitoring measures are highly sensitive to small changes in student performance over short periods of time.

6. Reliable. Student scores are relatively stable from one administration to the next. Further, teachers can consistently score the measures from one administration to the next.

7. Valid. The progress monitoring measures correlate highly with other measures of performance in a basic skills area (Fuchs & Fuchs, 1992; Jenkins & Jewell, 1993; Marston, 1989; Shin, Deno, & Espin, 2000). The measures also distinguish between high- and low-performing students as well as students across different grades (Fuchs & Deno, 1994; Fuchs,

Figure 16–7   Sample progress monitoring graph

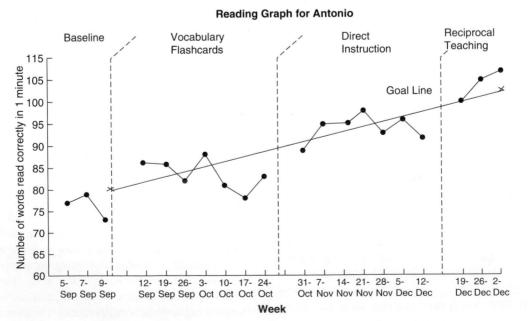

Fuchs, Hamlett, Walz, & Germann, 1993; Shinn, Tindal, Spira, & Marston, 1987).

8. Standardized. The measures are administered consistently each time the teacher collects student data.

Based on these characteristics, progress monitoring measures have been researched and developed for many basic skills areas. Next, we discuss the measures developed for the basic skills areas of reading, written expression, and math. After briefly reviewing the research for each measure, we describe how to create and administer the measures. The final section discusses how teachers can implement progress monitoring including collecting baseline data, graphing student data, and making instructional changes based on the data being collected.

Progress Monitoring Measures for Reading

Reading Aloud from Text One progress monitoring measure for reading that has extensive research to support its use is the number of words read aloud by a student in 1 minute. The research on this measure has shown it to have high criterion-related validity with respect to commercial, standardized measures of reading performance (Fuchs & Fuchs, 1992; Marston, 1989) as well as informal measures of reading such as Cloze procedures and passage recall (Fuchs & Fuchs, 1992; Fuchs et al., 1988). Further, reading aloud from text correlates highly with teachers' judgments of reading proficiency (Fuchs & Fuchs, 1992; Fuchs, Fuchs & Deno, 1982), which means that students who were rated as better readers by their teachers read more words in a minute than those rated as poorer readers. Finally, reading aloud from text has shown to have high discriminative validity. This means that the number of words read aloud in 1 minute can discriminate between students that receive special education services and those that do not (Marston, 1987; Shinn & Marston, 1985) as well as students in different grades (Fuchs & Deno, 1992; Fuchs, Fuchs, Hamlett, et al., 1993). Overall, the research on progress monitoring shows that the reading aloud measure has good technical characteristics that make it appropriate for monitoring student performance in reading.

Developing, Administering, and Scoring Reading Probes Before implementing progress monitoring, the teacher needs to create the materials that will be used to collect data on the students. Many times the materials that are created are referred to as probes due to the fact that the teacher is using them to "probe" student progress. Developing these probes is the first step in implementing progress monitoring.

Select the Reading Passages. The materials needed to create the reading probes are text passages. There are several options available for selecting the passages that will be used as probes. One option is to use passages from a reading curriculum that a student is currently using. A second option is to use text passages from a narrative text that is not being used by the students. Either way, the text passages that are used to create the probes must be novel to the students, which means that the students should not have read them before. In the case of using passages from a curriculum that students are currently being taught from, teachers have to select passages that the student has not yet studied and will not study over the course of the monitoring.

When selecting materials, teachers need to ensure that the reading level of the passages is not too difficult for the students who are going to be monitored. The students should be able to read approximately 80% of the words independently on any given probe. Further, teachers must ensure that each probe is long enough so that the student will be unable to finish it within a minute's time.

Develop the Reading Probes. For every probe that a teacher develops there should be a student copy and a teacher copy. The student copy should contain the text and be free of any pictures or figures. Further, it may be helpful to pick passages that are free from excessive numbers of pronouns (i.e., people's last names, titles, etc.). The teacher copy will be similar to the student copy except that it should have the cumulative number of words contained in the passage at the end of each line of text (see Figure 16–8 for an example of a student and teacher copy of a probe.) The number of probes you develop will depend on how long you will be monitoring the students and how many times per week you decide to administer the probes.

Administer the Reading Probes. The teacher randomly selects a reading probe to administer to the student. During each administration, the student is given 1 minute to read each probe. As the student reads aloud, the teacher follows along using his or her copy. If a student misreads or omits a word, the teacher places a slash mark through the word to indicate a miscue. If the student stops at a word that he or she cannot read, the teacher should wait 3 seconds. If the student still has not pronounced he word, the teacher should supply the word for the student and mark it as a miscue on the teacher copy. After 1 minute, the student is asked to stop and the teacher marks on the teacher copy where the student stopped.

FIGURE 16–8

Sample student and teacher copies of a read aloud probe

Student Copy

Little Jimmy slowly looked around the room. He remembered arriving from the airport late the night before but didn't remember how he had gotten to bed. The flight yesterday had been long. They had been stranded in Oakville airport for three hours because of bad weather. Since Jimmy didn't really want to visit his aunt in Middletown anyway, being stranded made him even more sullen. When they finally boarded the plane for Middletown, they were told that the bathrooms on the plane weren't working. Jimmy decided not to have anything to drink on the flight.

Teacher Copy

Little Jimmy slowly looked around the room. He remembered arriving from the	12
airport late the night before but didn't remember how he had gotten to bed. The flight	27
yesterday had been long. They had been stranded in Oakville airport for	40
three hours because of bad weather. Since Jimmy didn't really want to visit his	54
aunt in Middletown anyway, being stranded made him even more sullen. When	66
they finally boarded the plane for Middletown, they were told that the bathrooms	79
on the plane weren't working. Jimmy decided not to have anything to drink on	93
the flight.	95

Score the Reading Probes. The teacher uses the cumulative number of words on the teacher copy of the probe to determine how many words the student read. The number of errors the student made is subtracted from the number of words read. The student's final score on the probe is the number of words read − errors = student's score.

Progress Monitoring for Written Expression

Written expression probes can be either administered individually or to groups of students. The written expression measures used to monitor progress are timed writing samples from the students. Story starters are used to prompt and focus the writing of students on each probe. Simply put, a story starter is a sentence or sentence fragment based on a theme that will be familiar to the students being monitored. Examples of story starters are, "When I grow up I would like to be a . . . " or "One night when I was looking out of my window I saw . . . " Once the story starter is provided the students are given 5 minutes in which to write their responses. Figure 16–9 contains examples of story starters.

Several scoring options are available for calculating the score on the probes. These options will be discussed in the following text.

The development of progress monitoring measures in written expression has identified several measures that have acceptable reliability and validity for progress monitoring. At the elementary level, three measures have been identified that are reliable and valid indicators of overall student performance in written expression: the number of words written, the number of words spelled correctly, and the number of correct word sequences (Deno et al., 1980; Deno, Marston & Mirkin, 1982; Videen, Deno, & Marston, 1982). A correct word sequence is defined as two adjacent correctly spelled words that are correct in the context of the sentence according to a native speaker of the English language (Videen et al., 1982).

All three progress-monitoring measures have been found to correlate highly with standardized measures of writing (Deno et al., 1982; Videen et al., 1982). Finally, all three measures are sensitive enough to monitor progress over time (Deno et al., 1982; Marston et al., 1981; Tindal & Parker, 1991).

Although the number of words written, the number of words spelled correctly, and the number of correct word sequences are all appropriate progress monitoring measures at the elementary level, these measures have not been found reliable or valid for students at the secondary level (Tindal & Parker, 1989). Currently at the secondary level, the most reliable and valid measure for monitoring written expression is the number of correct word sequences minus the number of incorrect word sequences (Espin, Shin, Deno, Skare, Robinson,

FIGURE 16–9

Story starters and topic sentences

- One dark and scary night I walked outside and saw . . .
- I was walking outside when suddenly the wind started to blow and . . .
- One morning a strange light appeared in the sky and . . .
- In the morning I started to walk to school when suddenly . . .
- I was sleeping in my bed when the wind blew my window open and . . .
- I was about to open the door when somebody yelled, "Don't open that door."
- The room seemed to shake when . . .
- I couldn't believe my eyes when . . .
- Everybody started to run when . . .
- The music was so loud that . . .
- On Saturday we went to the carnival that came to town. We soon found out that it was a very strange carnival.
- You discover an old bottle. You rub it and a genie appears.
- You find a treasure map and follow it.
- You get into a magic car that will take you anywhere you want to go.
- We were out playing in the schoolyard when a helicopter landed . . .
- One morning you discover a big hole in your backyard big enough to crawl into. You climb down, down, down . . .
- You went on a trip in a rocket to outer space . . .
- If you were given a $100 bill, what would you do with it?
- One day you found an old key that unlocked a room in an old mansion . . .

& Brenner, 2000). The number of incorrect word sequences subtracted from the correct word sequences has strong alternate-form reliability and correlates well with ratings of the students' writing.

Developing, Administering, and Scoring Written Expression Probes

Develop a Set of Story Starters. Before teachers can begin collecting written expression data they must generate a list of story starters to use. A new story starter should be used for each probe administration. Additionally, teachers must be sure that the students will have some knowledge of the topics and that the topics are appealing to the students' developmental levels.

Administer the Written Expression Probes. To administer the written expression probes, the teacher randomly selects a story starter and reads it aloud to the students. The students are allowed 30 seconds to think about what they will write and then reread the story starter. The students have 5 minutes to write. At the end of five minutes, the teacher tells the students to stop and collects the probes.

Score the Written Expression Probes. How teachers score the written expression probes depends on which measure they choose to use. Once they have started using a scoring system they must continue to use it throughout the entire monitoring period. Changing scoring systems during monitoring will adversely affect the students' data.

Number of words written. Using this method, the teacher counts the total number of words written by the student whether they are spelled correctly or not. The score on the probe is the total number of all words written.

Number of words spelled correctly. Using this method, the teacher counts the total number of words written by the student that have been spelled correctly. The score on the probe is the total number of correctly spelled words.

Correct word sequences. Using this method, the teacher goes through several steps to attain the student's score. See Figure 16–10 for an example of this scoring method.

The teacher must follow these steps in scoring written probes:

Step 1: Read the entire passage before attempting to score it.

Step 2: Place a vertical line through the text where a sentence should end.

Step 3: Underline any words that are misspelled, misused, or grammatically incorrect.

Step 4: Place a caret above two words for a correct word sequence and below two words for an incorrect sequence.

Step 5: At the beginning of a sentence place a correct caret above the first word if it is capitalized and spelled correctly. If either is not correct, place an incorrect caret.

Step 6: At the end of a sentence place a correct caret above the last word and the end punctuation if the last word is spelled correctly and the end punctuation is correct. If either is not correct, place an incorrect caret.

Step 7: To calculate the word sequences score, count up the number of correct carets. For a correct minus

Example of scoring a writing probe using word sequences

Student's Writing Probe (story starter is in bold)

My favorite time of the year is . . . the winter. In winter you get to rode slads and make snowmans. I like it because it is cold and you loose your breth when you walk outside. sometimes I build a fort and hide inside it. Then I pop out and throw snow at my frends.

Student's Writing Probe Scored

My favorite time of the year is . . . ^ the ^ winter^. ^ In ^ winter^ you ^ get ^ to ˅ rode ˅ slads ˅ and ^ make ˅ snowmans ˅. ^ I ^ like ^ it ^ because ^ it ^ is ^ cold ^ and ^ you ˅ loose ˅ your ˅ breth ˅ when ^ you ^ walk ^ outside ^. ˅ sometimes ˅ I ^ build ^ a ^ fort ^ and ^ hide ^ inside ^ it ^. ^ Then ^ I ^ pop ^ out ^ and ^ throw ^ snow ^ at ^ my ˅ frends ˅.

Correct word sequences = 39

Correct—incorrect word sequences = 39–13 = 26

incorrect word sequences score, count the number of correct carets and subtract the number of incorrect carets.

Progress Monitoring for Math Computation

Similar to the written expression probes, the mathematics measures can be individually or group administered. Two types of mathematics probes have been developed: basic skills computation and concepts and applications. For either type of probe, math problems are selected from the entire curriculum being taught. Therefore, it is possible for math problems to appear on a probe even though the students have not yet been taught the math concept. Although this may seems unfair, it is important because mathematics measures are designed to monitor overall progress in math, not whether the students are mastering individual math concepts or applications. As the students become more competent in all aspects of the curriculum, their scores on the mathematics measures will increase.

The research on mathematics measures has focused primarily on basic facts for elementary students. Skiba et al. (1986) identified the number of digits written correctly in 2 minutes for probes that contained mixed facts as being technically adequate for monitoring student

progress in math. The measure was shown to be reliable (Tindal, Germann, & Deno, 1983) and valid (Skiba et al., 1986). Other measures have been developed that also sample computation skills as well as concepts and applications (see Fuchs, Fuchs, Hamlett, & Stecker, 1990; Fuchs et al., 1994 for information on these measures). Finally, research is currently being conducted examining estimation tasks (Foegen & Deno, 2001) that can be used to monitor student progress at the secondary level. In this chapter, we will focus on the basic facts probes used for elementary students.

Developing, Administering, and Scoring Mathematics Probes

Develop the Computation Probes. The mathematics probes are developed using problems representative of those that the students will be taught throughout the year. The probes should be long enough so that the students will be unable to finish them in 2 minutes. Also, teachers should leave enough space between problems on the probes for student work.

Several options are available for developing the probes. One option is to write a large selection of math problems on index cards (one problem per card). For each probe the teacher randomly selects problems using these cards and writes the problems on a sheet of paper. An example of a math probe can be seen in Figure 16–11. A second option is to use a computer program that will randomly select the problems. Many programs are available that can help generate the probes. The teacher inputs the math problems from the curriculum and the program randomly generates the probes. Although we do not advocate any specific programs, one free resource is available on the Internet at www.interventioncentral. org. Otherwise, we suggest that teachers perform an Internet search for worksheet generators in order to find a program that works best for them.

Administer the Computation Probes. To administer the computation probes, the teacher randomly selects a probe and places it face down in front of the students. The teacher tells the students they have 2 minutes to answer as many problems as they can. The students should move from left to right across rows of problems. If the students come to a problem they do not know how to do, the teacher tells them to skip it and move to the next problem. The students have 2 minutes to work on the probe. At the end of the 2 minutes the teacher collects the probe from the students.

Score the Computation Probes. The teacher has two options for scoring the computation probes: the number of problems correct or the number of correct digits.

Figure 16–11   Example of a scored mathematics computation probe (correct digits)

$$\begin{array}{r} 12 \\ +\ 20 \\ \hline 32 \end{array} \qquad \begin{array}{r} 13 \\ -\ 9 \\ \hline \cancel{22} \end{array} \qquad \begin{array}{r} 14 \\ +\ 25 \\ \hline 3\cancel{1} \end{array}$$

$$\begin{array}{r} 51 \\ -\ 19 \\ \hline 3\cancel{3} \end{array} \qquad \begin{array}{r} 18 \\ +\ 41 \\ \hline \cancel{6}9 \end{array} \qquad \begin{array}{r} 80 \\ -\ 37 \\ \hline 43 \end{array}$$

$$\begin{array}{r} 76 \\ -\ 9 \\ \hline \cancel{115} \end{array} \qquad \begin{array}{r} 75 \\ +\ 25 \\ \hline 1\cancel{1}\cancel{5} \end{array} \qquad \begin{array}{r} 88 \\ +\ 77 \\ \hline 1\cancel{5}5 \end{array}$$

Student Stopping Point

$$\begin{array}{r} 20 \\ -\ 12 \\ \hline 8 \end{array} \qquad \begin{array}{r} 42 \\ +\ 24 \\ \hline \cancel{88} \end{array} \qquad \begin{array}{r} 71 \\ -\ 56 \end{array}$$

Number of correct digits = 11

Either measure can be used for progress monitoring; however, the number of correct digits is more sensitive to small changes in growth. To score using the number of problems correct, the teacher counts the number of problems the students completed correctly. To score using the number of correct digits, the teacher counts each digit that is in the correct place value column. The probe score is the number of correct digits totaled across the entire probe. See Figure 16–11 for an example of a scored probe using the number of digits correct.

Implementing Progress Monitoring

Now that we have reviewed how to create, administer, and score the progress monitoring measures, we turn to how these measures can be used to set long-range instructional goals and monitor student progress. The following steps are the general procedure for implementing any of the measures previously discussed.

Step 1: *Collect baseline data.* Baseline data reflect the current functioning level of the student within a curricular area. By collecting baseline data, teachers can set an appropriate long-range goal. To collect baseline data, teachers should administer and score three randomly selected probes. Although these probes can be administered all on the same day, it is best to administer only one probe per session. After each administration, plot each probe score on a graph.

Step 2: *Determine the desired weekly growth rate of students.* This rate is how many more items (words read, words written, correct digits, etc.) the teacher believes a student will increase per week on the probes. Depending on how ambitious the teacher is, a good rule of thumb is setting the weekly growth at between 1 and 2 more items correct per week (e.g., increase words read per minute by 2 words per minute, increase correct word sequences written per minute by 1.5 words per week).

Step 3: *Set the long-range goal.* The long-range goal (LRG) is the performance level that the teacher wants the student to achieve by the end of the progress monitoring period. To set the LRG, the teacher needs the following information: the median (middle) baseline score, the number of weeks until the end of the progress monitoring period, and the rate of growth. Once the teacher has this information, he or she will set the LRG by multiplying weekly growth by the number of weeks in which the teacher will monitor the student and adding that number to the median baseline score. For example, if a student had the following three baseline scores on the reading aloud measures (60, 65, and 70) the median would be 65. If the annual IEP review would be held in 20 weeks and the teacher decided to set the students weekly growth rate at an ambitious 2 more words read correctly per week, the teacher would multiply the number of weeks (i.e., 20 weeks) times the rate of growth (i.e., 2 words per week) to get the increase in the number of words that the student will read correctly to achieve the goal (i.e., $20 \times 2 = 40$ words). The teacher would then add this number to the median baseline number to get the progress monitoring goal (i.e., $40 + 65 = 105$ words read correctly in 1 minute). Figure 16–12 is an example of a long-range goal worksheet.

Step 4: *Place the long-range goal line on the graph.* The teacher separates the graphed baseline data from where the progress monitoring data will begin by drawing a solid vertical line after the last baseline data point. On this vertical line he or she places an *X* at the median baseline score. On the last day that the teacher will be monitoring, he or she places an *X* on the LRG score and connects the two

FIGURE 16–12

Long-range goal worksheet

Information Needed:

Median baseline point _____

Short-term objective (weekly growth rate) _____

Number of weeks until the end of progress monitoring _____

Calculate Long-Range Goal:

Multiply number of weeks by short-term objective:_____ × _____ = _____

Add answer to median baseline score:_____ + _____ = _____

Long-Range Goal

---

*X*s to create the long-range goal line. A student's data are compared to this long-range goal line in order to determine whether he or she is making adequate progress toward the LRG. Figure 16–13 shows an example of an LRG graph.

Step 5: *Decide how often to monitor students.* The more often a teacher monitors his or her students, the quicker the teacher will be able to make changes in a student's instructional program. Students should be monitored minimally once per week.

Step 6: *Monitor the students.* At least once per week the teacher should administer a randomly selected probe and graph the data. Once the data is graphed, the teacher should examine the data using the data decision rules in step 7.

Figure 16–13   Example of graphing the long-range goal line

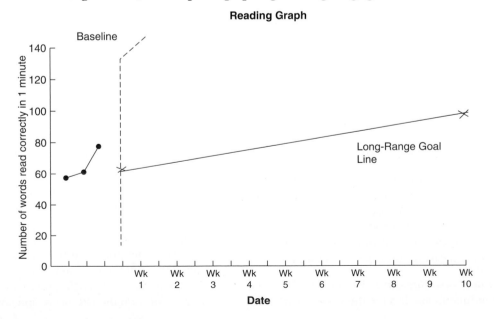

Reading Graph

Figure 16–14   Example of graphing an instructional change

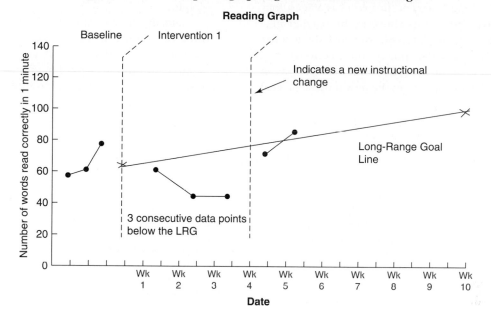

Step 7: *Implement decision-making rules and make instructional changes.* As a teacher collects a student's data, the teacher will compare it to the LRG line that has been drawn on the student's graph. If after 3 weeks of instruction the student has three consecutive data points that fall below the long-range goal line, the teacher should make an instructional change because the data indicate that the student is not progressing. To indicate when an instructional change is made, the teacher should draw a new vertical line on the student's graph and indicate the instructional change being made above it. Figure 16–14 shows an example of an instructional change graph.

Figure 16–15   Example of raising the long-range goal

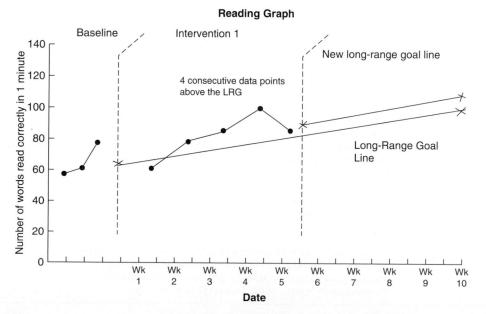

Conversely, if the student is consistently outperforming the long-range goal line and has at least four consecutive data points above it, the teacher may need to raise the goal. To raise the goal, the teacher takes the last three data points collected to use as a new baseline and then follows the instructions in steps 3 and 4 in order to set the new long-range goal line. Figure 16–15 shows an example of a raised goal graph.

Finally, if the student is making adequate progress toward his or her goal and neither of the two previous criteria has been met, the teacher should continuing implementing the current instruction and monitoring the student's progress.

Table 16–2   Web sites on curriculum-based measurement

Website	Description	URL
AIMSweb	AIMSweb is a Web-based, formative assessment system that informs the teaching and learning process by providing continuous student performance data via CBM in reading, written expression, mathematics, and spelling. AIMSweb reports CBM or DIBELS student progress in a 3-tier problem-solving model, including response-to-intervention (RTI), through a Web-based data management and reporting application.	www.aimsweb.com
Curriculum-Based Measurement for Early Literacy	This site contains curriculum-based materials developed for Project AIM (letter sound fluency, oral reading fluency) and includes normative data, examiner materials, and student materials. Project AIM (Alternative Identification Models) is a 3-year, longitudinal investigation funded by the U.S. Department of Education, Office of Special Education Programs.	www.glue.umd.edu/~dlspeece/cbmreading/index.html
Division for Learning Disabilities: Research to Practice Website	TeachingLD is a service of the Division for Learning Disabilities (DLD) of the Council for Exceptional Children. DLD is the largest international professional organization focused on learning disabilities. The site contains excellent resources, including tutorials on CBM.	www.teachingld.org
Dynamic Indicators of Basic Early Literacy Skills	The Dynamic Indicators of Basic Early Literacy Skills (DIBELS) are a set of standardized, individually administered measures of early literacy development. They are designed to be short (1 minute) fluency measures used to regularly monitor the development of prereading and early reading skills. The site contains the DIBELS measures, a data system for entering data and generating reports, and other valuable resources and links.	http://dibels.uoregon.edu/
Edcheckup	The Edcheckup site includes a progress monitoring system for students in Grades K–8 that evaluates student performance and measures student progress toward goals in reading, writing, and math. The site, which is based on CBM, can also be used for identifying children at risk for academic failure and can be used for a response to intervention problem-solving model.	www.edcheckup.com
Intervention Central	The Intervention Central site contains numerous free resources and tools for teachers and parents that will assist them to foster positive student behaviors and increase and monitor academic achievement.	www.interventioncentral.org
National Center on Student Progress Monitoring	The National Center on Student Progress Monitoring is a technical assistance center funded by the Office of Special Education Programs in the U.S. Department of Education. The site is a joint project of the American Institutes for Research and researchers at Vanderbilt University. In addition to training schedules, the site has many excellent resources for teachers and parents.	www.studentprogress.org
Research Institute on Progress Monitoring	The Office of Special Education Programs funds the Research Institute on Progress Monitoring to develop a system of progress monitoring to evaluate effects of individualized instruction on access to and progress within the general education curriculum. The institute is housed at the University of Minnesota.	www.progressmonitoring.org

Step 8: *Continue monitoring the students.* The teacher should continue to collect ongoing data for his or her students and revisit the decision-making rules in step 7. By constantly monitoring and adjusting instruction the teacher will be working to find the best instructional practices for students.

Table 16-2 lists Web sites that provide more information on student progress monitoring, CBM, and general outcome measurement.

MODIFYING INSTRUCTION USING START

When progress monitoring data indicate that an instructional program is not working with a student, his or her teacher needs to make an instructional change. When attempting to determine what changes to make a teacher is faced with the problem of what to modify. Clearly, it is difficult to predict what kind of modification will actually increase a student's success (Mirkin et al., 1981). A solution to this problem is to systematically make changes to a student's program and to continue monitoring his or her progress. In other words the teacher (a) forms a hypothesis, (b) makes the instructional changes, and (c) tests the effects of those changes using a technically adequate progress monitoring system. To successfully modify instruction in a meaningful and systematic manner, however, the original instructional plan must be outlined clearly so that a teacher can identify and alter a specific component of the plan and test the results of the instructional modification (Mirkin et al., 1981).

START is an excellent tool to help a teacher systematically alter or modify a student's instruction because the components and instructional activities are clearly described in the strategy. Thus, when START is used in conjunction with a progress monitoring system and the data indicate that a change in instruction is necessary, a specific component of START can be readily identified and altered. For example, if the teacher thought that the repeating readings strategy was useful, he or she may decide to increase the time devoted to the activity. In such a case, the teacher would increase the "Time" column (e.g., from 5 minutes to 10 minutes).

Changing a single part of START at a time is a good strategy because changing many parts of the plan at the same time would make it difficult to determine what produced the change in performance if, indeed, change did occur (Mirkin et al., 1981). For example, if increasing the student's repeated readings from 5 to 10 minutes increased his or her performance on the CBM it would be easy to attribute that improvement to the specific change. On the other hand, if the teacher decided to change everything at once (e.g., the teacher makes a change in every column) and the student's performance improves, it would be impossible to determine which component led to improved performance.

The type of progress monitoring data described in this chapter will allow a teacher to determine when an instructional change is necessary; however, the data do not tell the teacher what needs to be changed. It is up to the teacher, relying on his or her expertise, to make this determination. To select an effective program change it is important that a teacher select a substantial rather than an insubstantial change (Mirkin et al., 1981). That is, the change made should be one that is likely to cause a student's progress to improve in the particular area.

Chapter Summary

Teachers of students with EBD should pay as much attention to improving their students' academic performance as they do to improving their behaviors. This is because the evidence is clear that low academic achievement and school failure are primary characteristics exhibited by students with EBD. It is crucial, therefore, that when teachers instruct students with EBD they should use evidence-based strategies and procedures to increase their students' achievement. Teachers can increase the effectiveness of their instructional programs if they systematically plan their lessons and activities and monitor their students' progress. Planning entails developing long-range instructional plans and daily lesson plans. This chapter examined the nature of planning, how to plan, and how to monitor student progress. We suggested that teachers use the Systematic Teaching and Recording Tactic (START) procedure to become more systematic in their long-range and short-range lesson planning.

References

Achenbach, T. M., & Edelbrock, C. S. (1991). Child behavior checklist—teacher's report. Burlington, VT: University Associates in Psychiatry.

Adams v. Hansen, 632 F. Supp. 858 (N.D. Cal. 1985).

Adams, C., & Kelley, M. (1992). Managing sibling aggression: Overcorrection as an alternative to timeout. *Behavior Therapy, 23,* 707-717.

Adams, G. L., & Engelmann, S. (1996). *Research in direct instruction: 25 years beyond DISTAR.* Seattle, WA: Educational Achievement Systems.

Adams, M. J. (1988). *Beginning to read: Thinking and learning about print.* Cambridge, MA: MIT Press.

Adams, R. S., & Biddle, B. J. (1970). *Realities of teaching: Explorations with video tape.* New York: Holt, Rinehart & Winston

Al-Otaiba, S., & Fuchs, D. (2002). Characteristics of children who are unresponsive to early literacy interventions: A review of the literature. *Remedial and Special Education, 23*(5), 300-316.

Alberg, J., & Petry, C. (1993). *Approaches and choices to developing social competence in students with disabilities.* Research Triangle Park, NC: Research Triangle Institute.

Alberto, P. A., & Troutman, A. C. (2004). *Applied behavior analysis for teachers* (6th ed.). Upper Saddle River, NJ: Merrill/Prentice Hall.

Alberto, P. A., & Troutman, A. C. (2006). *Applied behavior analysis* for Teachers (7th ed.). Upper Saddle River, NJ: Merrill/Prentice Hall.

Alderman, G. L. (1997). Management traps: Recognizing and staying out of common behavior management traps. *Beyond Behavior, 8*(3), 23-26.

Algozzine, B., & White, R. (2002). Preventing problem behaviors using schoolwide discipline. In B. Algozzine and P. Kay (Eds.), *Preventing problem behaviors* (pp. 85-103). Thousand Oaks, CA: Corwin Press.

Algozzine, B., Ysseldyke, J., & Campbell, P. (1994). Strategies and tactics for effective instruction. *Teaching Exceptional Children, 26*(3), 34-36.

Algozzine, B., Ysseldyke, J., & Elliot, J. (1997). *Strategies and tactics for effective instruction* (2nd ed.) Longmont, CO: Sopris West.

Allen, L. D., Gottselig, M., & Boylan, S. (1982). Practical mechanisms for using free time as a reinforcer in classrooms. *Education and Treatment of Children, 5,* 347-353.

Allen, L. J., Howard, V. F., Sweeney, W. J., & McLaughlin, T. F. (1993). Use of contingency contracting to increase on-task behavior with primary students. *Psychological Reports, 72,* 905-906.

Allyon, T., & Azrin, N. H. (1968). *The token economy: A motivational system for therapy and rehabilitation.* New York: Appleton-Century-Crofts.

Allyon, T., Layman, D., & Kandel, H. J. (1975). A behavioral-educational alternative to drug control of hyperactive children. *Journal of Applied Behavior Analysis, 8,* 137-146.

Alverman, D. E., Smith, L. C., & Readence, J. E. (1985). Prior knowledge activation and the comprehension of compatible and incompatible text. *Reading Research Quarterly, 20,* 420-435.

American Psychiatric Association. (2000). *Diagnostic and statistical manual of mental disorders* (4th ed.rev.). Washington, DC: Author.

Anderson, C. A., & Jennings, D. L. (1980). When experiences of failure promote expectations of success: The impact of attributing failure to ineffective strategies. *Journal of Personality, 48,* 393-407

Anderson, J. A., Kutash, K., & Duchnowski, A. J. (2001). A comparison of the academic progress of students with EBD and students with LD. *Journal of Emotional and Behavioral Disorders, 9,* 106-115.

Anderson, L. M., Evertson, C. M., & Brophy, J. E. (1979) An experimental study of effective teaching in first grade reading groups. *The Elementary School Journal, 79,* 193-223.

Anderson, R. C., & Pearson, D. P. (1984). A schema-theoretic view of basic processes in reading comprehension. In R. Barr, M. L. Kamil, P. B. Mosenthal, & P. D. Pearson (Eds.), *Handbook of reading research* (Vol. 1, pp. 255-292). White Plains, NY: Longman.

Anderson, R. C., Reynolds, R. E., Schallert, D., & Goetz, E. (1977). Frameworks for comprehending discourse. *American Educational Research Journal, 14,* 367-381.

Ardoin, S. P., Witt, J. C., Suldo, S. M., Connell, J. E., Koenig, J. L., Resetar, J.L. et al. 2004. Examining the incremental benefits of administering a maze and three vs. one curriculum-based measurement reading probe when conducting universal screenings. *School Psychology Review, 33*(2), 218-233.

Arllen, N. L., Gable, R. A., & Hendrickson, J. M. (1994). Toward an understanding of the origins of aggression. *Preventing School Failure, 38*(3), 18-23.

Armstrong, S. W., & Kauffman, J. M. (1999). Functional behavioral assessment: Introduction to the series. *Behavioral Disorders, 24,* 167-168.

Ashlock, R. P. (1998). *Error patterns in computation: Using error patterns to improve instruction* (8th ed.). Upper Saddle River, NJ: Merrill/Prentice Hall.

Atkinson, T. S., Wilhite, K. L., Frey, L. M., & Williams, S. C. (2002). Reading instruction for the struggling reader: Implications for teachers of students with learning disabilities or emotional/behavioral disorders. *Preventing School Failure, 46*(4), 158–162.

Ausubel, D. P. (1960). The use of advance organizers in the learning and retention of meaningful verbal material. *Journal of Educational Psychology, 51*, 267–272.

Azrin, N.H., Holz, W.C., Hake, D. F. (1963). Fixed ratio punishment. *Journal of Experimental Analysis of Behavior, 6*, 141–148.

Azrin, N. H., Hutchinson, R. R., & Hake, D. F. (1966). Extinction produced aggression. *Journal of the Experimental Analysis of Behavior, 9*, 191–204.

Azrin, N. H., & Powers, M. (1975). Eliminating classroom disturbances of emotionally disturbed children by positive practice procedures. *Behavior Therapy, 6*, 525–534.

Azrin, V., Azrin, N. H., & Armstrong, P. (1977). The student-oriented classroom: A method of improving student conduct and satisfaction. *Behavior Therapy, 8*, 193–204.

Baber, G., & Bacon, E. H. (1995). Effect of instructional cues on memory for new words by poor readers. *Education and Treatment of Children, 18*(2), 117–127.

Babyak, A. E., Koorland, M., & Mathes, P. G. (2000). The effects of story mapping instruction on the reading comprehension of students with behavioral disorders. *Behavioral Disorders, 25*(3), 239–258.

Baer, D. M. (1984). Does research on self-control need more control? *Analysis and Intervention in Developmental Disabilities, 4*, 211–284.

Baer, D. M., Fowler, S. A., & Carden-Smith, L. (1984). Using reinforcement and independent-grading to promote and maintain task accuracy in a mainstreamed class. *Analysis and Intervention in Developmental Disabilities, 4*, 157–170.

Baer, D. M., & Wolf, M. M. (1970). The entry into natural communities of reinforcement. In R. Ulrich, T. Stahnik, & J. Mabry (Eds.), *Control of human behavior* (Vol. 2, pp. 319–324). Glenview, IL: Scott, Foresman.

Baer, D. M., Wolf, M. M., & Risley, T. R. (1968). Some current dimensions of applied behavior analysis. *Journal of Applied Behavior Analysis, 1*, 91–97.

Bagarozzi, D. A. (1984). Applied behavioral intervention in rural school settings: Problems in research design, implementation, and evaluation. *Clinical Social Work Journal, 12*, 43–56.

Bain, A., & Farris, H. (1991). Teacher attitudes toward social skills training. *Teacher Education & Special Education, 14*, 49–56.

Bain, S. K., & Garlock, J. W. (1992). Cross-validation of criterion-related validity for CBM reading passages. *Diagnostique, 17*(3), 202–208.

Baird, M. (2005). *IEPs: How the law transforms the process of developing IEPs.* (LRP Publications, VHS, 2005 release).

Bambara, L.M. (2005). Evolution of positive behavior support. In L.M. Barbara & L. Kern, *Individualized supports for students with problem behaviors: Designing positive behavior plans* (pp. 1–24). New York: Guilford Press.

Bandura, A. (1965). Influence of models' reinforcement contingencies on the acquisition of imitative responses. *Journal of Personality and Social Psychology, 1*, 589–595.

Bandura, A. (1977). *Social learning theory.* Upper Saddle River, NJ: Prentice Hall.

Bandura, A. (1978). The self system in reciprocal determinism. *American Psychologist, 33*, 344–358.

Bandura, A. & Walters, R. H. (1963). *Social learning and personality development.* Stamford, CT: International Thomson Publishing.

Barkley, R., Copeland, A., & Sivage, C. (1980). A self-control classroom for hyperactive children. *Journal of Autism and Developmental Disorders, 10*, 75–89.

Baron, J. B. (1991). *Performance assessment: Blurring the edges off assessment, curriculum, and instruction.* Waldorf, MD.: American Association for Advancement of Science.

Barriga, A. Q., Doran, J. W., Newell, S. B., Morrison, E. M., Barbetti, V., & Robbins, B. D. (2002). Relationships between problem behaviors and academic achievement in adolescents: The unique role of attention problems. *Journal of Emotional and Behavioral Disorders, 10*, 233–240.

Barrish, H., Sanders, M., & Wolf, M. M. (1969). Good behavior game: Effects of individual contingencies for group consequences on disruptive behavior in the classroom. *Journal of Applied Behavior Analysis, 2*, 119–124.

Barton-Arwood, S. M., Wehby, J. M., & Falk, K. B. (2005). Reading instruction for elementary-age students with emotional and behavioral disorders: Academic and behavioral outcomes. *Exceptional Children, 72*, 7–27.

Basso, D., & McCoy, N. (1996). *Study tools: A comprehensive curriculum guide for teaching study skills to students with special needs.* Columbia, SC: Twins Publications.

Bateman, B., & Golly, A. (2003). *Why Johnny doesn't behave: Twenty tips and measurable BIPs.* Verona, WI: Attainment Publications.

Bateman, B. D., & Herr, C. M. (2003). *Writing measurable IEP goals and objectives.* Verona, WI: IEP Resources.

Bateman, B. D., & Linden, M. A. (1998). *Better IEPs: How to develop legally correct and educationally useful programs* (3rd ed.). Longmont, CO: Sopris West.

Bateman, B. D., & Linden, M.A. (2006). *Better IEPs* (4th ed.). Verona, WI: IEP Resources.

Bauer, A. M., Keefe, C. H., & Shea, T. M. (2001). *Students with learning disabilities or emotional/behavioral disorders.* Upper Saddle River, NJ: Merrill/Prentice Hall.

Bauer, A. M., & Shea, T. M. (1988). Structuring the classroom through levels systems. *Focus on Exceptional Children, 21*(3), 1–12

Bauer, A. M., Shea, T. M., & Keppler, R. (1986). Levels systems: A framework for the individualization of behavior management. *Behavioral Disorders, 11*, 28–35.

Bazelon Center for Mental Health Law. (2003). *Suspending disbelief: Moving beyond punishment to promote effective interventions for children with mental or emotional disorders.* Washington, D.C.: Author.

Bean, A. W., & Roberts, M. W. (1981). The effect of time-out release contingencies on changes in child noncompliance. *Journal of Abnormal Child Psychology, 9,* 95–105.

Beaumont Independent School District, 21 IDELR 261 (SEA TX, 1994).

Beck, A. T. (1976). *Cognitive therapy and emotional disorders.* New York: International Universities Press.

Becker, R. E., & Heimberg, R. G. (1988). Assessment of social skills. In A. S. Belleck & M. Hersen (Eds.), *Behavioral assessment: A practical handbook* (3rd ed., pp. 365–395). New York: Pergamon.

Beidel, D. C., Turner, S. M., & Taylor-Ferreira, J. C. (1999). Teaching study skills and test-taking strategies to elementary school students. *Behavior Modification, 23*(4), 630–646.

Belfiore, P. J., Lee, D. L., Scheeler, M. C., & Klein, D. (2002). Implications of behavioral momentum and academic achievement for students with behavior disorders: Theory, application, and practice. *Psychology in the Schools, 39*(2), 171–179.

Benner, G. J., Nelson, J. R., & Epstein, M. H. (2002). Language skills of children with EBD. *Journal of Emotional and Behavioral Disorders, 10*(1), 43–57.

Berliner, D. (1991). What's all the fuss about instructional time? In M. Ben-Peretz & R. Bromme (Eds.), *The nature of time in schools: Theoretical concepts, practitioner perceptions.* New York: Teachers College Press.

Berliner, D., & Biddle, B. (1995). *The manufactured crises: Myth, fraud, and the attack on America's public schools.* New York: Addison-Wesley.

Bierly, C., & Billingsley, T. F. (1983). An investigation of the educative effects of overcorrection on the behavior of an autistic child. *Behavioral Disorders, 9,* 11–21.

Bijou, S. W., Peterson, R. F., & Ault, M. H. (1968). A method to integrate descriptive and experimental field studies at the level of data and empirical concepts. *Journal of Applied Behavior Analysis, 1*(2), 175–19.

Birnbrauer, J. S., Bijou, S. W., Wolf, M. M., & Kidder, J. D. (1965). Programmed instructions in the classroom. In L. P. Ullmann & L. Krasner (Eds.), *Case studies in behavior modification* (pp. 358–363). New York: Holt, Rinehart & Winston.

Birnbauer, J. S., Wolf, M. M., Kidder, J. D., & Tague, C. E. (1965). Classroom behavior of retarded pupils with a token economy. *Journal of Experimental Child Psychology, 2,* 219–235.

Blachman, B. A., Ball, E., Black, R., & Tangel, D. (1994). Kindergarten teachers develop phoneme awareness in low-income, inner-city classrooms: Does it make a difference? *Reading and Writing: An Interdisciplinary Journal, 6,* 1–17.

Blankenship, C. (1985). Using curriculum-based assessment data to make instructional decisions. *Exceptional Children, 52,* 219–232.

Blue-Banning, M., Summers, J., Frankland, H. C., Nelson, L., & Beegle, G. (2004). Dimensions of family and professional partnerships: Constructive guidelines for collaboration. *Exceptional Children, 70*(2), 167–184.

Board of Education of the Akron Central School District, 28 IDELR 909 (SEA NY 1998).

Board of Education of the Hendrick Hudson Central School District v. Rowley, 458 U.S. 176 (1982).

Board of Education of the Whitesboro Central School District, 21 IDELR 895 (SEA NY 1994).

Bornstein, P., Hamilton, S., & Quevillon, R. (1977). Behavior modification by long-distance: Demonstration of functional control over disruptive behavior in a rural classroom setting. *Behavior Modification, 1,* 39–49.

Bos, C. S. (1988). Process-oriented writing: Instructional implications for mildly handicapped students. *Exceptional Children, 6,* 521–527.

Bos, C. S., & Vaughn, S. (2002). *Strategies for teaching students with learning and behavior problems* (5th ed). Boston: Allyn & Bacon.

Bostow, D. E., & Bailey, J. (1969). Modification of severe disruptive and aggressive behavior using brief timeout and reinforcement procedures. *Journal of Applied Behavior Analysis, 2,* 31–37.

Bottge, B. A., & Hasselbring, T. S. (1993). A comparison of two approaches for teaching complex, authentic mathematics problems to adolescents in remedial math classes. *Exceptional Children, 59*(6), 556–566.

Bower, B. (1995). Criminal intellects: Researchers look at why lawbreakers often brandish low IQs. *Science News, 147,* 232–239.

Braaten, S., Simpson, R., Rosell, J., & Reilly, T. (1988). Using punishment with exceptional children: A dilemma for educators. *Teaching Exceptional Children, 20,* 79–81

Bradley, M. R. (2001). Positive behavior supports: Research to practice. *Beyond Behavior, 11*(1), 3–5.

Bradley, R., Henderson, K., & Monfore, D. A. (2004). A national perspective on children with emotional disorders. *Behavioral Disorders, 29*(3), 211–233.

Bradley-Johnson, S., & Lesiak, J. (1989). *Problems in written expression: Assessment and remediation.* New York: Guilford Press.

Brantley, D. C., & Webster, R. E. (1993). Use of an independent group contingency management system in a regular classroom setting. *Psychology in the Schools, 30,* 60–66.

Brantner, J. P., & Doherty, M. A. (1973). A review of timeout: A conceptual and methodological analysis. In S. Axelrod & J. Apsche (Eds.), *The effects of punishment on human behavior* (pp. 87–132). New York: Academic Press.

Braswell, L., & Kendall, P. C. (1988). Cognitive-behavioral methods with children. In K. S. Dobson (Ed.), *Handbook of cognitive-behavioral therapies* (pp. 167–213). New York: Guilford Press.

Brennan, A. D., Bridge, C. A., & Winograd, P. N. (1986). The effects of structural variations on children's recall of basal reader stories. *Reading Research Quarterly, 21,* 91–103.

Brett, J. (2005). *Compound words*. Retrieved June 11, 2005, from http://www.janbrett.com/piggybacks/compound.htm

Brigham, F., & Kauffman, J (1998). Creating supportive environments for students with emotional or behavioral disorders. *Effective School Practices, 17*(2), 8–24

Brigham, F. J., Bakken, J. P., Scruggs, T. E., & Mastropieri, M.A. (1992). Cooperative behavior management: Strategies promoting a positive classroom environment. *Education and Training in Mental Retardation, 27*, 3–12.

Brigham, F. J., Scruggs, T. E., & Mastropieri, M. A. (1992). Teacher enthusiasm in learning disabilities classrooms: Effects on learning and behavior *Learning Disabilities Research and Practice 7*, 68–73.

Brigham, F. J., Scruggs, T. E., & Mastropieri, M. A. (1995). Elaborative maps for enhanced learning of historical information: Uniting spatial, verbal, and imaginal information. *The Journal of Special Education, 28*, 440–460.

Brimmer v. Traverse City Area Public Schools, 872 F. Supp. 1994 (W.D. Mich. 1994).

Brisman, J., & Siegel, M.(1985). The bulimia workshops: A unique integration of group treatment approaches. *International Journal of Group Psychotherapy, 35*, 585–601.

Bristol, M. M., & Sloane, H. N., (1974). Effects of contingency contracting on study rate and test performance. *Journal of Applied Behavior Analysis, 7*, 271–285.

Broden, M., Hall, R. V., & Mitts, B. (1971). The effect of self-recording of the classroom behavior of two eighth grade students. *Journal of Applied Behavior Analysis, 4*, 191–199.

Broderick, C. B. (1993). *Understanding family process: Basics of family systems theory*. Newbury Park, CA: Sage Publications.

Brolin, D. (1989). *LCCE: Life Centered Career Education*. Reston, VA: Council for Exceptional Children.

Bronfenbrenner, U. (1979). *The ecology of human design: Experiments by nature and design*. Cambridge, MA: Harvard University Press.

Brooks, C. M. (1996). The law's response to child abuse and neglect. In B. D. Sales & D. W. Shulman (Eds.), *Law, mental health, and mental disorders*. (pp. 132–164). Pacific Grove, CA: Brooks/Cole.

Brophy, J. (1981). Teacher praise: A functional analysis. *Review of Educational Research, 51*, 5–32.

Brophy, J. (1988). Educating teachers about managing classrooms and students. *Teaching and Teacher Education, 4*, 1–18.

Brophy, J., & Evertson, C. (1976). *Learning from teaching: A developmental perspective*. Boston: Allyn & Bacon.

Brophy, J., & Good, T. (1986). Teacher behavior and student achievement. In M. Wittrock (Ed.), *Handbook of research on teaching* (3rd ed). New York: Macmillan.

Brophy, J. E. (1983). Classroom Organization and Management. *The Elementary School Journal, 83*, 264–285.

Brown, D., Reschly, D., & Saber, D. (1974). Using group contingencies with punishment and positive reinforcement to modify aggressive behaviors in a Head Start classroom. *Psychological Record, 24*, 491–496.

Brown, W., Bryson-Brockman, B., & Fox, J. (1986). The usefulness of J. R. Kantor's setting event concept for research on children's social behavior. *Child and Family Behavior Therapy, 8*, 15–25.

Brownell, M.T., & Smith, S.W. (1992). Attention/retention of special education teachers: Critique of current research and recommendations for retention efforts. *Teacher Education and Special Education, 15*, 229–248.

Brownell, M.T., Smith, S.W., & McNellis, J. (1997). Attrition in special education: Why teachers leave the classroom and where they go. *Exceptionality, 7*, 143–155.

Bulen, J., & Bullis, M. (1995). *Development of transition programs for adolescents with serious emotional disturbances*. Monmouth: Western Oregon College. (ERIC Document Reproduction Service No. ED385024)

Bulgren, J., & Lenz, K. (1996). Strategic instruction in the content areas. In D. D. Deshler, E. S. Ellis, & B. K. Lenz (Eds.), *Teaching adolescents with learning disabilities* (2nd ed., pp. 409–473). Denver, CO: Love.

Bulgren, J., Schumaker, J. B., & Deschler, D. D. (1994). Effectiveness of a concept teaching routine in enhancing the performance of LD students in secondary-level mainstream classes. *Learning Disability Quarterly, 11*, 3–17.

Bullis, M., & Cheney, D. (1999). Vocational and transitional interventions for adolescents and young adults with emotional and behavioral disorders. *Focus on Exceptional Children, 31*, 1–24.

Bullis, M., & Gaylord-Ross, R. (1991). *Moving on: Transitions for youth with behavioral disorders*. Reston, VA: Council for Exceptional Children.

Bullock, L., Gable, R., & Melloy, K. (2005). *Effective disciplinary practices: strategies for maintaining safe schools and positive learning environments for students with challenging behaviors*. Council for Children with Behavioral Disorders. (ERIC Document Reproduction Service No. ED495394).

Bullock, L. M., Ellis, L. L., & Wilson, M. J. (1994). Knowledge/skills needed by teachers who work with students with severe emotional/behavioral disorders: A revisitation. *Behavioral Disorders, 19*, 108–125.

Bullock, L. M., & Mendez, A. L. (1999). *Historical chronology of the council for children with behavioral disorders 1964–1999*. Reston, VA: Council for Children with Behavioral Disorders.

Bullock, L. M., Reilly, T. F., & Donahue, C. A. (1983). School violence and what teachers can do about it. *Contemporary Education, 55*, 40–44.

Burkell, J., Schneider, B., Pressley, M. (1990). Mathematics. In M. P. Pressley & V. Woloshyn (Eds.), *Cognitive strategy instruction that really improves children's academic performance* (2nd ed., pp. 147–177). Cambridge, MA: Brookline Books.

Burns, B. J., Howell, J. C., Wiig, J. K., Augimeri, L. K., Welsh, B. C., Loeber, R., et al. (2003). Treatment, services, and intervention programs for child delinquents. *Child Delinquency Bulletin* Series. Retrieved April 4, 2006 from http://www.ncjrs.gov/pdffiles1/ojjdp/193410.pdf

Bushell, D. (1978). An engineering approach to the elementary classroom: The behavior analysis follow-through project. In A. C. Catania & T. A. Brigham (Eds.), *Handbook of applied behavior analysis: Social and instructional processes* (pp. 525–563). New York: Irvington.

Cade, T., & Gunter, P. L. (2002). Teaching students with severe emotional or behavioral disorders to use a musical mnemonic technique to solve basic division calculations. *Behavioral Disorders, 27*, 208–214.

Calhoun, G. B., Glaser, B. A., & Bartolomucci, C. L. (2001). The juvenile counseling and assessment model and program: A conceptualization and intervention for juvenile delinquency. *Journal of Counseling & Development, 79*(2), 131–141.

Callahan, K., & Rademacher, J. A. (1999). Using self-management strategies to increase the on-task behavior of a student with autism. *Journal of Positive Behavior Interventions, 1*, 117–122.

Camp, B., Blom, G., Hebert, F., & van Doorninck, W. (1977). "Think aloud": A program for developing self-control in young aggressive boys. *Journal of Abnormal Child Psychology, 5*, 157–169.

Camp, B. W., & Bash, M. A. (1985). *Think aloud classroom programs.* Champaign, IL: Research Press.

Canter, L., & Canter, M. (1992). *Assertive discipline: Positive behavior management for today's classroom* (3rd ed.). Santa Monica, CA: Lee Canter & Associates.

Carnine, D. (2000). *Why education experts resist effective practices: And what it would take to make education more like medicine.* Washington, DC: Thomas B. Fordham Foundation.

Carnine, D. W., Silbert, J., Kame'enui, E. J., & Tarver, S. G. (2004). *Direct instruction reading* (3rd ed.). Upper Saddle River, NJ: Pearson/Merrill/Prentice Hall.

Carr, E. G. (1977). The motivation of self-injurious behavior: A review of some hypotheses. *Psychological Bulletin, 84*, 800–816.

Carr, E. G. (1988). Functional equivalence as a means of response generalization. In R. H. Horner, G. Dunlap, & R. L. Koegel (Eds.), *Generalization and maintenance: Lifestyle changes in applied settings* (pp. 221–241). Baltimore: Brookes.

Carr, E. G. (1997). The evolution of applied behavior analysis into positive behavior support. *Journal of the Association For Person with Severe Handicaps, 22*, 208–209.

Carr, E. G., Dunlap, G., Horner, R. H., Koegel, R. L.; Turnbull, A. P., Sailor, W., et al. (2002). Positive behavior support: Evolution of an applied science. *Journal of Positive Behavior Interventions, 4*(1), 4–16.

Carr, E. G., Durand, V. M. (1985). Reducing behavior problems through functional communication training. *Journal of Applied Behavior Analysis, 26*, 393–399.

Carr, E. G., Horner, R. H., Turnbull, A. P., Marquis, J., Magito-McLaughlin, D., McAtee, M. L., et al. (1999). *Positive behavior support for people with developmental disabilities: A research synthesis.* Washington, DC: American Association on Mental Retardation.

Carr, E. G., Levin, L. McConnachie, G., Carlson, J. I., Kemp, D. C., & Smith, C. E. (1994). *Communication based intervention for problem behavior: A user's guide for producing positive behavior change.* Baltimore: Brookes.

Carr, S. C., & Punzo, R. P. (1993). The effects of self-monitoring of academic accuracy and productivity on the performance of students with behavioral disorders. *Behavioral Disorders, 18*, 241–248.

Carter v. Florence County School District Four, 950 F.2d 156 (4th Cir. 1991).

Carter, J., & Sugai, G. (1989). Survey on prereferral practices: Responses from state departments of education, *Exceptional Children, 55* (4), 298–302.

Cartledge, G., & Kiarie, M. W. (2001). Learning social skills through literature for children and adolescents. *Teaching Exceptional Children, 34*(2), 40–47.

Cartledge, G., & Milburn, J. F. (1995). *Teaching social skills to children: Innovative approaches.* Boston: Allyn & Bacon.

Casazza, M. E. (1993). Using a model of direct instruction to teach summary writing in a college reading class. *Journal of Reading, 37*(3) 202–208.

Cates, D., Markell, M., & Bettenhausen, S. (1995). Child abuse. *Preventing School Failure, 39*(2), 6–10.

Cedar Rapids v. Garret F., 29 IDELR 966 (U.S. 1999).

Center, D. B., Dietz, S. M., & Kaufman, M. E. (1982). Student ability, task difficulty, and inappropriate behavior. *Behavior Modification, 6*, 355–375.

Center for Effective Collaboration and Practice (2000). *Improving services for children and youth with emotional and behavioral problems,* Retrieved from http://cecp.air.org/fba/problembehavior3/main3.htm on April 24, 2006.

Center on Positive Behavioral Interventions and Supports. (2001). *Defining positive behavior support.* Unpublished manuscript. Author.

Cessna, K. K., & Adams, L. (1993). Implications of a needs-based philosophy. In K. K. Cessna (Ed.), *Instructionally differentiated programming: A needs-based approach for students with behavior disorders* (pp. 7–18). Denver: Colorado Department of Education.

Cessna. K. K., & Borock, J (1993). Instructionally differentiated programming: Suggestions for implementation. In K. K. Cessna, *Instructionally differentiated programming: A needs-based approach for students with behavioral disorders* (pp. 7–18). Denver: Colorado Department of Education.

Cessna, K. K., & Skiba, R. (1996). Needs-based: A. responsible approach to inclusion. *Preventing School Failure, 40*, 117–123.

Champagne, J. F. (1993). Decisions in sequence: How to make placements in the least restrictive environment. *EdLaw Briefing Paper, 9 & 10*, 1–16.

Chandler, L. K., & Dahlquist, C. M. (2006). *Functional Assessment: Strategies to Prevent and Remediate Challenging Behavior in School Settings* (2nd Ed.). Upper Saddle River, NJ: Merrill/Prentice Hall.

Chard, D. J., & Kame'enui, E. J. (2000). Struggling first grade readers: The frequency and progress of their reading. *The Journal of Special Education, 34*, 28–38.

Charles, C. M. (2002). *Building classroom discipline* (7th ed.). Boston: Allyn & Bacon.

Cheney, D., & Sachs, J. J. (2000). What do members of the Council for Children with Behavioral Disorders say about inclusion? *Beyond Behavior, 10* (2), 18–23.

Child Abuse Prevention, Adoption, and Family Services Act, 42 U.S.C. § 5101 *et seq.* (1988).

Child Abuse Prevention and Treatment Act, 42 U.S.C. § 5101 *et seq.* (1992).

Christenson, S. L., & Ysseldyke, J. E. (1986, April). *Academic responding time as a function of instructional arrangements.* Paper presented at the Annual Meeting of the American Educational Research Association. San Francisco.

Christie, D. J., Hiss, M., & Lozanoff, B. (1984). Modification of inattentive classroom behavior: Hyperactive children's use of self-recording with teacher guidance. *Behavior Modification, 8*, 391–406.

Christle, C. A., Nelson, C. M., & Jolivette, K. (2004). School characteristics related to the use of suspension. *Education and Treatment of Children, 27*(4), 509–526.

Christle, C. A., & Schuster, J. W. (2003). The effects of using response cards on student participation, academic achievement, and on-task behavior during whole-class, math instruction. *Journal of Behavioral Education, 12*, 147–165.

Church, K., Gottschalk, & Leddy, J. N. (2003). 20 Ways to enhance social and friendship skills, *Intervention in School and Clinic, 38*(5), 307–310.

Clarizo, H. (1980). *Toward a positive classroom discipline* (3rd ed.). New York: Wiley.

Clark, C. M., and Yinger, R. J. (1980). *The hidden world of teaching: Implications of research on teacher planning* (Research Series No. 77). East Lansing: Michigan State University, Institute for Research on Teaching.

Clark, L. A., & McKenzie, H. S. (1989). Effects of self-evaluation training on seriously emotionally disturbed children on the generalization of their classroom rule following and work behaviors across settings and teachers. *Behavioral Disorders, 14*, 89–98.

Clyde K. v. Puyallup School District, No. 3, 35 F.3d 1396 (9th Cir. 1994).

Coalition for Evidence-Based Policy. (2002). *Bringing evidence-based policy to education: A recommended strategy for the U.S. Department of Education.* Washington, DC: Author. PDF available at http://www.excelgov.org/usermedia/images/uploads/PDFs/CoalitionFinRpt.pdf

Cocozza, J. J. (2005). *Mental health and juvenile justice: Issues, trends and needed directions.* Paper presented at the National Health Policy Forum, Washington, DC.

Coker, H. Lorentz, C. W., & Coker, J. (1980, April). *Teacher behavior and student outcomes in the Georgia study.* Paper presented at the American Educational Research Association Annual Meeting, Boston, MA.

Cole v. Greenfield-Central Community Schools, 657 F. Supp. 56 (S.D. Ind. 1986).

Coleman, M., Wheeler, L., & Webber, J. (1993). Research on interpersonal problem-solving training: A review. *Remedial and Special Education, 14*, 25–37.

Coleman, M. C., & Vaughn, S. (2000). Reading interventions for students with EBD. *Behavioral Disorders, 25*(2), 93–104.

Coleman, M. C. & Webber, J. (2002). *Emotional and behavioral disorders: Theory and practice* (4th ed.). Boston: Allyn & Bacon.

Colvin, G. (2004). *Managing the cycle of acting-out behavior in the classroom.* Eugene, OR: Behavior Associates.

Colvin, G., & Fernandez, E. (2000). Sustaining effective behavior support systems in an elementary school. *Journal of Positive Behavior Interventions, 2*(4), 251–253.

Colvin, G., Kame'enui, E., & Sugai, (1994). Reconceptualizing behavior management and school-wide discipline in general education. *Education and Treatment of Children, 16*, 361–381.

Colvin, G., & Lazar, M. (1997). *The effective elementary classroom: Managing for success.* Longmont, CO: Sopris West.

Colvin, G., Sugai, G., & Patching, W. (1993). Pre-correction: An instructional approach for managing predictable problem behaviors. *Intervention in School and Clinic, 28*, 143–150.

Colvin, G. T., & Sugai, G. M. (1988). Proactive strategies for managing social behavior problems: An instructional approach. *Education and Treatment of Children, 11*, 341–348.

Concerned Parents and Citizens for Continuing Education at Malcolm X v. The New York City Board of Education, 629 F.2d 751 (2nd Cir. 1980).

Conduct Problems Prevention Research Group. (1999a). Initial impact of the Fast Track prevention trial for conduct problems: I. The high risk sample. *Journal of Consulting and Clinical Psychology, 67*, 631–647.

Conduct Problems Prevention Research Group. (1999b). Initial impact of the Fast Track prevention trial for conduct problems: II. Classroom effects. *Journal of Consulting and Clinical Psychology, 67*, 648–657.

Condus, M. N., Marshall, K. J., & Miller, S. R. (1986). Effects of a keyword mnemonic strategy on vocabulary acquisition and maintenance by learning disabled children. *Journal of Learning Disabilities, 19*, 609–613.

Conroy, M., Clark, Gable, R., & Fox, J. (1999). A look at IDEA 1997 discipline provisions: Implications for change in the roles and responsibilities of school personnel. *Preventing School Failure, 43,* 64-70.

Conroy, M.A., & Brown, W. H. (2004). Early identification, prevention, and early intervention with young children at risk for emotional or behavioral disorders: Issues, trends, and a call for action. *Behavioral Disorders, 29*(3), 224-236.

Controlled Substances Act, 21 U.S.C. § 812(c).

Cook, L., & Friend, M. (1993). Co-teaching: An overview of the past, a glimpse at the present, and considerations for the future. *Preventing School Failure, 37*(4), 6-10.

Cooper, H. M., & Good, T. L. (1983). Classroom expectations: Definitions, past research, and the research model. In H. Cooper & T. Good, Eds., *Pygmalion grows up: Studies in the expectation communication process* (pp. 4-32). New York, NY: Longman.

Cooper, J. O., Heron, T. E., & Heward, W. H. (2007). *Applied behavior analysis* (2nd ed.). Upper Saddle River, NJ: Merrill/Prentice Hall.

Council for Exceptional Children. (1987). *The academy for effective instruction: Working with mildly handicapped students.* Reston, VA: Author.

Council for Exceptional Children. (2000). *Bright futures for exceptional learners: An action to achieve quality conditions for teaching and learning.* Reston, VA: Author.

Craighead, W. F. (1982). A brief clinical history of cognitive-behavior therapy with children. *School Psychology Review, 11,* 5-13.

Crockett, J. B. (2001). Exploring the meaning of science and defining rigor in the social sciences. *Behavioral Disorders,* 27, 7-11.

Crone, D. A., & Horner, R. H. (2003). *Building positive behavior support systems in schools: Functional behavioral assessment.* New York: Guilford Press.

Crone, D. A., Horner, R. H., & Hawkein, L. S. (2004). *Responding to problem behavior in the schools: The behavior education program.* New York: Guilford Press.

Cullinan, D. (2002). *Students with emotional and behavior disorders: An introduction for teachers and other helping professions.* Upper Saddle River, NJ: Merrill/Prentice Hall.

Cullinan, D., & Epstein, M. H. (2001). Comorbidity among students with emotional disturbance. *Behavioral Disorders, 26*(3), 200-213.

Curwin, R. L., & Mendler, A. N. (1998). *Discipline with dignity.* Merrill Education/ASCD College Textbook Series.

Curwin, R. L., & Mendler, A. N. (2000). *Discipline with dignity* (2nd ed.). Upper Saddle River, NJ: Merrill/Prentice Hall.

Custer, S., McKean, K., Meyers, C., Murphy, D., Olesen, S., & Parker, S. (1990). *SMARTS: Studying, memorizing, active listening, reviewing, test-taking, and survival skills. A study skills resource guide.* Longmont, CO : Sopris West.

Daggett, L. M. (1995). *Reasonable schools and special students: Tort liability of school districts and employees for injuries to, or caused by, students with disabilities.* Paper presented at the International Conference of the Council for Exceptional Children, Indianapolis, IN.

Dagley, D. L., McGuire, M. D., & Evans, C. W. (1994). The relationship test in the discipline of disabled students. *Education Law Reporter, 88,* 13-31.

Darch, C., Miller, A., & Shippen, P. (1998). Instructional classroom management: A proactive model for managing student behavior. *Beyond Behavior, 9*(3), 18-27.

Darch, C. B., & Kame'enui, E. J (2004). *Instructional classroom management: A proactive approach to behavior management* (2nd ed.). Upper Saddle River, NJ: Merrill/Prentice Hall.

Darveaux, D. (1984). The good behavior game plus merit: Controlling disruptive behavior and improving student motivation. *School Psychology Review, 13,* 510-514.

Davis, C.A., & Fox, J.J. (1999). Environmental arrangement, setting events, and applied research. *Journal of Behavioral Education, 9*(2), 77-96.

Davis, D. E. (1988). *My friends and me.* Circle Pines, MN: American Guidance.

Davis, R.W., & Hajicek, J. O. (1985). Effects of self-instructional training and strategy training on a mathematics task with severely behaviorally disordered students. *Behavioral Disorders, 10,* 275-282.

De la Paz, S. & Graham, S. (1997). Strategy instruction in writing: Effect on the writing performance and behavior of students with learning difficulties. *Exceptional Children, 63,* 167-183.

De Martini-Scully, D., Bray, M.A., & Kehle, T. J. (2000). A packaged intervention to reduce disruptive behaviors in general education students. *Psychology in the Schools, 37*(2), 149-156.

De Pry, R. L. & Sugai, G. (2002). The effect of active supervision and pre-correction on minor behavioral incidents in a sixth grade general education classroom. *Journal of Behavioral Education, 11,* 255-267.

Delbecq, A., Van de Ven, A., & Gustafson, D. (1986). *Group techniques for program planning: A guide to nominal group and Delphi processes.* Middleton, WI: Green Briar.

Delpit, L. (1995). *Other people's children: Cultural conflict in the classroom.* New York: New Press.

Delquadri, J. C., Greenwood, C. R., Whorton, D., Carta, J. J., & Hall, R. V. (1986). Classwide peer tutoring. *Exceptional Children, 52,* 535-542.

Deno, S. & Fuchs, L. S., (1987). Developing curriculum-based measurement systems for data-based special education problem solving. *Focus on Exceptional Children, 19,* 1-16.

Deno, S., Marston, D., & Tindal, G. (1986). Direct and frequent curriculum-based measurement: An alternative for educational decision making. *Special Services in the Schools, 2*(2-3), 5-27.

Deno, S. L. (1985). Curriculum-based measurement: The emerging alternative. *Exceptional Children, 52*(3), 219-232.

Deno, S. L. (1987). Curriculum-based measurement. *Teaching Exceptional Children, 20,* 21.

Deno, S. L. (1992). The nature and development of curriculum-based measurement. *Preventing School Failure, 36*(2), 5-10.

Deno, S. L. (1998). Academic progress as incompatible behavior: Curriculum-based measurement (CBM) as intervention. *Beyond Behavior, 9*(3), 12-17.

Deno, S. L. (2001). Curriculum-based measurement: Academics as incompatible behavior. *Beyond Behavior, 9*(3), 12-18.

Deno, S. L., Espin, C. A., & Fuchs, L. S. (2002). Evaluation strategies for preventing and remediating basic skill deficits. In Stoner, G., Shinn, M. R., & Walker, H. M. (Eds.), *Interventions for achievement and behavior problems* (pp. 213-242). Washington, DC: National Association of School Psychologists.

Deno, S. L., Marston, D., & Mirkin, P. K. (1982). Valid measurement procedures for continuous evaluation of written expression. *Exceptional Children, 48,* 368-371.

Deno, S. L., Mirkin, P. K., & Chiang, B. (1982). Identifying valid measures of reading. *Exceptional Children, 49,* 36-45.

Deno, S. L., Mirkin, P. K., & Marston, D. (1980). *Relationships among simple measures of written expression and performance on standardized achievement tests* (Research Report No. 22). Minneapolis: University of Minnesota Institute for Research on Learning Disabilities.

DePaepe, P. A., Shores, R. E., Jack, S. L. & Denny, R. K. (1996). Effects of task difficulty on the disruptive and on-task behavior of students with severe behavior disorders. *Behavioral Disorders, 21,* 216-225.

Department of Education. (n.d.) *The IDEA Amendments of 1997.* Retrieved from http://www.ed.gov./IDEA/amend95/prin2.html

Department of Education answers questions on regulations. (1997, November 21). *The Special Educator.* Horsham, PA: LRP Publications.

Devine, T. G. (1987). *Teaching study skills. A guide for teachers* (2nd ed.). Boston: Allyn & Bacon.

Dickens v. Johnson County Board of Education, 661 F. Supp. 155 (E.D. Tenn. 1987).

Dieker, L. A., & Barnett, C. A. (1996). Effective co-teaching. *Teaching Exceptional Children, 29,* 5-7.

DiGangi, S. A., & Maag, J. W. (1992). A component analysis of self-management training with behaviorally disordered youth. *Behavioral Disorders, 17,* 281-290.

DiGangi, S. A., Maag, J. W., & Rutherford, R. B., Jr. (1991). Self-graphing of on-task behavior: Enhancing the reactive effects of self-monitoring on on-task behavior and academic performance. *Learning Disability Quarterly, 14,* 221-230.

Din, F. S. (2000). Use direct instruction to improve reading skills quickly. *Rural Educator, 21*(3), 1-4.

Dinkmeyer, D. (1973). *Developing understanding of self and others (DUSO program).* Circle Pines, MN: American Guidance.

Dodge, K. A. (1985). Facets of social interaction and the assessment of social competence in children. In B. H. Schneider, K. H. Rubin, & J. E. Ledingham (Eds.), *Children's peer relations: Issues in assessment and intervention* (pp. 3-22). NY: Springer-Verlag.

Dougherty, B. S., Fowler, S. A., & Paine, S. (1985). The use of peer monitors to reduce negative interactions during recess. *Journal of Applied Behavior Analysis, 18,* 141-153.

Downing, J. E. (1999). *Teaching communication skills to students with severe disabilities.* Baltimore: Brookes.

Drabman, R. S., Spitalnik, R., & O'Leary, K. D. (1973). Teaching self-control to disruptive children. *Journal of Abnormal Psychology, 82,* 10-16.

Drasgow, E. (1997). Positive approaches to reducing undesirable behavior. *Beyond Behavior, 8*(2), 10-13.

Drasgow, E., & Yell, M. L. (2001). Functional behavioral assessment: Legal requirements and challenges. *School Psychology Review, 30*(2), 239-251.

Drasgow, E., & Yell, M. L. (2002). School-wide behavior support: Legal implications and requirements. In J. K. Luiselli & C. Diament (Eds.),. *Behavior psychology in the schools: Innovations in evaluation, support, and consultation* (pp. 129-146). New York: The Haworth Press.

Drasgow, E., Yell, M. L., Bradley, R., & Shriner, J. G. (1999). The IDEA Amendments of 1997: A school-wide model for conducting functional behavioral assessments and developing behavior intervention plans. *Education and Treatment of Children, 22,* 244-266.

Drasgow, E., Yell, M. L., & Robinson, T. R. (2001). Developing Legally and Educationally Appropriate IEPs: Federal Law and Lessons Learned from the Lovaas Hearings and Cases. *Remedial and Special Education, 22,* 359-373.

Drew, N. (1987). *Learning the skills of peacemaking: An activity guide for elementary-age children on communicating/cooperating/resolving conflict.* Rolling Hills Estates, CA: Jalmar.

Dunlap, G., Clarke, S., Ramos, E., Wright, S., Jackson, M., & Brinson, S. (1995). Self-monitoring of classroom behaviors with students exhibiting emotional and behavioral challenges. *School Psychology Quarterly, 10,* 175-177.

Dunlap, G., dePerczel, M., Clarke, S., Wilson, D., Wright, S., White, R., et al. (1994). Choice making to promote adaptive behavior for students with emotional and behavioral challenges. *Journal of Applied Behavior Analysis, 27,* 505-518.

Dunlap, G., Foster-Johnson, L., Clarke, S., Kern, L., & Childs, K. E. (1995). Modifying activities to produce functional outcomes: Effects on the disruptive behaviors of students with disabilities. *Journal of the Association for Persons with Severe Handicaps, 20,* 248-258.

Dunlap, G., Harrower, J., & Fox, L. (2005). Understanding the environmental determinants of problem behaviors. In L. M. Barbara & L. Kern, *Individualized supports for students with problem behaviors: Designing positive behavior plans* (pp. 25-46). New York: Guilford Press.

Dunlap, G., Kern, L., dePerczel, M., Clarke, S. Wilson, D., Childs, K. E., et al. (1993). Functional analysis of classroom variables for students with emotional and behavioral disorders. *Behavioral Disorders, 18*, 275-291.

Dunlap, G., & Koegel, R. L. (1999). Welcoming editorial. *Journal of Positive Behavior Interventions, 1*, 1, 2-3.

DuPaul, G. J., Ervin, R. A., Hook, C. L., & McGoey, K. E. (1998). Peer tutoring for children with attention deficit hyperactivity disorder: Effects on classroom behavior and academic performance. *Journal of Applied Behavior Analysis, 31*(31), 579-592.

DuPaul, G. J., Guevremont, D. C., & Barkley, R. A. (1992). Behavioral treatment of attention-deficit hyperactivity disorder in the classroom. The use of the attention training system. *Behavior Modification, 16*, 204-225.

Durand, V. M. (1990). *Severe behavior problems: A functional communication training approach.* New York: Guilford.

Durkin, D. (1981). Reading comprehension instruction in five basal reader series. *Reading Research Quarterly, 16*(4), 515-544.

Dush, D. M., Hirt, M. L., & Schroeder, H. E. (1989). Self-statement modification in the treatment of child behavior disorders. *Psychological Bulletin, 106*, 97-106.

Dustin, D., & Ehly, S. (1992). School consultation in the 1990s. *Elementary School Guidance and Counseling, 26*, 165-175.

D'Zurilla, T. J., & Goldfried, M. R. (1971). Problem solving and behavior modification. *Journal of Abnormal Psychology, 78*, 107-126.

Earle, R. S. (1992). Talk about teaching: New lamps for old. *Educational Technology, 32*(3), 35-37.

Eber, L., Nelson, C. M., & Miles, P. (1997). School-based wraparound for students with emotional and behavioral challenges. *Exceptional Children, 63*(4), 539-556.

Eber, L., Sugai, G., Smith, C. R., & Scott, T. M. (2002). Wraparound and positive behavioral interventions and supports in the schools. *Journal of Emotional and Behavioral Disorders, 10*, 171-180.

Elbaum, B., Vaughn, S., Hughes, M. T., & Moody, S. W. (1999). Grouping practices and reading outcomes for students with disabilities. *Exceptional Children, 65*, 399-415.

Elksnin, L. K., & Elksnin, N. (1998). Teaching social skills to students with learning and behavior problems. *Intervention in School and Clinic, 33*(3), 131-140.

Ellett, L. (1993). Instructional practices in mainstreamed secondary classrooms. *Journal of Learning Disabilities, 26*(1), 57-64.

Elliott, J. L., & Thurlow, M. L. (2003). *Improving test performance of students with disabilities . . . on district and state assessments.* Thousand Oaks, CA: Corwin Press.

Elliott, S. N., Busse, R. T. and Gresham, F. M., 1993. Behavior rating scales: Issues of use and development. *School Psychology Review*, 22, pp. 313-321.

Elliott, S. N., Witt, J. C., Galvin, G. A., & Peterson, R. (1984). Acceptability of positive and reductive behavioral interventions: Factors that influence teachers' decisions. *Journal of School Psychology, 22*, 353-360.

Ellis, A. (1973). Rational-emotive therapy. In R. Corsini (Ed.), *Current psychotherapies.* Itasca, IL: F. E. Peacock.

Ellis, A. (1994). *Reason and emotion in psychotherapy: Revised and updated.* New York: Birch Lane Press.

Ellis, E. S., Worthington, L. A., & Larkin, M. J. (1994). *Research synthesis on effective teaching principles and the design of quality tools for educators.* University of Oregon: National Center to Improve the Tools of Educators.

Emmer, E., Evertson, C. M., & Anderson, L. (1982). Effective classroom management at the beginning of the school year. *Elementary School Journal, 80*, 219-231.

Emmer, E. T., Evertson, C. M., & Worsham, M. E. (2003). *Classroom management for secondary teachers* (6th ed.). Boston: Allyn & Bacon.

Emmer, E. T., Evertson, C., & Worsham, M. E. (2006). *Classroom management for secondary teachers* (7th ed.). Boston: Allyn & Bacon.

Englemann, S. & Silbert, J. (1985). *Expressive writing 1.* Chicago; Science Research Associates.

Epanchin, B. C. (1991). Teaching social behavior. In J. L. Paul & B. C. Epanchin (Eds.), *Educating emotionally disturbed children and youth* (2nd ed., pp. 413-448). Upper Saddle River, NJ: Merrill/Prentice Hall.

Espin, C. A., Shin J. & Busch, T. W. (2000). *Focusing on formative evaluation.* Current Practice Alerts, 1(3), 1-4.

Espin, C. A., Shin, J., Deno, S. L., Skare, S., Robinson, S., & Benner, B. (2000). Identifying indicators of written expression proficiency for middle school students. *The Journal of Special Education, 34*, 140-153.

Espin, C. A., & Yell, M. L. (1994). Development of an empirically based methodology for evaluation of preservice teachers. *Teacher Education and Special Education, 17*, 154-169.

Etscheidt, S. (1991). Reducing aggressive behavior and improving self-control: A cognitive-behavioral training program for behaviorally disordered adolescents. *Behavioral Disorders, 16*, 107-115.

Etscheidt, S., Stainback, S., & Stainback, W. (1984). The effectiveness of teacher proximity as an initial technique of helping pupils control their behavior. *The Pointer, 28*, 33-35.

Evertson. C. (1989). Improving classroom management: A school-based program for beginning the year. *Journal of Educational Research, 83*(2), 82-90.

Evertson, C., Anderson, C., Anderson, L., & Brophy, J. (1980). Relationship between classroom behavior and student outcomes in junior high math and English classes. *American Elementary Research Journal, 17*, 43-60.

Evertson, C., & Emmer, E. (1982). Effective classroom management at the beginning of the school year in junior high classes. *Journal of Educational Psychology, 74*, 485-498.

Evertson, C., Emmer, E. T., & Worsham, M. E. (2006). *Classroom management for elementary teachers* (7th ed.). Boston: Allyn & Bacon.

Evertson, C. M., Emmer, E. T., & Brophy, J. E. (1980). Predictors of Effective Teaching in Junior High Mathematics Classrooms. *Journal for Research in Mathematics Education, 11*, pp. 167-178.

Evertson, C. M., Emmer, E. T., Sanford, J. P., & Clemens, B. S. (1983). Improving classroom management: An experiment in elementary school classrooms. *Elementary School Journal, 84*(2), 173-188.

Evertson, C. M., Emmer, E. T., & Worsham, M. E. (2003). *Classroom management for elementary teachers* (6th ed.). Boston: Allyn & Bacon.

Evertson, C. M., & Harris, A. H. (1992). What do we know about managing classrooms. *Educational Leadership, 47*(7), 74-78.

Eyer, T. (1998). Greater expectations: How the 1997 IDEA Amendments raise the basic floor of opportunity for children with disabilities. *Education Law Reporter, 126*, 1-19.

Fabry, B. D., Mayhew, G. L., & Hanson, A. (1984). Incidental teaching of mentally retarded students within a token system. *American Journal of Mental Deficiency, 89*, 29-36.

Falk, K. B., & Wehby, J. H. (2001). The effects of peer-assisted learning strategies on the beginning reading skills of young children with emotional or behavioral disorders. *Behavioral Disorders, 26*(4), 344-359.

Family Educational Rights and Privacy Act (FERPA), 20 U.S.C. § 1232, *et seq.* (1974).

Farmer, T. W., & Cadwallader, T. W. (2000). Social interactions and peer support for problem behavior. *Preventing School Failure, 44*, 105-109.

Federal Criminal Code, 18 U.S.C. § 930(g).

Federal Register (1993, February 10). Washington, DC: U.S. Government Printing office, 7938.

Feindler, E. L., & Fremouw, W. J. (1983). Stress inoculation training for adolescent anger problems. In D. Meichenbaum & M. E. Jaremko (Eds.), *Stress reduction and prevention*. New York: Plenum.

Feindler, E. L., Marriott, S. A., & Iwata, M. (1984). Group anger control training for junior high school delinquents. *Cognitive Therapy and Research, 8*, 299-311.

Feldman, D. (1990). *When do fish sleep? and other imponderables of everyday life*. New York: Perennial.

Ferraro v. Board of Education of the City of New York, 212 N.Y.S. 2nd 615 (1961).

Ferster, C. B., & Skinner, B. F. (1957). *Schedules of reinforcement*. Upper Saddle River, NJ: Merrill/Prentice Hall.

Fischer, L., Schimmel, D., & Stellman, L. (2002). *Teachers and the law* (6th ed.). Boston: Allyn & Bacon.

Fishbaugh, M. (1997). *Models of collaboration*. Boston: Allyn & Bacon.

Fishbein, J. E., & Wasik, B. H. (1981). Effect of the good behavior game on disruptive library behavior. *Journal of Applied Behavior Analysis, 14*, 89-93.

Fisher, C. W., Berliner, D. C., Filby, N. N., Marliave, R., Cahen, L. S., & Dishaw, M. M. (1980). Teaching behaviors, academic learning time, and student achievement: An overview. In C. Denham & A. Lieberman (Eds.), *Time to learn*. Washington, D.C.: National Institute of Education.

Fitzpatrick, K. A., & McGreal, T. L. (1983). The effect of training in classroom management on academic engaged time in secondary classrooms. *Illinois School of Research and Development, 20*(1), 20-32.

Fitzsimmons, M. K. (1998). *Violence and aggression in children and youth*. (ERIC Document Reproduction Service No. ED 429 419).

Flannery, D. J. (1997). *School violence: Risk, prevention, intervention, and policy*. Retrieved December 1997 from http://eric-web.tc.columbia.edu/monographs/uds109

Fleming, C. B., Harachi, T. W., Cortes, R. C., Abbott, R. D., & Catalano, R. F. (2004). Level and change in reading scores and attention problems during elementary school as predictors of problem behavior in middle school. *Journal of Emotional and Behavioral Disorders, 12*(3), 130-144.

Flower, L. and Hayes, J. R. (1981). A cognitive process theory of writing. *College English, 44*, 765-77.

Foegen, A., & Deno, S. L. (2001). Identifying growth indicators for low-achieving students in middle school mathematics. *The Journal of Special Education, 35(1)*, 4-16.

Foley, R., & Epstein, M. (1992). Correlates of the academic achievement of adolescents with behavioral disorders. *Behavioral Disorders, 18*(1), 9-17.

Foorman, B. R., Francis, D. J., Fletcher, J. M., Schatschneider, C., & Mehta, P. (1998). The role of instruction in learning to read: Preventing reading failure in at-risk children. *Journal of Educational Psychology, 68*, 70-74.

Foreman, S. G., (1980). A comparison of cognitive training and response cost procedures in modifying aggressive behavior of elementary school children. *Child Behavior Therapy, 2*, 49-57.

Forness, S. R., & Kavale, K. A. (1996). Training social skills deficits in children with learning disabilities: A meta-analysis of the research. *Learning Disability Quarterly, 19*, 2-13.

Forness, S. R., & Kavale, K. A. (2000). Emotional or behavioral disorders: Background and current status of the E/BD terminology and definition. *Behavioral Disorders, 25*(3), 264-269.

Forness, S. R., Kavale, K. A., Blum, I. M., & Lloyd, J. W. (1997). What works in special education and related services: Using meta-analysis to guide practice. *Teaching Exceptional Children, 29*(6), 4-9.

Fowler, S. (1986). Peer-monitoring and self-monitoring: Alternatives to traditional teacher management. *Exceptional Children, 52*, 573-582.

Fowler, S. A., & Baer, D. M. (1981). "Do I have to be good all day?": The timing of delayed reinforcement as a factor in generalization. *Journal of Applied Behavior Analysis, 14*, 13-24.

Fox J. J. & Gable, R. A. (2004). Functional behavioral assessment. In R. B. Rutherford, M. M. Quinn, and S. R. Mathur (Ed.), *Handbook of research in emotional and behavioral disorders* (pp. 143-162). New York: Guilford Press.

Foxx, R. M., & Bechtel, D. R. (1983). Overcorrection: A review and analysis. In S. Axelrod & J. Apsche (Eds.), *The effects of punishment on human behavior* (pp. 133-220). New York: Academic Press.

Foxx, R. M., & Shapiro, S. T. (1978). The timeout ribbon: A nonexclusionary timeout procedure. *Journal of Applied Behavior Analysis, 11*, 126-136.

Foxx, R. N. (1998). A comprehensive treatment for inpatient adolescents. *Behavioral Intervention, 13*, 67-77.

Franca, V. M., Kerr, M. M., Reitz, A. L., & Lambert, D. (1990). Peer tutoring among behaviorally disordered students: Academic and social benefits to tutor and tutee. *Education and Treatment of Children, 13*, 109-128.

Francis, D. J., Fletcher, J. M., Stuebing, K. K., Lyon, G. R., Shaywitz, B. A., & Shaywitz, S. E. (2005). Psychometric approaches to the identification of LD: IQ and achievement scores are not sufficient. *Journal of Learning Disabilities, 38*(2), 98-108.

Frantantoni, D. M. (1999). *The effects of direct instruction on sight vocabulary and how it can enhance reading rate and fluency.* M.A. Research Project, Kean University. (ERIC Document Reproduction Service No. ED427302).

Fraser, M. W. (1996). Aggressive behavior in childhood and early adolescence: An ecological-developmental perspective on youth violence. *Social Work, 41*, 347-362.

Fremouw, W. J., & Feindler, E. L. (1978). Peer versus professional models for study skills training. *Journal of Counseling Psychology, 26*(6), 576-580.

French, J. R. P., & Raven, B. (1960). The bases of social power. In D. Cartwright & A. Zander (Eds.), *Group dynamics in research and theory.* Evenson, IL: Row-Peterson.

Friend, M., & Cook, L. (2000). *Interactions: Collaboration skills for school professionals* (3rd ed). New York: Longman.

Frisby, C. (1987). Alternative assessment committee report: Curriculum-based assessment. *CASP Today, 36*, 15-26.

Fry, E. B. (1980). The new instant word list. *The Reading Teacher, 34*(3), 284-289.

Fuchs, D., & Fuchs, L. S. (2005). Peer-assisted learning strategies: Promoting word recognition, fluency, and reading comprehension in young children. *The Journal of Special Education, 39*(1), 34-44.

Fuchs, D., Fuchs, L.S., & Burish, P. (2000). Peer assisted learning strategies: An evidence based practice to promote reading achievement. *Learning Disabilities Research & Practice, 15*(2) 85-91.

Fuchs, D., Fuchs, L. S., Mathes, P. G., & Simmons, D. C. (1996). *Peer-assisted learning strategies in readings: A manual.* Available from http://kc.vanderbilt.edu/pals/

Fuchs, D., Fuchs, L. S., McMaster, K. L., Yen, L., & Svenson, E. (2004). Nonresponders: How to find them? How to help them? What do they mean for special education? *TEACHING Exceptional Children, 37*(1), 72-77.

Fuchs, L., & Fuchs, D. (1986). Effects of systematic formative evaluation: A meta-analysis. *Exceptional Children, 53*, 199-208.

Fuchs, L. S. (1989). Evaluating solutions: Monitoring progress and revising intervention plans. In M. R. Shinn (Ed.), *Curriculum-based measurement: Assessing special children* (pp. 153-181). New York: Guilford Press.

Fuchs, L. S., & Allinder, R. M. (1993). Computer applications in the schools for students with mild disabilities: Computer-assisted instruction and computer-managed instruction. In R. A. Gable & S. F. Warren (Eds.), *Advance in mental retardation and development disabilities* (pp. 49-70). Philadelphia: Jessica Kingsley Publishers.

Fuchs, L. S., & Deno, S. L. (1994). Must instructionally useful performance assessment be based in the curriculum? *Exceptional Children, 61*(1), 15-24.

Fuchs, L. S., & Fuchs, D. (1992). Identifying a measure for monitoring student reading progress. *School Psychology Review, 21*(1), 45-58.

Fuchs, L. S., & Fuchs, D. (2002). Curriculum-based measurement: Describing competence, enhancing outcomes, evaluating treatment effects, and identifying nonresponders. *Peabody Journal of Education, 77*(2), 64-84.

Fuchs, L. S., Fuchs, D., & Deno, S. L. (1982). Reliability and validity of curriculum-based informal reading inventories. *Reading Research Quarterly. 18*(1), 6-26.

Fuchs, L. S., Fuchs, D., & Hamlett, C. L. (1993). Technological advances linking the assessment of students' academic proficiency to instructional planning. *Journal of Special Education Technology, 12*, 49-62.

Fuchs, L. S., Fuchs, D., & Hamlett, C. L. (1994). Strengthening the connection between assessment and instructional planning with expert systems. *Exceptional Children, 61*, 138-146.

Fuchs, L. S., Fuchs, D., Hamlett, C. L., & Appleton, A. C. (2002). Explicitly teaching for transfer: Effects on the mathematical problem-solving performance of students with mathematical disabilities. *Learning Disabilities Research & Practice, 17*(2), 90-106.

Fuchs, L. S., Fuchs, D., Hamlett, C. L., Phillips, N. B., Karns, K., & Dutka, S. (1997). Enhancing students' helping behavior during peer-mediated instruction with conceptual mathematical explanations. *Elementary School Journal, 97*, 223-249.

Fuchs, L. S., Fuchs, D., Hamlett, C. L., & Stecker, P. M. (1990). The role of skills analysis in curriculum-based measurement in math. *School Psychology Review, 19*, 6-22.

Fuchs, L. S., Fuchs, D., Hamlett, C. L., Walz, L., & Germann, G. (1993). Formative evaluation of academic progress: How much growth can we expect? *School Psychology Review, 22*(1), 27-48.

Fuchs, L. S., Fuchs, D., & Karns, K. (2001). Enhancing kindergartener's mathematical development: Effects of peer-assisted learning strategies. *Elementary School Journal, 101*(5), 495-510.

Fuchs, L. S., Fuchs, D., & Maxwell, L. (1988). The validity of informal reading comprehension measures. *Remedial and Special Education, 9*(2), 20-28.

Fuchs, L. S., Fuchs, D., Yazdian, L., & Powell, S. R. (2002). Enhancing first-grade children's mathematical development with peer-assisted learning strategies. *School Psychology Review, 31*, 369-584.

Fuchs, L. S., Hamlett, C. L., & Fuchs, D. (1997). *Monitoring Basic Skills Program* [computer program]. Austin, TX: Pro-Ed.

Fulk, B. M., Lohman, D., & Belfiore, P. J. (1997). Effects of integrated picture mnemonics on the letter recognition and letter-sound acquisition of transitional first-grade students with special needs. *Learning Disability Quarterly, 20*, 33-42.

Furlong, M., & Morrison, G. (2000). The school in school violence. *Journal of Emotional and Behavioral Disorders, 8*, 71-82.

Gable, R., Hendrickson, J. M., & Sasso, G. M. (1995). Toward a more functional analysis of aggression. *Education and Treatment of Children, 18*, 226-242.

Gable, R. A. (1996). A critical analysis of functional assessment: Issues for researchers and practitioners. *Behavioral Disorders, 22*, 36-40.

Gable, R. A., Hendrickson, J. M., & Rutherford, R. B. (1991). Strategies for integrating students with behavioral disorders into general education. In R. B. Rutherford, Jr., S. A. DiGangi, & S. R. Mathur (Eds.), *Monograph in severe behavior disorders of children and youth* (Vol. 14, pp. 18-32). Reston, VA: Council for Children with Behavioral Disorders.

Gable, R. A., Hendrickson, J. M., Tonelson, S. W., & Van Aker, R. (2002). Integrating academic and non-academic instruction for students with emotional/behavioral disorders. *Education and Treatment of Children, 25*(3), 459-475.

Gable, R. A., Hendrickson, J. M., Young, C.C., & Shokoohi-Yekta, M. (1992). Pre-service preparation and classroom practices of teachers of students with emotional/behavioral disorders. *Behavioral Disorders, 17*, 126-134.

Gable, R. A., Quinn, M. M., Rutherford, R. B., Howell, K. W., & Hoffman, C. C. (2000). *Addressing student problem behavior. Part III. Creating positive intervention plans and supports.* Washington, DC: Center for Effective Collaboration and Practice.

Gable, R. A., & Strain, P. S. (1981). Individualizing a token economy system for the treatment of children's behavior disorders. *Behavioral Disorders, 1*, 39-45.

Gage, N. L. (1978). *The scientific basis of the art of teaching.* New York: Teacher's College Press.

Gall, M. D., Gall, J., Jacobsen, D. R., & Bullock, T. L. (1990). *Tools for learning: A guide to teaching study skills.* Alexandria, VA: Association for Supervision and Curriculum Development.

Gargiulo, R. M. (2006). *Special education in contemporary society.* Belmont, CA: Thompson Wadsworth.

Gartner, A., & Lipsky, D. (1992). Beyond special education: Toward a quality system for all students. In T. Hehir & T. Latus (Eds.), *Special education at the century's end: Evolution and theory and practice since 1970* (pp. 123-158). Cambridge, MA: Harvard Educational Review.

Gaskins, R. W. (1988). The missing ingredients: Time on task, direct instruction, and writing. *The Reading Teacher, 41*(8), 750-755.

Gaskins, R. W., Gaskins, I. W., Anderson, R. C., & Schommer, M. (1995). The reciprocal relationship between research and development: An example involving a decoding strand for poor readers. *Journal of Reading Behavior, 27*(3), 337-377.

Gast, D. L., & Nelson, C. M. (1977). Legal and ethical considerations for the use of timeout in special education settings. *The Journal of Special Education, 11*, 457-467.

Gelfand, D. M., & Hartmann, D. P. (1984). *Child behavior analysis and therapy* (2nd ed.). New York: Pergamon.

George, N. L., George, M. P., Gersten, R., & Grosenick, J. K. (1995). To leave or stay: An exploratory study of teachers of students with emotional and behavioral disorders. *Remedial and Special Education, 16*, 227-236.

Gerber, M. M., & Solari, E. J. (2005). Teaching effort and the future of cognitive-behavioral interventions. *Behavioral Disorders, 30*, 289-299.

Gersten, R. (1985). Direct instruction with special education students: A review of evaluation research. The *Journal of Special Education, 19*(1), 41-58.

Gersten, R., Carnine, D., & Woodward, J. (1987). Direct instruction research: The third decade. *Remedial and Special Education, 8*(6), 48-56.

Gersten, R., Keating, T., Yovanoff, P., & Harniss, M. (2001). Working in special education: Factors that enhance special educator's intent to stay. *Exceptional Children, 67*(4), 549-572.

Gettinger, M. (1986). Issues and trends in academic engaged time of students. *Special Services in the Schools, 2*(4), 1-17.

Giangreco, M. F., Edelman, S. W., Broer, S. M., & Doyle, M. B. (2001). Paraprofessional support of students with disabilities: Literature from the past decade. *Exceptional Children Children, 68*, 45-63.

Gibb, G. S., & Wilder, L. K. (2002). Using functional analysis to improve reading instruction for students with learning disabilities and emotional/behavioral disorders. *Preventing School Failure, 46*(4), 152-157.

Gibbs, J. (1987). *Tribes.* Santa Rosa, CA: Center Source Publications.

Gickling, E., & Havertape, J. (1981). *Curriculum-based assessment (CBA).* Minneapolis: National School Psychology Inservice Training Network.

Gickling, E., & Thompson, V. (1985). A personal view of curriculum-based assessment. *Exceptional Children, 52*, 205-218.

Giddan, J. J., Bade, K. M., Rickenberg, D., & Ryley, A. T. (1995). Teaching the language of feelings to students with severe emotional and behavioral handicaps. *Language, Speech, and Hearing in the Schools, 26*, 3-13.

Gillies, R. M., & Ashman, A. F. (2000). The effects of cooperative learning on students with learning difficulties in the lower elementary school. *The Journal of Special Education, 34*, 19.

Ginott, H. (1971). *Teacher and child.* New York: Macmillan.

Glang, A, Singer, G., Cooley, E., & Tish, N. (1992). Tailoring direct instruction techniques for use with elementary students with traumatic brain injury. *Journal of Head Trauma Rehabilitation, 7*(4), 93–108.

Glassberg, L. A., Hooper, S. R., & Mattison, R. E. (1999). Prevalence of learning disabilities at enrollment in special education students with behavior disorders. *Behavioral Disorders, 25*(1), 9–21.

Gleason, M. M. (1995). Using direct instruction to integrate reading and writing for students with learning disabilities. *Reading and Writing Quarterly: Overcoming Learning Difficulties, 11*(1), 91–108.

Glynn, E. L., Thomas, J. D., & Shee, S. M. (1973). Behavioral self-control of on-task behavior in an elementary classroom. *Journal of Applied Behavior Analysis, 6*, 105–113.

Goals 2000: Educate America Act of 1994, P.L. 103–227, 20 U.S.C. § 6301 *et seq.*

Goldstein, A. P. (1988). *The PREPARE curriculum.* Champaign, IL: Research Press.

Goldstein, A. P. (1999). *The PREPARE curriculum: Teaching prosocial competencies (Rev. ed.).*, Champaign, IL: Research Press.

Goldstein, A. P., & Glick, B. (1987). *Aggression replacement training: A comprehensive intervention for aggressive youth.* Champaign, IL: Research Press.

Goldstein, A. P., Sprafkin, R. P., Gershaw, N. J., & Klein, P. (1980). *Skillstreaming the adolescent.* Champaign, IL: Research Press.

Goldstein, B. A. (1997). Providing transition services. *Proceedings of the 16th National Institute on Legal Issues in Educating Individuals with Disabilities,* Alexandria, VA: LRP.

Goldstein, G., Shemansky, W. J., Cavalier, A. R., Ferretti R. P., & Hodges, A. E. (1997). Self-management within a classroom token economy for students with learning disabilities. *Research in Developmental Disabilities, 18*, 167–178.

Goldsworthy, C. L. (2003). *Developmental reading disabilities: A language based treatment approach* (2nd ed.). Clifton Park, NY: Delmar Learning.

Goleman, D. (1995). *Emotional Intelligence.* New York: Bantam.

Gonzalez, J. E., Nelson, R. J., Gutkin, T. B., Saunders, A., Galloway, A. & Shwery, C. S. (2004). Rational Emotive Therapy with Children and Adolescents. *Journal of Emotional and Behavioral Disorders; 12*, 222–235.

Good, R. H., & Salvia, J. (1988). Curriculum bias in published, norm–referenced reading tests: Demonstrable effects. *School Psychology Review, 17*(1), 51–60.

Good, R. H., Simmons, D. S., Kame'enui, E. J., Kaminski, R. A., & Wallin, J. (2002). *Summary of decision rules for intensive, strategic, and benchmark instructional recommendations in kindergarten through third grade* (Technical Report No. 11). Eugene: University of Oregon Press.

Good, T. L., & Brophy, J. E. (2003). *Looking in classrooms* (9th ed.). Boston: Allyn & Bacon.

Good, T. L., & Brophy, J. E. (2008). *Looking in classrooms* (10th ed.). Boston: Pearson/Allyn & Bacon.

Good, T. L., & Grouws, D. (1979). The Missouri mathematics effectiveness project: An experimental study in fourth-grade classrooms. *Journal of Educational Psychology, 71,* 355–362.

Gorn, S. (1998). *The answer book on individualized education programs.* Horsham, PA: LRP.

Gorn, S. (1999). *What do I do when . . . The answer book on discipline.* Horsham, PA: LRP.

Graesser, A., Golding, J. M., & Long, D. L. (1991). Narrative representation and comprehension. In R. Barr, M. L. Kamil, P. B. Mosenthal, & P. D. Pearson (Eds.), *Handbook of reading research* (Vol. 2, pp. 171–205). White Plains, NY: Longman.

Graham, S., & Harris, K. R. (1985). Improving learning disabled students' composition skills: Self-control strategy training. *Learning Disability Quarterly, 8*, 27–36.

Graham, S., & Harris, K. R. (1988). Instructional recommendations for teaching writing to exceptional students. *Exceptional Children, 6*, 506–512.

Graham, S., & Harris, K. R. (1997). It can be taught, but it does not develop naturally: Myths and realities in writing instruction. *School Psychology Review, 26,* 414–424.

Graham, S., & Harris, K. R. (2003). Students with learning disabilities and the process of writing: A meta–analysis of SRSD studies. In H. L. Swanson, K. R. Harris, & S. Graham (Eds.), *Handbook of learning disabilities* (pp. 323–344). New York: Guilford Press.

Graham, S., & Perrin, D. (2006). *Writing next: Effective strategies to improve writing of adolescents in middle and high school.* Alliance for Excellence in Education. Washington, D.C.

Graves, A., & Levin, J. (1989). Comparison of monitoring and mnemonic text-processing strategies in learning disabled students. *Learning Disability Quarterly, 12*, 232–236.

Green, S. K. (2001). Use of CBM oral reading in the general education classroom. *Assessment for Effective Intervention, 26*(3), 1–13.

Greenbaum, P. E., Dedrick, R. F., Friedman, R. M., Kutash, K., Brown, E. C., Lardieri, S. P., et al. (1996). National adolescent and child treatment study (NACTS): Outcomes for children with serious emotional and behavioral disturbance. In M. H. Epstein, K. Kutash, & A. Duchnowski (Eds.), *Outcomes for children and youth with behavioral disorders.* Austin, TX: Pro-Ed.

Greenberg, M. T., Domitrovich, C., & Bumbarger, B. (1999, July). *Preventing mental disorders in school-age children: A review of the effectiveness of prevention programs.* Retrieved October 28, 2001, from http://www.psu.edu/dept/prevention/CMHS.html

Greene, B. F., Bailey, J. S., & Barber, F. (1981). An analysis and reduction of disruptive behavior on school buses. *Journal of Applied Behavior Analysis, 14*, 177–192.

Greenwood, C., Delquadri, J., & Hall, R. (1983). *Opportunity to respond and student academic performance.* Kansas City: University of Kansas, Juniper Gardens Children's Project.

Greenwood, C. R. (1991). Longitudinal analysis of time, engagement, and achievement in at-risk versus non-risk students. *Exceptional Children, 57,* 521-535.

Greenwood, C. R., (1999). Reflections on a research career: Perspective on 35 years of research at Juniper Garden Children's Project. *Exceptional Children, 66,* 7-22.

Greenwood, C. R., Carta, J. J., & Hall, R. V. (1988). The use of peer tutoring strategies in classroom management and educational instruction. *School Psychology Review, 17,* 258-275.

Greenwood, C. R., Delquadri, J. C., & Hall, R. V. (1989). Longitudinal effects of classwide peer tutoring. *Journal of Educational Psychology, 81,* 371-383.

Greenwood, C. R., Horton, B. T., & Utley, C. A. (2002). Academic engagement: Current perspectives on research and practice. *School Psychology Review, 31*(3), 328-349.

Greenwood, C. R., Maheady, L., & Delquadri, J. C. (2002). Classwide peer tutoring. In G. Stoner, M. R., Shinn, & H. Walker (Eds.), *Interventions for achievement and behavior problems* (2nd ed., pp 611-649). Washington, DC: National Association of School Psychologists.

Gregory, K. M., Kehle, T. J., & McLoughlin, C. S. (1997). Generalization and maintenance of treatment gains using self-management procedures with behaviorally disordered adolescents. *Psychological Reports, 80,* 683-690.

Gresham, F.M. (1983). Use of a home-based dependent group contingency system in controlling destructive behavior: A case study. *School Psychology Review, 12,* 195-199.

Gresham, F. M. (1986). Conceptual issues in the assessment of social competence in children. In P. S. Strain, M. J. Guralnick, & H. M. Walker (Eds.), *Children's social behavior: development, assessment, and modification* (pp. 143-179). New York: Academic Press.

Gresham, F. M. (1989). Assessment of treatment integrity in school consultation and referral. *School Psychology Review, 18,* 37-50.

Gresham, F. M. (1991). Conceptualizing behavior disorders in terms of resistance to intervention. *School Psychology Review, 20,* 23-36.

Gresham, F. M. (1992). Social skills and learning disabilities: causal, concomitant, or correlational? *School Psychology Review, 21,* 348-60

Gresham, F. M. (1998a). Noncategorical approaches to K-12 emotional and behavioral difficulties. In D. Reschly, D. Tilly, & J. Grimes (Eds.), *Functional and noncategorical identification and intervention in special education.* Des Moines: Iowa Department of Education.

Gresham, F. M. (1998b). Social skills training: Should we raze, remodel, or rebuild.? *Behavioral Disorders, 24*(1), 19-25.

Gresham, F. M., & Elliott, S. N. (1993). Social skills intervention guide: Systematic approaches to social skills training. In J. E. Zins & M. J. Elias (Eds.), *Promoting student success through group interventions* (pp. 137-158). Binghamton, NY: Haworth Press.

Gresham, F. M., & Gresham, G. N. (1982). Interdependent, dependent, and independent group contingencies for controlling disruptive behavior. *The Journal of Special Education, 16,* 101-110.

Gresham F. M., & Kern, L. (2004). Internalizing Behavior Problems in Children and Adolescents. In R. B. Rutherford, M. M. Quinn, & S. R. Mathur (Eds.), *Handbook of research in emotional and behavioral disorders* (pp. 262-281). New York: Guilford Press.

Gresham, F. M., & Lambros, K. (1998). Behavioral and functional assessment. In T. S. Watson & F. M. Gresham (Eds.), *Handbook of child behavior therapy* (pp. 3-22). New York: Plenum.

Gresham, F. M., Lane, K., McIntyre, L. L., Olsen-Tinker, H., Dolstra, L., MacMillan, D. L., et al. (2001). Risk factors associated with the co-occurrence of hyperactivity-impulsivity-inattention and conduct problems. *Behavioral Disorders, 26*(3), 189-199.

Gresham, F. M., & MacMillan, D. L. (1997). Social competence and affective characteristics of students with mild disabilities. *Review of Educational Research, 67,* 377-415.

Gresham, F. M., Quinn, M. M. & Restori, A. (1999). Methodological issues in functional analysis: Generalizability to other disability groups. *Behavioral Disorders, 24,* 180-182.

Gresham, F. W., Watson, T. S., & Skinner, C. H. (2001). Functional behavioral assessments: Principles, procedures, and future directions. *School Psychology Review, 30,* 156-172.

Gross, A. M., & Wojnilower, D. A. (1984). Self-directed behavior change in children: Is it self-directed? *Behavior Therapy, 15,* 501-514.

Grossen, B. (2005). *Thirty years of research: What we now know about how children learn to read.* Retrieved June 11, 2005, from http://daisy.ym.edu.tw/~jrlee/30years .html#major.

Guernsey, T. F., & Klare, K. (1993). *Special education law.* Durham, NC: Carolina Academic Press.

Guetzloe, E. (1999). Violence in children and adolescents—a threat to public health and safety: A paradigm of prevention. *Preventing School Failure, 44,* 21-24.

Guido, B., & Colwell, C. G. (1987). A rationale for direct instruction to teach summary writing following expository text reading. *Reading Research and Instruction, 26*(2), 89-98.

Gunn, B., Biglan, A., Smolkowski, K., & Ary, D. (2000). The efficacy of supplemental instruction in decoding skills for Hispanic and non-Hispanic students in early elementary school. *The Journal of Special Education, 34*(2), 90-103.

Gunter, P. L., & Denny, R. K. (1996). Research issues and needs regarding teacher use of classroom management strategies. *Behavioral Disorders, 22*, 15–20.

Gunter, P. L., & Denny, R. K. (1998). Trends and issues in research regarding academic instruction of students with emotional and behavioral disorders. *Behavioral Disorders, 24*(1), 44–50.

Gunter, P. L., Denny, R. K., Jack, S. L., Shores, R. E., & Nelson, C. M. (1993). Aversive stimuli in academic interactions between students with serious emotional disturbance and their teachers. *Behavioral Disorders, 18*, 265–274.

Gunter, P. L., Denny, R. K., Kenton, R., & Venn, M. L. (2000). Modifications of instructional materials and procedures for curricular success of students with emotional and behavioral disorders. *Preventing School Failure, 44*(3), 116–121.

Gunter, P. L., Hummel, J. H., & Conroy, M. A. (1998). Increasing correct academic responses: An effective intervention strategy to decrease problem behaviors. *Effective School Practices, 17*, 43–50.

Gunter, P. L., Hummel, J. H., & Venn, M. L. (1998). Are effective academic instructional practices used to teach students with behavior disorders? *Beyond Behavior, 9*(3), 5–11.

Gunter, P. L, Jack, S., DePaepe, P., Reed, T. M. & Harrison, J. (1994). Effects of challenging behavior of students with EBD on teacher instructional behavior. *Preventing School Failure, 38*, 35–46.

Gunter, P. L., & Reed, T. M. (1996). Self-evaluation of instruction: A protocol for functional assessment of teaching behavior. *Intervention in School and Clinic, 31*, 225–230.

Gunter, P. L., Shores, R. E., Jack, S. L., Denny, R. K., & DePaepe, P. A. (1994). A case study of the effects of altering instructional interactions on the disruptive behavior of a child identified with severe behavior disorder. *Education and Treatment of Children, 17*, 435–444.

Gunter, P. L., Shores, R. E., Jack, S. L., Rasmussen, S. K., & Flowers, J. (1995). On the move: Using teacher proximity to improve students' behavior. *Teaching Exceptional Children, 28*, 12–14.

Hallahan, D. P., & Hudson, K. G. (2002). *Teaching tutorial 2: Self-monitoring of attention*. Retrieved December 15, 2005, from http://www.TeachingLD.org

Hallahan, D. P. & Kauffman, J. M. (2003). *Exceptional learners: Introduction to special education* (9th ed.). Boston: Pearson/Allyn & Bacon.

Hallahan, D. P., Lloyd, J. W., Kneedler, R. D., & Marshall, K. J. (1982). A comparison of the effects of self- versus teacher assessment of on-task behavior. *Behavior Therapy, 13*, 715–723.

Hallahan, D. P., Lloyd, J. W., Kosiewicz, M. M., Kauffman, J. M., & Graves, A. W. (1979). Self-monitoring of attention as a treatment for a learning disabled boy's off-task behavior. *Learning Disability Quarterly, 2*, 24–32.

Hallahan, D. P., Marshall, K. J. & Lloyd, J. W. (1981). Self-recording during group instruction: Effects on attention to task. *Learning Disability Quarterly, 4*, 407–413.

Halle, J. W., Bambara, L. M., & Reichle, J. (2005). Teaching alternative skills. In L. M. Barbara & L. Kern, *Individualized supports for students with problem behaviors: Designing positive behavior plans* (pp. 237–274). New York: Guilford Press.

Halle, J. W., & Drasgow, E. (2003). Response classes: Baer's contribution to understanding their structure and function. In K. S. Budd & T. Stokes (Eds.), *A small matter of proof: The legacy of Donald M. Baer* (pp. 113–124). Las Vegas, NV: Context Press.

Hallenbeck, B. A., & Kauffman, J. M. (1995). How does observational learning affect the behavior of students with EBD. *The Journal of Special Education, 29*, 45–71.

Hamblin, R. L., Hathaway, C., & Wodarski, J. (1974). Group contingencies, peer tutoring, and accelerating academic achievement: Experiment 1. In E. Ramp & B. L. Hopkins (Eds.), *A new direction for education: Behavior analysis* (pp. 41–53). Lawrence: University of Kansas Press.

Hamilton, S. L., Seibert, M. A., Gardner, R. III, & Talbert-Johnson, C. (2000). Using guided notes to improve the academic achievement of incarcerated adolescents with learning and behavior problems. *Remedial and Special Education, 21*(3), 133–140.

Handen, B. L., Parrish, J. M., McClung, T. J., Kerwin, M. E., & Evans, L. D. (1992). Using guided compliance versus time-out to promote child compliance: A preliminary comparative analysis in an analogue setting. *Research in Developmental Disabilities, 13*, 157–170.

Hanson, M. J., & Carta, J. J. (1995). Addressing the challenges of families with multiple risks. *Exceptional Children, 62*, 201–212.

Harp, B., & Brewer, J. A. (2005). *The informed reading teacher: Research-based practice*. Upper Saddle River, NJ: Pearson.

Harris, K. R. (1982). Cognitive-behavior modification: Application with exceptional students. *Focus on Exceptional Children, 15*, 1–16.

Harris, K. R. (1985). Definitional, parametric, and procedural considerations in timeout interventions and research. *Exceptional Children, 51*, 279–288.

Harris, K. R. (1986). Self-monitoring of attentional behavior versus self-monitoring of productivity: Effects on on-task behavior and academic response rate among learning disabled children. *Journal of Applied Behavior Analysis, 19*, 417–423.

Harris, K. R., & Graham, S. (1992). *Helping young writers master the craft: Strategy instruction and self-regulation in the writing process*. Cambridge, MA: Brookline Books.

Harris, K. R., & Graham, S. (1996). *Making the writing process work: Strategies for composition and self-regulation*. Cambridge, MA: Brookline.

Harrison, C., Killion, J., & Mitchell, J. (1989). Site-based management: The realities of implementation. *Educational Leadership, 46*(8), 55–58.

Harry, B., Rueda, R., & Kalyanpur, M. (1999). Cultural reciprocity in sociocultural perspective: Adapting the normalization principle for family collaboration. *Exceptional Children, 66*(1), 123–140.

Hartman V. Loudoun, County School District, 118 F3d 996 (4th Cir 1997)

Hartog-Rapp, F. (1985). The legal standards for determining the relationship between a child's handicapping condition and misconduct charged in a school disciplinary proceeding. *Southern Illinois University Law Journal, 2*, 243–262.

Hartwig, E. P., & Reusch, G. M. (2004). *Discipline in the schools* (2nd ed.). Horsham, PA: LRP.

Hawken, L.S, & Horner, R. H. (2003). Evaluation of a targeted intervention within a schoolwide system of behavior support. *Journal of Behavioral Education, 12*, 225–240.

Hawkins, J. D., Herrenkohl, T. I., Farrington, D. P., Brewer, D., Catalano, R. F., Harachi, T. W., et al. (2000). Predictors of youth violence. *Juvenile Justice Bulletin*, Office of Juvenile Justice and Delinquency Prevention, 1–11.

Hayes v. Unified School District No. 377, 669 F. Supp. 1519 (D. Kan. 1987).

Hayes, S. C., Brownstein, A. J., Haas, J. R., & Greenway, D. E. (1987). Instructions, multiple schedules, and extinction: Distinguishing rule-governed from schedule-controlled behavior. *Journal of the Experimental Analysis of Behavior, 46*, 137–147.

Hayes, S. C., Rosenfarb, I., Wulfert, E., Munt, E. D., Korn, Z., & Zettle, R. D. (1985). Self-reinforcement effects: An artifact of social standard setting? *Journal of Applied Behavior Analysis, 18*, 201–214.

Haynes, M. C., & Jenkins, J. R. (1986). Reading instruction in special education resource rooms. *American Education Research Journal, 23*, 161–190.

Hazel, J. S., Schumaker J. B., Sherman, J. A., & Sheldon, J. (1995). *ASSET: A social skills program for adolescents*. Champagne, IL: Research Press.

Hedges, L.V., & Olkin, I. (1985). *Statistical methods for meta-analysis*. Orlando, FL: Academic Press.

Heflin, J., & Bullock, L. (1999) Inclusion of students with EBD. *Preventing School Failure, 43*, 103–111

Heflin, L. J., & Simpson, R. L. (1998). Interventions for children and youth with autism: Prudent choices in a world of exaggerated claims and empty promises. Part I: Intervention and treatment option review. *Focus on Autism and Other Developmental Disabilities*, 13, 194–211.

Henderson, H. S., Jenson, W. R., & Erken, N. (1986). Focus article. Variable interval reinforcement for increasing on-task behavior in a classroom. *Education and Treatment of Children, 9*, 250–263.

Hendrickson, J., Gable, R., & Shores, R. (1987, Spring). The ecological perspective: Setting events and behavior. *The Pointer, 31*(3), 40–44.

Heward, W. L. (2000). *Exceptional children: An introduction to special education* (6th ed.). Upper Saddle River, NJ: Prentice Hall.

Heward, W. L., & Dardig, J. C. (1978). Improving the parent–teacher relationship through contingency contracting. In D. Edge, B. J. Strenecky, & S. I. Mour (Eds.), *Parenting learning-problem children: The professional educator's perspective*. Columbus: Ohio State University Press.

Hillocks, G., (1984). What works in teaching composition: A meta-analysis of experimental treatment studies. *American Journal of Education, 93* (1), 107–132.

Hillocks, G. (1987). Synthesis of research on teaching writing. *Educational Leadership, 44*, 73–83.

Hinshaw, S. P. (1992). Externalizing behavior problems and academic underachievement in childhood and adolescence: Causal relationships and underlying mechanisms. *Psychological Bulletin, 111*, 127–155.

Hirsch, E. J., Lewis-Palmer, T., Sugai, G., & Schnacker, L. (2004). Using bus discipline referral data in decision making: Two case studies. *Preventing School Failure, 48*(4), 4–9.

Hobbs, S. A., Forehand, R., & Murray, R. G. (1978). Effects of various durations of timeout on the noncompliant behavior of children. *Behavior Therapy, 9*, 652–656.

Hodge, J., Riccomini, P. J., Buford, R., & Herbst, M. (2006). A review of instructional interventions in mathematics for students with emotional and behavioral disorders. *Behavioral Disorders, 31*(3), 297–311.

Hodge, J. & Shriner, J. G. (1997). Mediation. *Beyond Behavior, 8*(2), 20–24.

Hofmeister, A., & Lubke, M. (1990). *Research into practice: Implementing effective teaching strategies*. Boston: Pearson/Allyn & Bacon.

Hogan, S., & Prater, M. A. (1993). The effects of peer tutoring and self-management training on on-task, academic, and disruptive behaviors. *Behavioral Disorders, 18*, 118–128.

Homme, L., Csanyi, A. P., Gonzales, M. A., & Rechs, J. R. (1970). *How to use contingency contracting in the classroom*. Champaign, IL: Research Press.

Homme, L. E. (1965). Perspectives in psychology: XXIV. Control of coverants, the operants of the mind. *Psychological Record, 15*, 501–511.

Hooper, S. R., Roberts, J. E., Zeisel, S. A., & Poe, M. (2003). Core language predictors of behavioral functioning in early elementary school children: Concurrent and longitudinal findings. *Behavioral Disorders, 29*(1), 10–24.

Hopewell (VA) Public Schools, 21 IDELR 189 (OCR 1994).

Hopps, H., & Walker, H. M. (1988). *CLASS: Contingencies for learning academic and social skills*. Seattle, WA: Educational Achievement Systems.

Horner, R., & Carr, E. (1997). Behavioral support for students with severe disabilities: Functional assessment and comprehensive intervention. *The Journal of Special Education, 31*, 84–104.

Horner, R. H., Albin, R. W., Sprague, J. R., & Todd, A. W. (2000). Positive behavior support. In M. E. Snell & F. Brown,

Instruction of students with severe disabilities (5th ed., pp. 207–243), Upper Saddle River, NJ: Merrill/Prentice Hall.

Horner, R. H., & Day, H. M. (1991). The effects of response efficiency on functionally equivalent competing behaviors. *Journal of Applied Behavior Analysis, 24*, 719–732.

Horner, R. H., Dunlap, G., Koegel, R. L., Carr, E. G., Sailor, W., Anderson, J., et al. (1990). Toward a technology of "nonaversive" behavioral support. *Journal of the Association of Persons with Severe Handicaps, 15*(3), 125–132.

Horner, R. H., O'Neill, R. E., & Flannery, K. B. (1993). Effective behavioral support plans. In M.E. Snell & F. Brown (Eds.), *Instruction of students with severe disabilities* (4th ed.) (pp 184–214). Upper Saddle River, NJ: Merrill/Prentice Hall.

Horner, R. H., Sugai, G., & Horner H. F. (2000). A schoolwide approach to student discipline. *The School Administrator, 24*, 20–23.

Horner, R. H., Sugai, G., Lewis-Palmer, T., & Todd, A. W. (2001). Teaching school-wide behavioral expectations. *Report on Emotional & Behavioral Disorders in Youth, 1*(4), 77–79.

Horner, R. H., Sugai, G., & Todd, A. W. (2001). Data need not be a four letter word: Using data to improve schoolwide discipline. *Beyond Behavior, 11*(1), 3–5.

Horner, R. H., Sugai, G., Todd, A. W., & Lewis-Palmer, T. (2000). Elements of behavior support plans: A technical brief. *Exceptionality, 8*, 205–216.

Horner, R. H., Todd, A. W., Lewis-Palmer, T., Irvin, L. K., & Boland, J. B. (2004). The school-wide evaluation tool (SET): A research instrument for assessing school-wide positive behavior support. *Journal of Positive Behavioral Interventions, 6*(1), 3–12.

Horner, R. H., Vaughn, B. J., Day, H. M., & Ard, W. R. (1996). The relationship between setting events and problem behavior: Expanding our knowledge of behavioral support. In L. K. Koegel, R. L. Koegel, G. Dunlap (Eds.), *Positive behavioral support: Including people with difficult behavior in the community.* Baltimore: Paul H. Brookes.

Hosley, N. S. (2003). *Survey and analysis of alternative education programs.* Harrisburg: Center for Rural Pennsylvania.

Hosp, J. L., & Ardoin, S. P. (2008). Assessment for Instructional Planning. *Assessment for Effective Intervention, 33*, in press.

Hosp, M. K., & Hosp, J. (2003). Curriculum-based measurement for reading, math, and spelling: How to do it and why. *Preventing School Failure, 48*(1), 10–17.

Huefner, D. S. (2001). The risks and opportunities of the IEP requirements under IDEA '97. *The Journal of Special Education, 33*, 195–204.

Huefner, D. S. (2005). *Getting comfortable with special education law: A framework for working with children with disabilities.* Norwood, MA: Christopher-Gordon Publishers.

Hughes, C. A. (1996). Memory and test-taking strategies. In D. D. Deshler, E. S. Ellis, & B. K. Lenz (Eds.), *Teaching*

adolescents with learning disabilities (2nd ed., pp. 209–266). Denver CO: Love.

Hughes, C. A., & Boyle, J. R. (1991). Effects of self-monitoring for on-task behavior and task productivity on elementary students with moderate mental retardation. *Education and Treatment of Children, 14*, 96–111.

Hughes, C. A., Korinek, L., & Gorman, J. (1991). Self-management for students with mental retardation in public school settings: A research review. *Education and Training in Mental Retardation, 26*, 271–291.

Hughes, C. A., & Maccini, P. (1997). Computer-assisted mathematics instruction for students with learning disabilities: A research review. *Learning Disabilities, 8*(3), 155–166.

Hughes, C. A., Ruhl, K. I., & Misra, J. W. (1989). An analysis of self-management. *Journal of Behavioral Education, 3*, 401–425.

Hughes, J. N. (1988). Cognitive behavior therapy. In L. Mann & C. Reynolds (Eds.), *The encyclopedia of special education* (pp. 354–355). New York: Wiley.

Hume, A. (1983). Putting writing research into practice. *Elementary School Journal, 84*, 3–18.

Humphrey, L. L., Karoly, P., & Kirschenbaum, D. S. (1978). Self-management in the classroom: Self-imposed response cost versus self-reward. *Behavior Therapy, 9*, 592–601.

Hunt, N., & Marshall, K. (2005). *Exceptional children and youth* (4th ed.). Boston: Houghton Mifflin.

Hupp, S. D., & Reitman, D. (1999). Improving sports skills and sportsmanship in children diagnosed with attention/deficit hyperactivity disorder. *Child and Family Behavior Therapy, 21*(3), 35–51.

Hyter, Y. D. (2003). Language intervention for children with emotional or behavioral disorders. *Behavioral Disorders, 29*(1), 65–76.

Idol, L., Nevin, A., & Paolucci-Whitcomb, P. (1986). *Models of curriculum-based assessment.* Rockville, MD: Aspen.

Imich, A. J. (1994). Exclusions from school: Current trends and issues. *Educational Research, 36*(1), 3–11.

Improving America's Schools Act of 1994, 20 U.S.C. § 16301 *et seq.*

Individuals with Disabilities Education Act (IDEA), 20 U.S.C. § 1400 *et seq.* (1997).

Individuals with Disabilities Education Act Regulations, 34 C.F.R. § 300 *et seq.*

Ingram, K., Lewis-Palmer, T., & Sugai, G. (2005). Function-based intervention planning: Comparing the effectiveness of FBA indicated and contra-indicated intervention plans. *Journal of Positive Behavior Interventions, 7*, 224–236.

Isaacson, S. L. (1987). Effective instruction in written language. *Focus on Exceptional Children, 19*(6), 1–12.

Iwata, B. A., & Bailey, J. S. (1974). Reward versus cost token systems: An analysis of the effects on students and teacher. *Journal of Applied Behavior, 7*, 567–576.

Iwata, B., Dorsey, M., Slifer, K., Bauman, K., & Richman, G. (1982). Toward a functional analysis of self-injury. *Analysis and Intervention in Developmental Disabilities, 3*, 138–148.

Iwata, B. A., Vollmer, T. R., & Zarcone, J. R. (1990). The experimental (functional) analysis of behavior disorders: Methodology, applications, and initiations. In A. C. Repp & N. N. Singh (Eds.) *Perspectives on the use of nonaversive and aversive interventions for persons with developmental disabilities* (pp. 301–330). Sycamore Press: Sycamore, IL.

Jackson, D., Jackson, N., Bennett, M., Bynum, D., & Faryna, E. (1991). *Learning to get along.* Champaign, IL: Research Press.

Jenkins, J. & Pany, D. (1978). Learning word meanings: A comparison of two procedures. *Learning Disability Quarterly, 1*, 21–32.

Jenkins, J. R., & Jewell, M. (1993). Examining the validity of two measures for formative teaching: Reading aloud and maze. *Exceptional Children 59*(5), 421–432.

Jensen, M. (2005). *Introduction to emotional and behavioral disorders: Recognizing and managing problems in the classroom.* Upper Saddle River, NJ: Merrill/Prentice Hall.

Jenson, A. (1966). The role of verbal mediation in mental development. *Journal of Genetic Psychology, 118,* 39–70.

Jenson, W. R., & Reavis, H. K. (1996). Reductive procedures: Time-out and other related techniques. In H. K. Reavis, S. J. Kukic, W. R. Jenson, D. P. Morgan, D. J. Andrews, & S. Fister (Eds.), *Best practices: Behavioral and educational strategies for teachers* (pp. 121–146). Longmont, CO: Sapris west.

Jitendra A., & Xin, Y. P. (1997). Mathematical word-problem-solving instruction for students with mild disabilities and students at risk for math failure: A research synthesis. *The Journal of Special Education, 20*(4), 412–438.

Johns, B., & Carr, V. (1995). *Techniques for managing verbally and physically aggressive students.* Denver, CO: Love.

Johns, B. V., Guetzloe, E. C., Yell, M. L., Scheuermann, B., Webber, J., Carr, V. C., et al. (1996). *Best practices for managing the behavior of adolescents with emotional/behavioral disorders within the school environment.* Reston, VA: Council for Children with Behavioral Disorders.

Johnson, D. W. & Johnson, R. T. (1987). *Learning together and alone: Cooperative, competitive, and individualistic learning.* Englewood Cliffs, NJ: Prentice Hall.

Johnson, D. W., Johnson, R. T., & Holubec, E. (1988). *Cooperation in the classroom.* Edina, MN: Interaction.

Johnson, M., Pugach, M., & Hawkins, A. (2004). School-family collaboration: A partnership. *Focus on Exceptional Children, 36*(4), 1–12.

Johnson, S., Agelson, L., Macierz, Tl, Minnick, M., & Merrell, T. (1995). *Leadership training institute: Interventions for youth with emotional/behavioral disorders who engage in violent and aggressive behavior.* St. Paul, MN: University of St. Thomas Press.

Johnson, S. M. (2000, June 7). Teaching's next generation. *Education Week,* 33–43.

Johnston, P. (1984). Prior knowledge and reading comprehension test bias. *Reading Research Quarterly, 19*(4), 219–236.

Jolivette, K., Wehby, J. H., Canale, J. & Massey, N. G. (2001). Effects of choice making opportunities on the behavior of students with emotional and behavioral disorders. *Behavioral Disorders, 26,* 131–145.

Jolivette, K., Wehby, J. H., & Hirsch, L. (1999). Academic strategy identification for students exhibiting inappropriate classroom behaviors. *Behavioral Disorders, 24,* 210–221.

Jones, V., & Jones, L. (2004). *Comprehensive classroom management: Creating communities of support and solving problems* (6th ed.). Boston: Allyn & Bacon.

Kabler, M. L. (1976). *Teaching fourth-grade children to use self-contracting as a form of self-control.* Unpublished doctoral dissertation, Ohio State University.

Kagan, S. (1994). *Cooperative learning.* San Juan Capistrano, CA: Kagan Cooperative Learning.

Kame'enui, E. J. (2002). *Effective instruction.* Paper presented at the Secretary's Reading Leadership Academy, Washington, DC, 20 February.

Kame'enui, E. J., & Simmons, D. C. (1990). *Designing instructional strategies: The prevention of academic learning problems.* Upper Saddle River, NJ: Merrill/Prentice Hall.

Kamps, D. (2002). Preventing problems by improving behavior. In B. Algozzine & P. Kay (Eds.), *Preventing problem behaviors: A handbook of successful prevention strategies.* Thousand Oaks, CA: Corwin Press.

Kamps, D. M., Ellis, C., Mancina, C., Wyble, J., Greene, L., & Harvey, D. (1995). Case studies using functional analysis for young children with behavior risks. *Education and Treatment of Children, 18,* 243–260.

Kamps, D. M., & Greenwood, C. R. (2003, December). *Formulating secondary level reading interventions.* Paper presented at the National Research Center on Learning Disabilities, Learning Disabilities Symposium. Kansas City, MO.

Kamps, D. M., & Tankersley, M. (1996). Prevention of behavioral and conduct disorders: Trends and research issues. *Behavioral Disorders, 22*(1), 41–48.

Kamps, D. M., Willis, H. P., Greenwood, C. R., Thorne, S., Lazo, J. F., Crockett, J. L., et al. (2003). Curriculum influences on growth in early reading fluency for students with academic and behavioral risks: A descriptive study. *Journal of Emotional and Behavioral Disorders, 2*(4), 211–224.

Kanfer, F. H., & Karoly, P. (1972). Self-control: A behavioristic excursion into the lion's den. *Behavior Therapy, 3,* 398–416.

Kaplan, J. S., & Carter, J. (1995). *Beyond behavior modification: A cognitive-behavioral approach to behavior management in the schools* (3rd ed.). Austin, TX: Pro-Ed.

Kartub, D. T., Taylor-Greene, S., March, R. E., & Horner, R. H. (2000). Reducing hallway noise: A systems approach. *Journal of Positive Behavioral Interventions, 2*(3), 179–182.

Kashani, J. H., Jones, M. R., Bumby, K. M., & Thomas, L. A. (1999). Youth violence: Psychological risk factors, treatment, prevention, and recommendations. *Journal of Emotional & Behavioral Disorders, 7*, 200-211.

Katsiyannis, A., Landrum, T. J., Bullock, L., & Vinton, L. (1997). Certification requirements for teachers of students with emotional or behavioral disorders: A national survey. *Behavioral Disorders, 22*, 131-140.

Katsiyannis, A., & Maag, W. J. (1998). Disciplining students with disabilities: Practice considerations for implementing IDEA '97. *Behavioral Disorders, 23*, 276-289.

Katsiyannis, A., & Smith, C. R. (2003). Disciplining students with disabilities: Legal trends and the issue of interim alternative education settings. *Behavioral Disorders, 28*(4), 410-418.

Katsiyannis, A., & Yell, M. L. (2000). The Supreme Court and school health services: *Cedar Rapids v. Garret F. Exceptional Children, 66*, 317-326.

Katsiyannis, A., Yell, M. L., Bradley, R., (2001). Reflections on the 25th anniversary of the Individuals with Disabilities Education Act. *Remedial and Special Education, 22*, 324-334.

Katsiyannis, A., Zhang, D., & Conroy, M. (2003). Availability of special education teachers: Trends and issues. *Remedial and Special Education, 24*(4), 246-253.

Katzenbach, J., & Smith, D. (1999). *The wisdom of teams: Creating the high-performance organization.* Boston: Harvard Business School Press.

Kauffman, J., Cullinan, D., & Epstein, M. (1987). Characteristics of students placed in special programs for the seriously emotionally disturbed. *Behavioral Disorders, 12*, 175-184.

Kauffman, J., & Lloyd, J. (1995). A sense of place: The importance of placement issues in contemporary special education. In J. Kauffman, J. Lloyd, D. Hallahan, & T. Astuto (Eds.), *Issues in educational placement: Students with emotional and behavioral disorders* (pp. 3-19). Hillsdale, NJ: Erlbaum.

Kauffman, J., & Wong, K. (1991). Effective teachers of students with behavioral disorders: Are generic teaching skills enough? *Behavioral Disorders, 16*, 225-237.

Kauffman, J. M. (2001). *Characteristics of emotional and behavioral disorders of children and youth* (7th ed.). Upper Saddle River, NJ: Merrill/Prentice Hall.

Kauffman, J. M. (2005). *Characteristics of emotional and behavioral disorders of children and youth* (8th ed.). Upper Saddle River, NJ: Merrill/Prentice Hall.

Kauffman, J. M., Brigham, F. J., & Mock, D. R. (2004). Historical to contemporary perspectives on the field of emotional and behavioral disorders. In R. B. Rutherford, M. M. Quinn, & S. R. Mathur (Eds.), *Handbook of research in emotional and behavioral disorders* (pp. 15-31.). New York: Guilford Press.

Kauffman, J. M., & Landrum, T. J. (2008). *Characteristics of emotional and behavioral disorders in children and youth* (9th ed.). Upper Saddle River, NJ: Merrill/Prentice Hall.

Kauffman, J. M., Mostert, M. P., Trent, S. C., & Hallahan, D. P. (2002). *Managing classroom behavior: A reflective case-based approach* (3rd ed.). Boston: Allyn & Bacon.

Kauffman, J. M., Pullen, P. L., & Akers, E. (1998). Classroom management: Teacher-child-peer relationships. In R. J. Whelan (Ed.), *Emotional and behavioral disorders: A 25 year focus* (pp. 363-376). Denver, CO: Love.

Kaufman, S. K., & O'Leary, K. D. (1972). Reward, cost, and self-evaluation procedures for disruptive adolescents in a psychiatric hospital school. *Journal of Applied Behavior Analysis, 5*, 293-309.

Kavale, K. A., & Forness, S. R. (1995). Social skills deficits and training: A meta-analysis of the research in learning disabilities. In T. E. Scruggs & M. A. Mastropieri (Eds.), *Advances in learning and behavioral disabilities* (Vol. 9, pp. 119-160). Greenwich, CT: JAI.

Kavale, K. A., Mathur, S. R., Forness, S. R., Rutherford, R. B., & Quinn, M. M. (1997). Effectiveness of social skills training for students with behavior disorders: A meta-analysis. In T. E. Scruggs & M. A. Mastropieri (Eds.), *Advances in learning and behavioral disabilities* (Vol. 11, pp. 1-26). Greenwich, CT: JAI.

Kavale, K. A., Mathur, S. R., & Mostert, M. P. (2004). Social skills training and teaching social behavior to students with emotional and behavioral disorders. In R. B. Rutherford, M. M. Quinn, & S. R. Mathur (Eds.), *Handbook of research in emotional and behavioral disorders* (pp. 446-461). New York: Guilford Press.

Kazdin, A., Mazurick, J., & Bass, D. (1993). Risk for attrition in antisocial children and families. *Journal of Clinical Child Psychology, 22*(1), 2-16.

Kazdin, A. E. (1977). *The token economy: A review and evaluation.* New York: Plenum Press.

Kazdin, A. E. (1982a). Current developments and research issues in cognitive-behavioral interventions: A commentary. *School Psychology Review, 11*, 75-82.

Kazdin, A. E. (1982b). *Single-case research designs: Methods for clinical and applied settings.* New York: Oxford University Press.

Kazdin, A. E. (1985). The token economy. In R. M. Turner & L. M. Asher (Eds.), *Evaluating behavior therapy outcomes* (pp. 225-253). Belmont, CA: Thomson/Wadsworth.

Kazdin, A. E. (1994). *Behavior modification in applied settings* (5th ed.). Pacific Grove, CA: Brooks/Cole.

Kazdin, A. E. (1995). *Conduct disorders in children and adolescence* (2nd ed.). Thousand Oaks, CA: Sage.

Kazdin, A. E. (2001). *Behavior modification in applied settings* (6th ed.). Upper Saddle River, NJ: Merrill/Prentice Hall.

Kelley, M. L., & McCain, A. P. (1995). Promoting academic performance in inattentive children. *Behavior Modification, 19*, 357-375.

Kelley, M. L., & Stokes, T. F. (1982). Contingency contracting with disadvantaged youth: Improving academic performance. *Journal of Applied Behavior Analysis, 15*, 447-454.

Kellum, S. G., Mayer, L. S., Rebok, G. W., & Hawkins, W. E. (1998). The effects of improving achievement on aggressive behavior and of improving aggressive behavior on achievement through two prevention interventions: An investigation of causal paths. In B. Dohrenwend. (Ed.), *Adversity, stress, and psychopathology* (pp. 486–505). Oxford: Oxford University Press.

Kendall, P. C. (1977). On the efficacious use of verbal self-instructional procedures with children. *Cognitive Therapy and Research, 4,* 331–341.

Kendall, P. C., & Finch, A. J. (1979). Developing nonimpulsive behavior in children's cognitive behavioral strategies on self-control. In P. C. Kendall & S. D. Hollan (Eds.), *Cognitive-behavioral interventions: Therapy, research and procedures.* New York: Academic Press.

Kendall, P. C., & Hollon, S. D. (1979). *Cognitive-behavioral interventions: Therapy, research and procedures.* New York: Academic Press.

Kennedy, C. H., (2005). *Single-case designs for educational research.* Boston: Allyn & Bacon.

Kern, L., Delaney, B., Clarke, S., Dunlap, G., & Childs, K. (2001). Improving the classroom behavior of students with emotional and behavioral disorders using individualized curricular modifications. *Journal of Emotional and Behavioral Disorders, 9*(4), 239–247.

Kern, L. & Dunlap, G. (1998). Curricular modifications to promote desirable classroom behavior. In J. K. Luiselli & M. J. Cameron (Eds.), *Antecedent control: Innovative approaches to behavioral support.* Baltimore: Paul H. Brookes.

Kern, L., Dunlap, G., Childs, K., & Clarke, S. (1994). Use of a classwide self-management program to improve the behavior of students with emotional and behavioral disorders. *Education and Treatment of Children, 17,* 445–458.

Kern, L., O'Neill, R. E., & Starosta, K. (2005). Gathering functional assessment information. In L. M. Barbara & L. Kern, *Individualized supports for students with problem behaviors: Designing positive behavior plans* (pp. 129–164). New York: Guilford Press.

Kern, L., Ringdahl, J. E., Hilt, A., & Sterling-Turner, H. E. (2001). Linking self-management procedures to functional analysis results. *Behavioral Disorders, 26,* 214–226.

Kerr, M. M., & Nelson, C. M. (2002). *Strategies for addressing behavior problems in the classroom* (4th ed.). Upper Saddle River, NJ: Merrill/ Prentice Hall.

Kerr, M. M., & Nelson, C. M. (2006). *Strategies for managing behavior problems in the classroom* (5th ed.). Upper Saddle River, NJ: Merrill/Prentice Hall.

Kerr, M. M. & Zigmond, N. (1986). What do high school teachers want? A study of expectations and standards. *Education and Treatment of Children, 9,* 239–249.

Kiewra, K. A., Benton, S. L., Kim, S., Risch, N., & Christensen, M. (1995). Effects of note-taking format and study technique on recall and relational performance. *Contemporary Educational Psychology, 20,* 172–187.

Kiewra, K. A., DuBois, N. F., Christian, D. McShane, A., Meyerhoffer, M., & Roskelley, D. (1991). Note-taking functions and techniques. *Journal of Educational Psychology, 83*(2), 240–245.

Kiewra, K. A., Mayer, R. E., Christensen, M., Kim, S., & Risch, N. (1991). Effects of repetition on recall and note-taking: Strategies for learning from lectures. *Journal of Educational Psychology, 83*(1), 120–123.

Kiewra, K. A., Mayer, R. E., DuBois, N. F., Christensen, M., Kim, S., & Risch, N. (1997). Effects of advance organizers and repeated presentation on students' learning. *The Journal of Experimental Education, 65*(2), 147–159.

Kilburtz, C. S., Miller, S. R., & Morrow, L. W. (1985) Structured learning using self-monitoring to promote maintenance and generalization of social skills across settings for a behaviorally disordered adolescent. *Behavioral Disorders, 11,* 147–55.

King-Sears, M. E., Mercer, C. D., & Sindelar, P. T. (1992). Toward independence with keyword mnemonics: A strategy for science vocabulary instruction. *Remedial and Special Education, 13,* 22–33.

Kleinert, H. L., Kearns, J. F., & Kennedy, S. (1997). Accountability for all students. *Journal of the Association for Persons with Severe Handicaps, 221,* 88–101.

Knapczyk, D. R. (1988). Reducing aggressive behaviors in special and regular class settings by training alternative social responses. *Behavioral Disorders, 14,* 27–39.

Knitzer, J. (1993). Children's mental health policy: Challenging the future. *Journal of Emotional and Behavioral Disorders, 1,* 8–10.

Knitzer, J., Steinberg, Z., & Fleisch, B. (1990). *At the schoolhouse door: An examination of programs and policies for children with behavioral and emotional problems.* New York: Bank Street College of Education.

Koegel, L. K., Harrower, J. K., & Koegel, R. L. (1999). Support for children with developmental disabilities in full inclusion classrooms through self-management. *Journal of Positive Behavior Interventions, 1,* 26–34.

Koegel, L. K., Koegel, R. L., & Dunlap, G. (1996). *Positive behavioral support: Including people with difficult behavior in the community.* Baltimore: Paul H. Brookes.

Koegel, R. L. & Frea, W. D. (1993). Treatment of social behavior in autism through the modification of pivotal social skills. *Journal of Applied Behavior Analysis, 26,* 369–377.

Koegel, R. L., & Koegel, L. K. (1990). Extending reductions in stereotypic behavior of students with autism through a self-management package. *Journal of Applied Behavior Analysis, 23,* 119–127.

Kohler, F. W., Strain, P., Hoyson, M. Davis, L., Donina, & Rapp, N. (1995). Using a group-oriented contingency to increase social interactions between children with autism and their peers. *Behavior Modification, 19,* 10–32.

Kortenkamp, K., & Ehrle, J. (2002). *The well-being of children involved with the child welfare system: A national overview* (No. B-43). Washington, DC: Urban Institute.

Kounin, J. S. (1970). *Discipline and group management in classrooms.* New York: Holt, Rinehart & Winston.

Kounin, J. S. & Obradovic, L. (1968). Managing emotionally disturbed children in regular classrooms: A replication and extension. *Journal of Special Education, (2)* 129-35.

Kouzes, J. L., & Posner, B. Z. (1987). *The leadership challenge: How to get extraordinary things done in organizations.* San Francisco: Jossey-Bass.

Koyanagi, C., & Gaines, S. (1993). *All systems failure: An examination of the results of neglecting the needs of children with serious emotional disturbance.* Washington, DC: National Institute for Mental Health and the Federation of Families for Children's Mental Health.

Krasnor, L. R., & Rubin, K. H. (1983). Preschool social problem solving: Attempts and outcomes in naturalistic interaction. *Child Development, 54,* 1545-1558.

Ladd, G. (1981). Effectiveness of a social learning method for enhancing children's social interaction and peer acceptance. *Child Development, 52,* 171-178.

Lake, S. E. (2002). *IEP procedural errors: Lessons learned, mistakes to avoid.* Horsham, PA: LRP Publications.

Landeen, J. J., & Adams, D. A. (1988). Computer assisted drill and practice for behaviorally handicapped learners: Proceed with caution. *Education and Treatment of Children, 11,* 218-229.

Landrum, T. (2000). Assessment for eligibility: Issues in identifying students with emotional or behavioral disorders. *Assessment for Effective Intervention, 26*(1), 41-49.

Landrum, T. J. (1997). Why data don't matter (guest editorial). *Journal of Behavioral Education, 7,* 123-129.

Landrum, T. J., & Tankersley, M. (1999). Emotional and behavioral disorders in the new millennium: The future is now. *Behavioral Disorders, 24,* 319-330.

Landrum, T. J., Tankersley, M., & Cook, B (1997, November). *Do data matter? Teachers' assessment of the intervention from different sources.* Paper presented at the 21st Annual Conference of Teacher Educators for Children with Behavior Disorders, Scottsdale, AZ.

Landrum, T. J., Tankersley, M., & Kauffman, J. M. (2003). What's special about special education for students with emotional and behavioral disorders? *The Journal of Special Education, 37,* 148-156.

Lane, K. L. (2004). Academic instruction and tutoring interventions for students with emotional and behavioral disorders: 1990 to the present. In R. B. Rutherford, M. M. Quinn & S. R. Mathur (Eds.), *Handbook of research in emotional and behavioral disorders* (pp. 15-31 and 462-486.). New York, NY: Guilford Press.

Lane, K. L., & Beebe-Frankenberger, M. (2004). *School-based interventions: The tools you need to succeed.* Boston: Allyn & Bacon.

Lane, K. L., Graham, S., Harris, K. R., & Weisenbach, J. L. (2006). Teaching writing strategies to young students struggling with writing and at-risk for behavioral disorders: Self-regulated strategy development. *Teaching Exceptional Children, 39,* 60-64.

Lane, K. L., Gresham, F. M., & O'Shaughnessy, T. E. (2002). Interventions for children with or at risk for emotional and behavioral disorders. Boston: Allyn & Bacon.

Lane, K. L., & Menzies, H. M. (2003). A school-wide intervention with primary and secondary levels of levels of support for elementary students: Outcomes and considerations. *Education and Treatment of Children, 26,* 431-451.

Lane, K. L., O'Shaughnessy, T. E., Lambros, K. M., Gresham, F. M., & Beebe-Frankenberger, M. E. (2001). The efficacy of phonological awareness training with first-grade students who have behavior problems and reading difficulties. *Journal of Emotional and Behavioral Disorders, 9,* 219-231.

Lane, K. L., & Wehby, J. (2002). Addressing antisocial behavior in the schools: A call for action. *Academic Exchange Quarterly, 6,* 4-9.

Lane, K. L., Wehby, J. H., Menzies, H. M., Gregg, R. M., Doukas, G. L., & Munton, S. M. (2002). Early literacy instruction for first-grade students at-risk for antisocial behavior. *Education and Treatment of Children, 25,* 438-458.

Langdon, T. (2004). DIBELS: A teacher-friendly basic literacy accountability tool for the primary classroom. *Teaching Exceptional Children, 37*(2), 54-58.

Lange, C. M., & Sletten, S. J. (2002). *Alternative education: A brief history and research synthesis.* Alexandria, VA: National Association of State Directors of Special Education.

Langland, S., Lewis-Palmer, T., & Sugai, G. (1998). Teaching respect in the classroom: An instructional approach. *Journal of Behavioral Education, 8,* 245-262.

Latham, G. (1992). Interacting with at-risk children: The positive position. *Principal, 72*(1), 26-30.

Laub, J. H., & Lauritsen, J. L. (1998). The interdependence of school violence with neighborhood and family conditions. In D. S. Elliot, B. Hamburg, & K. R. Williams (Eds.), *Violence in American schools: A new perspective* (pp. 127-155). New York: Cambridge University Press.

Layton, C. A., & Lock, R. H. (2008). *Assessing Students with Special Needs to Produce Quality Outcomes.* Upper Saddle River, NJ: Merrill/Prentice Hall.

Lazarus, B. D. (1993). Self-management and achievement of students with behavior disorders. *Psychology in the Schools, 30,* 67-74.

Lee, Y. Y., Sugai, G., & Horner, R. H. (1999). Using an instructional intervention to reduce problem and off-task behaviors. *Journal of Positive Behavior Interventions, 1*(4), 195-204.

Leedy, A., Bates, P., & Safran, S. P., (2004). Bridging the research-to-practice gap: Improving hallway behavior using positive behavior supports. *Behavioral Disorders, 29*(2), 130-139.

Lehr, C. (2004). Alternative schools and students with disabilities: Identifying and understanding the issues. *Information Brief: Addressing Trends and Developments in Secondary Education and Transition, 3*(6).

Leinhart, G., Zigmond, N., Cooley, W. (1980, April). *Reading Instruction and its effects*. Paper presented at the annual meeting of the American Educational Research Association. Boston.

Lennox, D. B., & Miltenberger, B. G. (1998). Conducting a functional assessment of problem behavior in applied settings. *Journal of The Association for Persons with Severe Handicaps, 14*, 304-311.

Lenz, K. B., Ellis, E. S., & Scanlon, D. (1996). *Teaching learning strategies to adolescents and adults with learning disabilities*. Austin, TX: Pro-Ed.

Lenz, M., Singh, N., & Hewett, A. (1991). Overcorrection as an academic remediation procedure. *Behavior Modification, 15*, 64-73.

Leone, P. E., Christle, C. A., Nelson, C. M., Skiba, R., Frey, A., & Jolivette, K. (2003). *School failure, race, and disability: Promoting positive outcomes, decreasing vulnerability for involvement with the juvenile delinquency system.* The National Center on Education, Disability, and Juvenile Justice. Retrieved March 11, 2006 from http://www.edjj.org.

Leone, P. E., & Cutting, C. A. (2004). Appropriate education, juvenile corrections, and no child left behind. *Behavioral Disorders, 29*(3), 260-265.

Leone, P. E., Mayer, M. J., Malmgren, K., & Meisel, S. M. (2000). School violence and disruption: Rhetoric, reality, and reasonable balance. *Focus on Exceptional Children, 33*(1), 1-20.

Leone, P. E., Rutherford, R. B., & Nelson, C. M. (1991). *Special education in juvenile corrections*. Reston, VA: Council for Exceptional Children.

Leslie, L., & Allen, L. (1999). Factors predicting success in an early literacy intervention project. *Reading Research Quarterly, 34*, 404-424.

Leslie, L., & Caldwell, J. (2001). *Qualitative Reading Inventory-3*. New York: HarperCollins.

Letter to Anonymous, 30 IDELR 707 (OSEP 1999).

Letter to McIntire, 16 EHLR 163 (OSEP 1989).

Levendoski, L. S., & Cartledge, G. (2000). Self-monitoring for elementary school children with serious emotional disturbances: Classroom applications for increased academic responding. *Behavioral Disorders, 25*, 211-224.

Levin, J. (1980). Lay vs. teachers perceptions of school discipline. *Phi Delta Kappan, 61*(5), 360-364.

Levin, J., & Nolan, J. F. (2004). *Principles of classroom management: A professional decision-making model*. Boston: Allyn & Bacon.

Levy, S. & Chard, D. J. (2001). Research on reading instruction for students with emotional and behavioural disorders. *International Journal of Disability, Development and Education, 48*(4), 429-444.

Lewis, C. T., & Short, C. (2006). *A Latin Dictionary*. Retrieved from http://www.perseus.tufts.edu/cgi-bin/ptext?doc=Perseus%3Atext%3A1999.04.0059%3Aentry%3D%239006&layout.reflookup=collaborate&layout.reflang=la

Lewis, R. B. & Doorlag, D. H. (1995). *Teaching special students in the mainstream*. Upper Saddle River, NJ: Merrill/Prentice Hall.

Lewis, T. J. (2001). Building infrastructure to enhance school-wide systems of positive behavior support: Essential features of technical assistance. *Beyond Behavior, 11*(1), 10-13.

Lewis, T. J., Colvin, G., & Sugai, G. (1998). Reducing problem behavior through a school-wide system of effective behavioral support: Investigation of a school-wide social skills training program and contextual interventions. *School Psychology Review, 27*, 446-459

Lewis, T. J., Colvin, G., & Sugai, G. (2000). The effects of precorrection and active supervision on the recess behavior of elementary school students. *Education and Treatment of Children, 23*, 109-121.

Lewis, T. J., Hudson, S., Richter, M., & Johnson, N. (2004). Scientifically supported practices in emotional and behavioral disorders: A proposed approach and brief review of current practices. *Behavioral Disorders, 29*(3), 247-259.

Lewis, T. J., Scott, T. M., & Sugai, G. M. (1994). The Problem Behavior Questionnaire: A teacher based instrument to develop functional hypotheses of problem behavior in general education classrooms. *Diagnostique, 19*, 103-115.

Lewis, T. J., & Sugai, G. (1999). Effective behavior support: A systems approach to proactive school-wide management. *Focus on Exceptional Children, 31*(6), 1-24.

Lewis, T. J., & Wehby, J. (1999). Building effective systems of support at the classroom level. In T. J. Lewis & G. Sugai (Eds.), *Safe schools: School-wide discipline practices*. Reston, VA: Council for Children with Behavioral Disorders.

Lewis-Palmer, T., Sugai, G., & Larson, S. (1999). Using data to guide decisions about program implementation and effectiveness. *Effective School Practices, 17*(4), 47-53.

Liberty, K. A., & Michael, L. J. (1985). Teaching retarded students to reinforce their own behavior: A review of process and operation in the current literature. In N. Haring (Ed.), *Investigating the problem of skill generalization* (3rd ed., pp. 88-106). Seattle: University of Washington Press.

Lienemann, T. O., & Reid, R. (2006). Self-regulated strategy development for students with learning disabilities. *Teacher Education and Special Education, 29*, 3-11.

Liles, J., & Rozalski, M. E. (2004). It's a matter of style: A plagiarism and style guide workshop for preventing plagiarism. *College and Undergraduate Libraries, 11*(2), 91-101.

Litow, L., & Pumroy, D. K. (1975). A brief review of classroom group-oriented contingencies. *Journal of Applied Behavior Analysis, 8*, 341-347.

Lloyd, J., Eberhardt, M., & Drake, G. (1996). Group versus individual reinforcement within the context of group study conditions. *Journal of Applied Behavior Analysis, 29*, 189-200.

Lloyd, J. W. (1980). Academic instruction and cognitive behavior modification: The need for attack strategy training. *Exceptional Education Quarterly, 8*, 53–63.

Lloyd, J. W., Bateman, D. F., Landrum, T. J., & Hallahan, D. P. (1989). Self-recording of attention versus productivity. *Journal of Applied Behavior Analysis, 22*, 315–323.

Lloyd, J. W., Forness, S. R., & Kavale, K. A. (1998). Some methods are more effective. *Intervention in School and Clinic, 33*(1), 195–200.

Lloyd, J. W., Hallahan, D. P., Kosiewicz, M. M., & Kneedler, R. D. (1982). Reactive effects of self-assessment and self-recording on attention to task and academic productivity. *Learning Disability Quarterly, 5*, 216–227

Lloyd, J. W., Kauffman, J. M., & Kupersmidt, J. B. (1988). Success of students with behavior disorders in regular education environments: A review of research and a systemic model for development of interventions. In K. Gad (Ed.), *Advances in learning and behavioral disabilities (Vol. 8)*. Greenwich, CT: JAI Press.

Lloyd, J. W., & Landrum, T. J. (1990). Self-recording of attending to task: Treatment components and generalization of effects. In T. E. Scruggs & B. Y. L. Wong (Eds.), *Intervention research in learning disabilities* (pp. 235–262). New York: Springer-Verlag.

Lochman, J. E., Nelson, W. M., & Sims, J. (1981). A cognitive-behavioral program for use with aggressive children. *Journal of Clinical Child Psychology, 19*, 146–148.

Loeber, R., & Farrington, D. P. (2000). Young children who commit crime: Epidemiology, developmental origins, risk factors, early interventions, and policy implications. *Development and Psychopathology, 12*, 737–762.

Lourie, I. S., & Hernandez, M. (2003). A historical perspective on national child mental health policy. *Journal of Emotional and Behavioral Disorders, 11*(1), 5–9.

Luiselli, J. K., & Rice, D. M. (1983). Brief positive practice with a handicapped child: An assessment of suppressive and re-educative effects. *Education and Treatment of Children, 6*, 241–250.

Luria, A. (1961). *The role of speech in the regulation of normal and abnormal behaviors*. New York: Basic Books.

Lynch, E. C., & Beare, P. L. (1990). The quality of IEP objectives and their relevance to instruction for students with mental retardation and behavioral disorders. *Remedial and Special Education, 11*, 48–55.

Lyon, S., & Lyon, G. (1980). Team functioning and staff development: A role release approach to providing integrated educational services for severely handicapped students. *Journal of the Association for the Severely Handicapped, 5*, 250–263.

Maag, J. W. (1999). *Behavior management: From theoretical implications to practical applications*. San Diego, CA: Singular.

Maag, J. W. (2001). Rewarded by punishment: Reflections on the disuse of positive reinforcement in schools. *Exceptional Children, 67*(2), 173–186.

Maag, J. W. (2003). *Behavior management: From theoretical applications to practical applications*. Belmont, CA: Wadsworth/Thomson Learning.

Maag, J. W. (2004). *Behavior management: From theoretical implications to practical applications* (2nd ed.). Belmont, CA: Wadsworth/Thomson Learning.

Maag, J. W., & Katsiyannis, A. (1996). Counseling as a related service for students with emotional or behavioral disorder: Issues and recommendations. *Behavioral Disorders, 21*, 293–305.

Maag, J. W., & Katsiyannis, A. (1998). Challenges facing successful transition for youths with E/BD. *Behavioral Disorders, 23*, 209–221.

Maag, J. W., & Katsiyannis, A. (1999). Teacher preparation in E/BD: A national survey. *Behavioral Disorders, 24*, 189–196.

Maag, J. W., Reid, R., & DiGangi, S. A. (1993). Differential effects of self-monitoring attention, accuracy, and productivity. *Journal of Applied Behavior Analysis, 26*, 329–344.

Maag, J. W., Rutherford, R. B., & DiGangi, S. A. (1992). Effects of self-monitoring and contingent reinforcement on on-task behavior and academic productivity of learning-disabled students. *Psychology in the Schools, 29*, 157–172.

Maag, J. W., & Swearer, S. M. (2005). Cognitive-behavioral interventions for depression: Review and implications for school personnel. *Behavioral Disorders, 30*, 259–276.

Mabee, W. (1988). The effects of academic positive practice on cursive letter writing. *Education and Treatment of Children, 11*, 143–148

Maccini, P., & Gagnon, J. C. (2000). Best practices for teaching mathematics to secondary students with special needs. *Focus on Exceptional Children, 32*(5), 1–22.

Maccini, P., & Hughes, C. (1997) Mathematics interventions for adolescents with learning disabilities. *Learning Disabilities Research and Practice, 12*, 168–176.

MacKinnon-Slaney, F. (1993). Theory to practice in co-curricular activities: A new model for student involvement. *College Student Affairs Journal, 12*, 35–40.

Madsen, C. H., Becker, W. C., & Thomas, D. R. (1968). Rules, praise, and ignoring. Elements of elementary classroom control. *Journal of Applied Behavior Analysis, 1*, 139–150.

Mager, R. (1962). *Preparing instructional objectives*. Palo Alto, CA: Fearon.

Mager, R. F. (1970). *Preparing instructional objectives* (2nd ed). Palo Alto, CA: Fearon.

Mager, R. F. (1997). *Preparing instructional objectives: A critical tool in the development of effective instruction* (2nd ed.). Atlanta, GA: Center for Effective Performance.

Maggs, A., & Morgan, G. (1986). Effects of feedback on the academic engaged time of behavior disordered learners. *Educational Psychology, 6*(4), 335–351.

Maheady, L., Harper, G. F., & Mallette, B. (2003). *Current practice alerts: A focus on classwide peer tutoring*. Reston, VA: Division of Learning Disabilities. Retrieved April 22, 2006 from http://www.teachingLD.org

Maheady, L., Harper, G. F., & Mallette, B. (2006). Four class-wide peer tutoring models: Similarities, differences, and implications for research and practice. *Reading & Writing Quarterly, 22*, 65-89.

Mahoney, K. S. (1995). School personnel and mandated reporting of child maltreatment. *The Journal of Law and Education, 24*, 227-239.

Malmgren, K., Edgar, E., & Neel, R. S. (1997). Post school status of youths with behavior disorders. *Behavioral Disorders, 23*(4), 257-263.

Malott, R. W. (2008). *Elementary principles of behavior* (6th ed.). Upper Saddle River, NJ: Merrill/Prentice Hall.

Malott, R. W., Malott, M. E., & Trojan, E. A. (2000). *Elementary principles of behavior* (4th ed.). Upper Saddle River, NJ: Merrill/Prentice Hall.

Malott, R. W. & Suarez, E. A. (2004). *Principles of behavior* (5th ed.). Upper Saddle Ricer, NJ: Merrill/Prentice Hall.

Marchand-Martella, N. E., Slocum, T. A., & Martella, R. C. (2004). *Introduction to direct instruction*. Boston: Pearson/Allyn & Bacon.

Margerison, C., & McCann, D. (2006). *Team management system*. Retrieved April 22, 2006 from http://www.tms.com.au/

Marshak, D. (1984). Study skills: Their values and why they should be taught. *NASSP Bulletin, 68*(468), 103-107.

Marston, D. (1987). The effectiveness of special education: A time series analysis of reading performance in regular and special education settings. *The Journal of Special Education, 21*(4), 13-26.

Marston, D., Lowry, L., Deno, S., & Mirkin, P. (1981). *An analysis of learning trends in simple measures of reading, spelling, and written expression: A longitudinal study*. (Research Report No. 49). Minneapolis: University of Minnesota, Institute for Research on Learning Disabilities.

Marston, D. B. (1989). A curriculum-based measurement approach to assessing academic performance: What it is and why do it. In M. R Shinn (Ed.), *Curriculum-based measurement: Assessing special children* (pp. 18-78). New York: Guilford Press.

Martella, R. C., Marchand-Martella, N. E., Young, K. R., & MacFarlane, C. A. (1995). Determining the collateral effects of peer tutor training on a student with severe disabilities. *Behavior Modification, 19*(2), 170-191.

Martella, R. C., Nelson, J. R., & Marchand-Martella, N. E. (2003). *Managing disruptive behaviors in the schools: A schoolwide, classroom, and individualized social learning approach*. Boston: Allyn & Bacon.

Martin, G. L., & Pear, J. J. (1996). *Behavior modification: What it is and how to do it* (6th ed.). Upper Saddle River, NJ: Merrill/Prentice Hall.

Martin, J. L. (1999, May). *Current legal issues in discipline of disabled students under IDEA: A section by section comment on § 1415(k), discipline regulations, and initial case law*. Paper presented at the LRP's Annual Conference on Special Education Law, San Francisco. LRP.

Martin, R. (1996). Litigation over the IEP. *Proceedings of the 16th National Institute on Legal Issues in Educating Individuals with Disabilities*, Alexandria, VA: LRP.

Martin, R. P. (1998). *Assessment of personality and behavior problems; infancy through adolescence*. New York: Guilford Press.

Mastropieri, M. A., Jenne, T., & Scruggs, T. E. (1988). A level system for managing problem behaviors in a high school resource program. *Behavioral Disorders, 13*, 202-208.

Mastropieri, M. A., & Scruggs, T. E. (1989). Constructing more meaningful relationships: Mnemonic instruction for special populations. *Educational Psychology Review, 1*, 83-111.

Mastropieri, M. A., & Scruggs, T. E. (1991). *Teaching students ways to remember: Strategies for learning mnemonically*. Cambridge, MA: Brookline Books.

Mastropieri, M. A., & Scruggs, T. E. (1998). Enhancing School Success with Mnemonic Strategies. *Intervention in School and Clinic 33*, 201-208.

Mastropieri, M. A., & Scruggs, T. E. (1998b). Increasing the content area learning of learning disabled students: Research implementation. *Learning Disabilities Research, 4*(1), 17-25.

Mastropieri, M. A., & Scruggs, T. E. (2000). *Teacher-Researcher Partnerships to Promote Success in Inclusive High School Science and Social Studies Classes*. Grant funded by the U.S. Department of Education.

Mastropieri, M. A., & Scruggs, T. E. (2004). *The inclusive classroom: Strategies for effective instruction*. Upper Saddle River, NJ: Prentice Hall.

Mastropieri, M. A., & Scruggs, T. E. (2007a). *Effective instruction for special education* (3rd ed.). Austin, TX: Pro-Ed.

Mastropieri, M. A., & Scruggs, T. E. (2007b). *The inclusive classroom: Strategies for effective instruction* (3rd ed.). Upper Saddle River, NJ: Merrill/Prentice Hall.

Mathes, M. Y., & Bender, W. N. (1997). The effects of self-monitoring on children with attention-deficit/hyperactivity disorder who are receiving pharmacological interventions. *Remedial and Special Education, 18*, 121-128.

Mathes, P. G., & Fuchs, L. S. (1994). The efficacy of peer tutoring for students with mild disabilities: A best evidence synthesis. *School Psychology Review, 23*(1), 59-80.

Mathur, S. R., Kavale, K. A., Quinn, M. M., Forness, S. R., & Rutherford, R. B. (1998). Social skills interventions with students with emotional and behavioral problems: A quantitative synthesis of single-subject research. *Behavioral Disorders, 23*, 193-201.

Mathur, S. R., & Rutherford, R. B. (1996). Is social skills training effective for students with emotional or behavioral disorders? Research issues and needs. *Behavioral Disorders, 22*, 21-28.

Matson, J. L., Esveldt-Dawson K., & Kazdin A. E. (1982). Treatment of spelling deficits in mentally retarded children. *Mental Retardation, 20*, 76-81.

Mattison, R. E., Hooper, S. R., & Glassberg, L. A. (2002). Three-year course of learning disorders in special education students classified as behavioral disordered. *Journal of the American Academy of Child and Adolescent Psychiatry, 41,* 1454-1461.

Mawdsley, R. D. (1993). Supervisory standard of care for students with disabilities. *Education Law Reporter, 80,* 779-791.

Mayer, G. R. (2002). School-wide behavior support: Legal implications and requirements. In J. K. Luiselli & C. Diament (Eds.), *Behavior psychology in the schools: innovations in evaluation, support, and consultation* (pp. 83-100). New York: Haworth Press.

Mayer, M., Lochman, J. E., & Van Acker, R. (2005). Introduction to the special issue: Cognitive-behavioral interventions with students with EBD. *Behavioral Disorders, 30,* 197-212.

McCaleb, J. L. and White, J. A. (1980). Critical dimensions in evaluating teacher clarity, *The Journal of Classroom Interactions, 15*(2), 27-30.

McCombs, J., Kirby, S. N., Barney, H., Darilek, S., & Magee, S. J. (2004). *Achieving state and national literacy goals, a long uphill road.* New York: Rand Corporation for the Carnegie Foundation.

McDougall, D., & Brady, M. P. (1998). Initiating and fading self-management interventions to increase math fluency in general education classes. *Exceptional Children, 64,* 151-166.

McFall, R. M. (1982). A review and reformulation of the concept of social skills. *Behavioral Assessment, 4,* 1-33.

McGinnis, J. C., Friman, P. C., Carylon, W. D. (2001). The effect of token rewards on "intrinsic" motivation for doing math. *Journal of Applied Behavior Analysis, 3,* 375-379.

McGinnis, E., & Goldstein, A. P. (1984). *Skillstreaming the elementary school child.* Champaign, IL: Research Press.

McIntyre, T. & Forness, S. R. (1996). Is there a new definition yet or are our kids still seriously emotionally disturbed? *Beyond Behavior, 7*(3), 4-9.

McLaughlin, T. F. (1981). An analysis of token reinforcement: A control group comparison with special education youth employing measures of clinical significance. *Child Behavior Therapy, 3,* 43-51.

McLaughlin, T. F. (1984). A comparison of self-recording and self-recording plus consequences for on-task and assignment completion. *Contemporary Educational Psychology, 9,* 185-192.

McLaughlin, T. F., Krappman, V. F., & Welsh, J. M. (1985). The effects of self-recording for on-task behavior of behaviorally disordered special education students. *Remedial and Special Education, 6,* 42-45.

McLaughlin, T. F., & Malaby, J. (1972). Intrinsic reinforcers in a classroom token economy. *Journal of Applied Behavior Analysis, 5,* 263-270.

McLaughlin, T. F., & Truhlicka, M. (1983). Effects on academic performance of self-recording and matching with behaviorally disordered students: A replication. *Behavioral Engineering, 8,* 69-74

McLoughlin, J. A., & Lewis, R. B. (2007). *Assessing students with special needs* (7th ed.). Upper Saddle River, NJ: Pearson/Merrill/Prentice Hall.

McMaster, K. L., Fuchs, D., & Fuchs, L. S. (2006). Research on peer-assisted learning strategies: The promise and limitations of peer-mediated instruction. *Reading & Writing Quarterly, 22,* 5-25.

Meadows, N., Neel, R S., Parker, G., & Timo, K. (1991). A validation of social skills for students with behavioral disorders. *Behavioral Disorders, 16,* 200-210.

Meadows, N, & Stevens, K. (2004). Teaching alternative behaviors to students with emotional and behavioral disorders. In R. B. Rutherford, M. M. Quinn & S. R. Mathur (Eds.), *Handbook of research in emotional and behavioral disorders* (pp. 424-486). New York: Guilford Press.

Meadows, N. B. (1991). Social competency, mainstreaming and children with serious behavioral disorders. *Monograph in Behavioral Disorders, 14,* 61-66.

Meadows, N. B. (1993). A philosophy of teaching, not just managing behaviors. *Teaching Education, 6(1),* 93-99.

Meadows, N. B. (1999). A university/public school collaborative project for including students with learning and behavior problems in general education classrooms. In J. R. Scotia & L. H. Meyer (Eds.), *New directions for behavioral intervention: Principles, models, and practices.* Baltimore: Paul H. Brooks.

Meadows, N. B. & Cavin, D. C. (1996). Teaching social skills to adolescents with behavior disorders: A social task approach. *Beyond Behavior. 7*(2), 22-25.

Meadows, N. B., Melloy, K. J., & Yell, M. L. (1996). Behavior management as a curriculum for students with emotional and behavioral disorders. *Preventing School Failure, 40,* 124-130.

Mears, D. P., & Aron, L. Y. (2003). *Addressing the needs of youth with disabilities in the juvenile justice system: The current state of knowledge.* Washington, DC: Urban Institute.

Meichenbaum, D. (1976). Cognitive factors as determinants of learning disabilities: A cognitive functional approach. In R. M. Knights & D. J. Baker (Eds.), *The neuropsychology of learning disorders: Theoretical approaches.* Baltimore: University Park Press.

Meichenbaum, D. (1977). *Cognitive behavior modification: An integrative approach.* New York: Plenum Press.

Meichenbaum, D. (1980). Cognitive behavior modification with exceptional students: A promise yet unfulfilled. *Exceptional Education Quarterly, 8,* 83-88.

Meichenbaum, D., & Asarnow, J. (1979). Cognitive-behavioral modification and metacognitive development: Implications for the classroom. In P. C. Kendall and S. D. Hollon (Eds.), *Cognitive-behavioral interventions: Theory, research, and procedures* (pp. 11-35). New York: Academic Press.

Meichenbaum, D., & Goodman, T. J. (1971). Training impulsive children to talk to themselves: A means of developing self control. *Journal of Abnormal Psychology, 77,* 115-126.

Meisel, S., Henderson, K., Cohen, M., & Leone, P. E. (1998). Collaborate to educate: Special education in juvenile correctional facilities. In R. Rutherford, M. Nelson, and B. Wolford (Eds.), *Building collaboration between education and treatment for at-risk and delinquent youth* (pp. 59–72). Richmond: National Juvenile Detention Association, Eastern Kentucky University.

Melloy, K. J. (1990). *Attitudes and behavior of non-disabled elementary-aged children toward their peers with disabilities in integrated settings: An examination of the effects of treatment on quality of attitudes, social status, and critical social skills.* Unpublished doctoral dissertation, University of Iowa, Iowa City.

Melloy, K. J., Davis, C. A., Wehby, J. H., Murry, F. R., & Leiber, J. (1998). *Developing social competence in children and youth with challenging behaviors.* Reston, VA: Council for Children with Behavior Disorders.

Mendel, R. A. (2000). *Less hype, more help: Reducing juvenile crime, what works—and what doesn't.* Washington, DC: American Youth Policy Forum.

Mercer, S. C., & Miller, S. P. (1991). *Strategic math series: Multiplication facts 0–81.* Lawrence, KS: Edge Enterprises.

Mercer, S. C., & Miller, S. P. (1992). Teaching students with learning problems in math to acquire, understand, and apply basic math facts. *Remedial and Special Education, 13*(3), 19–25.

Merrell, K. W. (1994). *Assessment of behavioral, social & emotional problems: Direct and objective methods for use with children and adolescents.* White Plains, NY: Longman.

Merrell, K. W., & Walker, H. M. (2004). Deconstructing a definition: Social maladjustment versus emotional disturbance and moving the field forward. *Psychology in the Schools, 41*(8), 899–910.

Meyers, A. W., Cohen, R., & Schlester, R. (1989). A cognitive-behavioral approach to education: Adopting a broad-based perspective. In J. N. Hughes & R. J. Hall (Eds.), *Cognitive behavioral psychology in the schools: A comprehensive handbook* (pp. 62–84). New York: Guilford Press.

Michaelson, L., Dilorenzo, T. M., Calpin, J. P., & Williamson, D. A. (1981). Modifying excessive lunchroom noise: Omission training with audio feedback and group contingent reinforcement. *Behavior Modification, 5,* 553–564.

Miller, D. (1998). *Enhancing adolescent competence.* Belmont, CA: Wadsworth.

Miller, D. L., & Kelley, M. L. (1994). The use of goal setting contingency contracting for improving children's homework performance. *Journal of Applied Behavior Analysis, 27,* 73–84.

Miller, M. D., Brownell, M. T., & Smith, S. W. (1999). Factors that predict staying in, leaving, or transferring from the special classroom. *Exceptional Children, 65,* 201–219.

Miller, S. C., & Mercer, C. (1993). Using a graduated word problem sequence to promote problem-solving skills. *Learning Disabilities Research and Practice, 8*(3), 169–174.

Miltenberger, R. G. (1997). *Behavior modification: Principles and procedures.* Pacific Grove, CA: Brooks/Cole.

Miltenberger, R. G. (2001). *Behavior modification: Principles and procedures* (2nd ed.). Pacific Grove, CA: Brooks/Cole.

Miltenberger, R. G. (2004). *Behavior modification: Principles and procedures* (3rd ed.). Belmont, CA: Thomson/Wadsworth.

Mims, A. (1991). Effective instruction in homework for students with disabilities. *Teaching Exceptional Children, 24*(1), 42–44.

Minner, S. (1990). Use of a self-recording procedure to decrease the time taken by behaviorally disordered students to walk to special classes. *Behavioral Disorders, 15,* 210–216.

Mirkin, P., Deno, S., Fuchs, L., Wesson, C., Tindal, G., Marston, D., et al. (1981). *Procedures to develop and monitor progress on IEP goals.* Minneapolis University of Minnesota, Institute for Research on Learning Disabilities.

Monroe, E. E., & Orme, M. P. (2002). Developing mathematical vocabulary. *Preventing School Failure, 46*(3), 139–142.

Mooney, P., Epstein, M. H., Reid, R., & Nelson, J. R. (2003). Status of and trends in academic research for students with emotional and behavioral disorders. *Remedial and Special Education, 24,* 273–287.

Moore, R. J., Cartledge, G., & Heckman, K. (1995). The effects of social skills instruction and self-monitoring on game-related behaviors of adolescents with emotional or behavioral disorders. *Behavioral Disorders, 20,* 253–266.

Morgan, D. P., & Jenson, W. R. (1988). *Teaching behaviorally disordered students: Preferred practices.* Upper Saddle River, NJ: Merrill/Prentice Hall.

Morrison, L., Kamps, D., Garcia, J., & Parker, D. (2001). Peer mediation and monitoring strategies to improve initiations and social skills for students with autism. *Journal of Positive Behavior Interventions, 3,* 237–250.

Mostert, M. P., & Kavale, K. (2001). Evaluation of research for usable knowledge in behavioral disorders: Ignoring the irrelevant, considering the germane. *Behavioral Disorders, 27,* 53–68.

Murphy, H. A., Hutchinson, J. M., & Bailey, J. S. (1983). Behavioral school psychology goes outdoors: The effect of organized games on playground aggression. *Journal of Applied Behavior Analysis, 16,* 29–36.

Muscott, H. S., Morgan, D. P., & Meadows, N. B. (1996). *Planning and implementing effective programs for school-aged children and youth with emotional and behavioral disorders within inclusive schools.* Reston, VA: Council for Exceptional Children.

Myles, B. S., & Simpson, R. L. (1994). Prevention and management considerations for aggressive and violent children and youth. *Education and Treatment of Children, 17,* 370–384.

Nagy, W. E., Herman, I. A., & Anderson, R. C. (1985). Learning words from context. *Reading Research Quarterly, 29*(2), 233–253.

National Association of State Directors of Special Education. (December, 2002). *Alignment of special and general* education reform in comprehensive school reform demonstration programs: Literature review. Alexandria, VA: author.

National Center for Education Statistics. (2002). *The condition of education 2002* (NCES 2002025). Washington, DC: U.S. Department of Education, Office of Educational Research and Improvement.

National Child Abuse Prevention and Treatment Act, 42 U.S.C. § § 5101–5107 (1974).

National Council of Teachers of Mathematics. (2000). *Principles and standards for school mathematics.* Reston, VA: Author.

National Institute of Child Health and Human Development. (2000). *Report of the National Reading Panel: Teaching children to read. An evidenced-based literature on reading and implications for reading instruction* (NIH Publication No. 00-4769). Washington, DC: NICHD Clearinghouse.

National Research Council. (2002). *Strategic education research partnerships.* Washington, DC: National Academy Press.

National Research Council Mathematics Learning Study Committee, J. Kilpatrick, & J. Swafford. (Eds.). (2003). *Helping children learn mathematics.* Washington DC: National Academy Press.

Neel, R., Meadows, N., Levine, P. & Edgar, E. (1988). What happens after special education: A statewide follow-up study of secondary students who have behavioral disorders. *Behavioral Disorders, 13*, 209-216.

Neel, R. S. (1988). Classroom conversion kit: A teacher's guide to teaching social competency. In R. B. Rutherford & J. W. Maag (Eds.), *Severe behavior disorders of children and youth* (Vol. 11, pp. 25-31). Reston, VA: Council for Children with Behavior Disorders.

Neel, R. S., Alexander, L., & Meadows, N. B. (1997). Positive outcomes and positive environments: new directions for students with serious emotional disturbance. *Journal of Emotional and Behavioral Disorders, 5*(1), 6-14.

Neel, R. S., & Cessna, K. K. (1993). Behavioral intent: Instructional content for students with behavior disorders. In K. K. Cessna (Ed.), *Instructionally differentiated programming* (pp. 31-40). Denver: Colorado Department of Education.

Neel, R. S., Cheney, D., Meadows, N. B., & Gelhar, S. (1992). Interviewing middle school students to determine problematic social tasks in school settings. *Monograph in Behavioral Disorders, 15*, 57-67.

Neel, R. S., Meadows, N. B., & Scott, C. M. (1990). Determining social tasks: A preliminary report. *Monograph in Behavioral Disorders: Severe Behavior Disorders of Children and Youth* (Vol. 13). Reston, VA: Council for Children with Behavior Disorders.

Nelson, C. M. (2000). Educating students with emotional and behavioral disabilities in the 21st century: Looking through windows, opening doors. *Education and Treatment of Children, 23*(3).

Nelson, C. M., & Rutherford, R. B. (1983). Timeout revisited: Guidelines for its use in special education. *Exceptional Education Quarterly, 4*(3), 56-67.

Nelson, C. M., Rutherford, R. B., & Wolford, B. I. (Eds.). (1996). *Comprehensive and collaborative systems that work for troubled youth: A national agenda.* Richmond, KY: National Coalition for Juvenile Justice Services.

Nelson, C. M., Scott, T. M., & Polsgrove, L. (1999). *Perspectives on emotional/behavioral disorders: Assumptions and their implications for education and treatment.* Reston, VA: Council for Children with Behavioral Disorders.

Nelson, J. R. (1996). Designing schools to meet the needs of students who exhibit disruptive behavior. *Journal of Emotional and Behavioral Disorders, 4*, 147-161.

Nelson, J. R. (2001). Designing schools to meet the needs of students who exhibit disruptive behavior. In H. M. Walker & M. H. Epstein (Eds.), *Making schools safer and violence free: Critical issues, solutions, and recommended practices* (pp. 58-72). Austin, TX: Pro-Ed.

Nelson, J. R., Benner, G. J., & Gonzalez, J. (2005). An investigation of the effects of a pre-reading intervention on the early literacy skills of children at risk of emotional disturbance and reading problems. *Journal of Emotional and Behavioral Disorders, 13*(1), 3-12.

Nelson, J. R., Benner, G. J., Lane, K., & Smith, B. J. (2004). Academic achievement of K-12 students with emotional and behavioral disorders. *Exceptional Children, 71*, 59-73.

Nelson, J. R., Benner, G. J., & Rogers-Adkinson, D. L. (2003). An investigation of the characteristics of K-12 students with comorbid emotional disturbance and significant language deficits served in public school settings. *Behavioral Disorders, 29*(1), 25-33.

Nelson, J. R., & Carr, B. A. (2000). *The think-time strategy for schools.* Longmont, CO: Sopris West.

Nelson, J. R., & Colvin, G. (1995). School-wide discipline: Procedures for managing common areas. In A. Deffenbaugh, G. Sugai, & G. Tindal (Eds.), *The Oregon Conference Monograph* (pp. 109-119). Eugene: College of Education, University of Oregon.

Nelson, J. R., Martella, R. M., & Galand, B. (1998). The effects of teaching school expectations and establishing consistent consequences on formal office disciplinary actions. *Journal of Emotional and Behavioral Disorders, 6*, 153-161.

Nelson, J. R., Roberts, M. L., Mathur, S. R., & Rutherford, R.B. (1999). Has public policy exceeded our knowledge base? A review of the functional behavioral assessment literature. *Behavioral Disorders, 24*, 169-179.

Nelson, J. R., Roberts, M. L. & Smith, D. J. (1998). *Conducting functional behavioral assessments in school settings: A practical guide.* Longmont, CO: Sopris West.

Nelson, J. R., Smith, D. J., & Colvin, G. (1995). The effects of a peer-mediated self-evaluation procedure on the recess behavior of students with behavior problems. *Remedial and Special Education, 16*, 117-126.

Nelson, J. R., Smith, D. J., Young, R. K., & Dodd, J. (1991). A review of self-management outcome research conducted with students who exhibit behavioral disorders. *Behavioral Disorders, 13*, 169–180.

Newcomer, P., Nodine, B., & Barenbaum, E. (1988). Teaching writing to exceptional children: Reaction and recommendations. *Exceptional Children, 54*, 559–564.

Newcomer, P.L. (1993). *Understanding and teaching emotionally disturbed children and adolescents* (2nd ed.). Austin, TX: Pro-Ed.

Newman, B., Buffington, D. M., O'Grady, M. A., Polson, C. L., & Hemmes, N. S. (1995). Self-management of schedule following in three teenagers with autism. *Behavioral Disorders, 20*, 190–196.

No Child Left Behind, 20 U.S.C. § 16301 *et seq.*

Noguera, P. (1995). Preventing and producing violence: A critical analysis of responses to school violence. *Harvard Education Review, 65*, 189–212.

Nolet, V. & McLaughlin, M. J. (2000). *Accessing the general curriculum: Including students with disabilities in standards-based reform.* Thousand Oaks, CA: Corwin Press.

Noll, M. B., & Simpson, R. L. (1979). The effects of physical time-out on the aggressive behaviors of a severely emotionally disturbed child in a public school setting. *AAESPH Review, 4*, 399–406.

Norlin, J. W., & Gorn, S. (2005). *What do I do when: The answer book on special education law.* Horsham, PA: LRP.

Novaco, R. W. (1975). *Anger control: The development and evaluation of an experimental treatment.* Lexington, MA: Lexington.

Novaco, R. W. (1979). The cognitive regulation of anger and stress. In P. C. Kendall & S. D. Hollon (Eds.), *Cognitive-behavioral interventions: Therapy, research and procedures* (pp. 241–285). New York: Academic Press.

Oberti v. Board of Education of the Borough of Clementon School District, 995 F.2d 1204 (3rd Cir. 1993).

O'Brien, T. P., Riner, L. S., & Budd, K. S. (1983). The effects of a child's self-evaluation program on compliance with parental instructions in the home. *Journal of Applied Behavior Analysis, 16*, 69–79.

Oden, S., & Asher, S. R. (1977). Coaching children in social skills for friendship making. *Child Development, 48*, 495–506.

Office of Technology Assessment (1992). *Testing in American schools: Asking the right questions.* (OTA-SET-519) Washington, D.C: U.S. Government Printing Office.

Ogle, D. S. (1986). K-W-L group instructional strategy. In A. S. Palincsar, D. S. Ogle, B. F. Jones, & E. G. Carr (Eds.), *Teaching reading as thinking* (Teleconference Resource Guide, pp. 11–17). Alexandria, VA: Association for Supervision and Curriculum Development.

O'Leary, K. D., Becker, W. C., Evans, M. B., & Saudargas, R. A. (1969). A token reinforcement program in a public school: A replication and systematic analysis. *Journal of Applied Behavior Analysis, 2*, 3–13.

O'Leary, S. D., & Dubay, D. R. (1979). Application of self-control procedures by children: A review. *Journal of Applied Behavior Analysis, 2*, 449–465.

Ollendick, T. H., & Matson, J. L. (1976). An initial investigation into the parameters of overcorrection. *Psychological Review, 39*, 1139–1142.

Ollendick, T. H., Matson, J. L., Esveldt-Dawson, K., & Shapiro, E. S. (1980). Increasing spelling achievement: An analysis of treatment procedures utilizing an alternating treatments design. *Journal of Applied Behavior Analysis, 13*, 645–654.

Olweus, D., Limber, S., & Mihalic, S. (1998). Bullying prevention program. In D. S. Elliott (Series Ed.), *Blueprints for violence prevention.* Boulder, CO: University of Colorado at Boulder, Institute of Behavioral Science, Center for the Study and Prevention of Violence.

Olympia, D. E., Sheridan, S. M., Jenson, W.R., & Andrews, D. (1994). Using student managed interventions to increase homework completion and accuracy. *Journal of Applied Behavior Analysis, 27*, 85–99.

O'Neill, R. E., Horner, R. H., Albin, R. W., Sprague, J. R., Storey, K., & Newton, J. S. (1997). *Functional assessments for problem behavior: A practical handbook* (2nd ed.). Pacific Grove, CA: Brooks/Cole.

O'Neill, R. E., Horner, R. H., Albin, R. W., Storey, K., & Sprague, J. R. (1997). *Functional analysis of problem behavior: A practical assessment guide* (2nd ed.). Pacific Grove, CA: Brookes/Cole.

Orlich, D., Harder, R. J., Callahan, R. C. Trevisan, M. & Brown, B. (2006). *Teaching strategies: A guide to effective instruction.* Boston: Houghton Mifflin.

Osborne, A. G. (1994). Procedural due process rights for parents under the IDEA. *Preventing School Failure, 39*, 22–26.

Osborne, S. S., Kociewicz, M. M., Crumley, E. B., & Lee, C. (1987, Winter). Distractible students use self-monitoring. *Teaching Exceptional Children, 19*, 66–69.

OSEP Center on Positive Behavioral Interventions and Supports. (1999). *Applying positive behavioral supports and functional behavioral assessments in schools.* Technical Assistance Guide #1-1999. Eugene: University of Oregon Press.

OSEP Discipline Guidance, 26 IDELR 923 (1997).

OSEP Memorandum 95-16, 22 IDELR 531 (1995).

OSEP Policy Letter, 18 IDELR 1303 (1992).

OSEP Policy Letter, 18 IDELR 627 (1991).

OSEP Questions and Answers. (1999, March 12). *Federal Register.* 12617–12632. Volume 64, No. 48.

O'Shaunessy, T. A., Lane, K. L., Gresham, F. M., & Beebe-Frankenberger, M. (2002). Students with or at risk for learning and emotional-behavioral difficulties: An integrated system of prevention and intervention. In K. L. Lane, F. M. Gresham, and T. E. O'Shaughnessy (Eds.), *Interventions for children with or at risk for emotional and behavioral disorders* (pp. 1–17). Boston: Allyn & Bacon.

Oswald, D., Coutinho, M., Best, A., & Sing, N. (1999). Ethnic representation in special education: The influence of school-related economic and demographic variables. *The Journal of Special Education, 32*, 194–206.

Paige, R. (2002, November). *Statement of Secretary Paige regarding Title I regulations.* Retrieved August 2002 from http://www.ed.gov/news/speeches/2002/11/11262002.html?exp=0

Paine, S., & Anderson-Inman, L. (1988). Teaching academic skills to behaviorally disordered students. In D. P. Morgan & W. R. Jenson, *Teaching behaviorally disordered students: Preferred practices.* Upper Saddle River, NJ: Merrill/Prentice Hall.

Paine, S. C., Radicchi, J., Rosellini, L. C., Deutchman, L., & Darch, C. B. (1983). *Structuring your classroom for academic success.* Champaign, IL: Research Press.

Pandey, J. B. (1991). *A sample of mathematics assessment.* Sacramento, CA: California Department of Education.

Parker, R., Hasbrouck, J. E., & Tindal, G. (1992). The Maze as a classroom-based reading measure: Construction methods, reliability, and validity. *The Journal of Special Education, 26*(2), 195–218.

Pasternak, R. (2002, March). *Testimony of Assistant Secretary Pasternak before the Senate Committee on Health, Education, Labor, and Pensions.* Retrieved November 2003 from http://www.ed.gov/news/speeches/2002/03/20020321.htm

Patrick, B. C., Hisley, J., & Kempler, T. (2000). What's everybody so excited about? The effects of teacher enthusiasm on student intrinsic motivation and vitality. *The Journal of Experimental Education, 68*, 217–236.

Patterson, G. R. (1982). *Coercive family process: A social learning approach.* Eugene, OR: Castalia.

Patterson, G. R., Forgatch, K. L., & Stoolmiller, M. (1998). Variables that initiate and maintain an early-onset trajectory for juvenile offending. *Development and Psychopathology, 10*, 531–547.

Peacock Hill Working Group. (1991). Problems and promises in special education and related services for children and youth with emotional or behavioral disorders. *Behavioral Disorders, 16*, 299–313.

Pearson, D. P., & Fielding, L. (1991). Comprehension instruction. In R. Barr, M. L. Kamil, P. B. Mosenthal, & P. D. Pearson (Eds.), *Handbook of reading research* (Vol. 2, pp. 815–860). White Plains, NY: Longman.

Pease, G. A., & Tyler, V. O. (1979). Self-regulation of timeout duration in the modification of disruptive classroom behavior. *Psychology in the Schools, 16*, 101–105.

Peck, A. F., Keenan, S., Cheney, D., & Neel, R. S. (2004). *Establishing exemplary personnel preparation programs for teachers of students with emotional and behavior disorders: Partnerships with schools, parents, and community agencies.* Arlington, VA: CCBD Mini-Library Series, Council for Children with Behavioral Disorders.

Petercsak, S. J., Jr. (1986). *Study skills: A resource book.* Columbus. Ohio State Department of Education.

Phillips, E. L., Phillips, E. A., Fixsen, D. L., & Wolf, M. M. (1971). Achievement place: Modification of the behaviors of pre-delinquent boys within a token economy. *Journal of Applied Behavior Analysis, 4*, 45–49.

Phillips, V., & McCullough, L. (1990). Consultation-based programming: Instituting the collaborative ethic in schools. *Exceptional Children, 56*, 291–304.

Pocatello School District #25, 18 IDELR 83 (SEA Idaho 1991).

Polsgrove, L. (2003). Reflections on the past and future. *Behavioral Disorders, 28*, 221–226.

Polsgrove, L. & Smith, S.W. (2004). Informed practice in teaching self-control to children with emotional and behavioral disorders. In R.B. Rutherford, & Quinn, M.M., Mathur, S.R. (Eds.) *Handbook of research in emotional and behavioral disorders* (pp. 399–425). New York: The Guilford Press.

Porterfield, J. K., Herbert-Jackson, E., & Risley, T. R. (1976). Contingent observation: An effective and acceptable procedure for reducing disruptive behavior of young children in a group setting. *Journal of Applied Behavior Analysis, 9*, 55–64.

Prater, M. A., Joy, R., Chilman, B., Temple, J., & Miller, S. R. (1991). Self-monitoring of on-task behavior by adolescents with learning disabilities. *Learning Disability Quarterly, 14*, 164–177.

Premack, D. (1959). Toward empirical behavior laws: I. Positive reinforcement. *Psychological Review, 66*, 233.

Premack, D. (1965). Reinforcement theory. In D. Levine (Ed.), *Nebraska symposium on motivation* (pp. 123–180). Lincoln: University of Nebraska Press.

President's Commission on Excellence in Education (2002). *A new era: Revitalizing special education for children and their families.* Retrieved from http://www.ed.gov/inits/commissionsboards/whspecialeducation/reports/images/Pres_Rep.pdfonJuly12, 2002.

Pressley, M. Symons, S., McGoldrick, A. J., & Snyder, T., &. (1989). Reading comprehension strategies. In M. Pressley & V. Woloshyn (Eds.), *Cognitive strategy instruction that really improves children's academic performance* (2nd ed.) (pp 19–56). Cambridge, MA: Brookline Books.

Price, K. M., & Nelson, K. L. (2007). *Planning effective instruction: Diversity responsive methods and management.* Belmont, CA: Thomson Wadsworth.

Proctor, M.A., & Morgan, D. (1991). Effectiveness of a response cost raffle procedure on the disruptive classroom behavior of adolescents with behavior problems. *School Psychology Review, 20*, 97–109.

Pullis, M. (1992). An analysis of the occupational stress of teachers of the behaviorally disordered: Sources, effects, and strategies for coping. *Behavioral Disorders, 17*, 190–201.

Putnam, M. L., Deshler, D. D., & Schumaker, J. S. (1993). The investigation of setting demands: A missing link in learning strategy instruction. In L. S. Meltzer (Ed.), *Strategy assessment and instruction for students with learning disabilities: From theory to practice* (pp. 324–354). Austin, TX: Pro-Ed.

Quay, H. C., Glavin, J. P., Annesley, F. R., & Werry J. S. (1972). The modification of problem behavior and academic achievement in a resource room. *Journal of School Psychology, 10*, 187–198.

Quinn, M. M., Gable, R. A., Rutherford, R. B., Nelson, C. M., & Howell, K. W. (1998). *Addressing student problem behavior: An IEP team's introduction to functional behavioral assessment and behavioral intervention plans* (2nd ed.) Washington, DC: Center for Effective Collaboration and Practice, American Institutes for Research.

Quinn, M. M., Rutherford, R. B., & Leone, P. E. (2001). *Students with disabilities in correctional facilities* (ERIC Digest No. EDO-EC-01-16). Arlington, VA: ERIC Clearinghouse on Disabilities and Gifted Education.

Quinn, M. M., Rutherford, R. B., Leone, P. E., Osher, D. M., & Poirier, J. M. (2005). Youth with disabilities in juvenile corrections: A national survey. *Exceptional Children, 71*(3), 339–345.

Rademacher, J. E., Callahan, K., & Pederson-Seelye, V. A. (1998). How do your classroom rules measure up? Guidelines for developing an effective rule management routine. *Intervention in School and Clinic, 33*(5), 284–289.

Raffaele-Mendez, L. M., Knoff, H. M., & Ferron, J. M. (2002). School demographic variables and out-of-school suspension rates: A quantitative and qualitative analysis of a large, ethnically diverse school district. *Psychology in the Schools, 39*(3), 259–277.

Rafoth, M. A., Leal, L., & DeFabo, L. (1993). *Strategies for learning and remembering: Study skills across the curriculum. Analysis and action series.* Washington, DC: National Education Association.

Rainforth, B., York-Barr, J., & MacDonald, C. (1992). *Collaborative teams for students with severe disabilities: Integrating therapy and educational services.* Baltimore: Brookes.

Ramp, E., Ulrich, R., & Dulaney, S. (1971). Delayed timeout as a procedure for reducing disruptive classroom behavior. *Journal of Applied Behavior Analysis, 4*, 235–239.

Rapport, M. L., Murphy, H. A., & Bailey, J. S. (1982). Ritalin vs. response cost in the control of hyperactive children: A within subject comparison. *Journal of Applied Behavior Analysis, 15*, 205–216.

Raubolt, R. R. (1983). Treating children in residential group psychotherapy. *Child Welfare, 62*, 147–155.

Recht, D. R., & Leslie, L. (1988). Effect of prior knowledge on good and poor reader's memory of text. *Journal of Educational Psychology, 80*(1), 16–20.

Reddy, M., Borum, R., Berglund, J., Vossekuil, B., Fein, R., & Modzeleski, W. (2001). Evaluating risk for targeted violence in schools: Comparing risk assessment, threat assessment, and other approaches. *Psychology in the Schools, 38*, 157–172.

Reed, H., Thomas, E., Sprague, J. R., & Horner, R. H. (1997). The student guided functional assessment interview: An analysis of student and teacher agreement. *Journal of Behavioral Education, 7*, 33–49.

Rehabilitation Act of 1973, 29 U.S.C., §§ 504 *et seq.*

Reid, R. (1996). Research in self-monitoring: The present, the prospects, the pitfalls. *Journal of Learning Disabilities, 29*, 317–331.

Reid, R., Gonzalez, J. E., Nordness, P. D., Trout, A., & Epstein, M. H. (2004). A meta-analysis of the academic status of students with emotional/behavioral disturbance. *The Journal of Special Education, 38*, 130–143.

Reid, R., & Harris, K. R. (1993). Self-monitoring of attention versus self-monitoring of performance: Effects of attention and academic performance. *Exceptional Children, 60*, 29–40.

Reilly, T. (1999). An inside look at the potential for violence and suicide. *Preventing School Failure, 44*, 4–8.

Reith, H., & Evertson, C. (1988). Variables related to the effective instruction of difficult to teach children. *Focus on Exceptional Children, 20*(5), 1–8.

Repp, A. C., & Dietz, D. E. D. (1979). Reinforcement based reductive procedures: Training and monitoring performance of institutional staff. *Mental Retardation, 17*, 221–226.

Repp A. C., & Dietz, S. M. (1974). Reducing aggression and self-injurious behavior of institutionalized retarded children through reinforcement of other behaviors. *Journal of Applied Behavior Analysis, 7*, 313–325.

Repp, A. C., & Horner, R. H. (1999). *Functional analysis of problem behavior.* Albany, NY: Wadsworth.

Reschly, D. J. (2000). Assessment and Eligibility Determination in the Individuals with Disabilities Education Act of 1997. In C. J. Tezrow & M. Tankersley (Eds.). *IDEA amendments of 1997: Practice guidelines for school-based teams* (pp. 65–104). Bethesda, MD: National Association of School Psychologists.

Resnick, M. J. (1987). The use of seriously emotionally disturbed students as peer tutors: Effects of oral reading rates and tutor behaviors. Unpublished doctoral dissertation. *Dissertation Abstracts International 49*(5), 1968. (University Microfilms No. 8813441).

Reynolds, L. K., & Kelley, M. L. (1997). The efficacy of a response cost-based treatment package for managing aggressive behavior in preschoolers. *Behavior Modification, 21*, 216–230.

Reynolds, W. M., & Coats, K. L. (1986). A comparison of cognitive-behavioral therapy and relaxation training for the treatment of depression in adolescents. *Journal of Consulting and Clinical Psychology, 54*, 653–660.

Rhode, G., Jenson, W. R., & Reavis, H. K. (1992). *The tough kid book: Practical classroom management strategies.* Longmont, CO: Sopris West.

Rhode, G., Morgan, D. P., & Young, K. R. (1983). Generalization and maintenance of treatment gains of behaviorally handicapped students from resource rooms to regular classrooms using self-evaluation procedures. *Journal of Applied Behavior Analysis, 16,* 171-188.

Rinaldi, C. (2003). Language competence and social behavior of students with emotional or behavioral disorders. *Behavioral Disorders, 29*(1), 34-42.

Rinehart, S. D., Stahl, S. A., & Erickson, L. G. (1986). Some effects of summarization training on reading and studying. *Reading Research Quarterly, 21,* 422-438.

Rivera, B. D., & Rogers-Adkinson, D. (1997). Culturally sensitive interventions: Social skills training with children and parents from culturally and linguistically diverse backgrounds. *Intervention in School and Clinic, 33*(2), 75-80.

Riveria, M. O., Al-Otaiba, S., & Koorland, M. A. (2006). Reading instruction for students with emotional and behavioral disorders and at risk of antisocial behaviors in primary grades: Review of the literature. *Behavioral Disorders, 31,* 323-339.

Roberts, M., McLaughlin, T. F., & White, R. (1997). Useful classroom accommodations for teaching children with ADD and ADHD. *B.C. Journal of Special Education, 21,* 272-284.

Roberts, M. W. (1984). The effects of warned versus unwarned procedures on child noncompliance. *Child and Family Behavior Therapy, 4,* 37-53.

Roberts, M.W., Hatzenbuehler, L. C., & Bean, A.W. (1981). The effects of differential attention and time out on child noncompliance. *Behavior Therapy, 12,* 93-99.

Roberts, M. W., & Powers, S. W. (1990). Adjusting chair time-out procedures for oppositional children. *Behavior Therapy, 21,* 257-271.

Robertson, L. M., Bates, M. P., Wood, M., Rosenblatt, J. A., Furlong, M. J., & Casas, J. M. (1998). Educational placements of students with emotional and behavioral disorders served by probation, mental health, public health, and social service. *Psychology in the Schools, 35*(4), 133-146.

Robin, A., Schneider, M., & Dolnick, M. (1976). The turtle technique: An extended case study of self-control in the classroom. *Psychology in the Schools, 12,* 120-128.

Robinson, D. H., & Kiewra, K. A. (1995). Visual argument: Graphic organizers are superior to outlines in improving learning from text. *Journal of Educational Psychology, 87*(3), 455-467.

Robinson, F. P. (1946). *Effective study.* New York: Harper.

Robinson, P. W., Newby, T. J., & Ganzell, S. L. (1981). A token system for a class of underachieving hyperactive children. *Journal of Applied Behavior Analysis, 14,* 307-315.

Robinson, T. R., Smith, S. W., & Miller, M. D. (2002). Effects of a cognitive-behavior intervention on responses to anger by middle school students with chronic behavior problems. *Behavioral Disorders, 27,* 256-271.

Robinson, T. R., Smith, S. W., Miller, M. D., & Brownell, M. T. (1999). Cognitive behavior modification of hyperactivity/impulsivity and aggression: A meta-analysis of school-based studies. *Journal of Educational Psychology, 27,* 256-271.

Rock, M. L. (2000) Effective crisis management planning: Creating a collaborative framework. *Education and Treatment of Children, 23*(3), 248-264.

Rogers, D. C., Deno, S. L., & Markell, M. (2001). The systematic teaching and recording tactic (S.T.A.R.T.): A generic reading strategy. *Intervention, 37*(2), 96-100.

Rogers-Adkinson, D. L. (2003). Language processing in children with emotional disorders. *Behavioral Disorders, 29*(1), 43-47.

Rogers-Adkinson, D. L., & Griffith, P. (1999). *Communication disorders and children with psychiatric and behavioral disorders.* San Diego: Singular.

Rogers-Adkinson, D. L., & Hooper, S. R. (2003). The relationship of language and behavior: Introduction to the special issue. *Behavioral Disorders, 29*(1), 5-9.

Rolider, A., Cummings, A., & Van Houten, R. (1991). Side effects of therapeutic punishment on academic performance and eye contact. *Journal of Applied Behavior Analysis, 24,* 763-773.

Rooney, K. J., Polloway, E. A., & Hallahan, D. P. (1985). The use of self-monitoring procedures with low IQ learning disabled students. *Journal of Learning Disabilities, 18,* 384-389.

Rosenberg, M. S. (1986). Maximizing the effectiveness of structured classroom management programs: implementing rule-review procedures with disruptive and distractible students. *Behavioral Disorders, 11,* 239-248.

Rosenberg, M. S., & Baker, K. (1985). Instructional time and teacher education: Training preservice and beginning teachers to use time effectively. *Teacher Educator, 20,* 195-207.

Rosenberg, M. S., & Jackman, L. A., (1997). Addressing staff and student behavior: the PAR model. *The Fourth R, 79,* 1-12.

Rosenberg, M. S., O'Shea, L. J., & O'Shea, D. J. (2005). *Student teacher to master teacher: A practical guide for educating students with special needs* (4th ed.). Merrill/Prentice Hall.

Rosenberg, M. S., O'Shea, L. J., & O'Shea, D. J. (2008). *Student teacher to master teacher: A practical guide for educating students with special needs* (4th ed.). Upper Saddle River, NJ: Merrill/Prentice Hall.

Rosenberg, M. S., Wilson, R., Maheady, L., & Sindelar, P. T. (2004). *Educating students with behavior disorders.* Boston: Allyn & Bacon.

Rosenshine, B. (1978). Academic engaged time, content covered, and direct instruction. *Journal of Education, 160*(3), 38-66.

Rosenshine, B. (1983). Teaching functions in instructional programs. *Elementary School Journal, 83*(4), 335-51.

Rosenshine, B. (1986). Synthesis of research on explicit teaching. *Educational Leadership, 43*(7), 60-69.

Rosenshine, B. (1987). Explicit teaching and teacher training. *Journal of Teacher Education, 38*(3), 34-36.

Rosenshine, B. (1997). Advances in research on instruction. In. J. W. Lloyd, E. J. Kame'enui, & D. Chard (Eds.), *Issues in educating students with disabilities* (pp. 197-220). Mahwah, New Jersey: Lawrence Erlbaum.

Rosenshine, B. (2002). Helping students from low-income homes read at grade level. *Journal of Education for Students Placed at Risk, 7*(2), 273-83.

Rosenshine, B., Meister, C., & Chapman, S. (1996). Teaching students to generate questions: A review of the intervention studies. *Review of Educational Research, 66*(2), 181-221.

Rosenshine, B., & Meyers, L. (1978). Staff development for teaching basic skills. *Theory into Practice, 17*(3), 267-271.

Rosenshine, B., & Stevens, R. (1986). Teaching functions. In M. C. Wittrock (Ed.), *The handbook of research and teaching* (pp. 376-391). New York: Macmillan.

Rosenthal, R., & Jacobson, L. (1968). *Pygmalion in the classroom: Teacher expectations and pupils' intellectual development.* New York: Holt, Rinehart & Winston.

Rozalski, M. E., Drasgow, E., & Yell, M. L. (In Press). Assessing the relationships among delinquent male students' disruptive and violent behavior and staff's proactive and reactive behavior in a residential treatment center. *Journal of Emotional and Behavioral Disorders.*

Rozalski, M. E., & Yell, M. L. (2004). The law and school safety. In J. Conoley & A. Goldstein, *School violence intervention: A practical handbook* (2nd ed., pp 507-526). New York: Guilford Press.

Rozalski, M. E., Yell, M. L., & Boreson, L. (2006). Using seclusion timeout and physical restraint: An analysis of state policy, research, and the law. *Journal of Special Education Leadership, 19*(2), 13-29.

Ruhl, K. L., & Berlinghoff, D. H. (1992). Research on improving behaviorally disordered students' academic performance: A review of the literature. *Behavioral Disorders, 17*, 178-190.

Ruth, W. J. (1996). Goal setting and behavioral contracting for students with emotional and behavioral difficulties: Analysis of daily, weekly, and total goal attainment. *Psychology in the Schools, 33*, 153-158.

Rutherford, R. B. (1992). *Teaching social skills: A practical approach.* Reston, VA: Exceptional Innovations.

Rutherford, R. B., Chipman, J., DiGangi, S., & Anderson, K. (1991). *Teaching social skills: A practical instructional approach.* Ann Arbor, MI: Exceptional Innovations.

Rutherford, R. B., & Nelson, C. M. (1982). Analysis of the response contingent time-out literature with behaviorally disordered students in classroom settings. In R. B. Rutherford, Jr. (Ed.), *Monograph in behavior disorders: Severe behavior disorders of children and youth* (pp. 79-105). Reston, VA: Council for Children with Behavioral Disorders.

Rutherford, R. B., & Nelson, C. M. (1998). Generalization and maintenance of treatment effects. In J. C. Witt, S. N. Elliott, & F. M. Gresham (Eds.) *Handbook of Behavior Therapy in Education* (pp. 277-324). New York: Springer.

Rutherford, R. B., Quinn, M. M., & Mathur, S. R. (1996). *Effective strategies for teaching appropriate behaviors to children with emotional/behavioral disorders.* Reston, VA: Council for Children with Behavioral Disorders.

Ryan, A. L., Halsey, H. N., & Matthews, W. J. (2003). Using functional assessment to promote desirable student behavior in schools. *Teaching Exceptional Children, 35*(5), 8-15.

Ryan, J. (1986). *The induction of new teachers.* Bloomington, IN: Phi Delta Kappa.

Ryan, J. B., Reid, R., & Epstein, M. H. (2004). Peer-mediated intervention studies on academic achievement for students with EBD: A review. *Remedial and Special Education, 25*, 330-341.

Ryan, J. B., Saunders, S., Katsiyannis, A., & Yell, M. L. (2007). Timeout: Best practices and legal guidelines. *Teaching Exceptional Children, 39*(4), 60-67.

S-1 v. Turlington, 635 F.2d 342 (5th Cir. 1981).

Sachs, D. A. (1973). The efficacy of time-out procedures in a variety of behavior problems. *Journal of Behavior Therapy and Experimental Psychology, 4*, 237-244.

Safer, D. J., Heaton, R. C., & Parker, F. C. (1981). A behavioral program for disruptive junior high school students: Results and follow-up. *Journal of Abnormal Child Psychology, 9*, 483-494.

Salend, S., & Maragulia, D. (1983). The timeout ribbon: A procedure for the least restrictive environment. *Journal for Special Educators, 13*, 9-15.

Salend, S. J. (1999). Facilitating friendships among diverse students. *Intervention in School and Clinic, 35*(1), 9-15.

Salend, S. J., & Gordon, B. D. (1987). A group-oriented timeout ribbon. *Behavioral Disorders, 12*, 131-137.

Salend, S. J., & Kovalich, B. (1981). A group response cost system mediated by free tokens: An alternative to token reinforcement in the classroom. *American Journal of Mental Deficiency, 86*, 184-187.

Salend, S. J., & Meddaugh, D. (1985). Using a peer-mediated extinction procedure to decrease obscene language. *Pointer, 30*(1), 8-11.

Salend, S. J., Tintle, L., & Balber, H. (1988). Effects of a student managed response cost system on the behavior of two mainstreamed students. *Elementary School Journal, 89*, 89-97.

Salend, S. J., Whittaker, C. R., & Reeder, E. (1992). Group evaluation: A collaborative, peer mediated behavior management system. *Exceptional Children, 59*, 203-209.

Salvia, J., & Hughes, C. (1990). *Curriculum-based assessment: Testing what is taught.* New York: Macmillam.

Salvia, J. & Ysseldyke, J. (2007). *Assessment in special and inclusive education* (10th ed.). Boston: Houghton Mifflin.

Sanger, D., Maag, J. W., & Shapera, N. R. (1994). Language problems among students with emotional and behavioral disorders. *Intervention in School and Clinic, 30*, 103-108.

Savage, T. V. (1999). *Teaching self-control through management and discipline* (2nd ed.). Boston: Allyn & Bacon

Scanlon, D. (1996) Social skills strategy instruction. In D. D. Deshler, E. S. Ellis, & B. K. Lenz (Eds.), *Adolescents with learning disabilities* (pp. 369–410). Denver, CO: Love.

Scheuermann, B. (1998). Curricular and instructional recommendations for students with emotional/behavioral disorders. *Beyond Behavior, 9*(3), 3–4.

Scheuermann, B., & Webber, J. (1996a). Best practices in developing level systems. In L. M. Bullock & R. A. Gable (Eds.), *Best practices for managing adolescents with emotional/behavioral disorders in the school environment* (pp. 21–30). Council for Children with Behavioral Disorders Mini-Library Series on Emotional/Behavioral Disorders. Reston, VA: Council for Exceptional Children.

Scheuermann, B., & Webber, J (1996b). Level systems: Problems and solutions. *Beyond Behavior, 7*(2), 12–17.

Scheuermann, B., Webber, J., Partin, M., & Knies, W. C. (1994). Level systems and the law: Are they compatible? *Behavioral Disorders, 19*, 205–220.

Schloss, P. J., Holt, J., Mulvaney, M., & Green, J. (1988). The Franklin-Jefferson program: Demonstration of an integrated social learning approach to educational services for behaviorally disordered students. *Teaching Behaviorally Disordered Youth, 4*, 7–15 .

Schloss, P. J., & Smith, M. A. (1998). *Applied behavior analysis in the classroom* (2nd ed.). Boston: Allyn & Bacon.

Schloss, P. J., Smith, M. A., & Schloss, C. N. (2001). *Instructional methods for secondary students with learning and behavioral problems* (3rd ed.). Boston. Allyn & Bacon.

Schmidt, G. W., & Ulrich, K. E. (1969). Effects of group contingent events upon classroom noise. *Journal of Applied Behavior Analysis, 2*, 171–179.

Scholtes, P. (1988). *The team handbook*. Madison, WI: Joiner Associates.

Schumaker, J. S., Hazel, J. S., & Pederson, C. S. (1988). *Social skills for daily living*. Circle Pines, MN: American Guidance Service.

Schumaker, J. S., Pederson, C. S., Hazel, J. S., & Meyen, E. L. (1983). Social skills curricula for mildly handicapped adolescents: A review. *Focus on Exceptional Children, 16*, 1–16.

Scott, T. M. (2001). Positive behavioral support: A school-wide example. *Journal of Positive Behavioral Interventions, 3*, 88–94.

Scott, T. M., & Barrett, S. B. (2004). Using staff and student time engaged in disciplinary procedures to evaluate the impact of school-wide PBS. *Journal of Positive Interventions, 6*(1), 21–27.

Scott, T. M., & Hunter, J. (2001). Initiating schoolwide support systems: An administrator's guide to the process. *Beyond Behavior, 11*(1), 13–16.

Scott, T. M., Liaupsin, C. J., Nelson, C. M. & Jolivette, K. (2003). Ensuring student success through team-based functional behavioral assessment. *Teaching Exceptional Children, 35*(5), 16–21.

Scott, T. M., & Nelson, C. M. (1999a). Universal school discipline strategies: Facilitating positive learning environments. *Effective School Practice, 17*(4), 54–64.

Scott, T. M., & Nelson, C. M. (1999b). Using functional behavioral assessment to develop effective intervention plans: Practical classroom applications. *Journal of Positive Behavioral Interventions, 1*, 242–251.

Scott, T. M., Payne, L. D., & Jolivette, K. (2003). Preventing predictable problem behaviors by using positive behavior support. *Beyond Behavior, 13*(1), 3–6.

Scott, T. M., & Shearer-Lingo, A. (2002). The effects of reading fluency instruction on the academic and behavioral success of middle school students in a self-contained classroom. *Preventing School Failure, 46*, 167–173.

Scruggs, T. E., & Mastropieri, M. A. (1986a). Academic Characteristics of Behaviorally Disordered and Learning Disabled Students. *Behavioral Disorders, 11*(3), 184–190.

Scruggs, T. E., & Mastropieri, M. A. (1986b). Improving test-taking skills of behaviorally disordered and learning disabled students. *Exceptional Children, 52*, 63–68.

Scruggs, T. E., & Mastropieri, M. A. (1988). Are learning disabled students 'test-wise'? A review of recent research. *Learning Disabilities Focus, 3*(2), 87–97.

Scruggs, T. E., & Mastropieri, M. A. (1992). *Teaching test-taking skills: Helping students show what they know*. Brookline, MA: Brookline Books.

Scruggs, T. E., & Mastropieri, M. A. (2000). The effectiveness of mnemonic instruction for students with learning and behavior problems. An update and research synthesis. *Journal of Behavioral Education, 10*, 163–173.

Scruggs, T. E., & Mastropieri, M. A. (2002). *Teaching tutorial: Mnemonic instruction*. Retrieved December 15, 2005, from http://www.TeachingLD.org

Scruggs, T. E., Mastropieri, M. A., & Tolfa-Veit, D. (1986). The effects of coaching on standardized test performance of learning disabled and behaviorally disordered students. *Remedial and Special Education, 7*, 37–41.

Searcy, S. & Meadows, N. B. (1994). Friendship issues of children and youth with behavior disorders. *Education and Treatment of Children, 17*(3), 255–266.

Senechal, M., & LeFevre, J. (2002). Parental involvement in the development of children's reading skill: A five-year longitudinal study. *Child Development, 73*(2), 445–460.

Senate Report on the Individuals with Disabilities Act Amendments of 1997 (P.L. 105-17). Retrieved March, 2002, from wais.access.gpo.gov.

Seuss. (1963). *Dr. Seuss's ABC: An amazing alphabet book*. New York: Random House.

Sexton, M., Harris, K. R., & Graham, S. (1998). Self-regulated strategy development and the writing process: Effects on essay writing and attributions. *Exceptional Children, 64*, 295–312.

Shapiro, E. S., & Cole, C. L. (1994). *Behavior change in the classroom: Self-management interventions*. New York: Guilford Press.

Shapiro, E. S. & Derr, D. F. (1987). An examination of overlap between reading curriculum and standardized achievement tests. *Journal of Special Education, 21*, 59–67.

Shapiro, E. S., DuPaul, G. J., & Bradley-Klug, K. L. (1998). Self-management as a strategy to improve the classroom behavior of adolescents with ADHD. *Journal of Learning Disabilities, 31*, 545–555.

Shin, J., Deno, S. L., & Espin, C. (2000). Technical adequacy of the Maze task for curriculum-based measurement of reading growth. *The Journal of Special Education, 34*(3), 164–172.

Shinn, M., Tindal, G., Spira, D., & Marston, D. (1987). Practice of learning disabilities as social policy. *Learning Disabilities Quarterly, 10*, 17–28.

Shinn, M. R. (1989). *Curriculum-based measurement: Assessing special children*. New York: Guilford Press.

Shinn, M. R., & Marston, D. (1985). Differentiating mildly handicapped, low-achieving and regular education students: A curriculum-based measurement approach. *Remedial and Special Education, 6*, 31–45.

Shinn, M. R., Walker, H. M., & Stoner, G. (2002). *Interventions for academic and behavior problems II: Preventive and remedial approaches*. Silver Spring, MD: National Association of School Psychologists.

Shisler, L., Top, B. L., & Osguthorpe, R. T. (1986). Behaviorally disordered students as reverse-role tutors: Increasing social acceptance and reading skills. *B. C. Journal of Special Education, 10*, 101–119.

Shores, R. E., Gunter, P. L., Denny, K., & Jack, S. L. (1993). Classroom influences on aggressive and disruptive behaviors of students with emotional and behavioral disorders. *Focus on Exceptional Children, 26*, 140.

Shores, R. E., Gunter, P. L., & Jack, S. L. (1993). Classroom management strategies: Are they setting events for coercion? *Behavioral Disorders, 18*, 92–102.

Shores, R. E., Jack, S. L., Gunter, P. L., Ellis, D. N., DeBriere, T. J., & Wehby, J. H. (1993). Classroom interactions of children with behavior disorders. *Journal of Emotional and Behavioral Disorders, 1*, 27–39.

Shores, R. E., & Wehby, J. H. (1999). Analyzing the classroom social behavior of students with ed. *Journal of Emotional and Behavioral Disorders, 7*(4), 194–199.

Shriner, J. & Salvia, J. (1988). Chronic noncorrespondence between elementary math curriculum and arithmetic tests. *Exceptional Children, 55*, 240–248.

Shriner, J. G. (2001). Legal perspectives on school outcomes assessment for students with disabilities. *The Journal of Special Education, 33*, 232–239.

Shriner, J. G. & Spicuzza, R. J. (1995). Procedural considerations in the assessment of students at risk for school failure. *Preventing School Failure, 39*(2), 33–39.

Shure, M. B. (1992). *I can problem solve*. Champaign, IL: Research Press.

Sidman, M. (1960). *Tactics of scientific research*. New York, Basic Books, Inc.

Sidman, M. (1989). *Coercion and its fallout*. Boston: Author's Cooperative.

Siegel, J. M., & Spivak, G. (1973). *Problem-solving therapy* (Research report 23). Philadelphia: Hahnemann Medical College.

Simmons v. Beauregard Parish School Board, 315 So. 2d, 883 (LA Ct. App. 1975)

Simpson, R. L., Whelan, R. J., & Zabel, R. H. (1993). Special educational personnel preparation in the 21st century: Issues and strategies. *Remedial and Special Education, 14*, 7–22.

Singh, N. N., & Singh, J. (1986). Increasing oral reading proficiency: A comparative analysis of drill and positive practice overcorrection procedures. *Behavior Modification, 10*, 115–130.

Singh, N. N., Singh, J., & Winton, A. S. (1984). Positive practice overcorrection of oral reading errors. *Behavior Modification, 81*, 23–37.

Skiba, R., Magnusson, D., Marston, D., & Erickson, K. (1986). *The assessment of mathematics performance in special education: Achievement tests, proficiency tests, or formative evaluation?* Minneapolis: Special Services, Minneapolis Public Schools.

Skiba, R. J. (2002). Special education and school discipline: A precarious balance. *Behavioral Disorders, 27*(2), 81–97.

Skiba, R. J., & Peterson, R. L. (1999). The dark side of zero tolerance: Can punishment lead to safe schools? *Phi Delta Kappan, 80*, 372–382.

Skiba, R. J., & Peterson, R. L. (2000). School discipline at a crossroads: From zero tolerance to early response. *Exceptional Children, 66*(3), 335–347.

Skiba, R. J., Peterson, R. L., & Williams, T. (1997). Office referrals and suspensions: Disciplinary interventions in middle schools. *Education and Treatment of Children, 20*, 295–315.

Skinner, B. F. (1938). *The behavior of organisms: An experimental analysis*. New York: Apple-Century-Crofts.

Skinner, B. F. (1953). *The science of human behavior*. New York: Macmillan.

Skinner, B. F. (1968). *The technology of teaching*. Upper Saddle River, NJ: Merrill/Prentice Hall.

Skinner, B. F. (1969). *Contingencies of reinforcement: A theoretical analysis*. New York: Apple-Century-Crofts.

Skinner, C. H., Bamberg, H. W., Smith, E. S., & Powell, S. S. (1993). Cognitive cover, copy, and compare: Subvocal responding to increase rates of accurate division responding. *Remedial and Special Education, 14*, 49–56.

Skinner, C. H., Ford, J. H., & Yuonker, B. D. (1991). A comparison of instructional response requirements on the multiplication performance of behaviorally disordered students. *Behavioral Disorders, 17*, 56–65.

Skinner, C. H., Turco, T. L., Beatty, K. L., & Rasavage, C. (1989). Cover, copy and compare: A method for increasing multiplication performance. *School Psychology Review, 18*, 412–420.

Smith, D. J., Young, K. R., West, R. P., Morgan R. P., & Rhode, G. (1988). Reducing the disruptive behavior of junior high school students: A classroom self-management procedure. *Behavioral Disorders, 13*, 231-239.

Smith, M., & Misra, A. (1994). Using group contingencies with students with learning disabilities. *LD Forum, 20*(1), 17-20.

Smith, S. W. (1990a). Comparison of individualized education programs (IEPs) of students with behavioral disorders and learning disabilities. *The Journal of Special Education, 24*, 85-100.

Smith, S. W. (1990b). Individualized education programs (IEPs) in special education—From intent to acquiescence. *Exceptional Children, 57*, 6-14.

Smith, S. W., & Farrell, D. T. (1993). Level system use in special education: Classroom intervention with prima facie appeal. *Behavioral Disorders, 18*, 251-264.

Smith, S. W., Lochman, J. S., & Daunic, A. P. (2005). Managing aggression using cognitive-behavioral interventions: State of the practice and future directions. *Behavioral Disorders, 30*, 227-240.

Smith, S. W., Siegel, E. M., O'Conner, A. M., & Thomas, S. B. (1994). Effects of cognitive-behavioral training on angry behavior and aggression of three elementary-aged students. *Behavioral Disorders, 19*, 126-135.

Smith, S. W., & Simpson, R. L. (1989). An analysis of individualized education programs (IEPs) for students with behavioral disorders. *Behavioral Disorders, 14*, 107-116.

Snow, C. E., Burns, M. S., & Griffin, P. (Eds.). (1998). *Prevention of reading difficulties in young children.* Washington, DC: National Academy Press.

Sobsey, D. (1990). Modifying the behavior of behavior modifiers. In A. Repp & N. Singh (Eds.), *Perspectives on the use of nonaversive and aversive interventions for persons with developmental disabilities* (pp 421-433). Sycamore, IL: Sycamore Publishing.

Speltz, M. L., Shimamura, J. W., & McReynolds, W. T. (1982). Procedural variations in group contingencies: Effects on children's academic and social behaviors. *Journal of Applied Behavior Analysis, 15*, 533-544.

Spencer, R. J., & Gray, D. F. (1973). A time-out procedure for classroom behavior change within the public school. *Child Study Journal, 3*, 29-38.

Spencer, V. G. (2006). Peer tutoring and students with emotional or behavioral disorders: A review of the literature. *Behavioral Disorders, 31*, 189-222.

Spivak, G., & Shure, M. B. (1974). *Social adjustment of young children.* San Francisco: Jossey-Bass.

Sprague, J., Sugai, G., & Walker, H. M. (1998). Antisocial behavior in schools. In T. S. Watson & F. M. Gresham, *Handbook of Child Behavior Therapy.* 451-474. New York: Plenum Press.

Sprague, J., & Walker, H. (2000). Early identification and intervention for youth with antisocial and violent behavior. *Exceptional Children, 66*(3), 367-379.

Sprague, J. R. & Horner, R. H., (1999). Low-frequency high-intensity problem behavior: toward an applied technology of functional assessment and intervention. In A.C. Repp & R. H. Horner (Eds.), *Functional analysis of problem behavior: From effective assessment to effective support.* Belmont, CA: Wadsworth.

Sprick, R., Sprick, M., Garrison, M. (1993). *Interventions: Collaborative planning for students at risk.* Longmont, CO: Sopris West.

Sprick, R. S., Borgmeier, C., & Nolet, V. (2002). Prevention and management of behavior problems in secondary schools. In M. A. Shinn, H. M. Walker, & G. Stoner, *Interventions for academic and behavior problems II: Preventive and remedial approaches.* Bethesda, MD: National Association of School Psychologists.

Stafford, R. T. (1978). Education for the handicapped: A senator's perspective. *Vermont Law Review, 3*, 71-79.

Stallings, J., & Kaskowitz, D. (1974). *Follow Through classroom observation evaluation, 1972-1973.* Menlo Park, CA: Stanford Research Institute.

Stanard, R. P. (2003). High school graduation rates in the United States: Implications for the counseling profession. *Journal of Counseling & Development, 81*(2), 217-222.

Stein, M., Kinder, D., Silbert, J., & Carnine, D. (2006). *Designing effective mathematics instruction: A direct instruction approach* (4th ed.). Columbus, OH: Merrill/Prentice Hall.

Stein, M. L. & Davis, C. A. (2000). Direct instruction as positive behavior support. *Beyond Behavior, 10*(1), 7-12.

Stenmark, J. K. (1991). *Mathematics assessment: Myths, models, good questions and practical suggestions.* Reston, VA. National Council of Teachers of Mathematics.

Stephens, T. M. (1992). *Social skills in the classroom.* Columbus, OH: Cedars Press.

Stewart, C. A. & Singh, N. N. (1986). Overcorrection of spelling deficits in mentally retarded persons. *Behavior Modification, 10*, 355-365.

Stichter J. P., Sasso G. M., & Jolivette, K. (2004). Including a student with EBD in a general education setting: Structural analysis as an evidence based practice. *Journal of Positive Behavioral Interventions, 6*, 166-177.

Stokes, T. F., & Baer, D. M. (1977). An implicit technology of generalization. *Journal of Applied Behavior Analysis, 10*, 349-376.

Stokes, T. F., & Osnes, P. G. (1986). Programming the generalization of children's social behavior. In P. S. Strain, M. J. Guralnick, & H. M. Walker (Eds.), *Children's social behavior: development, assessment, and modification* (pp. 407-443). Orlando, FL: Academic Press.

Stokes, T. F., & Osnes, P. G. (1989). An operant pursuit of generalization. *Behavior Therapy, 20*, 337-355.

Storey, K., & Gaylord-Ross, R. (1987). Increasing positive social interactions by handicapped individuals during a recreational activity using a multicomponent treatment package. *Research in Developmental Disabilities, 8*, 627-649.

Strachota, B. (1996). *On their side: Helping children take charge of their learning.* Greenfield, MA: Northeast Foundation for Children.

Strain, P. S., Kohler, F. W., Storey, K., & Danko, C. (1994). Teaching preschoolers with autism to self-monitor their social interaction: An analysis of results in home and school settings. *Journal of Emotional and Behavioral Disorders, 2*, 78–88.

Strickland, B. P., & Turnbull, A. P. (1990). *Developing and implementing individualized education programs* (3rd ed.). Upper Saddle River, NJ: Merrill/Prentice Hall.

Stuart, R. B. (1971). Behavioral contracting within the families of delinquents. *Behavioral Therapy and Experimental Psychiatry, 2*, 1–11.

Sugai, G. (2004). *South Carolina school-wide positive behavior interventions and supports: Leadership follow-up training on non-classroom settings.* Presentation to school leadership teams in the South Carolina State Improvement Grant. Available at http://pbis.org/english/powerpoints.htm.

Sugai, G., & Colvin, G. (1997). Debriefing: A transition step for promoting acceptable behavior. *Education and Treatment of Children, 20*, 209–221.

Sugai, G., Colvin, G., Hagan-Burke, S., & Lewis-Palmer, T., (2001). *Components and processes of school-wide discipline.* Eugene, OR: Center on Positive Behavioral Interventions and Supports.

Sugai, G., & Horner, R. H. (1999). Discipline and behavioral support: Practices, pitfalls, and promises. *Effective School Practices, 17*(4), 10–22.

Sugai, G., & Horner, R. H. (2001). The features of an effective behavior support at the school district level. *Beyond Behavior, 11*(1), 3–5.

Sugai, G., & Horner, R. H. (2002). The evolution of discipline practices: Schoolwide positive behavior supports. *Child and Family Behavior Therapy, 24*(1 & 2), 23–50.

Sugai, G., & Lewis, T. J. (1998). Preferred and promising practices for social skills instruction. In E. L. Meyen, G. A. Vergason, & R. J. Whelan (Eds.), *Educating students with mild disabilities* (pp. 137–162). Denver, CO: Love.

Sugai, G., Lewis-Palmer, T., & Hagan-Burke, S. (1998). Using functional assessment to develop behavior support plans. *Preventing School Failure, 43*(1), 6–13.

Sugai, G., Sprague, J. R., Horner, R. H., & Walker, H. M. (2001). Preventing school violence: The use of office disciplinary referrals to assess and monitor school-wide discipline interventions. In H. M. Walker & M. H. Epstein (Eds.), *Making schools safer and violence free: Critical issues, solutions, and recommended practices* (pp. 50–58). Austin, TX: Pro-Ed.

Sugai, G. M., & Lewis, T. (1990). *Using self-management strategies in classes for students with behavioral disorders.* Paper presented at the annual conference of Teacher Educators of Children with Behavioral Disorders. Tempe, AZ.

Sullivan, M. A., & O'Leary, S. G. (1990). Maintenance following reward and cost token programs. *Behavior Therapy, 21*, 139–149.

Sulzer-Azeroff, B., & Mayer, G. R. (1991). *Behavior analysis for lasting change.* Fort Worth, TX: Harcourt Brace.

Suritsky, S. K., & Hughes, C. A. (1996). Notetaking strategy instruction. In D. D. Deshler, E. S. Ellis, & B. K. Lenz (Eds.), *Teaching adolescents with learning disabilities* (2nd ed., pp. 267–312). Denver, CO: Love.

Sutherland, K. S. (2000). Promoting positive interactions between teachers and students with emotional and behavioral disorders. *Preventing School Failure, 44*, 110–115.

Sutherland, K. S., Alder, N., & Gunter, P. L. (2003). The effect of varying rates of opportunities to respond to academic requests on the classroom behavior of students with EBD. *Journal of Emotional and Behavioral Disorders, 2*(4), 239–248.

Sutherland, K. S., Copeland, S, & Wehby, J. (2001). Catch them while you can: Monitoring and increasing the use of effective praise. *Beyond Behavior, 11* (1), 46–49.

Sutherland, K. S., & Wehby, J. H. (2001a). The effects of self-evaluation on teaching behaviors in classrooms for students with emotional and behavioral disorders. *The Journal of Special Education, 35*, 161–171.

Sutherland, K. S., & Wehby, J. H. (2001b). Exploring the relationship between increased opportunities to respond to academic requests and the academic and behavioral outcomes of students with EBD. *Remedial and Special Education, 22*(2), 113–121.

Sutherland, K. S., Wehby, J., & Copeland, S. (2000). Effect of varying rates of behavior-specific praise on the on-task behavior of students with emotional and behavioral disorders. *Journal of Emotional and Behavioral Disorders 8*, 2–8.

Sutherland, K. S., Wehby, J. H., & Yoder, P. J. (2001). Examination of the relationship between teacher praise and opportunities for students with EBD to respond to academic requests. *Journal of Emotional and Behavioral Disorders, 10*, 5–13.

Swain, J. C., & McLaughlin, T. F. (1998). The effects of bonus contingencies in a classwide token program on math accuracy with middle-school students with behavioral disorders. *Behavioral Interventions, 13*, 11–19.

Swanborn, M. S. L., & de Glopper, K. (1999). Incidental word learning while reading: A meta-analysis. *Review of Educational Research, 69*(3), 261–285.

Swanson, H. L., Carson, C., & Sachse-Lee, C. M. (1996). A selective synthesis of intervention research for students with learning disabilities. *School Psychology Review, 25*, 370–391.

Swarts, L. (2003–2004). Alternative education accountability: Kentucky's approach. *Impact, 16*(3), 20–22.

Switzer, E. B., Deal, T. E., & Bailey, J. S. (1977). The reduction of stealing in second graders using a group contingency. *Journal of Applied Behavior Analysis, 10*, 267–272.

Symons, S. Carigula-Bull, B. L., Snyder, T., & Pressley, M. (1989). Why be optimistic about cognitive strategy instruction? In C. B. McCormick, G. E. Miller, & M. Pressley (Eds.), *Cognitive strategy research: From basic research to educational applications* (pp. 24–48). New York: Springer-Verlag.

Tankersley, M. (1995). A group-oriented contingency management program: A review of research on the good behavior game and implications for teachers. *Preventing School Failure, 40*, 19-24.

Tankersley, M., Landrum T. J., & Cook, B. G. (2004). How research informs practice in the field of emotional and behavioral disorders. In R. B. Rutherford, M. M. Quinn, & S. R. Mathur (Eds.), *Handbook of research in behavioral disorders* (pp. 98-113). New York: Guilford Press.

Tarver, S. (1999). Focusing on Direct Instruction. *Current Practice Alerts, 2*, 1-4.

Tauber, R. T. (1985). Power bases: Their application to classroom and school management. *Journal of Education for Teaching, 11*, 133-144.

Telzrow, C. F. & Naidu, K. (2000). Interim Alternative Educational Settings: Guidelines for Prevention and Intervention. In C. J. Tezrow & M. Tankersley (Eds.). *IDEA Amendments of 1997: Practice Guidelines for School-Based Teams* (pp. 199-240). Bethesda, MD: National Association of School Psychologists.

Thomas, C., Correa, V., & Morsink, C. (2001). *Interactive teaming: Enhancing programs for students with special needs.* Columbus, OH: Merrill/Prentice Hall.

Thomas, S. B. & Russo, C. J. (1995). *Special education law: Issues and implications for the 90's.* Dayton, OH: Education Law Association.

Thornton, T. N., Craft, C. A., Dahlberg, L. L., Lynch, B. S., & Baer, K. (2000). *Best practices of youth violence prevention: A sourcebook for community action.* Atlanta: Centers for Disease Control and Prevention, National Center for Injury Prevention and Control.

Thorndock v. Boise Independent School District, 767 P.2d 1241 (1988).

Thurlow, M. L., Elliott, J. L., & Ysseldyke, J. E. (2001). *Testing students with disabilities: Practical strategies for complying with district and state requirements.* Thousand Oaks, CA: Corwin Press.

Timberlake, E. M. (1981). Child abuse and externalized aggression. In R. J. Hunter & Y. E. Walker (Eds.), *Exploring the relationship between child abuse and delinquency* (pp. 43-51). Montclair, NJ: Allanheld, Osman.

Tindal, G & Crawford, M. (2002). Teaching writing to students with behavior disorders: Metaphor and medium. In K. L. Lane, F. M., Gresham, & T. E. O'Shaughnessy, T. E. (Eds.) *Interventions for children with or at risk for emotional and behavioral disorders* (pp. 104-124). Boston: Pearson/Allyn & Bacon.

Tindal, G., Germann, G., & Deno, S. L. (1983). *Descriptive research on the Pine County norms: A compilation of findings* (Research Report No. 132). Minneapolis: University of Minnesota Institute for Research on Learning Disabilities.

Tindal, G., & Parker, R. (1989). Assessment of written expression for students in compensatory and special education programs. *The Journal of Special Education, 23*, 169-183.

Tindal, G., & Parker, R. (1991). Identifying measures for evaluating written expression. *Learning Disabilities Research and Practice, 6*, 211-218.

Tindall, E. (1996). *Principal's role in fostering teacher collaboration for students with special needs.* Unpublished doctoral dissertation. College of William and Mary, Williamsburg, VA.

Tobin, T., & Sprague, J. R. (2000). Alternative education strategies: Reducing violence in school and the community. *Journal of Emotional and Behavioral Disorders, 8*(3), 177-186.

Tobin, T., Sugai, G., & Colvin, G. (2000). Using discipline referrals to make decisions. *NASSP Bulletin, 84*, 106-110.

Todd, A. W., Horner, R. H., & Sugai, G. (1999). Self-monitoring and self-recruited praise: Effects on problem behavior, academic engagement, and work completion in a typical classroom. *Journal of Positive Behavior Interventions, 1*, 66-76.

Todd, A. W., Horner, R. H., Sugai, G., & Colvin, G. (1999). Individualizing school-wide discipline for students with chronic problem behaviors: A team approach. *Effective School practices, 17*, 72-82.

Todd, A. W., Horner, R. H., Sugai, G., & Sprague, J. R. (1999). Effective behavior support: Strengthening school-wide systems through a team-based approach. *Effective School Practice. 17.* 23-37.

Tollefson, N., Tracy, D. B., Johnsen, E. P., & Chatman, J. (1986). Teaching learning disabled children goal implementation skills. *Psychology in the Schools, 8*, 194-204.

Torgeson, J. K. (1982). The learning disabled child as an inactive learner: Educational implications. *Topics in Learning and Learning Disabilities, 2*, 45-52.

Torgesen, J. K. (2004). Avoiding the devastating downward spiral: The evidence that early intervention prevents reading failure. *American Educator, 28*(3), 6-19, 45-48.

Touchette, P. E., MacDonald, R. F., & Langer, S. N. (1985). Scatterplot for identifying stimulus control of problem behavior. *Journal of Applied Behavior Analysis, 18*, 343-352.

Trap, J. J., Milner-Davis, P., Joseph, S., & Cooper, J. O. (1970). The effects of feedback and consequences on transitional cursive letter formation. *Journal of Applied Behavior Analysis, 11*, 381-393.

Trent, S., & Artiles, A. (1994). Overrepresentation of minority students in special education: A continuing debate. *The Journal of Special Education, 27*(4), 410-437.

Trice, A. D., & Parker, F. C. (1983). Decreasing adolescent swearing in an instructional setting. *Education and Treatment of Children, 6*, 29-35.

Trivette, C., Dunst, C., Boyd, K., & Hamby, D. (1995). Family-oriented program models, help giving practices, and parental control appraisals. *Exceptional Children, 62*, 237-248.

Trout, A. L., Nordness, P. D., Pierce, C. D., & Epstein, M. H. (2003). Research on the academic status of children and youth with emotional and behavioral disorders: A review of the literature from 1961 to 2000. *Journal of Emotional and Behavioral Disorders, 11*, 198–210.

Trovato, J., & Bucher, B. (1980). Peer tutoring with or without home-based reinforcement, for reading remediation. *Journal of Applied Behavior Analysis, 13*, 129–141.

Tucker, B. P., & Goldstein, B. A. (1992). *Legal rights of persons with disabilities: An analysis of federal law*. Horsham, PA: LRP.

Tuckman, B. W. (2003, August). *The Strategies-For-Achievement approach for teaching study skills*. Paper presented at the annual meeting of the American Psychological Association, Toronto, Canada.

Turnbull, A., & Turnbull, H. R. (2001). *Families, professionals, and exceptionality: Collaborating for empowerment* (4th ed). Columbus, OH: Merrill/Prentice Hall.

Turnbull, A. P., Turnbull, H. R., Shank, M., & Leal, D. (1995). *Exceptional lives: Special education in today's schools*. Upper Saddle River, NJ: Merrill/Prentice Hall.

Turnbull, R., Turnbull, A., Shank, M., & Smith, S. J. (2004). *Exceptional lives: Special education in today's schools* (4th ed.). Upper Saddle River, NJ: Merrill/Prentice Hall.

Twyman, J. S., Johnson, H., Buie, J. D., & Nelson, C. M. (1993). The use of a warning procedure to signal a more intrusive timeout contingency. *Behavioral Disorders, 19*, 243–253.

Tyroler, M. J., & Lahey, B. B. (1980). Effects of contingent observation on the disruptive behavior of a toddler in a group setting. *Child Care Quarterly, 9*, 265–274.

Umbreit, J. (1995). Functional assessment and intervention in a regular classroom setting for the disruptive behavior of a student with attention deficit hyperactivity disorders. *Behavioral Disorders, 20*, 267–278.

U.S. Department of Education. (1998). *Promising practices: New ways to improve teacher quality*. Retrieved July 4, 2006, from http://www.ed.gov/pubs/PromPractice/chapter6.html

U.S. Department of Education. (2001). *Expert Panel on Safe, Disciplined, and Drug-Free Schools*. Commissioned by U.S. Deptartment of Education's Safe and Drug-Free Schools Program (SDFS), in cooperation with the Office of Educational Research and Improvement. Retrieved from http://www.ed.gov/offices/OERI/ORAD/KAD/expert_panel/2001promising_sddfs.html August, 2006.

U.S. Department of Education. (2005). *Office of Special Education data analysis system (DANS)*. Retrieved August 24, 2006, from http://www.ideadata.org

U.S. Department of Education, Office of Special Education and Rehabilitation Services. (2003). *Twenty-fifth annual report to Congress on the implementation of the Individuals with Disabilities Education Act*. Washington, D.C.: Author.

U.S. Department of Health and Human Services (2001). *Report of the Surgeon General's conference on children's mental health: A national action agenda*. Washington, D.C.: Author.

Valente, R., & Valente, C. (2005). *Law in the schools* (6th ed.). Upper Saddle River, NJ: Merrill/Prentice Hall.

Van Acker, R., (1996). *Types of youth aggression and violence and implications for prevention and treatment*. Reston, VA: Council for Children with Behavioral Disorders.

Van Acker, R., Grant, S. H., & Henry, D. (1996). Teacher and student behavior as a function of risk for aggression. *Education and Treatment of Children, 19*, 316–334.

Vaughn, S., Gersten, R., & Chard, D. J. (2000). The underlying message in LD intervention research. *Exceptional Children, 67*, 99–114.

Vaughn, S., Levy, S., Coleman, M., & Bos, C. S. (2002). Reading instruction for students with LD and EBD: A synthesis of observation studies. *The Journal of Special Education, 36*(1), 2–13.

Venn, J. J. (2007). *Assessing Students with Special Needs* (4th ed.). Upper Saddle River, NJ: Merrill/Prentice Hall.

Videen, J., Deno, S. L., & Marston, D. (1982). *Correct word sequences: A valid indicator of proficiency in written expression* (Research Report No. 84). Minneapolis: University of Minnesota Institute for Research on Learning Disabilities.

Vygotsky, L. (1962). *Thought and language*. New York: Wiley.

Wacker, D. P., Berg, W. K., Asmus, J. M., Harding, J. K., & Cooper, L. J. (1998). *Experimental analysis of antecedent influences on challenging behaviors*. Baltimore: Paul H. Brookes.

Wagner, M., D'Amico, R., Marder, C., Newman, L., & Blackorby, J. (1992). *What happens next? Trends in post school outcomes of youth with disabilities: The second comprehensive report from the national longitudinal transition study of special education students*. Menlo Park, CA: SRI International. (ERIC Document Reproduction Service No. ED356603).

Wahler, R. G., & Fox, J. J. (1981). Setting events in applied behavior analysis: Toward a conceptual and methodological expansion. *Journal of Applied Behavior Analysis, 14*, 327–338.

Wald, J., & Losen, D. J. (2003). Defining and redirecting a school-to-prison pipeline. *New Directions for Youth Development, 99*, 9–16.

Walker, H., & Walker, J. (1991). *Coping with noncompliance in the classroom: A positive approach for teachers*. Austin, TX: Pro-Ed.

Walker, H. M. (1983). Applications of response cost in school settings: Outcomes, issues, and recommendations. *Exceptional Education Quarterly, 3*, 47–55.

Walker, H. M. (1995). *The acting-out child: Coping with classroom disruption*. Longmont, CO: Sopris West.

Walker, H. M., & Buckley, N. K. (1974). Teacher attention to appropriate and inappropriate classroom behavior. *Focus on Exceptional Children, 5*, 5–12.

Walker, H. M., Colvin, G., & Ramsey, E. (1995). *Antisocial behavior in school: Strategies and best practices*. Pacific Grove, CA: Brooks/Cole.

Walker, H. M., & Epstein, M. H. (2001). Preface. In H. M. Walker & M. H. Epstein (Eds.), *Making schools safer and violence free: Critical issues, solutions, and recommended practices* (p. 1). Austin, TX: Pro-Ed.

Walker, H. M., & Fabre, T. R. (1987). Assessment of behavior disorders in the school setting: Issues, problems, and strategies revisited. In N. Haring (Ed.), *Assessing and managing behavior disorders* (pp. 198–234). Seattle: University of Washington Press.

Walker, H. M., Forness, S. R., Kauffman, J. M., Epstein, M. H., Gresham, F. M., Nelson, C. M., et al. (1998). Macro-social validation: Referencing outcomes in behavioral disorders to societal issues and problems. *Behavioral Disorders, 24*, 7–18.

Walker, H. M., Horner, R. H., Sugai, G., Bullis, M., Sprague, J. R., Bricker, D., et al. (1996). Integrated approaches to preventing antisocial behavior patterns among school-age children and youth. *Journal of Emotional and Behavioral Disorders, 4*, 193–256.

Walker, H. M., McConnell, S., Holmes, D., Todis, B., Walker, J., & Goldin, N. (1983). *The Walker social skills curriculum: The ACCEPTS program.* Austin, TX: Pro-ed.

Walker, H. M., Ramsey, E., & Gresham, F. M. (2004). *Antisocial behavior in the school: Evidence-based practices* (2nd ed.). Belmont, CA: Thomson/Wadsworth.

Walker, H. M., Schwartz, I. E., Nippold, M. A., Irvin, L. K., & Noell, J. W. (1994). Social skills in school-age children and youth: Issues and best practices in assessment and intervention. *Topics in Language Disorders, 14*(3), 70–82.

Walker, H. M., & Severson, H. H. (1990). *Systematic screening for behavior disorders.* Longmont, CO: Sopris West.

Walker, H. M., Severson, H. H., & Fell, E. G. (1994). *The early screening project: A proven child-find process.* Longmont, CO: Sopris West.

Walker, H. M., Shinn, M. R., O'Neill, R. E., & Ramsey, E. (1987). A longitudinal assessment of the development of antisocial behavior in boys: Rationale, methodology, and first year results. *Remedial and Special Education, 8*(4), 7–16.

Walker, H. M., & Sprague, J. R. (1999a). Longitudinal research and functional behavioral assessment issues. *Behavioral Disorders, 24*(4), 335–337.

Walker, H. M., & Sprague, J. R. (1999b). The path to school failure, delinquency, and violence: Causal factors and some potential solutions. *Intervention in School and Clinic, 35*(2), 67–73.

Walker, H. M., Stieber, S., & O'Neill, R. E. (1990). Middle school behavioral profiles of antisocial and at-risk control boys: Descriptive and predictive outcomes. *Exceptionality, 1*, 61–77

Walker, H. M., Stieber, S., Ramsey, E., & O'Neill, R. E. (1991). Longitudinal prediction of the school achievement, adjustment, and delinquency of antisocial versus at-risk boys. *Remediation and Special Education, 12*(4), 43–51.

Walker, H. M., & Sylwester, R. (1991). Where is school along the path to prison? *Educational Leadership, 49*(1), 16.

Walker, H. M., Todis, B., Holmes, D., & Horton, G. (1988). *The ACCESS Program.* Austin, TX: Pro-Ed.

Walker, J. E. & Shea, T. M. (1999). *Behavior management: A practical approach for educators.* Upper Saddle River, NJ: Merrill/Prentice Hall.

Walsh (2005, February 22). *Congress improves IDEA: An overview.* Presentation to the South Carolina Council for Children with Behavioral Disorders.

Walther-Thomas, C., Korinek, L., McLaughlin, V. L., & Williams, B. T. (2000). *Collaboration for inclusive education: developing successful programs.* Boston: Allyn & Bacon.

Wangemann, P., Ingram, C., & Muse, I. (1989). A successful university-public school collaboration: The union of theory and practice. *Teacher Education and Special Education, 12*, 61–64.

Warner, L. A., & Pottick, K. J. (2003). Nearly 66,000 youth live in U.S. Mental health programs. In U. S. Departemnt of Health and Human. Services (Ed.), *Latest Findings in Children's Mental Health* (Vol. 2). New Brunswick, NJ: Institute for Health, Health Care Policy, and Aging Research, Rutgers University, Annie E. Casey Foundation.

Waters, V. (1982). In C. R. Reynolds & T. B. Gutkin, *The Handbook of School Psychology* (2nd ed.) (pp. 64–102). New York: Wiley.

Webber, J., Coleman, M., & Zionts, P. (1998). Reducing teacher stress with rational emotive behavior therapy. *Beyond Behavior, 9*(1), 21–26.

Webber, J., & Scheuerman, B. (1991). Managing problem behaviors: Accent the positive . . . eliminate the negative. *Teaching Exceptional Children, 24*(1), 13–19.

Webber, J., & Scheuerman, B. (1997). A challenging future: Current barriers and recommended action for our field. *Behavioral Disorders, 22*, 167–178.

Webber, J., Scheuermann, B., McCall, C., & Coleman, M. (1994). Research on self-monitoring as a behavior management technique in special education classrooms: A descriptive review. *Remedial and Special Education, 14*, 38–56.

Weber, M. C. (1992). *Special education law and litigation treatise* (2nd ed.). Horsham, PA: LRP Publications.

Weber, M. C. (2002). *Special education law and litigation treatise* (2nd ed.). Horsham, PA: LRP.

Webster, R. E. (1976). A time-out procedure in a public school setting. *Psychology in the Schools, 13*, 72–76.

Wehby, J. H., Dodge, K. A., & Valente, E. (1993). School behavior of first grade children identified as at-risk for development of conduct problems. *Behavioral Disorders, 19*(1), 67–78.

Wehby, J. H., Falk, K. B., Barton-Arwood, S., Lane, K. L. & Cooley, C. (2003). The impact of comprehensive reading instruction on the academic and social behavior of students with emotional and behavioral disorders. *Journal of Emotional and Behavioral Disorders, 11*(4), 225–238.

Wehby, J. H., Lane, K., & Falk, K. B. (2003). Academic instruction for students with emotional and behavioral disorders. *Journal of Emotional and Behavioral Disorders, 11*(4), 194–197.

Wehby, J. H., Symons, F. J., Canale, J. A., & Go, F. J. (1998). Teaching practices in classrooms for students with emotional and behavioral disorders: Discrepancies between recommendations and observations. *Behavioral Disorders, 24,* 51-56.

Wehby, J. H., Symons, F. J., & Shores, R. E. (1995). A descriptive analysis of aggressive behavior in classrooms for children with emotional and behavioral disorders. *Behavioral Disorders, 20,* 87-105.

West, R. P., Young, K. R., Callahan, K., Fister, S. Kemp, K., Freston, J, & et al. (1995). The musical clocklight: Encouraging positive classroom behavior. *Teaching Exceptional Children, 27*(2), 46-51.

Whelan, R. J., & Kauffman, J. M. (1999). *Educating students with emotional and behavioral disorders: Historical perspectives and future directions.* Reston, VA: Council for Children with Behavioral Disorders.

Whelan, R. J., & Simpson, R. L. (1996). Preparation of personnel for students with emotional and behavioral disorders: Perspectives on a research foundation for future practice. *Behavioral Disorders, 22,* 49-54.

White, G., & Greenwood, S. (1992). Empowering middle level students through the use of learning contracts. *Middle School Journal, 23,* 15-20.

White, O. R., & Haring, N. G. (1980). *Exceptional teaching* (2nd ed.). Upper Saddle River, NJ: Merrill/Prentice Hall.

White, R., Algozzine, B, Audette, B., Marr, M. B., & Ellis, E. (2004). Unified discipline: A school-wide approach for managing problem behavior. *Intervention in School and Clinic, 37,* 3-8.

White, R. B., & Koorland, M. A., (1996). Curses! What can we do about cursing? *Teaching, 28,* 48-51.

Wiggins, G. (1993). Assessment: Authenticity, context, and validity. *Phi Delta Kappan, 75*(3), 200-214.

Wilen, W., Ishler, M., Hutchinson, J. & Kindsvatter, R. (2003). *Dynamics of effective secondary teaching* (5th ed.). Boston: Pearson/Allyn & Bacon.

Wilen, W., Ishler, M., Hutchinson, J., & Kindsvatter, R. (2004). *The dynamics of effective teaching* (5th ed.). Boston: Allyn & Bacon.

Williams, J. P. (2005). Instruction in reading comprehension for primary-grade students: A focus on text structure. *The Journal of Special Education, 39*(1), 6-18.

Willoughby, T., & Wood, E. (1999). Mnemonic strategies. In E. Wood, V. Woloshyn, & T. Willoughby, *Cognitive strategy instruction for middle and high schools* (pp. 5-17). Cambridge, MA: Brookline Books.

Wilson, C. C., Robertson, S. J., Herlong, L. H., & Haynes, S. N. (1979). Vicarious effects of time-out in the modification of aggression in the classroom. *Behavior Modification, 3,* 97-111.

Wilson, C. L., & Sindelar, P. T. (1991). Direct instruction in math word problems: Students with learning disabilities. *Exceptional Children, 57*(6), 512-519.

Wilson, R., & Wesson, C. (1986). Making every minute count: Academic time in LD classrooms. *Learning Disabilities Focus, 2,* 3-19.

Winnett, R. A., Moore, J. F., & Anderson, E. S. (1991). Extending the concept of social validity: Behavior analysis for disease prevention and health promotion. *Journal of Applied Behavior Analysis, 24,* 215-230.

Witt, J. C., Cavell, T. A., Heffer, R. W., Carey, M. P., & Martens, B. K. (1988). Child self-report: Interviewing techniques and rating scales. In E. S. Shapiro & T. R. Kratochwill (Eds.), *Behavioral assessment in schools: Conceptual foundations and practical applications* (pp. 384-454). New York: Guilford Press.

Witt, J. C., Daly, E. M., & Noell, G. (2000). *Functional assessments: A step-by-step guide to solving academic and behavior problems.* Longmont, CO: Sopris West.

Witt, J. C., VanDenHeyden, A. M., & Gilbertson, D. (2004). Instruction and classroom management. In R. B. Rutherford Jr., M. M. Quinn, & S. R. Mathur, *Handbook of research in emotional and behavioral disorders* (426-451). New York: The Guilford Press.

Wittrock, M. (1986). *Handbook of research on teaching* (3rd ed). New York: Macmillan.

Wold, J. A., Fantuzzo, J., & Wolter, C. (1984). Student-administered group-oriented contingencies: A method of combining group-oriented contingencies and self-directed behavior to increase academic productivity. *Child and Family Behavior Therapy, 6*(3), 45-60.

Wolery M., Bailey, D. B., & Sugai, G. M. (1988). *Effective teaching: Principles and procedures of applied behavior analysis with exceptional students.* Boston: Allyn & Bacon.

Wolf, M. M., Giles, D., & Hall, R. V. (1968). Experiments with token reinforcement in a remedial classroom. *Behaviour Research and Therapy, 6,* 51-64.

Wolfe, D. A. (1999). *Child abuse* (2nd ed.). Newbury Park, CA: Sage.

Wolfe, J. A., Fantuzzo, J. W., & Wolter, C. F. (1984). Student-administered group-oriented contingencies: A method of combining group-oriented contingencies and self-directed behavior to increase academic productivity. *Child and Family Behavior Therapy, 6,* 45-60.

Wong, B. Y. L. (1989). On cognitive training: A thought or two. In J. N. Hughes & R. J. Hall (Eds.), *Cognitive behavioral psychology in the schools: A comprehensive handbook* (pp. 209-219). New York: Guilford Press.

Wong, H. K., & Wong, R. T. (2001). *The first days of school: How to be an effective teacher.* Mountain View, CA: Harry K. Wong Publications.

Wood, E., & Willoughby, T. (1999). Cognitive strategies for test taking. In E. Wood, V. Woloshyn, & T. Willoughby, *Cognitive strategy instruction for middle and high schools* (pp. 245-258). Cambridge, MA: Brookline Books.

Wood, E., Willoughby, T., & Woloshyn, V. (1999). An introduction to cognitive strategies in the secondary school. In

E. Wood, V. Woloshyn, & T. Willoughby, *Cognitive strategy instruction for middle and high schools* (pp. 1-4). Cambridge, MA: Brookline Books.

Wood, E., Woloshyn, V., & Willoughby, T. (1999). *Cognitive strategy instruction for middle and high schools.* Cambridge, MA: Brookline Books.

Wood, F. H. (1991). Cost/benefit considerations in managing the behavior of students with emotional/behavioral disorders. *Preventing School Failure, 35,* 17-23.

Workman, E. A. (1998). *Teaching behavioral self-control to students* (2nd ed.). Austin, TX: Pro-Ed.

Wright, P. W. D., Wright, P. D., & Heath, S. W. (2004). *No Child Left Behind.* Hartfield, VA: Harbor House Law Press.

Wu, H. (1999). Basic skills versus conceptual understanding. *American Educator, 23*(3), 14-19, 50-52.

Yell, M. L. (1988). The effects of three behavior reduction interventions on off-task behaviors of behaviorally disordered students. *Severe Behavior Disorders of Children and Youth, 11,* 167-174.

Yell, M. L. (1990). The use of corporal punishment, suspension, expulsion, and timeout with behaviorally disordered students in public schools: Legal considerations, *Behavioral Disorders, 15,* 100-110.

Yell, M. L. (1992). *A comparison of three instructional procedures on task attention, interfering behaviors, and achievement of students with emotional and behavioral disorders.* Unpublished doctoral dissertation. University of Minnesota, Minneapolis, MN.

Yell, M. L. (1994). Timeout and Students with Behavioral Disorders. Legal considerations. *Education & Treatment of Children, 17,* 293-301.

Yell, M. L. (1995). *Clyde K. and Sheila K. v. Puyallup School District:* The courts, inclusion, and students with behavioral disorders. *Behavioral Disorders, 20,* 179-189.

Yell, M. L. (1996a). Having to believe. In B. Brooks & D. Sabatino (Eds.), *Educating students with behavioral disorders: Personal perspectives* (pp. 442-462). Austin, TX: Pro-Ed.

Yell. M.L. (1996b). Managing student records: Legal requirements. *Preventing School Failure, 41,* 144-148.

Yell, M. L. (1996c). Reporting child abuse and neglect: Legal requirements. *Preventing School Failure, 40,* 136-140.

Yell, M. L. (1997). Teacher liability for student injury and misconduct. *Beyond Behavior, 8*(2), 7-10.

Yell, M. L. (2006). *The law and special education* (2nd ed.). Upper Saddle River, NJ: Merrill/Prentice Hall.

Yell, M. L., & Bradley, M. R (2000, February). *Beyond the schoolhouse door: The curriculum of control 10 years after Knitzer, Steinberg, & Fleisch.* Paper presented at the Midwest Symposium for Leadership In Behavior Disorders, Kansas City, MO.

Yell, M. L., Busch, T., & Drasgow, E. (2005). Cognitive behavior modification. In T. J. Zirpoli (Ed.), *Behavior management: applications for teachers* (pp. 226-266). Upper Saddle River, NJ: Merrill/Prentice Hall.

Yell, M. L., & Drasgow, E. (2000). Litigating a free appropriate public education: The Lovaas hearings and cases. *The Journal of Special Education, 33,* 206-215.

Yell, M. L., & Drasgow, E. (2005). *No Child Left Behind: A guide for professionals.* Upper Saddle River, NJ: Merrill/Prentice Hall.

Yell, M. L., Drasgow, E., Bradley, R., & Justesen, T. (2004). Critical legal issues in special education. In A. McCray Sorrells, H. J. Reith, & P. T. Sindelar, (Eds.), *Issues in special education* (pp. 16-37). Boston: Allyn & Bacon.

Yell, M. L., Drasgow, E., & Lowrey, K. A. (2005). No Child Left Behind and Students with Autism Spectrum Disorder. *Focus on Autism and Other Developmental Disabilities, 20,* 130-139.

Yell, M. L., Katsiyannis, A., Bradley, R., & Rozalski, M. E. (2000). Ensuring compliance with the discipline provisions of IDEA '97: Challenges and opportunities. *Journal of Special Education Leadership, 13,* 204-216.

Yell, M. L., Katsiyannis, A., & Shriner, J. A. (2006). The No Child Left Behind Act, adequate yearly progress, and students with disabilities. *Teaching Exceptional Children, 3*(4), 32-39.

Yell, M. L., & Peterson, R. (1995). Disciplining students with disabilities and those at-risk of school failure: Legal issues. *Preventing School Failure, 39*(2), 36-40.

Yell, M. L., Robinson, T. R., & Drasgow, E. (2001). Cognitive behavior modification. In T. J. Zirpoli & K. Melloy, *Behavior management* (4th ed.). (pp. 350-444). Upper Saddle River, NJ: Merrill/Prentice Hall.

Yell, M. L., & Rozalski, M. E. (2000). Searching for safe schools: Legal issues in the prevention of school violence. *Journal of Emotional and Behavioral Disorders, 8*(3), 187-196.

Yell, M. L., & Rozalski, M. E. (2001). Searching for safe schools: Legal issues in the prevention of school violence. In H. M. Walker & M. H. Epstein (Eds.), *Making schools safer and violence free: Critical issues, solutions, and recommended practices* (pp. 160-169). Austin, TX: Pro-Ed.

Yell, M. L., Rozalski, M. E., & Drasgow, E. (2001). Disciplining students with disabilities. *Focus on Exceptional Children, 33*(9), 1-20.

Yell, M. L. & Stecker, P. M. (2003). Developing legally correct and educationally meaningful IEPs using curriculum-based measurement. *Assessment for Effective Intervention, 28,* 73-88.

Young, K. R., Smith, D. J., West, R. P., & Morgan, D. P. (1987). A peer-mediated program for teaching self-management strategies to adolescents. *Programming for Adolescents with Behavior Disorders, 3,* 34-47.

Ysseldyke, J. E., & Christenson, S. (1993). *The Instructional Environment Scale –II* (TIES–II). Longmont, CO: Sopris West.

Zabel, M. K. (1986). Timeout use with behaviorally disordered students. *Behavioral Disorders, 12,* 15-21.

Zabel, M. K. (1992). Responses to control. *Beyond Behavior, 3,* 3-4.

Zabel, R. H. (1987). Preparation of teachers for behaviorally disordered students. In M. C. Wang, H. J. Wahlberg, & M. C. Reynolds (Eds.), *Handbook of special education: Research and practice.* Oxford, England: Pergamon Press.

Zabel, R. H., & Zabel, M. K. (1982). Factors involved in burnout among teachers of exceptional children. *Exceptional Children, 2,* 261-263.

Zettel, J. J., & Ballard, J. (1982). The Education for All Handicapped Children Act of 1975 (P.L. 94-142): Its history, origins, and concepts. In J. Ballard, B. Ramirez, and F. Weintraub (Eds.), *Special education in America: Its legal and governmental foundations* (pp. 11-22). Reston, VA: Council for Exceptional Children.

Zigmond, N., & Baker, J. M. (1996). Full inclusion for students with learning disabilities: Too much of a good thing? *Theory into Practice, 35,* 26-34.

Zigmond, N., Kerr, M. M., Schaeffer, A. L., Brown, G. M., & Farra, H. E. (1986). *School survival skills curriculum* (limited published circulation). Available from Department of Special Education, 5M30 Forbes Quadrangle, 230 Boquet Street, University of Pittsburgh, Pittsburgh, PA 15260.

Zionts, P. (1996). *Teaching disturbed and disturbing students.* Austin, TX: Pro-Ed.

Zionts, P. (1998). Rational emotive behavior therapy: A classroom mental health curriculum. *Beyond Behavior, 9*(1), 4-11.

Zirpoli, T. J. (2005). *Behavior management: Applications for teachers* (4th ed.). Upper Saddle River, NJ: Merrill /Prentice Hall.

Zirpoli, T. J., & Melloy, K. J. (1997). *Behavior management.* Upper Saddle River, NJ: Merrill/Prentice Hall.

Zirpoli, T. J., & Melloy, K. J. (2001). *Behavior management: Applications for teachers* (3rd ed.). Upper Saddle River, NJ: Merrill/Prentice Hall.

Name Index

Subject Index